UNDERSTANDING CROSS-CULTURAL MANAGEMENT

Third Edition

Marie-Joëlle Browaeys and Roger Price

PEARSON

Harlow, England • London • New York • Boston • San Francisco • Toronto • Sydney
Auckland • Singapore • Hong Kong • Tokyo • Seoul • Taipei • New Delhi
Cape Town • São Paulo • Mexico City • Madrid • Amsterdam • Munich • Paris • Milan

PEARSON EDUCATION LIMITED
Edinburgh Gate
Harlow CM20 2JE
United Kingdom
Tel: +44 (0) 1279 623623
Web: www.pearson.com/uk

First published 2008 (print)
Second edition 2011 (print and electronic)
Third edition published 2015 ([print and electronic])

© Pearson Education Limited 2008 (print)
© Pearson Education Limited 2011, 2015 (print and electronic)

The Financial Times. With a worldwide network of highly respected journalists, *The Financial Times*
provides global business news, insightful opinion and expert analysis of business, finance and politics.
With over 500 journalists reporting from 50 countries worldwide, our in-depth coverage of
international news is objectively reported and analysed from an independent, global perspective.
To find out more, visit www.ft.com/pearsonoffer.

ISBN: 978-1-292-01589-7 (print)
      978-1-292-01633-7 (PDF)
      978-1-292-01632-0 (eText)

British Library Cataloguing-in-Publication Data
  Browaeys, Marie-Joelle.
  Understanding cross-cultural management / Marie-Joelle Browaeys and Roger Price. -- Third edition.
    pages cm
  ISBN 978-1-292-01589-7
  1. Diversity in the workplace--Management.   2. Management--Cross-cultural studies.   I. Price,
Roger, 1946-   II. Title.
  HF5549.5.M5B75 2015
  658.3008--dc23

                                                                          2014042516

Library of Congress Cataloging-in-Publication Data
A catalog record for the print edition is available from the Library of Congress

10 9 8 7 6 5 4 3 2
18 17 16 15

Cover image © Getty Images

Print edition typeset in 10/12.5pt Minion Pro by 35
Print edition printed in Malaysia, CTP-PJB

Contents

Preface

Knowing is not enough; we must apply.
Willing is not enough; we must do.

Johann Wolfgang von Goethe

This third edition maintains the approach taken by its predecessors: it explores the many facets of cross-cultural management while allowing the reader to apply the many theories and ideas which have evolved in this area to actual practice. However, as the result of the feedback received from our readers as well as from the publisher's reviewers, we have given extra attention in this edition to particular areas. This has involved, in Part One for example, adding a number of theoretical issues which are now addressed in the form of *chapter prefaces*, extending our coverage of GLOBE's research findings and giving particular attention to the BRICS countries. In line with the feedback mentioned above, some of the topics in Part Two and Part Three have been replaced – or given less prominence – to allow other topics to be featured.

Updating has been an essential part of preparing this new edition. This has involved replacing a number of the newspaper articles used in the book, as well as including new case material based on recent research. This material not only facilitates the application of theory to practice, but also enables a more detailed examination of research methods used in the area of cross-cultural management.

Preparing for global business

Given the globalisation of business and increasing diversity within the workforce of so many industries and organisations, a cross-cultural component in management education and training can no longer be considered as a useful 'add-on' merely for those who might consider venturing abroad to pursue their career. Nowadays, more and more managers and professionals are required to work effectively across cultural borders. Even if they are confined to their offices, they are more and more likely to interact with people from other cultures. Training in cross-cultural management has therefore become a 'must', whatever the type of business education concerned, whether it be for aspiring graduates at the start of their career or for those senior managers who wish to increase their effectiveness in their present positions or their employability in the international market.

The approach of this book

This book is the result of our experiences in educating international executives and post-graduate students in the areas of cross-cultural management and cross-cultural business communication. It reflects the need we felt for a practical, hands-on approach to study in this area which:

- offers a broad, if selective, view of theories, models and ideas on culture in terms of management, organisation and communication. This is preferable to providing just one particular (theoretical) approach to cross-cultural studies or giving an encyclopaedic survey of the subject area;

- allows the theories and ideas mentioned to be applied to practice through the inclusion of examples and brief case studies from the business world, as well as activities that require some of the theories outlined to be applied to business situations and to the reader's own work situation.

Combining a concise overview of cross-cultural concepts and learning-by-doing activities is an approach to cross-cultural management we have found to be effective for both instructors and students, trainers and trainees. Students are exposed to approaches to cross-cultural aspects of business rather than being overwhelmed with detail about countries and their culture based on one theoretical framework. At the same time, they are asked to apply these approaches in a practical and relevant manner to a number of case studies, many of which are taken from the business media. When doing so, students are expected not only to use the concepts, but also to apply their own intuitive insights and cross-cultural experience. This can be a rewarding experience for those concerned because the learning-by-doing activities themselves can reveal cultural assumptions and attitudes of those undergoing the learning process.

The instructor will, it is hoped, appreciate the concise overview of theories and concepts relating to cross-cultural management while also being provided with activities to *facilitate learning*. Moreover, the material enables the instructor to make maximum use of the environment in which the learning is taking place. As a facilitator in the process, the instructor helps the students not only to 'construct' their own understanding based on their knowledge and experience, but also to take advantage of the informal learning process through those activities, which encourage interaction between trainees. Having said that, however, we believe that this book is also a valuable resource for self-study because it enables readers to extend and to deepen their cross-cultural awareness.

This approach to learning reflects a concern we had when writing a book that deals with culture: knowledge of oneself is as important as the knowledge of theory.

The structure of this book

This book is divided into three parts:

- **Part One. Culture and management** deals with the concept of culture, its facets and the levels at which culture operates. It explores cultural dimensions in the business context and examines the cultural dilemmas that arise for managers when making decisions. It finally presents a model of culture based on cultural value orientations that affect managerial and professional activities. Prior to the concepts presented, each chapter in Part One includes a short preface which introduces a theoretical issue.

- **Part Two. Culture and organisations** considers the influence of culture on aspects of organisations, including structures, corporate cultures and the role of leadership. The cultural factors involved in strategy and strategic alliances, as well as in fundamental organisational change, come to the fore. Culture and international marketing, along with the question of cultural diversity in organisations, are also addressed.

- **Part Three. Culture and communication** examines how culture affects the process of communication both within and between cultures. Various cross-cultural contexts are dealt with, including negotiations and international teamwork. Cross-cultural conflict is given particular attention, as are the skills required to be an effective intercultural communicator.

Each of these parts is made up of six chapters

The chapters in Part One each begin with a **preface**. The chapters in Parts One and Two each contain two **cross-cultural concepts** and those in Part Three each contain one. These concepts address key ideas and theories developed by leading researchers and practitioners in the area of cross-cultural management, and present our overviews of their work. **Spotlights** and **mini-cases** (with questions) improve the application of the theories described. Each chapter of the book ends with at least two **activities**. These allow the learner to apply the concepts through exercises of various kinds.

The **points for reflection** given after the concepts encourage the readers to go beyond their knowledge of the subject matter and apply their skills to certain cross-cultural issues. Following these are a list of publications for **further reading** and **references**. These are intended for readers who wish to read more detailed accounts, or extend their knowledge of the areas in question.

The **final activities** at the end of each part pull the strings together. Being more extended in nature and incorporating the elements of each part, they are intended to provide a broader perspective of the area in question.

A particular type of exercise which plays a prominent role in the book is case analysis. We have found case studies to be a very effective learning tool: confronted with a dilemma described in each case, students are forced to consider their potential behaviour in the context described and learn from the choices they make. Interaction with their peers and instructor when accounting for their choices compels them to *talk about their experiences* and feelings, as well as the insights they have gained from reading the cross-cultural concepts in the book. The cases deal with many cultural contexts, so students are confronted with different ways of thinking, thereby helping them to develop transcultural competence.

Flexibility of approach

The arrangement of material is such that it allows flexibility in the sequence to be followed. Although we would suggest that Part One be the starting point for any programme of study, the sequence of chapters in Part Two and Part Three, as given below, need not be followed slavishly. The chapters may be re-arranged according to the priorities of the instructor and/or student. For example, if Chapters 8 and 18 are studied one after another, then the cultural aspects of leadership can be examined in terms of the communicative skills considered appropriate and effective in different national/organisational cultures. A further example: Chapters 9 and 15 can be studied together and so allow the issue of company takeovers and mergers to be combined with the negotiating process involved.

Part One Culture and management	Part Two Culture and organisations	Part Three Culture and communication
1 Determinants of culture	7 Culture and corporate structures	13 Business communication across cultures
2 Dimensions of culture: Hofstede and GLOBE	8 Culture and leadership	14 Barriers to intercultural communication
3 Business cultures in the Western world	9 Culture and corporate strategy	15 Negotiating internationally
4 Business cultures in Asia, Africa and the Middle East	10 Cultural change in organisations	16 Working with international teams
5 Cultural dimensions and dilemmas	11 Culture and international marketing management	17 Conflicts and cultural differences
6 Culture and styles of management	12 Cultural diversity in organisations	18 Developing intercultural communicative competence

Acknowledgements

We would like to thank, first and foremost, Nyenrode Business University for encouraging us to prepare this book and to revise it for the third edition. We are particularly indebted to our colleagues in the university library who, through their patient dedication and efficiency, have allowed us to draw upon a considerable number of updated information sources.

We are also grateful to the editorial team at Pearson Education and their reviewers, for their unstinting professional support, to the readers/users of the previous editions for their advice and ideas, and to the *Financial Times*, whose coverage of international business has proved to be an indispensable source of recent business case studies for the new edition.

Our thanks also go out to the numerous contributors to the book. The contributions made by Fons Trompenaars and alumni from Nyenrode Business University deserve particular mention. Last, but by no means least, we would like to thank our respective partners, Wim and Anke, for their patience and encouragement while we undertook a further, time-consuming revision of the book.

Publisher's acknowledgements

We are grateful to the following for permission to reproduce copyright material:

Figures

Figure I.1 from *Managing Across Cultures*, Prentice Hall (Schneider, S.C. and Barsoux, J.L. 2003) p. 21 © Pearson Education Limited 2003; Figure I.2 from *Managing Across Cultures*, FT Prentice Hall (Schneider, S.C. and Barsoux, J.L. 2003) p. 34 © Pearson Education Limited 2003; Figure 2.1 from *Culture and Leadership Across the World: The GLOBE Book of In-Depth Studies of 25 Societies*, Lawrence Erlbaum Associates (Chhokar, S.J., Brodbeck, F.C. and House, R.J. (ed.) 2007) p. 108, Copyright 2007 by TAYLOR & FRANCIS GROUP LLC – BOOKS. Reproduced with permission of TAYLOR & FRANCIS GROUP LLC – BOOKS in the formats Textbook and Other Book via Copyright Clearance Center; Figure 2.2 from *Culture's Consequences*, 2nd ed., SAGE (Hofstede, G. 2001) p. 11, reproduced with permission; Figure on page 58 from Poster celebrating Europe Day, http://europa.eu/about-eu/basic-information/symbols/europe-day/index_en.htm; Figure 4.1 from Migration and business: weaving the world together, *The Economist*, pp. 72–74 © The Economist Newspaper Limited, London (Issue 8760) 19/11/2011; Figure 6.2 adapted from *Cultural Analysis – Towards Further Understanding*, Aalborg University Press (Gullestrup, H. 2006) p. 153, reproduced with permission; Figure 6.3 adapted from *Doing Business Internationally: The cross-cultural challenges – Participant Workbook*, Princeton Training Press (1992) 2.3, Reproduced by kind permission of TMC http://www.tmcorp.com/; Figure 6.4 adapted from *Understanding Cultural Differences*, Intercultural Press (Hall, E.T. and Hall, M.R. 1993) p. 103; Figure 7.1 from *International Dimensions of Organizational Behaviour*, 5th ed., South Western (Adler, N.J. with Gundersen, A. 2008) p. 128 © 2008 South-Western, a part of Cengage Learning Inc. Reproduced by permission. www.cengage.com/permissions; Figure 7.2 adapted from *Exploring Corporate Strategy*, 8th ed., FT Prentice Hall (Johnson, G., Scholes, K. and Whittington, R. 2008) © Pearson Education Limited 2008; Figure 7.3 from *Business Across Cultures*, Capstone (Trompenaars, F. and Woolliams, P. 2003) p. 106; Figure 8.2 from Six principles of effective global talent management, *MIT Sloan Management Review* (Stahl, Gunter K., Björkman, Ingmar and Farndale Elaine 2012) © 2012 from MIT Sloan Management Review/Massachusetts Institute of Technology. All rights reserved. Distributed by Tribune Content Agency; Figure 9.1 from *Breaking Through Culture Shock*, Nicholas Brealey (Marx, E. 1999) p. 12; Figure 10.1 adapted from *Diagnosing and Changing Organizational Culture*, Prentice Hall (Cameron, K.S. and Quinn, R.E. 1999) p. 32, reproduced by kind permission of Professor Cameron and Professor Quinn; Figure 11.2 from http://searchenginewatch.com/article/2329906/Only-52-of-Facebook-Ad-Spend-is-Outside-the-U.S.-tuy, reproduced with permission from Marin Software; Figure 11.4 from *Managing Cultural Differences:*

Strategies for Competitive Advantage, Addison-Wesley (Hoecklin, L. 1995) p. 101, © Pearson Education Limited 1995; Figure 12.1 from *International Management Ethics: A Critical, Cross-cultural Perspective*, Cambridge University Press (Jackson, T. 2011) p. 22; Figure 15.1 from 'Negotiating with "Romans"', Part 1, *Sloan Management Review*, 35 (2), p. 54 (Weiss, S.E. 1994); Figure 17.1 adapted from *Thomas-Kilmann Conflict Mode Instrument*, Xicom (Thomas, K.W. and Kilmann, R.H. 1974) p. 11; Figure 17.2 from *Handbook of International and Intercultural Communication*, SAGE (Gudykunst, W. and Mody, B. (eds.) 2002) Reproduced with permission of SAGE PUBLICATIONS in the format Republish in a book via Copyright Clearance Center; Figure 18.1 from *Experiential Learning: Experience as the Source of Learning and Development* Prentice-Hall (Kolb, D.A. 1984) p. 42, 1st ed., ©1984. Printed and Electronically reproduced by permission of Pearson Education, Inc., Upper Saddle River, New Jersey; Figure 18.2 from Foundations for the study of intercultural communication based on a third-culture model, *International Journal of Intercultural Relations*, 23 (1), pp. 91–116 (Casrnir, F.L. 1999), Copyright © 1999. With permission from Elsevier.

Map

Map 3.1 adapted from European Union, http://europa.eu/about-eu/countries/index_en.htm, © European Union, 1995–2014.

Tables

Table I.1 from *Cultural Anthropology: Tribes, States and the Global System*, Mayfield Publishing Co (Bodley J.H. 1994) p. 9, reproduced by kind permission of Dr J. Bodley; Table 1.1 adapted from *Understanding Organizations through Language*, SAGE (Tietze, S., Cohen, L., Musson, G. 2003) Reproduced by permission of SAGE Publications, London, Los Angeles, New Delhi and Singapore Copyright © SAGE Publications 2003; Table A1.1.2 adapted from Cross-border transfer of knowledge: cultural lessons from project GLOBE, *Academy of Management Executive*, pp. 59–76 (Javidan, G.K. 2005); Table 2.1 adapted from *Variations in Value Orientations*, Row, Peterson and Company (Kluckholn, F. and Strodtbeck, F. 1961) pp. 11–12; Table 2.8 adapted from *Culture, Leadership and Organizations: The GLOBE study of 62 societies*, SAGE (House, R.J., Hanges, P.J., Javidan, M., Dorfman, P.W. and Gupta, V. (eds.) 2004) p. 30, Global Leadership and Organizational Behavior Leadership effectiveness Research Program Reproduced with permission of SAGE PUBLICATIONS, INCORPORATED in the format Republish in a book via Copyright Clearance Center; Table 2.9 from *Culture and Leadership Across the World: The GLOBE Book of In-Depth Studies of 25 Societies*, Lawrence Erlbaum Associates (Chhokar, J.S., Brodbeck, F.C. and House, R.J. (eds) 2007) p. 993, Tab. 27.6, Copyright 2007 by TAYLOR & FRANCIS GROUP LLC – BOOKS. Reproduced with permission of TAYLOR & FRANCIS GROUP LLC – BOOKS in the formats Textbook and Other Book via Copyright Clearance Center; Table 2.11 from *Culture and Leadership Across the World: The GLOBE Book of In-Depth Studies of 25 Societies*, Lawrence Erlbaum Associates (Chhokar, J.S., Brodbeck, F.C. and House, R.J. (eds) 2007) p. 13, Copyright 2007 by

TAYLOR & FRANCIS GROUP LLC – BOOKS. Reproduced with permission of TAYLOR & FRANCIS GROUP LLC – BOOKS in the formats Textbook and Other Book via Copyright Clearance Center; Table 4.1 adapted from *Asian versus Western Management Thinking: Its Culture-Bound Nature*, Palgrave (Kase, K. Slocum, A. and Zhang, Y.Y. 2011) p. 105, Tab. 6.1, reproduced with permission of Palgrave Macmillan; Table 5.3 adapted from *Trompenaars, F. and Woolliams, P. 'Competency framework for the millennium manager' in Case Studies on Cultural Dilemmas*, Nyenrode University Press (Browaeys, M.-J. and Trompenaars, F. (eds.) 2000) pp. 21–28; Table 5.4 from The art of cross-cultural management: an alternative approach to training and development, *Journal of European Industrial Training*, 20 (1), p. 17 (Estienne, M. 1997); Table 8.1 adapted from Culture and Leadership in 25 Societies: Integration, Conclusions, and Future Directions in Chhokar, J.S., Brodbeck, F.C. and House, R.J. (eds.), *Culture and Leadership Across the World: The GLOBE Book of In-Depth Studies of 25 Societies*, Lawrence Erlbaum Associates (*Brodbeck, F.C., Chhokar, J.S. and House, R.J.* 2007) p. 1037, Copyright 2007 by TAYLOR & FRANCIS GROUP LLC – BOOKS. Reproduced with permission of TAYLOR & FRANCIS GROUP LLC – BOOKS in the formats Textbook and Other Book via Copyright Clearance Center; Table 10.1 from Organizational culture: what it is and how to change it in Evans, P., Doz, Y. and Laurent, A. (eds.), *Human Resource Management in International Firms*, Macmillan (Schein, E.H. 1989) pp. 83–94, reproduced with permission of Palgrave Macmillan; Table 14.1 from *Cadres français et communications interculturelles*, Editions Eyrolles (Gruère, J-P. and Morel, P. 1991); Table 15.1 from Cultural aspects of international business negotiations in Ghauri, N. and Usunier J.-C. (eds.), *International Business Negotiations*, 2nd ed., Elsevier (Usunier, J.-C. 2003) pp. 97–136; Table 16.2 from *The Blackwell Handbook of Global Management*, Blackwell (Maznevski, H.W., Mendenhall, M.L. and McNett, J.M.E. (eds.) 2004) pp. 232–234; Table 18.1 from Towards ethnorelativism: a developmental model of intercultural sensitivity in Paige, R.M. (ed.), *Education for the Intercultural Experience*, 2nd ed., Intercultural Press (Bennett, M.J. 1993) p. 29, reproduced by kind permission of Dr M.J. Bennett, http://www.idrinstitute.org; Tables 18.3, 18.4 and 18.6 from *Training for the Cross-Cultural Mind*, 2nd ed., SIETAR (Casse, P. 1981) pp. 140–146, Reproduced by kind permission of Professor Pierre Casse.

Text

Case Study A1.1 with permission from Robert Deidun and Javier Arias; Case Study A1.2 from *Galderma: a joint venture between L'Oréal and Nestlé An empirical study of cross-cultural relations between French, German and British managers in an international company* (Browaeys, M.-J. Price, R.L. and Seifert, C.R.); Activity A2.1 adapted from Masters Thesis, Nyenrode Business School (Sierkstra, E. and Stal, R. 2005); Activity A2.2 adapted from *The Challenge of Cross Cultural Management*, Nyenrode University Press (Browaeys, M.-J. (ed.) 1996); Extract on page 79 adapted from Jock Phillips. 'The New Zealanders – Multicultural New Zealand', *Te Ara – the Encyclopedia of New Zealand*, updated 13-Jul-12 http://www.teara.govt.nz/en/the-new-zealanders/page-13; Extract on pages 87–88 from Wiring design faulted for Airbus A380 production delays (Blog Article 14634), http://power.elecdesign.com (Davis S. 2007); Mini-Case 3.1 from German business culture should be a model for our own, *The Observer*, 15/08/2010(Sunderland, R.), Copyright Guardian News & Media Ltd. 2010; Spotlight 4.1 adapted with free translation from Paris supports the transfer of technology to India, *Le Monde*, 18/02/2013 (Follorou, J), reproduced with permission; Activity 4.2 adapted from *Cases Studies on Cultural Dilemmas*, Nyenrode University Press (Browaeys, M.J. and Trompenaars, F. (eds.) 2000) Case 10; Mini-Case 4.5 adapted from Celebrating business success in Africa in *Poverty matters* blog, *The Guardian* (the guardian.com) 09/06/2011 (Tran, M.), Copyright © Guardian News & Media Ltd. 2011; Extract on pages 135–137 from *Case Studies on Cultural Dilemmas*, Nyenrode University Press (Browaeys, M.-J. and Trompenaars, F. (eds.) 2000) pp. 29–33; Mini-Case 5.1 from *Case Studies on Cultural Dilemmas*, Nyenrode University Press (Browaeys, M.-J. and Trompenaars, F. (eds.) 2000) Case 7; Activity 5.1 from The practice of reconciliation in Browaeys, M.-J. and Trompenaars F. (eds.), *Case Studies on Cultural Dilemmas*, Nyenrode University Press (Trompenaars, F. 2000); Mini-Case 5.2 from *Case Studies on Cultural Dilemmas*, Nyenrode University Press (Browaeys, M.-J. and Trompenaars, F. (eds.) 2000) Case 5; Activity 5.2 from *Case Studies on Cultural Dilemmas*, Nyenrode University Press (Browaeys, M.-J. and Trompenaars, F. (eds.) 2000) Case 9; Spotlight 6.4 from Renault-Nissan and Mitsubishi agree co-operation deal, *Daily Telegraph* (telegraph.co.uk), 05/11/2013 (Hudson, P.), copyright © Telegraph Media Group Limited 2013; Activity 7.1 from *Cases Studies on Cultural Dilemmas*, Nyenrode University Press (Browaeys, M.-J. and Trompenaars, F. (eds.) 2000) Case 4; Spotlight 7.2 from Team learning on the edge of chaos, *The Learning Organization*, 17 (1), pp. 61–62 (Fisser, S. and Browaeys, M.-J. 2010); Activity 8.2 from Why multinationals struggle to manage talent (Retrieved from Business Source Complete database), *McKinsey Quarterly*, 4 pp. 10–13 (Guthridge, M. & Komm, A. 2008), This article was originally published in McKinsey Quarterly, www.mckinseyquarterly.com. Copyright © 2008 McKinsey & Company. All rights reserved. Reprinted by permission; Spotlight 8.3 from *Business Times*, Singapore, 05/10/2009, reproduced with permission; Activity 9.2 adapted from *The Challenges of Cross-Cultural Management*, Nyenrode University Press (Browaeys, M.-J. (ed.) 1996) pp. 41–50; Activity 11.1 from *Analysis of the Indian Truck Market*, Nyenrode University Press (Engelaer, F. and Vioet, D. 2005); Activity 11.2 adapted from *Cases Studies on Cultural Dilemmas*, Nyenrode University Press (Browaeys, M.-J. and Trompenaars, F. (eds.) 2000) Case 6; Extract on page 304 from A new unified competency framework for the millennium manager in Browaeys, M.-J. and Trompenaars, F. (eds.), *Case Studies on Cultural Dilemmas*, Nyenrode University Press (*Trompenaars, F. and Woolliams, P.* 2000) pp. 21–28; Spotlight 12.1 adapted from Companies apathetic about corruption, *The Telegraph* (telegraph.co.uk) 08/09/2013 (Roland, D.), copyright © Telegraph Media Group Limited 2013; Activity 12.1 adapted from *Diversity versus localization within a telecommunications company in Latin America*, Nyenrode Business University (Danker, R. 2006); Activity 13.1 from English names catch on amongst Chinese: young bridging a gap with West, *Boston Globe*, 01/10/2006 (Pocha, J.S.), Reproduced by permission of the author; Spotlight 13.2 from Meeting-room jargon: just fuel for buzzword bingo?, http://www.worldwidewords.org/articles/jargon.htm (Quinion, M. 2000); Mini-Case 14.1 from Unleash the power of the Hispanic market by avoiding these pitfalls, *Quirk's Marketing Research Review*, April (Baroutakis, M. 2010), http://www.quirks.com/articles/a2000/20000402.aspx?%20searchID=2071341 [accessed 01/09/2010], Reproduced by kind permission of Quirk's Marketing Research Review; Activity 14.2 from *Case Studies on Cultural Dilemmas*, Nyenrode University Press (Browaeys, M.-J. and Trompenaars, F. (eds.) 2000) Case 11; Spotlight 14.3 adapted from L'informatique a-t-elle un sexe?, *Le Monde Diplomatique*, 03/06/2007, p.3 (Collet, I.); Activity 17.1 from *Cases Studies on Cultural*

Dilemmas, Nyenrode University Press (Browaeys, M.-J. and Trompenaars F. (eds.) 2000) Case 1; Activity 17.2 from Untangling alliances and joint ventures, FT.com, 16/10/2006 (Manzoni, J-F. and Barsoux, J-L.); Activity 18.2 from *Cases Studies on Cultural Dilemmas,* Nyenrode University Press (Browaeys, M.-J. and Trompenaars, F. (eds.) 2000) Case 8.

The Financial Times

Spotlight 1.1 adapted from British phone-hacking inquiry calls for press regulation with force of law, *Financial Times*, 30/11/2012 (Budden, R., Fenton, B. and Stacey, K.), © The Financial Times Limited. All Rights Reserved; Activity 1.1 adapted from A rather civil partnership, *Financial Times* (FT.com), 20/01/2012 (Hill, A.), © The Financial Times Limited. All Rights Reserved; Activity 2.1 adapted from Masters of collaboration, *Financial Times*, 29/06/2007, p. 8 (Lester T.), © The Financial Times Limited. All Rights Reserved; Spotlight 2.2 adapted from A question of identity, *Financial Times* (FT.com), 23/11/2012 (Kuper, S.), © The Financial Times Limited. All Rights Reserved; Extract on page 87 adapted from Airbus and the damage done by economic patriotism, *Financial Times*, 02/03/2007 (Vives, X.); Extract on pages 89–90 adapted from For EADS partners, culture still matters, *Financial Times*, 27/09/2012 (Skapinker, M.), © The Financial Times Limited. All Rights Reserved; Mini-Case 3.2 from A tale of two Russian factories, *Financial Times*, 07/07/2006, p. 9, © The Financial Times Limited. All Rights Reserved; Activity 3.2 from Why financial scandals differ in the US and Europe, *Financial Times*, 13/04/2005, p. 12 (Skapinker M.), © The Financial Times Limited. All Rights Reserved; Mini-Case 3.3 from Turkey seeks influence in Africa, *Financial Times*, 07/01/2013 (Dombey, D.), © The Financial Times Limited. All Rights Reserved; Spotlight 3.7 adapted from Australia: Proud of its seat at the top table, *Financial Times*, 26/01/2010 (Smith, P.), © The Financial Times Limited. All Rights Reserved; Mini-Case 4.1 from Culture turned Fukushima from disaster to crisis 'made in Japan', *Financial Times*, 06/07/2012 (Dickie, M.), © The Financial Times Limited. All Rights Reserved; Mini-case 4.2 adapted from Pressure mounts on chaebol chiefs, *Financial Times*, 24/02/2013 (Song Jung-a), © The Financial Times Limited. All Rights Reserved; Mini-Case 4.3 adapted from Holiday groups target India's newly affluent travelling set, *Financial Times*, 03/03/2010, p.9 (Kazmin A.), © The Financial Times Limited. All Rights Reserved and Lloyd's of London hits at 'difficult' India, *Financial Times*, 04/03/2010 (Nakamotot M. and Leahy J.), © The Financial Times Limited. All Rights Reserved; Activity 4.4 from A new generation of family firm, *Financial Times*, 10/03/2007, p.12 (Lucas L.), © The Financial Times Limited. All Rights Reserved; Activity 7.2 adapted from The capital gained from culture, *Financial Times*, 17/08/2009, p. 10 (Simon, B.), © The Financial Times Limited. All Rights Reserved; Activity 8.1 from Le Patron, der chef and the boss, *Financial Times*, 09/01/2006, p.10 (Maitland, A.), © The Financial Times Limited. All Rights Reserved; Spotlight 8.2 from Gender diversity boosts company shares, *Financial Times* (FT.com), 18/04/2013 (Clarke, C.), © The Financial Times Limited. All Rights Reserved; Spotlight 4.5 adapted from Transfer of assets tarnished by elitism, *Financial Times*, 16/07/2009 (Lapper, R.), © The Financial Times Limited. All Rights Reserved; Mini-Case 4.6 from FT Report – Qatar, *Financial Times*, 18/05/2005, p.1 (Wallis W.), © The Financial Times Limited. All Rights Reserved; Spotlight 9.1 from China suspends India power projects, *Financial Times*, 23/03/2010 (Lamont, J.), © The Financial Times Limited. All Rights Reserved; Mini-Case 9.1 adapted from Carmakers' alliance faces cultural chasm, *Financial Times*, 07/04/2010 (Schafer, D. and Reed, J.), © The Financial Times Limited. All Rights Reserved; Activity 9.1 from Marriage after a century of cohabitation: Shell prepares for the next merger round, *Financial Times*, 28/06/2005, p. 21, © The Financial Times Limited. All Rights Reserved; Spotlight 10.1 adapted from The challenges facing leadership, *Financial Times* (FT.com), 12/11/2009 (Goffee, Rob and Jones, Gareth), with permission from authors; Mini-Case 10.1 from Brussels launches probe into secret accounts, *Financial Times*, 16/07/2003, © The Financial Times Limited. All Rights Reserved; Spotlight 10.2 from Decision-making, John Kay's way, *Financial Times*, 20/03/2010 (Kay, J.), © The Financial Times Limited. All Rights Reserved; Mini-Case 10.2 from GM and Chrysler steer different paths to recovery, *The Financial Times*, 14/08/2009 (Simon, B.), © The Financial Times Limited. All Rights Reserved; Activity 10.2 adapted from Samsung sows for the future with its garden of delights, *Financial Times*, 04/01/2008 (Fifield, A.), © The Financial Times Limited. All Rights Reserved; Mini-Case 11.1 from Cadbury to raise India's role, *Financial Times*, 01/06/2009, p.19 (Leahy, J.), © The Financial Times Limited. All Rights Reserved; Mini-Case 12.1 from Oil and gas has highest bribery rate, *Financial Times* (FT.com), 15/07/2012 (Chazan, G.), © The Financial Times Limited. All Rights Reserved; Activity 12.2 adapted from Ikea: against the grain, *Financial Times* (FT.com), 13/11/2012 (Milne, R.), © The Financial Times Limited. All Rights Reserved; Mini-Case 13.1 from Straight-talking, English-speaking culture brings communication problems, *Financial Times*, 09/11/2006, p.31 (Lau, J.), © The Financial Times Limited. All Rights Reserved; Activity 13.2 from Why English is de rigueur in many French boardrooms, *Financial Times*, 25/03/2008, p.8 (Braithwaite, T. and Smith, C.), © The Financial Times Limited. All Rights Reserved; Spotlight 13.3 from A matter of interpretation, *Financial Times*, 02/02/2010, p. 16 (Clegg, A.), © The Financial Times Limited. All Rights Reserved; Activity 14.1 from Germans aim for a World Cup surprise: they're fun, *Financial Times*, 22/05/2006, p.19 (Williamson, H.), © The Financial Times Limited. All Rights Reserved; Spotlight 16.1 from Global communication, *Financial Times*, 09/09/2004, p.13 (Maitland, A.), © The Financial Times Limited. All Rights Reserved; Activity 16.1 from Virtual teams: global harmony is their dream, *Financial Times*, 11/05/2005, p.8 (Murray, S.), reproduced with permission from the author; Spotlight 16.2 from Diversity in teams, *Financial Times*, 27/03/2007 (Maznevski, M.), © The Financial Times Limited. All Rights Reserved.

In some instances we have been unable to trace the owners of copyright material, and we would appreciate any information that would enable us to do so.

Part One

CULTURE AND MANAGEMENT

Introduction to Part One

Setting the scene

This introductory chapter will give an outline of the research in the field of culture and management, which in turn serves as a framework for Part One.

The concept of culture

Many experts in their fields have wracked their brains to come up with what they consider to be their concept of 'culture'. Those working in the field of cultural anthropology, alone, for example, have come up with a long list of definitions of the concept, based on their analysis of ethnological, social, psychological and linguistic data. The attempt made by Bodley (1994) to summarise these (Table I.1) gives an idea of all the facets of culture that need to be taken into account from an anthropological perspective.

Although acknowledging the multiplicity of cultures, the authors of this book consider that the fundamental aspect of culture is that it is something all humans learn in one way or another. It is not something people inherit, but rather a code of attitudes, norms and values, a way of thinking that is learnt within a social environment. Family, the social environment, school, friends, work – all these help to form this code and determine how people see themselves and the world. The national culture and the particular region which people live in also help to shape a person's cultural profile.

Although culture is reflected in individual behaviour, it is a way of thinking shared by individuals in a particular society that makes culture what it is.

Table I.1 **Diverse definitions of culture**

Topical	Culture consists of everything on a list of topics, or categories, such as social organisation, religion and economy
Historical	Culture is social heritage, or tradition, that is passed on to future generations
Behavioural	Culture is shared, learned human behaviour; a way of life
Normative	Culture is ideals, values, or rules for living
Functional	Culture is the way humans solve problems of adapting to the environment or living together
Mental	Culture is a complex of ideas, or learned habits, that inhibit impulses and distinguish people from animals
Structural	Culture consists of patterned and interrelated ideas, symbols, or behaviours
Symbolic	Culture is based on arbitrarily assigned meanings that are shared by a society

Source: Bodley, 1994: 9.

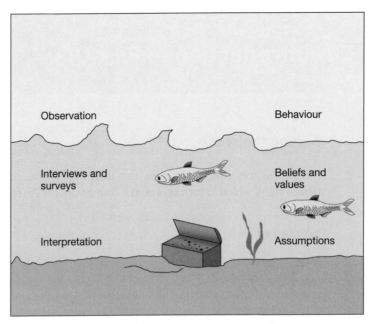

Figure I.1 **Navigating the seas of international business**
Source: adapted from Schneider and Barsoux, 2003: 21.

Culture operates on three levels

Culture operates on three levels, the first being on a level where it is observable and tangible. Here, **artefacts** and **attitudes** can be observed in terms of architecture, rituals, dress codes, making contact, contracts, language, eating and so on. Operating at a second level, culture is to do with norms and values. **Beliefs** – or **norms** – are statements of fact about the way things are. These are the cultural rules, as it were, which explain what is happening at level one and determine what is right or wrong. **Values** are to do with general preferences as to what is good or bad, how things should be. The third – and deepest level – has to do with **basic assumptions**. This level is difficult to explore and what lies there can only be construed through interpretation of what is happening at the other levels. Interpretation involves trying to explain why we act according to particular rules or in line with particular values. It is to do with the question 'Why?' and the attempt to answer it with more than just a 'Because!'

Figure I.1, based on one devised by Schneider and Barsoux (2003), gives a visual interpretation of these levels of culture and the ways they can be investigated. Exploring culture can be compared with exploring the ocean. On the surface, artefacts, rituals and behaviour can be seen. These give an idea of what may be below. The underlying norms and values can be ascertained through interviews and surveys. The assumptions lying at the very bottom can only be inferred through interpretation.

Giving dimensions to culture

Assumptions in the exploration of culture – the key dimensions – can be ascertained from the work of the anthropologists Kluckholn and Strodtbeck. In 1961, they developed a comparative model with six cultural orientations:

1. the nature of people;
2. the relationship to nature;
3. the relationship to other people;
4. the modality of human activity (doing and being);
5. the temporal focus of human activity (future, past, present);
6. the concept of space (private/public).

These cultural orientations have inspired researchers in culture and management, such as Schein, Adler, Hall, Hofstede and Trompenaars. These dimensions can help to define the cultural profile of people and discover the preferences that cultures have in relation to their environment.

Such dimensions are not to be considered as static but as being evolutionary in nature. The culture may change not only as a result of influences from outside the culture being depicted, but also from within, through changes to the orientations outlined above. Changes from within could, for example, occur as a result of the increasing multicultural nature of the society in question.

Understanding culture and management

The researchers referred to in Figure I.2 have developed models relating to this area:

- Edgar Schein examined the effect of the organisation on culture.
- Edward Hall was one of the first to study the role of communication in management.
- Nancy Adler pioneered the study of the influence of culture on organisational functions.
- Geert Hofstede and Fons Trompenaars both established dimensions to measure the impact of national culture on management.

Part One explores the effect of culture on management by examining the insights each of these researchers has developed. Work by other researchers in the same field is also discussed. Each chapter in Part One has a **preface** which introduces a theoretical issue related to the subject matter to be covered in the concepts. The approaches presented are intended not only to provide some understanding of culture and management in an international environment, but also to help develop the attitudes and behaviours desirable in a specific cross-cultural context.

The **concepts** presented in each chapter generally contain a number of spotlights and mini-cases. A **spotlight** is usually a short text that serves to illustrate a particular theme or subject developed in the concept in question. A **mini-case** is essentially a short case study taken from business life and which requires analysis by means of questions posed afterwards. Many of these cases are based on (edited) articles from the *Financial Times*. The **points of reflection** which follow the concepts are intended to consolidate the reader's learning by raising key issues arising from the subject matter presented. The **activities** which round off each chapter allow the reader to apply what has been learned from the preceding concepts to a particular scenario or extended case study. Two **final activities** will close Part One.

Part Two and Part Three are structured in a similar way and contain all the features described in the above paragraph.

Figure I.2 **Key dimensions of culture**

Source: Schneider and Barsoux, 2003: 34.

Chapter and concept overview

Chapter 1 Determinants of culture

Chapter 1 examines the very concept of culture, its facets as well as the role of norms and values. The levels at which culture operates – from family through organisation to society – are also described. Organisational culture as a 'metaphor' is briefly explored.

The chapter is divided into a preface and two concepts:

● **Preface:** organisational culture and ethnography.

● **Concept 1.1 Facets of culture.** After giving a short definition of the word 'culture' and its various 'layers', the concept will analyse the meaning of value systems for societies.

● **Concept 1.2 Levels of cultures.** This concept considers the levels of cultures ranging from national to organisational level and examines those elements that define them.

Chapter 2 Dimensions of culture: Hofstede and GLOBE

Chapter 2 explores cultural dimensions in the business context with particular reference to research by Geert Hofstede and GLOBE (Global Leadership and Organizational Behaviour Effectiveness), an ongoing research project. It also puts forward criticisms concerning the cultural dimension construct, particularly that devised by Hofstede.

The chapter is divided into a preface and two concepts:

- **Preface:** a model from social anthropology.

- **Concept 2.1 Hofstede's national cultural dimensions.** The five dimensions developed by Hofstede are explained, and the extremes of each characterised in terms of management and business. The criticisms made about Hofstede's research method as well as about the characterisation of national cultures are also outlined.

- **Concept 2.2 Cultural dimensions according to GLOBE.** The nine cultural practice dimensions devised by the GLOBE project are reviewed. A brief exploration of societal cultures practices ('As Is') and values ('Should Be') exemplifies how these values and practices affect organisational culture on all nine dimensions of organisational cultural practice.

Chapter 3 Business cultures in the Western world

This chapter, together with Chapter 4, gives an overview of business cultures in the world. The culture clusters as devised by GLOBE and presented in Chapter 2 are the starting point.

The chapter is divided into a preface and two concepts:

- **Preface:** two approaches to the concept of multiculturalism.

- **Concept 3.1 European cultures.** Elements in particular countries belonging to the European clusters are highlighted. One further country is included in this concept – Turkey. European business cultures are examined in cluster terms, and some similarities and differences between component countries noted. Attention has been paid to Central and East European emergent economies, particularly to Russia, the only BRICS country in Europe.

- **Concept 3.2 American and Australasian cultures.** This concept focuses on countries to which European cultures were 'exported' along with new immigrants. The countries covered include those in North America, Latin America, particularly Brazil (a BRICS country) and Australasia.

Chapter 4 Business cultures in Asia, Africa and the Middle East

The chapter will cover those clusters which were not covered in Chapter 3. The countries in these clusters are examined in terms of certain similarities that set them apart from Western business cultures. Attention is paid to three of these countries – China, India and South Africa – which share similarities with the clusters described in Chapter 3 while belonging to the BRICS group.

The chapter is divided into a preface and two concepts:

- **Preface:** two different cognitive approaches to management.

- **Concept 4.1 Asian cultures.** Two clusters are considered in Asia, the one influenced by Confucianism, the other – in Southern Asia – influenced by Hinduism. The significant role of the Chinese and Indian diasporas in business is explained.

- **Concept 4.2 African and Middle East cultures.** The importance of tribal identification among sub-Sahara countries in Africa is touched upon, together with the cultural diversity of one economically important country, South Africa, the newest BRICS country. Finally, an outline is given of the cultural elements shared by Arab countries in the Middle East.

Chapter 5 Cultural dimensions and dilemmas

Chapter 5 explores further cultural dimensions, particularly those from the work of Fons Trompenaars, and highlights the dilemmas these raise in management decision-making. The dilemma of motivation is addressed in the preface. Furthermore, the chapter deals with the issue of connecting people and organisations within a culture of innovation,

The chapter is divided into a preface and two concepts:

- **Preface:** motivation – needs and values.
- **Concept 5.1 Value orientations and dimensions.** This concept returns to the sources that inspired researchers in cross-cultural management. Particular attention is given to the Trompenaars' dimensions, which can be useful for the analysis of cultural differences in management. Hofstede's review of these dimensions is outlined, together with the reaction given by Hampden-Turner and Trompenaars to Hofstede's comments.
- **Concept 5.2 Reconciling cultural dilemmas.** This concept explains the method devised by Trompenaars and Hampden-Turner for finding a way to resolve dilemmas when doing business with different cultures.

Chapter 6 Culture and styles of management

This chapter proposes value orientations drawn from those presented in Chapters 1 to 5, as well as other value orientations taken from the work of Edward Hall, among others.

The chapter is divided into a preface and two concepts:

- **Preface:** the conceptualisation of culture – a static or dynamic approach.
- **Concept 6.1 Management tasks and cultural values.** This concept presents a model of culture based on cultural value orientations and examines their influence on managerial activities. This model is later used in the chapter in an activity during which readers can draw up their own cultural profile. Using this profile, readers are asked to outline strategies to enable them to operate effectively in a particular country.
- **Concept 6.2 Other views on cultural values.** This concept briefly examines other theories – which are relevant to managers who are involved in globalisation – where cultural values are regarded as being subject to change through interaction with other cultures. The concept then considers the idea that culture is not a set of values but the meaning which we as individuals attach to our environment.

Final activities

Part One ends with two extra final activities:

1. **The Alizee case.** Readers are asked to analyse the results of an investigation into online behaviour among airline consumers – from Brazil, Malaysia and the USA – in which the GLOBE cultural dimensions have been applied.
2. **The Galderma case.** Readers are asked to assess the research design of a research paper investigating the ways in which French, German and British managers in an international company cope with cultural differences when they are working together.

What you will gain

After working through Part One, you will gain more insight into:

● the link between culture and management;
● the effect of culture on the management of business;
● models and methods for analysing cross-cultural contexts;
● ways to develop cross-cultural effectiveness.

References

Bodley, J.H. (1994) *Cultural Anthropology: Tribes, States and the Global System*, Mountain View, CA: Mayfield.

Kluckholn, F. and Strodtbeck, F. (1961) *Variations in Value Orientations*, Evanston, IL: Peterson Row.

Schneider, S.C. and Barsoux, J.L. (2003) *Managing Across Cultures*, 2nd edition, Harlow: FT Prentice Hall.

Chapter 1

Determinants of culture

Culture is an integral part of all human societies. With the advent of globalisation, the notion of culture has taken on a broader meaning and has come to be an important element of organisations. These two aspects of culture will be developed in this chapter. Organisational culture as a 'metaphor' is also briefly explored.

Concept 1.1 will explore the notion of culture in society, while Concept 1.2 will consider the influence of culture on socio-economic realities such as the management of companies.

Learning outcomes

After reading this chapter, you will gain an understanding of:

- The concept of culture and the role of norms and values in determining culture.
- The relationship between culture, organisations and management.
- The concept of culture at various levels, both national and organisational.
- The role of ethnography in organisational research.

Preface: organisational culture and ethnography

As mentioned in the Introduction to Part One, there are different levels of culture and different methods used to explore and measure culture. The foundation of some of these methods was inspired by cultural anthropology – the study of the progress of human society and culture – which was developed in the first part of the twentieth century by renowned anthropologists. For their research, they used ethnographic (descriptive) data from various pre-industrial and small-size societies. The ethnography approach necessitates a continuous observation of a particular social group in order to understand the culture of this group from inside. The approach can explain norms and values and can provide understanding of the behaviour of the group. Nonetheless, the most difficult part remains the interpretation of these observations (Edgar and Sedgwick, 2002).

Recently, there has been a renewal in the field of anthropological research focusing on the organisation as subject of investigation. In the domain of organisational research, the ethnographic method is recognised as useful for managerial and organisational studies (Watson, 2012), such as the analysis of organisations through metaphors, which can help our understanding of organisational meaning (Tietze *et al.*, 2003). So, what implications does this have for exploring an organisational culture?

In his article, 'Making organizational ethnography' (2012), Watson argues that ethnography is more than a research method. He sees it more as a social science genre than as a social science method. This viewpoint provides researchers studying organisations with an important advantage since it allows them to adopt other methods – such as statistics and surveys – besides the necessary observation work inherent to ethnography.

To create organisational ethnographies successfully, it is essential to bear in mind that the notion of a 'cultural whole' is crucial in all ethnographic work and that organisations are an element of society. Watson (2012) explained this idea by giving an example of a student telling her tutor about the amazing organisational culture she had observed in a particular hotel in America. By doing so, she had fallen into the trap of seeing the hotel whose culture she had studied as unique. The tutor corrected her by explaining that most of the cultural characteristics she had observed were not typical for that hotel but exemplary for the entire hotel sector. Therefore, to appreciate fully the culture in a particular organisation, it is necessary to move the analysis up a level, to examine the sector of which the organisation is a part and the nation or society where it is situated.

Culture as organisational metaphor

Organisational culture can also be explored through metaphor. But, what does metaphor mean? Etymologically, the meaning of the term derives from the Greek – '(to) transfer or carry over' (Edgar and Sedgwick, 2002: 234). Although difficult to define, we can say that metaphor is a part of the human conceptual system; its function at the semantic (linguistic) and cognitive level is to help us understand through comparison. Metaphors are cultural and require interpretation, so the language and culture of speakers shape the way metaphors are constructed or decoded. For example, 'Time is money' is a most powerful metaphor in the Western world: paid work is associated with the time needed to do it, and this time can be quantified – people are paid by the hour, week, month, and so on (Tietze *et al.*, 2003).

Using Morgan's work, 'Images of organization' (1986), Tietze *et al.* (2003) compiled a summary of common metaphors used to describe organizations – their features and applications, values and weaknesses. Examples of such metaphors for organisations ('culture', 'organism', 'brain' and 'political system') are given in Table 1.1, below.

Table 1.1 **Common metaphors for organisations**

Metaphor	Features; applications	Value	Weaknesses
Culture	National cultures; corporate culture and subcultures; meaning systems; shared beliefs and values, norms and rule; enacting shared realities; organisational change; corporate culture writers	Quest for meaning	Underplays role of fragmentation, ambiguity and complexity of cultural dynamics; leads to mechanistic culture management
Organism	Open system; changeable; adaptation; relationship with environment; organisational needs; good fit; human relations approach; contingency thinking	Natural selection	Ascribes agency to the environment; ignores the role of conflict
Brain	Self-organisation and creative action; double-loop learning; learning throughout the organisation; holographic; decision-making; cybernetics; learning organisation	Learning	Overlooks realities of power and control; overlooks role of inertia as based on existing beliefs
Political system	Limited resources; conflicting interests; distribution of power; wheeling and dealing; negotiations; analysis of power and conflict; sources of power	Distribution of power	Can generate cynicism and mistrust; pursuit of personal interest; can overstate power of individuals

Source: adapted from Tietze *et al.*, 2003: 39.

Researchers or managers who make use of the metaphor approach work conceptually. When they apply this conceptual frame to organisations, they not only facilitate insight but also create new meanings and offer new perspectives. Ethnography seems the most appropriate methodology to use for this approach, because the study is performed in the organisation itself from a participant observer point of view. This provides a way of accessing organisational meaning systems.

Concept 1.1 Facets of culture

According to Fleury (2002), a society is an organised group of individuals who share functional relations. The complexity of present-day societies is increasing the roles for an individual and is, at the same time, diversifying the ways these roles can be interpreted. These roles are determined by culture. Each society defines its own norms and the ways in which they are realised. It can be said, therefore, that culture is a structure that gives form to behaviour and fixes the framework of exchanges between the people of this group. The function of culture is integration, adaptation, communication and expression. Societies are organised politically into nations, but within this national unity subcultures may exist with specific cultural characteristics. These groups use the society in which they are embedded as their framework of reference, and share their nationality, language and institutions, while being delineated by their socio-economic, historic or geographic characteristics.

What does culture really mean?

One can never use the word 'culture' without being obliged to give a range of definitions that contradict each other! Even if this term had only one meaning, irrespective of whether it was aesthetic, philosophical, national, organisational or managerial, it would only be a form of individual or collective representation. Genelot (1998: 195) stresses that 'men are products of their culture: their representations, their visions of what is good and what is wrong, their behaviour at work, their concepts of organisations are the fruit of the representations carried by their ancestors'. Can one state, therefore, that a change of culture would only be a change in representations? Anthropologists, sociologists, historians and philosophers have all put forward their definitions, but none of them seems to be sufficiently precise or inclusive.

Rather than look for an exact definition, it may be preferable to look for a meaning that is blurred but which somehow addresses the rather abstract idea of culture. Hofstede (1980: 25) refers to culture as 'the collective programming of the mind which distinguishes the members of one human group from another'. When elaborating on his definition, he says: 'Culture, in this sense, includes systems of values; and values are among the building blocks of culture.' This definition is frequently referred to in cross-cultural literature, probably because it is blurry enough to encompass other definitions, but sharp enough to reflect key elements of a culture.

Consider the implications of Hofstede's definition. Collective programming of the mind implies that members of a group are programmed by that group to perceive the world in a certain way, themselves and others included. In other words, the group shares meanings that hold them together. Furthermore, this definition implies that the group's culture is somehow learned rather than being innate. It is passed down from generation to generation and is the basis of the socialisation process in childhood when the norms of behaviour and the values on which these norms are based are learned. Finally, culture is to be seen as relative: no cultural group is 'better' in any absolute sense. There is no cultural standard whereby one group's perception of the world is intrinsically superior to another's.

The building blocks referred to earlier need to be examined more closely: the values that cultural groupings share and the resulting norms of behaviour.

Norms and values

Each culture can be seen as having three layers. The *first*, outer layer is the 'behavioural' or 'explicit' level. It is what you notice immediately when you go abroad for the first time: the language, the food, the architecture, the houses, the buildings and so on. But it is also the communication style: Latin cultures, for example, use exuberant body language and facial expressions. Other, less exuberant cultures, such as those in Nordic Europe consider this sort of behaviour to be 'over the top', but it is really just a matter of comparing the communication styles of one culture with those of another.

The *second* layer contains the 'norms and values'. Every culture has its own system of norms and values. Together, these form the national characteristics of a culture, and act as its framework of reference. Although norms and values are generally presented as a unit, a distinction must be made between the two. Norms are the rules of a society, determining what is good or bad with regard to behaviour. People are allowed, however, a certain individual freedom of choice between what 'you should always do' and what 'you should never do'. Norms are the written and unwritten rules of a society. Values are what is considered important or unimportant, beautiful or not beautiful, right or wrong. A value is something experienced inwardly and which is not up for discussion. The preference or aversion it contains is taken for granted by its bearers.

The *third* and innermost layer, and which lies at the core of 'culture' contains its assumptions and beliefs. These are difficult to describe or explain. When you are asked to justify why you do this or say that, the answer is often: 'I don't know'. Why, for example, do people eat with a knife and fork or with chopsticks? Well, that's the way people eat . . .

The system of values and norms not only varies from culture to culture, but also from one part of a society to another. Not every individual 'operates' from the same basis, nor do subcultures within a society. Moreover, a culture is never static, because norms and values are always changing. However, since every culture is so deep-rooted, the changes are never sudden or extreme and a certain constancy is maintained.

Sociologists who have compared the value systems of countries in terms of the way in which norms and values have developed in society, have concluded that there are four categories (Ruano-Borbalan, 2002: 339):

1. Traditional society, in which religion plays an important role [. . .] large families are encouraged, conformity is rewarded and individualism rejected. This is, for example, the case in many Arab countries.
2. Rational society, in which the interests of the individual come first, birth control is encouraged and the authority of the state is recognized. Germany [. . .] is a typical example.

3. A society in which survival is the primary concern, where the people are not happy and rather intolerant, where equality between the sexes has little chance [...] where materialism is predominant [...] This is often the situation in ex-communist countries.

4. Post-modern society [...] tolerant and democratic, such as those in Scandinavia and the Netherlands.

Politics and norms and values

The influence of politics on norms and values is obvious when it comes to bringing global unity to humanitarian norms and values. These are formally laid down in the 'Universal Declaration of Human Rights'. In a number of countries, however, politics also has a say in education, dress, manners and many other aspects of daily life. Recent reports from Iran, for example, show the degree of political interference in people's lives there. Students from Iranian universities heavily criticised their highest political leaders and the government's vice squad for persistently prescribing how Iranians should dress, how they should do their hair and how they should enjoy themselves.

Conversely, there are degrees of acceptance with regard to what politicians in each country may or may not do; what constitutes a scandal – and what does not. In Nordic Europe, for example, it is acknowledged that there is corruption in political life now and again, but in no way is it regarded as acceptable. If caught out, a politician must resign. In southern Europe, however, involvement in a corruption scandal does not necessarily mean the end of a politician's career. A politician may be involved for several years in corruption proceedings but stay in his/her post, despite being investigated for embezzlement for example. In Surinam, where corruption is regarded as an unavoidable evil, certain limits are nevertheless placed on wayward behaviour. Anyone who attempts to launch a coup d'état there, for example, will be severely punished.

The freedoms a politician may enjoy in his/her private life are also different according to country. When an affair came to light between a US president and an intern working in the White House, there was a call for the president to be impeached because he had lied about his relationship with the intern during a formal investigation. The impeachment process stumbled in the Senate and the president was allowed to complete his term of office. In France, however, sex scandals of this nature do not happen. 'Insiders' may have been aware of the double life being led by their country's president (an illegitimate daughter of his eventually emerged at his funeral) but, at the time, his extramarital relationship was regarded as a private matter. Homosexual politicians may not be accepted in many countries, but in the Netherlands, for example, a country where marriage between homosexuals is allowed by law, their sexual orientation is again regarded as a private matter.

Where a certain degree of economic, political and social integration is taking place between countries, can one talk of a movement towards a shared system of norms and values? Referring to the possibility of European countries sharing such a system, the French philosopher Edgar Morin (1987), declared that the creation of a European culture had nothing to do with dominant basic ideas (such as Christianity, humanism, rationalism, or science). It had to do instead with the opposition between ideas. Put another way, what is important in the forming process of European culture is the meeting of diversity, of opposite poles, the complementarity of ideas. This is what Morin calls 'dialogique': the union of two forms of logic, of two different principles, without their duality being lost. The association of contradictory terms or concepts can form one complex phenomenon.

British phone-hacking inquiry calls for press regulation with force of law

By Robert Budden, Ben Fenton and Kiran Stacey

An inquiry into the culture and ethics of the British press called for sweeping new regulation enshrined in law, reigniting a visceral battle between proponents of free speech and defenders of the individual right to privacy.

Concluding a nine-month investigation sparked by a scandal over the hacking of thousands of mobile phones by journalists, Lord Justice Leveson said that the government should introduce legislation to put the regulation of the press on a statutory footing.

His report, which rejected an industry proposal for stronger self-regulation, excoriated the press and politicians for fawning on them, and divided the political establishment.

While welcoming the call to tighten regulation of the UK's rumbustious press, David Cameron, prime minister, refused to back the proposal to underpin the system with new laws. Speaking to the House of Commons yesterday, two hours after the publication of the Leveson report, he said that he had 'serious concerns and misgivings' about the proposal.

'For the first time we will have crossed the Rubicon of writing elements of press regulation into the law of the land. We should think very, very carefully before crossing this line.' He added: 'I'm not convinced at this stage that statute is required to achieve Lord Justice Leveson's recommendations.'

The report called for a new independent self-regulating regime for the press, but backed by statutory measures that would incorporate an arbitration body for quick resolution of complaints.

Nick Clegg, deputy PM and leader of the Liberal Democrats, the junior partner in the UK's coalition government, backed his call for a statutory underpinning. 'A free press does not mean a press that is free to bully innocent people or free to abuse grieving families', he told MPs.

The report had harsh words for the fawning behaviour of some politicians who made themselves 'vulnerable to influences [by editors and proprietors of the media] which are neither known about nor transparent'. He also condemned the behaviour of an 'outrageous' element of the newspaper industry acting in the name of freedom of the press. Some papers had been reckless about facts and appeared to reject complaints, he said.

[. . .]

Mr Cameron commissioned the Leveson inquiry after a series of scandals in which journalists intruded into the privacy of celebrities and victims of crime, notably the hacking of the phone of Milly Dowler, a 13-year-old abducted and murdered in 2002.

Source: adapted from 'British phone-hacking inquiry calls for press regulation with force of law', *Financial Times* newspaper, 30/11/2012 (Budden, R., Fenton, B. and Stacey, K.), Copyright The Financial Times Limited 2012.

He takes mankind as an example: a human is both entirely determined biologically as well as culturally. This 'dialogique' can be found in every culture, but is particularly intensive within the European culture where there is an enormous amount of interaction and interference within areas to do with values, e.g. religion/rationality, mythical thought/critical thought, and humanism/science.

Cultural assumptions in management

After social norms and values comes the third layer of culture: assumptions. This layer is also identified by Schein. His work is a useful guide in the examination of cultural assumptions in a managerial context, and offers insights into the question of managing relationships. He defines culture as:

> a set of basic assumptions – shared solutions to universal problems of external adaptation (how to survive) and internal integration (how to stay together) – which have evolved over time and are handed down from one generation to the next.
>
> Schein, 2004: 14

In terms of external adaptation, this means, for example, asking: to what extent does management within a culture assume that it can control nature or to what extent is it controlled by nature? This question is allied to that of the nature of human activity: is doing more important than being, acting more important than reflecting? In terms of internal integration, this means asking a question such as: 'Are humans basically assumed to be good or evil', or trying to determine whether relationships at work are more important than the task itself.

The questions raised by Schein on cultural assumptions of organisations imply that management in an international context has not only to take account of the norms and values of the specific culture of a company, but also of its cultural assumptions.

Concept 1.2 Levels of cultures

According to Schein (1999), a culture starts developing in a context where a group of people have a shared experience. Members of a family, for example, share a life together and develop a certain togetherness through undergoing experiences inside and outside the home. Small groups without blood relations can develop the same closeness through sharing a pastime, a hobby or occupation; the experience they share may be rich enough to allow a culture to be formed.

In a business context, culture can develop at different levels – within a department or at the various ranks of a hierarchy. A company or organisation can develop its own culture, provided that it has what Schein calls 'sufficient shared history' (1999). This applies also for a collection of companies within a particular business or sector, or for organisations in, say, the public sector. This collective experience can be related to regions of a country, or regions across countries, or a grouping of nations themselves when they share a common experience, be it language, religion, ethnic origins or a shared historical experience in their development. In this concept we will try to distinguish levels at which cultures develop.

Culture and nation

When cross-cultural matters are under discussion, the terms 'culture' and 'nation' should be carefully distinguished, as Tayeb (2003) makes clear. She takes as an example the Kurds. Although they are a people with a distinctive cultural identity, they nevertheless live in three nation states – Turkey, Iraq and Iran. This is an obvious example of one culture straddling the political boundaries of two or more nation states.

This culture/nation distinction can, as Tayeb points out, have a bearing on the way organisations operate. If 'culture' is defined as a set of historically evolved, learned and shared values, attitudes and meanings, then this has an influence on organisations at both macro and micro level.

At the macro level, the nation, in terms of its laws and economic institutions, must be taken into account by organisations going about their business. They have to consider the measures taken by the state to protect its interests and those of its inhabitants. These can range from specific employment laws and safety legislation to general economic and social policies. These macro-level considerations are not only subject to change through political changes in government, but also through the desire of the nation's rulers to share legislation at social and economic level with other nations within some kind of association.

At the micro level, the organisation is influenced by cultural elements relating to employer–employee relationships and to behaviour among employees. Those wishing to introduce any changes with a view to improving management effectiveness or increasing productivity must take account of these elements when implementing such changes.

National culture

Although cultural make-up has many facets reflecting experience in life and membership of different groupings at different times in various environments, there is, as Tayeb (2003: 13) says, 'a constant thread [. . .] through our lives which makes us distinguishable from others, especially those in other countries: this thread is our national culture'. This national culture may be heterogeneous in nature, but it will contain enough elements which together enable a national culture to be created.

Tayeb (2003) gives a list of these elements and considers their effect at both micro and macro level. She starts with two elements that contribute to the building of a nation and the creation of a national culture:

- the physical environment;
- the history the nation has undergone.

She then refers to 'institutions' that contribute to the establishment of a national culture:

a) *Family.* The basic social unit where 'acculturation' takes place, where the culture of a particular environment is instilled in a human from infancy.

b) *Religion.* Religious beliefs can have a significant effect on a person's view of the world. This does not mean that people need to 'believe', but religion has helped in all sorts of direct and indirect ways to shape the environment in which people live.

c) *Education.* The value system on which education is based and the choices it makes in terms of the curriculum both help in the formation of a culture, particularly where educational institutions are well developed. At the micro level, the teaching approach used and the manner of learning can also affect future learning. This, in turn, can determine the quality and versatility of human resources in the labour market.

d) *Mass communication media.* Tayeb pays particular attention to the effect of recent advances in communication on the development of culture. The ever increasing presence of mass media has given a new meaning to shared experience: newspapers, magazines, television and radio, 'bring people closer together irrespective of their geographical locations, but also in terms of spreading values, attitudes, tastes, meanings and vocabulary – in short, culture' (Tayeb, 2003: 20). She does not regard this, however, as being a threat to the distinctive cultural characteristics of a nation. Instead, the mass media have created a new common dimension in which people can share experiences if they choose to.

e) *The multinational company.* This is a powerful culture-building institution, whose products and services can influence the way people live, whose operations can affect how and where they work. However, the multinational is also influenced by the preferences at national level with regard to product taste and form and the promotion of its goods and services.

Organisational culture

Edgar Schein (1999) refers to the *power* of culture on account of the extent to which it determines our behaviour individually and collectively. In organisational terms, he remarks on how cultural elements affect the way strategy is determined, goals are established and how the organisation operates. Furthermore, the key personnel involved are influenced by their own cultural backgrounds and shared experience since these have helped shape their own values and perceptions.

Schein (1990: 111) develops his definition of culture when defining organisational culture:

(a) a pattern of basic assumptions, (b) invented, discovered, or developed by a given group, (c) as it learns to cope with its problems of external adaptation and internal integration, (d) that has worked well enough to be considered valid and, therefore (e) is to be taught to new members as the (f) correct way to perceive, think, and feel in relation to chosen problems.

Drawing on this definition, we can say that organisational culture is the acceptance – in a tacit or formal way – of norms of specific behaviour by the members of an organisation.

Corporate culture

The term 'corporate culture' takes the question of organisational culture a step further. As Meschi and Roger (1994) point out, if an organisation develops into a multinational conglomerate, the culture at headquarters may influence that of subsidiaries abroad. In the same way, a firm involved in a joint venture with a company from another country may well find that the presence of the 'foreign' partners influences the underlying culture of the

SPOTLIGHT 1.2

Organisational cross-cultural challenges

Setting up joint ventures between East and West European companies has involved a number of cross-cultural challenges. A study made on joint ventures between the Netherlands, the Slovak Republic and Bulgaria revealed some key problems in the following areas:

1. Mutual support climate

When it comes, for example, to showing concern for colleagues, as well as offering mutual support and understanding, both in solving work and non-work problems, companies in the Slovak Republic appear to be much less supportive than those in Bulgaria and the Netherlands.

2. Innovative climate

The degree to which employees consider their organisation as being innovative is much higher among the Bulgarians and the Dutch than among the Slovakians. Slovak companies are considered to be less flexible, innovative and market-oriented than their Bulgarian or Dutch equivalents. Moreover, they are seen as less open to (self-) criticism and less likely to take risks.

3. Goal-directed climate

Bulgarian employees consider their companies to be particularly goal-directed, more so than their Slovak and Dutch counterparts. This is apparent in the way Bulgarian companies set clear goals, carefully measure the performance of the company and its employees, as well as monitor the efficient and effective use of materials.

The main conclusion of the study is that, to ensure the success of a joint venture between East and West European companies, the partners need to establish mutual trust as well as develop respect for their mutual differences.

Source: extract (adapted) from: Browaeys and Göbbels, 1999: 243–251.

firm. What evolves over time in terms of 'corporate culture' can have as its basis the 'original' organisational culture, or the national/regional culture – or a combination of the two.

The extent of the influence of corporate culture is disputed among experts in the field. Some regard a clearly defined corporate culture as key to a (multi)national company's success. Others consider a flexible culture to be the key to success because it can adapt to, and respond more effectively to, a local/national environment.

Although it is useful to know where the countries in question lie on the dimensions of national culture when working with other cultures, there are other factors at play, particularly the culture of the company itself. This is determined not just by external cultural factors such as the national and regional cultures, but also by internal cultural factors. The extent of cultural control, through company goals, manuals, instructions and the presence of long-standing employees, is important.

MINI-CASE 1.1

Tata

The values which a company adheres to are often explicitly stated in some form of *mission statement*, often to be found in its annual report.

Established as a trading company in Mumbai, India, in 1868, the Tata group has developed into a major multinational. It operates worldwide (Africa, Asia, Europe, the Americas) in a number of sectors, including steel manufacturing, IT, automobile production and financial services.

Examine the statements below, taken from the website of the Tata group – see source below – which describes the purpose and values of the Tata group.

Purpose

At the Tata group we are committed to improving the quality of life of the communities we serve. We do this by striving for leadership and global competitiveness in the business sectors in which we operate. Our practice of returning to society what we earn evokes trust among consumers, employees, shareholders and the community. We are committed to protecting this heritage of leadership with trust through the manner in which we conduct our business.

Core values

Tata has always been values-driven. These values continue to direct the growth and business of Tata companies. The five core Tata values underpinning the way we do business are:

- Integrity: we must conduct our business fairly, with honesty and transparency. Everything we do must stand the test of public scrutiny.
- Understanding: we must be caring, show respect, compassion and humanity for our colleagues and customers around the world, and always work for the benefit of the communities we serve.
- Excellence: we must constantly strive to achieve the highest possible standards in our day-to-day work and in the quality of the goods and services we provide.
- Unity: we must work cohesively with our colleagues across the group and with our customers and partners around the world, building strong relationships based on tolerance, understanding and mutual cooperation.
- Responsibility: we must continue to be responsible, sensitive to the countries, communities and environments in which we work, always ensuring that what comes from the people goes back to the people many times over.

Source: http://www.tata.com/aboutus/articles/inside.aspx?artid=CKdRrD5ZDV4 (extract), accessed 12/12/2012.

Questions

1. Which elements of the corporate culture of Tata group can you distinguish that relate to national culture (subsidiaries) and organisational culture (as defined by Schein)?

2. Look at another corporate website, for example Shell (www.shell.com). Click on 'About Shell', then 'who we are' to discover the company's purpose and values. Then, answer the above question, but in this case for Shell.

Professional culture

The nature of the line of business the company is in may have an important influence on the corporate culture as well as on the professional culture attached to key positions within the organisation. Professional culture is essentially to do with the set of values shared by people working together professionally. Schein (1996: 237) talks of three professional cultures in management. First, there are the 'operators' who are directly involved in production of goods or the provision of services. Second, there are the 'engineers', the people who design and monitor the technology behind the production and/or provision of services. Those who share this culture tend to show a preference for solutions where systems rather than people are involved. Third, there are the 'executives', the senior managers who share tacit assumptions regarding 'the daily realities of their status and role'.

The question of how these professional cultures co-exist within an organisation pre-occupies many scholars. How do the executives handle the 'operators' and 'engineers'? How best to manage conflict constructively? To what extent is delegation and empowerment desirable? What styles of management are appropriate?

Culture and management

At the basis of all the cultures mentioned lies the individual's culture. It is individuals who ultimately form the culture of an organisation. The values they embody as members of an organisation are formed partially through the family, social and national environment, and partially through the professional, organisational and corporate culture.

It is up to management to take into account the diversity of people in an organisation and to manage their cultural differences. In an international context, however, what does cross-cultural management mean?

Nancy Adler (2002: 11) gives a definition of what cross-cultural management is about:

> Cross-cultural management explains the behavior of people in organizations around the world and shows people how to work in organizations with employees and client populations from many different cultures. Cross-cultural management *describes* organizational behavior within countries and cultures; *compares* organizational behavior across countries and cultures; and, perhaps most important, seeks to understand and improve the *interaction* of co-workers, managers, executives, clients, suppliers, and alliance partners from countries and cultures around the world.

From another perspective, more oriented to the management tasks than the cultural differences, cross-cultural management can be defined as follows:

> The core task of cross-cultural management is to facilitate and direct synergistic action and learning at interfaces where knowledge, values and experience are transferred into multi-cultural domains of implementation.
>
> (Holden, 2002: 59)

In any case, the importance of cross-cultural management is evident in a world where all kinds of co-operation between companies in many countries is on the increase. Whether these are mergers, takeovers, partnerships or strategic alliances, they all need to be analysed in cultural terms, not only to determine where benefit can be gained, but also where difficulties may be encountered when companies are working together.

This chapter has given a brief overview of the levels at which culture operates. These will be dealt with in more detail in Chapter 2, particularly in Concept 2.2, which examines the influence of national culture on organisational culture. The question of business culture will be addressed in Chapters 3 and 4.

Conclusion

Chapter 1 has shown how difficult it is to give a definition of the word 'culture'. Apart from the multitude of definitions, culture can also be considered at various levels, the deepest of which, according to Edgar Schein contains 'assumptions'. This level, according to Schein, can also be found in the culture of an organisation.

This chapter also shows that the individuals in a group form a culture that can be national, organisational or professional. This implies that cross-cultural management has to take into account all of these contexts, not only within organisations, but also in relations with companies of different countries.

Points for reflection

1. The word 'culture' is used in many ways, such as when people talk about 'national culture', 'organisational culture', 'political culture' or 'youth culture'.

   In which ways do the meanings of culture differ?

2. Managing an organisation also involves managing human resources. These resources are not static: employees can move to another position, or leave an organisation, or be replaced. Ideally, any newcomers will adapt to the culture of the company or at least respect it.

   Give your comments on the statement given above. Then answer the question: Can a corporate culture be managed? If so, explain what needs to be done for it to be managed. If you believe it cannot be managed, explain why.

Further reading

Schneider, S.C. and Barsoux, J.-L. (2003) *Managing Across Cultures*, Harlow: Pearson Education, FT Prentice Hall. This book develops understanding of how culture influences management practice and also guides teams and organisations as to how to be more effective in international business. Theoretical foundations are linked to practical applications.

Tietze, S., Cohen, L. and Musson, G. (2003) *Understanding Organizations through Language*, London: Sage. The authors' starting point is that understanding how language works is indispensable when it comes to understanding organisational processes. They explain how language shapes social realities before showing how metaphors, narratives and discourse can give meaning to organisations. They go on to examine the connection between language and culture, particularly the issue of meaning making in different cultural contexts.

References

Adler, N.J. (2002) *International Dimensions of Organizational Behavior*, 4th edition, Ohio: South-Western, Thomson Learning.

Browaeys, M.-J. and Göbbels, M. (1999) 'Impact of national business cultures on East and West joint ventures', in Knapp, K., Kappel, B.E., Eubet Kasper, K. and Salo-Lee, L. (eds), *Meeting the Intercultural Challenge*, Berlin: Verlag Wissenschaft & Praxis: 243–251.

Edgar, A. and Sedgwick, P. (eds) (2002) *Cultural Theory, The Key Concepts*, London/New York: Routledge.

Fleury, J. (2002) *La culture*, Paris: Editions Bréa.

Genelot, D. (1998) *Manager dans la complexité*, Paris: INSEP Editions.

Hofstede, G. (1980) *Culture's Consequences,* London: Sage.

Holden, N.J. (2002) *Cross-Cultural Management,* Harlow: Financial Times/Prentice Hall.

Laurent, A. (1983) 'The cultural diversity of western conceptions of management', *International Studies of Management and Organization,* 13(1–2): 75–96.

Meschi, P.-X. and Roger, A. (1994) 'Cultural context and social effectiveness in international joint-ventures', *Management International Review,* 34(3): 197–215.

Morgan, G. (1986) *Images of organization,* quoted by Tietze, S., Cohen, L. and Musson, G. (2003) *Understanding Organizations through Language,* London: Sage.

Morin, E. (1987) *Penser l'Europe,* Paris: Gallimard.

Ruano-Borbalan, J.-C. (2002) 'Valeurs et cultures: allons-nous devenir post-modernes?' in Journet, N. (ed.), *La culture,* Auxerre: Sciences Humaines Editions: 335–342.

Schein, E.H. (1990) 'Organizational culture', *American Psychologist,* 42(2): 109–119.

Schein, E.H. (1996) 'Culture: the missing concept in organization studies', *Administrative Science Quarterly,* 41(2): 229–240.

Schein, E.H. (1999) *The Corporate Culture Survival Guide,* San Francisco, CA: Jossey-Bass.

Schein, E.H. (2004) *Organizational Culture and Leadership,* 3rd edition, San Francisco, CA: Jossey-Bass.

Schneider, S.C. and Barsoux, J.-L. (2003) *Managing Across Cultures,* Harlow: Pearson Education: FT Prentice Hall.

Tayeb, M. (2003) *International Management,* Harlow: Pearson Education.

Tietze, S., Cohen, L. and Musson, G. (2003) *Understanding Organizations through Language,* London: Sage.

Watson, T.J. (2012) 'Making organizational ethnography', *Journal of Organizational Ethnography,* 1(1): 15–22.

Examining an organisational culture in context

This activity focuses on the John Lewis Partnership. The 81,000 partners of this British company own John Lewis department stores and Waitrose supermarkets. The partnership has a constitution which defines the principles and rules of the company.

The first principle stated in the constitution has to do with the purpose of the company:

> The Partnership's ultimate purpose is the happiness of all its members, through their worthwhile and satisfying employment in a successful business. Because the Partnership is owned in trust for its members, they share the responsibilities of ownership as well as its rewards – profit, knowledge and power.
>
> Source: http://www.johnlewispartnership.co.uk/about/our-constitution.html, accessed 31/12/2012.

The newspaper article below describes the nature of the company in more detail, one which could be a model for organisational change.

Read the article and respond to the questions which follow it.

A rather civil partnership

By Andrew Hill

For nearly 150 years, John Lewis has had a shop on London's Oxford Street. Customer 'footfall' is steady. The department store group's carefully nurtured and increasingly well-marketed reputation for dependable quality and value for money, from picnic ware in the basement up to personalised stationery on the fifth floor, remains intact even as other UK retailers are failing.

But while the group's commercial success and enduring hold on middle-class Middle Britain are clear, the retailer also has a growing – and somewhat unlikely – role as a political talisman. Like unhappy couples seeking to make the home they cannot afford to leave more liveable, UK politicians are drawn to the John Lewis Partnership – owned by its staff and managed on democratic principles – as a model for economic and organizational reform.

From the US, where California has just enshrined in law new forms of socially aware 'flexible purpose' and 'benefit' corporations, to Spain, where the UN year of the co-operative has refocused attention on the Mondragon network of worker-led businesses, the leaders of crisis-hit economies are on a global shopping expedition. They are hunting for successful businesses run outside listed-company lines to help reinvent, rebalance and revive capitalism.

Nowhere does this urge to refurbish the economy seem more urgent than in the UK, where the influence of the shareholder-owned joint stock company is stronger and the dominance of financial capitalism greater than almost anywhere else. Speaking this week, Nick Clegg, deputy prime minister, told an audience at the Mansion House, in the heart of the City of London: 'We don't believe our problem is too much capitalism. We think it's that too few people have capital. We need more individuals to have a real stake in their firms. More of a John Lewis economy, if you like.'

[. . .]

But does it make sense for Britain to fetch a new economic model off the shelf, in the same way a consumer would drop into a department store to replace a faulty coffee-maker, a threadbare rug or a worn-out jacket? Even if it does, is John Lewis the right choice?

[. . .] John Spedan Lewis, son of the retailer's original founder, put his idealism into lasting action, pioneering a model of co-ownership that was, and remains, radical. In two chunks, in 1929 and 1950, he transferred his shares in the business to a trust. The company has an executive chairman and is governed under a set of principles and a constitution, with policy influenced by an elected council that represents the staff or 'partners'. Spedan Lewis ensured that all staff would benefit from an annual share of profits, and that pay would be regulated according to a ratio. The highest paid staff member cannot earn more than 75 times the average wage of the shop-floor salesperson. Staff are encouraged to air their concerns in the weekly *Gazette*, and senior managers are expected to respond. Generous pensions and holiday amenities are available for partners.

'Spedan's "big idea" was a simple one – employees work better if they feel they have a stake in their company', says Peter Cox, who wrote a history of the group after retiring from Waitrose in 2003. 'In the John Lewis case, they know that no nameless shareholders are taking a cut before they get their bonus. Unless a business distributes its profits to its employees, that subliminal motivational benefit is not replicable. But the

knowledge that they can appoint their own representatives, that they can complain and be listened to, is still a major advantage.'

It helps, of course, that John Lewis and Waitrose continue to demonstrate commercial success.

[. . .]

But even advocates of the John Lewis model point out that the form is no guarantee of success. A periodic accusation is that the management system tends towards bureaucracy, while employee-ownership impedes expansion and hinders productivity improvements. Charlie Mayfield, a suave former McKinsey consultant who is the group's executive chairman, says managers have to demonstrate their accountability to staff – the council can dismiss him if he fails in his duties – because the trust structure means employees cannot sell their shares. Low staff turnover improves the return on investment in training and encourages better service.

[. . .]

The elements of the formula – participative management style, employee ownership and profit-sharing – work best when applied together. David Erdal, author of *Beyond the Corporation: Humanity Working*, about employee-owned companies, says productivity can be increased by applying any of those approaches, but 'if you do all three, you have a knockout'.

[. . .]

Politicians' good intentions could still founder on the reefs of tax codes and the UK's engrained corporate culture. A change in the tax code to make it easier for entrepreneurs to transfer shares to staff would run up against the Treasury, traditionally a staunch backer of the shareholder-owned publicly listed company model, according to critics of the existing system. As one politician puts it: 'The Treasury's full of very clever, neoclassical economists who think the PLC was divinely created and handed down on tablets of stone to Moses.'

The fact that the financial sector is geared towards serving the stock markets and listed companies is a further obstacle to change, Prof Michie says. 'If you want to sell your family firm, and go to your bank or financial adviser for advice, they will tell you that you can sell it in a trade sale, or float it on a stock market. End of story', he says. 'They won't tell you that you can sell it to an employee trust. If you ask whether you can sell it to an employee trust, they will probably say "no".'

[. . .]

Questions

1. According to the author, there is growing support among UK politicians for partnerships such as that of John Lewis.

   What are the reasons for these politicians advocating the concept of a 'partnership' company?

2. What are the arguments against this form of partnership?

3. Schein (2004) defined culture as 'a set of basic assumptions – shared solutions to universal problems of external adaptation (how to survive) and internal integration (how to stay together) – which have evolved over time and are handed down from one generation to the next.

   Using this definition, try and detect the assumptions in the article with regard to (a) external adaptation (how to survive), and (b) internal integration (how to stay together).

ACTIVITY 1.2

Foreign influences: expats force locals to ask who they are

By Nada El Sawy

The United Arab Emirates (UAE) is unique in that expatriates constitute more than 80 per cent of the population. As the country continues to grow and accept foreigners at an astounding pace, Emiratis worry that their national identity and culture are at stake. The issue has become so pressing that President Sheikh Khalifa Bin Zayed al-Nahyan declared 2008 UAE national identity year.

'People here have the feeling that we are losing our own country if this double-digit [expatriate percentage of population] growth continues and if the government does not address the problem and address it squarely and urgently', says Abdulkhaleq Abdulla, a professor of political science at United Arab Emirates University in Al Ain.

Issues such as the demographic imbalance, the disappearance of the Arabic language, competition over jobs, lagging education and a lack of sensitivity towards Emirati cultural and religious values, have been discussed in the past, but are now taking centre stage.

Last month, a two-day forum on national identity took place in Abu Dhabi to debate such issues openly for the first time. The conference, organized by the Ministry of Culture, Youth and Community Development, featured more than 30 high-level government and private-sector speakers.

Participants spoke their minds. Ahmad al-Tayer, chairman of the National Human Resources Development and Employment Authority (Tanmia), said: 'Today, an Emirati student is being taught Islamic studies in English by a Pakistani. This is the state of our nation.'

Meanwhile, Dubai's police chief, Lieutenant General Dahi Khalfan Tamim, warned that there would be serious security issues if demographic balance was not restored. He advocated reducing foreign workers from any single country to a maximum 25 per cent of the population, according to press reports. He also suggested that property ownership be opened mostly to Emiratis and Arabs, and that increased childbearing should be a national strategy.

The UAE is a young country, created in 1971, but it attracted foreigners early on due to its strategic trade location and with the discovery of oil. During the period 1975 to 2004, the population of nationals increased 4.5 times while the expatriate population increased almost tenfold.

'We had this problem before. There were voices that were asking since the mid-70s [about the loss of national identity] when the country started construction', says Ebtisam al-Katbi, also a professor of political science at UAE University.

Prof. al-Katbi says several factors have exacerbated this problem. First, most foreigners coming to the UAE were initially Arab or Muslim, or from similar cultures. Today, more are coming from the west, Russia or the Balkan countries, where the cultural values are markedly different.

'It's not their fault. They come, they are not aware of the people's values, the culture, what should be done and what should not be done', she says. 'But they have misused their freedom here. I've never seen people who go to work or malls with this kind of dress. I'm not calling for conservative action, but this is still a Muslim country.'

'It's not a matter now of labour. You can limit labour. The problem now is that we are selling properties to expatriates. You cannot limit that', says Prof. al-Katbi. Foreigners should be welcomed on a temporary basis, not as permanent residents, she says. 'We are giving 99 years for those who are buying the properties to stay here. Why 99? Five years is enough.'

Some Emiratis, especially among the younger generation, say that expatriates are a part of the equation. Mishaal al-Gergawi, a 27-year-old, wrote an opinion piece in Abu Dhabi's *The National* headlined: 'If we Emiratis don't adapt, we'll become extinct', warning that there was a need for integration and dialogue between expatriates and locals.

He suggested promoting national culture through such activities as desert camps, traditional dance, fishing and diving trips, and visits to elders. Long-term residency should be open to foreigners who have made a strong contribution to the UAE and, ideally, have familiarized themselves with its values.

Other Emiratis advocate making Arabic the main language for communication, and improving the public education system so Emiratis do not feel the need to attend private international schools.

'We ought to note that we are not opposed to foreign nationalities and not opposed to the English language', says Bilal al-Bodour, assistant undersecretary at the Ministry of Culture. 'But this must not be instead of our nationality, and our language, and our identity.'

Several initiatives are already in place to help preserve national identity. Watani, a UAE social development programme, works with schools and universities to strengthen Emirati identity among youth. In March, students from more than 20 universities across the UAE participated in a conference on national identity at the University of Sharjah.

Questions

1. How would you describe the national identity of the UAE? How do they distinguish themselves from other Arab countries?

2. What do you think the inhabitants there need to do to 'preserve their own identity'?

ACTIVITY 1.3

The role of the manager

André Laurent (1983) carried out investigations in several countries into the attitudes of managers towards their organisation. A series of studies he made concerning national differences in concepts of management produced interesting results. Over a period of two years, questions were put to experienced international managers attending executive programmes at an international business school. The findings showed clear differences between countries with regard to the perception of organisations as political systems, authority systems, role-formalisation systems and hierarchical relationship systems.

The study was replicated among much younger and less experienced MBA students and in two multi-national companies, one being a US-based chemical firm with subsidiaries in France, Germany and Great Britain, and later in amended form to another multinational. The results from the replications were essentially the same as those from the first survey among executive programme participants. Although it might have been expected for those working in multinationals to have undergone some kind of homogenising effect in terms of managerial concepts, the results showed a surprising stability. Moreover, the results from the first multinational surveyed showed respondents' concepts to be even more entrenched.

Laurent's conclusion – that the management process in the ten countries surveyed is as much culture-bound as their cooking – is echoed in the results of the GLOBE project's survey among company employees working in their own society. The national culture remains dominant within the organisation. As Laurent explains, employees do not leave their national culture behind at the company entrance.

One of the questions which Laurent used in his surveys is given below. Respondents were asked to react to the following statement:

'It is important for a manager to have at hand precise answers to most of the questions that his subordinates may raise about their work.'

Examine the results and answer the questions below Figure 1.1.

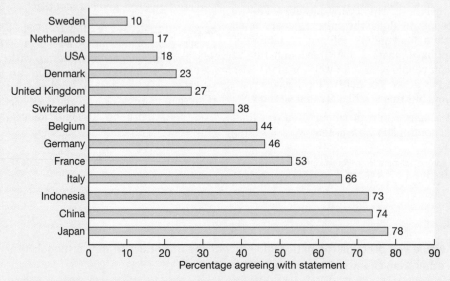

Figure 1.1 **Should a manager have precise answers?**

Source: based on figures given in Laurent, 1983: 86.

Questions

1. Using the percentages given in the above figure, how would you characterise the attitudes of Swedes, Germans and Japanese towards the role of the manager in an organisation?
2. How would you describe the research method Laurent used?

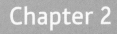

Chapter 2

Dimensions of culture: Hofstede and GLOBE

This chapter explores the conceptualisation of culture in terms of 'dimensions'. These are concepts that allow variations between the attributes of cultures to be quantified. Attention will be given to the reflection of these cultural dimensions in the business environment.

The chapter will first outline a model of value orientations drawn from social anthropology that has proved to be influential in the development of a dimensional approach to cross-cultural comparisons.

Concept 2.1 summarises the dimensions developed by Geert Hofstede who categorises national cultures in a binary way. These are applied in an organisational context. The concept will finally pinpoint some criticisms of Hofstede's research from fellows and other researchers around the world.

Concept 2.2 takes the notion of cultural dimensions a stage further by considering the more recent projection of cultural dimensions developed by the GLOBE project, as well as the methods used in the research to determine values and practices at both organisational and societal level. The concept gives particular attention to the project's findings with regard to the nine dimensions of societal cultural variation and introduces the notion of culture clusters, proposed by the GLOBE project.

Learning outcomes

After reading this chapter you will:

- Understand the concept of cultural dimensions.
- Be familiar, in particular, with the five-dimensional model developed by Hofstede as well as the culture construct definitions of more recent research by the GLOBE project.
- Have some insight into the relationship between societal values and practices and the culture of organisations working within a society.
- Become familiar with the idea of clustering cultures devised by the GLOBE project according to similarities between countries composing each culture cluster.

One important hypothesis underlying much research into culture is the stability of a culture's characteristics. Although cultural groupings all undergo change over time according to the ways they deal with the challenges laid down by their environment, they each remain constant in the sense that they maintain certain notions about the world and attitudes towards their fellow humans. We will necessarily focus on the stable elements of a culture while keeping in mind the evolutionary nature of culture in general, as indicated earlier in Chapter 1.

The characteristics that define each cultural group can offer international managers considerable insights when it comes, for example, to co-operating with companies from other cultural backgrounds. If awareness of cultural differences is consciously raised, then the ability to analyse the effectiveness of employing business policies in differing cultural environments is considerably improved.

Preface: a model from social anthropology

Before examining cultural differences in the business context, it is worthwhile considering a comparative model developed in the early 1960s that has been influential in other, more recent models relating to cross-cultural management. Kluckholn and Strodtbeck (1961) devised a model based on responses to questions concerning the human condition. An adapted version of this is given in Table 2.1, together with the possible range of responses.

This model, drawn from the field of social anthropology, suggests that a particular cultural grouping will display a certain orientation to the world in response to questions relating to those given in the table. It does not claim, however, that all individuals within a particular grouping will respond in the same way. Moreover, it does not account for so-called sub-cultural groupings or for the way organisations in a particular cultural environment respond to the questions. Nevertheless, it does enable a comparison to be made along certain variations of different cultures. Moreover, the model has proved to be the source of inspiration for many other researchers into cross-cultural matters, including Trompenaars (see Chapter 5) and Hofstede. These value orientations influence not only attitudes to work, but also to other concerns in life. As Diana Robertson (2002) suggests, if a culture has the future as its time focus, then it is likely to put more emphasis on the preservation of the environment for the sake of future generations than a culture that focuses on the past or present.

Table 2.1 **Variations in value orientations**

Basic questions	Range of responses		
What is the character of human nature?	Good	A mixture of good and evil	Evil
What is man's relationship to nature?	Man dominates	Harmony between man and nature	Nature dominates
What is the time focus of human activity?	Past	Present	Future
What is the modality of human activity?	Spontaneous expression of desires	All-round development of self	Achieving measurable goals
What is the relationship of man to man?	Hierarchical	Collectivist	Individualist

Source: adapted from Kluckholn and Strodtbeck 1961: 11–12.

Concept 2.1 Hofstede's national cultural dimensions

Geert Hofstede's research in the area of culture and management is known worldwide. His theories are not only frequently quoted and applied in cross-cultural research, but also used (often indiscriminately) in prescriptive works on dealing with other cultures. Despite, or maybe because of, its prominence, his work has provoked much criticism from theorists and practitioners alike, as we will see later. Nevertheless, consideration of Hofstede's work is indispensable to any study on culture and management.

Hofstede developed a dimensional approach to cross-cultural comparisons through his pioneering studies into how management is affected by differences between cultural groupings. He conducted extensive studies into national cultural differences, the first being across employees working in subsidiaries of a multinational corporation (IBM) in 64 countries. Hofstede, who had founded and managed the personnel research department of IBM Europe, took a database of scores resulting from attitude surveys among IBM employees worldwide and re-analysed the figures. The surveys had been developed as a management tool to examine issues relating to the work situation (determined beforehand through interviews with personnel). The original respondents in these surveys were matched groups (Hofstede, 1980) in seven occupational categories, five of them being non-managerial and two managerial.

The research set-up, as well as the statistical methods used by Hofstede, was applied by other researchers to other groups, including students in 23 countries, commercial airline pilots in 23 countries and civil service managers in 14 countries. These studies together identified and validated the first four dimensions of national culture differences described in this concept. Hofstede later developed a fifth dimension to account for value orientations that emerged from research carried out from a Chinese perspective.

Hofstede used the results of his research to produce a comparison between cultures on four and eventually five dimensions:

- *Power distance (high/low)*: attitudes to authority, the distance between individuals in a hierarchy.
- *Uncertainty avoidance (high/low)*: the degree of tolerance for uncertainty or instability.
- *Individual versus group orientation*: independence and interdependence, the loyalty towards oneself and towards a group.
- *Masculine versus feminine orientation*: importance of work goals (earnings, advancement) compared with personal goals (co-operation, relationships).
- *Short-term versus long-term orientation*: fostering virtues related to the past and present or virtues related to the future.

It should be stressed that these dimensions form a general model and are not necessarily applicable in specific circumstances. They describe tendencies within a certain cultural grouping; they present orientations adopted by the majority of members of a cultural grouping in normal situations. They do not account for cultural differences in absolute terms but in relative terms.

In the second edition of his publication *Cultures and Organizations* (2005), which he wrote with his son, Hofstede examines differences between cultures not only at society level, but also in terms of the family, education and the workplace. When examining these cultural dimensions this book will focus on the workplace, i.e. the business context.

Low/high power distance

'Power distance' refers to the extent to which members of a culture expect and accept that power is unequally distributed in society. It was developed by Hofstede on the basis of earlier research concerning preferences for power among different cultures and, in particular, on research identifying centralisation as a characteristic of organisations (Pugh, 1976).

As the Hofstedes' book says: 'Power and inequality, of course, are fundamental facts of any society and anybody with some international experience will be aware that all societies are unequal, but some are more unequal than others' (Hofstede and Hofstede, 2005: 137). Essentially, this dimension reflects how a culture relates to authority of one form or another. In relational terms, the comparisons made between cultures on this dimension convey the extent to which subordinates are dependent on their bosses. The extremes of this cultural dimension are characterised in Table 2.2.

In high power distance cultures, effective managers are essentially benevolent autocrats who are focused on the task. They are inaccessible and enjoy privileges their power gives them. If things go wrong, the subordinates – who are dependent on their superiors – are usually to blame. In low power distance cultures, on the other hand, effective managers are more oriented towards the people in an organisation and allow them to participate more in making decisions. The relations between subordinates and superiors are more horizontal than vertical: superiors are accessible and try to make out they are less powerful than they are. If anything goes wrong, the system is more to blame rather than the individuals involved.

Table 2.2 **Extremes of Hofstede's 'power distance' dimension**

Low power distance	High power distance
There should be a minimum of inequality since it can exploit others	Inequality is unavoidable and everyone has the place they deserve
If there is a hierarchy in an organisation it is only for the sake of convenience	Hierarchy in an organisation reflects natural differences
People who are superiors or subordinates are all the same	Superiors or subordinates are different kinds of people
Everyone should enjoy the same privileges; there should be no status symbols	Power-holders are entitled to privileges and status symbols
Subordinates should be consulted	Subordinates should be told what to do
Individuality is to be respected	Authority is to be respected
The manager should be a resourceful democrat	The manager should be a benevolent autocrat

Individualism/collectivism

This dimension concerns itself with the relationship between the individual and the group. To what extent are individuals in society autonomous and to what extent are they embedded in the group? This particular construct, apparent in ancient civilisations and to be found at the heart of much philosophical thought about the nature of the state and the individual, continues to be given much attention in many disciplines, particularly sociology, anthropology and psychology. It was Hofstede who subjected this construct to empirical investigation on a large scale and eventually produced a ranking of societies in individualistic/collectivistic terms. The extremes of this dimension are characterised in Table 2.3.

Table 2.3 **Extremes of Hofstede's 'collectivist/individualist' dimension**

Collectivist	Individualist
'We' mentality	'I' mentality
Identity is based on one's social group	Identity is based on the individual
Decisions are primarily made according to what is best for the group	Decisions are based primarily on individual needs
Relationships prevail over task	Tasks prevail over relationships
Focus is on belonging to an organisation	Focus is on individual initiative and achievement
Values differ according to the group (particularism)	Value standards apply to all (universalism)

This dimension is essentially about the importance that a cultural grouping attaches to relationships. Some cultures place more importance on personal relationships rather than the task to be performed or the deal to be completed. These relationships may well be within an extended family, so that blood-ties guarantee trust and loyalty. Relations outside the family need to be built on face-to-face social encounters. Loyalty to those within the circle of relations and friends is considered essential and is rewarded in many ways. Collective achievement is the focus, rather than the attainment of individual goals and careers. Indeed, some form of personal sacrifice may be necessary for the sake of the common good. In individualist cultures, the focus is more on rights and the achievements of the individual. Individuals are expected to achieve their own goals and to do so are willing, if necessary, to undergo contractual obligations. Managers expect employees to fulfil the terms of a contract and vice versa. Close ties may develop between the two, but this does not diminish the value of the contractual arrangements. Within this sort of environment, competition between individuals is encouraged, thus allowing them to meet their goals and needs, as long as these are in line with those of the organisation within which they are working.

Masculinity/femininity

From his initial studies at IBM, Hofstede developed a dimension whereby certain societies could be characterised as being either assertive and competitive (masculine in nature), or more caring and therefore more feminine. Hofstede does stress rather traditional roles of the sexes: masculine values such as achievement and exercise of power are used to characterise cultures along this dimension as are feminine values: caring for others, being less self-centred. Nevertheless, when a culture is examined in terms of the work environment, this dimension allows clear distinctions to be made between cultures in terms of their attitude to work. The characterisation of the two extremes of this dimension show how dramatic these distinctions can be (Table 2.4).

Table 2.4 **Extremes of the 'masculine/feminine' dimension**

Masculinity	Femininity
Distinct gender roles	Fluid gender roles
Men are assertive, women are nurturing	Men and women in nurturing roles
Stress on competition and performance	Stress on co-operation and environmental awareness
Acquisition of wealth	Quality of life
Ambition motivates	Service motivates
Live to work	Work to live
Sympathy for the successful achiever	Sympathy for the unfortunate
Independence ideal	Interdependence ideal
Managers are expected to be decisive and assertive	Managers use intuition and strive for consensus

Highly masculine cultures see work as a challenge, offering the possibility of high rewards and recognition. The stress is on performance, on competing with others to achieve goals. Highly feminine cultures give more attention to the broader picture, particularly to relationships with others in the workplace. Quality of life is a prime concern, not just in terms of how the work is performed but also in terms of what the work achieves.

This dimension is one that Hofstede (1998: 11) himself characterised later as 'taboo' since he saw the 'duality of male versus female' as a problem always under discussion, and answers to which cause wide-ranging discussion. The taboo was greatest, he felt, among 'masculine' countries where there was considerable stress on political correctness and concern about sexual harassment. Perhaps the very explicit use of the term masculine/feminine exacerbated matters, as evidenced in the tendency of other researchers exploring the phenomenon to talk of 'gender egalitarianism' (House *et al.*, 2004) or to incorporate features of this dimension into one relating to assertiveness.

Uncertainty avoidance

This fourth dimension measures the extent to which people in a certain culture avoid uncertainty. To what extent do they feel threatened by ambiguous, risky situations? To what extent do they prefer predictability in their lives, clearly prescribed rules and procedures in their work? Uncertainty-avoiding cultures perceive life as a battle against anxiety and stress. They may be willing to accept familiar risks but not the danger of the unknown. To that end they tend to resist innovation or anything that deviates from the known.

They appreciate authorities who have the 'right' answers, who lay down rules to prevent ambiguities. Cultures with low uncertainty avoidance are not disconcerted by ambiguity, and tolerate differences generally. They perceive that there are not always answers to problems and that laws are not always effective or necessary in dealing with deviation – they may be changed if deemed ineffective.

The two extremes of this dimension are characterised in Table 2.5.

Table 2.5 **Extremes for Hofstede's 'uncertainty avoidance' dimension**

Low uncertainty avoidance	High uncertainty avoidance
Uncertainty is a fact of life: take things as they come	Uncertainty in life is threatening and must be reduced
Deviance is not a threat	Intolerant of deviant persons and ideas
Ambiguity is tolerated	Predictability and clarity are preferable
Readiness to take risks	Concern about security
Toleration of innovation	Resistance to change
The fewer rules there are the better	Formal rules and regulations are necessary
Competition and conflict can be constructive	Consensus is better than conflict
Belief in generalists and common sense	Belief in experts and their knowledge
Hard work as such is not a virtue	There is an inner urge to work hard

Managers in uncertainty-avoiding cultures would be expected to maintain the rules and regulations of an organisation, to have precise answers to questions and to give exact instructions. Managers in cultures with low uncertainty avoidance would be expected to uphold or establish rules only as absolutely necessary (most problems can be resolved without strict rules anyway); managers cannot possibly be the source of all wisdom and may need to draw others into their decision-making who are more competent.

Hofstede's initial four dimensions have had an enormous influence on the development of management theories in many management areas, particularly those focusing on relations between the leader and the led. Two dimensions, power distance and uncertainty avoidance, are particularly important in this respect. As Hofstede and Hofstede themselves say:

> Both dimensions help answer two fundamental questions:
> Who should have the power to decide what?
> What rules or procedures should be followed in order to attain the desired ends?
>
> Hofstede and Hofstede, 2005: 63

The fifth dimension: short-term versus long-term orientation

The fifth dimension outlined below in Table 2.6 supplemented the other dimensions already given. It is based on the results of the Chinese Value Survey developed by Michael Bond and associates (The Chinese Culture Connection, 1987). They originally labelled it Confucian work dynamism since it reflected values upheld by Confucius and his followers. These values permeate those of a number of countries in Asia, as Chapter 4 will show.

Hofstede added the fifth dimension on the basis of the survey mentioned above, but gave it the label of short-term versus long-term orientation since the majority of the countries where the fifth dimension was found are 'unfamiliar with Confucius's teachings and anyway, *both* opposing poles of the dimension contain Confucian values' (2001: 55). According to Hofstede, non-Confucian countries such as Brazil and India have quite a high score on this dimension. Those values deemed short-term in nature are oriented towards the past and present and are more static; those deemed to be long-term are oriented towards the future and are more dynamic.

Table 2.6 **Hofstede's fifth dimension**

Short-term orientation	Long-term orientation
Need for achievement, self-determination	Need for accountability, self-discipline
Loyalty towards others can vary according to the needs of business	Develop and maintain lifelong personal networks
People should be rewarded according to their abilities	Large social and economic differences should not be tolerated
Stress is on short-term profits	Stress is on future market position
Managers and employees are in different camps	Owner-managers and workers share the same aspirations

A *short-term* orientation includes fostering virtues related to past and present, especially respect for tradition, preservation of face and fulfilling social obligations. A *long-term* orientation includes fostering virtues oriented towards the future, especially perseverance and thrift, ordering relationships by status, and having a sense of shame.

SPOTLIGHT 2.1

How the Chinese run their businesses outside China

When studying Chinese who were running businesses overseas, Gordon Redding (1990) shows how Confucian dynamism works. The companies are owned by the family and usually run by one dominant family member. They are kept small to enable this family control to persist since non-family employees are unlikely to have the necessary loyalty to the enterprise. If such companies decide to co-operate with other companies, they do so through a network of personal relations based on (extended) family members, village, clan or ethnic group within the Chinese population. The Confucian virtues of thrift and persistence are evident in their cost-conscious approach and in their patient accumulation of wealth. The two virtues are combined in the way the Chinese move their capital round the world to take advantage of low risk and high profitability.

Criticism of Hofstede's dimensions

The very simplicity of Hofstede's framework of analysis is seductive: he has come up with a minimum number of dimensions to enable cultural observers and analysts to pinpoint features to which they and their readers can relate. The fact that the results of replicated research often reflect those of Hofstede's original research has helped to increase his stature in the field.

However, since the publication in 1980 of his major work, *Culture's Consequences*, Hofstede has been subject to criticism from fellow researchers and from humble mortals who are wrestling with day-to-day problems arising from cross-cultural co-operation in an increasingly global world. Since 2000, this criticism has become more vocal.

Hofstede's research method

Scholars have put forward a number of general objections to the way Hofstede carried out his research. One in particular concerns the use of **attitude-survey questionnaires** alone. Since, they argue, culture manifests itself in so many different ways, the use of a single method approach cannot be considered to be a valid basis for inferring the values of respondents.

A number of critics question the **representative nature** of the respondents. How can those who completed the questionnaire be considered representative of a national culture if they come from only one location in each country and from only one company (IBM) and its carefully selected employees?

To make the assumption that there is **homogeneity** within IBM is, for many critics, a questionable one, particularly if, as Hofstede maintains, you can separate its organisational and occupational cultures from the national cultures present. Can one really talk of one organisational culture at IBM? One of Hofstede's staunchest critics, Brendan McSweeney, points out that Hofstede had not investigated this question carefully and acknowledged in his later work that organisations could contain different types of organisational culture (McSweeney, 2002). Even if the idea that IBM has one organisational culture is accepted, McSweeney asks whether such a culture, as Hofstede maintains, has to do with perceived common practices rather than the values of the employees concerned. Even if Hofstede has matched the results of the survey at IBM on an occupational basis, can one talk of a homogeneic occupational culture in the company? How can employees from different nations who share the same occupation really be said to share uniformity of culture: courses purporting to deliver similar qualifications can differ considerably between countries as well as within a country.

McSweeney also addresses the question of homogeneity with regard to national culture. If Hofstede were consistent in his research approach, he would maintain that each individual within a country shares the same national culture (McSweeney, 2002: 100). However, the IBM questionnaires produced responses within each country that were very different. What Hofstede did was to average the responses nationally and then compare them. The differences were then classified as national cultural differences. If the average tendency of IBM employees is considered to be nationally representative then

> it must also be assumed that this would be the same as the average tendency in every other company, tennis club, knitting club, political party, massage parlour, socialist party and fascist party within the same country.
>
> McSweeney, 2002: 101

The characterisation of national cultures

The dimensions Hofstede uses to delineate cultural differences have also undergone many critical reviews. Apart from questioning whether just five dimensions can really encapsulate all the complexities of a national culture, critics cast doubt on the independent nature of each of Hofstede's dimensions: how can we be sure, they argue, that these dimensions do not interact? There is also doubt expressed about the way Hofstede differentiates between cultures on each dimension according to their position on a continuum. Although this position reflects an **'average tendency'**, it does not account for which situations cause cultures to emphasise one extreme of a continuum rather than the other. Sinha *et al.* (2001), for example, demonstrate how collectivism co-exists with individualism in India and give a number of scenarios where one or the other comes to the fore, or where both intertwine. The fifth dimension has come in for particular criticism. Unlike the other dimensions, it does not appear to offer contrasting or opposing alternatives. However, according to Fang (2003), the Chinese do not consider long-term/short-term orientation as being opposite in nature, but instead as being 'rather closely interrelated with one another' (p. 354). The Chinese philosophical principle of paradox and dualism in the world embraces opposites as described in the fifth dimension.

Furthermore, there is the problem of characterising cultures which are **territorially bound**. Even though Hofstede himself acknowledges that this unit of measurement is not perfect, objections continue to be raised about the validity of national cultural profiles, particularly in the light of recent world developments. What is the status of Hong Kong's profile now that it has become part of China? Is it now to be regarded as a subculture within a much larger entity? What about the cultural profile of (former) Yugoslavia? Do all the independent states that once comprised the country now 'deserve' separate full-blown cultural profiles?

SPOTLIGHT 2.2

A question of identity

The nation-state is shrinking to just a flag, some sports teams and a pile of debts

By Simon Kuper

'The hour has come to exercise our right to self-rule', says Artur Mas, Catalonia's president, sounding like a 19th-century statue of a nationalist hero on horseback. Catalans vote tomorrow in what amounts to a referendum on independence from Spain. Scots are galloping down the same road: they vote on independence in 2014. And Flemish nationalists won big last month in Belgian local elections that you may have missed. If these characters get their way, the map of western Europe will undergo its first changes since Ireland became independent in 1922.

The nation-state is shrinking to just a flag, some sports teams and a pile of debts. Catalans, Scots and Flemings might as well get out.

They just shouldn't think their own little states will be more use. They appear aware of this. The game-plan is to couple glorious nationhood with the European superstate. When Scots and Catalans realised the European Union might not admit them, they cooled on independence.

In fact, the EU's recent rise exemplifies the demise of nationalism. During the economic crisis, the EU has been morphing into something of a federal state: central control over national budgets, European bailouts, perhaps banking union. Europeans have sulked, but they've mostly accepted this.

That doesn't mean they love the EU. Nobody ever ran into the street drunk, waving the European flag. The emotional choice now isn't between nation and Europe. Rather, people are gradually replacing nationalism with an array of transnational loyalties. Someone might identify with the global community of English-speakers, or as a Londoner, black person, Muslim, Justin Bieber fan, member of the global elite, or possibly all these things. Most people also still identify with a nation, but that's becoming just one identity among many.

In short, the validity and applicability of Hofstede's model is called into question by a number of critics, not only by scholars, but also by practitioners in the field of cross-cultural management training who feel uneasy when applying Hofstede's dimensions to 'the real world'.

Hofstede's response

As criticism has grown, so has the robustness of Hofstede's reactions to them, aided and abetted by the results of many follow-up research projects and the employment of facts and figures produced by economic institutions to back up his findings. Possibly tired of the occasional but persistent criticism of his work, Hofstede even lists a number of the reservations made about his work in the second edition of *Culture's Consequences* in 2001. These deal with the criticism that using surveys to measure culture is unsuitable, that using nations as units of analysis is not the most appropriate, that using only surveys at one company – IBM – as the basis of his research cannot yield information about entire national cultures. Finally, he responds to the reproach made that culture cannot be boiled down to so few dimensions.

Surveys are suitable, Hofstede maintains, but should not be the only method used. He agrees that nations are not always appropriate units of analysis, but they are the only sort of unit available. In response to the question as to why only one company was surveyed, Hofstede states that this was advantageous to his research: the company was homogeneous in nature, and so allowed a comparison to be made of cultural values across the subsidiaries. By ensuring that respondents to his questionnaires shared one organisational culture as well as one occupational culture (if their responses were matched), Hofstede believed he had been able to isolate nationality:

> The only thing that can account for systematic and consistent differences between national groups within such a homogeneous multinational population is nationality itself . . .
>
> Hofstede, 1991: 252

Furthermore, in response to criticisms of his research method generally, Hofstede emphasises the detailed and thorough nature of his research, the well-matched samples obtained and the correlations with other data, including many replications of his research.

When it comes to the reproach frequently made that his five dimensions cannot possibly tell the whole story, Hofstede's reaction is, basically: if others can find more dimensions that are independent of those he has devised and which can be validated – fine! As he puts it: 'Candidates are welcome to apply' (Hofstede, 2001: 73).

SPOTLIGHT 2.3

The 'happiness' dimension

The Hofstede research paradigm has been used in a large number of research projects over the years. The initial four dimension model has been applied most frequently even though, as we have seen, Hofstede added a fifth dimension in 1991.

In the 2010 edition of *Culture's Consequences*, Hofstede *et al.* added a sixth dimension as a result of the analysis done by his co-author, Michael Minkov, of the World Values Survey (http://www.worldvaluessurvey.org). This dimension is termed 'Indulgence versus Restraint'. According to Hofstede (2011), this extra dimension was included to cover aspects not covered by the other five and is one known from 'happiness research'. The literature on 'happiness', often referred to as 'subjective well-being' or 'subjective appreciation of life' has flourished in recent decades. A 'World Database of Happiness' (http://www1.eur.nl/fsw/happiness/index.html) registers the work carried out in this area.

This new dimension deals with the extent to which a society allows basic and natural desires to be gratified in its pursuit of happiness. The term 'indulgence' typifies societies which exercise little constraint in this pursuit; the term 'restraint' applies to societies which control desires for happiness and use strict social norms to do so. The differences relate to freedom of speech, the importance of leisure, the extent of obesity and the maintenance of social order.

According to Hofstede (2011: 16),

Indulgence tends to prevail in South and North America, in Western Europe and in parts of Sub-Sahara Africa. Restraint prevails in Eastern Europe, in Asia and in the Muslim world. Mediterranean Europe takes a middle position on this dimension.

Concept 2.2 Cultural dimensions according to GLOBE

Another work using dimensions is the Global Leadership and Organizational Behaviour Effectiveness research programme, in short, the GLOBE project. GLOBE is a long-term programme divided into four phases, designed to conceptualise, operationalise, test and validate a cross-level integrated theory of the relationship between culture and societal, organisational and leadership effectiveness. The results of the second phase of the project are described in House *et al.* (2004). The follow-up to the project can be found in a second publication entitled *Culture and Leadership Across the World: the GLOBE Book of In-Depth Studies of 25 Societies* (Chhokar *et al.*, 2008). These studies examine the historical, social and economic development of 25 countries (marked with an * in Table 2.9) which took part in GLOBE's extensive research.

Dimensions of societal cultural variation

During the first phase of the project, the investigators developed a range of dimensions of societal cultural variation, six of which have their origins in those identified by Hofstede, two are derived from Kluckhohn and Strodtbeck and one from McClelland (Performance orientation). These nine dimensions which GLOBE developed are given in the first column of Table 2.7, along with the definition of each. The dimensions were used to examine the practices/values construct at industrial, organisational and societal level. This was done by asking respondents questions as given in the second column of Table 2.7.

Table 2.7 **Culture construct definitions and sample questionnaire items**

Culture construct definitions	Specific questionnaire item
Power distance: the degree to which members of a collective expect power to be distributed equally	Followers are (should be) expected to obey their leaders without question
Uncertainty avoidance: the extent to which a society, organisation or group relies on social norms, rules and procedures to alleviate the unpredictability of future events	Most people lead (should lead) highly structured lives with few unexpected events
Humane orientation: the degree to which a collective encourages and rewards individuals for being fair, altruistic, generous, caring and kind to others	People are generally (should be generally) very tolerant of mistakes
Collectivism 1 (institutional collectivism): the degree to which organisational and societal institutional practices encourage and reward collective distribution of resources and collective action	Leaders encourage (should encourage) group loyalty even if individual goals suffer
Collectivism 2 (in-group collectivism): the degree to which individuals express pride, loyalty and cohesiveness in their organisations or families	Employees feel (should feel) great loyalty towards this organisation
Assertiveness: the degree to which individuals are assertive, confrontational and aggressive in their relationships with others	People are (should be) generally dominant in their relationships with each other
Gender egalitarianism: the degree to which a collective minimises gender inequality	Boys are encouraged (should be encouraged) more than girls to attain a higher education (scored inversely)
Future orientation: the extent to which individuals engage in future-oriented behaviours such as delaying gratification, planning and investing in the future	More people live (should live) for the present rather than for the future (scored inversely)
Performance orientation: the degree to which a collective encourages and rewards group members for performance improvement and excellence	Students are encouraged (should be encouraged) to strive for continuously improved performance

Source: House *et al.*, 2004: 30 (Table 3.1).

These questions reflect the two sides of culture: (1) the values, beliefs of a society or organisation, and (2) the practices of an organisation (not only a work organisation but also a family). They were phrased in terms of 'is' and 'are', so that the responses would indicate actual cultural practice(s), i.e. 'the way we do things'. The same questions were rephrased using 'should' and put to the respondents to enable a response that indicated the cultural value(s) held by each respondent (i.e. 'the ideal way of doing things').

One reservation concerning GLOBE's findings should be mentioned. Although a large number of respondents were involved in the project, multinational employees were excluded in the surveys in order to ensure that responses came only from representatives of the country in question.

Table 2.8 gives some of the scores on these dimensions for those countries that feature in the follow-up GLOBE publication (Chhokar et al., 2008). It shows the ranking of India where the scores of the country are compared with the highest and lowest scores from the original list of countries under investigation (as listed in Table 2.9).

Table 2.8 **Societal culture 'As Is' and 'Should Be'**

Societal culture 'As Is' and 'Should Be'			
Societal culture 'As Is'	India (rank)	Highest (country)	Lowest (country)
Assertiveness	3.73 (53)	4.80 (Albania)	3.38 (Sweden)
Institutional collectivism (Collectivism I)	4.38 (25)	5.22 (Sweden)	3.25 (Greece)
In-group collectivism (Collectivism II)	5.92 (4)	6.36 (Philippines)	3.53 (Denmark)
Future orientation	4.19 (15)	5.07 (Singapore)	2.88 (Russia)
Gender egalitarianism	290 (55)	4.08 (Hungary)	2.50 (South Korea)
Humane orientation	4.57 (9)	5.23 (Zambia)	3.18 (Germany)
Performance orientation	4.25 (23)	4.94 (Switzerland)	3.20 (Greece)
Power distance	5.47 (16)	5.80 (Morocco)	3.89 (Denmark)
Uncertainty avoidance	4.15 (29)	5.37 (Switzerland)	2.88 (Russia)
Societal culture 'Should Be'	India (rank)	Highest (country)	Lowest (country)
Assertiveness	4.76 (7)	5.56 (Japan)	2.66 (Turkey)
Institutional collectivism (Collectivism I)	4.71 (32)	5.65 (El Salvador)	3.83 (Georgia)
In-group collectivism (Collectivism II)	5.32 (50)	6.52 (El Salvador)	4.94 (Switzerland)
Future orientation	5.60 (29)	6.20 (Thailand)	4.33 (Denmark)
Gender egalitarianism	4.51 (36)	5.17 (England)	3.18 (Egypt)
Humane orientation	5.28 (44)	6.09 (Nigeria)	4.49 (New Zealand)
Performance orientation	6.05 (26)	6.58 (El Salvador)	4.92 (S. Africa Black sample)
Power distance	2.64 (38)	3.65 (S. Africa Black sample)	2.04 (Colombia)
Uncertainty avoidance	4.73 (29)	5.61 (Thailand)	3.16 (Switzerland)

Source: Chhokar et al., 2008: 993 (Table 27.6).

One point worth noting from the table is that India's scores in terms of 'As Is' are high for all dimensions except for Gender Egalitarianism and Assertiveness. Another point emerging from this table is the considerable discrepancy between the 'As Is' score and the 'Should Be' score for Power Distance. These and other issues are touched upon in Chapter 4 where features of non-Western societies are described. Such discrepancies come to the fore in many of GLOBE's findings, as exemplified in the second illustration taken from Chhokar *et al.* (2008). In Figure 2.1, the scores of societies on one particular dimension, that of *Power Distance*, are visualised.

The reader will see that all the scores in Table 2.8 show that the 'As Is' scores were higher than 'Should Be' scores in all countries. All the societies covered, it appears, want more equality than there actually is. This goes particularly for China. The discrepancy between this society's 'As Is' (5.04) score and its 'Should Be' (3.10) is the highest discrepancy of all the scores for China. Although Chinese managers show themselves to be very tolerant of inequality of power in society, they consider that power should be spread more equally. Chhokar *et al.* (2008) consider this to be a possible reflection of the two forces – one internal and one external – that are at play in Chinese society. Upholding traditional values entails superiors being held in great respect, which in turn can hold Chinese leaders back in their attempts to promote economic efficiency. Pressures from outside China, on the other hand, are forcing these leaders to become even more competitive, to consider merit rather than superiority of age or position. This question of competing values will be examined further in Concept 10.2 with regard to changing corporate culture.

This particular finding with regard to China reflects those of the GLOBE project generally: societal values and practices had a significant effect on organisational culture on all nine dimensions of organisational cultural practice. This went for all three industrial sectors and all the medium to large companies being investigated. As an example, let us analyse the results of practices and values on organisational culture in a 'flat country', as Chhokar *et al.* (2008) call the Netherlands, in the banking/financial, food and insurance sectors.

According to the GLOBE findings for three of the dimensions (performance orientation, gender egalitarianism and institutional collectivism) the Dutch scores are higher on values ('Should Be') than practices ('As Is'), while uncertainty avoidance score is lower. Thus, Dutch middle managers seem to prefer an organisational culture more focused on effective performance as well as humane and collective orientation. The study concludes that Dutch societal and organisational culture, while maintaining its classical values, tends to attach more importance to individual performance and innovation.

From the GLOBE Project's findings, it is clear that Dutch managers consider the Performance Orientation to be an important cultural dimension for business. What is also clear is that the distance between 'As Is' and 'Should Be' for this dimension is not only very high in the Netherlands, but also in most of the countries studied (Chhokar *et al.*, 2008: 1090). This is the case in Finland, a country which is influenced by both the West as well the East, where the scores show a gap between the perception of practices ('As Is') and values ('Should Be') for both Performance Orientation and Power Distance. Finnish managers think that they have to improve the current situation concerning these two dimensions in order to face future competition. To achieve this goal, they want to develop more efficiency and innovation.

After having developed nine societal dimensions, the GLOBE Project goes further in its research by proposing six 'leadership dimensions' (Chhokar *et al.*, 2008). These dimensions

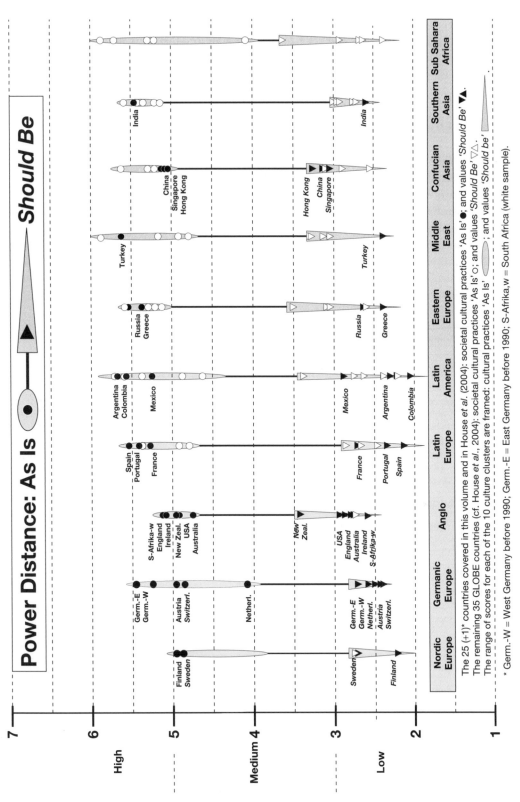

The 25 (+1)* countries covered in this volume and in House *et al.* (2004): societal cultural practices 'As Is' ●; and values 'Should Be' ▼▲.
The remaining 35 GLOBE countries (cf. House *et al.*, 2004): societal cultural practices 'As Is' ○; and values 'Should Be' ▽△.
The range of scores for each of the 10 culture clusters are framed: cultural practices 'As Is' ⬭; and values 'Should be' ◁.

* Germ.-W = West Germany before 1990; Germ.-E = East Germany before 1990; S-Afrika,w = South Africa (white sample).

Figure 2.1 GLOBE dimension of societal culture practices ('As Is') and values ('Should Be'): Power Distance

Source: Chhokar S.J. *et al.*, 2008: 108.

help to understand the commonalities and differences in leadership perceptions across countries (Chapter 8 will refer to this). In addition, this book keeps the original country-specific methodology of the research project and presents 25 countries classified in clusters (Table 2.9).

From dimensions to clusters

When faced with a cornucopia of cultures, it is natural to try to establish some sort of order that allows cultures to be clustered in terms of their similarities. Doing so enables those involved in multicultural operations to gain a perspective, be it a very general one, of similarities and differences between cultures. Religion, languages, geography and ethnicity are considered relevant factors, as are work-related attitudes and values. Historical developments and economic similarities are also seen as playing a crucial role in the clustering. The result shows a variety of countries classified into 10 clusters arranged according to calculations relating to the average distance in societal culture dimensions. The countries featuring in the clusters are given in Table 2.9:

Table 2.9 **The countries composing each culture cluster**

Anglo	Latin Europe	Nordic Europe	Germanic Europe

*Australia
Canada
*England
*Ireland
*New Zealand
*South Africa
  (White sample)
*United States
	*France
	Israel
	Italy
	*Portugal
	*Spain
	Switzerland
	  (French-speaking)
		Denmark
		*Finland
		*Sweden
			*Austria
			*Germany (former East)
			*Germany (former West)
			*Netherlands
			*Switzerland
			  (German speaking)

Eastern Europe	**Latin America**	**Sub-Saharan Africa**	**Middle East**
Albania Georgia *Greece Hungary Kazakhstan Poland *Russia Slovenia	*Argentina Bolivia Brazil *Colombia Costa Rica Ecuador El Salvador Guatemala *Mexico Venezuela	Namibia Nigeria South Africa (Black sample) Zambia Zimbabwe	Egypt Kuwait Morocco Qatar *Turkey
Southern Asia	**Confucian Asia**		
*India Indonesia Iran Malaysia Philippines Thailand	*China *Hong Kong Japan *Singapore South Korea Taiwan		

Source: Chhokar et al., 2008: 13.
* Countries dealt with at length in this book.

Conclusion

This chapter has explained the cultural dimensions of Hofstede and the relationship between national cultural values and those of organisational cultures. It has also outlined the many criticisms of Hofstede's research method, particularly the reliability and applicability of the findings. The chapter has also explained how the researchers involved in the GLOBE project have expanded this five-dimension model and the value orientation model (Kluckholn and Strodtbeck, 1961); and how they used a survey method which allows for a better understanding of the relations between organisational practices and social values. However, the above mentioned research is not exhaustive. Chapter 5 will go further with the value orientation and dimension approaches used in the business, including those of Trompenaars.

The significance of Hofstede's fifth dimension – short-term and long-term orientation – has also been described. This dimension is of special significance bearing in mind the increasing importance in current business of the relations between the Western countries and those in the East, especially China.

The clusters proposed by the GLOBE project (Table 2.9) will be the starting point for the following two chapters. Each chapter will take aspects of each cluster relating to history, religion and work-related values and practices. Chapter 3 will consider all European countries as well as the American and Australasian continents. Chapter 4 will cover the clusters in other parts of the world.

Points for reflection

1. This chapter has described cultural dimensions that can give insight into differences between national cultures.

   What are the advantages and limitations when using these dimensions to describe organisational cultures?

2. Hofstede's cultural dimensions were characterised in this chapter in relation to the business environment.

   Which of the dimensions mentioned in this chapter do you consider to be most relevant to the study of culture in the business context? Explain your choice.

3. The Hofstede's fifth dimension arose from research carried out by researchers with 'Eastern minds'.

   What added value does this dimension give to measuring the effect of culture in all business contexts around the world?

4. One criticism of Hofstede's work is that the scores on each dimension reflect only an 'average tendency' of a particular country and, therefore, inadequately reflect the wide range of responses given within a country to the survey, particularly from subcultures.

   Look up the profile of your country, as given on the Geert Hofstede website (www.geert-hofstede.com) and consider its analytical value, particularly with regard to any subcultures that you are aware of within your country.

5. On the basis of the results of its surveys, the GLOBE project arranged the countries in 10 clusters (see Table 2.9).

   What is your opinion concerning this kind of classification of countries?

Further reading

Hofstede, G. and Hofstede, G.J. (2005) *Cultures and Organizations: Software of the Mind*, 2nd edition, London: McGraw-Hill.

Hofstede, G., Hofstede, G.J. and Minkov. M. (2010) *Cultures and Organizations: Software of the Mind*, 3rd edition. New York: McGraw-Hill.

These two editions describe and analyse Geert Hofstede's research. The third edition describes the latest adjustments and additions to the cultural dimensions presented in earlier editions.

House, R.J., Hanges, P.J., Javidan, M., Dorfman, P.W. and Gupta, V. (eds) (2004) *Leadership, Culture and Organizations: the GLOBE Study of 62 Societies*, Thousand Oaks, CA: Sage.

Chhokar, J.S., Brodbeck, F.C. and House, R.J. (eds) (2008) *Culture and Leadership Across the World: the GLOBE Book of In-Depth Studies of 25 Societies*, New York, NY: Lawrence Erlbaum Associates.

These two volumes give an account of the GLOBE project as completed so far. They report the findings of the first two phases of GLOBE. Although the chapters are written by different groups of experts, the books offer a cohesive account of the theory underlying the GLOBE project. As Chhokar *et al.* (2008: 12) explain, the difference between the two volumes is as follows: 'Whereas House *et al.* (2004) provide a comparative understanding of all the GLOBE participating countries on all the nine societal cultural dimensions, 21 leadership scales, and their relationship with several socioeconomic indicators of these countries, Chhokar *et al.* (2008) provide much more detailed and comprehensive understanding of the 25 countries' (countries marked with an asterisk in Table 2.9).

References

Chhokar, J.S., Brodbeck, F.C. and House, R.J. (eds) (2008) *Culture and Leadership Across the World: The GLOBE Book of In-Depth Studies of 25 Societies*, New York, NY: Lawrence Erlbaum Associates.

Chinese Culture Connection (1987) 'Chinese values and the search for culture-free dimensions of culture', *Journal of Cross-Cultural Psychology*, 18: 143–164.

Fang, T. (2003) 'A critique of Hofstede's fifth national culture dimension', *International Journal of Cross Cultural Management*, 3(3): 347–368.

Hofstede, G. (1980) *Culture's Consequences*, 1st edition, Beverly Hills: Sage.

Hofstede, G. (1991) *Cultures and Organizations: Software of the Mind*, London: McGraw-Hill.

Hofstede, G. (1998) *Masculinity and Femininity: the Taboo Dimension of National Cultures*, Thousand Oaks, CA: Sage.

Hofstede, G. (2001) *Culture's Consequences*, 2nd edition, Thousand Oaks, CA: Sage.

Hofstede, G. (2011). 'Dimensionalizing cultures: the Hofstede Model in context', *Online Readings in Psychology and Culture*, 2(1). Retrieved from http://scholarworks.gvsu.edu/orpc/vol2/iss1/8.

Hofstede, G. and Hofstede G.J. (2005) *Cultures and Organizations: Software of the Mind*, 2nd edition, London: McGraw-Hill

House, R.J., Hanges, P.J., Javidan, M., Dorfman, P.W. and Gupta, V. (eds) (2004) *Culture and Organizations: The GLOBE study of 62 societies*, Thousand Oaks, CA: Sage.

Kluckholn, F. and Strodtbeck, F. (1961) *Variations in Value Orientations*, Evanston, IL: Row, Peterson.

McSweeney, B. (2002) 'Hofstede's model of national cultural differences and their consequences: a triumph of faith – a failure of analysis', *Human Relations*, 55(1): 89–118.

Minkov, M. and Hofstede, G. (2011) 'The evolution of Hofstede's doctrine', *Cross Cultural Management: An International Journal*, 18(1): 10–20.

Pugh, D.S. (1976) 'The "Aston" approach to the study of organizations', in Hofstede, G. and Kassem, M.S. (eds), *European Contributions to Organization Theory*, Assen, The Netherlands: Van Gorcum: 62–78.

Redding, G. (1990) *The Spirit of Chinese Capitalism*, Berlin and New York: Gruyter.

Robertson, D. (2002) 'Business ethics across cultures', in Gannon, M.J. and Newman, K.L. (eds), *Blackwell Handbook of Cross-Cultural Management*, Oxford: Blackwell: Chapter 18.

Sinha, J.B.P., Sinha, T.N., Verma, J. and Sinha, R.B.N. (2001) 'Collectivism coexisting with individualism: an Indian scenario', *Asian Journal of Social Psychology*, 4(2): 133–145.

Read the following article and answer the questions below it.

Masters of collaboration

By Tom Lester

Ants, those masters of collaboration, have made their species some of the most successful on the planet. In contrast, tigers walk alone, and are in grave danger of extinction. The message for business is this: in the modern world, we must collaborate or die.

Too often, however, in many UK companies, successful collaboration – both internal and external – happens by accident rather than design, contrasting vividly with many overseas rivals.

There are good reasons why effective collaboration is growing rapidly. Business operations are becoming steadily more flexible at every level of the organization. Non-core activities are outsourced, and procurement has become a worldwide activity centred on China. Satisfying customers at home demands an unprecedented level of co-operation unimpeded by rigid hierarchies and departmental boundaries.

Flatter organizations depend not on authority but on teamwork for effective action, and networks of individuals may stretch halfway round the globe and connect only electronically. The truly multinational executive, able to work effectively anywhere in the world with any nationality, remains a rare beast, and ordinary staff therefore need to understand and learn from different cultures to achieve the right level of collaboration.

A foreign joint venture or alliance, for example, may be agreed in Mumbai with great enthusiasm at board level, but the hoped-for results will only materialize if operating staff at all levels in Birmingham are ready and able to work with their opposite numbers.

Nationality, religion or corporate culture may be the big hurdle, but it is important to also realize that even within the same organization wider cultural gaps can exist between, say, R&D and finance as between the R&D teams of two partners. Wherever it occurs, the failure to understand can be disastrous. Rover is a tragic example. Back in the 1980s, when shop-floor collaboration in the UK car industry was near zero, Rover nonetheless managed to form a partnership with the Japanese group Honda to fill its vital new model programme.

But the arrogance of the Rover managers and the lack of a learning culture prevented them from obtaining the real benefits of the relationship, according to Professor Lord Bhattacharyya, head of the Warwick Manufacturing Group. Later, in 1992, when BMW bought the Rover business, communication with the German managers was even worse (exacerbated by political infighting on the German side).

Failure was the inevitable and bitter result. No doubt, ex-Rover patriots today will see the somewhat similar collapse of the DaimlerChrysler link as salve for wounded pride. Rather like Rover, DaimlerChrysler was dogged by poor collaboration and infighting, which stemmed in part from national cultural differences and traditions between German and US managers.

The outcome in both cases will have come as no surprise to Professor Geert Hofstede, who 30 years ago pioneered the study of cultural diversity in 56 countries using IBM's worldwide database. He has since been joined by others, notably a fellow Dutchman, Fons Trompenaars, and the American, Craig Storti.

Interest in their work is currently reviving after some big companies, including IBM, found that trying to impose a single corporate culture around the globe did not lead to better collaboration.

Two of the five 'cultural dimensions' that Prof. Hofstede derived from his database go some way to explaining the difficulties faced by Honda, BMW and Daimler-Benz managers in collaborating with their opposite numbers at Rover and Chrysler respectively.

One is individualism, defined as the degree to which ties between individuals – family as well as business colleagues – are loose or tight. The UK score as assessed by Prof. Hofstede is 89 out of a possible 100, indicating a high degree of individualism, exceeded only by the US with 91. Germany is a little above the European average at 67, but Japan scores 46.

On another dimension, uncertainty avoidance – the degree to which individuals feel uncomfortable in unstructured environments – the Japanese score 92, the Germans 65, the Americans 46 and the Brits 35. In real terms, the lack of precise rules and procedures at Longbridge, Rover's main factory, may have made the BMW team uncomfortable from the outset.

The cultural guru's great contribution may lie less in detailed analysis of deeply held cultural attitudes and more in helping companies anticipate and understand behaviour patterns that their foreign managers may display in their home territory, and the different patterns that they display when transferred to the UK.

As immigration grows, and London expands even further as an international financial centre, it becomes an important skill to be able to work effectively with and through executives of widely different backgrounds. Nationality, however, is not the only cause of non-communication, and not even the main cause, points out Kris Wadia, Accenture's executive partner for global sourcing.

'Put five English-speakers in a room to agree a set of tasks, and each will come away with a slightly different perspective', he says. Add in personal fiefdoms, ancient IT systems and complex and inappropriate organization and reward structures, and effective collaboration will sink rapidly.

Accenture's Mr. Wadia finds that with modern technology, companies can set up the infrastructure and telecommunications links between units relatively easily. What is more difficult and time-consuming are the soft issues, such as training UK managers to work together, and with foreign counterparts, and vice-versa.

The more sophisticated the communications systems, the more room there is for misunderstanding. Ants have no such problems.

Questions

1. 'Individualism' and 'Uncertainty Avoidance' are the two dimensions proposed by Hofstede which are mentioned in the text as influential factors in international collaboration. The text gives the 'scores' of the UK, USA, Germany and Japan on these dimensions to illustrate the differences.

   a) Look up the scores of these same countries on the remaining cultural dimensions on www.geert-hofstede.com

   b) How could score differences on these other dimensions also influence collaboration between the four cultures mentioned? Give concrete examples, if possible.

2. The text mentions that within the same organisation wider cultural gaps can exist between, say, R&D and finance as between the R&D teams of two partners.

   To what extent can Hofstede's cultural dimensions be used to explain such cultural gaps?

3. Now that Hofstede has proposed a new dimension that we called the 'sixth' dimension (see Spotlight 2.3), what added value does it offer when analysing this article?

ACTIVITY 2.2

Read the following article and answer the questions below it.

Hofstede versus the GLOBE project

On initial examination, the findings of the GLOBE project appear to be an ambitious and elaborate extension of Hofstede's research, a 'development of Hofstede's doctrine' and 'a corrective of Hofstede's model' (Minkov *et al.*, 2011: 14).

Although it may have led to a better understanding of Hofstede's work, the GLOBE findings challenged one of the basis tenants of the 'doctrine', namely Hofstede's perception of the phenomenon of culture. The definition which Hofstede devised ('the collective programming of the mind that distinguishes the members of one human group from another' – see Concept 1.1) has values at its core. These are the invisible elements which are reflected in three layers: rituals, heroes and symbols – the visible manifestations of culture. In short, Hofstede (2001: 11) sees cultural values as driving practices reflected as such in his version of the 'onion' metaphor: 'These are pictured as the layers of an onion around a core that consists of values' (Figure 2.2).

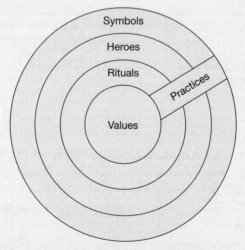

Figure 2.2 **The 'onion diagram': manifestations of culture at different levels of depth**

Source: Hofstede, 2001: 11.

The GLOBE approach followed a different line. As Javidan *et al.* (2006) explain, the project chose a different view of culture:

We followed Schein's (1992) view of culture as a product of a collective's attempts to address two sets of group issues: external adaptation and internal integration. Culture evolves as a collective adapts to ongoing challenges surviving in the face of external threats and opportunities and managing relations among its members.

Javidan *et al.*, 2006: 900

They view culture as a phenomenon which is not only to do with values but also the practices used to deal with challenges which their society faces.

This holistic view led to questionnaires being devised which were not focused on what the individual respondents considered desirable, but instead on what they considered the society in which they lived should desire. As described in Concept 2.2, the individuals were asked to describe their societies as they are and as they should be.

This approach put Hofstede's assumption to the test that cultural values drive cultural practices. The results of their research show that this assumption does not work. However counter-intuitive it may seem, the correlation between values and practices was found to be negative with regard to seven of the nine dimensions. Only Gender Egalitarianism shows a significant positive correlation. The idea, therefore, that people behave in a certain way because they hold particular values, that they have a particular view as to how things should be, does not hold water. As GLOBE's research shows, values and practices are each linked to different phenomena. Cultural practices are related to a number of societal features such as life expectancy and national competitiveness. Cultural values, however, are related to what the society in question considers to be outstanding leadership. In short:

. . . leaders' reported effectiveness is associated with the society's cultural values and aspirations, but the society's effectiveness is associated with its cultural practices.

Javidan *et al.*, 2006: 903

In his review of GLOBE, Hofstede makes a number of criticisms, many of which emanate from what he terms the 'unbridgeable differences' (Hofstede 2006: 885) between the GLOBE approach and that of Hofstede himself. The questionnaire items used come in for criticism: they are very abstract in nature, difficult to understand and 'may not have captured what the researchers supposed them to have captured'. The 'As Is' and 'Should Be' distinction is subjected to detailed criticism in the light of the distinction he makes between 'values as the desired' (what people actually and personally desire) and 'values as the desirable' (what they think they ought to desire). Hofstede (2006) believes that his values are measures of 'the desired' and therefore more predictive of practices. Unlike the questionnaire items in his surveys, none of the GLOBE items, he believes, measured 'the desired'.

GLOBE's response to this particular area of criticism is equally detailed and quite categorical:

. . . there is no empirical or theoretical justification for the assertion that GLOBE measures of values are too abstract or that the distinction between values as desirable versus values as desired is meaningful.

Javidan *et al.*, 2006: 903–904

Hofstede's review also includes a detailed re-analysis of GLOBE's dimension scores. Since the nine dimensions used by GLOBE were significantly correlated among each other, he set about simplifying the scheme using a factor analysis. His eventual conclusion was that the GLOBE dimensions could be reduced to five – 'and these show a family likeness with the Hofstede model' (Hofstede, 2006: 895).

In reaction to this claim, GLOBE gave a further explanation of the research procedures and retorted that Hofstede ignored state-of-the-art methods used to ensure reliability and validity. Furthermore, they pleaded for an end to what they term the 'Hofstedeian hegemony' (Javidan *et al.*, 2006: 910). However ground-breaking his work may be, it was time to move on. The results of their project allowed for a greater understanding of cultural dimensions to be developed, using constructs and scales which were 'more comprehensive, cross-culturally developed, theoretically sound, and empirically verifiable' (Javidan, 2006: 899).

GLOBE acknowledges that the results are not the only alternative to Hofstede: researchers may choose from a number of dimensions with which to pursue their cross-cultural work. They admit, however, that more research needs to be carried out with regard to the dynamics involved when cultures come into contact. There may well be cultural dimensions which play a key role when cultures come into contact.

Questions

1. What do you consider to be the essential differences between the approach taken by Hofstede and that taken by the GLOBE project towards determining cultural dimensions?

2. Which of the criticisms often made about Hofstede's work could be applied to that of the GLOBE project? Refer both to the above article as well as to the concepts.

3. Now that Hofstede has adopted a sixth cultural dimension (as a result of his work with Minkov – see Spotlight 2.3), to what extent do you think this invalidates the research which has been carried out using the original dimensions?

References used in this article

Hofstede, G. (2001) *Culture's Consequences*, 2nd edition, Thousand Oaks, CA: Sage.

Hofstede, G. (2006) 'What did GLOBE really measure? Researchers' minds versus respondents' minds', *Journal of International Business Studies*, 37: 882–896.

Javidan, M., House R.J., Dorfman, P.W., Hanges, P.J. and Sully de Luque, M. (2006) 'Conceptualizing and measuring cultures and their consequences: a comparative review of GLOBE's and Hofstede's approaches', *Journal of International Business Studies*, 37: 897–914.

Minkov, M. and Hofstede, G. (2011) 'The evolution of Hofstede's doctrine', *Cross Cultural Management: an International Journal*, 18(1): 10–20.

Schein E.H. (1992) *Organizational culture and Leadership*, 2nd edition, San Francisco CA: Jossey-Bass.

Chapter 3

Business cultures in the Western world

The clusters devised by the GLOBE project which were presented in Chapter 2 will be the starting point for this and the following chapter. These will take aspects of each of the GLOBE clusters relating to history, geography, languages, religion and work-related values and practices, and will feature certain countries within each cluster. Attention has been paid to emergent economies, particularly to Russia (the only BRICS country in Europe), and to Brazil, a 'founding member' of the BRICS group of emerging nations.

Chapter 3 will deal with clusters and the related cultures in European (concept 3.1), American, and Australasian countries (Concept 3.2). It will also consider three countries, Greece, Russia and Turkey, which have been placed in different clusters. We consider that Russia – along with the other countries placed in the East Europe cluster such as Greece – should be included in our deliberations concerning Europe as a whole. Turkey is a similar case: although the GLOBE project has positioned this country in the Middle East cluster, we believe that it should be included in this chapter, particularly on account of its application for membership of the European Union.

Learning outcomes

After studying Chapter 3 you will:

● Discover which characteristics bring together countries composing each of the clusters of the Western world.

● Gain awareness of some of the problems arising from co-operation between and within these clusters.

● Understand why Turkey has been included in this chapter along with countries in the European cluster.

● Improve your understanding of the notion 'multiculturalism'.

Before describing the business cultures in the Western world, it is important to highlight the phenomenon 'multiculturalism', also called 'ethnic diversity', which embodied a profound change in post-industrial societies. These societies, which represent a Western-centric economics concept, appeared at the beginning of the seventies when, for the first time, the service sector contributed more to the wealth of a number of countries than the manufacturing sector. Because of its history, the United States is considered to be the best example of this development. However, multiculturalism is no longer the preserve of Western societies. Countries such as Brazil and Mexico have also had ethnic minorities for a long time.

Preface: two approaches to the concept of multiculturalism

Political and economic factors have encouraged waves of immigration from one country to another, from one culture to another. The immigrants may be confronted with enormous differences at all levels of culture and need in some way or other to adapt. On the other hand, those cultures 'receiving' the immigrants may well find that a certain process of accommodation is required to enable the process of integration.

This integration process is at the heart of the multicultural issue. Andrea Semprini (2000) argues that in the US, it is the 'mass culture' that has been the major factor for the integration of immigrants coming 'from countries more distant from the European cradle'. For these groups, middle class values were involved in the process of acculturation (psycho-social adaptation of newcomers), the values which made up a strong frame of reference necessary when becoming familiar with their new home.

Joining a dominant culture, however, has entailed these groups giving up their own culture and recognising only one culture – that of the white middle class of European origin – as representative of the culture of 'Middle America'.

How can multiculturalism be addressed?

Conceptually, there are two major schools of thought which are opposed to each other, and even contradict each other, according to whether they promote a system of values belonging to monocultural or multicultural societies. In Table 3.1 we can see how their approaches differ with regard to their vision of the world, particularly their conception of the role of the human in a society.

Table 3.1 **Monocultural and multicultural visions compared**

Monocultural vision	Multicultural vision
Essentialist: existence of groups and identities, their internal consistency and cultural specificity is a given, accepted as such and unlikely to change	*Constructivist*: identities are the result of historical evolution, especially of interactions in a dynamic process with other groups present in a society
Universalist: values, moral judgements, behavioural choices are stated as absolute and can be applied to the whole of humanity	*Relativist*: as long as there are social groups and minorities interacting in the same social space, it is necessary to respect diversity
Proponents of '*equality*', found mainly in liberal societies, promote the equality of all citizens in terms of formal rights and legal administration	Proponents of '*differences*' argue that equality is a fiction that ignores cultural inequalities and specific ethnic identity; in short, the differences that make the heterogeneous social environment
Objective: supporters emphasise the positive role of competition and excellence. They demand objective standards of quality that permit integration or exclusion when work is being evaluated.	*Subjective*: multiculturalists emphasise the importance of 'recognition' in helping minorities to develop a sense of self-esteem. They demand appropriate criteria for evaluation of performance.

While the monocultural vision is illustrated by the metaphor of the *melting pot* – an optimistic and homogeneous process of integration, the multicultural vision is evoked by the image of the *salad bowl* representing the co-existence of a mosaic of cultures which each maintain their own particularities (Semprini, 2000).

Concept 3.1 | European cultures

According to French historian Jean-Baptiste Duroselle (2004), Europe is generally considered to be a community that is neither racially nor linguistically based but rather created on the events of its history.

Although Europe is traditionally designated as one of the world's seven continents its contours appear for the first time on a world map in 100–160 AD – its identity has never been clearly established either culturally, politically or geographically. As this chapter will show, current Europe's eastern borders in particular remain somewhat arbitrary, since these can also be seen as a part of Asia. Not having ever been a stable, autonomous entity, Europe has been portrayed in many different ways down the ages according to the cultural and political relations prevailing.

The most recent development in terms of relations within Europe is the European Union (EU). The historical roots of the EU lie in the Second World War, as do those of a parallel institution, the Council of Europe which was created in 1949 by West European nations. Six countries (Germany, France, Italy, Belgium, Luxembourg and the Netherlands) wishing to step up co-operation, signed a treaty whereby their coal and steel industries were to be run under a common management. This co-operation was developed further in other economic sectors and the creation of the European Economic Community (EEC), often referred to as the Common Market, was the result. As a result of the 1991 Maastricht treaty, the EEC became the European Union, paving the way for increased coordination in areas of foreign and security policy, criminal justice, judicial co-operation, as well as the creation of the euro currency. At the time of writing, the EU comprises 28 countries (see Figure 3.1), of which 18 share the euro currency (http://europa.eu/about-eu/eu-history/index_en.htm).

The Council of Europe and the European Union were both set up to bring peace and prosperity to a continent whose countries had been at war with each other. The Council has come to play a special role in the development of the EU by laying down economic, social and legal benchmarks for new applicant countries. By doing so, it is creating a European identity based on common values and practices.

However, to what extent can one talk of a European culture based on such values and practices? There is certainly an increasing uniformity in the way affairs are organised and in the way people run their lives, particularly thanks to the effects of the EU relating to the socio-economic domain. The 'Schengen Agreement', for example, allows free movement of persons within the majority of EU countries.

SPOTLIGHT 3.1

The Council of Europe and the European Union: different roles, shared values

United in diversity

9 May – Europe Day

A European Union poster celebrating Europe Day

The Council of Europe and the European Union share the same fundamental values – human rights, democracy and the rule of law – but are separate entities which perform different, yet complementary, roles.

Focusing on those core values, the Council of Europe brings together governments from across Europe – and beyond – to agree minimum legal standards in a wide range of areas. It then monitors how well countries apply the standards that they have chosen to sign up to. It also provides technical assistance, often working together with the European Union, to help them do so.

The European Union refers to those same European values as a key element of its deeper political and economic integration processes. It often builds upon Council of Europe standards when drawing up legal instruments and agreements which apply to its member states. Furthermore, the European Union regularly refers to Council of Europe standards and monitoring work in its dealings with neighbouring countries, many of which are Council of Europe member states.

Source: Council of Europe: http://hub.coe.int/web/coe-portal/european-union, accessed 12/9/2013.

Nevertheless, this organisation itself has a rather ambivalent attitude towards the concept of a European culture: while one EU body talks of its wish to develop a unified cultural entity, another talks of the need to preserve Europe's many cultures. Those who shout 'I am a European' may be essentially exclaiming an ideal based on a desire for European unity (or stating a fairly obvious geographical fact); those denying the existence of Europe see nothing more than institutional structures binding a hotchpotch of different cultures.

Despite the domination of Rome and the predomination of Christianity over centuries, despite increased co-ordination and co-operation between European countries, shared representation and legislation, and despite decolonization followed by a huge wave of immigrants from Africa and Asia to Europe, cultural differences between regions and countries have not been eradicated. Cultural values of a society are still being handed down from generation to generation in the same way as those of an individual. Some shifts may occur over time, but clear cultural differences still survive. Indeed, the case can be put forward that as a result of its increasing membership, the EU is becoming more heterogeneous.

Member states of the European Union are shown above. Candidate countries (FYROM, Turkey) are depicted in grey.

Figure 3.1 **The European Union**

Source: The European Commission ©.

Some historians have maintained that a much more united Europe existed in the Middle Ages (from around the ninth to twelfth centuries) when a number of its countries shared common features of a feudal society. With no strong central authority, political power was dispersed among lords who in turn granted vassals authority over particular lands. Those peasants who tended particular landholdings were obliged to supply the lord with labour and/or part of the land's output. This was a system essentially based on man-to-man relations, the one depending on the other, in an agrarian economy with limited money exchange. There was a clear convergence of civilisation and culture as those travelling on business felt at home, in Lübeck, Paris, London, Bruges, Cologne, Burgos, Milan or Venice (Braudel, 2008).

As Morin (1987) declares, the political, economic and cultural Europe of today is the result of the disruption of this feudal system and the ensuing conflicts. This, as well as the both complementary and conflicting cultural heritage of, Greek, Roman and Judeo-Christian cultures, is what makes Europe unique.

The regional differences mentioned earlier have a lot to do with the influences that events in history brought to daily life. The Roman Empire with its strict hierarchies and its codified system of laws was one; the later invasion of the Vikings who maintained local, largely independent communities with their own laws and hierarchies was another. These two influences will be the starting point for classifying the peoples of Europe in different *clusters*, in line with the terminology of the GLOBE project. However, in order to make clearer the differences between Western and Eastern European business cultures – especially on the economic level – the composition of the original GLOBE clusters has been modified.

Western Europe

Greece

Why is it not possible to talk about Europe without mentioning Greece? Historically speaking, Greek civilisation had a strong influence on the Romans and through the Latin language the Western world absorbed Greek culture (Duroselle, 2004). In contemporary terms, Greece, which became the tenth member of the EU in 1981, featured heavily in a recent major economic crisis involving the banking sector. Greece would have been bankrupt in 2011 if the states of the Eurozone and the International Monetary Fund (IMF) had not procured it financial assistance. Such help reflects the principle defined by Mario Draghi, President of the European Central Bank, in his speech in Munich (February 2013), with regard to EU countries which cannot succeed on their own: 'The ethical imperative when we see others in need is to help. It is to do what we can to limit their hardship'.

To try and understand why Greece ended up in this extreme situation we can refer to the analysis of Greek culture made by GLOBE, in particular concerning the 'perceived' and 'desired' results for several dimensions (see explanation of the methodology in Chapter 2, concept 2.2). There is a marked difference between the scores for organisational practices as perceived by managers and the scores for the personal preferred values of the organisation. In comparison with other countries, there is a substantial gap between what is happening now ('As Is') and what should be happening ('Should Be'), while both scores are low compared to the other cultures studied (Papalexandris, 2008: 780). This is reflected in the attitude towards the future orientation dimension where the Greeks are shown to be unwilling to make long-term plans. Nonetheless, when Greece was integrated into the EU and the European currency system, its government was asked – without respecting (or knowing) this cultural particularity – to adapt its practices in order to act in a more future-oriented way!

Latin Europe

Managing and organising in societies characterised by Romance languages close to Latin, by Roman-style legal systems and strong Roman Catholic churches, still differs from other societies where the Romans held little or no sway. The Roman Empire had the greatest effect on countries below the river Rhine. In Latin Europe, there is a more personal approach to managing and organising. There may be a highly developed bureaucracy present in Latin countries, but the layers of hierarchy and the procedures involved in getting things done are so formalised that working round them is quicker and in the end more efficient. That is why there is a reliance on family and personal relationships and connections to work around the system, to bend the rules.

Nevertheless, the boss is the boss, and the authority of that person rests on the need of a country's people for strong rule. There is often a tension between this dependence on and loyalty towards authoritarian figures and a distrust of authoritarian systems in general. Prominent figures may exploit this tension by showing their ability as leaders to impose their stamp, their will on unwieldy closed hierarchies.

As Boisot indicates (1993: 222) in his article on management in Spain:

> The need for a strong leader and a hierarchical leader, however, does not necessarily give the enterprise manager the kind of mandate that would allow him to play a proper co-ordinating role.

Managers lack the legitimacy to perform their role effectively and can be perceived as devious exploiters of the economic system. This problem of managerial legitimacy is one, he believes, prevalent in Latin culture because the economic dimension is perceived to be little more than an expression of the political culture.

In her book on Italian management, Vidal (1992) distinguishes two types of business leaders in Italy. A company is run by two people, a couple as it were, who share each other's confidence and complement each other. The one plays the role of leader and spends most of his time with external contacts in search of information that will allow him to adjust company objectives. While doing so, he keeps an eye on what is happening inside the company. The other assumes the role of manager in the traditional sense, focusing his attention on what is happening within the company while still keeping an eye on the world outside.

A leader in France, however, is alone at the top. Such power involves not only fulfilling contractual obligations, but also preserving the status of the position. If he is not moderate when enacting his power, if he lacks breadth of vision or is seen as mean-minded, then he is seen to belong to what Segal (d'Iribarne *et al.*, 1998) calls the category of 'little bosses', and so risks losing his status.

French leaders are tempted to apply the Anglo-Saxon management tools coming from American consultants, such as 'delegation' or 'team work', while it is obvious that the culture of power is the dominant element of the corporate culture in France.

France

Unlike the other countries in Latin Europe, France was formed by a wide range of peoples, consisting at the start mainly of Celts (the Gauls), Romans and Germans (the Franks). The country came into being after the separation of Francia Occidentalis (the West Frankish kingdom, now France) from Francia Orientalis (the East Frankish kingdom, now Germany). In the eighteenth century, France became the model of European culture, not only through the dissemination of the universal values – liberty, equality and fraternity – proclaimed during the French Revolution, but also through its language. It is perhaps the historical role of France as the upholder of universal cultural values that has made it reluctant to envisage a plurality of cultures, or to talk of one culture for one people. In any case, the French idea of universal culture and its concept of a unity of cultural communities within French society, contrasts strongly with the notion held in other European countries of a national culture essentially based on compromise (d'Iribarne *et al.*, 1998).

Another distinctive feature of France – compared to its neighbours – lies in its history as an old immigration country. Although European people migrated to various parts of the world to populate the colonies and the new countries, France took in more emigrants than the number of French people who went abroad. Nowadays, almost a quarter of the population has at least one of his/her four grandparents born in a foreign country. Therefore, it is difficult to talk about the 'identity of France' without referring to the cultural diversity of its original and immigrant peoples.

In the economic sphere, the number of companies with a state-owned majority shareholding – such as Renault, Air France and France Telecom, as well as the number of employees working in a public company have been declining in all sectors in the last decennia. Indeed, it has often been necessary to privatise enterprises to facilitate their growth through acquisitions or mergers with other European and global private companies. The state used to develop regulations concerning foreign ownership either to protect some large industrial companies against a hostile takeover bid or to preserve their 'national character'. Currently, although its participation already has greatly diminished, the state continues to sell its shares, particularly those in state-owned enterprises.

Examined in terms of the cultural dimensions put forward by House *et al.* (2004), the Latin European cluster is characterised as being low in terms of humane orientation practices, although humane orientation scores in terms of values more closely resemble those of other European clusters. This humane orientation construct addresses the degree of concern, tolerance and support extended to others. As a cluster with low humane orientation practices, self-interest is high, as is lack of consideration for others. However, in terms of consideration for family, the countries concerned are collectively inclined, showing greater loyalty and cohesiveness to their family. As will be seen later in concept 3.2 in this chapter, when looking at Latin America, the family concern is even more in evidence in the Latin countries of the New World.

Nordic Europe

The presence of the Vikings who swept down from Scandinavia and settled on a large part of northern Europe – occupied by Germanic peoples who maintained important trade relationships with the Romans – is still felt. Both merchants, sailors and warriors, they helped to reinforce the contrast between the cultural characteristics of the Northerners and those of the former Roman Empire. They had no overriding hierarchy, no elaborate systems of control. Instead, they maintained large independent communities, each with its own laws and governing bodies.

The Viking heritage of self-sufficiency, fairness, egalitarianism and democracy is reflected in the way present-day business is carried out in Scandinavian countries, i.e. in Norway, Sweden, Finland, Denmark, also including, broadly, Iceland. In most companies, bosses are seen more as team leaders and group facilitators as opposed to being decision-makers who delegate tasks to others. As such, employees are often encouraged to express

Table 3.2 **Scandinavian relationships within Europe**

Nordic countries	Council of Europe	EU member	Joined EU in	EFTA member	Schengen area	Euro currency
Denmark	Yes	Yes	1973		Yes	No
Sweden	Yes	Yes	1995		Yes	No
Finland	Yes	Yes	1995		Yes	Yes
Iceland	Yes	No	–	Yes	Yes	No
Norway	Yes	No	–	Yes	Yes	No

Source: adapted from http://en.wikipedia.org/wiki/European_Free_Trade_Association#EFTA_and_the_European_Union

their opinions freely at meetings and everyone's opinion is given consideration when making decisions. However, the final decision often lies in the hands of the team leader.

The countries of Nordic Europe share one distinctive feature – their approach to authority. Their inhabitants do not regard those in authority as remote persons whose word is to be accepted unquestioningly. They face up to them, question their decisions and expect to be consulted on issues affecting them. Those managing and being managed are less far apart socially than in Latin Europe, with more emphasis put on the job being done than the position in the hierarchy. Managers are not regarded as being expert in all matters but are expected to make effective use of the expertise among their co-workers. These characterisations are reflected in the position of Nordic European countries on the cultural dimensions relating to 'power distance' as described in Chapter 2.

However, on a socio-economic level, there are some differences between the Scandinavian countries. While Denmark, Finland and Sweden are state members of the European Union and the last two also of the Eurozone, Norway and Iceland are members of another organisation – the European Free Market Institution – and maintain a more complicated relationship with the EU. (See Table 3.2.)

Germanic Europe

House *et al.* (2004) admit that the cultural separation of Germanic and Nordic Europe is not as great as among other clusters. Along with the Nordic countries, Germanic countries show lower power distance than their other fellow Europeans. This is reflected in a general preference for company employees to work in groups rather than making solo efforts. However, this does not mean that, for example, the Germans are as informal as the Dutch (included as well as Austrian and Swiss German in the Germanic cluster) in their behaviour towards each other. In Germany, the hierarchical positions are not as easily separated from the persons occupying them as they are in the Netherlands. A respectful formality tends to prevail between company employees operating on different levels and in different areas of responsibility. The concern for detailed codes and written rules could be seen as reflecting not only the concept of 'universalism' as described by Trompenaars (see Chapter 5), but also Hofstede's dimension of uncertainty avoidance. German companies rely heavily on experts and their knowledge to minimise insecurity and, for the same reason, tend to adopt a longer-term perspective when making strategic decisions.

MINI-CASE 3.1

German business culture should be a model for our own

Germany's economic bounce-back is testament to its respect for manufacturing and a backbone of small- and medium-sized firms

By Ruth Sunderland

The Observer, Sunday, 15 August 2010

Germany has had plenty of troubles in the credit crunch. Some of its of the banks were pretty stupid and, as the strong man of the Eurozone, it has been riven by rows over its taxpayers having to bail out weaker nations such as Greece.

Its impressive bounce-back, with GDP growth of 2.2% in the second quarter, the strongest since unification, is unlikely to continue at this pace and it highlights the fact that much of the rest of the Eurozone is still struggling. But it is a testament to a business culture that has respect for manufacturing, and where exporters such as BMW or Bosch do not rely on a cheap currency to sell goods abroad but on the excellence of their products.

The backbone of the German economy is its *Mittelstand*, a core of small and medium-sized firms, many of which have existed for generations and have proved their durability and resilience. In the mid-noughties, I met a number of them in the industrial region of Nordrhein-Westfalen, and they were rightly sceptical about the UK's apparent economic miracle and about debt-based Anglo-Saxon capitalism in general.

Our government hopes smaller firms will create jobs and help rebalance the economy. In Germany it is starting to happen: according to its chambers of commerce, *Mittelstand* companies want to create up to 100,000 jobs by the end of the year, and are also pushing green technology.

We still have fantastic manufacturers, but that is in spite of the business culture of the past 30 years rather than because of it. Shouldn't we be asking what we can learn from the Germans?

Source: www.guardian.co.uk/business/2010/aug/15/german-growth-business-culture, accessed 8/2/2013.

Questions

1. To what extent do you think the unification of the West and East Germany played a role in building strong economy?

2. What are the best practices which the British and the Europeans in general should learn from the Germans?

Great Britain

It was Germanic peoples – the Angles, Saxons and Jutes – who, along with other tribes from Northern Europe, settled in large numbers in 'Britannia', the province that the Romans had established on the lowlands of the British mainland and later abandoned. With the eventual consolidation of the various settlements and kingdoms, this area became known as England. England eventually became the dominant part of a larger political entity, now known as the United Kingdom of Great Britain and Northern Ireland, which includes Wales, Scotland and the Northern part of the isle of Ireland. The use of the term 'British' reflects the union of the peoples of this extreme Western part of Europe and the amalgam of elements that constitutes their culture.

Because of their ethnic and linguistic similarities, the GLOBE project (House *et al.*, 2004; Chhokar *et al.*, 2008) placed these countries in the Anglo cluster along with North America and Australasia (concept 3.2). However, because of its common history with Europe, we will consider in this section Great Britain as being a country in the Western European cluster, even though its style of management is Anglo-Saxon. According to Péron (2002), this style is characterised by its pragmatic approach, which focuses more on action than analysis, thus more on the culture of 'how' than of 'why'. Using Hofstede's cultural dimensions, the British can be characterised as having less power distance and lower uncertainty avoidance than their European neighbours, while at the same time being more individualistic and more ambitious/aggressive than their counterparts on the continent.

The relaxed British approach to management contrasts strongly with the Latin and Nordic approach. Although bureaucracy is the most common form of organisation, and instrumental in creating Britain's economic success in the nineteenth century (the liberal principles of 'laissez-faire' and 'free trade' dominate the economic policy of this Victorian period), the British handle it in a very pragmatic way. As Hickson and Pugh (2001: 50) indicate:

> Characteristically, they balance its potential rigidities by day-to-day pragmatism, working things out as they go along, rather than taking bureaucratic prescription too far. They do not try to manage uncertainty by issuing regulations and declarations, of which they are sceptical. Hence it has been said that the British see an organization as a 'market' in which people negotiate what has to be done.

This ties in with the very individually oriented nature of the British. The job is a job, regarded as separate from one's personal life, a task to be performed impersonally. This can be seen in the way personnel are selected. Although the selection process may appear the same across European countries, the emphasis in British cultures is on the extent to which the individual concerned can contribute to the tasks of the organisation. That is why it is normal for intelligence and skills to be measured and assessment centres to be employed.

Compared to other European countries generally, Britain is reluctant to invest in training for the longer term. The very nature of its deregulated liberal market economy, where the goal is maximisation of profit in a relatively short time, entails less consideration being given to the employment needs in the longer term.

After losing its colonial empire, Great Britain had to face a dilemma concerning its role in Europe and the world: should it be bound to the European Community (Common Market at the time) or to the Commonwealth? (Braudel, 2008). Time was necessary to resolve this issue; but nowadays, the UK is currently one of the members of the EU just as it is one of the members of the Commonwealth of Nations – an intergovernmental organisation of member states that were mostly territories of the British Empire.

The UK joined the former European Union in 1973 and its relationship with the EU is illustrated by the speech delivered in 1988 by Margaret Thatcher, British Prime Minister at that time. This concerned (1) the European values: 'Nor should we forget that European values have helped to make the United States of America into the valiant defender of freedom which it has become'; (2) European cultural link with North-America: 'Some of the founding fathers of the community thought that the United States of America might be its model. But the whole history of America is quite different from Europe. People went there to get away from the intolerance and constraints of life in Europe. They sought liberty and opportunity; and their strong sense of purpose has, over two centuries, helped create a new unity and pride in being American – just as our pride lies in being British or Belgian or Dutch or German';

SPOTLIGHT 3.2

Selecting employees

Some comparisons between the British and countries from the Latin and Germanic clusters are relevant here to highlight differences with regard to recruitment and employment generally. In Latin countries, more focus is placed during the selection process on the extent to which the applicant will fit into the group of employees concerned. The emphasis, therefore, is on interpersonal skills and tests of personality and communicative competence.

French and UK methods of selection are more similar concerning the use of one-to-one interviews and the panel interviews. However it seems that the French make use of references much less than the British. The greatest contrast is the approach of the French, where the concern is not just about skills criteria but also about whether the applicants possess the behaviours desired by the organisation (Gilbert, 2008), with the approach of the British, where more reliance is placed on more objective criteria about

applicants' intellect or technical skills to determine whether they fit into the organisation.

In Germanic cultures, there is equal concern for the appropriate technical skills, but in a much broader and long-term context. As Hillmert (2002) indicates, the (potential) employer and employee are not just concerned with the present requirements of a company, but also with the longer-term occupational career of a candidate. Whereas the occupation of a British employee is closely connected to the firm where he/she works, that of the German employee is considered more as a step in the development of a career that involves further (state-supported) vocational training and inter-firm mobility. The stability of careers in Germany contrasts strongly with the job-hopping tendencies and short-term perspectives of British employees who do not benefit from a co-ordinated training provision from the state, employers and trade unions.

and (3) the vision of the role of Europe in the world: 'Let us have a Europe which plays its full part in the wider world, which looks outward not inward, and which preserves that Atlantic Community – that Europe on both sides of the Atlantic – which is our noblest inheritance and our greatest strength.' (Source: The Bruges Group, www.cvce.eu)

Currently, Britain's relationship with Europe on an economic level is particularly complicated, as illustrated in the spotlight below.

SPOTLIGHT 3.3

Norway option a 'clear choice' for Britain in Europe

There is a grouping of countries within Europe called the European Free Trade Association (EFTA). Although only now consisting of four countries – Iceland, Liechtenstein, Norway and Switzerland – EFTA is one of the off-the-shelf alternatives that exist for trading with EU countries. Another is the European Economic Area (EEA) which unites the 27 EU member states and the EFTA countries (excepted Switzerland) into an internal market for citizens and economic operators in EEA. Britain will stay in the EEA, and is tempted to take the 'Norway option', outside the EU but part of EFTA: by switching to the 'Norway option', Britain could

control its own affairs, save money, free business from unnecessary regulations and reduce unemployment, claims a think-tank. The EU countries are spending a lot of their time on the euro experiment, while other countries in the world are getting better managed and improving the lives of their people – what normal government is supposed to do.

Source: extract from Hugo van Randwyck on behalf of the Bruges Group think-tank in the UK. http://www.publicserviceeurope.com/article/3177/norway-option-a-clear-choice-for-britain-in-europe, accessed 12/3/2013.

Whatever agreements may be reached at economic or social level with countries that already are or aspire to EU membership, co-operation of whatever sort can clearly only work if there is a willingness to do so at cultural level. Observers of the developments in Europe have noted this from the start, including one of the founders of the original European Community, Jean Monnet. He was asked what he would do differently if he had the chance to start over again with the development of the community. It is often suggested that he replied: 'I would start first through culture' (http://www.ecb.int/press/key/date/2011/html/sp110602.en.html). These words resound as strongly nowadays as they did when first reported.

Eastern Europe

The GLOBE researchers have placed most of the former communist countries in the Eastern Europe cluster (see Concept 2.2) rather than including the countries there in one of the Western European clusters. It is clear that the aftermath of the Second World War involved Europe being divided into two, with Eastern Europe becoming closed off, thrown back on itself and dependent on Soviet communism. Western Europe, on the other hand, fell under the very strong influence of the US, its enterprising mind, its taste for risk and championing of individual rights. However, after the fall of the Berlin Wall (9 November 1989), Western and Eastern Europe were no longer separated and the restructuring of the East German economy began, along with that of the Soviet Union and the satellite states of the communist bloc.

Another incongruity in the GLOBE project's classification is that Turkey, which is placed in the Middle East cluster, has been an associate member of the European Union since 1963 and is striving to become a full member.

Emergent economies

Although the economies of the Eastern and Central European countries, including Russia and Turkey, have been growing rapidly, these countries have some similarities with other countries around the world, which are called 'emerging markets' and defined by Cavusgil, Ghauri and Akcal (2013: 5) as follows:

Emerging markets are countries which are in a transition phase from developing to developed markets due to rapid growth and industrialization.

Different indices classify the countries in emerging markets according to *inter alia* their development level, the size of the companies and their openness to foreign ownership and trade.

In terms of this definition, a number of EU members (Poland, Czech Republic, Hungary, and Romania) can be considered as 'emerging markets'. It is therefore important from a 'developed markets' point of view to take into consideration cultural differences when conducting business with these countries.

East and Central Europe

The Austro-Hungarian Empire, the Russian Empire and the Soviet hegemony have had a major influence on East and Central European cultures. The post-revolution regimes in particular had a profound effect on these countries. Before the Iron Curtain eventually fell, countries under Soviet sway were characterised by highly autocratic, centralised organisations with many bureaucratic levels, reflecting the presence of a dual hierarchy (politics and business worked hand-in-hand) and an obsession with state planning. The legacy of the communist system of administration is what the societies of East and Central Europe have had to contend with since the early 1990s, when Western political and economic practices were introduced. The transformation of highly bureaucratic and centralised economies has taken much longer than anticipated. The withdrawal of centralised control has increased feelings of uncertainty and helplessness. Individuals and companies can no longer rely on the 'system' to help them out; instead they must battle their own way through, develop self-confidence and learn how to deal with a more open, less merciful environment. This transition has, however, caused considerable unrest, and there is still a longing for how things used to be among those unwilling to adapt to the new environment.

The opportunity to take on roles and responsibilities similar to those of their Western neighbours is still seen as a threat, especially by those who grew up and worked under the old regimes.

Russia, a BRIC country

With the political collapse of the Soviet Union, 15 republics emerged, of which Russia itself is a collection of smaller republics, hence, its official name: The Russian Federation. This 'new' country, which spans Europe and Asia, has also been struggling since 1991 to replace the social, political and economic features of the Communist era with a more democratic political system and a market-oriented economy. Close association with the EU is seen as an important way of developing the Russian economy, but membership is a step too far for many Russians who fear their independence being swallowed up in a greater Europe. Is the country really a European nation? If, in geographic terms, the border of Europe is considered to be the Urals mountain range, can that part of Russia to the west of the Urals, and where most of the population is centred, be considered as 'European Russia'?

In economics terms, Russia not only belongs to the category of European emergent markets but is also classified as one of the BRIC countries, along with emerging countries from other continents – Brazil (concept 3.2) plus India and China (Chapter 4). The BRIC countries are seen as rapidly developing, with a potential to overshoot the world's largest economies in the future. A high level of power distance enables the BRIC companies to make decisions quickly since only a small percentage of individuals are involved in the process (Cavusgil *et al.*, 2013). Recently, South Africa (Chapter 4) joined this organisation of the largest emerging and developing economies – so the acronym was changed to BRICS, thus representing 40 per cent of the Earth's population.

Although the EU and Russia have been exploring the idea of developing a common European economic space, competing political and economic aims and interests appear to have gained the upper hand. Even if Russia's presence on the European business stage is becoming increasingly dominant, there are many who question whether Russians have the same regard for essential values (such as democracy, human rights and freedom) as countries in and close to the EU. Russia and Europe, they argue, are unlikely ever to share such cultural values.

MINI-CASE 3.2

The joint venture GM-AvtoVAZ

GM-AvtoVAZ is going to export about 4,000 vehicles in 2013, the press office of joint venture informed AUTOSTAT agency. 2,744 Chevrolet Niva vehicles were delivered in foreign markets for 2012, which is a 31.9% increase on a year-to-year basis.

Source: http://eng.autostat.ru/news/view/7462, accessed 13/3/2013.

Just a few years ago . . .

A tale of two Russian factories

It takes less than 10 minutes to drive from Avtovaz, maker of Lada cars, to its joint venture with General Motors. But to make the journey feels like crossing the border between the Soviet Union and the West 20 years ago.

On one side are grey and crumbling concrete factories, military-style security and unsmiling workers. An office block towers over the plant, with a top-floor restaurant reserved for managers.

On the other is a modern-looking factory, with low-key security, welcoming workers in blue overalls and a canteen where managers and workers eat at the same tables.

Workers in both places are Russian and live in the same city. But one factory is stuck in the Soviet era while the other is part of the modern world.

Inside, the differences do not lie in technology: Avtovaz has a new assembly line, equipped with the latest German and Italian machinery, to produce its slick-looking Kalina model. But as one foreign executive puts it: 'What these guys do not understand is that it is not about a car, it is about people. Spending $5bn or even $10bn in the same environment will not make a good carmaker.'

The real distinctions between Avtovaz and its joint venture lie in management approaches and relations between managers and workers. 'Here everything is different: the work culture, the discipline, the attitude,' says Evgeny Berezin, assembly manager at GM-Avtovaz. 'You can build the same factory as the one here, but it is all in the mind', he adds.

He says all workers at GM-Avtovaz are encouraged to show initiative and make suggestions, which can be quickly taken on board. Any suggestion at Avtovaz usually gets lost in bureaucracy.

'Avtovaz makes the same model for 10 years – almost unchanged. The car we make here today is different from the one we made a couple of years ago. I like working here because I can see the result of my work. People here have real responsibility.'

Vadim Klassen, who has worked in both plants, says: 'If we learn from [foreign carmakers] we will catch up quickly. If we go down our own path, we never will. But you have to want to learn and know how to learn.'

Questions

1. Could you explain what the foreign executive means by saying: 'What these guys do not understand is that it is not about a car, it is about people.'

2. Comment on the last paragraph of the case. Do you agree with Vadim Klassen?

SPOTLIGHT 3.4

Russia: a decline in collectivist values?

Findings from the GLOBE project, as drawn up by Grachev *et al.* (2008), show what the authors consider to be a severe decline in traditional collectivistic values in Russia. They reveal a considerable difference between the 'As Is' and 'Should Be' scores for institutional collectivism. The authors see the country as moving along the path to increasing individualism and social fragmentation.

The findings also reflect a trend evident in many other societies: a move towards lower power distance. However, the gap between 'As Is' and 'Should Be' remains substantial, leading the authors to question whether Russia can balance moves towards democracy with the maintenance of order in society.

Finally, they also detect a striking contrast between increasingly individual behaviour and low social responsibility, on the one hand, and the active networking used for survival on the other hand. The latter, they note, is often exploited by criminal structures.

The 'active networking' referred to in Spotlight 3.4 appears to be one feature of society in Russia that has survived the recent transition and which continues to play an important role in Russian life. This is a form of social networking called *blat*, which enabled individuals to deal with the scarcity of goods and services of a centrally planned economy. Although the word *blat* was originally associated with small crime, it came to be more associated with caring and sharing, with helping and being helped through a network of personal relationships. These relationships were built up over time, and mutual trust, common understandings and (implicit) rules of behaviour were established which allow favours of many kinds to be reciprocated. With the increased uncertainties of post-Soviet reforms, *blat* has continued to flourish, essentially to reduce the uncertain nature of a society where services at social, educational, financial and legal levels are weak, scarce, or non-existent. Michailova and Worm (2003: 517) argue that its nature has changed:

> [*Blat*] is becoming increasingly materialized, dominated by pragmatism and market-governed. The transformation of its nature from being based on moral and ethical considerations to having an explicit financial expression is a phenomenon in itself. *Blat* is becoming a negative word again with criminal undertones.

They point out that the perception there of bribery and corruption is a different one: people are more tolerant of wayward practices, and employees and managers consider it an important element of conducting business.

Nevertheless, bribery and corruption are not only an unethical way for doing business in the emerging countries. The developed countries also have their responsibilities when the Western managers – wishing to do business in these markets – offer bribes to bureaucrats or corporate buyers for succeeding their business deals (Cavusgil *et al.*, 2013).

Turkey

Turkey is often seen as the bridge or crossroads between Europe and Asia. Its largest and most populated part, together with its capital Ankara, lies in Asia; its smaller western part in Europe. The country's largest city, Istanbul, straddles the Bosphorus, the traditional border between Europe and Asia.

Although negotiations for it to become a full member of the European Union began in 2005, a number of EU countries have made it clear that they do not consider that Turkey would be a suitable member. Their one fundamental concern is that Turkey is not European, culturally or geographically.

Proponents of Turkey's membership argue that the country is European: it is successor state to the partitioned Ottoman Empire which stretched from the Red Sea to the gates of Vienna and included most of South Eastern Europe; as such it played an influential role in the history of Europe for over four centuries. Opponents maintain that if Turkey eventually became a full member of the EU, its large, mainly Muslim, population would threaten the Judeo-Christian cultural homogeneity of the continent.

MINI-CASE 3.3

Sub-Saharan focus – Turkey seeks influence in Africa

By Daniel Dombey in Istanbul

Selim Bora had never been south of the Sahara before the call came to design and build the conference centre for an African Union summit in just six months.

But a week later the 43-year-old Turkish businessman was in Equatorial Guinea. His family-owned company, Summa, built the 13,000-square-metre complex in time for the 2011 AU summit in Malabo.

'We had no clue about the country when we went there', Mr Bora says. 'We had to figure it all out.'

His story is part of a concerted push by Turkey deep into Africa, as it follows China, Brazil and India in seeking to secure economic and political influence on the continent.

As Ankara looks to diversify away from the stuttering European economy, it is searching not only for new markets but also a more prominent role on the world stage. In the past three years, Turkey has opened 19 new embassies on the continent. It now has 26 south of the Sahara and will have opened new delegations in Chad, Guinea and Djibouti by the end of this month, as Recep Tayyip Erdogan, prime minister, visits Gabon, Niger and Senegal.

'The aim is to develop ties, to close gaps, to go to places where we have never been', says a Turkish official. Travelling to the region is becoming easier.

Last month, Turkish Airlines, a 49 per cent state-owned company, announced the start of direct flights to Niamey, Ouagadougou, Yaoundé and Douala, bringing the number of destinations in sub-Saharan Africa to 24. Underpinned by such diplomatic and transport ties, Ankara's commerce with sub-Saharan Africa jumped from $742m in 2000 to almost $7.5bn in 2011.

Today, Mr Bora says, the region accounts for 40 per cent of his group's business – total revenues are $300m a year – and he is interested in developing further ties with countries ranging from Niger to Angola. He adds that the Turkish construction sector as a whole is expanding from North Africa to the oil and gas rich countries of western Africa.

He highlights Turkish executives' willingness to work in challenging or unusual circumstances, including for regimes such as Equatorial Guinea, which was criticised for spending €500m on the summit complex and carried out arrests before the event.

'For us, it's really the same, regardless of the regime, regardless of the geographical conditions, regardless of the climactic conditions', Mr Bora says. 'For us the important thing is to get the job done.'

Such projects have broader economic consequences, as well. In a recent *Financial Times* interview, Erdem Basci, the governor of Turkey's central bank, grouped Africa together with Russia and the Middle East as a region with a fast-growing appetite for imports that could help Turkey diversify away from the EU. 'Our businessmen are extremely rapid and flexible moving into these markets', he said.

With 55 countries, Africa represents more than a quarter of all UN members: a potential repository of votes for a state willing to invest politically in the region. Mr Ulgen a former Turkish diplomat now at Carnegie Europe, depicts Turkey's stance as a halfway house between the EU and China.

It does not tie aid to governance conditions but sees the relationship as more than merely economic. Its aid agency, which delivered more than $150m to countries in sub-Saharan Africa last year, says denying aid to human rights violators risks punishing those most in need of help. Mr Ulgen cautions that the biggest danger for Turkey is to overpromise: Ankara's $800bn economy cannot match the resources of Brussels and Beijing.

Moreover, commerce with sub-Saharan Africa still represents only a fraction of Turkey's $376bn overall trade. While Arcelik, a Turkish white-goods manufacturer, acquired Defy, a South African equivalent, for $325m in 2011, most of the country's investments in the region are considerably smaller.

Nevertheless, Turkey's businessmen and politicians are increasingly looking to Africa. Erbil Oksuz, a Turkish construction subcontractor who has been working in Uganda for a year, complains about health risks and the entrenched position of Chinese companies. But he enthuses about the country's infrastructure needs and its discovery of oil. 'It is worth the effort . . . Africa is riskier but we make more money', he says. 'More Turks are coming.'

Additional reporting by Funja Guler

 Source: 'Sub-Saharan Focus – Turkey seeks influence in Africa', *The Financial Times* 7/1/2013, (Dombey, D.), Copyright ©The Financial Times Limited 2013.

Questions

1   How could you describe the business culture of Turkey?

2   What are the main reasons for Turkey doing business in Africa?

We now move from the European clusters to the American and Australasian clusters. From an historical point of view, it would be more exact to say that we are moving from the 'European Old World' to the 'New World'. European peoples, first Portuguese and Spaniard, then the British, Dutch, French and Swedes, brought their cultures to colonies that they founded on the American continent and called: New Spain, New England, New Amsterdam, New France, New Sweden. It was also Europeans who set up New Holland (Australia) and New Zealand.

Concept 3.2   American and Australasian cultures

This concept will focus on the cultures in the Americas, Australia and New Zealand where European colonists established trading settlements which evolved into formal colonies and eventually achieved independence.

United States of America

The original 13 British colonies in what would become the USA, unilaterally declared their independence of the British throne. This act of defiance led to the revolutionary war between these colonists and Great Britain, the defeat of the mother country and the eventual creation of the USA.

Uniting the 13 colonies, now states, involved a Constitutional Convention basically inventing a nation through devising a constitution and creating a suitable form of central government, all based on the principle of equality. A workable balance of power had to be established between a central authority and the states who were proud of the independence they had enjoyed for many years. Within the government itself the notion of equality was reflected in the way a number of institutions checked and balanced each other. The president was to check the power of Congress and Congress to check the power of the president, and the Supreme Court to check the power of both by referring to the rule-book of the Constitution. However, as Alistair Cooke (1973: 147) remarks,

> There might have been no workable Constitution and no all-powerful Court if the Founding Fathers (the Constitutional Convention) had not listened to the missing giant [...] Thomas Jefferson.

It was Jefferson who, as Minister to France, had himself experienced assaults on personal liberty and who managed to persuade members of the convention that they should specify exactly what the human rights were which Americans should enjoy in terms of the 'unalienable right to liberty'. Ten amendments listing these rights, known as the Bill of Rights, were eventually added to the constitution. The Supreme Court's task was then, as now, to protect the rights of the citizen through interpretation of the US constitution.

The 'pursuit of happiness' was also enshrined in the Declaration of Independence. Although the exact meaning of this phrase is still disputed, it essentially reflected the desire of future Americans for a better, richer and happier life. This is what James Adams called 'the American dream', a term used for the first time in his history of America published in 1931 and entitled *The Epic of America*. This phrase reflects the essential optimism which many Americans still have regarding their personal progress in life as well as the progress of their nation. Realising this dream entailed hard work, however, and the early settlers and those immigrants who followed had the 'work ethic' needed.

The term used by present-day Americans to loosely describe the founders of the USA is 'White Anglo-Saxon Protestants' or WASPs. The many immigrants who followed the early settlers were not all in any sense Protestant in their religious beliefs, but they adopted what Max Weber referred to as the Protestant work ethic. In his influential book *The Protestant Ethic and the Spirit of Capitalism*, first published in German in 1905 and translated into English in 1930, Weber studied the psychological conditions underpinning the development of capitalist civilisation. He argued that modern capitalism was born from the spirit of Christian asceticism in its specifically Protestant form. He saw a link between the self-denying ethos of the Protestant sects and the behaviour patterns associated with capitalism, above all those to do with hard work. It was this work ethic which spurred on the first Americans and their successors to realise the 'American Dream'.

This work ethic is still regarded as being a driving force within US business. However, the US constitution, as interpreted by the Supreme Court, guards the rights of the citizen and determines whether businesses are operating against the interests of the individual. The aggressive will to succeed in business is tempered by a detailed framework of legislation and within companies themselves there are strict rules and procedures to be followed. The 'impersonal organisation' is predominant, with a clearly defined hierarchy. This is not to be seen as inflexible, however. Just as the constitution can be 'interpreted', so can the rules and regulations. A common sense, pragmatic approach is needed to deal with uncertainty. Hickson and Pugh (2001: 50) refer to the US organisation as a 'negotiated order'. There may be a clearly defined hierarchy with explicit responsibilities for all concerned, but those higher on the ladder can be addressed by those on the lower ranks and the rules questioned. After all, the overriding concern is the advancement of the company; without it, self-advancement is itself in danger.

A strong, shared commitment among a company's employees allows for considerable delegation and decentralisation to be established more easily. This makes it easier for a company to contend with uncertainty and allows for an attitude towards the vicissitudes of the market that is more relaxed than, say, among British organisations. Thriving on competition is a feature: strong competition keeps a company on its toes and encourages innovation.

A vital indicator of success for US businesses is the 'bottom-line'. Although financial results are crucial to all those pursuing business in the Anglo-Saxon way, Americans are much more concerned about the bottom-line in the short term. This attitude engenders considerable criticism, especially among those who believe that investments of whatever kind often need time to bear fruit. On the other hand, US companies are continually aware of the interests of shareholders. Money engenders money, and time is the key instrument. Time must be harnessed as effectively as possible to enable progress, advancement and continuing commitment to the company.

One clear difference that is frequently referred to when British and American businesses are being compared is the way they look at the future. The general optimism prevalent in US business concerning the future – and future success – is said to contrast strongly with the more nuanced view of British business about future developments.

The 'new' immigrants

Until the 1960s the main source of immigrants had been Europe. From then on, however, Latin America became the larger source, thanks to the easing of immigration laws, the removal of national quotas and the need for extra labour in the rapidly expanding economy of the USA. Latin American immigrants made up over 16 per cent of the US population in 2011, equivalent to 52 million inhabitants (Motel and Patten, 2013). By that time, however, the numbers of immigrants from Asia, especially India, Japan and South Korea, exceed even those of Latin America. These Asian immigrants will be referred to in detail in Chapter 4.

Well over half of the Mexican immigrants are to be found in California and Texas, states which share the 2000-mile-long border with Mexico. The social and economic impact on these and other states and others where large numbers of Latin American immigrants have settled has been considerable. The complaints of a number of US citizens, especially in these areas, recall those made in previous centuries when large waves of German and Irish immigrants were thought to be a major threat to US society. Many of these comparatively recent immigrants are still undergoing the process of assimilation. One particular factor which adds a new dimension to this process is the fact that millions of Mexican immigrants live close to their mother country. Unlike the earlier immigrants from Europe, Mexicans living in the USA can maintain close cultural ties with their mother country, and many choose to do so. This is facilitated by an abundance of Spanish-language media. Even US companies make full use of these to promote their products and services, many of which are tuned to the needs and aspirations of the immigrants and their families. To add to this cross-cultural mixture, Mexican – and even Brazilian – companies have entered the market, taking advantage of the economic boom in their domestic markets. They have poured billions of dollars into the USA to start up and take over businesses in the USA which not only cater for the needs of their fellow countrymen but for Americans generally. With a number of banks, TV stations and construction companies now being run by Latin Americans, all kinds of federal and state agencies, as well as service industries now have to deal with the Latin American way of doing business.

SPOTLIGHT 3.5

Telenovelas for US tastes

There was a time, not too long ago, when melodramatic scenes of heartbreak and passion were the exclusive realm of midday soap operas broadcast to millions of housewives and domestic staff throughout Latin America.

Not any more: last month, Televisa, the Mexican master of the telenovela, announced a big push into the English-language market as part of its expansion into the US market.

Televisa USA, as the company's new Los Angeles-based studio is called, launched with multiple broadcast network deals, including a joint venture with Lionsgate, the global entertainment company, to develop new content for television audiences all over the US.

'Our content travels well', Carlos Madrazo, who heads Televisa's investor-relations department, told the *Financial Times*. 'It transcends language and culture.'

The strategy, he explained, involves complementing new material with content adapted from Televisa's existing library of Spanish-language soap-opera titles, which is the biggest in the world.

 Source: extracts from 'North of the border', *The Financial Times*, 23/8/12 (Thomson, A.), Copyright © The Financial Times.

Recent investigations into this process in the south-western states have shown how assimilation varies in economic terms. Valdez refers to the classic assimilation theory which foresees 'a pattern of gradual convergence to the socioeconomic outcomes of middle-class, non-Hispanic whites' (2006: 397). However, when analysing the 2000 census of Mexican Americans, she found that those who were poorly educated and earned low wages experienced a 'downward assimilation' to the permanent US underclass. Only those who were highly educated and with higher wages underwent an upward trend towards Anglo-conformity.

Canada

Canada, originally the territory of the Indians and Inuit, was first explored by the French who set up their first colony around Quebec. The British also set up colonies and it was they who eventually took control of Canada through settlement, warfare and the Treaty of Paris in 1763. Although the British were to reign over a francophone majority for 80 years, they formally granted these 'Canadiens' the right to practice Catholicism as well as French civil law through the Act of Quebec (1774). As Dufour (1990: 42) notes:

> The Act took into account that the Canadiens were not English – and never would be, at least not in the foreseeable future. The genius of this Act was in letting the Canadiens be themselves while remaining British subjects. According to some historians these were the beginnings of the Commonwealth.

Although the number of Anglophone immigrants increased rapidly and with it the number of Canadian provinces, Canada maintained clear French Canadian and Anglo Canadian identities up to and beyond 1867 when the country became independent. French and English are the two official languages of Canada, with the province of Quebec containing the majority of French speakers. There have been frequent political clashes between Quebec and central government and it was the Québecois who almost succeeded in getting the province separated from the rest of Canada in 1995.

Canada may remain officially bilingual, but since 1971 the country has implemented a number of policies to address the increasing plurality of cultures resulting from the waves of immigrants from many parts of the world. It was in that year that the then Prime Minister, Pierre Elliott Trudeau, proclaimed:

> There is no official culture, nor does any ethnic group take precedence over any other. No citizen or group of citizens is other than Canadian, and all should be treated fairly.
> http://www.multiculturalcanada.ca/Encyclopedia/A-Z/m9/1, accessed 4/8/2013.

This statement boldly summarised the respect for cultural diversity and cultural pluralism which was eventually enshrined in the Canadian Multiculturalism Act of 1988. This legislation has been a source of inspiration for other countries coming to terms with a diversity of cultures. Nevertheless, many Canadians are still concerned about who they actually are: can Canada be said to have a single national identity?

One way of clarifying who you are is to try and ascertain who you are not. When dealing with Americans, Canadians are only too aware of the need to stand their own ground, to counter the tendency of Americans to assume that Canadians are just like them, despite the fact that they speak the same language, have similar lifestyles and share a similar frame of reference.

Relations between the USA and Canada have proved to be very fertile ground for many Canadian writers and commentators. One of the most famous, Northrop Frye, observes that:

> American students have been conditioned from infancy to think of themselves as citizens of one of the world's greatest powers. Canadians are conditioned from infancy to think of themselves as citizens of a country of uncertain identity, a confusing past and a hazardous future.
> www.liveabroad.com/articles/canada.html, accessed 1/9/2010.

This comment reflects the contrast often made between the pushy, boastful, optimistic American and the low-key, modest and cautious Canadian. Pierre Trudeau, the Canadian prime minister referred to earlier, spoke of another aspect of US–Canadian relations:

> Americans should never underestimate the constant pressure on Canada which the mere presence of the United States has produced. We're different people from you and we're different people because of you. Living next to you is in some ways like sleeping with an elephant. No matter how friendly and even-tempered is the beast, if I can call it that, one is effected [*sic*] by every twitch and grunt. It should not therefore be expected that this kind of nation, this Canada, should project itself as a mirror image of the United States.
>
> http://www.cla.ca/issues/cla_buildingtheknowledgeeconomy_final.pdf, accessed 13/3/13.

SPOTLIGHT 3.6

Love thy neighbour

In 2003, the Canadian Department of Foreign Affairs and International Trade launched a 'Dialogue on Foreign Policy' in the form of a public discussion paper and an extensive programme of consultations. While the dialogue was underway, it published a bulletin online (no longer accessible) in which it gave advice on Canada–US relations:

1. The increase in American investment and the prevalence of American cultural products in Canada are a threat to Canadian identity. They lead Canadians to expect institutions and policies that replicate those of the US rather than being representative of Canada.
2. Canada should avoid a 'holier than thou' approach to relations with the US and treat its relationship with the US with greater respect.
3. Canada should be seeking common ground with the US. Working to maintain a stable relationship with the US is in Canada's economic and security interests.
4. Canada should reduce its economic dependence on the US and stop using the US as a reference point in defining Canadian culture.
5. The security of the Canada–US border should be maintained, but not at the expense of trade.
6. US foreign policy positions are constantly evolving. Canadian policy towards the US should not be based solely on the realities of the current administration. Policies should be created with the long term in mind.

A final report on the dialogue was eventually published in the same year on: http://dataparc.com/projects/www.foreign-policy-dialogue.ca/en/final_report/index.html#relations, accessed 13/3/2012.

Most participants in the dialogue acknowledged that the values and interests of the two countries frequently coincide, but that there were some issues where Canada had to go its own way.

The Canadian style of management can contrast strongly to that of the USA in that it is less formalised, less driven by individual goals and more aware of society as a whole. It is often considered to be more conservative in fiscal issues and its expertise in financial management is well-regarded internationally.

Australia and New Zealand

Australia and New Zealand were both colonies of the UK. Britain claimed Australia as a colony in 1788 and New Zealand became a separate UK colony in 1840 after first being administered by the Australian state of New South Wales. The lives of the early inhabitants of this remote part of the world, the Australian Aborigines and the New Zealand Maoris, were irrevocably changed by the European settlers. In Australia these were first convicts from the UK and later free immigrants. In New Zealand these were predominantly UK whalers and traders.

When both countries became independent of the UK, they still retained their essential Anglo-Saxon identity. Further waves of British migrants were welcomed with open arms, while other Europeans of non-British origin were expected to shed their particular cultural identities and integrate with the host population. Australia, however, has been the first to acknowledge the increasing ethnic diversity created by more recent waves of immigration from other non-European countries, particularly from countries in South-East Asia. With its present population of circa 23.5 million, the country now sees multiculturalism as being at the heart of its society.

New Zealand's population of around 4.5 million is now predominantly European, although immigration policy has focused more on the micro-states of the South Pacific and, most recently, on migration flows of professionally qualified South Africans and East Asians. A prerequisite for selection for immigration is still proficiency in English.

MINI-CASE 3.4

Australia, New Zealand and cultural diversity

Both Australia and New Zealand have taken a similar path in the development of policies regarding cultural diversity.

Up until the mid-1960s, Australia's concern was maintaining homogeneity through assimilation. The vision of Australia as a racially white nation entailed not only the exclusion of non-European immigrants but also the forced assimilation of the indigenous population of Aborigines. The move towards integration came with a reduction of immigrants from Europe and a reduction in the barriers to immigration from other parts of the world. The new cultures present in Australian society had some influence on the dominant culture, but everyone was expected to adopt the integrated culture. Ongoing cultural diversity was not encouraged.

The notion of multiculturalism was gradually developed and now stands at the forefront of government policy. In 1999, The National Multicultural Advisory Council published a report entitled 'Australian Multiculturalism for a new century: towards inclusiveness' which emphasises the culturally diverse nature of Australian society and recognises that all sectors of the community will need to make some adjustments in order to absorb newly arrived people. These in turn will be required to accept Australian law, the democratic form of its government and English as the national language. However, Australian multiculturalism recognises that many migrants and their children will choose to retain many of their customs and cultural traditions, some of which will be adopted by other Australians.

In New Zealand, the original inhabitants of the country – the Maori – had negotiated a treaty whereby they challenged the domination of the white settlers. From the late 1960s, there were many protests at the loss of Maori land and the Maori pushed for recognition of their own values and traditions. It was in the 1980s that the term 'biculturalism appeared' and the idea of that New Zealanders could exist in one nation but as two peoples each with their own language, education system, social services and businesses.

However, during the 1970s, the pattern of immigration started changing and this pushed the country towards multiculturalism. The following extract from *Te Ara, The Encyclopaedia of New Zealand*, published by Matanū Taonga, the New Zealand Ministry of Culture and Heritage, gives an overview of developments (http://www.teara.govt.nz/en/the-new-zealanders/page-13, accessed 14/2/13).

The multicultural idea

Many of these people, from a wide range of cultures, settled down, took up citizenship and brought up New Zealand-born children. This was a major challenge to the idea of who New Zealanders were. Initiated in Canada and picked up in the 1970s in Australia, the concept of multiculturalism quickly spread to New Zealand. It was proposed that people could be legitimate members of the New Zealand nation while retaining their own language, foods and traditions.

Non-British New Zealanders

As the numbers of non-British people increased, their cultural differences became more evident. In South Auckland, Pacific Islanders congregated and evolved a distinctive New Zealand Pacific culture which was more than the sum of their different cultures. Large Asian communities who had originally been settled throughout the country came together in areas with their own schools and styles of housing.

Challenge for a new century

At the beginning of the 21st century it was not easy to define the New Zealander, nor even to explain the origin of many New Zealand characteristics. The character of the country's people had been in part shaped by the physical environment – the outdoor climate, the proximity to beach and bush, the location in the South Pacific. No less important were the very different cultures brought to the country by waves of settlers – Maori who arrived some 700 years ago from the Pacific, the British and Irish who dominated the population for over a century from 1850, and more recent immigrants from Asia and the Pacific. All of these groups would have agreed that each were New Zealanders. All would have accepted that New Zealanders were no longer 'Better Britons'. But the cultural meaning of the New Zealander had become uncertain. How it would evolve was one of the major issues for the new century.

Questions

1. What differences can you detect between the two countries in the path taken towards multiculturalism?

2. The extract from the New Zealand encyclopaedia refers to the cultural meaning of the New Zealander as having become uncertain. What do you think are the issues at play behind this statement?

Australia and New Zealand are both aware of their isolation. As the Secretary-General of ASEAN, the Association of Southeast Asian Nations, said of Australia, when addressing the Southeast Asia Institute at the Australian National University:

For a long time, Southeast Asian states, and even Australians themselves, viewed Australia as something of an aberration – a European country that just happened to be located in the Asia Pacific:

http://www.aspistrategist.org.au/australia-an-asean-perspective/, accessed 14/2/13.

Thanks, in part, to the financial crisis which beset many countries in the early twenty-first century, one from which the country emerged relatively unscathed, Australia was able to make its presence felt at international level, as Spotlight 3.7, written in 2010, shows.

SPOTLIGHT 3.7

Australia: proud of its seat at the top table

By Peter Smith

The (Australian) economy has been a top performer in the developed world during the downturn. After skirting technical recession, it is into its 18th year of uninterrupted economic growth.

Its fortunes were boosted by a large federal government budget surplus quickly deployed to stimulate the economy, a robust banking sector, rising exports of key commodities such as iron ore and coal, deepening trade ties with China, and an unemployment rate a little more than half the 10 per cent plaguing the US and Eurozone. Just as importantly, Australia's long-term goal to have a stronger international voice was boosted when the crisis elevated the G20 to the dominant economic grouping.

The Australian government is also lobbying to win a seat on the UN Security Council, is an advocate of nuclear disarmament and championed a new Asia-Pacific community grouping that includes the US, unlike a rival Japanese proposal.

However, Australia has encountered problems, particularly in its regional backyard where it relies on strong trading ties. Relations with China, which last year regained its position as the country's biggest two-way trading partner, have been strained. [. . .]

Canberra has also had to repair relations with New Delhi following a string of brutal attacks on Indians studying in Australia. And the government continues to ban uranium exports to India. Japan, Australia's longest-standing regional trading partner, has also been irritated by Canberra's focus on China and a lack of action on activists targeting Japanese whaling boats in the Antarctic.

Michael McKinley, a political scientist at the Australian National University, sees problems ahead. 'Our foreign economic policy is about turbo-charged free trade. If you get that it will lead to social dislocation', he says. He believes dislocation leads to instability and social problems, and will promote religious fundamentalism. He adds that Australia's international influence is often overstated.

'If you look at who is powerful it is the Bric countries [Brazil, Russia, India and China], Australia talks up its role but without the substance to back it up', he says, adding that Australia lacks membership of important regional groupings such as the 10-country Association of Southeast Asian Nations (ASEAN).

[. . .]

Compared with structural problems besetting many developed nations as they claw their way back from recession, Australia's appear much more manageable.

Both Australia and New Zealand continue to increase their involvement in South East Asia at a number of levels, thereby helping to promote their own well-being as well as to help shape the future prosperity of the region. One recent development has been the establishment of a free trade area, completed in 2013, between Australia and New Zealand and ASEAN countries. This has allowed interregional trade in goods and services to be liberalised, investment to be facilitated and investment in the educational sector to be developed. Along with this increased engagement has come increased liberalisation in the immigration rules for both Australia and New Zealand, thereby making both societies more multi-ethnic and multi-cultural.

The business culture in Australia and New Zealand remains very much Anglo-Saxon in nature. However, the work environment tends to be more collaborative than in the UK or US, which means decision-making can be rather slow and drawn-out. The typical hierarchies are in place in most organisations, but since there is a general distrust of authority, particularly of people who tend to 'flaunt' it, a modest, egalitarian approach is preferred when colleagues are dealing with each other. They can, however, be more direct and critical than their British counterparts, although may not take so kindly towards outsiders joining in the criticism. Humour is an indispensable ingredient of communication, with a preference for teasing others, particularly those whom they consider to be 'tall poppies', the term used to denote arrogant people who 'show off' by talking frequently of their own accomplishments.

Latin America

As happened with the British colonists in North America and Australasia, the arrival of conquistadores/colonists from Spain and Portugal, and to a smaller extent from France, brought their cultures to Central and Southern America, and implanted them in foreign soil. The common linguistic, cultural and religious heritage is still strong and is seen in the many activities shared between the 'mother country' Spain and its former colonies, ranging from intensive trade to football tournaments. Latin American companies which are eager to expand abroad are using Spain as a springboard and a number of them are investing in Spanish companies – more Latin American companies are investing in their Spanish peers, or choosing Spain as a base from which to expand abroad. These recent developments have led to some commentators regarding this as a sort of colonisation in reverse.

There are similar developments between Portugal and Brazil. The latter was a Portuguese colony before being given independence in the nineteenth century and Portuguese is the official language. Economic, social and cultural ties with the European ex-ruler are still strong.

The term 'Latin' is believed to have been devised by the French in the nineteenth century to reflect the difference between Anglo-Saxon North America and Spanish/Portuguese South America. The term allowed for France, also a Latin country, to claim a role in the development of a continent where a number of countries were demanding independence from their Spanish masters.

This other America, the first rich America, is a deeply divided continent that has not been able to emulate its northern neighbours. Although recent attempts to create some sort of unity at trading level have apparently been successful, conflicts between the many countries of the continent are still prevalent. Furthermore, conflicts within some of these countries, often arising from clashes of interest between the indigenous and 'Hispanic' parts of society have prevented countries developing economically and socially in the way they would prefer.

There have been a number of attempts to bring some or all of the countries together into some sort of formal grouping. The latest and broadest union is The Community of Latin American and Caribbean States (CELAC), founded in December 2011 and comprising 33 states, including Cuba. Although seen as a further attempt to foster unity in the region, observers see it as an attempt to stand up to the United States in its own 'backyard'. In many respects it can be seen as an alternative to the OAS (The Organization of American States), founded in 1948 to promote solidarity and collaboration between Latin American countries, and to defend their sovereignty, their territorial integrity, and their independence. The major difference, however, is that two OAS members, the United States and Canada, do not belong to the CELAC organisation.

Despite the differences between the countries of Central and South America, cultural values are shared. Strong belief in the Catholic religion is a facet of South American society that reflects the importance of the family as well as the distinct male and female roles in society. These features were clearly evident in the Iberian peninsula until recently, but have been watered down through increasing industrialisation, the end of authoritarian, centralistic regimes and increasing exposure to other European cultures. In South America, however, such values still predominate.

House *et al.* (2004) characterise Latin America as a collectivist culture, which places great value on pride, loyalty and interdependence in families, but less value on institutional collectivism, i.e. collective distribution of resources and collective action.

Central governments are strong and societies are generally highly stratified. The gulf between rich and poor is considerable and difficult to bridge. Those in the lower social classes are poorly educated and lack the skills that countries still in the throes of industrialisation badly need. This stratification, however, appears to have changed in nature with increased economic activity and the rise of the middle classes. According to the World Bank report (Ferreira *et al.*, 2013), Latin America's middle class expanded by 50 per cent, from 103 million to 152 million, between 2003 and 2009. This expansion led to the point where the number of people in poverty is equal to the size of the middle class.

The main reasons given by Ferreira *et al.* (2013) for Brazil's strong economic performance in recent years has been its poverty reduction policies, new work opportunities, and a better-educated workforce. They talk of a consumption boom being in full swing thanks to the strong purchasing power of the middle class. However, they also warn of the economy slowing down in the long term since the country's middle-class households are saving too little and risk becoming over indebted. Their warning materialised more quickly than they anticipated. By 2013, Brazil was struggling with sluggish growth, inflation and lack of competitiveness. The middle class even expressed frustration about their thwarted ambitions in unprecedented street protests generated by the use of social media.

The rise of the middle class in Brazil is a phenomenon shared with other BRICS countries. Brazil was a 'founding member' of the BRICS group of emerging nations, when this category was first devised in 2003, since it was one of the largest high-growth emerging economies at the time and expected to be wealthier than major economic powers by 2050. However, just like two other BRICS members (India and Russia), Brazil has had to face demonstrations by the middle class as a result of the economic slowdown.

SPOTLIGHT 3.7

In Brazil, an emergent middle class takes off

Jorge Sinésio de Almeida, a 52-year-old construction worker, has bad memories from all of the bus trips he has taken from São Paulo to his hometown in Paraiba. 'It is a three-day journey on terrible roads. Passengers are always at the risk of getting robbed on the way.'

He currently counts the days until his first airplane trip, in December. 'I can't wait to board. The flight will be just three hours long', he says. 'I don't fear. My friends loved it.'

'I feel that Brazil and my life are better than they were when I first arrived in São Paulo 26 years ago', comments Almeida, after buying his plane tickets. These are one of the most purchased items among Brazil's emergent middle class. Between July 2011 and July 2012 alone, 9.5 million Brazilians flew for the first time, according to Data Popular, a think-tank based in São Paulo.

Source: adapted from http://www.worldbank.org/en/news/feature/2012/11/13/middle-class-in-Brazil-Latin-America-report, accessed 2/3/13.

These developments seem to reflect the idea put forward by Ferreira *et al.* (2013) that the rising middle class did not appear to pursue an ideological agenda in terms of equality or democracy but tended to operate out of pragmatic self-interest.

The essentially authoritarian nature of Latin American society is still present: the *patron* in whatever form still exerts considerable power in all aspects of daily life, whether it be in politics, the church, agriculture or business generally. With his high status he can command unquestioning loyalty from those beneath him. According to Romero (2004) the 'patron' is the traditional Latin American leader who can be described as autocratic and directive and is expected to be assertive and aggressive. He seldom delegates work or uses teams, prefers a formal top-town communication as the normal mode of communication while being very relationship-oriented and conflict-avoiding. According to McIntosh and Irving (2010), this predominant leadership style in Latin America is said to come from the Spanish and Portuguese conquests, a style which persisted through the colonial and early independence periods.

Whether this style of leadership is changing as a result of the ongoing economic development and modernisation is as yet unclear. Romero (2004) envisaged a possible shift from the 'patron' to a modern-style leader through high levels of interaction with multinational firms and more economically developed countries. The rapid rise of 'multilatinos' – internationally operating companies in Latin America – entails increasing exposure to leadership styles in other countries, could well result in changes in the long term. A further factor could also bring significant changes to the nature of leadership through domestic social unrest – exemplified by the street protests in Brazil – which bypasses political parties and movements.

Conclusion

This chapter has examined some of the characteristics that bring together a number of European countries as well as other countries in the world which are historically linked to Europe. It has also shown that countries which may share certain similarities do not necessarily enjoy a harmonious co-existence.

The first concept of this chapter considered culture clusters in Europe, including East Europe. It gave examples of the cultural features that countries within each cluster share. It showed how the European clusters in question, although aligned within European institutions, remain ambivalent concerning the extent to which countries should strive for some kind of unity. The difficulties involved in drawing Europe's boundaries were also addressed, particularly with regard to countries such as Russia and Turkey. The second concept of this chapter gave a brief overview of the Americas and Australasia, highlighting key cultural features of the regions and their reflection in business practice.

Points for reflection

1. Mention has been made in the two concepts of the Anglo-Saxon approach to business.

   How would you summarise this approach? Why do you think this approach often comes under criticism? Refer to any current business and/or political events.

2. It has been argued that, since both countries span the continents of Europe and Asia, Russia and Turkey are each in fact two countries: one belonging to Europe, the other belonging to Asia.

   Can Russia and Turkey, therefore, each be assigned to a particular cultural cluster? Give arguments to explain your answer.

3. Do you think the whole continent of America could be seen as having one business culture? Refer to the information in the chapter.

4. Which of those multicultural societies mentioned in this chapter do you consider to have been most successful in dealing with the issue of multiculturalism. Give your reasons.

Further reading

Chhokar J.S., Brodbeck, F.C. and House, R.J. (eds) (2008) *Culture and Leadership Across the World: the GLOBE Book of In-Depth Studies of 25 Societies*, New York, NY: Lawrence Erlbaum Associates. This is the second volume of articles to emerge from the GLOBE project (described in Chapter 2). The first (House, R.J., Hanges, P.J., Javidan, M., Dorfman, P.W. and Gupta, V. (eds) (2004) *Leadership, Culture and Organizations: the GLOBE Study of 62 Societies*, Thousand Oaks, CA: Sage) was referred to in Chapter 2. This second volume focuses on quantitative and qualitative data from 25 of the countries covered in the first volume and contains in-depth analyses of these cultures from different perspectives. It provides a detailed understanding of similarities and differences between these cultures in terms of leadership practices and values.

References

Boisot, M.H. (1993) 'Spain: the revolution from outside: Spanish management and the challenges of modernization', in Hickson, D.J. (ed.), *Management in Western Europe: Society, Culture and Organization in Twelve Nations*, Berlin: Walter de Gruyter: 205–228.

Braudel, F. (2008) *Grammaire des civilisations*, Collection Champs. Paris: Flammarion.

Cavusgil, S.T., Ghauri, P.N. and Akcal, A.A. (2013) *Doing Business in Emerging Markets*, 2nd edition, London: Sage.

Chhokar, J.S., Brodbeck, F.C. and House, R.J. (eds) (2008) *Culture and Leadership Across the World: the GLOBE Book of In-Depth Studies of 25 Societies*, New York, NY: Lawrence Erlbaum Associates.

Cooke, A. (1973) *Alistair Cooke's America*, London: British Broadcasting Corporation.

Davis, S. (2007) 'Wiring design faulted for Airbus A380 production delays', http://power.elecdesign.com, article 14634, accessed 1/10/2010.

d'Iribarne, P., Henry, A., Segal, J.P., Chevrier, S. and Globokar, T. (1998) *Cultures et mondialisation*, Paris: Editions du Seuil.

Dufour, C. (1990) *A Canadian Challenge – le défi québecois*, Lanzville, BC: Oolichan Books & Halifax NS: Institute for Research on Public Policy.

Duroselle, J.-B. (2004) *L'Europe: Histoire de ses peuples*, Collection Pluriel Paris: Hachette Litératures.

Ferreira, F.H.G., Messina, J., Rigolini, J., López-Calva, L.-F., Lugo, M.A. and Vakis, R. (2013) *Economic Mobility and the Rise of the Latin American Middle Class*, Washington, DC: World Bank. © World Bank. https://openknowledge.worldbank.org/handle/10986/11858 License: CC BY 3.0 IGO.

Gilbert, P. (2008) 'Panorama des théories et outils de la gestion des ressources humaines', in Schmidt, G. (ed.) *Management*, Auxerre: Sciences Humaines Editions.

Grachev, M.V., Rogovsky, N.G. and Rakitski, B.V. (2008) 'Leadership and culture in Russia: the case of transitional economy', in Chhokar, J.S., Brodbeck, F.C. and House, R.J. (eds), *Culture and Leadership Across the World: the GLOBE Book of In-Depth Studies of 25 Societies*, New York, NY: Lawrence Erlbaum Associates: 803–822.

Hickson, D.J. and Pugh, D.S. (2001) *Management Worldwide*, London: Penguin.

Hillmert, S. (2002) 'Labour market integration and institutions: an Anglo-German comparison', *Work, Employment & Society*, 16: 675–701.

House, R.J., Hanges, P.J., Javidan, M., Dorfman, P.W. and Gupta, V. (eds) (2004) *Leadership, Culture and Organizations: the GLOBE study of 62 societies*, Thousand Oaks CA: Sage.

McIntosh, T.A. and Irvin, J.A. (2010) 'Evaluating the Instrumento de Contribución al Liderazgo de Siervo (ICLS) for Reliability in Latin America', *The Journal of Virtues & Leadership*, 1.1: 30–49.

Michailova, S. and Worm, V. (2003) 'Personal networking in Russia and China: *blat* and guanxi', *European Management Journal*, 21: 509–519.

Morin, E. (1987) *Penser l'Europe*, Paris: Gallimard.

Motel, S. and Patten E. (2013) *Statistical Portrait of Hispanics in the United States, 2011*, Pew Research Hispanic Center, http://www.pewhispanic.org/2013/02/15/statistical-portrait-of-hispanics-in-the-united-states-2011/, accessed 10.3.2013.

Papalexandris, N. (2008) Greece: 'From ancient myths to modern realities', in Chhokar J.S., Brodbeck, F.C. and House, R.J. (eds) *Culture and Leadership Across the World: the GLOBE Book of In-Depth Studies of 25 Societies*, New York, NY: Lawrence Erlbaum Associates.

Péron, M. (2002) 'Réflexion sur la transdisciplinarité dans la pensée managériale' in Péron, M. (ed.), *Transdiciplinarité: fondement de la pensée managériale Anglo-Saxonne?* Paris, Economica.

Romero, E.J. (2004) 'Latin American leadership: el patrón & el líder moderno', *Cross Cultural Management: An International Journal*, 11(3): 25–37.

Semprini, A. (2000) Le multiculturalisme, Paris: Presses Universitaires de France.

Valdez, Z. (2006) 'Segmented assimilation among Mexicans in the Southwest', *The Sociological Quarterly*, 47: 397–424.

Vidal, F. (1992) *Le management à l'italienne*, Paris: InterEditions.

Chapter 3 Activities

ACTIVITY 3.1

Airbus

This activity involves examining developments which have taken place since 1970 within Airbus – and its mother-company – which involve a number of issues, many of which could be considered to be cultural in nature.

You will be asked to address a number of questions relating to:

- the problems experienced by Airbus in developing its new aircraft;
- a proposed merger between a British company (BAE Systems) and EADS, the European consortium of which Airbus is the major component.

Read first the account given below, as well as the various articles included.

1. Airbus: from consortium to company

Airbus SAS, based in Toulouse, France, is a major airplane manufacturer, producing around half of the world's jet airliners. It was formally established in 1970 as a European consortium whose goal was to gain a share of the aircraft construction market dominated till then by the US. It began as a consortium of French and German companies, to be joined later by Spanish and British companies.

In 2000, the Airbus consortium became an integrated company, 80 per cent of it being owned by **EADS**, the European Aeronautic Defence and Space Company NV. EADS itself came into being in the same year as a result of a merger between a German aerospace and defence company, a Spanish aircraft company and a French aerospace company. EADS develops and markets civil and military aircraft, as well as communications systems, missiles, space rockets, satellites, and related systems. The remaining 20 per cent of Airbus was at the time owned by **BAE** systems (the acronym is derived from British Aerospace Engineering), successor to a number of British aircraft, defence electronics and warship manufacturers.

The Airbus website (http://www.airbus.com) gives a detailed account of the development of the company and of the aircraft it has produced. The company has become global in nature, with fully owned subsidiaries in the United States, China, Japan and in the Middle East, spare parts centres in Hamburg, Frankfurt, Washington, Beijing and Singapore, training centres in Toulouse, Miami, Hamburg and Beijing, and more than 150 field service offices around the world. Apart from the importance of technology, the website refers to the special experience and expertise that come from more than 100 nationalities represented among its 59,000 employees.

For an Airbus employee it is usual to work side by side with people from a range of cultures. Career advancement within the company can take an employee not just to another floor or another building – but to another country.

Airbus takes pride in the diversity of its employees, valuing the special experience and expertise people from different backgrounds bring to the industry. The company thrives on the mix of ideas, vision and knowledge such a combination of cultures creates. At the same time, it encourages employees to develop their individual talents and experience and to be proud of their roots.

Source: http://www.airbus.com/company/people-culture/, accessed 1/3/13

The company has produced a series of successful aircraft, including the world's first twin-engine wide-body double-deck A380, the most technologically advanced plane in the world today.

The development of such highly sophisticated aircraft required a reorganisation of the company to improve co-ordination, reduce the costs of production and the time between conception of planes and their introduction into service. The French, German, British and Spanish partners, who had operated independently, merged their plane-making assets in 2001 to form Airbus SAS.

2. Delays in production

Nevertheless, there were considerable problems in bringing a major new product, the A380, to the market. A two-year delay and a consequent loss in profits of €2 billion forced the company to make drastic cuts in the size of its workforce, to close plants and to outsource many more aircraft parts.

The extract below is taken from an article written by Xavier Vives, a professor of economics and finance at IESE Business School, Barcelona, Spain, It focuses on the role of 'economic patriotism' in the running of Airbus.

Traditionally, the workforce at the aircraft manufacturer is geographically distributed in proportion to national ownership stakes. It is hard to make sense of this from the point of view of productive efficiency. It is an instance of economic nationalism, whereby governments distort private transactions among economic actors by discriminating against foreigners in the name of the national interest.

Economic motives include the preservation of employment or the attraction of economic activity to a certain area. Strategic motives include national security or attempts to capture rents abroad in monopolistic markets. In many circumstances the patriotic approach proves ineffective because it conflicts with economic efficiency, but its endurance derives from protection of the interests of local lobbies. Politicians benefit from the revolving door between political office and the boardroom or by catering to a clientele with a view towards re-election. [. . .]

The damage caused by economic nationalism includes inefficiency and poor corporate governance. When EADS, parent company of Airbus, was created, it was headed by two chief executives, German and French. In spite of the fact that tensions flourished, the twin-headed structure was maintained even after the crisis caused by problems in the development of the A380 began. As a result, Airbus's reputation has been dented and it has fallen behind Boeing. In other cases, cost-cutting measures are delayed as state aid comes to the rescue of the champion, or competition is distorted because government-supported companies have privileged access to infrastructure and procurement contracts. The market for corporate control suffers as takeover threats from potentially more efficient foreign companies are removed. Finally, national efforts end up being self-defeating as other countries react in kind, neutralizing the initial attempt to gain an advantage.

Source: extract from 'Airbus and the damage done by economic patriotism', 2/3/07,
Financial Times (Vives, X.)

One of the causes of the delay in the production of the A380 was the design of the complex wiring system for the aircraft. Sam Davis gives an insight into co-ordination problems.

You wouldn't expect a wiring problem to delay delivery of an airplane, but that is what has happened.

To understand why wiring is critical, you have to know that there are almost 1,200 functions to control the plane, which takes 98,000 wires and 40,000 connectors. The digital design system has 500,000 models, and all those must be kept in sync by mismatched computer-design systems in different countries.

Further complicating aircraft design – nose sections are built in France, fuselages in Germany, wings in Great Britain and tails in Spain, Airbus' A380 aircraft sections will be transported on a special ship from sites in Broughton (UK), Hamburg (Germany), Puerto Real (Spain) and St. Nazaire (France) for final assembly in Toulouse (France).

As reported in the January 2007 IEEE Spectrum article, 'Manufacturing Mayday,' by Alexander Hellemans, designing the aircraft was much more difficult than anticipated. Engineers in Germany and Spain used the older V4 version of the CAD program to design the wiring whereas engineers in France and England used the newer V5 version. Although the software developer said the two versions were compatible, data was lost when transferring files from one system to the other. Another complication: the French were familiar with the software whereas the Germans did not have as much experience with it.

Because of the wiring design software compatibility issues, problems arose when incorporating wiring changes in the fuselage sections in Germany.

Source: Davis, S. (2007) 'Wiring design faulted for Airbus A380 production delays,' http://power.elecdesign.com/Articles/index.cfm?ArticleID=14634&stylename=maroon, accessed 1/3/13

3. A proposed merger

In 2012, EADS devised a plan to merge with BAE systems, the company which had once owned 20 per cent of EADS's Airbus subsidiary. BAE had taken partial ownership when Airbus became an integrated company in 2000. EADS took the remaining 80 per cent. In 2006, however, BAE had sold its stake in Airbus. At the time, UK commentators generally considered this to be a smart move since it looked as if the civil aircraft business was about to enter a cyclical decline. The sale would allow BAE to increase its funding of acquisitions, especially of companies in the massive US defence sector. Some observers also considered BAE's withdrawal to be related to its inability to have a real say in the way EADS was being run. EADS was said to be too heavily influenced by the national interests of the dominant French and German partners. Although heavily involved in the construction of Airbus aircraft, BAE's influence on decision-making in the boardroom was limited. There was also, it was felt, one more factor involved in BAE's departure: the UK's 'special relationship' with the USA. The company wanted to maintain and extend this relationship: wasn't a tie-up with US concerns preferable to a partnership within a European consortium?

So BAE left Airbus and went its own way to become a major defence, security and aerospace company with operations worldwide. It is, at the time of writing, one of the largest suppliers to the United States Department of Defence. However, it still maintains its important manufacturing role in Airbus, being responsible for the construction of the wings for all Airbus aircraft.

In 2012, the British government rethought its position with regard to the future of BAE systems. The following article from the *Financial Times* describes the circumstances surrounding the British change of mind.

UK hopes BAE deal will seal Airbus role

Politicians of all parties regret BAE's decision to sell its Airbus stake six years ago

Airbus is a rare example of pan-European industrial collaboration turning into a global success story.

Conceived by the French, German and UK governments in the 1960s as the only way to challenge the US hegemony in the aerospace industry, Airbus has over the past 40 years become Boeing's main rival in the passenger jet market.

Airbus's factory in Broughton, north Wales, makes all the wings for its jets but the UK's longstanding ambivalence towards the company has left the country vulnerable to efforts by partner nations – notably Germany – to poach work off Britain.

One of the reasons why David Cameron, UK prime minister, has given conditional backing to plans by EADS, Airbus's parent company, to combine with BAE Systems, the British defence group, is the belief that the €34.7bn tie-up could safeguard and even strengthen Britain's position at Airbus. 'The feeling is that this deal could once again give Britain an interest in Airbus', says one UK government insider.

The French and German governments in effect control EADS through a mixture of direct and indirect shareholdings but Tom Enders, group chief executive, wants to use the BAE deal to curb political interference at the company.

He is proposing that the French, German and UK governments each have a golden share in the enlarged group but no additional veto rights. London broadly supports this governance change, partly because it could reduce the opportunity for Paris and Berlin to try to take Airbus work from Britain.

 Source: 'UK hopes BAE deal will seal Airbus role', 4/10/2012, FT.com (Parker, A. and Pickard, J.).

The *Financial Times* summarised the advantages for both sides of the proposed merger as follows:

Despite the daunting political hurdles, EADS says a deal would let it solve three big problems at a stroke: end its heavy reliance on the cyclical Airbus passenger jet business; give it entry to the until now impenetrable US defence market; and cancel the Franco-German shareholder pact that has stunted its international ambitions. For BAE, the merger would be a sharp about-turn, letting it back into the Airbus business six years after it marched into a strategic cul-de-sac by becoming a defence-only business.

Source: extract from 'BAE-EADS TALKS – Q&A – Big questions surrounding defence tie-up', 21/9/2012, *The Financial Times* (Boxell, J. and Sakoui, A.)

There were many comments and analyses made in both the European and American media on the economic and political implications of the proposed merger. Boeing expressed its concern about the complex industrial and national security concerns involved. Some American observers questioned the need for Paris and Berlin to be involved in the running of the USA defence systems. Some British commentators raised objections similar to those made in 2006 concerning the power of the Franco-German voting bloc in the proposed new company. The French, in particular, were considered to be hanging on to their 'dirigiste' policies, attempting to use the French company holding to steer EADS's future strategic path in favour of the country. This would jeopardise the UK's strategic position.

The cultural aspects were also dealt with at length in the media, particularly with regard to the ability of the three main partners – the French, the Germans and the British – to work together effectively.

For EADS partners, culture still matters

I found the French-German-British combination in the old Airbus fascinating. I always marvelled, when I visited an aircraft factory, that these huge contraptions could carry hundreds of passengers tens of thousands of feet in the air. That the Airbus aircraft were put together by this multi-national Babel seemed more marvellous still.

How did it work? I interviewed Airbus leaders many times at their Toulouse headquarters, as well as executives of the three principal companies in their home countries and at international air shows.

What always struck me was that the French and, particularly, the Germans seemed more comfortable with the British than they were with each other.

German managers told me that the relationship with the French was not a natural one. A senior

French executive said his message to the British was: 'Please don't leave us in the room on our own with the Germans.' He was talking about the wider European Union project rather than Airbus because there was little thought at the time that BAE would leave. But it did, finally selling its 20 per cent Airbus stake in 2006.

I wondered how the French and Germans would get on without the Brits. Badly, as it turned out. After BAE left, a former French executive described EADS as a 'house of conflict'. The giant Airbus A380 suffered delays because the Germans and French were using different software so that some of the electrical harnesses didn't fit.

An interesting article in the *Journal of Business and Behavioral Sciences* used the work of Geert Hofstede to analyse the A380 fiasco [. . .] He found that French managers tended to be distant from their subordinates, while British and German employees felt they had greater freedom to talk back. Indeed, the British and German 'power distance' scores were identical. By contrast, the British had higher tolerance for uncer-

tainty than the Germans or the French. While the French and German scores weren't the same, they both showed less comfort with ambiguity and a greater desire for procedures. The British were good at coming up with ideas, but weaker at implementation.

One could object that Prof. Hofstede's work relies on stereotypes and ignores large differences within countries. But, as he pointed out in his book, *Culture and Organizations: Software of the Mind*, we cannot escape the families, school systems and societies that formed us. His schema helps us understand why the British-French-German mix, with its complementary traits, appeared to work better than the last two alone.

The proposed EADS-BAE tie-up faces many obstacles and may yet fall to the objections of one of the three governments, or of the US.

But Airbus old timers will see the attraction. Princess Diana once complained of the destructive effect of having three people in her marriage. EADS, on the other hand, may work better as a *ménage à trois*.

After a short period of intensive negotiations, the proposed deal collapsed. The parties involved each gave their particular version of events, each essentially blaming the other. Diplomatic reaction was muted, but German and French officials made it clear that the size of the French state shareholding of the enlarged company remained a stumbling-block to the end. Fears on all sides were expressed, directly or indirectly, about having insufficient control of the new company. Even BAE shareholders had their doubts about the strategic value of merging with EADS.

There was the general feeling among observers that if the three government leaders involved had really wanted the merger to take place they could have enabled it to happen. However, as James Blitz notes in his *Financial Times* article:

All three could see the industrial logic behind the deal. But at a time of acute political and economic pressures in Britain and the Eurozone, they also saw the pitfalls. They wanted the deal to happen. But they did not want it enough to close ranks and sweep away the obstacles on the table.

Source: extract from 'Leaders' lack of enthusiasm hits BAE-EADS', 10/10/2012, FT.com (Blitz, J.)

As a postscript, it is worth noting that in 2013 EADS decided to give itself a new name – **the Airbus group**. In a press release, the Airbus CEO, Tom Enders, gave the basic reason for the change:

The renaming simply gathers the entire company under the best brand we have, one that stands for internationalisation, innovation and integration – and also for some two thirds of our revenues. It reinforces the message that 'we make things fly'.

Source: http://www.airbus-group.com/airbusgroup/germany/de/presse/
press.20130731_eads_h1.html, accessed 3/1/14

Questions

1. How would you define the concept of 'economic patriotism'? What role do you think it may have played in the problems besetting Airbus and the decision not to go ahead with the EADS–BAE merger?

2. To what extent do you consider that the wiring problems with the A380 were a reflection of the way the Airbus company was organised, despite the merger of the national components in 2001?

3. The author of the article 'For EADS partners, culture still matters' refers to Hofstede's 'power distance' and 'uncertainty avoidance' scores for the major countries involved in the Airbus project. To what extent do you consider it valid for these scores to be used to support the author's arguments?

4. When examining the culture of its company, Airbus mentions on its website (see above) that it 'thrives on the mix of ideas, vision and knowledge such a combination of cultures creates'.

   How do you imagine the way in which the company has exactly thrived, despite the events described in this activity?

5. What elements in these texts about the Airbus consortium are reflected in the description of the culture clusters in this chapter?

6. What other explanations can you find for the change in name from 'EADS' to 'Airbus'?

ACTIVITY 3.2

Why financial scandals differ in the US and Europe

By Michael Skapinker

'Does Europe hate us?' Thomas Friedman, the *New York Times* columnist, asked in a documentary on the Discovery Channel last week. The answer, he concluded after pottering around the Continent looking increasingly worried, was 'yes'.

From the war on terror to attitudes to maternity leave, Mr Friedman's film made it plain that Europeans inhabited a different world from Americans. When it came to business, he portrayed a Europe whose bureaucrats plotted endlessly to make life difficult for US companies. Brussels was banning pharmaceutical ingredients regarded as perfectly safe in the US. European competition authorities had stamped on the ambitions of US companies from Microsoft to Coca-Cola.

His narrative punctuated by the sort of menacing soundtrack film-makers reserve for those moments before dad opens the door to discover that his family has been murdered by machete-wielding maniacs, Mr Friedman asked: 'Is this the end of the west?'

Quite possibly – and it gets worse. According to a recent paper by John Coffee of Columbia law school, the US and Europe are so far apart that they even suffer from fundamentally different corporate scandals.[1]

Take two emblematic examples: Enron in the US and Parmalat in Europe. The Enron misdeeds were aimed at boosting and maintaining the energy trader's share price. At Parmalat, the dairy group, by contrast, money appears to have been siphoned off for the benefit of particular individuals.

[1] John Coffee, 'A theory of corporate scandals: why the US and Europe differ', http://papers.ssrn.com/sol3/papers.cfm?abstract_id=694581.

The divergence reflects underlying differences in the way US and European companies are organized, Prof. Coffee argues. In the US, the typical company's shareholders are a widely dispersed group. Being too fragmented to exercise day-to-day control over executives, they attempted to align top managers' interests with theirs by granting them share options.

In 1990, the average chief executive of an S&P 500 Industrial company earned $1.25m (£660,000), of which 92 per cent was in cash and 8 per cent in equity. By 2001, the average chief executive was earning more than $6m, of which 66 per cent was in equity.

The prevalence of share options substantially changed US chief executives' attitudes to presentation of their companies' earnings. 'During early periods, US managements famously employed "rainy day reserves" to hold back the recognition of income that was in excess of the market's expectation in order to defer it until some later quarter when there had been a shortfall in expected earnings', Prof. Coffee writes.

'Managers engaged in income smoothing, rolling the peaks in one period over into the valley of the next period. This traditional form of earnings management was intended to mask the volatility of earnings and reassure investors who might have been alarmed by rapid fluctuations.'

By the late 1990s, chief executives, stuffed with share options, were doing something different: 'stealing' earnings from future periods to create an 'earnings spike' to meet market expectations and prevent the share price from taking a dive.

'Although such spikes may not be sustainable, corporate managers possess asymmetric information and, anticipating their inability to maintain earnings growth, they can exercise their options and bail out', Prof. Coffee writes. He cites studies demonstrating a relationship between how extensively companies use options and the likelihood of their falling victim to fraud.

European companies, on the other hand, often have controlling shareholders or groups of shareholders, who do not need indirect mechanisms such as share options to control management.

They can simply tell them what to do. European chief executives have less freedom to manipulate their earnings. But they also have less incentive to do so.

Fraud still occurs in Europe, but it is a different sort of fraud and different people perpetrate it. Instead of executives manipulating earnings, dominant shareholders use their control to help themselves to the company's assets.

Because European and US companies are vulnerable to different types of fraud, they should adopt different ways of preventing it. While US corporate governance reforms have concentrated, for example, on ensuring that independent audit committees deal with the auditors, this might be less effective in Europe where the board struggles to escape the controlling shareholder's influence.

'Although diligent auditors could have presumably detected the fraud at Parmalat . . . one suspects that they would have likely been dismissed at the point at which they began to monitor earnestly', Prof. Coffee says.

He confesses he does not have a simple suggestion on how to prevent European-style frauds. Regulators could require auditors to report to minority shareholders, he says, but he appears to accept this is unlikely to have many takers.

A second objection to his argument that European fraud is different from the American variety is that there are prominent exceptions. What about Ahold and Vivendi? Were not these European companies whose scandals involved earnings manipulation? They were, Prof. Coffee says, but that manipulation either happened in their US subsidiaries or in companies such as Vivendi that turned themselves into US-style conglomerates and therefore took an American form.

What of Tyco, a US company where the top managers allegedly appropriated assets for themselves? Prof. Coffee acknowledges that the differences between US and European companies are overall tendencies rather than iron-clad rules.

In the polarized world described by Mr Friedman, I suppose we should take some comfort from the small number of Europeans and Americans imitating one another's misbehaviour.

Question

Fraud seems to be a universal phenomenon. In this case, however, the author underlines the difference between committing fraud in the US and Europe. Can you explain how this difference comes about?

ACTIVITY 3.3

Read the following case study about the problems of exporting flowers to Russia and then answer the questions.

To Russia with love

Jan de Rover sat back in his chair, his feet resting on the piles of paperwork on his desk. He watched a jet flying low over the greenhouses as it came in to land at Amsterdam airport. He was thinking about his next trip to Moscow, where he was trying to sell flowers, which his company grew under glass. 'I'm not looking forward to going', he told his financial director Rob, who was also watching the plane. 'It's frightening over there, you know?' Sitting up, he leaned over his desk and said: 'You won't believe what the Russian mafia gets up to. Their tentacles are everywhere. And you never know where you are with them, they're so unpredictable. Do you know there was a shooting incident last week – about flowers, would you believe it!'

Jan's company is all about flowers – acres of greenhouses, a dozen trucks to transport the flowers to the flower auction just round the corner, two hundred employees, including seasonal workers, and the office building where everything is managed. He exports 120 million flowers to all parts of the world, including Eastern and Southern Europe, North and South America. Forty dozen flowers are sent to Russia each week. The time factor plays an important role here since flowers will not survive any long transport delay.

The prices of flowers sent to Russia are automatically set 30 per cent higher. The difference in price is given to the mafia, otherwise the flowers would never arrive at their destination on time. For Jan this is the only way to overcome the problems caused by the poor infrastructure. Bribes are the only way, for example, to make sure that the flowers get loaded on to local transport before they start wilting. Even then, however, as Jan explains to his financial director, you never know beforehand whether they're going to accept the bribe.

Rob is not happy with these 'facilitation payments' either. Nor is he happy about the fact that the eventual payments for the flowers take ages to reach Holland. In some cases it has taken over a year before the money has been transferred – and then without any excuse or apology. If this happened in his own country, the company would stop any further deliveries. 'If you ask me', said Rob to his boss, 'I reckon the Russians and the mafia are in it together.' Jan nodded his head in reluctant agreement.

Questions

1. Jan believes that paying bribes is the only way to overcome the problems caused by the poor infrastructure in Russia. Is this really the only way of tackling these problems?
2. How do you explain Rob's comment that 'the Russians and the mafia are in it together'?

Chapter 4

Business cultures in Asia, Africa and the Middle East

The previous chapter discussed the Western clusters which comprised the European, American and Australasian clusters. The chapter also took into consideration the emerging markets, including Turkey, Russia and Brazil, the last two of which are classified as BRICS countries together with India, China and South Africa. The latter three countries will be discussed in this chapter.

Chapter 4 will cover aspects of the other clusters and countries as outlined in the GLOBE project. This will be done in a similar way to that used in the previous chapter: a cultural feature will be described which relates to the history, geography and/or religion of one or more countries from each cluster, and which is reflected in work-related values and business practices. Concept 4.1 will discuss Asia and the role played by diasporas in the rapid globalisation of business; Concept 4.2 will discuss Africa and the Middle East.

Learning outcomes

After reading this chapter you should:

- Be able to distinguish essential differences and similarities between four culture clusters devised by GLOBE, viz. Confucian Asia, Southern Asia, Sub-Saharan Africa and the Middle East.
- Have some insight into the cultural factors that have an influence on business.
- Gain initial insight into the cognitive approach to management taken in the East and that taken in the West.

When comparing business management styles across countries it is important to be aware that differences in management thinking affect the way business is done in the Eastern, Western, Northern and Southern parts of the world. In other words, the ideas about 'how to do business' may differ between people and influence their thinking and acting in their respective managerial environments.

Preface: two different cognitive approaches to management

According to Kase *et al.* (2011: 40), most researchers assume that the process of 'scientific' managerial thinking is universal. With this assumption they (1) reduce different management practices to 'one common scientific approach' and (2) consider business at international level only in terms of being able to 'identify the differences between empirical phenomena and situational contexts'.

However, Kase *et al.* are convinced that there are different epistemological approaches to thinking (which they define as 'the science of knowing'):

> There are internal, cognitive reasons that lead managers to approach strategic problems, and arrive at conclusions about outcomes, differently.

Kase et al., 2011: 41

They suggest that managers can be divided into two main categories at macro level: Eastern (Eastern Asian) and Western (Europe and North America).

1. Western managers: deal with managerial issues using a 'deductive thinking' approach which is 'defined as a process of drawing logical consequences from premises. In this way, consequences or outcomes are derived from what is assumed' (p. 51).

2. Eastern managers: deal with managerial issues using an 'inductive thinking' approach which 'is a process of seeking new knowledge which starts with a generalization and concludes with a particular' (p. 48).

Besides inductive reasoning (bottom-up logic) and deductive reasoning (top-down logic), there is a third type of logic called 'abduction' (rational perspective). However, because abduction is also the process of explaining what is known, Kase *et al.* (2011) argue that abductive reasoning could culturally be considered as an element of the inductive thought process. They therefore categorise abduction along with induction, deduction being the opposite.

Table 4.1 outlines the general schemas (categories) and the main differences in these two thinking approaches. This can help in understanding how the managers from different backgrounds resolve their problems and challenges.

Table 4.1 **Main differences between inductive and deductive thinking**

Categories	Deductive	Inductive
Temporality (how time is perceived)	Anticipation of predictability and linearity of time	Anticipation of unpredictability and circularity of time
Predictability (how future uncertainty is coped with)	Guarantees in projected future	Probable truth in projected future
Recursivity (causes are simultaneously effects and vice versa)	Not admitted: there must be observability of linear actions	Real existence of unobservable and recursive actions
Approach to learning	Learn by memorising	Learn by understanding
Approach to thinking and restructuring of problems	Apply solution habits from past experience, try until it works	Create new solution to new situation, rearrange problem elements
Approach to categorisation (of social surroundings)	Categories are determinate, with definite boundaries and clear structures	Categories are an experimental epistemology. Boundaries are not definite
Cognition (about the validity of empirical facts derived from the mental realm)	To be legitimate, key decision makers' perceptions in issue diagnosis and problem formulation must represent innate, real and demonstrable capability	Links between environment, strategy, structure can legitimately be cognitive and socially constructed
Use of metaphor	Metaphors are concrete and verbally coded	Metaphors can be abstract, and verbally or non-verbally coded
Perception of reality	Objective-absolute	Subjective-relative

Source: adapted from Kase *et al.*, 2011: 105–106 (Table 6.1: Twelve schema categories related to inductive and deductive thinking).

Concept 4.1   Asian cultures

This first concept will examine the two Asian clusters featuring in the GLOBE culture clusters: Confucian Asia and Southern Asia. According to Chhokar *et al.* (2008), a clear distinction needs to be made between these two clusters. The Confucian Asia cluster, as its name implies, has undergone the influence of Confucian ideology. The Southern Asia cluster, on the other hand, contains many different religions and ethnic groups which live in peaceful co-existence.

There is, however, one feature which both clusters share and that is to do with the way relationships are managed. Unlike the West, business in Asian countries is as much to do with the relationship between the parties concerned as the actual transaction itself. This entails paying considerable attention to building trust and establishing respect while displaying the utmost courtesy, particularly towards those in senior positions. Harmony between the participants of any meeting is required, so everything must be done in a courteous, deferential manner to ensure that nobody is offended or loses face. If harmony is maintained, confidence and trust will build and this in turn will form the basis of consensus and eventual agreement on a deal. Patience is of the essence: time is needed to establish a relationship, to decide whether a deal can be made and, if it can, to actually make the deal.

All these elements cause Westerners considerable frustration when trying to do business in Asia. They often have to try to make deals under time pressure, so go for the hard sell, assuming that vigorous handshakes and tales of past successes will immediately put them in a good light. Egocentric, brash behaviour does not encourage the establishment of a harmonious relationship, let alone any attempt by the Westerner to impose a deadline on any deal.

Nevertheless, deals are made, relationships between Asia and the West do develop, and more and more joint ventures or partnerships are formed. Asians are always interested in a good deal. The basis has to be right: trust is the key component for establishing a good relationship as is illustrated in Spotlight 4.1 on a deal between French and Indian industries.

SPOTLIGHT 4.1

India–France: strengthening long-term economic partnership

France is prepared to share its industrial secrets with the emerging superpower India, in sensitive, but profitable sectors such as the nuclear, military and high-tech industries.

During a two-day state visit to India, the President of France justified the move towards technology transfer on the basis of the trust credited to India as to how it would use missiles and submarines purchased from France: 'Since India has shown confidence in France for its defence material, France has confidence in its utilisation.'

For the president, this co-operation is also justified by the sharing of the same values. 'India will remain a peaceful power for ever', he explained. While stressing their common democratic culture, thus ruling out India's Chinese neighbours, he added: 'India and France speak a common language in global issues'.

During the second day of an India–France economic conference held in Mumbai, the president of the Confederation of Indian Industry, Dhruv Sawhney, considered that the president of France 'is looking for a new paradigm that could provide a link between his country and our companies'.

A director of Safran[1] added: 'Even if developments are faster in China, intellectual property is a new concept in that country whereas India maintains a legal system that offers real security.'

His counterpart from another French company in the same sector said: 'Indians accept negotiating and the idea of a balanced outcome.'

Paul Hermelin, CEO of Cap Gemini – representative of the French Foreign Affairs Ministry for economic relations between France and India – explained: 'China claims to be the factory of the world, while India seeks partnerships'. According to him, 'China moves slowly and alone, remains difficult to deal with compared to India, which is a country easier for Westerners to tackle since British colonisation left well-known customs and an essential tool for business: the English language'.

According to Paul Hermelin, India's divergences with China are underestimated and the positive European attitude towards India, and vice versa, is explained by a common distrust of China. In his view, India considers Europe to be a long-term partner.

1 Safran is a French multinational company divided into three main branches: aerospace propulsion, aircraft equipment, and defence security.

Source: free translation of 'Paris supports the transfer of technology to India', *Le Monde*, 18/2/2013 (Follorou, J).

We will examine the question of relationship-building a little more closely in the two Asian clusters. We will first address this issue in China, Japan and (South) Korea.

Confucian Asia

Confucianism is a philosophy developed from the teachings of Confucius. Born in 551 BC in the province of Lu, China, Confucius was a political figure, educator and philosopher who lived during a time when China was divided into small states locked in endless conflicts and power struggles. His teachings over peace and universal love among humankind were preserved by his followers and established the basis of subsequent Chinese thought on how the ideal man should live and interact, as well as how society and government should be formed. Confucianism eventually spread from China to other parts of Asia, to Korea, Japan and Vietnam. Even today Confucian values still have an important role in East Asian life, even as the pace of modernisation increases.

Referring to the preface of this chapter, we can assume that Confucianism – like other Asian philosophies – differs on the whole from Western philosophies. However, even within Confucianism we can distinguish two different schools: the theory-oriented school (subjective) and the practice-oriented school (objective). Where the first school ascribes importance to the achievement of virtue (*ren*) through reflection, the second believes in the value of acts and the practice of propriety (*li*) (Kase *et al.* 2011).

The Chinese and *guanxi*

Relationships in China are the key to business success. Building up a strong network of such relationships, referred to as *guanxi*, is the preoccupation of Chinese businessmen. Trust and confidence are vital elements of such relationships, so that transactions made between people in close relationship do not need to be made in contractual form. In fact, *guanxi* goes much further than an elaborate network of relationships. Those in the network both grant favours and expect eventually to receive favours in return. As Westerners have discovered, it can be difficult setting up relationships without using others who are themselves owed favours. When *guanxi* with someone has been achieved, then the business of penetrating the Chinese market is made easier.

Such a network is indispensable as a source of information and expertise, as a way of developing new relationships, finding business partners and eventually new deals. Its origins are disputed, although it does reflect many of the features of traditional village life in China. It appears to have developed on a large scale as a way of dealing with the state bureaucracy, and to have flourished during the recent opening up of China and consequent economic development.

Those Western companies in business in China are aware of the continual need to develop and maintain these special relationships and will pay them explicit attention in the organisation of their activities. A member of staff or whole department will be concerned with *guanxi* or public relations administration. This entails maintaining good relations not just with customers and suppliers, but also with local authorities, financial institutions and tax offices (Burns, 1998).

Related to this is the notion of *mianzi*, meaning 'face'. The need to maintain your own dignity and that of others has already been mentioned as a general characteristic of relationships in Asia. In China this is taken a step further. Here, it is to do with your personal and public reputation, to be maintained at all cost and to be used to influence other people in their decision-making. Direct criticism or confrontation of anyone related to business activities is not only an invitation for some kind of damaging retribution, but also results in damage to the *mianzi* of the person who has made the criticism and thereby harmed the other.

The parallels between *guanxi* and the Russian *blat* (as described in Chapter 3) are immediately apparent, although there are differences. As Michailova and Worm (2003) indicate, *guanxi* is a much older tradition and the reflection of Confucianism's notions that individuals, as social beings, each have their place in a hierarchy of relationships. As such, helping friends within a network is a moral and social obligation; not doing so entails loss of face and prestige. *Blat*, although it also entails making commitments, is more to do with emotions and self-serving pleasure. It is more analytical in nature, confined to smaller networks and more often pursued on a one-to-one basis.

Has Western democracy had an influence on the norms of younger present-day Chinese? Fu *et al.* (2008) suspect that this may well be the case. Their research in Shanghai using the GLOBE constructs produced some interesting results, particularly with regard to the cultural dimension Power Distance ('As Is' and 'Should Be'). The discrepancy between the 'As Is' and 'Should Be' scores was the highest of all the nine pairs of scores, showing a strong wish among the respondents for greater equality. However, when compared with the scores of all 61 countries surveyed in the GLOBE project, the Chinese 'As Is' result puts their managers in forty-first position and the 'Should Be' result in twelfth. According to Fu *et al.* (2008), this may indicate that Chinese managers are more tolerant of power inequality in society, despite their wish for less inequality. Moreover, Fu *et al.* suggest that there may well be opposing forces at play: internal pressures to conform to traditional Confucian values are vying with external pressures to be competitive. Although the traditional respect for and obedience to seniority and authority are still deep-rooted, reforms within the system now allow people to seek their own employment rather than the authorities telling them where to work.

SPOTLIGHT 4.2

China, a global business player

China is becoming more and more active in global business. It is no longer confining itself to business with the West. Apart from its rapidly expanding activities in Africa, China is also increasing business with its Central Asian neighbours, including Kazakhstan, Uzbekistan and Turkmenistan – all republics of the former Soviet Union (USSR). According to the French newspaper *Le Monde* (Pedroletti, 2009), these countries were particularly impressed by the 'wisdom' shown by China during negotiations over the trans-Asian oil pipeline. The same newspaper reports (Truc, 2010) that countries belonging to the Arctic Council (including Russia, Canada, USA, Denmark, Greenland and Norway) were equally impressed by China's pragmatic approach when participating as observer in a recent Arctic Frontiers conference on circumpolar resources.

Wisdom and pragmatism are words often used when describing China's role in present-day global business and its business culture generally. The Confucian nature of this culture is apparent in its focus on building relationships, on the importance China gives to establishing harmonious relationships.

The Japanese and *wa*

Harmony is also a term that can be applied to the culture of Japanese society. The concept of *wa*, the spirit of harmony, is a principle of Japanese thought, one applied to all relationships – even to the relationship with nature. This spirit is reflected in the considerable degree of collaborative behaviour and consensus-building within an organisation. This behaviour is fundamental to decision-making in business and involves proposals being discussed informally on the work-floor before being pushed up through the organisation's hierarchy where each level of management gives its input and suggestions. The managers are to be seen more as facilitators in making decisions rather than the actual decision-makers. Building a consensus within the organisation may take time through the need to go into detailed discussion and to give everyone the feeling that they are participating in the decision-making process. Eventually, the proposals reach the top and are acted on.

The idea of *wa* is also reflected in the relationship between the organisation and its employees. In return for an employee's loyalty and commitment to an organisation, the employer will provide job security. In some larger industrial companies this mutual commitment can be for life. This interdependent relationship follows on from other, similar, relationships which the working Japanese have experienced in their lives – with family, school and university. All of them require mutual commitment and loyalty. Some observers see a greater loyalty behind these relationships, that of loyalty to the country. The individual employee identifies with his/her colleagues who, as a group, identify with the company, which in turn identifies with the economic needs of Japan.

The whole process of consensus-building may seem long and drawn out to Western eyes. It must, however, be taken into account when doing business in Japan, along with the Japanese disdain of individualism and self-assertion. Moreover, when the implementation phase of a deal is reached, everything happens quickly and enthusiastically.

MINI-CASE 4.1

Culture turned Fukushima from disaster to crisis 'made in Japan'

By M. Dickie

The chairman of an investigation ordered by Japan's parliament into the Fukushima nuclear disaster has declared that it was a crisis 'made in Japan' resulting from the 'ingrained conventions of Japanese culture'.

Kiyoshi Kurokawa, chairman of the Diet's Nuclear Accident Independent Investigation Commission, said the crisis was the result of 'a multitude of errors and wilful negligence' by plant operator Tokyo Electric Power, regulators and the government.

In an English language summary of the commission's final report, Mr Kurokawa blamed the plant's failure on 'our reflexive obedience; our reluctance to question authority; our devotion to "sticking with programme"; our groupism; and our insularity. What must be admitted – very painfully – is that this was a disaster "made in Japan"', he added. 'Had other Japanese been in the shoes of those who bear responsibility for this accident, the result [might] well have been the same.'

In his preface to the Japanese version of the report, however, Mr Kurokawa offered a more measured critique of the cultural background to the crisis, blaming one-party rule, seniority systems and lifetime employment rather than the nation's culture as a whole.

Mr Kurokawa's commission is leading one of three large-scale investigations into the failure of Fukushima Daiichi, which suffered multiple reactor meltdowns and hydrogen explosions after its safety systems were knocked out by the earthquake and tsunami that hit Japan's north-east coast on 11 March 2011. All three have criticized Tepco, politicians and bureaucrats.

The Diet commission was intended to bring a broad range of perspectives to analysing the causes of the crisis.

Mr Kurokawa's commission also included a former diplomat, two lawyers, a chemist, a seismologist and a science journalist.

The report, in effect, accuses Tepco of covering up possible earthquake damage to Daiichi.

Asked on state television about the Diet report, Naomi Hirose, Tepco president, said he had not yet read it.

The commission blames poor communication by the utility and bureaucrats responsible for nuclear safety for causing Naoto Kan, Japan's then prime minister, to lose trust in them and attempt to manage the crisis directly.

Questions

1. How do you believe Japanese readers of the report would have reacted if the report in Japanese had contained the criticism of Japan's culture which was given in the English summary?

2. The Tepco president claimed on television that he had not yet read the report. How would you interpret this reaction?

3. Look at the final paragraph of the text. What do you think the term 'trust' means to the prime minister and what lies in the phrase 'poor communication' which led that trust to be lost?

The South Koreans and the *chaebol*

Throughout most of its history, Korea has been invaded, influenced and fought over by its larger neighbours, including China and Japan. The Second World War, and Japan's eventual defeat, meant the end of Korea's last occupation but also the division of the country into the communist, USSR-backed North Korea and the US-backed South Korea. North Korea remains outside the global business environment, so South Korea will be the focus here.

One invader that changed Korean norms and values was China. Its Choson Dynasty ruled the country for more than five hundred years and made Confucianism the state 'religion'. Its focus on family life and the need to protect family members and to enhance family fortunes has in turn influenced the way South Korea has developed its economy.

The meteoric rise of the South Korean economy since the 1960s is in no small part due to the role of the extended family in the development of a network of conglomerate businesses. These conglomerates, or *chaebols*, are each active in a large number of business sectors. They are owned by families and run by family members.

SPOTLIGHT 4.3

'Korean model triumphs over West'

This was the headline of an article published on *Asia Times* Online (17 November 2009) to describe how South Korea has emerged relatively unscathed from the global financial crisis which began in 2008. The author of the article sees the role in the economy of the chaebol as being one of the possible factors. The government spent many years building up and coordinating the activities of key industries which focused on the manufacturing of products for which there is a high demand. Although, according to the journalist, Western experts have questioned South Korea's status as a developed economy because of this very 'dirigiste' policy, the approach appears to have given the country a comparative advantage during the crisis.

Source: http://www.atimes.com/atimes/Korea/ KK17Dg01.html , accessed 1/9/2010.

Each *chaebol*, of which there are around 60, is a combination of companies held together by cross-ownership and cross-subsidies. As with any family in this part of the world, the leader is autocratic and at the head of a very strict hierarchy. At the same time, relations between members of the clan are strongly communitarian.

MINI-CASE 4.2

Pressure mounts on chaebol chiefs

Capturing the voice of minority shareholders is crucial for improving the woeful corporate governance standards in the country, which is said to be one of the biggest factors behind the so-called 'Korean discount'. Korean companies are undervalued by about 20 per cent relative to their Asian peers.

At the centre of the push is Navistock, a small listed company running an online community website for minority shareholders. Navistock has become a

➡

significant force in pushing for better corporate governance, nurturing an online group of 35,000 minority shareholders.

'Our biggest aim is to improve corporate governance, which often means better decision-making by management', says Kim Jung-hyun, chief executive of Navistock. 'The problem in Korea is that key management decisions are often made for the benefit of the founding families or the senior management of those companies rather than general shareholders.'

But the country's chaebol, the huge family-run conglomerates, are facing growing shareholder calls for bigger payouts, spurred by stalling growth in capital investment and new president Park Geun-hye, who has promised to attack corporate governance failings.

The cross-shareholdings between chaebol companies, which enable the founding families to maintain control, have reduced the clout of other shareholders and their appetite to challenge management. Only about 0.5 per cent of votes went against proposals at shareholder meetings in the first half of last year.

The result, however, has been speedy decision-making among the country's big family-run conglomerates, which Mr Kim admits has quickened South Korea's rapid economic development over the past several decades. But he warns that this is causing serious governance problems, such as irregular transfers of wealth, with control being passed on to second and third generations.

Navistock has already had some successes in improving corporate governance. With its help, minority shareholders have replaced senior executives at BNB Sungwon, a stainless steel pipe maker, which was delisted in May, and stopped Samyang Optics from being delisted last year by staging street protests.

Mr Kim expects the power of minority shareholders to accelerate in Korea amid growing calls for 'economic democracy', although he believes it will be a bumpy ride. To make that ride easier he plans to join forces with institutional investors in urging the push for better corporate governance standards.

 Source: from 'Pressure mounts on chaebol chiefs', *Financial Times*, 24/2/2013 (Song Jung-a), © The Financial Times Ltd. All Rights Reserved.

Questions

1. Why is Navistock trying to improve the corporate governance of the chaebol companies?
2. How have the chaebol managed so far to limit the power of shareholders?
3. In what way have the conglomerates benefited the country despite the fact that their value is much lower than that of equivalent companies elsewhere in Asia?

Southern Asia

The phenomenon of family businesses is one that India shares with the other Asian cultures. Whether you are in India, in Malaysia or in Indonesia, you will find the same preponderance of family firms, and this holds true in all the economic sectors. However, this does not mean that these companies are not without their problems, especially when they break with tradition.

Apart from India, Thailand also has a business culture that embraces the principles of the Buddhist religion. These two countries are characterised below.

The Indians and karma capitalism

According to an article entitled 'Karma Capitalism' in the US magazine *Business Week* (30 October 2006), a trend in the business world is the development of a certain infatuation with Indian philosophy. This is due in no small part to the influence of a number of the world's leading business gurus who are of Indian descent, such as C.K. Prahalad, Ram Charan and Vijay Govindrajan. Their work contains common themes, including the basic notion that executives should be motivated by more than money alone. The same article quoted C.K. Prahalad: 'It's the idea that corporations can simultaneously create value and social justice.' Companies should not be shareholder-driven, but stakeholder-focused, showing concern for society and the environment as well as those directly involved in their activities. A capitalism needs to be developed that, according to Prahalad, 'puts the individual at the centre of the universe'.

India's culture, while displaying many of the features shared in Asia, places particular emphasis on the family. Every company employee works for the family to maintain and enhance its fortunes. Loyalty to the (extended) family takes priority over loyalty to the company, although here, too, a strong loyalty may develop towards the professional group involved. Loyalty to both family and group can become entwined: success in your profession will give your family added status. This goes, of course, particularly for those who are engaged in a family business.

It is in the family business environment that the hard-working nature of Indians is particularly evident. Material success is important, not so much for the individual, but more for the sake of maintaining the family's honour and ensuring a sound future for the family's offspring. To be successful involves not just working long hours but also being creative, coming up with new ideas and trying them out with panache. There may be failures but this is less to do with personal competence, more to do with fate. The Hindu religion, shared by three-quarters of the population (1.22 billion in 2013), has engrained a deep sense of fatalism into its followers, and as Lewis notes (1996), this removes any stigma attached to failure. This attitude is reflected in business where, generally speaking, Indians are not reluctant to take risks.

Just as Indians accept the hierarchy of gods in their religion, so they accept the strict social hierarchy in their society and the hierarchies in the business environment.

SPOTLIGHT 4.4

The birth of India and Pakistan

After a long campaign of civil disobedience India was eventually granted independence by the British Parliament in July 1947 and Jawaharlal Nehru, leader of the National Congress Party, became its first prime minister. Along with independence came also partition: in accordance with the demands of the Muslim League led by Muhammad Ali Jinnah, the areas where Muslims formed the majority of the population, were partitioned to form the separate state of Pakistan. The mainly Hindu dominated areas became India, although a substantial Muslim minority still lived within the new borders.

After the accelerated departure of the British, India and Pakistan were left to deal with the problems resulting from the path of the border between the two countries. Even today the area of Kashmir, where around three-quarters of the population is Muslim, is in dispute.

They show considerable respect towards their seniors in all aspects of their lives, but also expect these to fulfil the obligations that power bestows. The father is obeyed, but is expected to do everything to promote the family's well-being; the manager may behave in an authoritarian way, but is expected in turn to show care and consideration towards his employees.

During research carried out among Indian companies it was remarked that 'many of senior executives mentioned that the levels of hierarchy had to be respected and were an important consideration in relationship-building in North India' (Zhu *et al.*, 2005).

MINI-CASE 4.3

Business in Today's India

Tourist industry woos India's newly affluent travelling set

By Amy Kazmin in New Delhi

The full-page, colour newspaper advertisement looks irresistible – top Bollywood stars romancing against the stunning backdrop of Swiss mountains and meadows.

Sponsored by Switzerland Tourism, the city of Lucerne and the Indian arm of Kuoni Travels, the advertisement urges Indians to 'experience the magic' themselves, by visiting the locations where the well-known Bollywood films were shot.

On the very next page of the same paper, Cox & Kings, the newly listed Indian travel company, has its own full-page advert promoting tours to a wide range of destinations, including the US, Europe, Egypt, Turkey, Australia and Kenya.

The duelling ads reflect the new competition among countries and global travel companies to catch the fancy of Indian travellers, who are increasingly using their new-found affluence to take overseas family holidays – once the preserve of a privileged few.

'Indians are tired of seeing Manhattan only in Hindi films', says Suhel Seth, managing director of Counselage. 'Today, he can be part of the scene by going there – so he is going. It's no longer impossible. The average Indian is discovering a world beyond.'

Indian overseas travel still lags far behind the 45m Chinese travelling abroad each year. But the World Tourism Organisation estimates that by 2020, about 50m Indians will be taking foreign holidays each year. It may represent a tiny proportion of India's population but it is a huge new market for the global travel industry.

Industry professionals say overseas travel is often far better value. 'It's cheaper for me to travel abroad', Mr Sanjeet says. 'A five-star hotel is cheaper in Macao and Holland than New Delhi and Mumbai. Plus it's great "show-off" value. In your peer group, that's a great status symbol to go out and see what is happening in other parts of the world.'

For all the desire of Indians to see the world, however, travel executives say they can be finicky about some things, especially first-time travellers from India's less cosmopolitan smaller cities.

'The most important is the Indian food', says Kashmira Commissariat, chief operating officer for SOTC, an Indian subsidiary of Kuoni. 'Wherever they would go, they require that.'

Lloyd's of London hits at 'difficult' India

By Michiyo Nakamoto in Tokyo and Joe Leahy in Mumbai

India is among the most protectionist countries in the insurance industry in the fast-growing Asian region, the chairman of Lloyd's of London said, in a forthright criticism of the country's regulatory system.

India, which imposes a 26 per cent ownership limit on foreign investors in insurance companies, is reviewing raising this to 49 per cent but legislation has become bogged down in parliament.

India is 'the one place I would complain about. India is a very, very difficult market', Lord Levene said in an interview on Thursday. 'It's one of the few places in the world where I blame regulation [for keeping foreign insurance companies out]'.

Lord Levene, who was in Tokyo to open the Lloyd's insurance market's new office there, said he hoped to increase its business in Asia from about 8 per cent of total premium income to about 15 per cent over the next decade. 'It would

be nice, in 10 years' time if we had 15 per cent in Asia', he said.

However, while Lloyd's expects moderate growth in Japan, one of its top 10 markets, and China, where it opened an office two years ago, it has failed even to obtain a licence in India.

Lloyd's opened an office in India several years ago but soon scaled it down after realising that regulatory change was unlikely to come quickly.

Like many other industries, India's insurance sector is mired in red tape relating to foreign-ownership restrictions. Overseas companies complain these are onerous, but domestic operators view them as necessary to allow them to get a foothold in their respective industries.

In China, Lloyd's also faced tough negotiations but after two or three years of difficult talks it was able to obtain a re-insurance licence.

'In China you need patience, in India you need more patience', Lord Levene said.

Source: adapted from 'Lloyd's of London hits at "difficult" India', *Financial Times*, 4/3/2010 (Nakamotot, M. and Leahy, J.), © The Financial Times Ltd. All Rights Reserved.

Questions

1. How could business in India be characterised?
2. What differences between other Asian countries mentioned in the mini-case are apparent?

Chhokar (2008), who reports the India-specific findings of the GLOBE project, refers to the many ongoing changes in the nature of Indian society as reported by Indian surveys. He refers to the weakening of the caste system, as well as the liberalisation and restructuring of the economy. Nevertheless, a manager has to contend with both collectivist and individualist values within a formal system of management. With its high 'As Is' scores on Power Distance and In-Group Collectivism (see Figure 2.1), Indian culture is typified as 'vertical collectivist'.

According to Gelfand *et al.* (2004), in vertical collectivist cultures, people emphasise the integrity of the in-group, are willing to sacrifice their personal goals for the sake of in-group goals, and support competition between the in-groups and out-groups.

Although they may accept the hierarchies of religion, society and business, the Indians do not accept their lot without showing their feelings – unlike other Asian cultures. Indians are renowned for their readiness to express their frustration if their efforts in life are not successful, or the joy experienced when their hopes or ambitions come true. The emotive dialogue in the many films from India's Bollywood film industry is testament to this extensive verbosity. This is a feature of Indian behaviour that foreign business representatives have encountered when pushing their products or services in India, particularly when their audience has the impression that these people are being patronising. Equivalent products in India may not be as well produced or delivered, but it is not the role of foreigners to tell them this.

This behaviour became manifest in a recent incident in the pharmaceutical industry sector – India occupies the third place worldwide – when a patent claim for a cancer drug from the Swiss company Novartis (second place) was rejected by India's Supreme Court: 'This drug does not add any new elements which can justify the protection by a patent and the high price'. Thus, India authorised generic drug manufacturers to continue making cheap versions when the Western multinationals accused them of counterfeiting (*NRC Handelsblad*, 2 April 2013). By taking this attitude, India clearly shows the overbearing nature of its institutions and its boldness in confronting the Western world.

Thailand and karma

Unlike Cambodia, Laos, Vietnam and Malaysia, Thailand was not colonised by a European country. One reason for this was its role as a buffer state between the French and British colonies. Thailand, originally called Siam and then changed to Thailand in 1949 (Thai meaning freedom and also the name of the main ethnic group) has a long tradition of commerce, particularly with Western countries. At the beginning of the twentieth century it developed a new social class composed of merchants and functionaries.

Buddhism plays a dominant role in the values of Thai society. This religion is practised by more than 90 per cent of the population and for its lay followers it is pragmatic in nature, prescribing more than it proscribes. Although *nirvana*, with its sublime ideals, is the ultimate goal, many Buddhists are content to improve their lives by pursuing ethical principles and by asserting personal and social responsibilities to ensure peace and serenity. By doing so, they hope to accumulate sufficient positive *karma* (action and result) and so ensure their rebirth in another, happy, state of existence.

This notion of *karma*, defined succinctly by Scarborough (1998: 82) as 'the cumulative net effect of merit and demerit over the span of an individual's lives that determines his intermediate and ultimate fates', contributes to the development of a particular kind of paternalism evident in Thailand. The person in a position of leadership is considered to have attained that status thanks to the accumulation of good rather than bad karma. Leadership requires exercising personal responsibility towards the community, being its leader and servant.

In an interview with Chamlong Srimuang, former Bangkok governor, at the East Asia economic summit in Kuala Lumpur (*Bangkok Post*, 9/10/2002, p. 11), the question of leadership comes to the fore. Chamlong Srimuang considers that leadership – whether in politics or business – requires:

> **Self-sacrifice or selflessness in one way or another. Such leadership or power over the people lasts longer than the leader's life. Jesus Christ, Mohammed and Buddha, to name a few, are clear examples of such long-lasting spiritual leadership.**

In his view, people are not trained/formed to become leaders, but good leaders, which means being able to see clearly the benefit of being hard-working, economical, honest, self-sacrificing and grateful. Trying to be the best is not the key to success. Having personal gain as the only goal is useless or even dangerous. Being the best is about 'being true to oneself, one's conscience'.

The newspaper article in Mini-case 4.4 describes the development strategy in Thailand based on Buddhist principles, an approach approved by the United Nation's main development agency.

MINI-CASE 4.4

Thai Buddhist economic model

By Kalinga Seneviratne

In the last two decades, Buddhism's appeal has grown in the West, drawing people seeking a calm not found in the fast-paced world of Internet-driven commerce and communications. Its economic model has been endorsed by the United Nations.

Bangkok, Thailand – while *bhavana* (Buddhist meditation), has become a form of modern psychotherapy and influenced Western lifestyles, is there anything in the religion's 2,500-year-old teachings that could influence modern economics?

According to Thailand's much revered King and lately members of the [new military installed] government and a growing number of economists and grassroots development activists, the answer is, yes, there is. They call it 'Sufficiency Economics', a term coined by King Bhumibol Adulyadej in the midst of Thailand's economic meltdown in 1997. It embraces the three pillars of Buddhism – *dana* (giving), *sila* (morality) and *bhavana* (meditation) – and is based on the Buddhist principle of the 'Middle Path', that is avoidance of extremes (of greed).

The Thais have recently got a strong endorsement of this Buddhist development strategy from the United Nation's main development agency. In a report released in January, the United Nations Development Programme (UNDP) hailed Thailand's new 'Middle Path' development model as a key to fighting poverty, coping with economic risk and promoting corporate social responsibility [. . .]

For communities, Sufficiency Economics principles are fundamental to empowerment and building resilience, such as setting up savings groups, revolving credit lines, and local safety nets. For private business it means, 'taking corporate responsibility to the next level' by using this approach as a guide to management and planning.

'This approach encourages them to focus on sustainable profit, to adhere to an ethical approach to business, to pay special attention to their employees, to respect nature, to have careful risk management, and to grow where possible from internal resources', the report explains. And for the third pillar, the government, the Sufficiency Economy is central to alleviating poverty, promoting good governance, and guiding macroeconomic policies to immunise against shocks. The UNDP report gives many examples of how the Sufficiency Economy model has been implemented in many parts of Thailand, encouraged by models set up under royal patronage across the country.

One such example is of Chumphon Cabana resort, which shows that the benefits of the sufficiency approach are not just confined to the agriculture sector. In the crisis of 1997, this resort on the east coast of the peninsula suffered financial difficulties like so many other businesses. In a desperate attempt to stay afloat, the owner took inspiration from the sufficiency approach.

As a start, she began to plant rice, vegetables, flowers and fruit trees on land within the resort project. To improve the sandy land without the cost of chemicals, she experimented with making organic fertiliser from hotel waste and other materials.

She planted a local variety of rice and installed a rice mill. The husk was used in making the fertiliser and for animal feed. As the resort's land was not enough to supply all its needs, she got the co-operation of surrounding villages to supply the deficit, and also helped train them in making fertiliser and other practices of organic farming. The employees of the resort were especially encouraged to participate.

Next she invented a just-in-time system of supply by posting the following day's requirements of various articles on the local school's notice board. Local production expanded beyond food to include various cleaning materials made from local materials.

As production increased, these articles were also supplied to other resorts in the area. The resort benefited from low production costs and reliable supplies. Surrounding farmers had a secure market and good prices because there were no middlemen.

Soon the resort gained a reputation with the result that other resort owners, farmers, NGOs, and government officials came to learn – which gave the employees a sense of pride. As the owner concluded, 'I think this is a kind of development which makes everybody happy.'

In a 1998 statement on the essence of the Sufficiency Economics model, King Bhumibol said: 'Sufficiency' is moderation. If one is moderate in one's desires, one will have less craving. If one has less craving, one will take less advantage of others. If all nations hold to this concept, without being extreme or insatiable in one's desires, the world will be a happier place.'

Source: Seneviratne, K., 2007.

Questions

1. In what way does the Chumphon Cabana resort illustrate the Sufficiency Economy model?

2. Which characteristics of this model relate to Buddhism?

3. In what way does the notion of 'corporate responsibility', referred to twice in the text, reflect Buddhist values? How is this notion being applied in concrete terms?

Chinese and Indian diasporas

Diasporas have played a significant role in the rapid globalisation of business, particularly those of two countries featured in this concept: China and India. The numbers of migrants involved have increased substantially, with *The Economist* (2011) estimating that in 2011 there were 215 million first-generation migrants in the world, a 40 per cent increase on figures for 1990. Both the Chinese and Indian diasporas have helped connect their mother countries to the world, thanks essentially to the advent of modern communication channels combined with the trust which they place in their fellow-countrymen. *The Economist* (2011) gives a stark example of the way in which diasporas operate by describing how a Chinese businessman in South Africa who sees a demand for plastic vuvuzelas will quickly inform his cousin who runs a factory in China:

> That Chinese factory-owner will believe what his cousin tells him, and act on it fast, perhaps sealing a deal worth millions with a single conversation on Skype.

Economist, 2011: 72

Figure 4.1 shows the geographical range of the Indian and Chinese diasporas as well as the numbers involved with regard to the 20 countries where most of them live. *The Economist* (2011) estimates, for example, that the number of Chinese living outside China exceeds the population living in France (+/−65 millions).

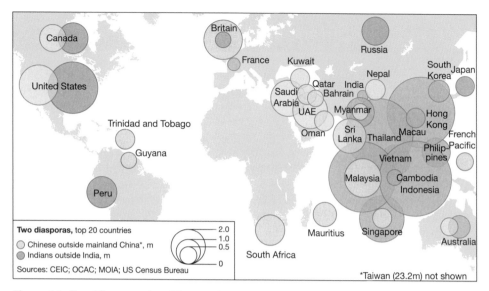

Figure 4.1 Two Diasporas, top 20 countries
Source: 'Migration and business', *Economist* 19/11/2011, Vol. 401, Issue 8760: 72–74.

This matter of trust has also played an important role in facilitating business between foreigners and the mother countries concerned. In this respect, research carried out by Foley and Kerr (2013) suggest that US-based innovators who have a particular ethnicity can help US concerns to start up and expand their activities in countries which are associated with that particular ethnicity. Chinese American innovators, for example, with their connections and knowledge, can foster trust during their company's attempts to gain or increase access to the Chinese market.

China and India, BRICS countries

Before concluding this concept, it is worth reminding the reader that both China and India belong to the BRICS group of emerging countries. As already indicated in Chapter 3, these countries are expected to account for much of the world's economic growth in the decades to come. While sharing the same BRICS platform, both countries call for far-reaching changes in the global and financial order, changes which allow for the increased representation of emerging economies and developing countries.

The frequent meetings between representatives of these giant neighbours at BRICS conventions, as well as regular summit meetings, have certainly helped the development of economic relations between the two countries. However, a number of historical disputes are holding back the creation of what could be a full-blown trading partnership. Border disputes are a factor: despite recent pacts being signed, distrust between the two countries remains.

This first concept has highlighted some features of the two culture clusters in Asia and has mentioned a few of the countries in these clusters. Nevertheless, it is hoped that clear differences between these cultures have become apparent, as well as the contrast with the Western cultures dealt with in Chapter 3.

Concept 4.2 African and Middle East cultures

For the purposes of this concept, we will consider Africa in terms of Sub-Saharan Africa, including South Africa. This has been done because North Africa is seen as closer culturally to the Middle East.

Africa

African countries had their frontiers defined by West European colonists who divided the continent between themselves at the start of the nineteenth century. Ethnic groupings, or tribes, found themselves divided by political boundaries drawn on a map. National identities are difficult to pinpoint, with various tribes inhabiting one arbitrarily defined country.

Besides the former colonial languages of English, French, German, Portuguese and Spanish, there are 20 official languages at national level in Africa. The establishment of the colonial borders resulted in the phenomenon of 'cross-border languages', which may falsely suggest that the speakers did cross borders. In fact, it describes a reality for many African countries, resulting in linguistic and cultural divergence between the ethnic groups on either side of a border, especially because the official languages are often different. Some prominent Africans have referred to cross-border languages as a factor that can promote African unity (http://www.acalan.org).

Sub-Saharan Africa

Africa's inhabitants are diverse in every way – languages, religions, dwellings and economic activities. They live in a wide range of societies, some archaic, others advanced.

The majority of its peoples live outside towns and cities in primitive cultures where archaic, animist religions determine the social order. This organisation is based on the patriarchal family following a strict hierarchy in which the patriarch has absolute authority over the whole community of the lineage or clan. This authority is generally handed down through the lineage of the patriarch (Braudel, 2008).

With increasing economic activity and improved local transportation, people migrated to towns from the country to get work and to support their families back in the countryside. Education, imported Christian religions and Islam have often supplanted animist religions in developing urban areas. Despite this increased mobility there is still identification with tribes, although this is weakening over time.

Europeans to some extent developed the lands they colonised, but since moving to independence the dictatorships that arose in individual countries have nullified most of the economic advantages created by development. Only recently has the continent started to make the transition to democratically elected governments and privatised businesses.

An example of a country that has recently been undergoing rapid business development is Nigeria. Here a Western-style 'professional' order has been imposed on relations between co-workers in companies. The workers have responded positively to the hierarchical organisation, which runs parallel to the hierarchy within their family. Despite their flexible, easy-going attitude to time they are also responding to the need for regularity and punctuality in work routine.

Shepherd Shonhiwa, a Zimbabwean expatriate and fellow of the Institute of Directors in Southern Africa recently pleaded for Europe to re-assess its view of Africa's business. In a contribution to the *Financial Times* series, 'Mastering Management', he noted that African culture had distinctive feelings of communalism rather than separatism. He went on to describe what he considered to be fundamental African personality traits:

- In the main, African culture is non-discriminatory and does not promote prejudice. This explains the readiness with which Africans embrace reconciliation in politics and business.

- Africans have a mentality of inherent trust and belief in the fairness of human beings.

- They have high standards of basic morality, based on historical precedent. These are bolstered by the close kinship observed through totem or clan names and the extended family system.

- A hierarchical political ideology, but based on an inclusive system of consultation. Labour relations and people management practices will optimise this trait.

- A perpetual optimism is an integral part of the African, mainly due to strongly held religious beliefs.

MINI-CASE 4.5

Celebrating business success in Africa

Given the growing importance accorded to the private sector in development, Mossadeck Bally winning Africa's business leadership award is a sign of the times

Africa's movers and shakers sipped fruit cocktails on Wednesday in the glitzy Ritz Four Seasons hotel in Lisbon as they celebrated a homegrown business success story.

The man they came to honour was Mossadeck Bally, the softly-spoken founder and chairman of the Azalai hotel group in west Africa. Bally received the African business leadership award at a side event of the African Development Bank's annual meeting taking place in the Portuguese capital.

The occasion at the Ritz represented a different side of Africa, one of high economic growth, growing private equity interest, and successful entrepreneurs. Given the growing importance accorded to the private sector in development – something that was also much in evidence at last month's UN conference on least developed countries in Istanbul – Bally's award is indeed a sign of the times.

Born in Niger to Malian parents, Bally, 50, studied in France and the US before returning to Mali. He started his hotel business in 1994 by buying the Grand Hotel de Bamako when it was privatized by the government. Other hotel acquisitions followed as he established the Azalai chain, which expanded into Burkina Faso, Guinea Bissau and, most recently, Benin. Azalai is now the first African private hotel chain in west Africa, employing 700 people directly and more than 3,500 indirectly.

In his acceptance speech, Bally expressed his confidence in Africa's potential, oozing quiet optimism. This is the image of Africa that African policymakers are keen to project, a counterpoint to that of conflict, coups and hunger Westerners so often associate with the continent.

Increasingly, African leaders speak of self-reliance and of the need for homegrown solutions to development challenges, moving beyond aid to financing from local capital markets and private equity, and finding growth through regional co-operation.

Fine sentiments, but there are hard facts to overcome. They can be found in the African Development Bank's 2011 review. Take the obstacles to private sector development: 'African business is held back by excessive and poorly designed regulation, limited access to finance and a lack of legal mechanisms for enforcing contracts and protecting property rights. Competitiveness is undermined by insufficient access to basic infrastructure such as roads, port facilities, information and communications technology, power and water [. . .] all of this limits the ability of the private sector to invest and grow.'

And despite talk of regional co-operation, trade between African countries remains low, the review notes. Trade within Africa grew from $48 billion in 2005 to $76 billion in 2009, but continues to be held back by cumbersome regulations and poor transport. Africa still looks primarily for markets in the north with only 10–12 per cent bound for African countries. This is half the level in other emerging markets. Moreover, half of Africa's interregional trade occurs in the southern Africa development community (SADC), in which South Africa trades with its smaller neighbours.

Such constraints make Bally's success all the more remarkable, and it is unsurprising that he was lionised in Lisbon. He really did succeed against the odds. But it could have been so different. When Bally returned from the US from his studies to work in his father's business, he was unhappy and wanted to leave during the first six months of his homecoming.

'I wasn't intellectually at ease, things were a mess and I applied for a visa to go back to the US', he told *The Guardian*. 'But I thought again, and realised I was being selfish and that my place was to help my father.'

Bally says he has absolutely no regrets about staying. 'In America, I would have been just a social security number', he said. 'And I see more émigrés returning to Africa because they see the place is at a turning point. And despite all the difficulties – a predatory and corrupt state sector – things are really changing. It is much less difficult to do business in Africa now than it was 26 years ago. The private sector really has a historic role to play.'

Source: Tran, 2011.

Questions:

1. To what extent do these views reflect any of the African characteristics put forward by Shepherd Shonhiwa, particularly with regard to the importance of the patriarchy?

2. In what way does the critical review of the Africa Development Bank and the general optimism expressed by Bally and African leaders reflect the essential dilemma which Africa faces, viz. choosing between tradition and modernity?

Mutabazi (2001: 100) underlines the characteristics put forward by Shonhiwa by emphasising that 'the cultural unity of African societies exceeds their diversity'. These societies share a collection of values and beliefs as a result of which every village or town, local administration or company displays the same social phenomena and behaviour. This shared cultural basis of values and rules will have been passed down through many generations within the tribes and passed on through networks of families and friends to communities living in other 'countries'.

Cultural models imported from the West did not succeed in replacing this common African cultural base, one which, according to Mutabazi (2001) is characterised by its relationship to time and (organised) work, as well as its relationship with other people (family, hierarchy, colleagues, subordinates, outsiders). These relations are the same in regions that may be geographically very distant from each other, or very different to each other in terms of climate, religion or language. Mutabazi gives the Ivory Coast and Rwanda as examples of very different countries where, at business level, there are similar attitudes as to how decisions should be made, how managers should give orders. There are also similarities in the way employees behave towards the company. This can be witnessed, for example, in their low rate of attendance, their frequent absenteeism and their lack of initiative.

Furthermore, the great majority of local companies reject the idea of interpersonal competition among employees, as encountered in the North American model. They therefore, for example, do not allocate bonuses to individuals for extra performance or productivity. Certain bureaucratic procedures dating from the French colonial period, such as contracts and other written directives, are also rejected by the Africans. They place greater value on verbal commitments.

South Africa, the Rainbow Nation

The rainbow, South Africa's recently adopted symbol, reflects the country's huge cultural diversity. Apart from the indigenous black peoples there are the white Europeans, Indians, Chinese and other immigrants from various countries in Asia.

The white population is not ethnically homogeneous and descends from many ethnic backgrounds. Culturally and linguistically, they are divided into the Afrikaners, who speak Afrikaans (language from the original Dutch settlers) and English-speaking groups, many of whom are descended from the ensuing British settlers. Officially there are eleven languages which are formally equal, but some languages are spoken more than others by the population. While about 65 per cent of White residents speak Afrikaans at home and 35 per cent speak English, only 0.7 per cent of Black residents speak Afrikaans and 0.5 per cent English at home.

Since the dismantling of the policy of apartheid, which not only allowed the white minority to maintain its domination of the country through control of its economic and social system but also institutionalised racial discrimination, South Africa has confidently promoted its multicultural society and is attempting to draw diverse ethnic, cultural and religious groups into the social and economic development of the country.

The increasing migration to towns from the country, as mentioned earlier concerning Africa as a whole, has helped create a sharp urban/rural contrast in South African society. In the rural areas traditional values still apply: the head of the family determines the manner in which business takes place and the way it is carried out. Tribal/family connections can play an important role in this process, even when it comes to doing business with companies in neighbouring countries. Those who have moved into urban areas are subjected to the many influences of the others living there, including the large inflow of migrants from neighbouring countries. At the same time they may well encounter a professional, top-down managerial style one which is more task-focused.

This brings us to the nature of management generally in South Africa. As Booysen and van Wyk (2008) indicate, it is difficult to talk of a particular approach to management in this multi-ethnic country. They refer to the dilemma facing managers in this country: choosing between the 'Eurocentric' approach and the 'Afrocentric' approach. Using the original GLOBE findings on the white male manager in South Africa and subsequent research among white and African black management, they typify both approaches in terms of the GLOBE dimensions. They typify the 'Eurocentric' approach as one reflecting

SPOTLIGHT 4.5

Black empowerment

By Richard Lapper

Few areas of life in contemporary South Africa excite quite so much controversy as black economic empowerment (BEE), a set of government policies and business agreements designed to give the country's disadvantaged majority greater influence over trade, finance and industry.

Voluntary codes stipulating minimum levels of black ownership in finance, mining and other key sectors have been reinforced by legislation. Although compliance is not compulsory, businesses unwilling to follow the new rules – monitored by the department of trade and industry – will lose out in any dealings with the public sector.

Perhaps because of the scale of this shift, BEE has been hugely controversial. Conservative critics allege that it has triggered emigration of skilled professionals from minority white, Indian and coloured communities, undermining overall economic performance.

They argue that, worse still, the policy has fostered cronyism and corruption, by allowing an elite of politically well-connected and poorly qualified 'black tycoons' to make fortunes while bringing no appreciable benefit to the poor.

Despite efforts to broaden the focus of BEE beyond a simple transfer of ownership to include issues such as management, board representation and procurement policies, left-wingers still rail against the way the 'new rich' flaunt accumulated wealth.

 Source: adapted from 'Transfer of assets tarnished by elitism', *Financial Times*, 16/7/2009 (Lapper, R.), © The Financial Times Ltd. All Rights Reserved.

high performance orientation on the individual level as well as high assertiveness. The 'Afrocentric' approach, on the other hand, reflects high collectivism and, humane orientation, as well as below-average assertiveness. Although Booysen and van Wyk (2008: 470) call for both approaches to be embraced, they argue that:

> [. . .] with the changes taking place in the new South Africa, even corporate culture has started to realize that we are all in Africa, and that the average South African is 15 years old and black and they, with their sense of values and perceptions, and frames of reference, will be the workforce of tomorrow.

While pursuing their business goals, managers should be intent on conciliation rather than confrontation, thus reflecting the need to maintain social harmony in this multicultural environment.

South Africa, the newest member of BRICS

South Africa was welcomed into the informal club of developing countries in 2011. Its presence in the group has been called into question, not least by Jim O'Neill, the chairman of Goldman Sachs Asset Management International, who originally devised the acronym for the group of booming economies. In an interview with the *Mail & Guardian*, O'Neill said that the inclusion of South Africa did not make any sense. Its economy was too small and its rate of growth low, even compared to the rest of Africa. In his view, Mexico, South Korea and Turkey would be more eligible members of the BRICS club (http://mg.co.za/article/2012-03-23-sa-presence-drags-down-brics, accessed 20/3/2013). Nevertheless, we may assume that South Africa has, in common with other classified BRIC's countries, a growth potential which should permit it in the future to equal the largest economies. (See Chapter 3.)

Why was South Africa chosen to become a member? A number of observers, including a *Le Monde* journalist writing in the *Weekly Guardian*, consider the choice to have been more of a political one.

> This is no longer an artificial body founded on comparable economic performance, but increasingly a political club representing the developing world, determined to counterbalance western influence in major international forums.
>
> Source: Hervieu, 2011

The Middle East

The Middle East, stretching from Iraq through the Arabian peninsula and along the north coast of Africa, has for centuries been the crossroads where West and East have met. Here, the inhabitants have successfully traded between the two, buying and selling the goods from other countries, as well as their own.

Five of these countries in North Africa – Mauritania, Morocco, Algeria, Tunisia and Libya – are often referred to collectively by the Arab word Maghreb. All these countries are often clustered together because of the many cultural features they share.

Language and culture are unifying factors, with the Islam religion providing an overarching body of belief and a strong sense of identity and community. Islam spread in the seventh century and along with it the Arab language, which had once been a tribal language in the Arab peninsula. The present Arab states were formed following the break-up of the Ottoman Empire during the First World War (1914–18). We will focus specifically on the Arabs of the Middle East, the geographical term created in the West to describe the group of countries in this part of the world.

The family remains at the basis of Arab social structure. As already witnessed in Asia, this means the broader notion of family, a kin group or clan involving several households and cousins on the father's side. The welfare of the family is of primary concern. Family ties bring security but also commitments. These can override the interests of close members in favour of nephews or cousins if the interests of the clan as a whole are better served.

The family is run in a disciplined way by an authoritarian father. The head of the family clan is usually the oldest, competent member of the grouping and runs the clan in an equally authoritarian way. A large proportion of Arab businesses are family-owned and discipline is maintained by a leader having strong central control and a strict hierarchy.

The considerable awareness that Arabs have of their social and economic environment is a noticeable feature of their business culture. They are highly sensitive towards traders and may turn down a lucrative business deal because they dislike the people they

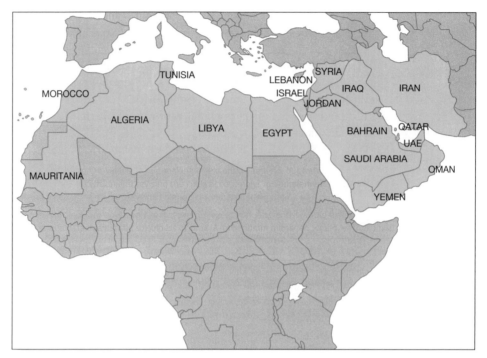

Figure 4.2 **Middle East and North Africa**

Source: *Financial Times* (FT.com), 2 February 2011 (adapted).

are dealing with, particularly if these people do not enhance their personal reputation. This is of utmost importance, since damage to one member of the family damages the whole family. It is often contended that when a family concern has to deal with the government it is more often than not a question of two family businesses coming to terms with each other. Recent upheavals in a number of Arab states have, however, undermined the many traditional relationships between business and government 'families'.

The phrase 'Inshalah', often translated as 'God willing' or 'if Allah so wishes', is one often used in everyday conversation and reflects deep-rooted beliefs in predestination and fatalism. Its use also emphasises the extreme sensitivity shown to the context of any discussion. Its exact meaning depends on the subject in hand, the particular purpose of the discussion, and the relationships between the individuals involved. On some occasions it can mean 'yes', on others 'no'; sometimes it can mean 'I'll arrange it', other times 'Don't discuss this further'. Communication, therefore, can be a hazardous affair for not only outsiders but also for any translators involved, particularly because they must also take account of the intonation and body language used.

Keeping face is often referred to with regard to Arab society and is related to this question of reputation. Admiration and respect are sought after as much as, if not more than, financial success. And this prestige is not for the individual concerned, but for the family to whom the individual belongs. The face or image conveyed to others, especially in public, is therefore given considerable attention, even when this involves dealing with relative strangers. The Arabs are renowned for their generosity and hospitality, but these 'duties' may also be a prelude to seeking some kind of commitment or request.

These comments on family and face highlight a paradox which Hickson and Pugh (2001: 221) refer to when discussing the Arab model of management:

> Arabs are disposed to handle authority centrally with high power distance, yet at the same time they aspire to an 'open door' for all comers, high or low, and to consultation in the manner of the sheikhs.

The door is now wide open in many parts of the Middle East, and aspects of Western culture have made their way into many Arab countries. More and more Middle Easterners are also participating in management education programmes in the West and applying the knowledge and skills to their native business environment. This process, however, is being controlled not only by those implementing changes, but also by the guardians of Arab society who wish to prevent its norms and values, as enshrined in civil and religious law, from being abused. In short, we can say that Arabic companies are facing a dilemma that brings the globalisation of the economy into conflict with affection for cultural values of the past.

However, a middle class is becoming apparent in a number of Middle East countries which is trying to reconcile the process of economic modernisation with the development of new values, such as tolerance, individualism and concern for the future.

The changes happening in the Gulf emirate of Qatar, as shown in the following text, exemplify this process.

MINI-CASE 4.6

How has Qatar come to play such a significant role in Europe?

Qatar is a small state with enormous wealth which has rapidly become a major diplomatic and cultural player on the world stage. In the financial world too it has become a major investor, particularly in Europe. *The Huffington Post* (2013) gives a few examples of its funding role: 'After the creation of mutual funds in France and Italy, Qatar signed a similar agreement with Greece for investing up to €1 billion in local SMEs (small and medium enterprises).'

The Guardian (2012) reports on its acquisitions in London: 'Qatar Holdings and the Qatar Investment Authority, have been on a long shopping spree, spending more than £13 billion in recent years on purchasing Chelsea Barracks, Harrods and the Olympic Village. Qatar is the largest shareholder in Barclays Bank.'

Its heady ambitions and rapid development were already pinpointed in the following article, written in 2005.

A different breed of foot soldier

By William Wallis

A strange kind of revolution is taking place in the tiny, energy-rich Gulf emirate of Qatar. Until relatively recently a fiercely conservative peninsular state living in the long shadow of Saudi Arabia, Qatar is asserting itself with global ambitions. Women are flocking to universities. Skyscrapers are sprouting from the desert and foreigners and investors are pouring in in search of business. At a time when the Arab street is seen to be stirring in pursuit of change, the transformations under way in Qatar have

been engineered not so much by its population as by Sheikh Hamad bin Khalifa al-Thani, the absolute ruler.

In Doha, the foot soldiers of change are a different breed from those crowding other Arab capitals. They are more likely to be from public relations firms and management consultancies, hired from abroad to help promote and develop the emir's 'vision'. Slogans such as 'modernisation without westernisation', or 'modern but Muslim' emerge from PowerPoint presentations rather than street pamphlets or radical preachers. 'His highness', explains one enthusiastic subject from Qatar's academic community, 'is way ahead of his society. He is trying to position us to benefit from the changes in the world. What's good for the world is also good for Qatar. We are not some kind of freak nation.'

By the standards of the conservative autocracies of the Gulf, Qatar is, however, becoming distinct in more ways than one even if it shares many of the same challenges. The emir says he wants to build a nation rich in human as well as natural resources, strategically positioned for its service industries, as well as its energy wealth. To achieve this, he is not just changing the skyline in Doha. He is also attempting to remould the mind-set of its inhabitants. In the first 24 years of independence from Britain, when other oil rich Gulf societies were assembling the trappings of modernity, Qatar remained a comparative backwater.

From the smallest financial sector in the immediate vicinity, Qatar wants to develop the region's preferred banking centre and has tailored regulations for the purpose. It wants more tourists, more skyscrapers, more international sporting and cultural events and more skills and know-how. Behind these ambitions, say government officials, is a desire on the part of the emir to shake off the apathy that characterised times past.

He and his influential wife, Sheikha Moza, are going out of their way to empower women and instil entrepreneurialism in a population accustomed to being looked after in style by the state, they say. There is also, says Mohamed al-Thani, the economy and commerce minister, a will to invest at home money that might previously have gone abroad. Expense is of little concern. But the tiny size of the local population is, together with a desire not to be seen to compromise the deeply held Islamic beliefs of Qatar's strict Wahabbi culture.

Although there are a growing number of exceptions, most Qatari women do not work and 60 per cent of the population is under the age of 21. 'Qatar is looking to do things that require global experience right from the guy operating the crane, to the engineer, to the financier trying to pull together investors', says an expatriate government adviser who himself fits the category. In the process, some Qataris complain that the roads are clogging up with traffic, rents have risen by 100 per cent in the past year and the composition and size of the population is changing by the day. About 10,000 labourers have been brought in from south-east Asia for one project alone.

The government wants a booming tourism industry but without the trashier trappings. It is liberalising the economy and wants a world class financial sector. But there is little scrutiny of business and data on public debt, foreign reserves or local population size are not disclosed. Most paradoxical of all, the government wants to develop its non-energy economy without jeopardising the culture and proportion of the local population. Its approach in this respect is far more cautious than nearby Dubai's, where you can now buy a beer with your fish and chips on the beach.

But the larger the non-Qatari population becomes, the harder it may be to stem the flow of unwanted aspects of foreign influence. With so many projects at stake, this appears to be a price the emir believes worth paying. As a non-elected leader with almost limitless funds at his disposal he has the luxury of thinking big and planning long term.

Questions

1. What are the contradictions and resulting cultural dilemmas which the inhabitants of Qatar had to face?

2. What elements in the mini-case support the statement that the modernisation of Qatar is the result of previous colonisation?

3. Are there any clues in the mini-case that could predict the success of Qatar as described in the introduction?

This second concept has focused on further clusters drawn from the GLOBE project outlined in Chapter 2. Fundamental traits of the business cultures in Africa and the Middle East have been highlighted and examples given to illustrate similarities and differences.

Conclusion

Chapter 4 has presented some key features of the (business) culture of countries within the Asian, African and Middle East clusters. It has highlighted the importance of relationships and networks in these clusters, expressed, for example, in the form of *guanxi* in China and the karma in India and has shown generally how Confucianism and Buddhism influence economic activity.

It now seems appropriate to go deeper into the value systems inherent to every culture in a business context, and to bring forward some of the dilemmas these contradictory values can generate. This is the aim of the next chapter, Chapter 5.

Points for reflection

1. Concept 4.1 underlined the importance of Confucianism and Buddhism in Asian societies. The differences between these two religions or philosophies have caused GLOBE to create two clusters, one containing China, for example, the other containing India.

   To what extent do you believe that Confucianism and Buddhism still play an important role in the business cultures of these countries?

2. Sub-Saharan Africa could be characterised as a region of contrasts: on the one hand there is modernity and Western influence, and on the other hand tradition and local cultural values.

   How do you account for these contrasts? Could the Middle East be characterised in the same way? Explain why.

Further reading

Kase, K., Slocum, A. and Zhang, Y.Y. (2011) *Asian versus Western management thinking. Its culture-bound nature*, Hampshire: Palgrave Macmillan. This book attempts to address the important question concerning the extent to which theories of management are universally applicable principles and the extent to which they are specific to particular cultural, national and temporal contexts. In the foreword of the book, Robert M. Grant remarks: 'By addressing differences in management thinking between the West and the East, the authors embark on an exciting journey with the hope of expanding the scope and depth of management theory and practice by inquiring into its cultural specificity.'

References

Booysen, L.A.E. and Van Wyk, M.W. (2008) 'Culture and leadership in South Africa', Chhokar, J.S., Brodbeck, F.C. and House, R.J. (eds), *Culture and Leadership Across the World: the GLOBE Book of In-Depth Studies of 25 Societies*, New York, NY: Lawrence Erlbaum Associates.

Braudel, F. (2008) *Grammaire des civilisations*, Paris: Arthaud-Flammarion.

Browaeys, M.-J. and Trompenaars, F. (eds) (2000) *Cases Studies on Cultural Dilemmas*, Breukelen, Netherlands: Nyenrode University Press.

Burns, R. (1998) *Doing Business in Asia: A Cultural Perspective*, Australia: Addison Wesley Longman.

Chhokar, J.S. (2008) India: 'Diversity and Complexity in Action', in Chhokar, J.S., Brodbeck, F.C. and House, R.J. (eds) in *Culture and Leadership Across the World: the GLOBE Book of In-Depth Studies of 25 Societies*, New York, NY: Lawrence Erlbaum Associates.

Chhokar, J.S., Brodbeck, F.C. and House, R.J. (eds) (2008) *Culture and Leadership Across the World: the GLOBE Book of In-Depth Studies of 25 Societies*, New York, NY: Lawrence Erlbaum Associates.

Engardio, P. with McGregor, J. (2006) 'Karma Capitalism', *Business Week*, 30/10/ 2006: 84–87.

Foley, C.F. and Kerr, W.R. (2013) 'Ethnic Innovation and U.S. Multinational Firm Activity', *Management Science*, 59(7): 1529–1544.

Follorou, J. 'Paris supports the transfer of technology to India', *Le Monde*, 18/2/2013.

Fu, P.P., Wu, R. and Yang, Y. (2008) 'Chinese culture and leadership', in Chhokar, J.S., Brodbeck, F.C. and House, R.J. (eds), *Culture and Leadership Across the World: the GLOBE Book of In-Depth Studies of 25 Societies*, New York, NY: Lawrence Erlbaum Associates.

Gelfand, M.J., Bhawuk, D.P.S., Nishii, L.H. and Bechtold, D.J. (2004) 'Individualism and Collectivism' in House, R.J., Hanges, P.J., Javidan, M., Dorfman, P.W. and Gupta, V. (eds), *Culture, Leadership and Organizations: the GLOBE Study of 62 Societies*: 437–512, Thousand Oaks, CA: Sage.

Hervieu, S. (2011) 'South Africa gains entry to Bric club' in *Guardian Weekly*, 19/4/2011, http:// www.theguardian.com/world/2011/apr/19/south-africa-joins-bric-club, accessed 2/4/2013.

Hickson, D.J. and Pugh, D.S. (2001) *Management Worldwide*, 2nd edition, London: Penguin.

Kase, K. Slocum, A. and Zhang, Y.Y. (2011) *Asian versus Western Management Thinking: Its Culture-Bound Nature*, Hampshire: Palgrave Macmillan.

Lewis, R.D. (1996) *When Cultures Collide*, London: Nicholas Brealey.

Michailova, S. and Worm, V. (2003) 'Personal networking in Russia and China: *blat* and *guanxi*', *European Management Journal*, 21(4): 509–519.

Mutabazi, E. (2001) 'Multiculturalisme et gouvernement des sociétés africaines', in Dahan-Seltze, G. and Pierre, P. (eds), *Mondialisation: les cultures en questions*, Sociologies Pratiques, Paris: APSE: 95–118.

Pedroletti, B. (2009) *Le Monde*, Edition internationale, Paris, France: Société éditrice du Monde (SA), 19/12/2009: 5.

Scarborough, J. (1998) *The Origins of Cultural Differences and Their Impact on Management*, London: Quorum.

Seneviratne, K. (2007) 'Thai Buddhist economic model', *Lanka Daily News*, 20/3/2007, www.dailynews.lk/2007/03/20/fea03.asp, accessed 1/9/2010,

Srimuang, Chamlong: interview in *Bangkok Post*, 09/10/2002: 11.

The Economist (2011) 'Weaving the world together', 11/19/2011, 401 (8760): 72–74.

Tran, M. (2011) 'Celebrating business success in Africa' in Poverty matters blog, *Guardian* 9/6/2011, http://www.theguardian.com/global-development/poverty-matters/2011/jun/09/africa-private-sector-mossadeck-bally, accessed 2/4/2013.

Truc, O. (2010) *Le Monde*, Edition internationale, Paris, France: Société éditrice du Monde (SA), 6/2/2010: 4.

Zhu, Y., Bhat, R. and Nel, P. (2005) 'Building business relationships: a preliminary study of business executives' views', *Cross Cultural Management*, 12(3): 63–84.

Chapter 4 Activities

ACTIVITY 4.1

Read the case study and answer the questions below.

Pulling out all the stops

A Canadian packaging company wished to extend its activities in the area of convenience foods. It had pin-pointed one particular area where it could supply pizza boxes to half a dozen chains of pizza restaurants which operated home delivery services. These chains relied on local suppliers for their pizza boxes and were unhappy with the products supplied, the irregular delivery and, above all, the cost.

Through intensive online research and consultation with the commercial section of the embassy of the People's Republic of China, the Canadians had managed to find a packaging manufacturer near Shanghai that could provide pizza boxes at a very reasonable price in line with the specifications and quantities required – and deliver them within the deadlines set.

Negotiations by e-mail and phone had taken place and a deal seemed imminent. Before contracts could be signed, however, it was agreed that both the Chinese and Canadians should visit each other's headquarters and meet face-to-face to establish complete confidence in their venture and to settle final details. The Chinese were to visit Canada and the Canadians were to fly to China two weeks later.

The Canadian company decided to pull out all the stops to give their visitors a reception they would never forget. They arranged an elaborate welcome ceremony in a five-star hotel, to be followed by an authentic Chinese dinner. Considerable attention was paid to all the details involved – some of the ingredients for the meal had even been specially imported for the occasion.

Eventually, the big day came and the Chinese guests were whisked by limousine to the hotel where they were greeted by the Canadian company's president and management team. Despite the lavish words of praise from the Canadians in front of the hundred guests present, and the bonhomie everyone tried to engender, the Chinese remained reticent and very formal in their behaviour. During the meal the Chinese did not seem to appreciate the effort put into the food they were served. Moreover, they said very little and the attempts by the Canadians to keep the social conversation going eventually ended in silence on both sides. Despite being promised an exotic Chinese floor-show after the dinner, the delegation made their excuses (they were tired after their journey) and quietly retired to their rooms. The Canadians were surprised and disappointed. What had gone wrong?

Questions

1. Why were the Canadian hosts surprised by the behaviour of the Chinese? How do you think the Canadians expected the Chinese to behave?
2. Why do you think the Chinese behaved the way they did?
3. If you had to choose a word to describe Chinese culture, what would that word be?
4. Read the information on the fifth dimension one more time. Try to explain the Chinese author's analysis by using the values described in Concept 2.1.

ACTIVITY 4.2

In the case study below, a Dutch business consultant gives his account of a problem that he was called in to resolve. The problem involved a South Korean company and a Dutch advertising agency. Before reading the text and answering the questions, re-read both Chapters 3 and 4.

This activity also prepares the ground for Chapter 5, which examines cultural dilemmas.

My negotiating dilemma

One of my clients was a South Korean company established in the Netherlands. The sales targets that the company had been given by the headquarters in Seoul were very high. To help the company reach these targets, it hired an advertising agency. The agency went to work and came up with a total media campaign which the South Korean company accepted and allowed to be set in motion. One ingredient of the campaign was a simple but innovative slogan that quickly caught on.

The advertising agency continued the campaign, which appeared to maintain its success. The initial euphoria within the company, however, had evaporated. Its managers thought the agency's bills were too high, not only because the agency had been working with them for two years, but also because they were suspicious about the actual hours that the agency was spending on producing the advertising. They knew it was difficult to check on the time needed to come up with brilliant ideas, but still they felt that the Dutch were taking advantage of the situation. As I discovered later, a comment which was frequently heard at the top of the company was: 'You have to be careful with those Dutch.'

The Korean company started to withhold payments. The director of the Dutch agency saw this as a typical tactic of the Koreans to get lower prices. He shared the view held by some businesses that Koreans easily breach contracts, a perception that usually comes about because people are generally unaware of how Koreans interpret the word 'trust'. Having tried to explain this to him, it was not really a surprise to hear from the Koreans that they intended to break their contract with the agency. I told them it could damage their name in the market if they did so, and reminded them that all the slogans used to promote their products remained the (intellectual) property of the advertising agency.

Well, the agency threatened to take the Korean company to court to recover the money it was owed. They did so, despite being eager to continue with the contract. Losing it would mean disaster for a company that had only started up a few months before getting the Korean contract.

A meeting took place between the two sides without my presence. During it the Koreans made it clear that they were not going to pay. The young manager representing the agency told the Koreans that they would not be allowed to use the slogans any more if the contract was terminated.

The Korean management called me in and asked me to help.

I had a dilemma. It was in my clients' interest to continue the contract. Breaking it would mean putting an end to the whole advertisement campaign that they needed so much (since they were new in the market). The Dutch had good arguments for the amounts they had charged and were really afraid of losing the contract. If the advertising agency started legal proceedings, the Koreans would have no chance of winning the case.

Source: Browaeys and Trompenaars, 2000: case 10, adapted.

Questions

1. What exactly is the dilemma referred to in the last paragraph?
2. How would you describe the contrast between the South Koreans and the Dutch when they are doing business?
3. How do you think the dilemma could be resolved?

ACTIVITY 4.3

Read the following text and answer the questions.

Where are the workers?

The following incident took place in a company based in South Africa and which had a Dutch management team. Those employed in the production department were black.

The general manager was pleased with the performance of the production workers, and as is usual in his own country, the Netherlands, he awarded them a bonus at the end of the year equivalent to two weeks' wages.

The Christmas holidays came and went and the New Year started. However, none of the production workers turned up for work, even though the factory was open. Eventually, on 15 January they re-appeared.

The general manager was perplexed. What had gone wrong?

Questions

1. Why was the factory empty for the first two weeks of January?
2. Analyse the attitude of the workers using the relevant 'culture construct definitions' given in Table 2.7 as well as relevant data in Table 2.8 (Chapter 2).

ACTIVITY 4.4

Read the following case study about Asian family businesses and then answer the questions.

A new generation of family firm

By Louise Lucas

All happy families are the same, to paraphrase Leo Tolstoy. But even unhappy ones are not bad for business.

A 'family index' produced by Credit Suisse shows that companies in which the founding family has a stake of 10 per cent or more are good for shareholders' wealth. According to analysts at the Swiss bank, European stocks with a significant family influence have outperformed their respective sectors by an average 8 per cent a year over the past decade.

The US experience is similar. Small wonder that several US companies, including the retailer, Gap, are going back to their family roots, five decades or so after the model was nudged aside in favour of public ownership.

Asia, of course, never gave up on family businesses. Mainland entities aside, family-owned companies dominate Hong Kong's Hang Seng Index. South Korea's corporate dynasties are flourishing, even after those pesky scandals. The Lee family has tightened its grip on the Samsung group by elevating the son of chairman Lee Kun-hee. And Chung Mong-koo 'retains full operational control and decision-making authority for long-term strategic issues affecting Hyundai Motor', the carmaker says – in spite of being handed a three-year prison sentence for embezzlement.

Dynasties proliferate across south-east Asia: the Malaysian Kuoks, whose interests span hotels and media; Indonesia's Salims in noodles; and the same country's Bakries in mining and telecoms. Taiwan has the Wangs, of Formosa Plastics fame, and the Koos, its oldest business dynasty, now in a spot of bother over the antics of heir apparent Jeffrey Koo junior. Even Singapore, whose corporate landscape is partly in government hands, has family empires.

Does that mean Asian investors have more chance of outperforming benchmarks? Sadly, Credit Suisse has not developed an Asian version of its index.

However, consistent out-performance does not apply to all the region's best-known family companies. Korea's Samsung Electronics underperformed its benchmark in two of the past four years, while Hutchison lagged behind every year. In Singapore, state-controlled DBS outperformed its family-owned banking peers. Other Asian dynasties move in lockstep with their peers – a reflection of the fact that many are rooted in cyclical industries such as property development.

But there are plenty of stars in the family-controlled universe. Henry Yeung Wai-Cheung, an associate professor at the National University of Singapore who has researched Asian family businesses, sees grounds for optimism. Corporate governance and transparency – once conspicuous by their absence – have improved, he says, along with greater globalisation of operations.

Younger generations are moving family businesses into different areas. 'This new phenomenon is leading to a new kind of family firm, more driven by emerging operations, especially in technology', he says. 'That's a good development – extracting more from the existing franchise.'

And what of the unhappy families? The spat in India between Reliance's Ambani brothers, who engaged in a power struggle when their father died, briefly sent Reliance shares tumbling. But it did shareholders a favour in the long run – the subsequent division of the company unlocked value and pushed both brothers into expansion mode.

Stanley Ho, the Macao casino kingpin, disowned his sister over a row about dividend payments and shareholdings in his gambling empire. But his dynasty continues to produce fabulous returns for shareholders. His son Lawrence's casino joint venture with the son of Australian media magnate Kerry Packer recently listed on NASDAQ and shareholders saw gains of up to 32 per cent on day one.

Perhaps the most startling family rift was last year's bid by Li Ka-shing, the Hong Kong billionaire, to help bankroll an acquisition of his son's telecoms business. Mr Li's proposal, ultimately rejected by shareholders, probably owed more to repairing political relations than sparing his son's blushes. Richard Li's plans to sell PCCW's telecom assets to private equity firms were scuppered by Beijing. But it set back the cause of family businesses. A pity, since it was Mr Li who wrote the epitaph for keeping wealth in the family, in a speech last September entitled 'My third son' – which is how he refers to his charitable foundation.

Mr Li said: 'In Asia, our traditional values encourage and even demand that wealth and means pass through lineage as an imperative duty. I urge and hope to persuade you, especially all of us in Asia, that if we are in a position to do so, that we transcend this traditional belief.'

Questions

1. How can an unhappy family be good for business?

2. How does an Indian family differ from the other family types in Asia? Refer to Concept 4.1.

Chapter 5

Cultural dimensions and dilemmas

Figure I.2 in the introduction to Part One mentioned the names of two social scientists, Kluckholn and Strodtbeck. Their book, *Variations in Value Orientations* (1961), has served as a primary source of reference for many researchers into culture and management, including Schein, Adler, Hall, Hofstede and Trompenaars. These researchers developed cultural value orientations when investigating the phenomenon of culture and developed cross-cultural management models for a business context.

Some insight was given in Chapter 2 into the relationship between national cultural values and management. Trompenaars also developed dimensions to measure cultural differences and to gain further understanding about cultural diversity in business. What is particularly original about his work is that he presents opposing cultural values in the form of dilemmas.

Concept 5.1 goes further by developing the value orientation model addressed in Chapter 2. It then gives an overview of Trompenaars' dimensions and the ensuing dilemmas which a manager may encounter in an intercultural environment. It also highlights some of the differences between Trompenaars' and Hofstede's dimensions. In addition, it deals with the culture of innovation in organisations.

Concept 5.2 explains the method and the process for reconciling the dilemmas outlined in Concept 5.1. The dilemma of motivation is addressed in the preface.

Learning outcomes

After reading the chapter you should:

- Understand the concept of value orientations.
- Have gained insight into Trompenaars' seven dimensions.
- Have explored some cultural dilemmas in business.
- Have learned how cultural differences can be reconciled.
- Have acquired an initial insight into the theories of motivation.

One experiences a dilemma (the notion of two opposing values) when answering the question 'What should I do?' by saying 'I don't know, but I can't ignore the problem' (Tahssain-Gay and Cherre (2012): 18).

Preface: motivation – needs and values

When considering the problem just raised, Gullestrup (2006) sees it as a possible dilemma in ethical terms for what he calls a 'cultural actor', i.e. the person seeking intercultural understanding when interacting with people from other cultures. He considers such dilemmas as occurring at two levels. At an *abstract* level, a dilemma is related to the question whether something like an ideal, universally valid culture actually exists, one which can be applied to any local culture. At an *emotional* and *personal* level, a dilemma may occur when the cultural actor is trying to modify certain behaviour or values in a given culture. Gullestrup illustrates the latter by referring to an exporter who is attempting to change the habits of people in a particular culture to enable him to sell them more products.

Dilemma of motivation

This type of second-level dilemma is one experienced by many managers working in an international context experience who are dealing with people from different cultural backgrounds. One of the most important dilemmas such managers have to face is what it is called, the dilemma of motivation. Acknowledging that people work in different ways is not enough; what needs to be recognised is that they may have different motivational systems. Finding out what systems are at play is not an easy matter since there are various systems which may improve the quality of individual working life as well as group behaviour.

The dilemma of motivation may arise when a manager is searching an appropriate strategy for motivating people with different needs and values. As Todes *et al.* (1977: 165) emphasise: 'The success or failure of motivation rests not on the technique itself but on management's ability to match the needs of people with appropriate incentives.' This implies that a manager should possess an interdisciplinary knowledge of several disciplines comprising psychology (personality of the individual) and motivational theories.

Motivation theories: human versus cultural perspectives

There are many theories of motivation, most of which come from the Western world. Below is a brief overview of some of them in terms of two approaches to motivation: human needs and cultural values.

Human needs

Todes *et al.* (1997: 166) classify the needs of people according to four motivational perspectives:

1. The sociological view: people's actions are governed by the customs and the values of the society.
2. The biological view: human's actions are determined by their physical needs.
3. The psychoanalytic view: human actions are driven by mostly unconscious processes.
4. The behaviourist view: human behaviour is the response to various motivating stimuli.

At the organisational level, other scholars add psychological and spiritual needs, needs which are not only more complex to understand because these are not just to do with human needs, but are also related to the cultural background of the organisation in question.

Cultural values

Adler with Gundersen (2008) argue that the motivation theories which emanate from the US are more a reflection of American values than a universal description of motivation. She is referring in particular to Maslow's well-known hierarchy of five basic needs, and to Herzberg's two-factor motivation theory. The latter can be briefly described as one involving (1) intrinsic factors or motivators that influence the employee's job satisfaction (the need for personal growth) and (2) extrinsic factors that influence the employee's job dissatisfaction (the need to avoid disagreement).

However, when considering Vroom's expectancy theory of motivation, in which motivation depends 'on the extent to which people believe they have control over the outcomes of their efforts as well as on manager's abilities to identify desired rewards', Adler (2008: 189) notes its 'universal' character. This is because the theory does not stipulate the nature of the rewards that motivate a specific culture. This suggests that the managers themselves have to discover which type of reward is the most adequate for a specific group. Nevertheless, this theory, like the ones mentioned earlier, still reflects the values related to the culture where the theory has been developed.

However, as Adler with Gundersen (2008: 192) point out, more recent motivation theories take into account the cultural component. This goes particularly for the cultural intelligence theory, developed originally by Earley and Ang (2003), which refers to a person's capability to adapt when interacting with people from different cultural contexts. One of the three constituents or 'motivational aspects' of cultural intelligence comprises values such as confidence, persistence, and, not least, the level of affinity with a new culture. Having confidence, persistence and the required affinity may improve a manager's performance effectiveness in an international context, even though the manager maintains an unconscious ethnocentrism.

Concept 5.1 Value orientations and dimensions

The concepts of cultural theory have inspired researchers, particularly those relating culture to management, to examine the effect of the norms and values of a society on the individual.

Parsons, an American sociologist who attempted to integrate all the social sciences into a science of human action, argued in his ground-breaking work, *The Structure of Social Action* (1937), that the action of the individual is totally integrated into a social system. Individuals passively follow the rules of conduct of the specific society in which they are living. The norms of the society are institutionalised and internalised by the individuals in it through a process of socialisation. These norms steer their actions and subordinate individuals to the social order, reducing the uncertainty they experience when interacting. Without this social mechanism, interaction would be much less predictable, the motives and reactions of those involved much less certain.

The value-orientation approach

Kluckholn and Strodtbeck (1961: 4) define value orientations as being complex principles that are the result of interaction between three elements: the cognitive, the affective and the directive. This final element is of particular interest since it orders and conducts human thoughts and actions 'as these relate to the solution of "common human" problems'.

They put forward a classification of the universal components of value orientations, including some intracultural variations. To enable this classification to be made, Kluckholn and Strodtbeck (1961: 10) formulate three assumptions:

1. 'There are a limited number of common human problems for which all peoples at all times must find some solution'. This forms the essentially universal nature of value orientations.

2. There are many ways of solving problems.

3. Societies have different preferences when it comes to choosing solutions.

These assumptions allow them to determine five problems common to all human groupings. On the basis of these problems they established the variations in five orientations, which have been integrated into Chapter 6 dealing with cultural values in management.

To enable a clearer understanding of these value orientations, Kluckholn and Strodtbeck (1961: 11–20) illustrate their definitions with examples, many of which relate to the culture prevailing in the US at that time.

1. *Human nature orientation* (goodness or badness of human nature): 'Some in the United States today incline to the view that human nature is a mixture of Good and Evil. These would say that although control and effort are certainly needed, lapses can be understood and need not always be severely condemned' (p. 12).

2. *Man–nature orientation* (harmony-with-nature and mastery-over-nature): 'In the conceptualization of the man–nature relationship is that of harmony; there is no real separation of man, nature and supra-nature [. . .] The mastery-over-nature position is the first-order [orientation] (that is, the dominant orientation) of most Americans. Natural forces of all kinds are to be overcome and put to the use of human beings' (p. 13).

3. *Time orientation* (past, present and future): 'Americans place an emphasis upon the future – a future which is anticipated to be bigger and better [. . .] The ways of the past are not considered good just because they are past, and truly dominant [. . .] Americans are seldom content with the present. This view results in a high evaluation of change, providing the change does not threaten the existing value order – the American way of life' (p. 15).

4. *Activity orientation* (being, being-in-becoming and doing): 'The doing orientation is so characteristically the dominant one in American society [. . .] "Getting things done" and "Let's do something about it" are stock American phrases' (p. 17).

5. *Relational orientation* (man's relation to other men): 'The Lineal, the Collateral and the Individualistic 'relational' alternatives are analytical concepts for the purpose of making fine distinctions both within and between systems rather than generalizing concepts for the specification of the gross differences between systems' (p. 17).

The US, with its many ethnic groups, serves as an ideal example to illustrate the degrees of variation in value orientations. These variations result from the presence of subgroups in every society whose behaviour is more or less patterned according to the value orientations of the dominant group. These subgroup variations contribute to the creation of what Kluckhohn and Strodtbeck (1961: 28) call a 'web of variation' in a society.

SPOTLIGHT 5.1

Ubuntu

This term, which refers to the spirit of community in Africa, comes from traditional African culture. It can be translated in several ways, but means essentially 'I am because you are'. It reflects a way of life in which collective responsibility is considered more important than individual concerns. It is the group which ensures the survival of the individual as long as the individual remains loyal to the collective cause. In the many townships in South Africa *ubuntu* means that those in need are helped by others who have the means, without any obligation to give in return.

Trompenaars follows the same line of reasoning as Kluckhohn and Strodtbeck by proposing dimensions based, in particular, on the orientation of societies with regard to their relations with other people, with time and with nature. However, he goes beyond the framework of anthropology and sociology to show how these dimensions also affect the process of managing across cultures.

Trompenaars' seven dimensions

The standpoint of Fons Trompenaars is that each culture has its own specific solutions for universal problems. In his surveys he presented his respondents with a number of dilemmas and asked them to choose one of a number of solutions. In the first edition of his book, *Riding the Waves of Culture* (1993), Trompenaars attempts to show the effects of culture on management by describing different cultural orientations based on academic and field research carried out in several countries. He rejects the notion that there is one 'best way' of doing business and advocates a better understanding of the cultural dilemmas faced by international companies. Furthermore, if there is a large number of products and services on world markets, attention should be given to 'what they mean to the people in each culture' (1993: 3). Trompenaars examines culture within seven dimensions divided into three main categories: people, time and environment. Some of the dimensions produced reflect those of the authors mentioned above and these are relevant to business.

Five of the seven dimensions of culture as presented by Trompenaars in *Riding the Waves of Culture* are outlined in Table 5.1. This first set of dimensions is based on the five relational orientations borrowed from Parsons (1951) which describe 'the ways in which human beings deal with each other' (Trompenaars, 1993: 8).

Table 5.1 **Relations to the other people**

1. *Universalism versus particularism:* • societal versus personal obligation	*Universalism*: absolute rules apply, irrespective of circumstances and situations *Particularism*: circumstances and relationships are more important considerations than absolutes Example in business: the role of the contract
2. *Individualism versus collectivism (communitarianism):* • personal versus group goals	*Individualism*: personal welfare and fulfilment *Collectivism*: social concern and altruism Example in business: goals of negotiating and decision-making
3. *Neutral versus affective relationships:* • emotional orientation in relationships	This dimension concerns the contexts and ways that cultures choose to express emotions. Should emotion be exhibited in business relations?

4. *Specific versus diffuse relationships:*
  • contact versus contract
  • rapport versus report
	Specific: company employees are hired in contractually to be part of a system which performs efficiently
	Diffuse: company employees are members of a group working together. Their relations with each other and the organisation determine how the company functions

5. *Achievement versus ascription (doing/being):* • legitimating power and status	In achievement-oriented cultures, business people are evaluated by how well they perform an allocated function. In ascriptive cultures, status is attributed, for example, to older people, those who are of good family or highly qualified

Source: adapted from Trompenaars (1993: 8–11) and his other publications.

Let us have a look at an example, which could be analysed with the dimensions: 'relations to other people'.

MINI-CASE 5.1

Statements of commitment

One of my tasks as financial manager was to implement a customer profitability system at a Swedish company located in Amsterdam. The system required a team of people from different parts of the company to aggregate and analyse information related to customer activities. Under my direction, this team of workers had created all the necessary processes and analyses for the customer profitability model. The new system had already succeeded in helping the company's account managers to derive more profits from their existing customers.

Pleased with the results of my team's customer profitability system, the Swedish head of the branch asked me to ensure that the system remained in place even after I had returned to the US. With this in mind, I wrote a formal document that stated the individual commitments of everyone on the team in terms of the profitability system over the next year. My intention was to have each member of the team individually sign up to these commitments. My Swedish branch head believed that the idea to have all the team members agree to their commitments on paper was an excellent one because he believed that the project might otherwise fall apart after I had left Amsterdam.

Upon presenting my commitment document to one Dutch manager with whom I had worked closely, I was surprised by his unease when signing the document. He said that having individuals sign a document in this manner was very 'un-Dutch'. However, if I failed to gain some kind of formal commitment to the project, I felt sure that my Swedish manager would be dissatisfied.

Source: adapted from Browaeys and Trompenaars, 2000: case 7.

Questions

1. What do you think the financial manager should do to get the team's formal commitment?

2. How can this situation be analysed using Trompenaars' dimensions as given in Table 5.1?

Trompenaars added two dimensions of particular interest to management and business. The dimensions he delineated are to do with time and the environment (Table 5.2).

Table 5.2 **Relations to time and the environment**

6. *Sequential versus synchronic time* (monochronic/polychronic)	*Sequential*: time is tangible and divisible. Only do one activity at a time
	Synchronic: time is flexible and intangible. Appointments are approximate and subject to 'giving time' to significant others
7. *Inner versus outer directed* • Internal or external control to the environment	*Internal control*: one's personal conviction is the starting point for every action and this may result in conflict with others and resistance to nature
	External control: Sensitive to the environment and seeks harmony. Often flexible attitude, willing to compromise

Source: see Table 5.1.

Although it is important to know the dimensions based on value differences in societies to compare cultures, it is nevertheless necessary for management to define what these dimensions mean in concrete terms, the differing attitudes that result. A useful way of demonstrating these differences is by examining the ways in which dilemmas are approached. Details of these dimensions and the related cultural dilemmas are presented below.

A framework for the new millennium manager

These seven dimensions were essentially the result of Trompenaars' research based on the question 'Where are you coming from?' Are the value-systems of a person predominantly universalistic or particularistic; is that person an individualist or communitarian person? Does the status of that person derive from what (s)he does or who (s)he is? This approach:

> helps to identify and model the source of not only national cultural differences, but related issues of corporate culture as well as dealing with a diverse work force. This has served to help managers structure their real world experiences. The Trompenaars' database of 50,000 managers worldwide continues to be a rich source of social constructs for identifying and explaining and predicting culture clash.
>
> Trompenaars and Woolliams, 2000: 22

Trompenaars and Woolliams (2000: 25–27) developed a framework for the 'millennium manager' by combining these seven dimensions with a range of dilemmas identified by Hampden-Turner. By using a factor analysis, they reduced the variety of behaviours to seven core competencies defined on the basis of the dimensions on which the values of diverse cultures vary. The same framework can be used to consider many business dilemmas (Table 5.3). These concepts are abstract but all exhibit bifurcation. Effective behaviours can be defined for each dimension.

Table 5.3 **A framework for the 'millennium manager'**

1. Universalism–particularism
A high-performing manager recognises, respects and reconciles allegiance to rule-bound activity or unique circumstances. In practice, dilemmas are typically between: ● legal contracts and loose interpretations; ● emphasis on globalism or localism; ● human rights or special relationships; ● low-cost strategies or premium strategy; and ● extending rules or discovering exceptions. Thus, effective management lies not in the values of rule-making or exception-finding, but between these. How else can the rules be improved except by noting each exception and revising the rules accordingly? In complementarity, how else can exceptional abilities be developed than by noting the highest defined standards and exceeding them? To their annoyance, managers promulgate a rule only to discover an exception. A scientist would believe he had failed. A boss would feel defied. A moralist would be against the sinfulness of it all. A 'millennium manager' would learn from it!
2. Individualism–communitarianism (collectivism)
A high-performing manager recognises, respects and reconciles the individual employee's development, enrichment and fulfilment or the extent to which the corporation and customers should be the beneficiaries of personal efforts. In practice, dilemmas are typically between: ● profit or market share strategy; ● rights or duties; ● egoism or altruism; ● responsibility for self or others; and ● originating ideas or refining useful products.
3. Neutral or affectivity
A high-performing manager recognises, respects and reconciles the legitimacy of showing or controlling emotions. Dilemmas can arise from: ● being detached or enthusiastic; ● long pauses or frequent interruptions; and ● being professional or engaged.
4. Specific-diffuse
A high-performing manager recognises, respects and reconciles the tendency to analyse and break down the field of experience or to synthesise, augment and construct the experience. Dilemmas can arise from: ● the bottom line or general good will; ● data and codification or concepts and models; ● being results-oriented or process-oriented; and ● facts or relationships.
5. Achieved or ascribed status
A high-performing manager recognises, respects and reconciles why status is conferred on people. Dilemmas can arise from: ● pay for performance or vindication for worth; ● status following success or status preceding success; ● head-hunting or developing in-house; and ● learning at school or learning through life.

Table 5.3 *(continued)*

6. Sequential or synchronic time
A high-performing manager recognises, respects and reconciles different meaning and priority given to time passing in sequence or coming around and around.
Dilemmas can arise from:
• highly rational, standardised production or just-in-time production; • keeping to schedule or being easily distracted; and • winning the race or shortening the course.

7. Inner or outer directed
A high-performing manager recognises, respects and reconciles whether the locus of control is inside or outside the people involved. For the latter, it is the environment to which people must adapt.
Dilemmas can arise from being:
• driven by conscience or responsive to outside influence; • strategically oriented or fusion oriented; and • dauntless entrepreneur or public benefactor.

Source: adapted from Trompenaars and Woolliams, 2000: 25–27.

Mini-case 5.2 is a typical example of the cultural dilemma of achievement versus ascription.

MINI-CASE 5.2

In search of status

An English friend of mine had finished her studies in the most famous *grande école* of commerce in France. She did both her undergraduate and her MBA studies there and then she was hired by a well-known consulting firm in London.

She worked there for four years and reached the level of senior consultant by the age of thirty-three. She was then given an assignment with an oil company based in Saudi Arabia. Until then she had had no problems in communicating with the client's team members and had always produced successful results. However, with this particular client, she had enormous difficulties.

She worked as hard as she could to figure out the structure of the company, its problems and possible solutions. Despite her efforts, however, she could feel that her opinions were not being taken seriously, and that senior managers of the client usually tried to avoid discussing issues with her. Moreover, she had difficulty in getting vital information from employees lower down in the hierarchy, so she was unable to come up with the analyses she wanted.

Although she felt she could really help the company with her knowledge and experience, she found it difficult to persuade the client to put her ideas into practice. In fact, the better and more innovative her ideas were, the more difficult it was to get them over to the managers in Saudi Arabia.

Source: adapted from Browaeys and Trompenaars, 2000: case 5.

Questions

1. Which particular aspects of status relate to the consultant and to the company for whom she was working?

2. How do you think the consultant could try to improve her situation?

Trompenaars' dimensions versus Hofstede's dimensions

Fons Trompenaars, a compatriot of Geert Hofstede's – but with a French mother – has on several occasions acknowledged his indebtedness to Hofstede. The seven dimensions he has developed may, at first glance, even look as if they are 'more of the same'. However, as this concept has shown, the nature of these dimensions is different and reflects irreconcilable differences in approach between these two Dutch stalwarts. This is very clear from the response which Trompenaars and co-author Charles Hampden-Turner (1997) gave to the review made by Hofstede (1996) of Trompenaars' model of national culture differences.

Having carried out an empirical analysis of Trompenaars' own data, Hofstede comes to the conclusion that the questionnaire used by Trompenaars is essentially measuring Hofstede's own individualism dimension by using dimensions that are interrelated. Hofstede questions Trompenaars' research method, claiming among other things that the latter had started his research using preconceived notions taken from mid-twentieth century US literature and had not changed these concepts using the database Trompenaars compiled. Hofstede (1996: 198) had concluded his review by implying that Trompenaars was less interested in scholarship, more in commerce: 'He tunes his messages to what he thinks the customer likes to hear.'

In their measured response to Hofstede's review, Hampden-Turner and Trompenaars (1997) concede that Hofstede has taught them a lot and that they basically respect the results of his research. However, they staunchly defend their approach by giving a detailed account of the statistical methods used and which, they say, Hofstede should consider more carefully. They insist that he does not have the right when assessing their results to view his 'independent variables' as sovereign and to claim that other cultural concepts are derived from them. As for the question of 'preconceived notions' and implied lack of rigour, Hampden-Turner and Trompenaars strongly defend the US research literature, rejecting the idea that the many researchers whose work they drew on did no empirical research. If anything, it is continental Europe that is more concerned with 'an excess of rationalism and grand theories'. They then turn to the questions Hofstede himself uses in his questionnaires: these are, they argue, borrowed from (or disguised versions of) questions used in various psychological profile tests used during the 1950s and 1960s in the US, a time when personality research was extremely popular.

As for the dimensions themselves, they consider Hofstede's pursuit of the least number of dimensions to account for observed differences to be 'one dimensional thinking' (1997: 158). Hampden-Turner and Trompenaars see cultures as 'dancing' from one preferred end of a dimension to another when encountering various dilemmas. In that sense, cultures are more like circles with 'preferred arcs joined together' rather than being Hofstede's linear forms where cultures are positioned high or low or in the middle. Faced with dilemmas, they argue, cultures attempt to integrate and reconcile values to come up with a satisfactory response. Their dimensions, they believe, are essentially 'heuristic devices' or speculative formulations that serve as a guide when investigations are being made into 'family resemblances' between cultures when they are faced with dilemmas.

Rather than being 'the perfect model', which Hofstede is still seeking, Hampden-Turner and Trompenaars see theirs as a 'model-to-learn-with'. They can learn from their respondents – and vice-versa. Hofstede's search for perfection has, they maintain, slowed his learning and hindered renewal. Hampden-Turner and Trompenaars say they have moved on, as can be seen in Trompenaars' recent publications, including *Riding the Whirlwind* (2007). In this book, he suggests connecting people and organisations within a culture of innovation. He discusses not only the dilemmas and their reconciliation (as explained in Concept 5.2), but also how a culture of innovation can be created to harness creativity.

Innovation and culture of the organisation

According to Genelot (2011), innovation not only refers to the creation of products or services. Innovation in the areas of methods of management and production can also be facilitated and conditioned through scientific developments and evolutionary thinking. He distinguishes three levels of innovation – (1) science and culture, (2) organisation and production, (3) consumption of products and services. These three levels are all interactive, so innovation is itself an extremely complex process which requires complex actions.

Two essential conditions contribute to the success of an innovation process:

1. The ability to produce new ideas, which is particularly dependent upon the culture created by the company and its openness *vis-à-vis* the external and cultural environment.

2. The ability to transform these ideas into effective projects, which requires a wide variety and flexibility in the methods of management.

The innovation process starts at the individual level and is stimulated and engendered by the culture of the organisation. This culture must also be open to the outside world, open to, and bringing together communication and exploration, a culture which invites the mind to innovation and encourages the emergence of ideas.

Openness is crucial to generating ideas, to facilitating communication and to allowing influences from the external world. The ability to produce new ideas, therefore, depends less on rules, regulations and procedures, and more on the ability to create an environment in which people are allowed to regulate themselves and in which ideas are left to emerge 'bottom up'.

Concept 5.2 Reconciling cultural dilemmas

The dilemmas outlined in Trompenaars' seven-dimensional model of culture in the previous concept, require some kind of resolution. Hampden-Turner has explored and conceived a methodology which aims to reconcile what appear to be opposing values within each of the dimensions.

In his article, 'The practice of reconciliation', Trompenaars (2000: 29–33) gives more consideration to the question of cultural dilemmas in the business context. He proposes a model that can be used to reconcile what appear to be values that conflict with each other:

A model of reconciliation

When businesses cross cultures there are many potential situations in which the reconciliation of differences may be both desirable and necessary. The success of the business being conducted may depend on it. Reconciliation is part of building transcultural competence. There are three essential components of transcultural competence: awareness, respect and reconciling cultural differences.

Especially important are the processes of reconciliation. Without the confidence that reconciliation is possible, awareness can bring pain and frustration can emerge from respect. However, awareness and respect are necessary foundations for reconciling cultural differences. If people lack sufficient awareness of the differences that may exist between cultures, they may easily damage a relationship without intending to do so.

Cultural awareness is understanding states of mind, your own and the person being encountered. You can never be fully informed, since the permutations of options are countless. The seven-dimensional model of culture provides frames of reference for analysing ways in which people attribute meaning to the world.

Respect is most effectively developed once people recognize that most cultural differences are in themselves, but they have not recognized most of them. One could say that Westerners think the Japanese are mystics, at times even unreliable. It is difficult to know what they feel or think, they always say 'yes', even in cases where they might feel or think negatively about it. Yet, consider the case where a child has given a nervous and halting performance in her first solo in a school concert. She must go on again after the interval. Might her father not say 'Wonderful, darling' to give her confidence, although he did not actually believe her performance was good?

To sum up, both awareness and respect are necessary steps toward developing transcultural competence. But even their combined powers may not always suffice. People often ask questions such as: 'Why should only we respect and adapt to the other culture? Why don't they respect and adapt to ours?' Another, perhaps more interesting problem is that of mutual empathy (Bennett, 1979). What happens when one person attempts to shift to another culture's perspective when at the same time the other person is trying to do the same thing?

Motorola Solutions Learning prepared carefully for a presentation in China. After considerable thought, it was entitled: 'Relationships do not retire.' The gist of the presentation was that Motorola had come to China to stay and help the economy to create wealth. Relationships with Chinese suppliers, sub-contractors and employees would constitute a permanent commitment to building Chinese economic infrastructure and earning hard currency through exports.

The Chinese audiences listened politely to the presentation, but were quiet when invited to ask questions. Finally, one manager put up his hand and said: 'Can you tell us about pay for performance?'

What was happening here is very common. Even as the Americans moved towards the Chinese perspective, the Chinese started to move towards theirs, and the two sides passed each other invisibly, like ships in the night. Remember that the Chinese who turn out for a presentation by a Western company, may already be pro-Western and see Western views as potentially liberating. This dynamic is especially strong when a country is small and poor. When a drug salesman from a US company meets with a health minister from Costa Rica, the former's salary may be ten times the latter's. The temptation to 'sell out' one's own culture is overwhelmingly strong and, of course, such encounters only harden prejudices. 'See, they all want to be like us.'

However, foreign cultures have integrity, which only some of its members will abandon. People who abandon their culture often become weakened and corrupt. Companies need foreigners to be themselves if partnership is to work. It is this very difference that makes the relationship valuable. This is why people need to reconcile differences, to be themselves, but at the same time see and understand how the other's perspectives can help their own.

Once one is aware of one's own mental models and cultural predispositions, and once one can respect and understand that those of another culture are legitimately different, then it becomes possible to reconcile differences. Why do this? Because business people aim to create wealth and value, not just for themselves, but also for those who live in different cultural worlds. People need to share the value of buying, selling, of joint venturing, of working in partnership.

How does reconciliation work?

In essence, the process of reconciliation leads to a dynamic equilibrium between seemingly opposed values, which make up a dilemma. In fact, reconciliation results in the integration of values through synergy. There are many ways of achieving synergy. The first one is *processing*, the activity in which a dilemma is made into two processes. So if the dilemma is central versus decentral it has to be turned into centralizing versus decentralizing. It is easier to reconcile verbs than nouns.

The second approach is called *contextualizing*. Here, one has to decide what is text and what is context. For example, compare the names of two luxury hotels located in Amsterdam:

Le Meridien Apollo Hotel	AMSTEL HOTEL InterContinental

Figure 5.1 **Text and context: two examples**

The Apollo Hotel is a member of the Le Meridien hotel group and uses the group's name as its main logo. The Amstel Hotel uses its name in capital letters, and shows its membership of the InterContinental hotels group after its name. Text and context change.

A third option is *sequencing*. You can first centralise and later decentralise. Every process of reconciliation is also a sequence. Finally, the process of *synergizing* is a way to reconcile. Synergizing is best explained by adding the word 'through' between the two opposite orientations. It is the answer to the question: 'How can we increase the quality of our central offerings through better learning from our decentralised operations?'

Reconciliation is preferred over other methods for dealing with cultural differences such as conflict, in which both parties may not benefit. Even compromise has its problems, because in a compromise both parties may still not get what they expected. Reconciliation permits both parties to maintain what is important to them, yet recognize the needs of the other.

Source: adapted from Trompenaars, 2000: 29–33.

Stages of the reconciliation process

Marion Estienne (1997) sees five stages to the reconciliation process as developed by Trompenaars. These are given in Table 5.4, as well as the methods she proposes for moving from one stage to the next. The first mandatory stage involves the relevant parties showing their commitment to developing their relationship. There then follows a rigorous search for clear differences and similarities among the parties during which dialogue plays a key role. Those involved discuss openly not only the conflict itself but also their relationship.

The skills mentioned in Table 5.4 will be elaborated upon in later chapters, particularly in Part Three, but these go hand-in-hand with knowledge of the cultures involved.

As Estienne (1997) indicates, going through these stages is itself a way of developing skills for global business. Those involved need to maintain a rapport despite all the cultural differences encountered. The focus needs to be not on getting things done, but rather on developing and maintaining a rapport, despite the tensions involved, which eventually enables effective action to be undertaken by the parties involved.

Table 5.4 **Framework for the reconciliation of cross-cultural conflict**

	Stages of the reconciliation process	Method employed to arrive at next stage
1	Reaffirm our commitment to the ongoing relationship and its benefit to both parties	Think 'win–win' and concentrate on the benefits of collaboration to each culture
2	Recognise where and how we differ	Develop a global mind-set Legitimise diversity Acquire knowledge of other cultures Display 'acceptance' when appropriate
3	Continue by searching for similarities	Employ dialogue
4	Synthesise our solutions or create outcomes which utilise the most appropriate elements of the opposing cultural dimensions	Practise creative thinking Demonstrate a willingness to learn Dialogue
5	Review the learning process, capture it, and make available for the future	Practise experience-based learning Articulate what has been seen and known Act on learning at a later stage

Source: Estienne, 1997: 17.

The reconciliation approach opens the door to a third dimension, unblocks in some way the duality of the dilemma. In an intercultural business context, recourse to reconciliation may well avoid a situation ending in an impasse. Getting to know the cultural framework of reference of one's interlocutors seems to be the best way of adapting to their culture(s) and their way of working. Chapter 6 offers an instrument to assist in this exploration.

Conclusion

This chapter has outlined the cultural dimensions devised by Trompenaars. These allow cultures to be classified according to certain values, as expressed in the way they confront dilemmas. These dimensions reflect the value-orientation concept proposed by Kluckholn and Strodtbeck since they take into account the relations with others, with nature and with the environment. These dimensions serve not only to distinguish national cultures, but also to show how the values they reflect can affect relations in business and management.

The cross-cultural manager has to face dilemmas. Dilemmas are universal, but the way they are resolved is determined culturally. Chapter 5 gives examples to demonstrate this point as well as the means to resolve them through the principle of reconciliation. The approach to dilemmas by means of reconciliation remains an interesting approach, especially since it takes into account the dynamics of cultures, i.e. the interaction between the interlocutors. Rather than the dimensions themselves, it is the model of reconciliation that distinguishes the work of Trompenaars and Hampden-Turner from that of Hofstede.

Points for reflection

1. Many researchers in the area of cross-cultural management refer to authors whose disciplines are in the field of social sciences. These researchers appear to rely more on cultural theory than theories of management.

   Why do you think this is the case?

2. In their response to Hofstede, Trompenaars and Hampden-Turner consider their dimensions to be essentially 'heuristic devices' or speculative formulations that serve as a guide for investigations into 'family resemblances' between cultures when faced with dilemmas. Their perception of dimensions contrasts with what they term the linear nature of Hofstede's dimensions.

   In what other ways do the two sets of dimensions differ? To what extent do they resemble each other?

3. For cultural dilemmas in business, Trompenaars proposes the reconciliation method as a way of dealing with opposing values. If the definition of 'dilemma' is taken as 'a situation that requires a choice between options that are or seem equally unfavourable or mutually exclusive' (www.thefreedictionary.com/dilemma), **to what extent do you believe the reconciliation method can be used to resolve all dilemmas?**

4. Referring to the relationship between the culture of an organisation and innovation, discuss Trompenaars' statement: 'a culture of innovation can be created to harness creativity'.

Further reading

Trompenaars, F. (2007) *Riding the Whirlwind*, **Oxford: Infinite Ideas Limited.** Inspired by the humour and John Cleese's vision of creativity, Trompenaars describes in his book how to connect people (individuals and teams) and organisations in a culture of innovation.

Trompenaars, F. and Hampden-Turner, C. (1997) *Riding the Waves of Culture*, **2nd edition, London: Nicholas Brealey.** Fons Trompenaars first published this book in 1993. Additions to the second edition are significantly influenced by Charles Hampden-Turner's way of thinking. The authors added three new chapters: one on methodology for reconciling cultural dilemmas and two in which they discuss diversity within, rather than between, countries.

Trompenaars, F. and Woolliams, P. (2003) *Business Across Cultures*, **Chichester, England: Capstone.** The aim of this book is to provide executives with a cross-cultural perspective on how companies meet the diverse needs of customers, investors and employees.

Website

Trompenaars Hampden-Turner, Culture for Business, www.thtconsulting.com, website of the firm run by Trompenaars and Hampden-Turner. The firm provides consulting, training, coaching and (un)learning services to help leaders and professionals manage and solve their business and culture dilemmas.

References

Adler, N.J. with Gundersen, A. (2008, 2002) *International Dimensions of Organizational Behavior*, 5th edition, Mason, OH: Thompson/South Western.

Bennett, M.-J. (1979) 'Overcoming the golden rule: sympathy and empathy', in Nimmo, D. (ed.), *Communication Yearbook 3*, Austin, TX: International Communication Association.

Browaeys, M.-J. and Trompenaars, F. (eds) (2000) *Case Studies on Cultural Dilemmas*, Breukelen, Netherlands: Nyenrode University Press.

Earley, P.C. and Ang, S. (2003) *Cultural Intelligence: Individual Interactions Across Cultures*, Stanford, CA: Stanford University Press.

Estienne, M. (1997) 'The art of cross-cultural management: an alternative approach to training and development', *Journal of European Industrial Training*, 20(1): 14–18.

Genelot, D. (2011) *Manager dans la complexité.* 4th edition. Paris: INSEP Editions.

Gullestrup (2006) *Cultural Analysis*, Aalborg, Denmark: Aalborg University Press.

Hampden-Turner, C. and Trompenaars, F. (1997) 'Response to Geert Hofstede', *International Journal of Intercultural Relations*, 21(1): 149–159.

Hofstede, G. (1996) 'Riding the waves of commerce: a test of Trompenaars', *International Journal of Intercultural Relations*, 20(2): 189–198.

Kluckhohn, F. and Strodtbeck, F.L. (1961) *Variations in Value Orientations*, CT: Greenwood.

Parsons, T. (1937) *The Structure of Social Action*, New York, NY: McGraw Hill.

Parsons, T. (1951) *The Social System*, New York, NY: Free Press. Quoted in Trompenaars, F. (1993) *Riding the Waves of Culture*, London: Economist Books, p. 8.

Tahssain-Gay, L. and Cherre, B. (2012) 'Le comportement éthique est-il mesurable? Réflexion autour des dilemmes', *Gestion 2000*, septembre–octobre.

Todes, J.L., MacKinney, J. and Ferguson Jr., W. (1977) *Management and Motivation*, New York: Harper and Row.

Trompenaars, F. (1993) *Riding the Waves of Culture*, London: Economist Books.

Trompenaars, F. (2000) 'The practice of reconciliation', in Browaeys, M.-J. and Trompenaars F. (eds), *Case Studies on Cultural Dilemmas*, Breukelen, Netherlands: Nyenrode University Press, pp. 29–33.

Trompenaars, F. (2007) *Riding the Whirlwind*, Oxford: The Infinite Ideas.

Trompenaars, F. and Hampden-Turner, C. (1997) *Riding the Waves of Culture*, 2nd edition, London: Nicholas Brealey.

Trompenaars, F. and Woolliams, P. (2000) 'Competency framework for the millennium manager', in Browaeys, M.-J. and Trompenaars, F. (eds), *Case Studies on Cultural Dilemmas*, Breukelen, Netherlands: Nyenrode University Press, pp. 21–28.

Chapter 5 Activities

ACTIVITY 5.1

Individual and group bonus plans: a case for reconciliation

The dilemma below explores the issue of reconciling a cultural dilemma in a business environment (adapted from Trompenaars, 2000: 31–32).

Jeff Mate was the human resources director of an Australian company in household appliances. In the last couple of years, Matehold had internationalised its operations. First, some activities had been transferred to the Mid-West of the USA and some research and development work was being done in the UK because of its excellent education system. Sales were promising, especially in the Pacific Rim markets. A subsidiary had been set up in Japan to develop operations there.

During an international human resources meeting, Jeff raised the question of the need for greater consistency among his colleagues. In the past, the Japanese had worked in Japan and the Americans had worked in the US. Now, however, multicultural teams were slowly being formed, with US, British, Japanese and Australian employees working together. The US HR manager and Jeff proposed an individual incentive system worldwide that would increase the staff's productivity. Mr Kataki from Japan saw big difficulties in implementing the individualised bonus system in the light of the predominantly team-oriented value system of the Japanese. This led to a heated discussion involving all the HR directors present.

In the evening, Jeff was asked to make a decision that would be respected by all.

Question

What would you do if you were in Jeff's position? Choose one of the options given below. Check your answer with your instructor.

1. I would implement the individual incentive programme. After all, everyone responds to individualised monetary rewards. The programme would be based on the success of the Australian employees who produced more effort since they had been recognised for their individual work. And it would improve consistency between the international operations.

2. a) I would recognise that the individual incentive programme alone would not be effective, given the communitarian orientation of some Asian staff.

   b) I would allow the company employees in Asia to choose a group-oriented incentive system in Asia and those working in the more individualistic parts of the world to choose a system based on individual incentives.

3. I would discuss the idea further with the HR staff, asking them to tell me what aspects of the incentive programme they thought would be worthwhile. I would then implement a worldwide programme in which one of the major individual incentives is based on how people support the group.

4. I would introduce a consistent plan worldwide that rewards the group, but which makes the team responsible for looking after individuals either who do not optimally support the group's production goals or who support individual inventiveness.

ACTIVITY 5.2

Read the following case and answer the questions that follow.

Expatriate's first job in Switzerland

Marcus, an American whose parents had been born in India, arrived in Zurich with his Swiss wife. They were both excited about starting a new chapter in their life together. After spending four years in San Diego, they were keen for a change, although Marcus had mixed feelings about job prospects for himself in Switzerland. Four months into their new environment they were elated when Marcus found a challenging new position at Kraft Jacobs Suchard, managing its international assignments programme.

Though this was now a US company (Jacobs Suchard having been acquired three years before) and quite a few expatriates of varying backgrounds worked in the Zurich regional head office where Marcus was posted, there were nevertheless some strong Swiss work attitudes that pervaded the work environment, much to the confusion and chagrin of Marcus.

One area of confusion and some conflict had to do with teamwork and the boundaries of job descriptions. A newcomer to a function or a department, as Marcus was, will have a rather steep learning curve for the first few months on the job. From this perspective, Marcus presumed that his new Swiss colleague Heidi would help with the vast amount of learning that he faced, particularly as there was no formal training for this posting. This was a natural assumption given that this is what he had experienced in various jobs in the US.

However, this was not to be the case in Zurich. Although Heidi did lend some assistance to Marcus (by telling him, for instance, when she normally had lunch), she made it plain that she considered giving any sort of training to Marcus to be beyond her job description. And she stuck to this position adamantly. This left Marcus in a quandary. How could he gain the knowledge he needed to be effective in this new job?

Another point of contention was overtime. Since the Zurich regional head office was in frequent contact with the head office in New York, Zurich staff had to stay later because of the time difference (Zurich is seven hours ahead of New York). During Marcus' interviews for the position, it was made clear that overtime would be required because of this time difference. Marcus did not feel this was unusual for someone in a salaried position, particularly since he had had similar experience dealing with different time zones when working in the US. Heidi, however, did not feel the same way. Her work responsibilities, she felt, ended at 5 p.m., prompt. Naturally, this left Marcus having to deal most evenings with the less uptight (relatively speaking, of course) New Yorkers.

But was this fair? And how could Marcus achieve a more equitable work balance while at the same time build a working relationship with Heidi, whose knowledge he needed to become proficient in his job?

Source: Browaeys and Trompenaars, 2000: case 9.

Questions

1. After reading the case, refer to Concept 5.1 and try to identify in which of the seven dimensions you can categorise the dilemma in question. Justify your choice.

2. Using the Trompenaars' model of reconciliation, how can Marcus and Heidi resolve the dilemma in order to enable them to work together efficiently and effectively?

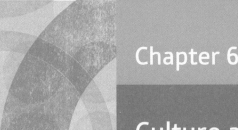

Chapter 6

Culture and styles of management

This chapter examines cultural values from different angles. They are first characterised in bipolar terms and their influence on everyday business activities discussed. The conceptualisation of such cultural values is then considered, particularly the notion that they, just as cultures in general, are inherently dynamic and subject to influence through mutual interaction.

In Concept 6.1, cultural values that have been extracted from the dimensions examined in earlier chapters are presented as a model of culture. The influence which these values may have on managerial activities is then examined. The reader will later be asked to apply this model in an activity which involves devising cultural profiles as well as outlining strategies for effective management in a particular country.

In Concept 6.2, the stability of cultural values, as well as their very existence, are given consideration. The notions – relevant to cross-cultural managers – of integrating values and sharing patterns of meaning and interpretation are examined in brief, as is the rejection of culture as a set of values.

Learning outcomes

After reading this chapter you should:

- Gain a clearer appreciation of the effect cultural values have on the way managers work.
- Understand how a number of management practices are shaped according to the cultural preferences of the managers concerned.
- Be aware of different ideas regarding the notion of cultural values.

Preface: the conceptualisation of culture – a static or dynamic approach

The cross-cultural theories such as those devised by Hofstede and Trompenaars, and which were examined in earlier chapters, use criteria for their classification of cultures which can be considered as essentially **static** and assumed to be absolute or universal. Such theories are often criticised for encouraging a very general comparison of (the beliefs, values of) cultures, using predetermined characteristics. More consideration is being given instead to the possibility that culture itself is a dynamic phenomenon. Those who embrace its dynamic nature see culture as ever changing and multilayered, subject to both internal and external forces. An increasing number of scholars argue that the interaction between diverse cultural groupings, particularly in the context of increasing globalisation of much human activity, has the potential to affect respective norms and values. As a result, intercultural theory has emerged which is focused on what happens at individual, group and international level when there is interaction between cultures.

Søderberg and Holden (2002), for example, refer to a recent dynamic approach to the way culture is conceptualised in terms of relations between people rather than in terms of stable sets of values. The cultural identity of people is determined by the context:

> This relational approach to culture and to cultural complexity and the idea of cultural complexity suggest that every individual embodies a unique combination of personal, cultural and social experiences, and thus that ultimately any communication and negotiation is intercultural.
>
> Søderberg and Holden, 2002: 112

The consequence of this standpoint is that making a standard cultural profile is impossible because it ultimately reflects only constructs based on 'the practitioners' and the researchers' own cultural thought patterns, and the concepts and categories to which they are socialised.

Gullestrup (2003a) argues that culture is such a complex phenomenon that no single specific paradigm can be used to study it. He proposes instead the creation of theoretical and analytical models to act as frame models which enable different paradigms to:

a) perceive and understand what the important elements of culture are, as well as the inter-relation between them. The factors involved are the culture in focus, the aim of the study and the research method used.

b) perceive and understand the complexity of cultural studies as well as the complexity of cross-cultural studies. The factors involved here are the relativity of each culture, the coincidence of cultures, a culture's changeability and ethical problems related to cross-cultural studies.

> Gullestrup, 2003a: 3

The model he proposes includes both static and dynamic elements. It consists of a horizontal cultural dimension, a vertical dimension and a dynamic cultural dimension. At the core of the **horizontal dimension** are eight cultural segments which are vital when it comes to understanding a culture:

A. The way in which nature is processed – technology

B. The way in which the output is distributed – economic institutions

C. The way in which individuals live together – social institutions

D. The way in which someone controls others – political institutions

E. The way in which knowledge, ideas and values are disseminated among individuals and groups – language and communication

F. The way in which individuals and the unity are integrated, maintained, and developed – reproduction and socialization

G. The way in which a common identity is created and preserved – ideology

H. The way the view of the relationship between life and death is manifested – religious institutions.

> Gullestrup, 2003b: 38

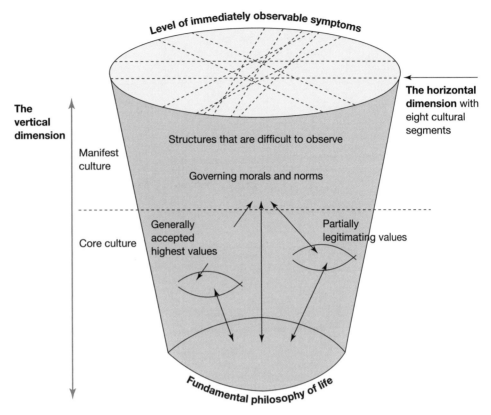

Figure 6.1 The semi-static cultural model
Source: Gullestrup, 2003b: 41, adapted.

The **vertical dimension** focuses on the value system of a culture which defines its inner direction. At the base is the *core culture* containing the fundamental philosophy of life and the norms and values passed on from previous to future generations. Above these are the manifestations of the core culture. If carefully researched, the more visible (manifest) levels can offer what Gullestrup considers to be a sort of gateway to understanding what lies at the core of any culture, including our own. Figure 6.1 presents the model where the more accessible horizontal segments of culture (described above) are combined with the vertical culture dimension.

Gullestrup goes further, however. His model includes a third dimension, **the dynamic cultural dimension**. This accounts for the notion that the foundations of a culture can be influenced by mutual interaction both internally and externally. Those internal and external factors which subject it to change are outlined in the model below.

What Gullestrup calls **change-initiating factors** are those factors which may put pressure on the culture to change, but may not succeed in doing so. These can be *internal* pressures which have come about through developments in research, technology, trade and industry or even through changes in the political/social arena. They may also be *external* factors involving changes in nature influenced by humans or otherwise. Furthermore the internal changes in other cultures may also have the potential to bring about change in another culture.

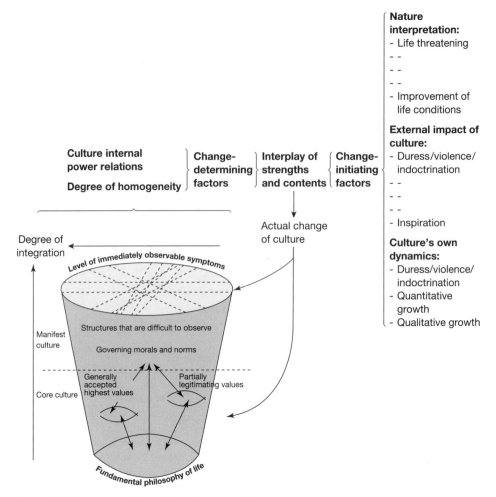

Figure 6.2 **The general dynamics culture model**
Source: Gullestrup, 2006: 153, adapted.

As to whether actual change is realised depends on **change-determining factors**. These are:

a) the degree of integration within a culture: the extent to which there is conformity of values within a given culture;

b) the degree of homogeneity within a culture: the width and depth of the total knowledge and insight shared; and

c) the power structure present within the culture.

This model is an attempt to combine the perspective of the participant of a culture with that of the observer of that culture. The core culture featured in it can only be considered as a reality for those belonging to the culture and as such not easily accessible to outsiders, i.e. observers. Combining the outsider and insider view enables a participant in a particular culture to gain insight into the culture at a particular point in time, as well as into its relations to other cultures.

Concept 6.1 Management tasks and cultural values

There are many activities performed by managers and professionals across all societies on which cultural values have a considerable effect. The activities chosen below will be discussed in the light of cultural values.

Management tasks

The following management tasks and Tables 6.1 to 6.8 are based on material in the participant workbook of *Doing Business Internationally* (1992).

1. **Planning**. This has to do with how the goals and objectives of a company or department are established, as well as determining what actions on an individual level are needed to achieve them.

2. **Organising**. This is a big responsibility of managers. They need to decide how the work involved is to be divided up and how it is to be co-ordinated or executed in order to achieve the organisational objectives. The use of the resources involved also requires careful organisation to ensure effectiveness and efficiency.

3. **Staffing**. The task of hiring employees and allocating them particular positions within a company is a demanding one, whether it is the concern of HRM, the line manager or team manager. Consideration needs to be given to enabling people to fulfil their potential within the company.

4. **Directing**. This has to do with leading the organisation and its employees towards its goals. How do managers relate to the employees, how they do they communicate with them, how do they supervise them?

5. **Controlling**. Monitoring the performance of a company or department is a task for which different cultures may use different systems and approaches. This goes also for the ways used to prevent problems or to resolve them. The differences reflect the relations between the levels of organisational hierarchy as well as the way performance is perceived.

The way the above tasks and responsibilities are performed will be examined in the light of cultural values.

The effect of cultural values on management

A number of cultural values have emerged in previous chapters when cultural dimensions were being presented and discussed. Since the terminology used often varied, we have used the value concepts presented so far to compile our own list of cultural value orientations which we judge as having a considerable influence on the way managers perform their activities. This list has been supplemented by other value orientations based on the works of other scholars, Hall in particular, whose ideas on time, space and communication have proved to be especially relevant to management activities.

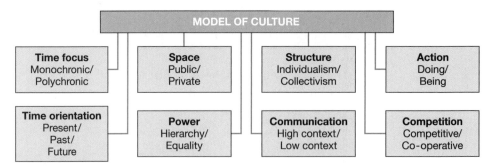

Figure 6.3 **A model of culture**

Source: adapted from *Doing Business Internationally*, Participant Workbook: 2.3.

Figure 6.3 presents the value orientations and characterises the related values in bipolar terms to clarify the differences. It is intended to be used as a framework of reference when readers are attempting to understand some of the differences they may encounter when doing business internationally and when managing across cultures. This framework will also be used in Activity 6.2, an activity aimed at developing cross-cultural effectiveness in an international context.

The eight cultural value orientations featured in the model will now be examined in turn.

1. Time focus (monochronic and polychronic)

Time is related to the rhythm of nature. Different cultures have different perceptions of time according to their environment, history, traditions and general practices. Time, therefore, is one of the fundamentals on which all cultures rest and around which all activities revolve.

Hall and Hall (1990) analyse differences in time systems among cultures. These authors distinguish two prominent time systems of particular relevance to management: monochronic and polychronic. In cultures where a monochronic perception of time prevails, time is experienced and used in a linear way. People tend to do one activity at a time and dislike having to move away from a schedule. They are more focused on information than people, and their relations with others may suffer because they do not fit into the schedule of things to be done. In cultures where polychronic time is preferred, people tend to focus on several tasks and are less dependent on detailed information when performing these tasks. Schedules, if kept, are much more approximate and may be changed at any time. What is more important is involvement with other people – they take priority over schedules. That explains why polychronic cultures may well have problems respecting timings within the international working environment.

The differences in time focus as characterised in Table 6.1 can be seen in the role given to formal meetings. These may be used more to determine action points and deadlines or more as an opportunity to reflect on the company generally and to sound each other out on the way things are going or should be going. Actual decisions may come later through further (informal) consultation.

SPOTLIGHT 6.1

Keeping time and using time

International students in a European business school were asked to keep a diary in which to give an account of their experiences when working in small multicultural groups.

An Indian student spoke euphorically about the joys of getting to know other nationalities. However, there was one issue which she and her colleagues from the Indian subcontinent and South America found a real challenge: punctuality. Arriving in time for the start of group meetings was still a problem for her, even after several months into the programme. Those who regularly arrived promptly showed a certain understanding during the first few meetings as she and her fellow latecomers walked apologetically into the room, but their goodwill soon turned into frustration. Angry words were spoken and the latecomers promised to be more 'business-like' and to do everything to arrive on time. Their punctuality had improved, Ali admitted: they often arrived late, but no later than five minutes after the official start of the meeting. This margin of time now seemed to have been accepted by those who always arrived on time.

Another student from Finland, Mikael, gave an account of the positive experiences when working with other cultures, but expressed his frustration when some of his colleagues, he felt, did not always stay focused on the small-group tasks they had to complete by a certain deadline. During their work he regularly saw a Lebanese and a Brazilian student in the group reading and responding to e-mails and tweets which clearly had nothing to do with the task at hand. Discussions were often interrupted by phone signals and even by phone calls to the two students concerned.

Mikael expressed his concern frequently during the first group-work sessions and the phone calls eventually ceased. However, as he noted in his diary, the two students still continued to busy themselves now and again with other matters on their laptops during their intensive group work. They were sometimes even seen writing other reports for other assignments. He gradually realised, however, that they were still tuned into the discussions and made valuable contributions to the task set.

Table 6.1 **Characteristics of two attitudes to time**

	Monochronic cultures	Polychronic cultures
1. Planning	The focus of activity is more on the task itself and making schedules	The focus of activity is more on relationships when planning
2. Organising	The approach used is structured, linear and task-focused	The approach is a less structured one, more holistic in nature and people-focused
3. Staffing	Concerns are focused on the shorter term, meeting immediate needs and requirements	The focus is on the longer term, with concern for building relationships over time
4. Directing	The emphasis is on making and following plans, managing the inflow and distribution of detailed information	The emphasis is on being flexible, reacting according to (changed) circumstances, giving priority to people over plans, relying more on the sharing of implicit knowledge and information
5. Controlling	Tendency to use control systems that depend on detailed information and involve strict deadlines	Tendency to use more flexible control systems involving people as well as information

Cultures can also be categorised according to another aspect of time, namely a culture's orientation towards the past, present and future.

2. Time orientation (past, present and future)

Cultures focused on the past value the upholding of tradition. Changes and plans are made according to whether or not they are in line with the history of the company and the way it usually does things. Those cultures concerned with the present are out for quick results and short-term gain. Those with a view towards the future are more likely to give up short-term gains when there is the prospect of more substantial long-term benefits. Any changes or plans are therefore assessed in the light of expected future benefit.

Hall and Hall (1990) emphasise the importance of knowing which parts of the time frame are given prominence in which areas of the world. They see that countries in the Far East, as well as India and Iran, have cultures oriented towards the past. On the American continent, however, they consider the culture of the urban US to be more oriented towards the present and short-term future, while the cultures of Latin America, are both past and present-oriented.

SPOTLIGHT 6.2

How to plan your time

Without planning, you'll never have the time for anything. Yes, initially, you may have to spend even more time to make time – but that is a sensible, positive investment. You have to take control of the time at your disposal and decide how you want to spend it. Time is a resource to be husbanded in the same way as you would treat raw materials or finished goods or stock in the business. Time also costs money. So if you have only a finite amount of time, and that time is expensive, it is crucial to plan out how it's going to be spent to most effect. This means clarifying the main purpose of your job.

Ask yourself: what am I here for? Those whose answers identify or match the purpose of the organization for which they work can award themselves several gold stars. Yes. Your purpose is to assist the organization in achieving its objectives, regardless of whether your job function is that of data processing manager, senior welfare officer, sales director or typing pool supervisor. Being organized will help you to achieve those objectives. Having a plan is the first step on the way to that achievement.

Source: Video Arts (1984) *So You Think You Can Manage?* London: Methuen: 20.

These differences in values (Table 6.2) can be perceived in many activities, particularly when it comes to negotiations. Those who are 'past-oriented' may be more intent on compensating for previous losses or regaining past successes rather than aiming for a resolution that all those involved find acceptable. Plans for the future will tend to be based on past experiences rather than expectations whereby employees are entrusted with responsibility for what happens in the future.

Table 6.2 **Time orientation and management skills**

	Past orientation	Future orientation
1. Planning	The emphasis is on continuing traditions and building in long-term time frames if the plan is for a change process	The emphasis is on longer-term plans and long-term results
2. Organising	Organisational decisions are made within the context of the customs of the society. Past goals and precedents guide the process of organising	Work and resources are divided and co-ordinated to meet longer-range goals and projections for the future
3. Staffing	Management are slower in adapting the criteria by which they select and train employees	Management select and train employees to meet long-term business goals
4. Directing	Tendency to develop vision and mission statements that emphasise the continuation of the company's values and reputation	Tendency to develop vision and statements which focus on achieving long-term benefits
5. Controlling	Tendency to develop performance objectives in keeping with customary goals	Tendency to develop performance objectives in the context of long-term goals

3. Power (hierarchy and equality)

The power value orientation is to do with the extent to which the less powerful members of a society expect and accept that power is distributed unequally. As Mead indicates (1994: 66) it is in this area that a culture shows the extent to which it 'tolerates and fosters pecking orders, and how actively members try to reduce them'.

In some cultures, inequality is a given and no attempt is made to make any compensations on a socio-economic level for intellectual or physical inequalities. In other cultures, inequality is regarded as undesirable, necessitating some form of correction through legal, political and economic means.

At work, the level of power and authority are strictly marked out by cultures oriented to hierarchy. There, the employees do their work according to the directives of their boss. In their eyes, the role of the manager is to allocate tasks and to take decisions. During negotiations, title, status and formal position have less influence in cultures oriented towards equality. There, the hierarchy exists essentially to facilitate the relations between the people in an organisation. Managers see their role as more participative than directive. They are more likely to consult employees before taking decisions (Table 6.3).

In companies oriented towards equality there will be more informal structures based on expertise or focused on certain projects. However, hierarchy may still be there below the surface. When risks have to be taken or when there is a budgetary crisis, those with formal authority may well re-assert their power. An organisation with a formal hierarchy that adopts certain features of equality in the way it is run will always feel the tension between control and empowerment.

Table 6.3 **Effects of hierarchy**

	Hierarchy	Equality
1. Planning	More autocratic or paternalistic planning is displayed, in which managers make decisions without consulting employees	Employees may implement the plan in the way they believe is the most appropriate. More participative planning is displayed
2. Organising	The organisational structure is tightly controlled. Authority and responsibility are centralised	The organisational structure encourages individual autonomy. Authority is decentralised to the lowest possible level
3. Staffing	Subordinates expect bosses to take the initiative to train, develop and promote them	Work relationships should not be strictly prescribed in terms of appropriate/inappropriate behaviours and roles
4. Directing	Leaders are expected to behave in ways that reinforce their importance. Employees like being closely supervised and feel comfortable with a directive supervisor	Managers exhibit participative or consultative styles. In boss–subordinate communications, employees are not afraid to disagree with their managers
5. Controlling	Employees prefer the personal control of superiors over impersonal control systems	Subordinates tend to like working with their bosses to develop, implement, monitor and alter performance objectives

SPOTLIGHT 6.3

Culture and airline safety

The controversial Canadian journalist, Malcolm Gladwell, dedicates a chapter of his recent book *Outliers* (2008) to an examination of the role of culture in air crashes. He focuses in particular on one crash involving Colombian pilots and another involving pilots from South Korea. He maintains that, apart from the weather conditions and fatigue, the pilots in question were struggling with a cultural legacy: the hierarchical relationship between the crew members. In both cases, the subordinates had to be deferential towards the captain and felt unable to warn him that the plane was about to crash. Planes such as those built by Boeing and Airbus, Gladwell argues, must be flown by two equals because of their complex nature.

4. Competition (competitive and co-operative)

Management may well encourage competition in an organisation, particularly where the environment is that of a 'free market'. It encourages employees to take responsibility for the organisation's survival and can be crucial in stimulating innovation and developing markets. When competitiveness is valued, the culture is focused on acquiring wealth, performing well and achieving ambitions. The success of a project is determined only by the profit it makes. In other cultures, however, job satisfaction has less to do with making money and more to do with working in a pleasant environment. Here, competition is not so highly valued and not considered to be the main purpose of business. Instead, co-operation is preferred, with the stress on the quality of life, relationships and consensus (Table 6.4).

Table 6.4 **Co-operation and competition**

	Competitive	Co-operative
1. Planning	The emphasis is on speed and task performance when implementing plans	Emphasis is on maintaining relationships in plan implementation
2. Organising	Individual achievement is allowed and encouraged in organising the work. Managers have more of a leadership role	Group integration is permitted, together with maintenance of a positive working environment and convenient schedules. Managers have more of a facilitating role
3. Staffing	Employees are selected on their ability to act independently	Employees are selected for their ability to work well in groups
4. Directing	The leader's role is to track and reward achievement. The stress involved in the work is generally higher	The leader's role is to facilitate mutually beneficial relationships
5. Controlling	Systems that are predominantly performance-based are preferred	Task performance is recognised as a standard for success; however, other standards are also considered important, including team effectiveness

SPOTLIGHT 6.4

Co-operating competitively

Despite the fierce competition between car-makers in the global market, there are many examples of rival companies working together to promote their individual interests. This is particularly the case where new technologies which are being developed require considerable financial investment.

The Daily Telegraph reports on a recent extension of an already existing joint venture between French and Japanese car companies.

Renault-Nissan and Mitsubishi agree co-operation deal
The Renault-Nissan Alliance and Mitsubishi Motors Corporation have announced that the current co-operation between Nissan and Mitsubishi could be expanded to include Renault.

It is expected that the existing Nissan/Mitsubishi NMKV joint-venture company will be extended to develop a new small car including an electric version that can be sold worldwide. The basis for this will be from a jointly-developed 'kei car' platform of the type of diminutive vehicle popular in the Japanese market.

Renault-Nissan and Mitsubishi also confirmed their intention to share technologies and product assets related to electric vehicles and latest-generation platforms.

It is expected that two new saloons based on Renault vehicles would be launched as Mitsubishis. The first, to compete in the full-size D-segment markets of the United States and Canada, would be manufactured at the Renault-Samsung plant in Busan, South Korea.

The second saloon is intended to compete in the global C-segment, although that market in Europe at least is dominated by hatchbacks such as the top-selling Volkswagen Golf and Ford Focus. The manufacturing location for this model remains under discussion.

Carlos Ghosn, the president and CEO of the Renault-Nissan Alliance, said: 'Nissan and Mitsubishi Motors have jointly benefited from several collaborations in the past, most recently the successful joint-venture on *kei* cars in Japan. I welcome the direction being taken towards this broader co-operation, creating new opportunities for Renault in addition to further leveraging the productive relationship between Nissan and Mitsubishi Motors.'

Osamu Masuko, the president of Mitsubishi Motors Corporation, said: 'As a result of the development of collaborative projects with Nissan Motor up to now, Mitsubishi Motors is pleased to work again with Nissan and now Renault towards achieving further collaborations. The new opportunities could be described as evidence that the ongoing collaborative projects between Mitsubishi Motors and Nissan have brought positive results.'

The existing Nissan/Mitsubishi NMKV company was established in June 2011 to co-develop a range of *kei* cars for both brands. The first of these, the Nissan Dayz and Mitsubishi eK wagon, went on sale in Japan this year. Both are built by Mitsubishi in Japan.

Renault and Nissan have been strategic partners since 1999.

Source: Renault-Nissan and Mitsubishi agree co-operation deal, *Daily Telegraph*, 5/11/2013 (Hudson, P.), http://www.telegraph.co.uk/motoring/news/10427480/Renault-Nissan-and-Mitsubishi-agree-co-operation-deal.html.

A company operating in a competitive, dynamic market, but which is keen to maintain or develop co-operation among its staff, will experience a tension between opposing values similar to that felt during other management activities mentioned earlier. Nevertheless, the company will wish to promote innovation (Chapter 5) among its employees through competition while, at the same time, encouraging co-operation between its employees to ensure effective running of the organisation.

5. Action (activity: doing and being)

Kluckholn and Strodtbeck (1961) place 'activity' in their value orientation system because they consider this to be one of the universal human problems. They see every method of human expression as resulting in some form of activity (not in the active or passive sense) which, in turn, shows a preference towards a 'being' or 'doing' orientation (Table 6.5).

If the orientation is towards being, then this is 'a spontaneous expression of what is conceived to be "given" in the human personality'. The 'doing' orientation, on the other hand, prefers 'a kind of activity which results in accomplishments that are measurable by standards conceived to be external to the acting individual' (Kluckholn and Strodtbeck, 1961: 17).

The stress in 'doing' cultures is placed on challenge and achieving personal goals. Prime motivators are recognition of achievement and promotion. In 'being' cultures, the stress is placed on working for the moment and living the experience rather than achievement itself. The prime motivator is the promise of future rewards while maintaining social harmony.

Table 6.5 **Two approaches to 'action'**

	Doing cultures	Being cultures
1. Planning	Tends to be done by developing measurable, time-framed action steps	Tends to be done with a strong focus on the vision or ideal a company wishes to attain
2. Organising	Involves developing action-oriented documentation for project management in which task responsibilities are clearly spelled out	Based more on the assumption that implementation is not so much dependent on action steps as on common vision and personal trust
3. Staffing	Account is not necessarily taken of a person's worth beyond his or her ability to carry out organisational tasks	Career development is usually based not only on performance but also on other standards, such as personal or social criteria
4. Directing	Managers are considered to be effective if they have the necessary expertise and competence	Managers are considered to be effective if their personal philosophy, values and style are seen as compatible
5. Controlling	The focus is not only on the tasks to be done, but also on the ways in which they are done. Management of performance is carried out systematically	The focus is less on efficiency and more on effectiveness and adaptability. Management of performance measurement tends to be less systematic

The meeting

The contrast between these two types of culture can come clearly to the fore when decisions are being taken during meetings. In a 'being' culture, the status of the 'boss' is unquestioned: it is he who makes the decision. In a 'doing' culture, everybody attending the meeting has a role to play, and these roles can change according to the type of decision, the expertise and experience available. The 'boss' may take the final decision on the basis of the information and analysis emerging during the meeting, or may even delegate the decision to those he considers more competent.

6. Space (private and public)

One aspect of space orientation relates to what is to be regarded as private and public space (Table 6.6). In some cultures, a house, car or refrigerator is not open to public view, in others some or all of these are. Another aspect relates to the invisible boundary around every person, a 'comfort zone'. If this zone is encroached upon, people feel uneasy or even under threat. In some cultures, this zone is much narrower than in others. The proximity of people in conversation, for example, may be much closer in one culture than in another.

This concept of space can be seen in terms of personality, as Hoecklin (1995: 44) notes when reviewing Trompenaars' dimension of 'specific versus diffuse relationships':

> Every individual has various levels to their personality, from a more public level to the inner, more private level. However, there can be cultural differences in the relative size of people's public and private 'spaces' and also in the degree to which they feel comfortable sharing those parts of their personality with other people.

Table 6.6 **The influence of personal space at work**

	Private	Public
1. Planning	Tendency to use more individualistic or systematic forms of planning	Public space cultures tend to use more group-oriented or authoritative forms of planning
2. Organising	The approaches used tend to centre on tasks	The approaches used tend to be more centred on relationships
3. Staffing	The information about how staff are to be employed is more explicit	The information about how staff are to be employed is more implicit
4. Directing	Managers and employees do not share the same office	The location or size of the place where an employee works does not necessarily reflect that person's rank in the company
5. Controlling	Since managers are separated spatially from their employees, they need to use more explicit measures of performance	Managers can use more informal checks on performance

SPOTLIGHT 6.6

Private business

A European manager may find himself getting invited by his Chinese business partner to the latter's home, his private space. By doing so, the Chinese is hoping to get to know his partner well with a view to establishing a close relationship. This can prove to be an important basis for (more) business deals.

In cultures that are more specific in nature, there are large public spaces or spheres where personal matters are openly discussed, where family worries and individual failings are revealed for all to comment on. Private spheres, however, are very small and not easily penetrated.

In more diffuse cultures, public spaces are smaller and more formal, access to which is not easy for strangers. However, once a member of a diffuse culture accepts someone, then that person will be given access to a larger private sphere.

7. Communication (high-context and low-context)

When investigating communication between different cultures, Hall (1976) introduced the concept of context and described the role it plays in the communication process (Table 6.7). Context relates to the framework, background and surrounding circumstances in which communication or an event takes place. He distinguishes between high-context and low-context messages:

Table 6.7 **Communication and context**

	Low context	High context
1. Planning	Low-context cultures develop plans that are explicit, detailed, quantifiable and information-based	High-context cultures develop plans that are more implicit and less detailed in terms of instructions
2. Organising	Task-responsibility guidelines are explicit: they are detailed and understood through verbal or written instruction	Assigning tasks and responsibilities are implicit and understood according to the context
3. Staffing	Detailed contracts of employment and explicit performance appraisals	The criteria and methods for recruitment, selection, pay and firing are not explicit, nor is the appraisal process
4. Directing	Managers get work done through others by outlining specific goals and ways to achieve them. Instructions are explicit and conflict is depersonalised	In high-context cultures, managers get work done through others by giving attention to relationships and group processes. Conflicts must be resolved before work can progress
5. Controlling	Control is more task-driven in accordance with monitoring and control procedures used to ensure performance objectives	Control is more process-driven. Information regarding the various aspects of control is embedded in the cultural context

> A high context (HC) communication or message is one in which most of the information is already in the person, while very little is in the coded, explicit, transmitted part of the message. A low context communication (LC) is just the opposite, i.e., the mass of the information is vested in the explicit code.

> Hall and Hall, 1990: 6

When applying this concept to cultures, he sees the US as a low-context country, because the messages conveyed generally, and in business in particular, are usually clear and explicit. Japan, however, is a high context country, where the most important part of any information is 'hidden' in the text; the situation in which the communication takes place carries most of the information.

SPOTLIGHT 6.7

The office

To illustrate the contrast between the two ends of this context spectrum, Hall and Hall (1990) describe a typical routine in a US office and compare it with one in a French and Japanese office. When an American company director is in his office, he has to work through a stream of pre-arranged appointments, with visitors usually entering the office one at a time. The information needed to do the job comes from a small group of people seen through the day as well as from memos and reports he reads. The flow of information is controlled by supervisors and assistants. According to Hall and Hall (1990), the equivalent office day in a high-context country such as France or Japan is very different. People are constantly entering and leaving the office, both requesting and passing information on. The organisation itself is dependent on the collection and distribution of information so that everyone in the business knows about every aspect and who is the best informed about which subjects.

Although Hall does not rank countries in terms of their degree of LC or HC, Figure 6.4 reflects the qualitative insights of Hall himself as well as of other scholars in cross-cultural

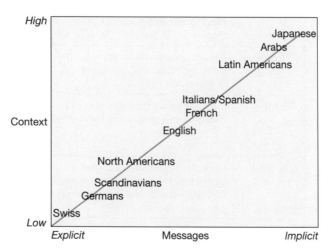

Figure 6.4 **Messages and context (adapted from Hall)**
Source: Usunier, 1993: 103.

communication as to where certain countries lie on the context dimension. At one end of the dimension are a number of countries in Asia, at the other a number of Northern European countries, as well as the US.

Part Three of this book will deal with this high/low context orientation in more detail.

8. Structure (individualism and collectivism)

The term 'structure' refers to a social structure or, in business terms, a company structure, which allows management to distinguish uncertain situations, ambiguity, stress and risk (Table 6.8). This particular value orientation concerns the relation between the individual and the group as described by Hofstede (Chapter 2) and Trompenaars (Chapter 5).

According to Kluckholn and Strodtbeck (1961), individualism shows the extent to which cultures elevate the role of the individual over the role of the group. When individualism is valued, the 'I' predominates over the 'We'. Individual goals, initiative and achievement are most important and people are encouraged to be independent and self-reliant. There is less need to conform to a group and less distinction made between in-groups and out-groups. Individuals frequently acquire and change their friends and do not hesitate to establish preferred relationships among family relatives.

Collectivism shows the extent to which the interests of the group prevail over individual interests. Each person in a collectivist society is encouraged to conform, to do what is best for the group and to avoid expressing opinions or beliefs that go against it. Reluctance to work together with the group or eagerness to stand out is frowned upon. Clearer distinctions are made between in-groups and out-groups. Relationships are more constant both within and outside the family.

Table 6.8 **Structure and business activities**

	Individualism	Collectivism
1. Planning	It is expected that those involved in planning will take the initiative to present their views	Plans are developed within the shared values used for measuring and justifying activities in the organisation
2. Organising	Organisational structures emphasise the individual in tasks assignments and resources allocation	Organisational structures emphasise the group; the team is assigned tasks and resources
3. Staffing	Organisations are not expected to look after their employees' career development	Promotion is based primarily on seniority. Managers are evaluated according to how well they conform to organisational or group norms
4. Directing	Leaders expect employees to meet or exceed their responsibilities and defend their own interests. Management entails managing individuals	Leaders expect loyalty in exchange for protection. Group or top-down decisions are the norm, with the leader in quiet control
5. Controlling	Control tends to be exerted by individual standards of excellence. Fear of losing self-respect discourages deviance from standards	Deviation from standards and expectations is discouraged through group-oriented pressure

SPOTLIGHT 6.8

An in-tray task

Christopher Earley, a US management researcher, gave 48 management trainees from southern China and a matched group of 48 management trainees from the US an 'in-tray task' consisting of 40 items requiring between two and five minutes each (Earley, 1989). The task involved such activities as writing memos evaluating plans and rating job candidates' application forms. Half of the participants from each country were given an individual goal of 20 items; the other half were given a group goal of 200 items to be completed in one hour by 10 people. In addition, half of the participants from either country, both from the group and from the individual goal subsets, were asked to mark each item with their name; the other half turned them in anonymously. The Chinese, collectivist, participants performed best when operating with a group goal and anonymously. They performed worst when operating individually and with their name marked on their work. The individualist US participants performed best when operating individually and with their work attributed to them personally, and performed very poorly when operating as a group and anonymously.

Source: Hoecklin, 1995: 37.

This concept has led to a number of cultural value orientations and presented extreme differences between the values within each orientation. Sometimes, of course, the differences between (some) cultural values may not be as extreme as the differences presented here, so that some sort of accommodation can be made between the representatives of the cultures in question. On the other hand, the contrasts may be such that working together is extremely difficult.

Concept 6.2   Other views on cultural values

The previous concept outlined the cultural values and the way they are reflected in management. Values are what people essentially share in a particular culture, what helps them co-exist. Hofstede (1991) emphasises their durability, as does Trompenaars. The latter's dilemma approach, however, acknowledges that in dealing with foreign cultures it may be necessary to talk of reconciliation whereby the parties involved recognise each other's needs while maintaining their own values.

Integrating values

As we have seen in Chapter 5, this reconciliation process may, according to Trompenaars, entail the development of a third dimension in which the values of the parties concerned are integrated through close synergy. This is a much more productive way of addressing the either/or nature of a cultural dilemma than trying to resolve it through making weak compromises. This idea of **integrating values** is much less clear-cut in nature than that of trying to find a trade-off of values during cultural collisions. The complex and unpredictable nature of this integration process, however, seems to reflect much more faithfully the nature of present-day international business and the increasing interdependence between countries and business sectors across the globe.

Cultural patterns

The notion of cultures and their related values being subject to their mutual interaction has received increasing consideration. Søderberg and Holden perceive culture as a sharing of 'patterns of meaning and interpretation' (2002: 112). Rather than there being stable cultural communities, there are groups sharing such patterns who, when interacting with others whose patterns they can identify with, may take them on board, be it in adapted form, and/or negotiate a shared meaning and interpretation. In their view, managers who are involved in globalisation may relate to this concept much more readily than to the fixed dimensions of culture as described in Part One. They will see their role as more to do with ensuring that the interaction within multicultural teams is effective and reaping synergetic rewards. Rather than being a matter of dealing with cultures in isolation, their work is 'the management of multiple cultures' (Søderberg and Holden, 2002: 110), thereby ensuring that 'knowledge, values and experience are transferred into multicultural domains of implementation' (idem: 113).

Culture is not a set of values

Earley (2006) is another scholar who sees the concept of culture as being related to the context, to interaction with others. He is adamant about wanting to avoid what he calls the 'cultural quagmire' of the cultural dimension construct whereby cultural values are an aggregate of individual perceptions and therefore contradict the construct itself (idem: 924). 'Culture', Earley claims, 'is not a value or set of values; culture is the meaning which we attach to aspects of the world around us' (idem: 925). Values as culture remains what Earley calls the 'obsession' of cross-cultural researchers. They should, he maintains, be more focused on meaning as culture. Values are only one element allowing meaning to be attached to the environment. Rather than developing even more value-based classifications on a grand scale, he proposes (more) research based on the concept of culture as a psychological construct whereby an individual is subject to a number of influences. Earley shows how this ties in with a definition of culture made by Rohner (1984: 119–120):

> The totality of equivalent and complementary learned meanings maintained by a human popu-lation, or by identifiable segments of the population, and transmitted from one generation to the next.

What is needed, Earley says, is the development of theories and framework that 'link culture to action', which can be used to understand 'the linkage among cultures, percep-tions, actions, organizations, structures, etc.' (Earley, 2006: 928). At the heart of this lies the individual, not societies and their 'average tendencies' (the term used by Hofstede to describe the nature of cultural dimension scores).

After reviewing work done to establish the linkage described above, Earley (2006) points to the work done by several authors, including Earley himself, on the '**cultural intelligence**' construct. This approach to studying cultural differences examines the extent to which individuals are able to adapt to cultural settings. The focus moves from the context of interaction (such as shared values and meanings) to the behaviour of the individual and the (meta-) cognitive processing involved. Earley admits this approach needs considerable development, but believes it offers a promising way to examine how individual actions are affected by culture.

Conclusion

This chapter has presented a model of culture, the development of which is based on definitions drawn from research in the field of culture and management. This model has been applied to the world of international business and the daily tasks of a manager examined in terms of cultural values. The assumption underlying this study is that an individual's framework of cultural preferences influences the way in which their tasks are executed. The case given in Activity 6.1 will demonstrate this influence.

This chapter has also considered the question whether cultures – and their values – are dynamic rather than stable in nature. It has done so by briefly reviewing the notion of values being subject to modification through interaction in and between cultures, as well as the idea that culture is to do with sharing patterns of meaning and interpretation. Finally, Chapter 6 touches on the belief that culture has nothing to do with shared values, but rather to with the individual.

Activity 6.2 will provide readers with the opportunity to reflect on their own cultural values and to develop, it is hoped, a clear definition of their own style of working. Furthermore, the activity allows a comparison to be made between the cultural values and related work styles with those from other cultures.

Points for reflection

1. The concept gives a range of eight cultural values that could affect five management skill areas.

   Can you suggest other cultural value ranges that could be applied? Are there other management skill areas to which these values could apply?

2. There are those who think that when doing business internationally it is necessary to follow certain professional codes of behaviour, such as keeping to deadlines, meeting delivery dates and obeying terms of contract. There are others, however, who consider that business culture rather than business convention has a greater influence on the way people work internationally or otherwise. Managers operating internationally therefore need to take cultural differences into account.

   Which standpoint do you support? Explain why and give examples on the basis of your experience or analysis.

3. You have seen how culture can affect management.

   Apart from being aware of this, what else do you think is needed to perform successfully in a cross-cultural context?

4. Earley argues that culture has less to do with determining values and more to do with meanings. When doing so, he refers to Rohner's definition of culture: 'The totality of equivalent and complementary learned meanings maintained by a human population, or by identifiable segments of the population, and transmitted from one generation to the next.'

   Compare this definition of culture with that made by Hofstede (Chapter 1): 'The collective programming of the mind which distinguishes the members of one human group from another'.

   In which ways do you consider these definitions to be complementary and/or oppositional in nature?

5. Gullestrup sees the General dynamics culture model which he has created (see Figure 6.2 – which includes Figure 6.1) as being a frame for further research. It is to be seen as a skeleton to which data and information has to be added according to the specific nature of the study being carried out.

   How useful do you consider this model to be if you are about to carry out a cross-cultural research project?

Further reading

Earley, P.C. and Mosakowski, E. (2004) 'Cultural intelligence', *Harvard Business Review*, 82 (October): 139–146. This article describes what the authors claim to be the three sources of cultural intelligence. After giving six cultural intelligence profiles to enable readers to assess which one describes them, the authors suggest ways in which cultural intelligence can be cultivated.

Hall, E.T. and Hall, M.R. (1990) *Understanding Cultural Differences*, Yarmouth, ME: Intercultural Press. Although this book was written primarily for business people, it is oriented towards interpersonal relations with foreigners. It is useful, therefore, for many other people whose lives involve contact with foreign nationals, either in their personal or professional lives.

Gullestrup, H. (2006) *Cultural Analysis – towards further understanding*, Aalborg: Aalborg University Press. This book examines the nature of cross-cultural understanding and co-action. The author presents a way of considering intercultural plurality and complexity in abstract terms. He then proposes an empirical model for the analysis of intercultural co-action before discussing ethical issues relating to intercultural co-action.

References

Doing Business Internationally: the Cross-Cultural Challenges (1992) Participant Workbook, Princeton, NJ: Princeton Training Press.

Earley, C.P. (1989) 'Social loafing and collectivism: a comparison of the United States and the People's Republic of China', *Administrative Science Quarterly*, 34: 565–581.

Earley, P.C. (2006) 'Leading cultural research in the future: a matter of paradigms and taste', *Journal of International Business Studies*, 37: 922–931.

Gullestrup, H. (2003a) 'The Complexity of Intercultural Communication', *Intercultural Communication*, 6: 1–19.

Gullestrup, H. (2003b) 'The Challenges facing the International Managers in the Future', Dwumiesiêcznik 'Zarządzanie Zasobami Ludzkimi' (Human Resource Management bi-monthly Polish journal): 6/2003.

Gullestrup, H. (2006) *Cultural Analysis – Towards Further Understanding*, Aalborg: Aalborg University Press.

Gladwell, G. (2008) *Outliers: the Story of Success*, London: Penguin.

Hall, E.T. (1976) *Beyond culture*, New York, NY: Anchor Books.

Hall, E.T. and Hall, M.R. (1990) *Understanding Cultural Differences*, Yarmouth, ME: Intercultural Press.

Hoecklin, L. (1995*) Managing Cultural Differences: Strategies for Comparative Advantage*, Wokingham: Addison-Wesley.

Hofstede, G. (1991) *Cultures and Organizations: Software of the Mind*, London: McGraw-Hill.

Kluckholn, F. and Strodtbeck, F.L. (1961) *Variations in Value Orientations*, Westport, CT: Greenwood.

Mead, R. (1994) *International Management: Cross-cultural Dimensions*, Oxford: Blackwell Business.

Rohner, R.P. (1984) 'Toward a conception of culture from cross-cultural psychology', *Journal of Cross-Cultural Psychology*, 15(2): 111–138.

Søderberg, A.-M. and Holden, N. (2002) 'Rethinking cross cultural management in a globalizing business world', *International Journal of Cross Cultural Management*, 2(1): 103–121.

Usunier, J.C. (1993) *Marketing Across Cultures*, Hemel Hempstead: Prentice-Hall.

Video Arts (1984) *So You Think You Can Manage?* London: Methuen.

Yoshino, M.Y. and Rangan, U.S. (1995) *Strategic Alliances: an Entrepreneurial Approach to Globalization*, Cambridge, MA: Harvard Business School Press.

Read the case study below, based on the experiences of Larry Zeenny in the Lebanon. It concerns a football agent's attempt to make a deal for his client. When you have read it, answer the questions that follow.

An own goal

The taxi arrived at the impressive mansion in Faqra and I made my way through the blistering sun towards the entrance. I was met by two servants and directed to Mr Haider's room. He had faxed me a contract, the terms of which were ridiculously low, and I was determined to get a better deal for my client.

A peek at my watch revealed it was 11.30. I'd arrived just in time, despite the flight delays at Frankfurt and the queues at Beirut airport. In front of Haider's door I cleared my throat, tightened my tie, gathered all my courage and entered the room. 'Mr Haider, I am delighted to meet you', I said, rather too exuberantly. 'Ahlan Wilhelm, welcome my friend', said Haider. 'I just have to say goodbye to my important visitors. Please make yourself at home while you're waiting.'

A servant led me to a large room where there were two men and, in the far corner, a beautiful oriental woman. I sat down in a chair and waited for Mr Haider. An elaborate clock chimed twelve, but there was still no sign of him. By now the other three were thoroughly enjoying their lunch, which I had refused out of politeness. To keep my nerves steady I had only accepted a glass of arak. By 12.15 my patience had started to desert me. I was going to be too late for my next meeting. How could I trust Mr Haider if he had already broken his promise beforehand?

Eventually, at 12.30, Mr Haider entered the room. He looked extremely relaxed in his traditional dress and I jumped up to greet him. Before approaching me he first kissed both men and had a brief conversation with the woman. I had prepared myself well for this moment. I gave him a firm handshake and seated myself.

'Ahlan Wilhelm, welcome to Lebanon', he said. Looking at the table, he added: 'I hope you enjoyed your delicious lunch with my beloved sons, Alain and Elie, and of course with my habibi, Charlotte.'

'Mr Haider', I replied, 'Thank you for your warm reception, but I ate on the plane. My client is extremely pleased about your interest and he is looking forward to playing for such an illustrious club as Al Ansar. Shall we come to terms as quickly as possible so we can finalise this matter in the best interest of both parties?'

'Shouf Wilhelm', he retorted. 'Please call me Hashem. But why the rush? We have the time for business until the sun walks out on us! When will your client arrive?'

I told him that my client, a goalkeeper who had played for German, Italian and British teams, as well as for his home country, Denmark, would be unable to attend the negotiations. 'The thing is . . .' (I hesitated: how could I call him by his first name and show my total respect?) 'It's usual for a player to leave such dealings to his agent.'

Mr Haider seemed disgruntled, but agreed to talk. He called his two sons over while his wife quietly headed for the door. As she passed by I respectfully looked her in the eye and wished her a pleasant day.

The bargaining process began and, quite disconcertingly, Mr Haider's sons joined in. Was he hoping to get the upper hand through force of numbers? Could I trust his sons to honour the confidentiality aspect of the negotiation? I was concerned details would leak out to the predators from the international press. After an hour we had reached an impasse, but I couldn't really understand why. Mr Haider refused to provide me with a bank guarantee with respect to my client's salary and signing-on fee. In fact, Mr Haider persistently refused to go into financial matters. These could be discussed the next day, he insisted, since they would not be a problem as far as he was concerned.

But for me they *were* the problem. And that was why we had reached a stalemate.

Questions

1. What is the significance of the title of this case?
2. How would you define the problem from your perspective?
3. What do you think has caused the so-called stalemate? Refer to the cultural values outlined in this chapter that have had an impact on the way the agent handled his encounter with Mr Haider. Mention, in particular, issues relating to:
   - time focus;
   - competition;
   - action;
   - space;
   - communication; and
   - structure.
4. How do you think Wilhelm can rescue the deal?
5. How can Wilhelm best prepare for any future negotiations in the Middle East on behalf of his football clients?

ACTIVITY 6.2

Developing your cross-cultural effectiveness

The concepts presented in Part One have allowed a framework of reflection and knowledge to be developed about national cultures and businesses cultures. It has also shown how close the relations are between culture and management. Such insights are essential for working and succeeding in an environment different to one's own. However, it is not enough to learn the different styles of doing business inherent to certain culture(s). International managers or professionals also need to develop personal capabilities, particularly cultural analysis skills which will enable them to operate effectively in a variety of cultural contexts.

The aim of this activity is to help you to develop your cross-cultural effectiveness by enabling you to:

- gain insight into your own culture by defining your own management/professional style with respect to the eight cultural variables as represented in Figure 6.3: A model of culture.
- develop understanding of the national and business culture of another society/country by determining its preferences in terms of the same Figure 6.3.
- determine how you need to adapt your professional skills to the culture and working style of this other society or country.

Task 1: developing your self-awareness

Identify your own cultural values by making a cultural profile of yourself.

To facilitate this task, you can use a Microsoft Excel file entitled 'Cultural Profile' which your instructor can download on your behalf from the website dedicated to this book.

1. Refer to Figure 6.3 as well as the eight parameters shown in Concept 6.1.
2. Make your own cultural profile in Figure 6.5 by giving a score for each of the eight cultural parameters concerned. Enter a score in Table 6.9 against each parameter that reflects your own value on a range of 1 to 5.

Table 6.9 **Make your own profile**

Parameter	Value = 1	Value = 5	Your score (from 1 to 5)
Time focus	monochronic	polychronic	
Time orientation	past	future	
Space	private	public	
Power	equality	hierarchy	
Structure	individualism	collectivism	
Competition	co-operative	competitive	
Communication	low context	high context	
Action	being	doing	

These values can be plotted on a 'Step-one profile' diagram (Figure 6.5).

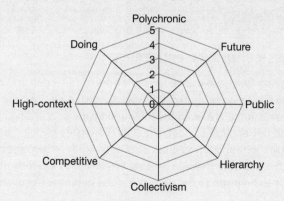

Figure 6.5 **Step one profile**

Task 2: developing cross-cultural understanding

Now you are asked to make a comparison of the differences between your own culture and another culture. This will involve preparing a profile of the culture in question.

1. Choose a country where you know some of its inhabitants and/or where you intend to do business. Using Chapters 3 and 4 (and/or referring to other relevant documentation), try to work out how you perceive the culture of this country,

2. Make up the cultural profile of the country you have chosen in the same way as you did when preparing your own profile: giving a score for the eight cultural parameters in the same cultural profile document (Figure 6.5). Examples of completed cultural profiles are given below in Table 6.10 and Figure 6.6.

Table 6.10 **Example: your cultural profile score and that of chosen country**

Parameter	Value = 1	Value = 5	Your score	Score of country chosen
Time focus	monochronic	polychronic	1	5
Time orientation	past	future	3	3
Space	private	public	1	4
Power	equality	hierarchy	2	5
Structure	individualism	collectivism	1	4
Competition	co-operative	competitive	5	1
Communication	low context	high context	1	5
Action	being	doing	4	2

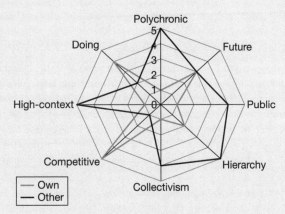

Figure 6.6 **Step two profile: own and chosen country**

3. Compare the two profiles and determine the difference and similarities in the parameters.

4. Define what you believe are the critical issues when representatives of the two cultures profiled work together?

Task 3: adapting your professional skills

This final task is one where you are asked to determine the strategies needed to make a success of your job in the country chosen:

1. Look at the eight tables in Concept 6.1 entitled 'Management tasks and cultural values', then work out what impact of the main differences in the eight cultural values are between you and the country chosen on five tasks: planning, organising, staffing, directing and controlling (Table 6.11).

2. Reflect on how you can adapt to operate in the business environment of the chosen country taking into account individual, national and professional cultural differences in Table 6.11 given at the end of this activity.

To help you complete Task 3, an example is given below which explains differences between the Netherlands and Japan in terms of cultural values regarding management tasks (1) and the strategies needed (2) for the launching of a new product.

Planning

1 Differences in cultural values regarding management tasks

Japanese customer relationships are based on trust and long-term perspectives. When the introduction of a product in this market is being planned, it is necessary to exercise patience: time is needed to build relationships and this has to be taken into account when sales targets and market share objectives are being established. The marketing plan needs to emphasise long-term relationship building. The planning should be schedule-driven, but not with too many detailed instructions. On the other hand, the goals and objectives set should be very detailed and quantifiable, and accepted as a shared objective by all involved.

2 Management strategies

As manager, one should have concrete ideas on what the plan has to be. Top-down planning is expected. Plans should be challenging to motivate sales people. If the Dutch approach was used, and employees were allowed the room to discuss and participate in the planning, the Japanese would set very conservative goals to avoid risk. The initiative clearly has to come from the manager.

Organising

1 Differences in cultural values regarding management tasks

Once staff have been hired, they need to be organised: tasks need to be allocated, geographical areas assigned and a reporting structure put in place. Japanese people are used to a relatively strong hierarchical structure. Since informal and casual management communication is characteristic of the Dutch, the expected flexibility in an organisation, therefore, will be lacking. Procedures and protocols will need to be followed if goals are to be achieved in the long run.

In contrast to the focused, step-by-step approach to planning, where adherence to time schedules is very important, the task does not need to be specified in such great detail. Relationships rather than detailed plans are more important for selling the product. Tasks will nevertheless need to be clearly assigned to a specific person or a team. If there is any ambiguity, people will react defensively.

2 Management strategies

The assignment of specific customers to specific, reliable salespeople could be of crucial importance. Each salesperson or sales-team needs to be the right 'fit' for the customers concerned, so that the best possible relationships can be built.

Staffing

1 Differences in cultural values regarding management tasks

Bearing in mind the above-mentioned emphasis on building long-term relationships, people should be hired who have the social skills required. For a product launch in Japan to be successful, local sales and marketing people who are reliable and trustworthy need to be recruited.

2 Management strategies

To motivate employees, a manager should show that he takes care of their interests. To ensure their co-operation, he needs to apply a system of seniority that employees will accept. Salaries can be lower than in the Netherlands (owing to differences in Japanese living standards), but achievements should be rewarded with bonuses. Training is to be initiated by the manager although the score on competitiveness would suggest differently.

Directing (Leading)

1 Differences in cultural values regarding management tasks

Japanese sales employees are used to strong directive control and detailed instructions on how to proceed. Absence of this directive attitude or a sudden casual form of management can confuse employees, cause uncertainty and lead to undesirable behaviour.

Marketing people familiar with the local market can avoid cultural mistakes in communication about the product. However, since the Japanese are not used to participative management, they should be instructed carefully as to the expectations of the Dutch management. If an idea is put forward, it may well be accepted because the Japanese are reluctant to show their disagreement and cause possible conflict. As a result, the wrong ideas can end up being taken on board.

2 Management strategies

Group coherence is very important in the Japanese culture and therefore the best results probably will be achieved if this value is applied. This can be done, for example, by making the group responsible for meeting sales targets.

Again, time based management is expected and therefore the Dutch manager should adapt his directives accordingly.

Controlling

1 Differences in cultural values regarding management tasks

Conflicts must be resolved before work can progress. That means that, whenever a deviation to the plan has been observed, the feedback given should be carefully communicated, preferably in an indirect way. Japanese people are used to security in their job through lifetime employment. Any corrective measures should therefore be carefully considered.

2 Management strategies

Strategies should involve building good relationships with employees.

Table 6.11 **Cultural differences summary**

Management tasks	1. Differences in cultural values regarding management tasks 2. Management strategies
Planning Defining goals and objectives	1. 2.
Organising Defining tasks and relationship structures	1. 2.
Staffing Acquiring appropriate human resources	1. 2.
Directing (leading) Leading the employees towards the goals of the organisation	1. 2.
Controlling Monitoring performance and giving feedback on achievements	1. 2.

Reference

Doing Business Internationally: the Cross-Cultural Challenges (1992) Participant Workbook, Princeton, NJ: Princeton Training Press.

Part One Final activity A1.1

This final activity concerns a case based on a research project carried out for an international airline company, which has its headquarters in Europe. The research focused on obtaining knowledge and insights in order to understand the cultural differences – if any – in the buying behaviour of consumers in a digital environment. This case draws particular attention to a number of cultural variables developed by the GLOBE programme (see Chapter 2) and their impact on the online behaviour of consumers and non-consumers of the airline company from Brazil, Malaysia and the USA.

The airline company in question has been given the fictitious name 'Alizee'.

Learning objectives

After completing the assignment, you should

- Be in a position to make an analysis based on the preliminary results of a research project.
- Have improved skills in drawing conclusions.
- Be able to formulate a critical opinion regarding the application of the cultural dimensions to business.

YOUR ASSIGNMENT

After having read the Alizee airlines case, carry out the following tasks:

Task 1 Establish the research framework: complete the form below with information you find in each section of the Alizee case.

Section	What is the main objective of this section? Which information is the most relevant?
1	
2	
3	
4	
5	
6	

Task 2 Make an analysis of the results from the in-depth interviews of the two groups: Alizee consumers and non-Alizee consumers for Brazil, Malaysia and the USA (see section 5).

A. Summarise the results concerning the five variables in the table below:

1. Determine whether each of the five variables given is relevant or irrelevant. For each variant which you consider relevant, mention the common responses and the aspects these reflect.

Variables	Brazil		Malaysia		USA	
	Consumers	Non-consumers	Consumers	Non-consumers	Consumers	Non-consumers
Future orientation						
Performance orientation						
Institutional collectivism						
Power distance						
Uncertainty avoidance						

2. Write an analysis based on the completed table.

B. 1. Compare the results from consumers and non-consumers for each of the countries involved in this case, regarding their perceptions of online efforts and preferences for online channels, such as:

- performing channels
- e-mail: Alizee campaign 'luggage tag'
- display: banners of an online advertisement.

2. Write a separate analysis by country.

Task 3 Discuss the conclusions.

A. Complete the table below using the results concerning the relevance of cultural dimensions for Alizee for the three countries, i.e. the combined results for consumers and non-consumers from task 2. Use the terms 'relevant', 'moderately relevant' or 'irrelevant' for each variable.

	Brazil	Malaysia	USA
Power distance			
Performance orientation			
Uncertainty avoidance			
Future orientation			
Institutional collectivism			

B. In section 6 of the case, the authors make the following statement: 'It seems that when consumers approach airline services in the online environment, they do so on the basis of cultural constructs that do not necessarily follow the GLOBE study's results'.
Compare the completed table above with Table A1.1.2 (Relevance of cultural dimensions according to GLOBE study) and write a conclusion for each of the countries.

C. Short essay: discuss the following statement: 'Research methods using cultural dimensions (e.g. those from the GLOBE project) are not relevant to the study of international business issues.'

Alizee airlines case

Cultural dimensions and their impact on online behaviour and consumption of digital channels among airline consumers from Brazil, Malaysia and the USA

Shortened and adapted from a thesis written by **Javier Arias** (Costa Rica) and **Robert Deidun** (USA), MBA graduates (2012) of Nyenrode Business University, the Netherlands

1. INTRODUCTION

This case study focuses on understanding the cultural differences in terms of what generates sales in the digital environment among Alizee consumers from the USA, Brazil and Malaysia.

Online channels within the airline industry have grown significantly as a source of revenue and a way of engaging with consumers. Therefore, it is very important for Alizee to understand all the variables that influence customer behaviour in the online environment. So far, Alizee has successfully implemented campaigns in Brazil, the USA and Malaysia through online channels such as mobile, display advertising, e-mail, metasearch, affiliation and social media. All of these campaigns have engaged consumers through increasing brand awareness, promoting transactions or allowing interaction with the brand. Nonetheless, the competitive airline environment obliges the company to constantly look for ways to improve its connection with consumers.

Alizee is aware of the need to understand this behaviour in order to take its online marketing efforts to the next level. To this end, this case study aims to reveal insights into the markets mentioned to help Alizee in its efforts to develop engaging and effective online marketing initiatives.

Research into consumer behaviour has shown that cultural dimensions still play an important role in the decision-making process. That is why Alizee wants to know more about the cultural similarities and differences that affect buying behaviour for Alizee services through different online channels in the USA, Brazil, and Malaysia. By becoming more aware of how cultural dimensions affect the online behaviour of consumers in each of these three countries, Alizee can optimise online marketing activities which are specific to each.

However, due to time limitations, the research on which this case is based does not provide a representative sample of the whole population in each market, since only a limited number of consumers and non-consumers will be approached. The conclusions of this report, therefore, cannot be applied to all consumers of each market or to other markets where Alizee operates.

2. COMPANY ENVIRONMENT

Global airlines offer consumers the quickest and most time-convenient method of transportation, making them a key player in transporting the world's globetrotters. As can be seen in the Air Transport Association of America's 2010 Economic Report, commercial aviation plays a major role in today's modern economy, providing economic activity as well as millions of jobs in the global work force.

The general landscape of today's airline industry requires players in the markets to offer high levels of customer service among their clients (Wiseman, 2012). The digital environment provides the airline industry with a plethora of opportunities to develop products which meet the growing needs of its customers. To take advantage of these opportunities, it is necessary to understand the markets where an airline company is operating and, in particular, to understand the differences between these markets from a cultural standpoint.

One useful way for Alizee to measure the effectiveness of cultural variables within the online processes of airline services is to use as benchmarks the home carriers in the markets where the company operates. In this regard, the following airlines have been defined by Alizee as relevant players in the markets investigated in this study: Airline B (in Brazil), Airline U (in the USA) and Airline M (in Malaysia).

3. RESEARCH METHODS

In order to understand the behaviour of online consumers in the different markets, a qualitative exploratory approach was used for this study. According to Patton (2002):

> Qualitative methods typically produce a wealth of detailed information about a much smaller number of people and cases. This increases the depth of understanding of the cases and situations studied.

> Patton, 2002: 14

That is why this project makes use of non-numerical research tools to gain a deeper understanding of the cultural drivers, artefacts and attitudes of consumers' online behaviour and their interaction with different online channels.

Different research methods will be used to understand the different variables that play a role in the decision-making process of consumers in the three markets mentioned above. Two groups of variables – as defined by the GLOBE project – were made. The first group included variables to be explored via in-depth interviews. These variables include: power distance, uncertainty avoidance, institutional collectivism, future orientation and performance orientation. The second group of variables were investigated via analysis of information displayed on the Facebook profiles of each airline. This group of variables includes: in-group collectivism, assertiveness, gender egalitarianism and humane orientation. (See section 4, Table A1.1.1.)

This adaptation of the original thesis will only focus on the results of the first group of variables which were obtained via in-depth interviews. These in-depth interviews were carried out with airline consumers as well as stakeholders from each of the markets. These stakeholders provided an understanding of Alizee's operations in the markets selected. Their responses served as a means not only to understanding the business, but also to defining some of the questions for the consumer interviews.

According to Boyce and Neale (2006):

> In-depth interviews are useful when you want detailed information about a person's thoughts and behaviours or want to explore new issues in depth.

> Boyce and Neale, 2006: 3

This research method helped to obtain insights into the beliefs and values that determine the interaction between consumers and airlines through different digital channels. It also provided an overview of the norms that determine the perception and efficiency of Alizee's digital communications. Hence, additional questions were asked during the consumers' interviews about performing channels and two Alizee campaigns:

- Where do you prefer to buy your airline ticket, i.e. through your computer, iPad, mobile phone, others? Why?

- I would like to know what you think about this e-mail. What would you change in it? (The interviewee was shown an e-mail about an Alizee campaign which offered the consumers the possibility to personalise a luggage tag with predetermined pictures or pictures uploaded by the user, plus text.

- I will present you with an online advertisement. (The interviewee was shown the banners of an online display advertisement whereby Alizee promotes low fares for specific destinations.) What did you like about it? What would you change in it?

Both researchers conducted the in-depth interviews. In the case of the consumers' interviews, a pilot survey was carried out with an airline consumer in order to validate the comprehensibility of the questionnaire and to minimise room for misinterpretation. However, the international scope of the case study implied some local interpretation of questions, especially in Brazil where English is not the mother tongue.

The interviews with airline consumers were conducted on a one-on-one basis by one of the researchers and took place in a comfortable environment. The closed environment used was intended to promote trust and to encourage the interviewees to be more open when giving their responses.

Interviews with airline consumers from Malaysia were run in Alizee's local offices in Kuala Lumpur. Interviews in Brazil were conducted in Sao Paulo in the presence of a Portuguese-speaking interpreter. The interviews with USA consumers were conducted at Amsterdam's Schiphol Airport.

The interviewees were people who could provide information related to the content of the research project. In this case, the most relevant players who provided the insights regarding the role of cultural dimensions of each market were:

a) Airline consumers: ten consumers from the USA, Brazilian, and Malaysian markets were used as a primary source of information. Two main groups of interviewees were approached – Alizee consumers and non-Alizee consumers for each market; five of the interviews were conducted with Alizee consumers and five with non-Alizee consumers.

b) Stakeholders related to Alizee online operations: country managers from different departments in the Brazil, Malaysia and USA markets.

4. VARIABLES

Table A1.1.1 **Conceptual, instrumental and operational definitions of each cultural variable**

Cultural variables (House *et al.*, 2004)		Conceptual definition (House *et al.*, 2004)	Instrumental definition	Operational definition
In-depth interviews	Power distance	'The extent to which a community accepts and endorses authority, power differences, and status privileges'	This variable is considered to be relevant for Alizee's online marketing communications if the interviewees refer to at least three of the following aspects: privileges, status, power, equality, differences between economy and business classes, exclusivity and social mobility.	This variable is included in the questionnaire of the in-depth interviews.
	Uncertainty avoidance	'The extent to which a society, organisation, or group relies on social norms, rules, and procedures to alleviate the unpredictability of future events'	This variable is considered to be relevant for Alizee's online marketing communications if the interviewees refer to at least three of the following aspects: formality in interaction, risk taking, change, planning, structure, reaction to events (expected and unexpected), self-protection and social norms.	This variable is included in the questionnaire of the in-depth interviews.
	Institutional collectivism	'The degree to which organisational and societal institutional practices encourage and reward collective distribution of resources and collective action'	This variable is considered to be relevant for Alizee's online marketing communications if the interviewees refer to at least three of the following aspects: group loyalty, autonomy, friendship, organisation (interdependence/ independent), individualism, social fairness, decision-making.	This variable is included in the questionnaire of the in-depth interviews.
	Future orientation	'The degree to which a collectivity encourages and rewards future-oriented behaviours such as planning and delaying gratification'	This variable is considered to be relevant for Alizee's online marketing communications if the interviewees refer to at least three of the following aspects: gratification, wealth management, long-term/short-term, connection between wealth and fulfilment, flexibility to reach goals, treating yourself, 'the now'	This variable is included in the questionnaire of the in-depth interviews.
	Performance orientation	'Reflects the extent to which a community encourages and rewards innovation, high standards, excellence, and performance improvement'	This variable is considered to be relevant for Alizee's online marketing communications if the interviewees refer to at least three of the following aspects: innovation, excellence, performance, 'high standards', materialism, value of self, self-improvement.	This variable is included in the questionnaire of the in-depth interviews.

Table A1.1.1 *Continued*

Cultural variables (House *et al.*, 2004)		Conceptual definition (House *et al.*, 2004)	Instrumental definition	Operational definition
Analysis and data-processing (Facebook)	In-group collectivism	'The degree to which individuals express pride, loyalty, and cohesiveness in their organisations or families'	This variable is considered to be relevant for Alizee's online marketing communications. In the Facebook pages at least two of the following aspects are displayed four times in a two-month period: social endorsement, pride, loyalty, pace of life, relations.	This variable is considered in the matrices for the data-gathering of Facebook fan pages.
	Assertiveness	'The degree to which individuals are assertive, confrontational, and aggressive in their relationships with others'	This variable is considered to be relevant for Alizee's online marketing communications. In the Facebook pages at least two of the following aspects are displayed four times in a two-month period: complaints, competition, personal environment (control/harmony), ambiguity, trust building.	This variable is considered in the matrices for the data-gathering of Facebook fan pages.
	Gender egalitarianism	'The degree to which a collective minimises gender inequality'	This variable is considered to be relevant for Alizee's online marketing communications. In the Facebook pages at least two of the following aspects are displayed four times in a two-month period: gender segregation, women, societal roles, gender interdependence; and economic participation.	This variable is considered in the matrices for the data-gathering of Facebook fan pages.
	Humane orientation	'The degree to which an organisation or society encourages and rewards individuals for being fair, altruistic, friendly, generous, caring, and kind to others'	This variable is considered to be relevant for Alizee's online marketing communications. In the Facebook pages at least two of the following aspects are displayed four times in a two-month period: social responsibility, friendliness, caring, tolerance for mistakes, well-being.	This variable is considered in the matrices for the data-gathering of Facebook fan pages.

5. RESULTS OF THE INTERVIEWS WITH AIRLINE CONSUMERS

The interviews were accomplished successfully for each of the markets. The same questionnaire was used for both Alizee consumers and non-Alizee consumers in each country, including two questions for each of the first five cultural variables given in Table A1.1.1. All of the interviewees agreed to respond to all of the questions.

5.1 Results from Brazil

5.1.1 Alizee consumers

For the variable Future Orientation, four of the interviewees said that they decided which flight to take on the basis of cost. There was some flexibility involved in their decision. One of the interviewees even said: 'It really depends on what is on offer: if it was really a good offer maybe I would change my mind'. Alizee consumers mentioned that the next preferred place to fly to on their list was the factor that defined their trip; the season was also a consideration in this matter and they started planning their trips well in advance. Consumers mentioned at least three of the aspects defined in the 'instrumental definition' (section 4) as relevant to this cultural dimension.

The Performance Orientation variable proved to be relevant for only two people. The most important factor for four of the interviewees when choosing to buy an airline service online was the price. Some interviewees mentioned the flight connections as well. Three individuals perceived the innovations introduced by the airline as user-friendly.

For the Institutional Collectivism variable, all of the five consumers said that external sources were their main reference when looking for information about airline services. These sources included forums, blogs and other travel-related websites. One of the interviewees said: 'I use an internet forum to share information with people who are planning to travel'. Three of the interviewees would also ask friends if they did not find enough information online. When watching the video 'Alizee's Trip planner campaigns', four of them had the impression 'it reminds me of me and my friends'. Four of the five consumers showed at least three aspects defined in the 'instrumental definition' (section 4) as relevant to this variable.

With respect to the Power Distance variable, consumers had different views regarding whom Alizee's online efforts such as newsletters and e-mails with promotions, were targeting. Three of the interviewees said that they were aimed at everyone, while one added that Alizee was moving towards a much larger audience. She stated that: 'From my experience, I would say that Alizee is trying to expand the range of people who travel with them . . . because nowadays younger people have more opportunity to travel due to the economic situation in Brazil'. Interviewees mentioned that Alizee's efforts targeted 'people like me'. However, when it came to Alizee's apps and social media, four of the interviewees replied that only young people used them.

Of the aspects defined in the 'instrumental definition' (section 4) of the Power Distance variable, at least three were mentioned by just one of the interviewees. Still, three of the consumers referred to the 'social mobility' aspect in Brazil.

For the Uncertainty Avoidance variable, three of the interviewees stated that they would buy an Alizee ticket online because that was what they had always done. In addition, two of them mentioned that they did so because it was safe. When asked for the reasons for buying a ticket through another party, just one of the interviewees mentioned safety as the reason for doing so.

All five interviewees mentioned at least three aspects of the Uncertainty Avoidance variable (see the instrumental definition, section 4). Most of them referred several times to expected versus unexpected situations, self-protection and avoiding taking risks. One of the consumers said: 'If I had a problem with the ticket I would want to talk directly to the airline company'.

When it came to choosing a channel for buying online services, all five consumers said they preferred using a website. They considered this channel more trustworthy and easy to use. Two of the interviewees said they thought that using a mobile phone channel might not be safe. Three of them considered using a tablet as a possible option. Still, some of them referred to the extra functionality which a desktop offered to be preferable in this sense.

With respect to Alizee's e-mail campaign, five consumers said they liked the initiative. They found the personalised gadgets to be very attractive. Three of them mentioned that the message was clear. However, three of them also said that the message or images could be even clearer. One of the consumers added: 'The idea is very good but the font is very small and there is no explanation as to how the promotion works'.

The reactions of the consumers to the display advertisements from Alizee's campaign were very positive. Three of them said they liked the idea and that the banners were very clear. Two consumers spoke positively about the use of the design elements in the banners, as well as the message given in the text. However, most of the consumers preferred the vertical versions of the banners to the horizontal ones. The latter were more attractive and easier to understand.

5.1.2 Non-Alizee consumers

For the first variable, Future Orientation, the decision about taking a flight involved several different considerations. Three non-Alizee consumers mentioned all of the following: a spontaneous decision, a decision based on cost, a seasonal decision and a decision based on the next place to fly to on their list. Three interviewees mentioned that they plan their trips one month in advance. One of these said that she planned her trip only one month in advance because: 'I travel with my son, who travels a lot, so my decision is based on the place where he is and whenever he has time'.

For four of the interviewees, the aspects related to Future Orientation were relevant in the decision to plan a trip. Among the aspects mentioned more frequently were the flexibility to reach goals, long-term versus short-term orientation and giving yourself a treat.

The aspects related to Performance Orientation did not prove to be very relevant for this group. However, the five consumers said that the range of prices on offer was a key consideration for choosing to buy an airline service online. Reliability was mentioned by two of the interviewees as a relevant factor as well. With respect to the innovations made by airlines online, the answers were very diverse. They ranged from 'I like them but it doesn't satisfy my needs' to 'They are user-friendly'.

Just like Alizee consumers, most of the non-Alizee consumers said they looked for external sources when they wanted to access other people's opinions regarding an airline or a destination. Three of them also mentioned that asking friends could be a source of information. Non-Alizee consumers' impressions of one of Alizee's initiatives were very diverse. Most of them were positive and included answers such as 'it reminds me of me and my friends', 'I would totally do it' and 'I would do it if some things were different'.

All five non-Alizee consumers mentioned the aspects considered to be relevant to the Institutional Collectivism dimension. Among the most relevant aspects revealed are the autonomy, organisation (independence), friendship, individualism and decision-making. Regarding the autonomy of the decision, one of the consumers remarked: 'I believe it is important to get all the information possible, both positive and negative . . . both positive and negative have to be filtered with respect to what I want'.

For the Power Distance dimension, three of the interviewees said that they perceived Alizee's online efforts as being directed towards rich people. Two said that they were aimed at business people. Moreover, non-Alizee consumers believed that rich people and young people used Alizee's apps and social media. Even when several respondents associated Alizee with wealthy travellers, the interviews did not show high indicators for the Power Distance variable.

As for Uncertainty Avoidance, three of the non-Alizee consumers answered that they would buy an Alizee ticket online because it was safe to do so. In the case of other airlines or online travel agents, three of the interviewees mentioned that they used meta-research or online travel agents to look for information but not to book a ticket. Additional fees and unwillingness to deal with an intermediary were the reasons mentioned for not using these to buy a ticket.

Four of the interviewees revealed aspects related to Uncertainty Avoidance. The aspects which were mentioned the most were expected versus unexpected situations, self-protection and risk-taking. One of the interviewees said: 'I would buy an Alizee ticket because Alizee is a company that I have always heard of and I have heard that everything always works as expected . . . I would buy online because I already feel confident about Alizee'.

With respect to the means used by non-Alizee consumers to buy their online tickets, the website was also the preferred method. Some of the reasons mentioned include convenience and 'I'm used to doing it there'. Using a mobile phone was one option for accessing for information but they preferred not to use it for buying tickets because it was not convenient.

Regarding the e-mail from the luggage-tag campaign, three of the interviewees liked the images and three of them liked the initiative. One of them even said that she liked the initiative because: 'Brazilian airlines do not do things like this'. Two of the consumers liked the fact that it was a personalised promotion.

After being exposed to the different banners used in an Alizee campaign, non-Alizee consumers said that they liked the fact that the banners were very clear and clean. Two of them specifically liked the idea and two of them the design elements. As with the Alizee consumers, the vertical banners were preferred to the horizontal banners. One of the interviewees said: 'The horizontal is difficult to understand but this [the vertical] is easy because it is bigger, it is nice . . . this [the vertical banner] is the best for me'.

5.2 Results from Malaysia

5.2.1 Alizee consumers

Results from the interviews with Alizee consumers in Malaysia showed that – for the Future Orientation variable – four of the interviewees determined their journey on a cost basis. Three of them mentioned that referring to the next location on their list of places to fly to played a role in their travel decisions. Four of the five consumers said they planned their trips well in advance. Three interviewees mentioned at least three of the aspects defined in the variables section as relevant to this cultural dimension. Wealth management, long-term orientation, and searching for gratification were among the aspects which these consumers mentioned most.

As for the Performance Orientation variable, four of the interviewees said they made their decision according to ease of use. In addition, three of them said they made their decision on the basis of the airline's reputation and reliability. However, this variable did not appear to be relevant to the interviewees.

With respect to the Institutional Collectivism variable, all five interviewees said that they came to a decision after asking friends or family. Four of the five Alizee consumers mentioned aspects relevant to this cultural variable. These included group loyalty, friendship, organisation (dependence) and decision-making.

The aspects of the Power Distance variable seemed irrelevant to those interviewed. Still, consumers showed a mixture of responses concerning the people towards whom Alizee's efforts were directed. Two of them mentioned business people. One stated that these efforts 'are not directed towards groups'. As to whom Alizee was targeting its social media and mobile efforts, three respondents stated that they were for everyone while two said the target was people who travel often.

With respect to the Uncertainty Avoidance variable, three current consumers mentioned that they would buy an Alizee ticket because they had always done so. Two of them said 'Because there won't be any unexpected situations'. However when asked why they would purchase airline services with a different airline, all five respondents said that they would do so if another airline was cheaper. Three of them mentioned relevant aspects related to this dimension: risk-taking, planning, structure, and expected vs. unexpected.

When asked where they preferred to purchase their airline services, consumers presented different answers. Three interviewees preferred to purchase their airline services on a computer or laptop via Alizee's website. One person referred to using the Alizee app on their smart phone. Two people said they preferred booking their travel on a tablet, such as an iPad. Consumers also mentioned occasionally booking by telephone or through a travel agent if they were travelling in groups.

When presented with the e-mail from an Alizee campaign, interviewees provided different responses. One consumer said: 'I do not care about this initiative'. Another person did not like the idea behind it, stating that: 'it is not for Malaysians, it is only for students'. Two consumers liked the personalised nature of the initiative. When asked what they would change, two of the interviewees said that they did not like the use of pictures; one stated that the pictures were unclear and another said they should use warmer pictures. Two consumers said that they would make the textual message clearer.

When campaign banners were shown to Alizee consumers, one consumer ignored it, saying 'It is not important for me'. Three people did not like the idea. When asked what they would change, one consumer said 'everything'. Three people said they would change the message, while the other two consumers mentioned changing the colours and pictures.

5.2.2 Non-Alizee consumers

With respect to Future Orientation, all five non-consumers mentioned cost as the leading factor they considered when making their travel decisions. Three people mentioned a promotion as well. Two respondents said that they made their decision according to the next place on their list of places to fly to. Four of the five consumers said that they planned their trips well in advance. Nonetheless, the consumers displayed only two aspects relating to this dimension during the interviews (long/short term and wealth).

For the Performance Orientation variable, all five respondents considered ease of use to be the most important consideration when purchasing airline services online. Three people said that reliability was important to them. Two interviewees said that they liked to see different prices being offered. Three of the five interviewees mentioned aspects relevant to this cultural variable: innovation, excellence, performance and high standards were among the aspects which the consumers mentioned most.

With respect to Institutional Collectivism, two of the five respondents stated that they valued the opinions of friends, family and co-workers in making their travel decisions. The other three respondents said they made decisions on their own. As for the Alizee campaign video, two interviewees said that it reminded them of their friends, two said that it was nothing like them and their friends. Not enough aspects around this dimension were displayed by the consumers. The aspects of Power Distance variable were not considered relevant to the interviewees either. Still, three interviewees said that they felt that Alizee's efforts spoke to everyone. Two people felt that Alizee's efforts were more directed towards business people, while only one said 'to people like me'. Regarding social media and mobile applications, two interviewees felt that they were directed towards everyone, two felt that they were only for people who travelled often, and two said that they were for business people.

As for the Uncertainty Avoidance variable, non-consumers gave a mixture of different responses concerning why they would purchase an Alizee ticket online. Two people said this was because they had always done it this way. Four people stated that they would do so because of price. With respect to buying with another airline, all five respondents said that they would use another airline if it was cheaper. Most of the aspects of the Uncertainty Avoidance variable were mentioned by this group in Malaysia: risk-taking, planning, structure, expected reaction to events and self-protection were among the most popular aspects.

On the subject of where Alizee consumers preferred to purchase their airline services online, four of the respondents stated that they preferred booking through a website via a computer or laptop. Two people said that they would book through their mobile phone, and two people preferred to book through a tablet such as an iPad. Interviewees unwilling to book through a mobile phone said that they were worried about the security of the transaction.

When presented with the e-mails that Alizee sent out for one of its campaigns, two non-consumers liked the initiative. One person liked the images, another liked the textual message. Two respondents liked their personalised nature and another liked their clarity.

When asked if they could change anything in this e-mail campaign, four of the non-consumers said that they would change the images since they were cold or boring. Three people said that they would make the textual message clearer. Two people said that in general they would make the overall message clearer.

When presented with an Alizee online advertisement, three of the interviewees did not like the initiative, and two people did like it. Two of the respondents liked its clarity.

If it were possible to change any of the elements in this initiative, two respondents said that they would change the images. Three people said that they did not like the use of colours and three people would change the message to make it clearer. One observation from a respondent was that they would make it more 'attention-getting' or even 'controversial' by including more Asian elements.

5.3 Results from the USA

5.3.1 Alizee consumers

For the Future Orientation variable, three of the interviewees said that they made their decision to travel according to the next destination on their list. Most of the consumers started planning their trips well in advance. The aspects for this variable which were mentioned most included wealth management and long-term thinking when planning trips.

The aspects of the Performance Orientation variable were popular for Alizee consumers as well. Reliability and safety were key considerations for consumers when making an online transaction with an airline. Among the most frequently mentioned aspects were excellence and performance. However, the attitude of these consumers towards airline innovations was not positive. Two of them said 'I really don't care about them' and two felt that they were complicated.

Not enough aspects of the Institutional Collectivism variable were mentioned by Alizee consumers in the USA. When asked about whose opinion they considered important, most of them referred to friends or family. However, consumers displayed an individualistic approach towards making the final decision. One of them said: 'I still do what I want'. Their impressions about one of Alizee's campaigns were very diverse. However, four consumers did say that they would definitely use Alizee to book a flight or they would do so if some things were different.

The aspects related to the Power Distance variable were not popular among Alizee consumers. When asked about which people they thought Alizee's online efforts were directed at, the interviewees said either everybody or business travellers. One of the consumers said: 'To people who are looking to travel to the Netherlands'. Four of the consumers said emphatically that it was only people who travelled often who used Alizee's mobile applications and social media pages.

As for the aspects related to the Uncertainty Avoidance variable, four interviewees referred to at least three related elements. Four Alizee consumers mentioned that they would buy an Alizee ticket online because they had always done so. Structure and avoidance of unexpected events were mentioned. Still, three consumers stated that they would buy tickets online with another airline or online service if they were cheaper.

With respect to the preferred channel for buying online services, the website was mentioned by three of the consumers. Convenience and ease of use were among the reasons given. Using a mobile phone was considered to be unsafe. One of the consumers said: 'not only is the screen very small, but it is also not safe to use the credit card [with it]'. Positive reactions were made about tablet devices but they were still not used very much for this purpose.

With respect to the e-mails from an Alizee campaign, the five consumers said they liked the initiative. Four of them also liked the fact that they were personalised. However, four also mentioned that they could be clearer.

The display advertisements shown did not generate very positive reactions. Three of the consumers said that they did not like the idea. One of them said: 'they don't really stand out for me'. Some of the changes they would make would be to the images and the colours used.

5.3.2 Non-Alizee consumers

For the Future Orientation variable, interviewees said they made their decision to travel on the basis of cost or on available promotions. The majority of non-Alizee consumers began planning their trips well in advance. This dimension was not shown to be relevant to the non-consumer group. Only two aspects were mentioned frequently: long-term orientation and flexibility to reach goals.

Aspects of the Performance Orientation were mentioned by Alizee non-consumers. Reliability and safety were major considerations for this group when making their transaction online with an airline. Excellence, performance, and high standards were aspects mentioned by this group. They showed, however, a negative attitude towards airline innovations.

Institutional Collectivism was not relevant to Alizee non-consumers in the USA. When asked whose opinion they considered important to them, the majority of them said their family's. Interviewees displayed a rather individualistic approach to making their travel decision. One mentioned: 'When planning a group trip, it might be cheaper to call the "group" department of the airline.' Impressions of one of Alizee's campaigns were positive – three of them said that they would definitely make use of Alizee's promotion.

The Alizee non-consumers did not really refer to the aspects of the Power Distance variable. As for the question about the people whom they thought Alizee's online efforts were targeting, these respondents mentioned either business travellers or everybody. One of the non-consumers said: 'Alizee seems more for business people'. Four of them said outright that only frequent flyers used Alizee's social media pages and mobile applications.

Regarding Uncertainty Avoidance, five interviewees referred to at least three elements related to the variable. Three interviewees from the non-Alizee consumer group said that they would purchase a ticket with Alizee online because 'there won't be any unexpected situations'. Risk-taking and unexpected events were most mentioned among the non-consumer group. Nonetheless, four interviewees from this group said that they would purchase a ticket with another airline if it was cheaper.

With respect to the preferred channel for purchasing online, websites were mentioned by all five non-Alizee consumers. Security was the most popular reason mentioned. Using a tablet is also popular among most of the non-consumers, while using a mobile phone is less of a possibility for this group. One of the interviewees said, 'I feel safer buying directly online with the airline and I know if something happens I can deal with the airline'.

Regarding the e-mail campaign, all five of the non-consumers liked the initiative, although three of them said that they would change the images. Display advertisements shown generated positive reaction. The non-consumer group would like to see a different use of images. One of them said: 'It would be nice if the pictures helped to get the message across better'.

6. GENERAL CONCLUSIONS

The conclusions of our research are a result of the combination between conceptual frameworks, literature findings, interviews, online observation and data analysis. The findings, conclusions and recommendations relate only to Alizee for the markets that this study covers. Furthermore, the qualitative approach to this research does not provide a statistically representative sample to allow general conclusions to be made for the whole population of each market studied.

On the basis of the research findings, a number of conclusions can be made with respect to the cultural dimensions that influence the online behaviour of online consumers. Firstly, it would appear that the cultural dimensions as defined by the GLOBE project are a good instrument for understanding the social components, personal components and psychological components of individuals in a country. Secondly, however, it seems that when consumers approach airline services in the online environment, they do so on the basis of cultural constructs that do not necessarily follow the GLOBE study's results.

As can be seen in Table A1.1.2, Javidan *et al.* (2005) refer to the GLOBE results for each of these countries: Brazil (cluster Latin America), Malaysia (cluster Southern Asia) and the USA (cluster Anglo). The data used in this table is based on findings of the GLOBE study with respect to the perception of society 'As Is', and only gives the scores for the first group of variables which were explored in the present case.

Table A1.1.2 **Relevance of cultural dimensions according to GLOBE study (Javidan, 2005)**

Dimensions	Brazil	Malaysia	USA
Power Distance	High	High	High
Performance Orientation	Low	Average	High
Uncertainty Avoidance	Low	Low	Low
Future Orientation	Low	Low	Low
Institutional Collectivism	Low	Average	Low

Using just the results of the in-depth interviews, the case shows which cultural dimensions are relevant for Alizee when it comes to using online channels.

In short, the cultural differences that influence consumer interaction with digital channels and stimulate transactions in the USA, Brazil and Malaysia markets for the airline industry have been explored throughout this research. Each of the markets presents a different profile of consumption of digital channels on the basis of its cultural dimensions and the dynamics of the airline industry in the market. The conclusions of this research are intended to provide Alizee with a cultural-based perspective of how cultural effectiveness can be applied when these different markets are approached.

We stated earlier that this research is intended to provide input on the three focus markets for Alizee. The cultural differences found in these markets that stimulate conversion cannot be extrapolated and applied to other markets. However, we consider it absolutely necessary to continue studying those differences in the markets where the company operates since these cultural dimensions can help Alizee to improve the efficiency of its online operations. We also recommend keeping track of the online activities of the home carriers in their markets to understand the differences between what they do and what Alizee does. Moreover, we recommend that Alizee's best practices be examined and compared with the cultural profiles of the countries covered in this research. Finally, we believe it is important for Alizee to maintain contact with consumers using a qualitative approach, thereby enabling ongoing input on the basis of their cultural perspective.

References

Air Transport Association of America (2010) *Economic Report*. (http://www.airlines.org/Documents/economicreports/2010.pdf)

Boyce, C. and Neale, C.B. (2006) *Conducting In-Depth Interviews: a Guide for Designing and Conducting In-Depth Interviews for Evaluation Input*, Watertown, MA: Pathfinder International.

House, R.J. *et al.* (eds) (2004) *Culture, Leadership and Organizations: the Globe Study of 62 Societies*, Pennsylvania: Sage.

Javidan, G.K. (2005) 'Cross-border transfer of knowledge: cultural lessons from project GLOBE', *Academy of Management Executive*, 59–76.

Patton, M.Q. (2002) *Qualitative Research and Evaluation Methods* (3rd edition), Thousand Oaks, CA: Sage.

Wiseman, D.B.-B. (2012) *The State of Social Business: the Airline Industry 2012*, Darlinghurst, Australia: Headshift Asia Pacific.

Part One Final activity A1.2

This final activity is based on a research paper which takes a practical approach towards investigating cultural relations. This approach could be used as a framework for readers who intend to study the relations between employees from different cultural backgrounds who are working in one company.

Learning outcomes

After reading the research paper and doing your assignment you will:

- Gain insight into how cultural sensitivity can be assessed through careful, sensitive questioning.
- Understand how essentially qualitative data can be interpreted in a reflective manner by a team of interviewers from different cultures who have themselves undergone considerable international exposure.

YOUR ASSIGNMENT

The research paper below investigates how representatives of three European cultures cope with each other's cultural differences when they are working together.

The assignment involves the following tasks:

Task 1. Make the research design of this paper: methodology (why), gathering data (who, how, what) and represent the results (section 4) by means of a graph.

Task 2. Discuss the representation of the data, as well as the analysis and interpretation that the researchers made.

Task 3. Compare the categorisation used in section 7 of the paper with other research methods described in Part One and indicate their respective advantages and/or disadvantages.

Final Task (optional). Devise a small-scale research task on cross-cultural behaviour, as explained at the end of this activity.

Now read the paper below.

RESEARCH PAPER

Galderma: a joint venture between L'Oréal and Nestlé

An empirical study of cross-cultural relations between French, German and British managers in an international company.

By M.-J. Browaeys, R.L. Price and C.R. Seifert
Revised research paper no. 8, Nyenrode University Press

1. INTRODUCTION

In the light of continuing European integration – economic and otherwise – the aim of the investigation was to gain insight into how three dominant members of the present-day European Union – the German, French and British – cope with each other's cultural differences when working together. The starting-point was one company in which the three cultures mentioned were working together, and had been doing so since the company came into being. It was hoped that the results of the investigations, outlined below, would lead to a framework that could be used when examining other companies operating internationally.

2. GALDERMA INTERNATIONAL

Galderma International is the first co-operative venture between L'Oréal and Nestlé. Started in 1981, it is an international company selling skin preparations and products to dermatologists on the world market. The company's initial range of products consisted of those produced by Alcon, Nestlé's US subsidiary, and those developed by L'Oréal. As well as having research and development centres in France, the US and Japan, Galderma produces products at its plants in France and Canada. Galderma's parent company is in Switzerland, with corporate services in Paris. Galderma employs 2,300 people in 33 fully owned subsidiaries worldwide. Among its European subsidiaries are those in France, Germany and the UK.

The management of the holding company is staffed by several nationalities, as is the laboratory. The interviews carried out by the researchers (who each represented one of the three cultures under investigation) took place at the Paris headquarters, at the R&D centre at the technology park of Sophia Antipolis near Nice in southern France, and at the German subsidiary. In Paris, the chief executive (président-directeur général) of the company was interviewed, as well as all members of the board of management. In Nice, all those people in managerial positions were interviewed, with one exception; in Germany, the director and product portfolio manager. In total, 13 managers were interviewed.

3. INTERVIEW METHOD

The interviews revolved around open-ended questions about how the managers in question interacted with managers from other nations within their specific working environment. In particular, they were asked to give their perceptions of the two other cultures involved in the research and to give their own perceptions of their own cultures in the eyes of the other cultures.

The interviewees were not asked a standard list of questions, although a number of basic questions were composed beforehand to serve as a framework for each interview. The interviews were carried out in the interviewee's native tongue in such a way that the experiences of the subjects were drawn upon to a maximum, with minimum influence from the interviewers as to the nature of the answers given.

The responses were then considered, reflected upon and analysed by the interviewers, each of whom represented one of the three cultures in question. During this stage of the research, the interaction of the differing perceptions relating to the researchers' cultural backgrounds acted as a control on the subjectivity of the final analysis.

4. THE MANAGERS IN QUESTION

4.1. Their background

All the managers interviewed had undergone a university education in science and/or management studies, part or all of which had been taken abroad. They had all worked outside their home country before coming to work at Galderma. The majority of them had worked in two foreign countries, one of which was the US, one in Europe. All had English as their native or second language.

4.2. Their perception of other cultures

During the interviews the various nationalities present in the managers' working environment came up for discussion. The comments that the interviewees made are given below, arranged in terms of the particular cultural aspects touched upon.

a) The French view of the British

All the French managers interviewed in the company commented on how the British communicate. The comments ranged from 'their soft expression' through 'they don't always say what they mean' to 'you have to decode what they say'. These comments applied to situations where the code of communication was English or French. Some remarks focused specifically on the communicative behaviour of the British when operating in English. One particular comment reflects the tenor of others given: 'They tend to bring considerable nuance to their expression, which frequently begs the question: "What are you trying to say exactly?" '

This behaviour led one of the French interviewees to say that it was sometimes necessary to treat the British in a gingerly fashion, to use kid gloves, to be less direct in communication with them than they would wish. If criticism had to be given or disagreement expressed, the interviewee felt obliged to be very careful in finding a form that would not cause the British to feel too offended.

Another interviewee concluded that there was a general lack of understanding between the two nations. Deep in the collective unconsciousness of the French, he said, there was an incomprehension of the British that has to do with the feeling that they still remain the traditional enemy of the French, despite 'ententes cordiales', 'rapprochement' and other diplomatic manoeuvres.

Most interviewees commented on the need for the British to make their presence felt, to be regarded as important within the company. 'They enjoy a position of power and enjoy reminding others of the power they possess', was one typical comment. One interviewee talked of their wish to 'recreate the world', i.e. the tendency to fantasise about how the department/company/country/world would be like if they had total control. This was something they tended to do in the company of other Anglo-Saxons when drinking in a local bar after finishing work. Several interviewees described the behaviour of the British in the company as *fanfaron*, which implies that they display a certain boastfulness when talking of their role in the company.

As for their general effectiveness in the company's operations, the general impression drawn from the interviews was not positive. Several respondents made the point that, although they may be effective in helping to determine policies, they lack effectiveness when carrying them out. One person talked of how her English colleague preferred to delegate implementation of a policy if it was likely to meet resistance among members of the department. Another talked of a lack of courage in seeing matters through. He talked of a lack of *rigueur* – the British being 'wishy-washy', either because they did not know what they really wanted, or because they were afraid to commit themselves to an action or decision that might later rebound on them. Another interviewee went further by saying that the British were known to have gone back on decisions they made or supported earlier. This view was contested by another respondent who maintained that if the Brits made a 'gentleman's agreement', they always stuck to it.

Comments made by three interviewees on the British attitude to work shed further light on the question of the general effectiveness of the British in the company. One said bluntly: 'They don't work'; another said they were not *travailleur*; another: 'They stop work at 4 p.m.' (the French tendency being to work until 6–7 p.m.). All three were positive about the essential friendliness of their British colleagues, but essentially wished they would talk less and work more.

Another aspect concerning working with colleagues is highlighted by two comments on the difficulty the British have in dealing with female colleagues. The Brits, they maintained, were not used to dealing with women who occupied a similar position to themselves in the hierarchy, and have even greater problems with women who are above them.

One interviewee summed up his experiences with the British by saying that they were not international, but rather members of an exotic island race that just went its own way – on the left-hand side of the road!

b) The British view of the French

A common thread in all the comments given by the British interlocutors was the bureaucratic administration of the French. The headquarters of Galderma as well as the laboratory are situated in France, and both are subject to French law. The criticisms relate to the bureaucratic nature of public employees in civil administration and the health sector in particular.

For one respondent, the battle with French bureaucracy is the focus of his activities with the company, although he is rarely in face-to-face contact with the bureaucrats themselves. Instead, he devises strategies to outsmart his adversaries, and uses French nationals to carry them out. A number of respondents referred to their experiences with bureaucracy elsewhere in the world and conceded that the problems they had undergone or were undergoing in France caused no particular irritations.

In relation to the above, one respondent talked of the 'bloody-mindedness' of the French, another of their individualistic nature. The former explained that this had to do with excelling within a very rigid hierarchical system; the latter explained that working together with others was not a particular strength of the French. He attributed this to the fact that, unlike the British, the French did not have sport as part of their school curriculum. 'Sport encourages team-play', he added, 'and this is something which the British are good at doing'.

The same two respondents talked about dealing with the French at meetings. Although both considered themselves proficient in the French language, there were times, they admitted, when it was more convenient for them to go into English if they wished to communicate effectively. This often put the French at a considerable disadvantage: the subtlety of the English language was something only native speakers of English could use, and something the French colleagues could neither use nor appreciate. The result was, they admitted, occasional miscommunication and misunderstanding.

A further respondent, who said he made a point of speaking in French at all times, found that the French could display strong emotions at such meetings: one moment they were 'up in the air', the next they were calm. This 'roller-coaster' of emotions was something he found difficult to deal with: 'When I explode – which isn't very often – I tend to stay up in the air for the rest of the meeting. When this happens the French sometimes find it difficult to deal with me.'

Another interviewee would not be drawn into defining what was typically French in the behaviour of his colleagues. 'There are no French,' he maintained. He acknowledged, however, that to become partially integrated into French society it was essential to have some knowledge of French culture. He meant essentially French classic literature and referred specifically to Voltaire, Racine and La Fontaine.

Just as the French see the British as being imperious in nature, so the British see the French as being nationalistic. One manager added that they were protectionist about their presence in this international company – a recent round of staff cuts involving French employees had provoked considerable local publicity, although a further round involving non-French employees had caused hardly any reactions. Another manager added that the French encourage the non-French to take an active interest in their culture and language – 'they need to justify their culture'.

c) How the British think the French see them – and vice versa

Not all respondents were able to deal with this area, preferring instead to talk in terms of personalities. One manager, however, did make remarks concerning the French view of the British. The French, he said, tend to think of the British as being rather pragmatic in their ideas – they prefer the concrete to the 'airy-fairy'. This point was pursued by another respondent who said that the French found it difficult to talk in English with the British about 'concepts'. They considered French a much more suitable language for discussing more abstract matters than English. A third manager thought his French colleagues found him rather phlegmatic. While they expressed their opinions/feelings in no uncertain terms, he tended to hold himself back.

As for the French, one respondent talked of the British reaction in the UK to his critical comments about the role of Britain in the EU. 'They were scandalized by my open criticism', he said, adding that he felt the British thought he was being much too outspoken. Moving on, he talked of certain prejudices the British have towards the French – 'a certain envy' was how he put it, particularly of their lifestyle.

d) The French view of the Germans

Two contrasting views appeared to predominate in the company, one based on the stereotype image of the Germans, the other on the presence of one German manager who was seen as the very opposite.

The stereotype image is reflected in comments such as 'their authoritarian character', 'their pride in themselves', 'their rigidity', 'their imperious nature' and 'their monolithic presence'. Despite these remarks, there was a general feeling, expressed and implied, that working with the Germans was not too unpleasant an experience. This is based on comments such as 'they may be somewhat rule-bound, but at least they are easier to understand (than the British)', 'you can count on them, even if they are rather direct'. 'My contacts with the Germans may not have been very warm, but at least they get things done.'

Several respondents raised the matter of lack of warmth in day-to-day contact. One manager commented on the tone of voice used by the Germans as being sometimes unpleasant. She referred in particular to requests which a German manager makes in French on the phone. These tended to sound more like orders, particularly with the more direct modal forms being used. The same respondent said this would be bearable were it not for the lack of 'chit-chat' preceding the request. The expectation on the French side is, therefore, that the channel of communication be carefully prepared. If not, the imperative nature of the request is all the stronger.

One particular feature of the Germans that received some attention in the interviews was their very careful approach to business, careful both in the sense of being very precise and accurate, as well as in the sense of being conservative, reluctant to take risks. One interviewee gave a concrete example of this behaviour in relation to the sales forecasts of the German subsidiary for one particular product. He said the subsidiary had been told to sell this product, although the Germans had doubts about its potential success as a result of their own marketing research. Their reservations were clearly expressed in the low sales forecast for this product they sent to headquarters. 'When actual sales turned out to be ten times the number forecast', he added, 'the Germans were delighted and proud to have achieved such wonderful sales figures!'

The interviewee in question called such conservative forecasting 'sandbagging', thus implying that the Germans were prepared for the worst by presenting such modest sales forecasts. This sort of behaviour naturally put the Germans in a good light, he said somewhat scornfully, when the estimated and actual sales were compared at headquarters. The downside, however, was the fact that the German subsidiary ran out of stock after a while, and could not meet demand.

This essential prudence, as it was called, contrasted strongly with what the same respondent called the French preference for 'bold strokes'. Several other managers talked admiringly about the German *Gründlichkeit*, but at the same time remarked upon the disadvantages this brings: 'stick-in-the-mud attitudes', a 'reluctance to take our [French] creativity seriously', the need to 'argue till the cows come home before you can convince them'.

One manager said that this view of the Germans predominated and that the Germans were aware of this. As a result 'they work twice as hard to prove that this [authoritarian, inflexible] image is not a true one'.

As said earlier, one German member of the management team was considered to be different. He was regarded by several French interviewees as 'soft', thus an anti-authoritarian figure, a 'Green' who was ecologically aware.

e) The German view of the French

The comments recorded in this area were limited and further interviews need to be made. Nevertheless, the following observations are worth noting.

'The French', one interviewee remarked, 'are more concerned with ideas than with detail. They are not particularly thorough, have a certain disdain for detail – and this can be somewhat vexing for someone who is concerned with getting things right.' Related to this was the following comment: 'The French are very good at defining goals, but are not particularly concerned as to how the goal should be reached.'

Favourable comments were expressed by three interviewees about the French lifestyle, although the fact that life is family-oriented makes it difficult to integrate. The less disciplined ways of the French were also commented on – the lack of punctuality was appealing to one, more of an irritation to another. One German commented on the influential role of the French *grandes écoles* and the preponderance of their graduates in top management not so much on the basis of merit, more as a result of their simply being graduates of these schools.

f) The British view of the Germans

The views expressed by the French on the contrasting German images were frequently reflected in the observations made by the British managers. One manager, when talking about his German colleague said: 'X is the exception to the rule' – and went on to give the stereotype image of the Germans as portrayed by John Cleese, the British comedy actor who has portrayed the Germans as goose-stepping, authoritarian, Hitleresque figures. Other descriptions of the typical German were: 'the regimented, inflexible type', 'the worker who goes by the book – if it's not in there, he doesn't know what to do'.

In line with the French observations made earlier, two managers talked of the immense effort made by the Germans to integrate. One said that despite all these efforts, X is still perceived as being Germanic in character; the other said that Y was pursuing with some success an 'affiliatory style of management'.

One gut reaction made to the question concerning Germans and their colleagues in general was: 'The French do not like the Germans.'

g) The German view of the British

One interviewee expressed exasperation with the British. They were seen as great fun to be with – their social lifestyle and sense of humour being very enjoyable. They were masters of communication in their own tongue, and it was fascinating to see how they used their language to such great effect. On the other hand, on the basis of experiences with the British subsidiary, it was not always possible to rely on them. The managers there, he remarked, were extremely co-operative and 'promised you heaven', but the realisation of these promises depended on others who lacked the same commitment. Promises were therefore not always kept. Moreover, their skill in English was frequently used to conceal their real thoughts, so it was occasionally necessary to read between the lines to get at what they were really thinking. A very difficult task.

5. A CLASSIFICATION OF THE INTERVIEWEES AT GALDERMA

5.1. Graphical representation of interview results

On the basis of their individual reflections on the responses, each interviewer allotted a score ranging from 1 (low) to 5 (high) to the persons interviewed. The score consisted of two numbers: the first represented the degree of perception which, it was felt, each interviewee had acquired concerning his/her own culture; the second number reflected the degree of perception that the interviewee was judged to have reached vis à vis other cultures. Once the interviewers had deliberated with each other over the individual scores they had allotted, a median score was awarded to each interviewee and plotted (Figure A1.2.1).

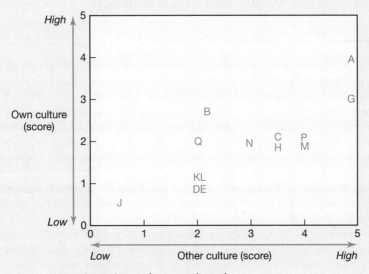

Figure A1.2.1 **Interviewees' scores plotted**

5.2. Initial observations on the graph

The graph shows that the majority of the interviewees have, in our judgement, a rather high score when it comes to their perception of other cultures. When it comes to their own culture, however, the degree of perception is generally lower.

The top left of the graph, where a high degree of perception of one's own culture and a low degree of perception of other cultures is marked, is scarcely occupied.

The scores allotted to the majority of their managers at Galderma tend to be clustered around the centre of the figure.

5.3. Categorisation of the scores

The field on which the scores are plotted can be divided up into quadrants (Figure A1.2.2).

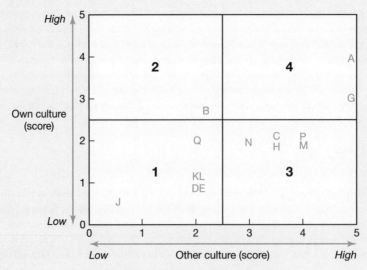

Figure A1.2.2 **Shared characteristics of interviewees**

The interviewees to be found in each quadrant can be said to share certain characteristics with regard to their cultural awareness.

Those in quadrant **1**, such as interviewee J, show great interest in the question topics, but became aware of the intercultural phenomenon only as the interview progressed. In quadrant **3**, interviewees such as M are able to analyse their own culture, but do so in an implicit manner by indicating ways in which another culture differs from their own. They talk at length about other cultures and display a high degree of perception, frequently using detailed examples drawn from their own experiences to support their analysis. They also attempt now and again to give explanations for the cultural attitudes that they have described.

In quadrant **4**, the two interviewees plotted – A and G – are both able to make a critical analysis of companies which are representative of their own culture. They explain how necessary it is to adapt one's manner of communication to that of the host country.

Just like the interviewees in quadrant 3, they are able to talk at length about other cultures, citing many examples. They go further, however, by characterising the cultures in terms of their professional activities and by explaining why they prefer to work with one culture rather than another.

Quadrant 2 has not yet been referred to since only one interviewee has been plotted there, B. This subject is, however, clearly set apart from the others. He deals with his own culture in terms of opinions and observations, but does not make any attempt to analyse it. He does show a certain interest in his culture, but his remarks are based more on intuition rather than reflection. He knows the other cultures which he presents in terms of clichés and *idées reçues*. He is very descriptive and categorical in his judgement.

After further reflection concerning the responses of these interviewees, according to the quadrants in which they have been plotted, it is possible to come to a concise definition of each of these four categories. This can serve as a framework for further study of managers working in international companies.

6. PERCEPTIONS OF THE MANAGERS: SOME CONCLUSIONS

6.1. The cultures remain

The responses to the questions and reflections upon them lead to a conclusion that, whatever insights they have displayed concerning themselves and their international colleagues, the interviewees remain essentially French, German and British.

This is an obvious conclusion, perhaps, but one that counters the comments of a number of those interviewed. One proclaimed: 'I'm a European'; another (French) interviewee stated: 'There are no French'; a third remarked: 'There are no differences between cultures; it's only a question of personality.' Such comments are not necessarily a denial of the culture in question, but more, we believe, a wish to show that the interviewee is able to exist, even flourish, in another culture and is not being dragged down by the ballast of his/her own culture.

Nevertheless the 'Frenchness', 'Germanness' and 'Britishness' remain, even though the interviewees had been exposed to other cultures, were living in other cultures and taking on board many of that culture's ways. Many respondents may be unable to say explicitly what it is to be French, German or British, i.e. to describe features of their cultural identity. These features are, however, implicit in the way they describe the other culture with which they are working.

6.2. Cultural sensitivity

Although section 4 presented the comments in such a way as to highlight some of the common threads woven through the individual comments on the cultures in question, it does not make clear to what extent the degree of cultural sensitivity varies from one respondent to another. This was therefore to be the next stage to the analysis.

This stage involved returning to the raw material of the interviews, reflecting on it carefully as individual interviewers and as a group of interviewers and assessing as carefully as possible the cultural sensitivity of each person interviewed. The questions which, it was decided, the interviewers should ask themselves were the following:

- To what extent is the interviewee aware of the cultural background of the colleagues with whom (s)he is dealing?
- To what extent is the interviewee aware of his/her own cultural background?

7. THE FOUR CATEGORIES: DISCUSSION

7.1. Definitions and comments

The four categories defined below correspond to the four quadrants on the graph in Figure A1.2.2.

Category 1

> People who have given little or no reflection to their own culture and therefore have minimal knowledge or awareness of it. The question of cultural differences has not occurred to them.

This category accounts for those who display a minimal degree of cross-cultural awareness. Such people have never considered what it is to be a member of a culture, are unable to describe what being French, German or British is all about. The fact that their culture may be different from others is not something they have ever had to deal with.

We encountered few representatives of this category during our interviews. This is not surprising bearing in mind that we were dealing with a collection of managers who had all had experience of living and working abroad. We would, however, expect to find many more representatives of this category in national companies with international ambitions.

Category 2

> People who have some knowledge of their own culture, but who have little or no awareness of the other culture(s) in question. They tend to be judgemental when there are cross-cultural differences.

A person belonging to this category is usually able to make general comments about his/her own culture and can refer to what (s)he considers to be typical features of the behaviour displayed. As for the other culture(s), the person in question is aware that (s)he is dealing with someone from a different cultural background, is familiar with some of the features of that background. When it comes to working with representatives of the culture(s) in question, the person is not aware of the influence that his/her cultural background has on their working together. Instead, the person tends to make judgemental remarks and opinionated comments on the other culture(s) without showing understanding of them.

Although only one respondent is clearly placed in this category, we would expect to come across many more representatives of this category in other companies.

Category 3

> People who are trying to adapt fully to the other culture, but do not reflect on their own culture while doing so.

The people in question here have clearly gained insight into the cultural background of the people with whom they are working. Their comments are perceptive and non-judgemental. They have adapted to their working environment. However, they have not gained insight into their own cultural background, have not perceived how the other cultures perceive them. Interaction with other cultures is perceived by their standpoint only, no account is taken of the other culture's perception of themselves and the reasons for this.

Category 4

These people adapt consciously to the other culture(s) while reflecting critically on the culture(s). They can function effectively in the other culture(s) while reflecting critically on their own.

A person in this category has reflected on both his/her own culture and the culture(s) encountered. A degree of awareness has been reached which enables questions to be asked such as:

'Why is X reacting that way?'
'Why is X causing me to react in this way?'

On the one hand, the person is attempting to account for what (s)he may consider to be abnormal behaviour in terms of the other's cultural background. This implies relating such behaviour to what may be 'normal' for the culture in question. On the other hand (s)he is also attempting to consider why (s)he considers this behaviour abnormal anyway. This therefore implies that the person is trying to elicit what (s)he considers to be 'normal' behaviour, i.e. behaviour that corresponds to his/her cultural norm.

This does not imply that such questions can be answered, but the fact that they are asked shows that the person is busy reflecting on his/her situation, on the interaction with those around. This very attitude puts that person in a position where (s)he is taking stock, coming to terms with the culture(s) in question and adapting where possible. If this is not possible, the person can ask 'Why cannot I adapt?' This critical reflection and further experience with(in) the culture in question may lead to an enhanced understanding of the person's own culture and the other culture. In short, one can talk of the person moving along a spiral of experiential learning, referring constantly to the person's own culture and that of the other(s).

7.2. Some reservations

The problem with such a categorisation is, of course, its seductive simplicity. People are forever attempting to characterise facets of human behaviour, and this could be seen as another vain attempt. Moreover, these categories of cultural awareness cannot adequately deal with the process each individual undergoes when dealing with other cultures. The interviewers themselves recognise the complex nature of this process, one which involves posing questions about one's own culture as well as about the other(s), coming up with hypothetical answers to these questions, trying them out, finding other answers if the original answers do not appear to be valid, trying these out and so on. Gaining awareness, then, is an erratic to-and-fro between one's perception of one's own culture and the other culture, during which differences are determined, reflected upon and in some way accounted for.

Nevertheless, the categorisation does give some indicators of what the interviewers believe to be the degree of sensitivity attained by the subjects questioned. Moreover, this categorisation can be used as a somewhat primitive instrument with which to examine the degree of cross-cultural awareness of individual managers as well as the composition of a management team when other companies active in international business are being investigated.

FINAL TASK (OPTIONAL)

Imagine you are asked to do a small-scale research project aimed at exploring one particular aspect of cross-cultural differences within a small group of people from different cultural backgrounds. The cross-cultural difference could relate to one of the management tasks featured in Concept 6.1. Assume that you need to combine both qualitative and quantitative elements in your approach to the task.

Prepare an outline proposal for your project to include the following:

1. The background to the research project

2. The problem statement

3. The research question(s)

4. The conceptual model which you intend to apply

5. The research methods which you intend to use (how you will collect the data needed).

Part Two

CULTURE AND ORGANISATIONS

Introduction to Part Two

By examining the effect of culture on organisations, this part aims to develop the cross-cultural competence you need for working in international business. This cross-cultural competence involves being aware of:

- the impact of culture in the international business environment, particularly the issue of cultural diversity.
- the influence of culture on companies operating in the global market-place, particularly on the way they are led.

A small case study for starters

An appropriate way of starting the examination of managerial competence within a context of cultural diversity is to consider the case of Mr Takahashi and the perfume.

Mr Takahashi and the perfume

Lekan, a large wholesaler specialising in interior furnishings, needed to boost its sales. Its domestic market was stagnant and its export sales, although increasing gradually, were not delivering the anticipated volume. The company desperately needed to make a large deal, preferably in the expanding Asian market.

After intensive efforts by its marketing department, Lekan was eventually contacted by a Japanese company, Ligato, which was interested in purchasing floor coverings. The two companies met on several occasions in Tokyo and a large deal was finally made. A dinner was arranged to celebrate the successful conclusion of business.

Mr Roberts, the senior sales manager who had headed the Lekan team of negotiators, had brought along gifts for Mr Takahashi, his Japanese counterpart. With heartfelt expressions of gratitude, Mr Roberts handed over a bottle of 25-year-old malt whisky and then Chanel perfume which, he said, was intended for Mrs Takahashi.

Mr Takahashi did his best to conceal his anger and disappointment. He left the celebrations, however, without signing the contract.

Why did Mr Takahashi react the way he did?

It was not the malt whisky that upset Mr Takahashi, but the present for his wife. In Japan it is not done to buy perfume for a woman because it implies that she has an unpleasant odour. Mr Roberts' present had been unintentionally insulting. Had he known how the Japanese perceived such a gift, then the deal could have been signed and sealed. Before we ask ourselves how best to prepare for this kind of situation, we need to look more closely at the context of cultural diversity and cultural competence.

The context in which a manager operates

It has been known for some time that the process of globalisation is a reality for business. The same is true of cultural diversity. People from different cultures interact with each other more and more frequently, not only on an international level, but also nationally and at local level.

Bearing this continuing globalisation in mind, Bartlett and Ghoshal (1989) came up with a model for the organisation of the future: the *transnational organisation*. As Concept 12.1 will describe in detail, this model has both the managers at company headquarters but also those in charge of the subsidiaries abroad being responsible for the co-ordination of units within the whole organisation. The transnational company, which combines the abilities of the multinational, global and international firm, now represents the territory of the modern manager.

Managers and professionals in such an organisation perceive the cultural diversity present as an opportunity, as long as they are able to handle it. This means that they need to learn about the methods and tools that will help them to optimise their skills. In this way they can eventually adopt the most appropriate attitude in a specific cross-cultural context. This acquired complex of skills is referred to as 'transcultural' competence.

Acquiring transcultural competence

To define a competence of this nature in detail, consider Figure II.1 based on the concept developed by Le Boterf (1994).

This model shows *knowledge* on one side and *know-how* on the other. People develop competence via a combination of knowledge and know-how, which when combined through the channels of communication and human interaction helps to form the desired level of competence. To sum up, competence involves a full range of resources related to knowledge, skills and cognitive abilities. The ability to integrate these resources represents the key to

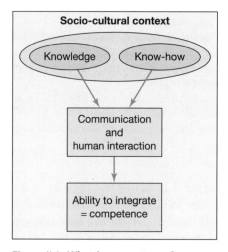

Figure II.1 **What is competence?**

competence. For Le Boterf, competence is at the heart of the complexity surrounding the ordinary and cannot only be defined as the capacity to solve a problem. In the context of management, Le Boterf sees this competence in the following terms:

> [. . .] the good manager is not the one who exhibits the same behaviour in all circumstances, but the one who knows how to modify management strategy according to the situations encountered.
>
> Le Boterf, 1994: 24

To return to Mr Roberts and the perfume, he will make sure that he is not confronted with the same situation again. He will investigate why Mr Takahashi did not sign the contract and learn more about Japanese business culture generally. Integrating this with his managerial know-how when he is interacting with his counterpart, Mr Roberts will then modify his behaviour according to the situation, especially since knowledge itself entails learning from experience.

Learning about cultures

An effective way of learning from experience is by studying examples. Just as in medicine and in human sciences, the objective of case studies is, in the first place, the development of the capacity to reason and not the achievement of a precise solution. Bearing this in mind, the primary function of the case study method is to learn how to deal with complex and non-structured problems. After an analysis of the situation, the effect can then be imagined of different actions in line with one's own experience in comparable situations.

The case study approach is directed at the development of cognitive abilities of an individual such as structuring knowledge, reasoning and problem-solving, as well as the learning process itself. The most important factor, however, is 'memory' because it provides individuals with the ability to store information. All situations heard, read or studied, put together in the form of case studies, will find a place within a database. This database will form the knowledge of an individual. Know-how is all about calling on the right knowledge at the right moment to identify a problem.

This implies that the competence of a transnational manager will involve possession not only of the knowledge or experience in the field of cross-cultural relations, but also the development of a 'memory of cases'. A manager will draw on this memory to adopt the appropriate attitude in a given situation. This will eventually permit individuals to act at the right moment without thinking.

A special form of case study is the 'critical incident', such as the one given at the start of this introduction. Here, there is no need for a comprehensive case analysis. Instead, the reader is confronted with a specific situation, in a context with its own particular dynamics whereby the interaction between the people concerned is unique.

As Bosche (1993) remarked, we learn much more about culturally different people in the dynamics of their interaction than by learning about their cultural backgrounds; it is this interaction that is the motor of learning. Critical incidents are therefore particularly suitable for learning about cultures and, just as in Part One, will continue to be present in the activities of this part of the book.

We will now outline the various components of Part Two.

Chapter and concept overview

Chapter 7 Culture and corporate structures

This chapter examines the places that national culture and the business environment occupy in the notion of corporate culture.

- **Concept 7.1 Organisational structures.** This concept shows how models of organisational structure evolve in line with the changes in context and with the influence of cultural differences.
- **Concept 7.2 Corporate cultures.** The focus of this concept is corporate culture and its constituents. Various forms of classification are described which take account of the business environment and the national cultural setting. The notion of the cultural web as a metaphor for corporate culture is also reviewed.

Chapter 8 Culture and leadership

This chapter looks at the evolution of thought with regard to leadership, cultural elements involved in defining the role of leaders as well as attributes of leadership within and between cultures.

- **Concept 8.1 Different conceptions of leadership.** Having outlined the developments in Western ideas on leadership this concept looks at present-day thinking on the subject, particularly the influence of Japan and Eastern philosophies.
- **Concept 8.2 Leadership in a global context.** This concept considers cultural variables that may be contingent on leadership effectiveness. It then considers the question as to whether there are attributes reflecting 'good' leadership in the West that are to be found in all cultures. The global context of leadership is examined further, particularly with regard to the management of (potential) leadership talent.

Chapter 9 Culture and corporate strategy

This chapter addresses the role culture plays in determining strategy, especially strategic alliances in the global marketplace.

- **Concept 9.1 Cultural view of strategy.** The cultural factors involved in strategy are explored, as is the way national culture influences a company's strategy.
- **Concept 9.2 Strategic alliances and business cultures.** This concept deals with human factors – such as cross-cultural adaptation – when merging company cultures, as well as with the difficulties in all kinds of co-operation on the cultural front.

Chapter 10 Cultural change in organisations

Fundamental organisational change involves changing the culture of the organisation concerned. This chapter examines the role of culture in this process.

- **Concept 10.1 Organisational change as a cultural process.** Once the process of organisational change and the mechanisms involved have been presented, the concept considers the cultural insights needed for change to succeed.

● **Concept 10.2 Organisational change in a global environment.** This concept examines how external factors influence the culture of an organisation and presents an assessment instrument for diagnosing discrepancies between its culture and its business environment.

Chapter 11 Culture and international marketing management

This concept investigates the influence of culture on the marketing management of companies operating in an international and social networking environment.

● **Concept 11.1 Marketing in a cross-cultural environment.** Once the present-day approach to marketing has been addressed, one which involves the whole company, the question of intercultural marketing is discussed. This involves adapting products and marketing strategies to the international consumer.

● **Concept 11.2 Marketing communication across cultures.** The question of brands is addressed, their relation to national images, and how their meaning is managed across cultures, especially in commercial as well as social marketing advertising.

Chapter 12 Cultural diversity in organisations

This chapter addresses the general question of cultural diversity in organisations, the nature of the transnational organisation and the management of cultural diversity. It also considers particular problems which may occur at an ethical level in a multicultural environment.

● **Concept 12.1 Managing diversity in a global environment.** The concept examines ways in which managers can deal with cultural diversity as well as turn it to their advantage.

● **Concept 12.2 Diversity and transcultural competence in organisations.** The notion of transcultural competence is addressed, an essential component for managing cultural diversity effectively.

Final activities

Part Two contains two final activities:

1. **Making cultural profiles of brands.** The first of the final activities requires you to create cultural profiles of brands of your choice. Before doing so, you will read a study in which the cultural profiles of a range of brands are developed. The models used are adapted from the cultural model referred to in Part One.

2. **A case study** about a joint venture between two chemical manufacturers in South Africa presents strategic and cultural issues involved in such a venture.

What you will gain

After working through Part Two you will gain more insight into:

● The influence of culture on all aspects of the organisation: its structure, its leadership, strategy and marketing.

● The skills necessary for dealing competently with cultural diversity when operating in international business.

References

Bartlett, C.A. and Ghoshal, S. (1989) *Managing across Borders: The Transnational Solution*, Boston, MA: Hutchinson.

Bosche, M. (1993) 'La problématique interculturelle', in Bosche, M. (ed.), *Le management interculturel*, Paris: Editions Nathan: 31–48.

Le Boterf, G. (1994) *De la compétence*, Paris: Les Editions d'Organisation.

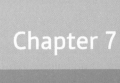

Chapter 7

Culture and corporate structures

This chapter describes the relation to be found between the structure and the culture of an organisation. This relation is a very close one because structure is not independent of culture but an element of the organisation's culture. To gain a better understanding of this relation, structure and culture have been separated into two concepts.

Concept 7.1 focuses on the forms of organisational structure and how these have evolved. This is because models change or adapt in line with new forms of organisation that emerge over time according to the context and influence of cultural differences.

Concept 7.2 refers to the classifications of corporate culture proposed by experts in the area of organisational culture. Such classifications are useful, although different forms should be put forward to reflect the different facets of an organisation's culture. It is this range of ideas that gives particular interest to this concept.

Learning outcomes

After reading this chapter you will gain an understanding of:

- The relation between the structure and the culture of an organisation.
- Forms of organisational structure.
- The levels and values of corporate cultures.
- The notion of the cultural web as a metaphor for corporate culture.

Concept 7.1 Organisational structures

The term 'organisational structure' describes the way an institution is organised to carry out its objectives and pursue its projects. It allows relations within the organisation to be formalised by describing the tasks, jobs and positions of its personnel, as well as the limits and responsibilities of the work units. It also indicates the kind of hierarchy within the organisation, the levels of authority and power as well as the formal lines of communication between the employees. In short, organisational structure forms the frame of the organisation's culture. That is why the structure of an organisation is used to analyse its culture.

Several variables influence the structure of an organisation. Size is one: if a company is small, it can be flexible and engage the whole staff in a range of activities. The business environment is another: the structure of a large-scale organisation, for example, will need to be more decentralised if it sells its products in many markets, whether they be regional or international. Another important variable is the influence internal and external factors can have on the organisational structure. Fatehi (1996) makes a distinction between internal requirements (the choice of technology, the type of activity being undertaken, the particular strategy pursued) and the external environment (external forces such as economic conditions, host governments and product-market characteristics) that influence an organisation's fate. The way internal and external forces are combined gives each enterprise a different structure, one that allows it to realise its particular goals.

Fatehi (1996), however, does not see any fundamental differences between multinational organisations and domestic ones, apart from the fact that multinationals need to take account of factors such as the physical distance between headquarters and the subsidiaries, their mutual relations and the legislation of the countries where the subsidiaries operate. The fact that multinationals operate across national borders means that the need for co-ordination and integration will be greater than in domestic organisations.

Forms of organisational structure

Generally speaking, two main types of organisational structures can be distinguished: a traditional hierarchical structure and a structure with several lines of reporting. In the former, the staff is divided up according to function, product, service or location; in the latter, the structure takes the form of a project team or assumes a matrix structure. For several years now, another form of structure has been making its appearance, one that has assumed increasing importance – the network structure. This form facilitates partnerships between organisations.

According to Fatehi (1996: 104): 'Functions, products and geographic areas remain the three basic models of organizational structure.' Bearing in mind these domains, he puts forward a detailed classification of five organisational structures which he defines as follows:

1. *Geographic structure.* In this structure, employees are grouped according to region in the broad sense (or country/continent if they are multinationals). At the head of each division there is a senior-level executive who shares responsibility for the area with the human resources manager. Headquarters maintains control of 'strategic planning' as well as control of the operations of each company. A number of regional divisions may retain the possibility of producing and selling according to local needs.

2. *Functional structure.* Here, responsibilities are arranged according to functional areas: at the head of each function – marketing, finance, research and development, etc. – is a senior manager who reports directly to the company's chief executive. Where a company has several product lines, the 'functional managers' do not always have the same objectives. These differences of opinion may be passed to headquarters, where executives could spend more time resolving such conflicts than they do making strategic decisions.

3. *Product structure.* The organisations using this model organise their staff according to product lines, which are in turn grouped according to product divisions. All the functions relating to the product being sold and the market being served are controlled by the

divisions. This structure allows a product to be launched simply through the creation of a new division. Although the rest of the company may be less destabilised as a result, such autonomous units can pose problems relating to control and co-ordination.

4. *Mixed structure.* This structure is often preferred by organisations that wish to extend their international business activities. They are looking for a form that allows different structures to be combined. Multinationals may wish, for example, to combine:

- area knowledge with product and functional skills; or
- the functional divisions with product divisions; or
- the geographic areas with product lines; or
- the functional skills with the geographic divisions.

5. *Matrix structure.* A matrix organisation does not follow the traditional hierarchy since it does not respect the principle that each employee has just one superior. Moreover, the management of this type of organisation acknowledges a lateral authority. The two 'lines' – functional and project – share responsibility. In general, this system facilitates the co-ordination and integration of projects, but it also has the disadvantage of relying on more managers (thus increasing costs) and of possibly increasing internal competition. This may, in turn, create conflict among people in the organisation.

SPOTLIGHT 7.1

Accountability: where does the buck stop?

A classic bureaucracy usually has a number of relatively independent business units reporting to head office. Head office prescribes the strategy for each of these components and checks that the strategy is being carried out. A certain decentralisation may be allowed, whereby the units fill in elements of the overall strategy and are responsible for monitoring the process but, essentially, the buck stops at HQ.

Philips, the Dutch electronics multinational, with a vast range of products and a growing number of markets worldwide, was one of the first companies to adopt a matrix structure. Hindle (2006) points out that the company superimposed geographical 'silos' on the company structure that cut across the traditional functional units. This meant that: 'The boss of the washing-machine division in Italy, say, would report to the head of Philips in Italy as well as to the washing-machine supremo in the Netherlands.' The basic problem Philips encountered with this sort of organisation was to do with accountability. Was the country boss (in the case of washing-machines the one in Italy) responsible for the profit-and-loss account, or was it the head of that product division in the Netherlands?

The tug-of-war between country bosses and product heads eventually resulted in Philips reorganising itself again in the late 1980s. Businesses were grouped together into units (built around products such as consumer goods, lighting and medical products). These units were based at Philips' headquarters and local operations ('national offices') were to report to the director of the unit in question.

Hindle (2006) points out that this structure has been modified slightly as a response to criticism that too much attention was being given to technology and the development of new products and not enough to the company's customers. Changes include the creation of the position of chief marketing officer. Moreover, collaboration between units is being encouraged and incentives have been put in place to get employees to move between geographical regions or product areas. This need to cross organisational boundaries has also been reflected in the running of workshops for top managers across the company to discuss issues that are of concern to the whole company.

Current thinking on other organisational structures

The organisational structures described above are still common. However, the phenomenon of globalisation has brought about the appearance of new organisational forms or adaptations of existing forms to keep pace with economic reality.

Network structure

This form of organisational structure has gained considerable favour, thanks mainly to developments in technology and a network's apparent ability to deal more effectively with global competition. Rather than being a pyramid hierarchical structure, a network has company units with a horizontal system of communication. This implies that responsibility and decision-making is dispersed to local subsidiaries and alliances (Deresky, 2003).

Network structures also have to do with managing the cross-cultural transfer of knowledge. Holden (2002) considers networking as an activity of cross-cultural exchanges of knowledge. This activity has the shape of a negotiation involving interlocutors being chosen and, at the same time, allowing access to the resources of organisations that are culturally or geographically different.

The practice of networking facilitates organisational learning and is the essential characteristic of a 'learning organisation' (see Concept 8.1 for a definition). Networking uses 'socio-interactive communication' to support the strategy and the mission of the organisation. This network is indispensable for companies needing to learn about the rapidly changing business environment in which they are involved.

SPOTLIGHT 7.2

Dealing with a network of individuals

The asset management division at Delta Lloyd changed a policy that affected organisational structures in an attempt to improve its performance and market position. Within the division, that was originally hierarchically structured in pillars, a 'shadow' organisational structure rose that would centre around six, so called 'business teams'. These teams were extracted from the existing six business lines.

Setting up business teams

At this division of Delta Lloyd, it was considered important that the business teams had a cross-functional character. Therefore, the teams were composed of various business functions: portfolio managers and information specialists of the specific 'business line', combined with sales representatives of fund sales and institutional sales, a marketer, a back-office co-worker and a technical product manager. The portfolio manager as representative of the business line was chosen as the captain of the team. The business teams had to function as autonomous internal think tanks demonstrating an open and accountable process of problem analysis, research, decision-making, implementation and evaluation. The teams were supposed to co-operate, to share visions and dilemmas with the 'established' organisation and to hold each other accountable for results and performance.

Source: extract from Fisser, S. and Browaeys, M-J., 2010: 61–62.

Transnational structure

Bartlett and Ghoshal (1989: 59) were among the first to propose a new structure that corresponded more effectively to the strategy of internationalisation among companies: the transnational structure. They argue that international enterprises must adopt a multifaceted strategy to respond to the complex environment within which they operate. In other words, they must opt at the same time for international, multinational and global strategies to become what the authors call a 'transnational company'. In such a company 'innovations are regarded as an outcome of a larger process of organizational *learning* that encompasses every member of the company'.

Such a company has the following characteristics:

- It is dispersed, interdependent and specialised.
- National units make differentiated contributions to integrated worldwide operations.
- Knowledge is developed jointly and shared worldwide.

Fifteen years after the emergence of the transnational organisation, the authors asked themselves about the future of this model: how must the transnational model evolve to respond to the needs of the future? (Bartlett *et al.*, 2004: 756). This question addressed predictions that the end of large worldwide companies was in sight, to be replaced by either more flexible small companies, or by 'virtual corporations' thanks to the evolution of technology. While maintaining the concept of the 'transnational company', the authors suggested that 'large companies' should no longer be described in terms of a formal structure divided into business, geographic and functional units, but in terms of processes. This description reflects more accurately a style of business management that involves the entrepreneurial process, the integration process and the renewal process. The influence of culture is to be found not only in the choice of structure, but also in the sum of processes occurring within the organisation. This implies that the managers have to adapt their attitudes and skills to their new roles.

Cultural diversity and organisational structure

In this sphere of internationalisation, relations between people from various cultural backgrounds are increasing and companies have to manage these differences. How does the organisational structure affect these differences? To what extent is cultural diversity reflected in organisations? Furthermore, how does cultural diversity affect a firm's strategy?

To address these questions, we can refer to the work done by Adler with Gundersen (2008, 2002). They investigated the impact of national culture and cultural diversity on organisations and the stages that organisations need to go through before they can call themselves global. One of the key observations they made was that, in present-day business, 'firms frequently skip phases in order to more rapidly position themselves to maximize their global competitive advantage' (Adler with Gundersen, 2008: 9).

They describe four kinds of organisation, each of which is not only an independent structure, but also one of the phases of development when going global. In addition, they give the results of their investigation on the importance of cultural diversity in these organisations. The order of the phases can vary from country to country; Figure 7.1 represents the most common evolution of North American firms.

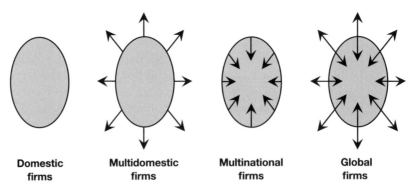

Figure 7.1 Organisational location of global cross-cultural interaction: internal and external

Source: Adler with Gundersen, 2008: 128.

1. Domestic structure

   Up to now, most firms with this structure have offered their products or services almost exclusively to the domestic market. If they sell their products abroad, it is because foreign customers want to buy their products. Such firms can therefore be said to have an ethnocentric perspective where no sensitivity towards cultural differences is apparent: 'Worldwide cultural diversity traditionally has not affected domestic firms' internal organizational culture' (Adler with Gundersen, 2008: 128).

2. Multidomestic structure

   The organisation is presented as a set of sub-units in several countries which operate autonomously. Unlike those with a domestic structure, each of these firms must take into account the particularities of the local market in which it is operating. Sensitivity towards cultural differences is therefore important when the implementation of corporate strategy is being considered. 'Cultural diversity strongly affects relationships external to the organization, given that it has both clients and employees in other countries' (2008: 128).

3. Multinational structure

   Owing to the geographical spread of this structure, diversity is inherent to the organisation concerned. Unlike a multidomestic firm, a company with a multinational structure has an internal organisation whose culture is affected by the cultural diversity present. That is why these companies attach great importance to managing multinational diversity within the firm rather than to managing cultural differences external to the firm.

4. The transnational (or global) structure

   Although many present-day companies may consider the multinational phase to be the final phase of development, and so continue operating according to its norms, there is a fourth phase into which competitive companies are moving. This final type of structure – the transnational structure, as described by Bartlett and Ghoshal (1989) – gives enterprises their 'global' status. This structure differs from the others through the fact that it generates its own evolution without having to rely on forces outside the enterprise. Heterogeneity, and all the problems it may bring, is indispensable. In this structure the global strategies of human resources become essential and the diversity present allows mutually beneficial relations to be created.

This classification takes account of the importance of cultural diversity when it is tied to a certain type of organisational structure. However, to be able to assess the effect on organisations of cultural diversity, it is necessary to explore this phenomenon in greater depth – see Chapter 12.

It must be said that the types of organisational structure given above are based principally on the Western model, which does not necessarily reflect practices and traditions elsewhere. Nevertheless, it is hoped that new structures will emerge – transnational as well as network structures – that allow organisations to respond more effectively to a complex global environment.

Concept 7.2 Corporate cultures

Concept 7.2 discusses models proposed by various writers that allow national culture to be given shape. It also examines the place national culture occupies in the notion of corporate culture. The focus is on the 'corporate' element of culture and on two key criteria: the business environment and the national cultural setting.

According to Deal and Kennedy (2000: 13), 'The business environment is the single greatest influence in shaping a corporate culture.' In other words, the types of industry in question, as well as the type of product and the markets involved, play an important role.

The national cultural setting also has an influence on how companies manage their business. The cultural assumptions with regard to the relations between employees and their organisation, the hierarchical system in place, the company's mission and aims, all these elements have an influence on the preference for a particular organisational culture.

Corporate culture and management

Most domains of management use the concept of culture. For strategy, culture is a diagnostic element and also acts as a framework of reference for instigating strategy. It is also a framework of reference in human resource management for the implementation of change and the involvement of the people in the process. Marketing has to do with the commercial culture of the firm and even finance shows the relation between cultural values and accounting systems. However, according to Thévenet (1999), it is still not clear whether the implicit values inherent in every management system are the same as those of the corporate culture.

If management is defined as an activity based on three aspects – action, the management of people, and the achievement of objectives – to what extent does culture affect management?

First, culture is of interest to management if it offers the possibility of increasing efficiency at various levels. If culture is taken into account, then the potential for analysis is greater and this allows the manager to explain how an organisation works before deciding whether it needs to be changed.

Second, culture helps to understand the organisation as an entity, as a collection of individuals who have together created a heritage of references based on the experience of the group. This serves as a framework of reference for situations in the future.

Finally, the company has a raison d'être: it is there to achieve certain objectives, to reach certain targets. It is management's task to achieve these by looking for behaviours that allow the best performance. Culture is also a source of behaviour and, therefore, a source of performance.

Levels of corporate culture

To define 'corporate culture', Schein (1999, 2009) starts with his general definition of culture and its three layers. According to him: 'The levels of culture go from the very visible to the very tacit and invisible' (2009: 21). He calls the first level 'artefacts', i.e. everything visible in an organisation: the structure, the way the offices are arranged, the office doors (are they open or closed?), the frequency of meetings, the way people dress. However, what is easily visible or observable does not always explain why things are as they are. Answers to questions such as 'why do they do what they do' allow people to gain only a certain understanding about the 'artefacts' and behaviour patterns. 'The first things you learn when you start asking questions is that the organization has certain values that are supposed to create an image of the organization.' (2009: 23). It is the second level, 'espoused values', that reveals the strategies, objectives and philosophies of the organisation.

Still, according to Schein, it could be that two organisations share certain values such as integrity, teamwork, customer orientation and product quality, without having the same visible behaviour. This shows there is a deeper level of thought and perception driving the overt behaviour. This is the third level, 'shared tacit assumptions'. The history of the company, all the values, beliefs and assumptions of its founder(s) and 'key leaders', as well as certain individuals or small teams that have made the company successful, all these elements form the culture of an organisation. If the organisation continues to perform well, then these beliefs and values are shared with newcomers and, through 'a joint learning process', they become tacit assumptions about the nature of the world and how to succeed in it.

In conclusion, Schein (2009) insists that cultural assumptions consist not only of the internal workings of a company, but also above all of how an organisation sees itself in relation to its environment. This forms the culture content of the organisation, which must:

- survive in the external environment (mission, strategy, structure, processes . . .);
- integrate human aspects (common language, relationships . . .); and
- take account of the national culture in which it is operating.

Corporate values

Other writers stress the importance of values. Deal and Kennedy (2000: 21), for example, consider that values – which they define as being 'the basic concepts and beliefs of an organization' – form the basis of corporate culture: 'Values provide a sense of common direction for all employees and guidelines for their day-to-day behaviour.' They add that 'rational' managers show little concern for the system of values of an organisation; they are more interested in its structure, policies and procedures, strategies or budgets. This lack of concern undermines both the leadership of the organisation as well as commitment. The everyday business environment, however, requires that choices be made and values are an indispensable guide for making such choices.

According to the same authors, three characteristics emphasise values and distinguish companies from each other:

1. The organisations have an explicit philosophy as to why they are conducting business.

2. The management places great importance on communicating the values that shape the company in terms of the economic choices and the business environment of the company.

3. These values are shared at all levels of the organisation, from the shop floor to the board room.

Identifying corporate cultures

Deal and Kennedy (2000: 15–16) are among the first to examine in detail the phenomenon of corporate culture. Their book is intended primarily to serve as a primer on cultural management for business leaders. Using concrete examples taken from companies that, according to them, know how to manage their culture, they examine the role of the leader as a 'mediator of behaviour' and the positive effects of building culture. The main belief is that a company is not only a place where things are produced, but also an institution whose principal resources are people. And it is these people who manage themselves by using 'the subtle cues of a culture'. A strong culture – which they see 'as a system of informal rules that spells out how people are to behave most of the time' – allows the behaviour of people to be guided and to 'feel better about what they do, so they are more likely to work harder'.

As stated in the introduction to this concept, the business environment in which a company operates has a considerable influence on the culture of the company. That is why Deal and Kennedy (2000) present a classification of the types of cultures on the basis of a study they made of various firms and their business environment. Using two factors – how much risk is involved in the firm's activities, and how much time is needed before a company and its employees know how successful their decisions or strategies have been – they distinguish four categories of culture. These categories provide a useful framework for classifying organisational cultures.

● *The tough-guy, macho culture.* This culture takes a lot of risks and quickly finds out whether its actions have been successful. A police force or a hospital can be seen as representatives of this type of culture. The construction or cosmetics industries, or even management consulting and the whole entertainment industry, are other examples, particularly since they have to deal with a lot of internal competition. This type of culture puts great emphasis on youth and speed. Decisions must be made quickly, even if there is a risk that they may not be the right ones.

● *Work hard/play hard culture.* This is a 'fun' and action culture with a tendency to pursue low-risk activities that give quick feedback. This culture is to be found in the sales department of a company or in a factory. The feedback is gained rapidly and everyone knows whether or not the work has been carried out according to the rules. There is a strict control system preventing big risks. This culture attaches particular importance to consumers and their needs. In contrast to the 'tough-guy' culture, which is 'find a mountain and climb it', the 'the work hard/play hard' culture rests on 'find a need and fill it'.

● *Bet-your-company culture.* This form favours high risk, but in an environment where feedback is slow. A lot of time passes – maybe months and years – before the employees see the benefit of the decisions taken by the company. This type of organisation may invest millions in a project that will take years before it is completed – or not. The risk of the company going bankrupt is considerable. That is why relations within the company are such that discussions are encouraged to make sure that the right decision is taken.

- *The process culture.* There is little feedback within this sort of culture, and the activities are low-risk. This is typical of banks, insurance companies and financial departments, as well as in highly regulated industries such as pharmaceutical companies. As in the work/play culture, the financial interests are low but, unlike that culture, the employees receive no feedback. This lack of feedback forces employees not to worry about what they are doing but how they are doing it.

Analysing organisational cultures: the 'cultural web'

Any attempt to gain a clearer understanding of a culture of whatever kind involves identify-ing phenomena 'that are powerful in their impact but invisible and to a considerable degree unconscious' (Schein, 2010: 14). However, an examination of the artefacts, the visible structures and processes, may help to discern what Paton *et al.* (2000: 41) call a 'unique cultural blueprint which dictates how it interacts with its environment and manages its people'.

The 'cultural web', as devised by Johnson *et al.* (2008), is a tool which may help in the analysis of 'the behavioral, physical and symbolic manifestations of a culture that inform and are informed by the taken-for-granted assumptions, or paradigm, of an organization' (Johnson *et al.*, 2008: 197). The 'web' metaphor (see Chapter 1) is an apt one since it evokes an image of interwoven strands (elements), all of which are linked to the central idea (paradigm) of an organisation.

As Figure 7.2 shows, the **paradigm** is at the centre of the web and is the set of assump-tions which are taken as given within the organisation. To gain clearer insight into the paradigm it is necessary to draw upon the manifestations as depicted in the external ring of the figure. **Routines** are particular practices which occur as a matter of course in the organisation and which allow it to run smoothly. These are reinforced by **rituals**, certain formal events or activities such as in-company training courses, staff evaluation procedures, or less formal ones such as the Friday afternoon drinks with management. **Stories** are those told by employees to each other or to new recruits or outsiders, usually about past events in the organisation and the people involved. They can be about success as well as failure, but in essence 'summarize the meaningful and key aspects of an organization's past and tell people what counts as acceptable conduct today' (Capon, 2009: 151). **Symbols** of various kinds can have a functional purpose (furnishings, office size and layout, means of transport, etc.), but can also carry a meaning about a person's status or the power of (a group of) individuals. The **power structures** in place may reflect the importance attached to seniority, length of service and/or expertise. The **control systems** used show how the organisation is being monitored and so emphasise what is considered important. This can be through the way people are rewarded and/or the particular activities which are checked. The **organisational structures** display the hierarchies, both formal and informal, which are used and which identify the (power) relationships within management.

This web metaphor is useful in that it shows not only how the interdependency of cultural aspects but also how entangled these elements are. Furthermore the cultural web can also serve as a diagnostic tool when organisational strategy is being devised since it can

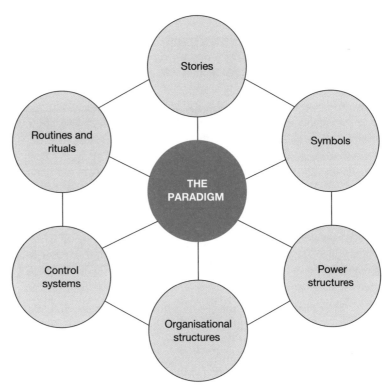

Figure 7.2 **The cultural web**
Source: Johnson *et al.*, 2008: 198 (adapted).

bring to light the cultural aspects which need to be addressed. It can help management determine which new cultural values, assumptions, attitudes and behaviours are needed for a new paradigm or mission for the organisation.

The issues around cultural change in organisations are dealt with in further detail in Chapter 10 where further diagnostic tools are explained. Suffice to say for the moment that the notion of the cultural web is not always regarded as an adequate image of organisational culture, particularly when it comes to change. Geertz (1973), for example, argues that if an image of organisational change is needed, an appropriate one is more that of the octopus:

> [. . .] whose tentacles are in large part separately integrated, neurally quite poorly connected with one another and with what in the octopus passes for a brain, and yet who nonetheless manages both to get around and to preserve himself, for a while anyway, as a viable if somewhat ungainly entity.
>
> Geertz, 1973: 408

Stereotyping corporate culture

Deal and Kennedy's classification model described earlier, whereby organisational culture is divided into four groups, has been taken up by other writers. Other criteria, however,

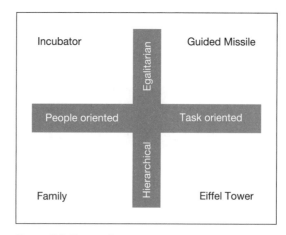

Figure 7.3 **Four culture types**
Source: Trompenaars and Woolliams, 2003: 106.

have been used for the classification. Trompenaars and Woolliams (2003: 101) dedicate a whole chapter of their book, *Business Across Cultures*, to corporate culture. They describe it as the 'driver' of the organisation: '"Management of culture" is now about creating a corporate culture in which people will work together to achieve the organization's goals, reconciling dilemmas that originate from issues of corporate culture.'

Just as in a society, an organisation is composed of individuals with different personalities who form and share a culture. Trompenaars and Woolliams (2003: 106–111) put forward a model based on 'organisational relationships' – those between employees, between employees and their superiors and the relations within the group as a whole. By using a model that combines two dimensions – task or person (high versus low formalisation), hierarchical or egalitarian (high versus low centralisation), they come up with four culture types:

- *The incubator* is like a team without a leader. Its main characteristics are that it is person-oriented and focused on self-realisation, commitment to oneself and professional recognition.

- *The guided missile* has a low degree of centralisation and a high degree of formalisation. It is task-oriented with a management by objectives approach and a focus on the power of knowledge/expertise, commitment to tasks and pay for performance.

- *The family* culture is characterized by a high degree of centralisation and a low degree of formalisation. It is power-oriented, with a stress on personal relationships (affinity/trust) and an entrepreneurial character.

- *The Eiffel Tower* has a high degree of formalisation together with a high degree of centralisation. It is role-oriented, with power attached to the position or role. The formality is reflected in the importance given to job descriptions and evaluations, rules and procedures, order and predictability.

To conclude this concept, Delavallée's standpoint (2002) appears correct, in that globalisation of trade, identical management and production techniques have narrowed the differences between companies. What remains different is the culture of each company. That culture exists in its own right and, being the result of the company's history, belongs to it alone. Unlike a production method, a corporate culture cannot be copied. That culture is a way a company can differentiate itself from its global competitors. Therefore, if the company has adapted to the demands of its environment, culture remains the most effective way of maintaining a lasting competitive advantage.

This chapter has presented two ways of categorising companies according to their structure or culture. It would be worthwhile investigating a possible correlation between the two to see if certain types of organisation are more suited than others to developing specific corporate values inherent to a particular type of culture.

Conclusion

According to this chapter, in order to analyse the culture of an organisation, it is necessary to take into account its structure. There are many organisational structures, ranging from geographical and matrix structures through to network and transnational structures. The last two seem to lend themselves more to the globalisation of business. The choice of structure depends on the strategy and the mission of the organisation, as well as its cultural diversity. While cultural diversity has little impact on national organisations, it can affect structure at all levels in international organisations.

However, an organisation is not only characterised by its structure, but also by its specific corporate culture, one which can be analysed by means of the 'cultural web' metaphor. Deal and Kennedy (2000) show that the culture of a company is strongly influenced by its history, by the people who compose it, and also by its attitude towards the business environment. Therefore, the corporate culture of a company – even if it is somehow classifiable – has unique characteristics that differentiate it from others.

Points for reflection

1. An organisation's structure and culture are often seen as one and the same. Its structure is often given more serious consideration than its culture. If the size of the company increases or decreases, or if the business environment evolves, any consequent change – internal or external – often involves a change to the organisation's structure. Its culture, on the other hand, is often ignored or seems to be the last resort for dealing with the company's problems.

   Discuss the above statement and answer the question. What do the structure and the culture have in common?

2. Even if their classification systems differ, the scholars who introduced the concept of corporate culture, such as Deal and Kennedy, and Schein, describe the basis of corporate culture using the same criteria as those used for the concept of culture. As indicated in Part One, each culture can be seen as having three layers: the 'behavioural' or 'explicit' level; a second layer containing the 'norms, beliefs and values'; and a third containing its assumptions.

Because the systems of norms (what is right or wrong), values (what is good or bad) and assumptions appear to vary from company to company, what do you consider to be the possible purpose of organisational culture?

3. Johnson uses the 'web' metaphor to analyse organisational culture, since a web has interwoven strands all linked to the central idea (paradigm) of an organisation. Geertz, however, prefers the 'octopus' metaphor because of its ungainly nature and poorly connected parts.

Which metaphor do you consider to be a more appropriate reflection of organisational culture? Give your reasons.

Further reading

Bartlett, C.A., Ghoshal, S. and Birkinshaw, J. (2004) *Transnational Management*, 4th edition, New York, NY: McGraw-Hill. This edition reviews the overall content of the 1989 edition. The authors discuss transnational management and focus on cross-border companies and management. It provides a fulfilling and realistic approach to the management of today's multinationals.

Deal, T.E. and Kennedy, A.A. (2000) *Corporate Cultures: The Rites and Rituals of Corporate Life*, Cambridge, MA: Perseus. Despite the changes of business in the past two decades, this book, written in 1982, remains relevant. In their new introduction, the authors argue that the basics – the artefacts of organisational life and the shared values – are as strong as they were in organizations 20 years ago. Their work remains, as they say, 'still deeply committed to the embryonic ideas, launched a while ago and still viable today'.

References

Adler, N.J. with Gundersen, A. (2008, 2002) *International Dimensions of Organizational Behaviour*, 5th edition, Mason: South-Western Cengage Learning.

Bartlett, C.A. and Ghoshal, S. (1989) *Managing Across Borders; the Transnational Solution*, Boston, MA: Hutchinson.

Bartlett, C.A., Ghoshal, S. and Birkinshaw, J. (2004) *Transnational Management*, 4th edition, New York, NY: McGraw-Hill.

Browaeys, M.-J. and Trompenaars, F. (eds) (2000) *Cases Studies on Cultural Dilemmas*, Breukelen, Netherlands: Nyenrode University Press.

Capon, C. (2009) *Understanding the Business Environment*, 3rd edition, Harlow: Pearson.

Deal, T.E. and Kennedy, A.A. (2000) *Corporate Cultures: the Rites and Rituals of Corporate Life*, 2nd edition, Cambridge MA: Perseus.

Delavallée, E. (2002) *La culture d'entreprise pour manager autrement*, Paris: Editions d'Organisation.

Deresky, H. (2003) *International Management: Managing Across Borders and Cultures*, 4th edition, Upper Saddle River, NJ: Prentice Hall.

Fatehi, K. (1996) *International Management: a Cross-cultural Approach*, Upper Saddle River, NJ: Prentice Hall.

Fisser, S. and Browaeys, M.-J. (2010) 'Team learning on the edge of chaos', *The Learning Organization*, 17(1): 58–68.

Geertz G. (1973) *The Interpretation of Cultures: Selected Essays*, New York, NY: Basic Books.

Hindle, T. (2006) 'The matrix master', *Economist*, 21/01/2006, pp. 3–5.

Holden, N.J. (2002) *Cross-Cultural Management*, Harlow: Pearson Education.

Johnson, G., Scholes, K. and Whittington, R. (2008) *Exploring Corporate Strategy*, 8th edition, Harlow: FT Prentice Hall.

Paton, R.A. and McCalman, J. (2000) *Change Management: a Guide to Effective Implementation*, 2nd edition, London: Sage.

Schein, E.H. (1999, 2009) *The Corporate Culture Survival Guide*, new and revised edition, San Francisco, CA: Jossey-Bass.

Schein, E.H. (2010) *Organizational Culture and Leadership*, 4th edition, San Francisco, CA: Jossey-Bass.

Thévenet, M. (1999) *La culture d'entreprise*, Paris: PUF Que sais-je?

Trompenaars, F. and Woolliams, P. (2003) *Business Across Cultures*, Chichester: Capstone.

Chapter 7 Activities

ACTIVITY 7.1

Read the case study below about a joint venture between a Saudi Arabian and a German company, then answer the questions.

Bad blood

Our group, the Venture Group – a mother company in India, with as branch head, Mr Soota – received an offer to invest $2 million in a joint venture between Brigitte Zankyl GmbH in Munich and DXB-Al Fayed Corporation in Saudi Arabia. The proposed project was to build a plant in a small town near Riyadh to make blood transfusion tubes to sell in the Middle East. The German company had the technical expertise; the knowledge, capital and funding required was to be provided by our company. At this point, Venture was in the process of negotiating the contract.

DXB-Al Fayed was a partner in the business because it had managed to negotiate and win a favourable contract with the government for the purchase of the plastic tubes. The Saudi Arabian company was in a very comfortable position: it had no financial stake in the project and was a 35 per cent partner in the business by virtue of its good contacts with the Saudi government and its in-depth knowledge of the local market.

A few senior managers from our company were asked to go to Riyadh to explore the viability of the investment. Two weeks later, after our managers had returned, the company was more convinced than ever that this was going to be a wonderful project. We only had to wait for another three weeks since the German negotiating party was going to negotiate and conclude the contract after having received the necessary approval from us.

A large delegation of nine people, including lawyers from Germany, prepared themselves for the negotiations. On the first evening after negotiations had started, we heard by phone from the German side that things were looking good.

The next day, however, we received a call from the Saudi party. They informed us that they were not willing to sign any contract with the German party and, if possible, we should try instead to team up with them. Mr Habib commented on the phone: 'I am sure that we can work with you, but Mr Zankyl and Mr Kirchdorfer are people we do not trust! We get the feeling that they are trying to fleece us. They are trying to pretend they are doing us a big favour; they think they are lords, but Allah is there watching us all. There is no place for being crooked. We have tried to work with Westerners before and they always try to be difficult. The only solution I can see is that we contract with you: you run the project. We don't care if you outsource the technology and expertise from Brigitte Zankyl, but our only condition is that they do not become a partner in our business!'

Mr Soota was becoming concerned and, to try and diffuse the situation, asked Mr Habib to calm down. 'Mr Habib', he said, 'I apologise on behalf of my business partners in case there has been any misunderstanding. I am sure we can resolve the matter. Would you like me to fly down there early tomorrow morning so that we can resume discussions using a clean slate?'

Mr Habib appreciated Mr Soota's remarks, adding: 'I wish the German side could understand us as much as we understand each other. They do not care about what we think! All that matters to them is dollars, dollars and more dollars. Our esteemed minister Mr Sherrif gave us his word and promised us that, Insha'Allah, the government would sign the purchase contract next month, but the German lawyers told us that they would only like to see contracts in black and white and said that our word was not enough. Do they want to imply that, I, Sheikh Habib, am a liar? If they don't trust us, then I have to be honest and admit that we do not even trust them since business should be for mutual benefit and not dictated. I am sorry, but please do not expect me to respect somebody who thinks that we are dishonest and unprofessional in our approach. Mr Kirchdorfer said that our small family concern needs to gear up and act more professionally to manage the new project! But we know how to run our business – we don't need the Germans for that!'

Source: adapted from Browaeys and Trompenaars, 2000: case 4.

Questions

1. Why do you think Mr Habib did not want to do business with Brigitte Zankyl GmbH?

2. In his analysis, the author of the case proposes four reasons for explaining what happened. What do you think is the most likely reason?

   a) The two contracting parties had perhaps agreed on the first level of organisational integration but had unfortunately ignored the interpersonal and cultural integration aspect of organisational synthesis, which very much provides the necessary foundation for the success of any strategic alliance. Had both parties made a conscious and deliberate effort to understand one another as individuals with an appreciation for one another's cultural bearing, perhaps the matters would not have got out of hand.

   b) The Germans and the Arabs are at opposite extremes on the monochronic–polychronic scale, therefore communication did not take place in a normal manner. Furthermore, the exigencies of the Muslim religion often complicate the interchange of ideas even more. Yet, Arabs are used to dealing with foreigners and readily forgive them for not behaving like Arabs as long as they do not feel personally challenged and insulted.

   c) In the negotiations, when the German experts in finance, marketing and law met their Arabic counterparts, the Germans' approach was perhaps to try and clarify facts and determine who held the decision power. To the Germans, the Arabs appeared to be evasive and secretive, not revealing anything. For the Arabs, it was not just the 'facts' that the Germans seemed to be prying into, but also the mutual understandings between the leaders and themselves.

   d) Having a 'specific' culture, the German managers perhaps found it particularly easy to insult their opposite 'diffuse' Arab partners. This is because they do not understand the principle of losing face, which is what happens when something is done that people perceive as being private. It can be inferred from the scenario that perhaps Mr Habib would have felt very insulted in front of his colleagues if the German contracting party had demanded proof of his claims about the government order.

3. What would have been the most appropriate attitude for the Germans to adopt? Explain your choice.

   a) One serious pitfall for 'universalist' cultures (Germans) in doing business with the more 'particularist' ones (Saudi Arabians) is that the importance of the relationship is often ignored. The Germans saw the contract as definite, whereas the Arabs perhaps regarded it as only a rough guide or approximation. For the Arabs, relationships have a flexibility and durability that contracts often lack. Particularists get suspicious when hurried. It is important to create a sound rational and trustworthy basis that equates the quality of the product with the quality of the personal relationship.

215

b) As close working relations develop among the alliance participants, psychological contracts, based on trust and shared goals, replace the formal alliance agreement. Firms that are adept at managing strategic alliances use a flexible approach, letting their alliances evolve as conditions change over time. They not only allocate adequate resources and management attention to these relationships, but also integrate the organisations so that the appropriate points of contact and communication are managed.

c) The only solution for good communication for the 'linear-active' Germans should have been to make some concessions towards extroversion. Many find this difficult, even painful, but the rewards for doing so can be considerable. If people keep their distance, just like the Germans did in Riyadh, the Arabs will think that their own physical presence is considered distasteful, or that these people are cold individuals. Arabs speak volubly and earnestly to someone they like, so the contracting party should have also attempted to do the same. When talking business with Arabs, one must always do so against an intensely personal background.

4. What would you do next if you were in Mr Soota's position? Explain why.

ACTIVITY 7.2

Read the following article which examines the corporate culture at the Royal Bank of Canada. Answer the questions that follow.

The capital gained from culture

By Bernard Simon in Toronto

Gordon Nixon makes a point of escaping Canada's frigid winter each January for a Caribbean cruise. But the excursion is more work than pleasure for Royal Bank of Canada's chief executive. His 700 fellow passengers are RBC tellers, administrative staff, junior employees and middle managers who are being rewarded for superior performance.

Mr Nixon joins the cruises to put into practice the teamwork and mutual respect he has tried to foster among RBC's 73,000 employees in eight years at the helm of Canada's biggest bank. As he sees it, that culture has played a crucial role in RBC's ability – rivalled by only a handful of other large banks – to ride out the storms that have battered the financial services industry during the past two years. 'We don't tolerate fiefdoms and so forth', Mr Nixon says. 'Those are the sort of things that brought down a lot of organizations.'

Teamwork and 'doing the right thing for the organization' are non-negotiable elements of RBC's culture, Mr Nixon says. 'We can have the hottest-shot trader in the world, but if he doesn't comply with the culture and values of the organization, we don't want that person being part of the [bank].'

None of Canada's big five banks – the others are Toronto-Dominion, Bank of Nova Scotia, Bank of Montreal and Canadian Imperial Bank of Commerce – has escaped the turmoil unscathed. Even so, the Canadian banks are emerging from the crisis in better shape than most of their rivals elsewhere in the world. They have survived without any infusion of government money, and have relied far less on liquidity support than US and European lenders. All five have maintained their dividends.

Mr Nixon, 52, has a reputation as a level-headed manager. He joined Dominion Securities – at the time Canada's biggest brokerage firm – 30 years ago and stayed on after RBC acquired it in 1987.

He has spent most of his career in investment banking, including a three-year stint in Tokyo. RBC is gearing up to take advantage of its strong position. 'I think we've got a period here that's going to last at least two to five years where banks around the world are going to be shrinking their balance sheets when we have the ability to invest in all of our businesses', he says.

Asked what RBC will look like five years from now, Mr Nixon is noncommittal. 'In many ways that's a dangerous question because it was at the root of some of the problems that some banks had in the early part of this decade', he says. 'There's no hurry because there are going to be lots of opportunities and lots of restructuring in the financial services industry over the next five years. So if you do something, you want to make sure it's very sensible and very strategic.'

On the capital markets side, however, Mr Nixon says: 'We're not going to make an acquisition. We're going to grow it by continuing to do what we've been doing for the past five years – which is to hire people, hire teams, extend our balance sheet, build our customer base.'

A great believer in having the right person running each business

Gordon Nixon, Royal Bank of Canada chief executive, traces RBC's good fortune to its conservative culture. In the late 1990s and early this decade, he says, there was a 'pretty significant shift'. The bank wanted to make sure that 'where we were extending our balance sheet, we were being paid for it' and that in each case the client decision was sensible. 'We weren't going to lend our balance sheet to a customer in Europe who Royal Bank had no relationship with simply because there was an opportunity to lend money and to earn a return.'

Mr Nixon says he is 'a great believer in ensuring that you've got the right person running your businesses and giving them the rope to make mistakes but also to do the right thing'. But, he adds: 'You can't be afraid to make changes even when you've got good people.'

The former chief operating officer is now head of strategy. She has been replaced by a thirteen-strong operating committee.

Questions

1. Define the corporate culture of RBC using the models presented in Chapter 7.

2. To what extent does the behaviour of the RBC management reflect the Canadian business culture as outlined in Chapter 3, where this is compared to that of the US?

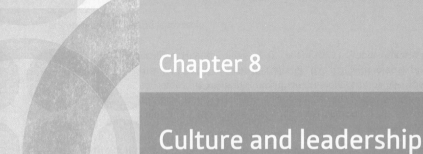

Chapter 8

Culture and leadership

The previous chapter examined types of company structure and the range of corporate cultures to be found within them. By gaining insight into a company's culture, managers can see more effectively how a company works and how it can improve its performance. It is this role of management in the cultural context that Chapter 8 will examine in detail. This involves looking briefly at (Western) theories of leadership and the recent influence of Eastern ideas on them, before considering the notion that assumptions about leadership are shared across all cultures. The global context of leadership is examined further, particularly with regard to the management of leadership talent.

Learning outcomes

After reading this chapter, you will gain an understanding of:

- Evolving ideas with regard to leadership, particularly those Western ideas influenced by Asian concepts of leadership.
- The notion that there are attributes of leadership shared across all cultures, even though these are perceived differently in different cultures.
- How (potential) leadership needs to be managed, both in the global and national context.

Concept 8.1 Different conceptions of leadership

Before examining the role of leader, it is necessary to look at the concept of leader. A number of theories about leadership have been devised over the years, most of which emanate from the US and Europe. They contain many definitions of the term in the business context, but most assume that leadership has to do with an individual intentionally exerting influence on others to structure the relationships in an organisation. Where definitions differ is with regard to how the influence is exerted and the outcome of the attempt to influence.

The first leader

The prototype leader in a business context is the entrepreneur who founds a company. That person will have a strong influence from the start. He/she will determine the mission of the company and the environmental context in which it operates. However, as the company grows, the company culture takes on a life of its own. The leader's pioneering work may have resulted in the establishment of routines in all aspects of the company's operations. Such routines/habits may, however, be difficult to break if there is felt to be need for change in response to a dynamic environment. The increasing size of a successful company and the consequent decentralisation of its operations may water down the power and influence exerted by those who have replaced the leader. This management team may not recognise the need for change when the company undergoes some sort of decline and may instead cling to power, preferring to keep things going as they have always done and blaming the environment for the change in its fortunes. Then it is up to the leader to re-assert his position and to instigate changes to revitalise the company. Or hand over the reins to a successor or new leader from the management team.

In recent history, it is the industrial revolution that spawned the founder/leader as well as the study of organisations. The next section will give a brief account of the development of organisation theory with emphasis on the role of the leader/manager.

The theories evolving around the leader

Research on organisations and the decision-makers focused originally on the organisation of work systems. The production process, including the increasing specialisation and division of labour emerging from the industrial revolution, was the focus of attention. What was the best way for a leader to get the job done in the most efficient way possible? This led to the development of **principles of scientific leadership**, whereby the questions of planning, organising, leading and controlling a group of employees were approached in a scientific way. Standard methods for doing a job were developed – the worker was not required to think, only the leader. Chapter 6 touched on these issues when examining cultural elements relating to the tasks of the manager.

Bureaucratic organisations were the eventual product of this approach to managing production processes, particularly as a response to much larger companies. In such bureaucracies the leader heads a carefully designed hierarchy of authority, where responsibilities are clearly defined. Functions within the organisation become specialised, information and control – centralised. The totally rational approach of this model is emphasised by the uniform application of standard rules and procedures. All employees play a role in this bureaucratic world that is totally separate from the one they play in their private lives. Examples of bureaucracies include not only government departments, the police and military, but also large companies.

Alongside these process-focused theories emerged ideas about the ideal leader. The first clearly definable trend was the **trait approach**, which took many ideas from historians, psychologists and sociologists. The theory was developed that some people have traits – and skills – which will make them seek out and reach positions of leadership and be effective in them, whatever the situation, whoever the 'followers'. Great leaders throughout history were examined and the features they had in common. Stogdill (1974), for example, reviewed studies of leader attributes and made a list of characteristics of a successful leader from different countries. These included:

- high intelligence;
- considerable verbal fluency;
- overall knowledge;
- considerable initiative involving energy, ambition and persistence;
- height: tallness implies authority!

The question of **human relations** within organisations only began to achieve prominence as a result of research carried out in the late 1920s and early 1930s. Attempts were also made to marry the scientific and human approaches by focusing on the role of the decision-makers. If they are to operate successfully, they need to find a compromise between rational, goal-oriented behaviour and non-rational behaviour among an organisation's employees.

Task orientation versus relationship orientation

With the shift to the human factor came a shift in emphasis with regard to the recipe for leadership success. The style of leadership behaviour became the base for analysis, particularly as to how leaders interacted with groups under various conditions. While a leader needs to remain task-oriented to ensure effective performance of the organisation, he has to be a relationship-oriented leader to ensure greater satisfaction among subordinates. The successful leader, it was maintained, managed to balance both task and relationship concerns. Maintaining this balance was necessary to ensure the effectiveness of the group.

The **X and Y theory** of McGregor (1960) gave a startling contrast between the task-oriented view and human-oriented view. The message accompanying this theory was that managers should take a more positive approach towards employees, delegate authority, making jobs more challenging, providing rewards for superior performance, and treating workers with respect.

Theory X is based on a pessimistic assumption that people have an inherent dislike of work and will do a lot to avoid it. They generally lack ambition, avoid responsibility and seek security in the workplace, lack imagination, creativity and initiative. The theory X manager is results-driven, demands rather than asks, has little interest in human issues, and shows little concern for the morale of the workforce. The X manager does not listen to suggestions for improvement, sees criticism as threatening, holds responsibility but is the first to hold subordinates accountable for failures.

Theory Y is based on an optimistic approach and assumes that people actually like working under suitable conditions; they are self-starters, willing to accept responsibility, are creative and imaginative. The Y manager believes people, under the right conditions, want to learn to accept and to seek responsibility. The Y manager wants employees to participate in decision-making and problem-solving – people's creativity can be used to solve problems and further the organisation's success.

One drawback to this approach was that it gave little consideration to the influence of different situations in which a leader may operate and how these affect the effectiveness of the leader. Theories were developed to try to establish the factors determining an appropriate match between leadership style and demands of the situation. The implication of this approach is that there is no universal answer as to what makes an effective leader. If there is one answer that can be given, it is 'it depends . . .'

Therefore, in the search of leadership effectiveness, the focus of the research being done in North America shifted from the person to the context in which leadership takes place. Fiedler (1967) established a new perspective on the study of leadership, and many studies since have adopted a similar approach.

Fiedler's **contingency theory** considers how performance of the workers in an organisation is the result of the interaction of two factors: leadership style and situational favourableness. Leadership effectiveness is the result of interaction between the style of the leader and the characteristics of the environment in which the leader works. This environment is characterised by three factors:

- Leader–member relationship: the degree of confidence, trust and respect.
- Task-structure: the extent to which it is necessary to spell out the goals, procedure and guidelines to the workers.
- Position power: the extent to which the leader or the group holds the power. The leader's power may be boosted by the expertise shown and the authority to reward or punish.

Fiedler (1967) presents two extreme situations, describing all the contingent factors:

- A highly favourable situation in which everyone gets along well, the task performed is clear and the leader enjoys considerable power. In this situation, all that is needed is someone to take charge and show direction.
- A highly unfavourable situation in which the leader has a battle of wills with the workforce and the task is not clearly structured. The leader needs to be strong to counterbalance the power of the workforce and to show direction in an ambiguous environment.

Cultural contingency factors

The one contingency not taken account of explicitly in Fiedler's theory, and that is culture: leaders may not be able to exercise all the variables described because of cultural constraints. Instead of being in a position to influence the workforce and the dominant culture, they may be forced to alter their own leadership behaviour to conform to the cultural realities they face. Managers working in an international environment may need to take account of cultural differences and adapt their style of leadership accordingly.

Two areas where cultural attitudes and values can obviously have a big effect on styles of leadership have already been touched upon in Part One: the wielding of power and the handling of uncertainty.

In those societies where **power** is more evenly distributed among the members, the difference between the more powerful members and the least powerful members is small. In those societies where there is a wide variation in power distribution, the difference between the most powerful and least powerful is large. Here, large differences in power are legitimate and acceptable. Should an attempt be made to reduce the distance between the leader and the workforce by increasing accessibility between the two and attempting to engender a friendly interaction, the subordinates concerned may well feel uncomfortable with these changes and may indeed attribute some sinister motive to the actions. In such an environment, subordinates' expectations have a considerable influence on whether certain leadership behaviours are feasible. In cultures where there is a large power distance, an ideal leader may well be expected to display great authority, but to do so to the benefit of those being led. A benevolent autocrat or paternalist is not expected to ingratiate himself gratuitously with his subjects. Age, experience and accumulated wisdom will account for more than the actual ability to do the job.

The second factor is to do with the way cultures handle **uncertainty**. This ties in with the question of task structure as a contingency factor raised by Fiedler (1967). Cultures with strong uncertainty avoidance are unwilling to take risks and to assume heavy responsibilities. In the workplace they prefer to work by the book, to rely on rules, regulations and instructions. They avoid ambiguities in their tasks and prefer to be told how to carry out their tasks. In Fiedler's terms, therefore, the leader may well need to show direction and make sure that tasks are unambiguous and well structured.

Bearing these factors in mind, the cultural profile of the actual leader will inevitably play a role in the way the leader functions. If, for example, he is himself risk-averse by nature, can he be expected to lead a company to success in a competitive environment, particularly if the employees in that company are similarly risk-averse?

The Japanese way

The context within which the contingency theory was developed was that of (North American) companies running bureaucratic systems whereby the core functions of planning, organising and controlling workforces could be exercised efficiently to ensure maximum economies of scale and increased output.

This way of functioning had indeed appeared to be working well: the growth and profitability of the US economy had soared during the 1950s, 1960s and most of the 1970s. By that time, however, the increasing presence of Japanese products in the US domestic market was beginning to take its toll. The car and electronics sectors in particular were being hit hard by innovative, well-made and well-priced products from Japan. The attention of researchers in management inevitably turned increasingly to the Japanese way of doing business and their approach to management.

Ouchi (1981) describes the basic elements of the Japanese management approach and explains what US business people can learn from their Japanese counterparts. The **Z theory** which he introduced and developed reflects the Japanese concept of *wa*, referred to in Chapter 4. This is the notion of harmony, reflected in the considerable degree of collaborative behaviour and consensus-building within an organisation.

Ouchi's theory assumes that employees are disciplined, have a strong moral obligation to work hard and want to establish close, co-operative working relations with their colleagues as well as with those for whom they are working. They can be trusted to work hard as long as management can be trusted to give them maximum support and to show concern for their well-being. This entails the organisation giving consideration to the workers' families and traditions since these are as important as work itself. Management's job is to ensure that employees increase their knowledge of the company through training and job rotation. Rather than becoming specialists, the employees develop a range of skills that can be applied in many parts of the company's operations. Through gaining considerable familiarity with these operations while being trained to develop their skills and decision-making competence, the workers are expected to develop a loyalty to the company and to devote themselves to it for their working life. If they are eventually promoted to a high managerial position, they will be very knowledgeable about the company and the way it operates and will in turn be in a position to use the management Z approach with new employees.

The role of the leader in a 'learning organisation'

The concept of **the learning organisation** is one heralded by the Z theory and at the same time a response to the increasing uncertainty and complexity of global business. Peter Senge, one of the architects of the concept, saw that learning, or rather the rate of learning, could offer organisations an immense, sustainable advantage in a world where competition is becoming increasingly stronger. In his seminal work, *The Fifth Discipline*, Senge (1990: 3) defines learning organisations as:

> [...] organizations where people continually expand their capacity to create the results they truly desire, where new and expansive patterns of thinking are nurtured, where collective aspiration is set free, and where people are continually learning to see the whole together.

The main task of a leader in such an organisation is to bring about a fundamental shift of mind among its members. This entails designing learning processes, creating, fostering and managing a shared vision, and helping people to understand what brings about change. Such leaders have to counter the 'mental models' that hold back members of an organisation from participating fully in its operation. People need tools and guiding ideas to cope with and give real meaning to the situations they face. Senge (1990) advocates the mastery of disciplines that enable people to gain a broader view of the organisation's operations, to see themselves not as powerless figures in the corporate landscape but as participants who shape that very landscape.

A transformational rather than a transactional leader

Ouchi's work moves the focus away from the manager's viewpoint, as presented in the X and Y theory, towards the attitudes and responsibilities of subordinates. This shift has contributed towards changes in the Western perception of leadership whereby nowadays less emphasis is placed on planning, allocating responsibilities and controlling, and more emphasis given to motivating and inspiring subordinates, creating change and empowering others. This new focus is embodied in the **transformational leader** who creates, communicates and embodies a vision that can influence changes in the attitudes and assumptions of subordinates, builds their commitment to the organisation and inspires trust, confidence and loyalty. This type of leader contrasts strongly with the traditional leader who has more of a 'business-like' relation with subordinates, a give-and-take approach whereby, through various kinds of exchange, the concerns of the company as well as the employees are protected. In short, this **transactional leader** (Bass, 1985) appeals to the self-interest of all parties.

Bass and Avolio (2002) make it clear that there is need in business for both types of leadership. In their view, the most effective leaders are both transformational and transactional in their leadership style. Spotlight 8.1 considers the notion of 'charisma' in leaders.

SPOTLIGHT 8.1

A gift from the gods?

Max Weber, a German sociologist, used the term 'charisma' when describing the qualities some leaders have that enable them to motivate others to achieve outstanding performance. This term – a Greek word meaning 'a gift from the gods' – is used frequently when describing transformational leaders. Robert House (1977) tried to define the charismatic leader by referring to:

- personality, which has a profound effect on the leaders' followers;
- the need for power, which motivates them to be leaders;

- leaders' strong feeling of self-efficacy: they feel they are essentially capable; and
- leaders' conviction in the moral rightness of their beliefs.

One crucial element is their ability to inspire those around them to create a dedicated, loyal workforce by articulating a clear, compelling vision.

Republican politician George Bush (senior), when campaigning for the US presidency, was asked why he focused on the short-term objectives and not on the longer term. Bush's reaction was: 'Oh, the vision thing.'

This concept has offered a framework of reference on leadership by outlining the development in thought with regard to leadership. It has shown how many of the theories developed came from North America and Western Europe, but also how recent ideas have been heavily influenced by the approach taken by Japanese management. The next concept will take some of these ideas on leadership further, consider some of the cultural implications and go in search of attributes of leadership that can be applied across cultures. Meanwhile, Mini-case 8.1 summarises the concept of a 'new leadership model' as conceived recently by the World Economic Forum.

MINI-CASE 8.1

The new leadership

Over a six-month period in 2011–2012, members of the Global Agenda Council on New Models of Leadership met in Abu Dhabi and Davos, as well as virtually, to discuss and agree on a collective view of a new model of leadership. The model presented in Figure 8.1 describes the Council's collective assumptions about new models of leadership.

- There is a **quantum change** in the context in which leadership is taking place. This emerging context is defined by significant demographic and societal changes, fundamental technological advances and continuous globalisation, as well as complex multistakeholder issues and resource scarcity.
- These changes are opening up a **new leadership space** that contains tensions and balances. This space can be defined by a leader's profound sense of purpose, which can be described in three ways: through the emotional capacity of the leader (values, courage, self-awareness, authenticity); by their intellectual and cognitive development (creativity, innovation, world view, systems thinking); and by the extent and depth of their social relationships and networks (community building, alliances, collaboration, virtual worlds).

- Developing this new leadership space will require a profound **leader journey**. At the heart of this journey is an inner and outer journey. The inner journey describes how the leader learns through reflection, mentoring and practice. The outer journey describes the crucible experiences in which leadership is forged and includes challenge, risk and working at the 'edge of the system'.

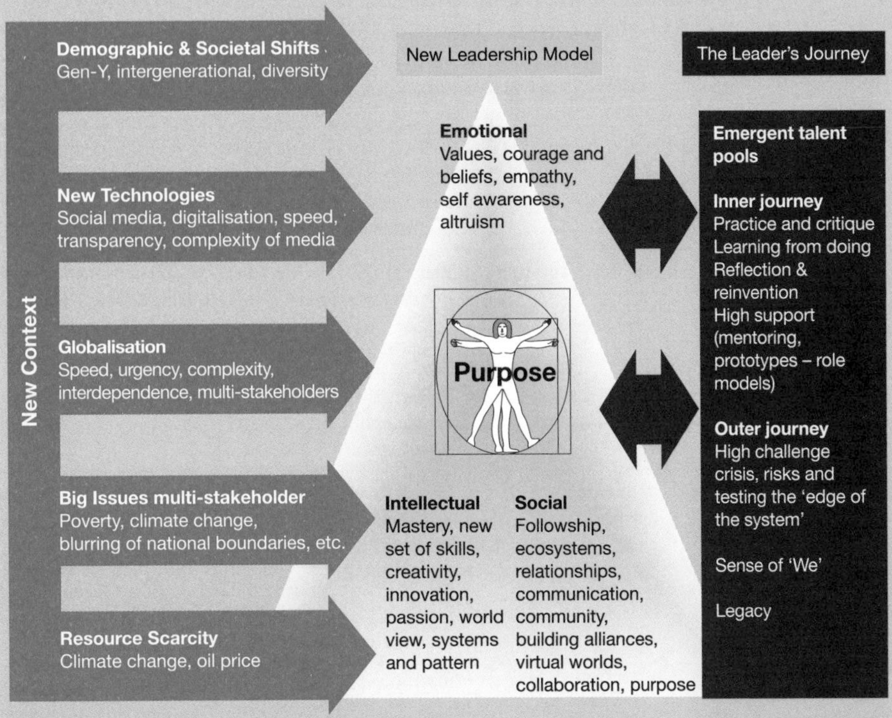

Demographic & Societal Shifts
Gen-Y, intergenerational, diversity

New Technologies
Social media, digitalisation, speed, transparency, complexity of media

New Context

Globalisation
Speed, urgency, complexity, interdependence, multi-stakeholders

Big Issues multi-stakeholder
Poverty, climate change, blurring of national boundaries, etc.

Resource Scarcity
Climate change, oil price

New Leadership Model

Emotional
Values, courage and beliefs, empathy, self awareness, altruism

Purpose

Intellectual
Mastery, new set of skills, creativity, innovation, passion, world view, systems and pattern

Social
Followship, ecosystems, relationships, communication, community, building alliances, virtual worlds, collaboration, purpose

The Leader's Journey

Emergent talent pools

Inner journey
Practice and critique
Learning from doing
Reflection & reinvention
High support (mentoring, prototypes – role models)

Outer journey
High challenge crisis, risks and testing the 'edge of the system'

Sense of 'We'

Legacy

Figure 8.1 Model of the new leadership

Source: World Economic Forum Report: Global Agenda Council on New Models of Leadership 2012, http:// reports.weforum.org/global-agenda-council-on-new-models-of-leadership/#, accessed 10/2/2014.

Questions

1. Bearing in mind the developments in leadership theory described so far in this concept, to what extent do you consider the 'new leadership' to be actually '*new*'?

2. The text refers to a 'profound leader journey' – 'journey' being a term which implies a destination. What do you consider the leader's destination to be?

Concept 8.2 | Leadership in a global context

This concept will examine firstly the question as to whether there are attributes of leadership that can be found in all cultures. It will then consider the role of leaders when managing global talent.

Universal attributes and cultural variables

The question of the **universality of leader behaviours** is one of a number of issues dealt with in the Global Leadership and Organizational Behaviour Effectiveness (GLOBE) research programme. The research carried out so far has determined six global leadership dimensions which summarise the characteristics perceived culturally to further or to impede effective leadership. These dimensions are given in Table 8.1.

Table 8.1 **Global leadership dimensions**

Charismatic/value-based leadership	Reflects the ability to inspire, to motivate, and to expect high performance outcomes from others based on firmly held core values. It includes six sub-scales labelled visionary, inspirational, self-sacrificial, integrity, decisive, and performance oriented
Team-oriented leadership	Reflects effective team-building and implementation of a common purpose or goal among team members. It includes five sub-scales labelled team collaborative, team integrator, diplomatic, malevolent (reverse scored) and administratively competent
Participative leadership	Reflects the degree to which managers involve others in making and implementing decisions. It includes two sub-scales labelled autocratic (reverse scored) and participative
Humane-oriented leadership	Reflects supportive and considerate leadership but also includes compassion and generosity. It includes two sub-scales labelled humane orientation and modesty
Autonomous leadership	Refers to independent and individualistic leadership. This is a newly defined leadership dimension that has not previously appeared in the literature. It includes a single sub-scale labelled autonomous
Self-protective leadership	Focuses on ensuring the safety and security of the individual. This leadership dimension includes five subscales labelled self-centred, status-conscious, conflict inducer, face saving and procedural

Source: Brodbeck *et al.*, 2008: 1038 (adapted).

As Brodbeck *et al.* report (2008: 1037), the project's findings reveal that most of the characteristics of Charismatic/Value-based Leadership and Team-Oriented Leadership were seen as *positively* contributing to leadership in societies and clusters around the world. The authors propose that a number of the cultural dimensions referred to in Chapter 2 (Table 2.7) can give a strong prediction regarding which of these two types of leadership are regarded positively by a particular society or organisation.

As Table 8.2 indicates, societies and organisations that highly value improved performance and innovation are most likely to require leaders who are visionary, inspirational, trustworthy and decisive. Those societies and organisations which value loyalty and cohesiveness, which encourage fairness and concern for each other, and which need to avoid uncertainty are most likely to require leaders who are team oriented.

The other leadership dimensions in Table 8.1 are far from being universal since there are considerable variations between societies with regard to their perceived effectiveness. Using GLOBE's country-specific investigations, Brodbeck *et al.* (2008) detail key differences on these dimensions which appear to be based on differing cultural practices and values.

Table 8.2 **Cultural dimensions as predictors of leadership style**

Global leadership dimension	Cultural dimension as predictor
Charismatic/value-based leadership	Performance orientation
Team-oriented leadership	In-group collectivism, humane orientation, uncertainty avoidance

Although Participative Leadership is found to contribute to effective leadership in all the cultures and clusters studied, Brodbeck *et al.* (2008: 1042) detect four different types (or 'species') of this particular facet:

a) **as an opposition to non-participative, autocratic or directive leadership (e.g. Finland, Argentina, France);**

b) **as a legal principle to organise interactions at work between labour and capital (or management) manifest in societal and organisational cultural practices and values (e.g. Austria and other Germanic countries);**

c) **as a set of personal characteristics in modern North American leadership conduct that surface, for example, in treating others as equals, being informal and not pre-occupied with oneself (e.g. United States);**

d) **as a set of communication behaviours like listening and inviting suggestions from others that aligns with societal cultural resentment against formal rules and a preference for open exchange (e.g. Greece).**

Their findings concerning Humane Oriented Leadership, the fourth leadership dimension, show that this dimension has an impact on effective leadership varying from very positive to neutral. As with Participative Leadership, the authors are able to derive a number of 'species' on the basis of the country-specific findings of the GLOBE project (Brodbeck *et al.*, 2008: 1043):

a) **as a set of values and behaviours that espouse equanimity, egalitarianism and not flaunting one's status as a leader (evident in several Anglo countries);**

b) **as friendly, open, generous interpersonal conduct; in times of crisis direct and clear (in New Zealand), compassionate (in the United States) or aggressive (in Australia);**

c) **as a Confucian principle of moderation and maintaining harmonious social relationships (China, partly in Singapore);**

d) **as a traditional principle of humanity reposing faith and confidence in followers, giving them freedom, and taking personal care of their well-being (India).**

As for Autonomous Leadership, the culture-specific findings show the greatest variation of the six dimensions, both between individual societies and between culture clusters. This dimension is perceived, for example, as contributing slightly to organisational effectiveness in Germanic Europe, but perceived as ineffective in Anglo countries. The findings relating to Germany reflect the value given to autonomous leaders with considerable technical expertise: they negotiate their involvement in activities to ensure the highest possible standards. In the Netherlands, however, autonomous leadership is considered to be a facet of Autocratic and Self-centred Leadership. As Brodbeck *et al.* (2008) indicate, the findings for this country very much reflect those of Anglo countries concerning Humane-Oriented

Leadership: 'leaders should not flaunt their authority and should behave in an egalitarian way' (2008: 1046).

The findings concerning the final leadership dimension in Table 8.1, Self-protective Leadership, also show considerable variation, although the range of scores is less extreme than those for Autonomous Leadership. Those societies scoring high on the cultural dimensions of Power Distance and Uncertainty Avoidance tend to have scores that show that Self-protective Leadership has either no impact on effective leadership or contributes slightly to it. Elsewhere, Self-protective Leadership is considered to inhibit effective leadership.

One question that remains when examining leadership dimensions across cultures has essentially to do with the meaning of the terms used to describe aspects of leadership. House *et al.* (2004: 727) address this issue succinctly by referring to the term 'integrity', an attribute that is considered desirable in all the cultures studied:

> [. . .] does it mean the same thing to a Chinese as it does to an American. How do people in different cultures conceptualize, perceive and exhibit behaviour that reflects integrity?

These thoughts echo those of Bass (1997) who proposed that transformational/charismatic leadership may be universal, but this does not exclude the possibility that the way transformational attributes are expressed may differ between cultures. The concept of charisma, for example, may well be shared among all cultures, but what each culture perceives as charismatic behaviour may differ.

Gender can be regarded as just one of many social differences that play an important role in the development of leadership styles. Developing an appropriate, effective style of leadership may be hampered by *gender stereotypes* clouding the perception subordinates have of what makes a successful leader. Overcoming these stereotypes, while focusing on the characteristics appropriate to the position, remains key for any candidate for leadership, whether male or female.

SPOTLIGHT 8.2

Gender diversity boosts company shares

By Charlotte Clarke

The under-representation of women at senior levels in companies continues to divide opinion, with Angela Merkel, the German chancellor, facing a revolt by women parliamentarians over statutory quotas for women on boards and Viviane Reding, EU commissioner for justice, forced to adapt her proposed quota plan to sanctions.

But a study by Michel Ferrary, professor of human resource management at Skema Business School in France, suggests companies with at least 35 per cent women on the management team perform better during financial crises. Analysing the stock performance of each company in the CAC40, the Parisian stock index, he composed the Femina Index, a separate index of 10 companies whose management teams consisted of 35 per cent women. These include Danone, L'Oréal, LVMH and Société Générale.

The professor then compared both indexes for six years, from 2007 to 2012, and found the CAC40 lost 34.70 per cent of its value, whereas companies in the Femina Index, lost only 5.28 per cent.

'This shows that if you design an investment strategy based on gender diversity, you will beat the market', says Prof. Ferrary.

One reason for this, according to the professor, is that diversity leads to a better understanding of the market. For example, female engineers at Renault were asked to design a car and consequently came up with one that could be driven with a flat tyre. 'A man would never have thought of this', he says 'as it is part of the male psych to know how to change a tyre!'

Another reason is that gender diversity creates better decision-making processes with more balanced risk-taking. At BNP Paribas, for example, one of the 10 companies in the Femina Index, 44 per cent of the management is female and it is considered one of the best banks in France, he says. Meanwhile, Dexia, the only French bank to go bankrupt, has only 18 per cent of women in management.

However, the professor also points out that one negative reason for this outcome is salary differences. 'Women are paid less than men [which] saves money and increases the profitability of a company', he explains.

The results contrast significantly with a paper published by Germany's central bank this month that challenges the popular idea that the global financial system would be intrinsically safer if run by women. But Prof. Ferrary believes his research approaches the issue from a different angle, by considering the stock performances of companies with the number of women on the whole management team of a company as opposed to just their board.

'The 35 per cent threshold I have used makes a difference', he says, explaining that a minority of less than this has little influence on company performance.

 Source: 'Gender diversity boosts company shares', *Financial Times*, FT.com 18/4/2013 (Clarke, C.) © The Financial Times Ltd. All Rights Reserved.

Do the considerations outlined above concerning gender and leadership apply across cultures?

Although international research in this area is thin on the ground, one survey carried out across a number of countries – both in the East and West – still has a certain resonance. In Judy Rosener's (1990) survey, members of the International Women's Forum, together with matched male counterparts, were asked to describe, among other things, their leadership performance as well as the ways they used to influence those with whom they worked. Male respondents generally saw their job performance as a series of transactions with subordinates whereby rewards were given for satisfactory performance, and punishments given for inadequate performance. They saw the power they used as coming from their formal, hierarchical position within the company. Female respondents, on the other hand, saw their leadership role as getting subordinates to see the bigger picture, to move beyond self-interest and consider the interest of the group as a whole. Female leaders considered their power to come less from their position in the organisation and more from their own character – their charisma, their interpersonal skills and their ability to work hard. Rosener summarises the differences between male and female leaders in terms of the transactional and transformational behaviour referred to earlier.

Rosener's survey (1990), as well as other limited research carried out in the area where leadership, gender and culture interact, suggests that differences between genders in one culture are also found in other cultures. Male and female leaders, it appears, display differing behavioural tendencies whatever their country of origin. Although leadership style may be based on gender, differences in the leadership style employed are based more on culture than on gender.

The management of global talent

The earlier discussion on universal attributes of effective leadership and the cultural variables involved highlights the inherent tension in global management between local and international effectiveness. This tension is also apparent when it comes to strategic decisions about ensuring the (further) success of an enterprise operating in the global market through the recruitment, development and retention of management talent. Account needs to be taken of global priorities as well as of national contexts in which this talent operates (McDonnell and Collings, 2011).

In a sense this involves the leaders of global companies being able to reflect on their own strengths and shortcomings when attempting to ensure that their successors are capable of addressing the demands of the global and national contexts in which the companies they are to lead are engaged. The many 'templates' devised in the field of international human resource management to facilitate the identification and evaluation of talent reflect many of the issues already raised. McDonnell and Collings (2011: 57) give an example suggested by Ulrich (2006) whereby talent should be identified in terms of a mix of:

a) competence: possessing the necessary knowledge, skills and values;
b) commitment: applying the above in the workplace, engaging employees with their work role;
c) contribution: giving value to the organisation (promoting its success) and gaining value from it (self-fulfilment in terms of meaning and value in their work).

However, local considerations need to be made even when a global template is used. Stahl *et al.* (2007: 24) suggest that local subsidiaries should be able to adapt such a template to meet the circumstances specific to their context. Although their research shows that the degree of global integration and local adaptation involved differs widely, the authors argue that not paying sufficient attention to local demands could lead to a shortage of talent in the company since global competitors are becoming more adept at adapting to local circumstances. Furthermore, although a company may be able to create a strong talent pool through applying global standards, the people involved may lack the diversity needed for the company to deal with a rapidly changing business environment (Stahl *et al.*, 2007: 23). On the other hand, by developing strong local talent pools to increase diversity, the company may find itself limited in its ability to maximise economies of scale in the recruitment, training and retention of potential leaders. Clearly, finding a successful balance between setting global standardisation and implementing it in accordance with local requirements is the key to leaders ensuring quality management in the future.

Other factors involved in managing global talent are given in Figure 8.2. One worth noting is that of senior/line management involvement. Their active participation in

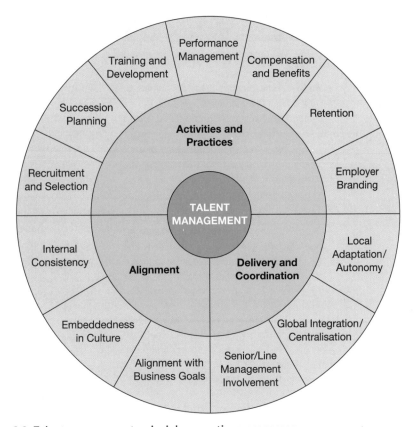

Figure 8.2 Talent management: principles, practices, processes

Source: Stahl, G. *et al*, 'Six Principles of Effective Global Talent Management', *Sloan Management Review*, © 2012 from MIT Sloan Management Review/Massachusetts Institute of Technology. All rights reserved. Distributed by Tribune Content Agency.

leadership development through coaching and mentoring, as well as through encouraging movement throughout the company will not only help these potential leaders to increase their awareness of the company's activities and international management skills, but also break down the 'silo mentality' whereby departments and subsidiaries are reluctant to share knowledge and information with other parts of the company.

A number of the issues mentioned above – as well as others featured in Figure 8.2 – come to the fore in Spotlight 8.3, which concerns the management of international talent in 'Asia-focused' companies.

It is clear that the leader of a global company must take a leading role in the planning and execution of the whole talent management process and so ensure the quality of future managers and the (ongoing) success of the company.

This concept has briefly described cultural variables that apply to conceptions of leadership. It has also shown that there are consistent elements of leadership recognised across cultures but whose form may vary between cultures. Moreover, this concept has indicated that some modern concepts of leadership generated in the West appear to have their antecedents in the East. Different cultures, it seems, can generate similar perceptions of leadership, even if the contexts within which leadership is affected are very different. The issue of managing talent in a global company has also been briefly addressed.

SPOTLIGHT 8.3

Talent retention is vital

The Business Times Singapore asked a number of executives from multinationals operating in Asia to pinpoint the key workforce-related issues that affect Asia-focused organisations today. They were also asked to describe some of their key 'people strategies' for Asia. Here is the response from Charles M. Ormiston, Director Bain & Company, a global management consulting firm.

I think it would be difficult to exaggerate the enormous people-development challenges facing Asia. The gap between organisations who 'get it' and those who don't is tremendous. There are MNCs where the bulk of their Asian senior management is of Asian origin, many 'Asian expatriates' who have spent years of their life working in different markets and who are fully comfortable with working in either the 'East' or the 'West'. Citibank, Standard Chartered, Hewlett-Packard, Schlumberger and Unilever are examples of great companies that attract and develop talent in the local markets they work in, and then deploy the best talent globally. And yet there are still MNCs dominated by foreign expatriates on three-year rotations from head office, who seem to begin thinking about how to return to New York or Chicago within weeks of arriving in Singapore.

There are 'local firms' who have also mastered the art of working with talent from a range of sources – SingTel is doing an impressive job with diverse assets in Australia, India and the Philippines as well as in their home market;

Temasek is one of the most innovative institutions I have come across in terms of flexible work practices and creating opportunities for employee development. And yet there are local firms who have visibly failed with virtually all attempts to diversify their talent base.

Mr Ormiston then outlines fundamental shifts which he believes most 'Asia-focused' corporations will need to undertake in their thinking. These include the following:

Create diversity in your senior ranks. If your senior ranks are primarily people from one nationality or ethnic group, you will never be an attractive workplace for people who are from other backgrounds – no matter what platitudes you convey. You have to take visible risks with non-traditional employees to be credible.

Employers need to actively coach their employees on their careers. When I talk to employees of the best employers in Asia, they focus on the fairness and objectivity of their performance appraisal systems and the 'good advice' they receive from key mentors over the years. With the firms that 'don't get it' in Asia, this type of system is often non-existent – the rotating expatriates in MNCs simply don't take the time to bond with the local employee base in a productive way and the poorly run local firms have a tremendous wall between the 'top team' and the up-and-coming generation.

Source: *Business Times Singapore*, 5/10/2009.

Conclusion

The concept of leadership in the West has evolved. Based originally on scientific principles, it has taken on a much more human orientation, reflecting the influence of the way leaders behave in Asia. There now appears to be a consensus across cultures as to what makes an effective leader (including integrity, charisma, decisiveness and being team-oriented). However, the way in which these attributes are expressed in actual behaviour can vary considerably from culture to culture. The same applies in a way to the question of gender and leadership: the differences in leadership style between males and females observed in one country are also seen in other countries, but the ways in which behaviour tends to reflect these differences is based more on culture than gender. Ensuring effective future leadership of an internationally operating company is also a concern of those presently leading. A number of strategic decisions need to be considered, particularly with regard to the leader's ability to pursue global integration while maintaining or increasing adaptation to local markets.

Points for reflection

1. Ouchi put forward the Z theory to explain how Japanese management works and to show the Americans what they could learn from their Japanese counterparts. Many advocates of the theory indicate that type Z companies are among the most successful types of US companies.

   How do you account for their success, bearing in mind that the principles of scientific leadership still predominate in that country?

2. One element of transformational leadership referred to in this chapter is charisma. Research shows that it is a universal attribute of good leadership. However, certain facets of charisma are valued differently in different countries.

   Pinpoint which aspects of the leadership dimension outlined in Table 8.1 prevail in your country, especially in domestic companies.

3. Companies are becoming increasingly aware of the need for relation-oriented skills in their global endeavours. Female managers working for Western companies, for example, could generally be regarded as potentially effective managers in, say, Asia because of their person-oriented leadership skills. The consideration women show others, as well as their ability to empathise, are features that are said to be held in high esteem in that part of the world.

   Why do you think that some multinationals nevertheless tend not to give serious consideration to female candidates for managerial positions in, for example, the Middle East?

4. When addressing the issue of global talent management, mention is made of the need to find a successful balance between setting global standardisation and implementing it according to local requirements. This is said to be the key to leaders ensuring quality management in the future.

   What other key ways do you think leaders could use to ensure the same result?

Further reading

House, R.J., Hanges, P.J., Javidan, M., Dorfman, P.W. and Gupta, V. (eds) (2004) *Leadership, Culture and Organizations: the GLOBE study of 62 societies*, Thousand Oaks, CA: Sage. One of the aims of this book, as described in Concept 8.2, is to find out how leadership is understood differently across cultures. The GLOBE project is a long-term research programme based on an integrated theory of the relationship between culture and societal, organisational and leadership effectiveness. Apart from proposing a range of cultural dimensions (dealt with briefly in Part One), the book gives an interesting review of leadership theories.

Scullion, H. and Collings, D.G. (eds) (2011) *Global Talent Management*, New York, NY: Routledge. Using recently developed theories dealing with global talent management, this book critically addresses the key issues facing multinational companies. The perspective it uses is both theoretical and practical, particularly since it deals with issues which are emerging in key economies such as China, India, the Middle East and Eastern Europe.

References

Bass, B.M. (1985) *Leadership and Performance Beyond Expectations*, New York, NY: Free Press.

Bass, B.M. (1997) 'Does the transactional-transformational paradigm transcend organizational and national boundaries?', *American Psychologist*, 52 (2): 130–139.

Bass, B.M. and Avolio, B.J. (eds) (2002) *Developing Potential Across a Full Range of Leadership: Cases on Transactional and Transformational Leadership*, Mahwah, NJ: Lawrence Erlbaum Associates.

Brodbeck, F.C., Chhokar, J.S. and House, R.J. (2008) *Culture and Leadership in 25 Societies: Integration, Conclusions, and Future Directions*, in Chhokar, J.S., Brodbeck, F.C. and House, R.J. (eds), *Culture and Leadership Across the World: the GLOBE Book of In-Depth Studies of 25 Societies*, New York, NY: Lawrence Erlbaum Associates.

Fiedler, F.E. (1967) *A Theory of Leadership Effectiveness*, New York, NY: McGraw-Hill.

House, R.J. (1977) 'A 1976 theory of charismatic leadership', in J.G. Hunt and L.L. Larson (eds), *Leadership: The Cutting Edge*, Carbondale, IL: Southern Illinois University Press: 189–207.

House, R.J., Hanges, P.J., Javidan, M., Dorfman, P.W. and Gupta, V. (eds) (2004) *Leadership, Culture and Organizations: the GLOBE Study of 62 Societies*, Thousand Oaks, CA: Sage.

McDonnell, A. and Collings, D.G. (2011) 'The identification and evaluation of talent in MNEs', in Scullion, H. and Collings, D.G. (eds) (2011) *Global Talent Management*, New York, NY: Routledge: 56–73.

McGregor, D. (1960) *The Human Side of Enterprise*, New York, NY: McGraw-Hill.

Ouchi, W.G. (1981) *Theory Z: How American Business Can Meet the Japanese Challenge*, New York, NY: Avon.

Rosener, J.B. (1990) 'Ways women lead', *Harvard Business Review*, 68(2): 119–125.

Scullion, H. and Collings, D.G. (eds) (2011) *Global Talent Management*, New York, NY: Routledge.

Senge, P.M. (1990) *The Fifth Discipline: the Art and Practice of the Learning Organization*, New York, NY: Currency Doubleday.

Stahl, G., Björkman, I., Farndale E., Morris, S.S., Paauwe, J., Stiles, P., Trevor, J. and Wright, P.M. (2007) *Global Talent Management: How Leading Multinationals Build and Sustain Their Talent Pipeline*, INSEAD Research Paper 2007/34/OB, http://www.insead.edu/facultyresearch/research/details_papers.cfm?id=17506, accessed 1 Feb. 2014.

Stogdill, R.M. (1974) *Handbook of Leadership: a Survey of Theory and Research*, New York, NY: Free Press.

Ulrich, D. (2006) 'The talent trifecta' in *Workforce Management*, 10/9/2006: 32–33.

ACTIVITY 8.1

Read the following article which describes the results of a survey among British, German and French managers. Answer the questions which follow the article.

Le patron, der Chef and the boss

By Alison Maitland

Have you heard the one about the three captains of industry? The Brit insists he is happy to have his decisions challenged. The German stresses the importance of humility. And the Frenchman enjoys wielding power without having to consult first.

Far from being a joke, these are the revealing findings of a new survey of 200 chief executives, chairmen and directors in the UK, Germany and France. It is often assumed that rules about leadership apply regardless of culture or nationality. But the survey suggests this is an oversimplification. It highlights big differences in national attitudes to responsibility, status and decision-making that global companies would do well to understand.

The research, co-ordinated by MORI for DDI, an international human resources consultancy, labels French captains of industry as 'autocrats', Germans as 'democrats' and British as 'meritocrats'.

In support of these catchy generalizations, it finds that fewer than three in 10 French bosses are happy to be challenged about the decisions they make, compared with half of Germans and more than nine out of 10 business leaders in the UK. The French prize the autonomy they gain from the job. Nearly two-thirds count 'the freedom to make decisions with minimum interference' as one of the three best things about being a leader.

'I enjoy the decision-making without having to confer with others', says one Gallic captain of industry. Only 46 per cent of bosses in Germany and 39 per cent in the UK regard this as being important.

The ability to hand-pick their team is another perk of the job for the French, but one that is less highly rated in Germany and Britain.

For business leaders in the UK and Germany, the best thing about the job is developing talent in the company. Seventy per cent of British bosses and nearly 50 per cent of Germans – but only 14 per cent of French ones – rate this among the top three benefits of leadership.

Although few of the 200 captains of industry choose 'being in a position of power' as one of the three best things about the job, the French are three times more likely than the British, and eight times more likely than the Germans, to regard this as important, the survey finds.

'In Germany, you accept the responsibility of authority but you don't talk about it, whereas typically in France, if you belong to the upper echelons of management, or if you own a company, it's a badge of success that you wear in every aspect of your life', says Steve Newhall, managing director of DDI Europe.

Public recognition is more important in France, reflecting the kudos attached to a senior position in business, he says. Just over 30 per cent of

French chief executives and directors rate this as one of the three best things about being a leader, compared with 16 per cent in Germany and just two per cent in the UK.

Is it possible that these differences simply reflect greater honesty from the French about enjoying the exercise of power, while the British and Germans consider this would be politically incorrect? Mr Newhall admits it is hard to be sure, but he says the anonymity of the interviews makes it likely these are genuine differences.

'The intention was to get as honest an answer as possible and to probe behind the PR', he says. 'The French are more likely to respond in that way because it's something that's acceptable within their cultural norms. We know about the *grandes écoles* system where the elite are prized. In the UK, "the establishment" is used more as a derogatory than a positive term.'

He says he is not suggesting that one leadership style is better than another. But executives of international companies need to be like chameleons, able to adapt to the corporate and national culture in which they are working, while not abandoning their individualism.

'The danger for any leader is only being able to operate within one of these styles. If you take an autocratic style into a culture that expects a more democratic or meritocratic style, the chances are that you will trip up.'

German leaders stand out in the survey for their social conscience and their concern about the responsibility that goes with power. Nearly half say that one of their top three concerns is having to make tough decisions that affect people's futures – compared with only 28 per cent of leaders in the UK and 20 per cent in France.

'Sometimes the amount of influence I have frightens me', says one German boss. 'I have to be very cautious and thoroughly weigh up the pros and cons of any decision.' Another comment: 'You have to remain humble: personal vanity and over-estimating your ability will lead to the downfall of the enterprise.'

Given such modest responses, it is perhaps paradoxical that deference is strongest in Germany, with nearly 60 per cent of business leaders saying their decisions are likely to go unchallenged. Four in 10 German bosses cite fear of failure as a top concern, compared with just over two in 10 in Britain. Mr. Newhall believes this reflects the lingering stigma of failure in Germany, which contrasts with the Anglo-American preference to see failure as an opportunity to learn and move on.

Leaders in the UK appear the most upbeat, perhaps because of the more stable economic environment, the research finds. What keeps them awake at night are external pressures, such as new legislation and corporate governance issues.

For French leaders, warring egos in the management team are a big concern. While this may simply reflect Gallic style, the DDI report suggests that French chief executives' fondness for independent decision-making may lead to friction.

Despite the many differences, some worries and beliefs are shared across all three countries. Lack of personal time is a common concern. The importance of the team is widely appreciated.

'Again and again, in private one-to-one interviews, whether face-to-face or on the phone, captains of industry stated their focus to be on responsibility rather than power, and on their team's success rather than their own', says Mr Newhall.

This emphasis on collaboration is epitomized by a German boss who says: 'I see myself as a service provider in a company run as a democracy, where everyone pulls together to achieve the strategies we have worked out together.' A French respondent concurs: 'We are working in an ever more complex environment, and working efficiently within a team is the best way.'

A final common theme is that the risks increase the higher you get, and that nothing can fully prepare you for the challenge of running a company. Enjoy it while it lasts. As a German respondent puts it: 'It is a long hard climb to the top of the mountain. There is a nice view, but it is quite windy.'

 Source: from 'Le Patron, der Chef and the boss', *Financial Times*, 9/1/2006, p. 10 (Maitland, A.),
© The Financial Times Ltd. All Rights Reserved.

Questions

1. Look again at the text and try to determine what questions were used in the survey.

2. Enter key examples in the table below of behaviour or attitudes that reflect the label given to each type of leader at the beginning of the article.

Le patron: the autocrat	*Der Chef:* the democrat	*The boss:* the meritocrat

3. How reliable in your opinion, are the results of the survey? Refer in particular to the comments made in the text about the 'honesty' of the respondents.

4. If you were asked to classify the business leaders in your country, which of the above labels would you use to describe them? Give examples of behaviours that reflect your labelling.

5. If the title of the article had been '*La patronne, die Chefin* and the female boss', how valid do you think the results of the survey would have been? What behavioural or attitudinal differences – if any – would you have expected to see in the survey?

ACTIVITY 8.2

Read the article below and answer the questions that follow.

Why multinationals struggle to manage talent

By Matthew Guthridge and Asmus B. Komm

Managing talent in a global organization is more complex and demanding than it is in a national business – and few major worldwide corporations have risen to the challenge.

A McKinsey survey of managers at some of the world's best-known multinationals covered a range of sectors and all the main geographies. Our findings suggest that the movement of employees between countries is still surprisingly limited and that many people tempted to relocate fear that doing so will damage their career prospects.

Yet, companies that can satisfy their global talent needs and overcome cultural and other silo-based barriers tend to outperform those that don't.

We've long observed that global corporations grapple with a more difficult talent agenda than their domestic counterparts – partly because they need to share resources and knowledge across a number of business units and countries, partly because of the especially demanding nature of global leadership. To find out more, we undertook in-depth interviews with executives at 11 major global corporations and separately invited senior managers at 22 global companies to participate in an online survey investigating how effectively they manage their talent. More than 450 people, ranging from CEOs and other directors to senior managers, including HR professionals, took part in the survey.

The responses confirmed impressions from the interviews that companies now struggle on a number of talent-management fronts, such as achieving greater cultural diversity, overcoming barriers to international mobility, and establishing consistent HR processes in different geographical units.

Despite the value companies claim to place on international management experience, the senior managers who took the survey had made, on average, only 1.5 cross-border moves during their careers, as against an average of 2 for managers at the top-performing companies. Interestingly, we found that the respondents had also moved, on average, 1.7 times between different divisions within the same geography but only 1.3 times between different functions – another sign that movement from silo to silo is still limited.

Participants cited several personal disincentives to global mobility, but one of the most significant was the expectation that employees would be demoted after repatriation to their home location. 'Overseas experience is not taken seriously and not taken advantage of', commented one senior manager. 'Much valuable experience dissipates' because companies have a habit of 'ignoring input from returnees, and many leave.' The quality of the support for mobility a company provides (for instance, assistance with housing and the logistical aspects of a move) also plays a decisive role in determining how positive or challenging an overseas assignment is for expatriates.

Perhaps the most provocative finding from the research was the relationship between financial performance, as measured by profit per employee[1], and 10 dimensions of global talent management. Companies scoring in the top third of the survey (when all 10 dimensions were combined) earned significantly higher profit per employee than those in the bottom third. The correlations were particularly striking in three areas: the creation of globally consistent talent evaluation processes, the management of cultural diversity, and the mobility of global leaders. Companies achieving scores in the top third in any of these three areas had a 70 per cent chance of achieving top-third financial performance. Companies scoring in the bottom third of the survey in these three areas had a significantly lower probability of being top performers, particularly if the company had inconsistent global talent processes. Although providing no evidence of true causality and lacking a longitudinal perspective, the strong associations between company financial performance and these global-talent-management practices strengthen our belief that these are important areas on which businesses and HR leaders should focus their attention.

Global consistency in a company's talent evaluation processes is important, because for mobility to succeed, line managers need to feel confident that employees transferring into their units from other parts of the organization meet the same standards that their own people do. Moreover, company support and training is vital to the promotion of diversity. HR managers stressed the need for expatriates to learn more about the culture of the countries they transfer to than just the local language. 'If you have to choose', explained one HR director, 'it's more important to have an open-minded leader than to have someone with the right language skills.'

In our view the key implication of the research is that companies should focus hard on rotating talent globally across divisions and geographies. Not only will this rotation support the development of company talent, it will also promote greater cultural awareness and diversity. The research further examined why some companies are better than others at developing global talent in this way. It found that those with top managers and promotion systems that actively encourage their people to gain international experience –

and provide managers with incentives to share their talent with other units – were roughly twice as likely to have effective global mobility practices than those that don't.

Global companies should consider devoting more resources and senior-management time to liberating talent 'trapped' in national silos and more wholeheartedly supporting global-mobility programs. Instilling a common set of talent evaluation processes throughout the world – especially standardized individual performance evaluations – will underpin this effort and build the confidence of line managers.

More and more companies are stepping up their international revenues, their overseas customer base, and their non-domestic workforce. What our research suggests is that many of them need to match these achievements with truly global talent-management attitudes and practices.

[1] See Lowell L. Bryan (2007) 'The new metrics of corporate performance: profit per employee', *McKinsey Quarterly*, No. 1: pp. 56–65.

Source: Guthridge, M. and Komm, A. (2008), 'Why multinationals struggle to manage talent', *McKinsey Quarterly*, 4: 10–13. Retrieved from Business Source Complete database.

Questions

1. Summarise the cultural factors that according to the survey, correlate strongly with strong financial performance. Which do you consider to be the key factor? Explain your reasons.

2. On the basis of the survey's findings, how can the cultural experiences of managers returning from working abroad best be used for the company's benefit?

3. What, in your opinion should be the shared 'talent evaluation processes' which could liberate 'talent trapped in national silos'?

Chapter 9

Culture and corporate strategy

Strategy is not only an element of managing organisations, it is found in all areas of management, from marketing through human resources to communication. This chapter takes the concept of strategy as it is used generally in business and addresses the relationship – if one exists – between strategy and culture.

Concept 9.1 addresses this issue, while Concept 9.2 deals with human factors in strategic alliances between companies and attempts to explain the influence of culture – whether organisational or national – in strategic applications such as mergers and acquisitions.

Learning outcomes

After reading this chapter you will gain an understanding of:

● The relationship between strategy and culture.

● The role of national culture in the formation of company strategy.

● The effect of strategy on international mergers and acquisitions.

● The broad-spectrum theory of cross-cultural adaptation.

Concept 9.1 Cultural view of strategy

Since the 1960s, companies have been looking for strategies to use in their competitive environment and so help realise their objectives. The question is: what link, if any, can be made between strategy and culture?

Strategy and corporate culture

Is culture used to formulate strategy, or is it just a component of strategy? According to Schoenberger (1997), the relationship between company culture and strategy is closer than would appear. Strategy can be seen as less to do with making decisions and more to do with knowledge, i.e. what the organisation knows or what it thinks it knows. This knowledge also includes the way it interprets the world and its position in it. It is the company's imagination that determines how this world could or should be. This means strategy undergoes the influence of culture since it is through its culture that a company creates an understanding of itself as well as an interpretation of the world. When this world presents new problems or changes, then culture devises a company's strategic response to them.

If it is examined from this standpoint, strategy is a product of culture. At the same time, however, since the strategic orientation of the company has in the past moulded specific practices, relations and ideas, culture is also a product of strategy. Culture and strategy, therefore, are inextricably connected. What companies need to resolve, says Schoenberger (1997: 14), 'is not so much how to *adapt* the corporate culture to a new strategy as to understand how culture *produces* strategy'.

Schneider and Barsoux (2003) also underline the relationship between culture and strategy. They argue that their definition of culture – a solution to the problems of external adaptation and internal integration – could also be used as the definition of strategy. The process is the same: strategic decisions are made to adapt to the environment and these are implanted and integrated within the company by means of human resources. The actual departments where strategic plans are made, as well as the tools, models and jargon used, are simply cultural artefacts. The application by management of the strategies chosen have created beliefs and values, and behind these managerial practices are assumptions. But do these assumptions have the same meaning in different cultures?

Cultural models of strategy

Deresky (2003) argues that most companies use strategic planning to evaluate their future prospects and in this way decide on strategies to be taken to accomplish their objectives in the long term. Although the strategic planning process is an ideal way for doing so, this does not prevent decisions being influenced by the personal judgement, experience and motivation of the managers who make them. This implies that a change in management can radically change the eventual strategy of the company. This is what Schneider and Barsoux (2003: 122) emphasise when they say:

> Assumptions regarding internal integration are relevant to questions such as who is involved and who takes the decision.

Furthermore, when it comes to strategic management, Schneider and Barsoux (2003) divide management from different countries into two types according to their behaviours, values and assumptions (concerning uncertainty, control, power, human activity and time):

- Controlling model: the departments responsible establish strategic plans and present them to top management or to the board for their consideration. The company's reports are the main source of information about its environment, and these are fairly quantitative and objective in nature.

- Adapting model: responsibility for strategic decisions lies with all levels of the organisation. The information obtained is qualitative and subjective in nature because it comes from personal sources, friends and colleagues.

Cultural factors of strategy

Following the same line as the previous authors, Fatehi (1996) adds that formulating strategy is not just a question of collecting information, but also of deciding what is to be done with it. Such decisions are in no way 'free of human biases' and in fact the whole process of collecting and examining information is a perceptual one based on culture. If this is so, in what way is the formulation of strategy affected by cultural differences?

Fatehi (1996) suggests that two areas in particular are influenced by culture.

- *Relationship with the environment.* To illustrate cultural differences in this area, Fatehi (1996) uses what he refers to as the 'mental framework' of two types of person. The first is 'engineering-oriented' and goes looking for information to support a strategy (change) whereby the environment can be altered to the benefit of the company. This orientation rests on the belief that humans can control their surroundings. The second is 'symbiotic-oriented', believes in close ties with nature and therefore looks for another, non-destructive strategy for dealing with the environment. Fatehi (1996) refers to the fatalist beliefs of Buddhists and the conviction among Muslims that events are predetermined. Both recognise the limits humans have when trying to control their environment.

- *Relationships among people.* Fatehi also distinguishes differences in the question of interpersonal relationships within a company. Formulating strategy is just one of the functions of management involving a predictable pattern of relationships. Within a certain hierarchy the reaction of a subordinate to the order of a superior will be in line with expected modes of behaviour. To show differences in attitude among employees towards a company's strategy, Fatehi contrasts US and Japanese companies. The former consider possibilities of success as 'environmental opportunities'. They formulate their strategies in such a way that they do not have to demand individual sacrifice of their employees. Japanese companies, on the other hand, may demand a number of strategic choices, of which one or more could involve personal sacrifice from their personnel. The individual employee, however, does not see this demand as a self-sacrifice since it is made for the benefit of the company.

Trice and Beyer (1993) also take up the question of the role played by cultural factors in corporate strategy. They too dwell on the differences between US and Japanese companies. Although there is intense competition between the two, the way they compete is shaped by cultural differences. Competition is inherent to US culture: companies in the US compete fiercely for market domination. Neither the laws in place nor the managers and their way of thinking make it easy for companies from different sectors to co-operate with each other, not even outside the US. The Japanese culture, however, is more to do with co-operation and harmonious relations – as was described in Part One. Nevertheless, they can be as competitive as their US counterparts. The difference is that Japanese companies practise competition to achieve collective goals against 'outsiders'. This type of competition preserves internal harmony and benefits the country as a whole.

The effect of national culture on strategy

In what way can national culture affect strategy? Not only on the choice of strategy but also on the way it is realised. So, this is about leadership and the decision-making process. Tayeb (2003) describes how, for example, Swedish managers spend more time making decisions than their British counterparts. The British, on the other hand, require more interaction and consultation with experts. Schneider and Barsoux (2003) also refer to the cultural elements of decision-making: who makes the decisions, who is involved, where the decisions are taken (in a formal meeting, or elsewhere). Nor should the matter of time be forgotten: how quickly the decisions are made. The whole process reflects different cultural assumptions.

Tayeb (2003) mentions another area where national culture impinges on strategy: the product and services sectors. Consumer demand for certain products will differ from country to country, from region to region, and this will influence the different markets. The needs and preferences of the consumers need to be taken into account when analysing the resources and capacities of the organisation, particularly when business overseas is concerned.

Finally, the question of national culture comes to the fore when a multinational has to make strategic decisions about the maintenance – or otherwise – of the national culture in its local subsidiaries. As Bartlett *et al.* (2003: 672) indicate, if a corporate strategy is used, managers at headquarters will not necessarily have a clear insight into the business environment and the cultural differences at play in the foreign markets where the multinational operates. They underline the importance of the role of the country manager in the implementation of company strategy. This manager is at the centre of the strategic tension between defending the company's market positions against global competitors on the one hand, and satisfying the demands of the local subsidiary on the other. These demands usually include meeting the requirements set by the host government, responding to the specific needs of local consumers and reinforcing the company's competitive position with local (potential) resources. The country manager assumes the role of 'cultural interpreter' who is expected to be able to give information about the national situation to 'those whose perceptions may be obscured by ethnocentric biases'. In short, it is necessary to understand the national culture of the host country, to respect the local cultural norms and, at the same time, to understand the corporate goals, strategies and values and communicate them effectively to the local employees.

Global market strategy

Why is it that one company succeeds in the global market and not another? Some analysts claim that success is due to strategy, others say it is as a result of structure or technological innovation. Black *et al.* (1999) argue that the key to success is the people involved. It is they who formulate the strategy and implement it, it is they who create and shape the organisational structures and it is they who invent and use the technology.

In this regard, global assignments can be very important strategically for the company. The managers sent from headquarters to the subsidiary abroad are not only able to concentrate on the specific needs of the local market but can also analyse the tendencies in the global market for the benefit of the whole company. By going on an international assignment, the managers involved can also develop their individual knowledge and competencies, particularly since they need to understand and work with people from another culture.

But how is a manager to gain insight into the attitudes of those involved in a cross-cultural situation and modify the management strategy accordingly? This does not mean that the manager has to have a fixed 'new' strategy for whatever circumstances. She/he will realise that the strategy is not to have the same strategy, but to modify it according to the situations encountered – especially since knowledge itself entails learning from experience. This learning is therefore to do with applying skills and knowledge learned in one context

SPOTLIGHT 9.1

China suspends India power projects

By James Lamont in New Delhi

Last year, India introduced new limits on the use of foreign labour. Only 1 per cent of a project's workforce can be foreign. On power projects the limit is 40 skilled workers.

Parvesh Minocha, the managing director of the transport division of Feedback Ventures, an infrastructure consultancy, said India would be forced to turn to expatriates, particularly experts in project management, to help it meet goals in an environment in which cost and time overruns are the norm.

China, India's largest trading partner, is a big supplier of power equipment and other infrastructure. It also has a reputation for building power stations faster than its neighbour. McKinsey, the management consultancy, estimates that it takes double the time to build a power station in India as it does in China.

Some Chinese companies, such as Huawei, are making efforts to localise their operations to be seen more as an Indian company. Its executives say they need a strategy to overcome prejudice against China's low-cost contractors and equipment in spite of their wide application across India's fast-growing telecommunications industry.

 Source: from 'China suspends India power projects', *Financial Times*, 23/3/2010 (Lamont, J.), © The Financial Times Ltd. All Rights Reserved.

to another context. Once a manager has acquired this competence, then she/he is able to make judgements and adapt to different situations.

This cultural understanding is particularly important in alliances such as mergers and acquisitions, as the following concept shows.

Concept 9.2   Strategic alliances and business cultures

To develop strategies for the global market, companies are turning to alliances. Strategic alliances can create considerable advantages. First, they can help realise increased economies of scale and reduced marketing costs. Furthermore, they can result in access to new markets, know-how and technology. Moreover, if the alliance is a close one, a takeover or merger, risks can be shared and products developed jointly. Through carefully managed co-operation, the results of rapprochement between companies can be seen relatively quickly. Not that everything is necessarily plain sailing: extra problems may well arise – especially those relating to culture.

This is an area of concern to managers only when things are not running smoothly. The focus is often first on the business advantages, including the merging of products and/or services, strategic fit in the market, and the financial savings. The matter of cultural fit is given relatively little attention at the start. Only when problems arise, particularly when they interfere with the business goals established through an alliance, are they given real attention.

MINI-CASE 9.1

Carmakers' alliance faces cultural chasm

By Daniel Schäfer in Frankfurt and John Reed in London

When the chief executives of Renault-Nissan and Daimler kicked off a strategic tie-up at a picture-perfect signing ceremony in Brussels on Wednesday, both quoted philosophers from their partner's respective countries.

It was meant to demonstrate the Franco-German corporate bridge their partnership was building, but the quotations instead suggested big differences in how Carlos Ghosn and Dieter Zetsche viewed it – and pointed to potential future friction between their companies.

Renault-Nissan's Mr Ghosn spoke about creating a 'technological powerhouse', and quoted Hegel: 'Nothing great has ever been accomplished without passion', he declared. Daimler's Mr Zetsche, who chose to emphasise the tie-up's practical side and the hard work it had taken to conclude, cited Voltaire with 'Work is the father of pleasure'.

Mr Ghosn has long been an advocate of cross-shareholdings in an industry facing growing pressure to be present in every market and vehicle segment. He had long spoken of adding a third partner to the eleven-year-old Renault-Nissan alliance.

But Daimler was burnt badly in past misalliances with three other mass-market carmakers: America's Chrysler, Japan's Mitsubishi and South Korea's Hyundai. Max Warburton, analyst with Sanford Bernstein, said: 'Daimler is clearly still scared by the Chrysler disaster, so it will see attractions in a much looser co-operation.'

As Mr Ghosn acknowledged, the 'strategic partnership' announced on Wednesday falls short of the cross-shareholding alliance between Renault and Nissan. However, it goes well beyond the smaller, time-limited collaborations on cars, engines or plants favoured by competing carmakers.

The talks began in 2009 when Daimler approached Renault about working together on its Smart small-car brand and smaller four-cylinder engines. Daimler had said it was talking to other potential partners on small cars, but Renault seems to have been its best option.

The two companies will build three Smart and Renault Twingo models in France and Slovenia together, and co-operate on small engines, in addition to joining forces on vans. But analysts said that the partnership – while helping to solve Daimler's problem in small cars – would yield more obvious benefits for Renault and Nissan, including by giving the Japanese carmaker's Infiniti brand access to Mercedes' expertise in engines.

To make the company share knowledge with Renault and Nissan, Mr Zetsche will have to push through a big cultural shift in the lower ranks of the engineering-driven, technology-loving Stuttgart company.

Paul Newton, analyst at IHS Global Insight, said: 'The opportunities for Daimler are many and obvious, but Daimler's engineers and corporate culture may have to undergo a radical change for this to truly succeed.'

Speaking in his German philosophical vein on Wednesday, Mr Ghosn sought to dismiss scepticism about the partnership by quoting Nietzsche's remark that what does not kill you makes you stronger.

When Renault and Nissan started their alliance in 1999, he said, some thought the alliance 'would probably kill both companies'.

'Here we are', he said. 'We are not dead, and we are much stronger than we were 11 years ago.'

Questions

1. Referring to the text, explain what the author means by the phrase 'cultural chasm' as used in the title.
2. How can you explain the fact that the Renault and Nissan alliance is still alive? What factors have helped to make the alliance stronger?

Merging cultures

As Delavallée (2002) points out, an alliance between companies – whether through a merger or a takeover – is one area where the most serious cultural problems arise. Only a major organisational change within a company causes a similar amount of anguish and conflict. The success or failure of an alliance is down to the human factor, not the bottom line.

And the human factor is all to do with how people come to terms with each other, how the employees of two companies work together to help realise the goals of the alliance: the cultural dimension, therefore. However, as Delavallée (2002) stresses, this is often ignored or forgotten about. The systems that make up the organisation of the two companies that are coming together must harmonise, if not become one. The merger process involves making a coherent whole out of the subsystems of the organisation of each partner-to-be. These subsystems comprise goals, structures, techniques and culture. The merger process, therefore, has three levels: strategic, organisational and human.

On the strategic level, Delavallée (2002) uses the work of Cartwright and Cooper (1993) to explain the strategies used during company mergers. According to them, there is not just one merger strategy but four: assimilation, deculturalisation, separation and integration. The type of merger strategy used depends on:

- how strong the buyer's influence is on the culture of the company being absorbed; and
- the degree to which the company to be absorbed is bound to its own culture.

Compatibility between cultures is rarely taken into account while the merger process is under way. When the two sides are highly incompatible – a discovery often made months later when people actually start working together – the shock can be overwhelming.

If a merger between two national companies can lead to a culture shock when the two teams have to work together, what can be expected when there is a merger between companies from different countries or cultures? Furthermore, what will happen when a manager is going to work abroad, which implies a cross-cultural adaptation?

Culture shock

The notion of 'culture shock' refers generally to the unpleasant experience that can be had when coming into contact with other cultures. Marx (1999) has developed a model to describe this notion, one adapted from that of the anthropologist Oberg (1960). According to Marx, international managers experience culture shock psychologically at three levels. She uses what she calls the 'culture shock triangle' to describe these levels (Figure 9.1).

Marx (1999) insists on the fact that the culture shock phase is an integral part of the adaptation phase and, as such, should have no negative connotations. This is a normal reaction of people who confront the strange, the unknown, the foreign, but who have no indication of future success.

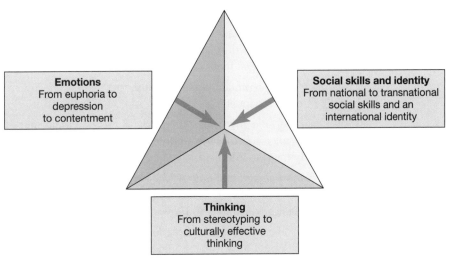

Figure 9.1 **Culture shock pyramid**
Source: Marx, 1999: 12.

Cross-cultural adaptation

When attempting to theorise cross-cultural adaptation, Kim (2005: 377) refers to the lack of coherence in the work of different researchers in this domain who not only use various terms – for example, acculturation, adjustment or assimilation (Spotlight 9.2) – but also use divergent perspectives to describe the phenomenon. According to her, the literature on cross-cultural adaptation misses 'a systemic insight into what happens when someone crosses cultural boundaries'.

SPOTLIGHT 9.2

Adaptation embraces other similar terms

Adaptation is a compromise – a vector in the internal structure of culture and the external pressure of the environment. Adaptation is placed at the intersection of the person and the environment, and embraces other similar but narrower terms:

From:
Assimilation: the acceptance of mainstream cultural elements of the host society by the individual.

And *Acculturation*: the process commonly defined as the acquisition of some, but not all, aspects of the host cultural elements.

To:
Coping and *adjustment*: both of which are often used to refer to psychological responses to cross-cultural challenges.
And *Integration*: often defined as social participation in the host society.

Source: text adapted from Kim, 2005: 380.

Kim proposes a broad-spectrum theory on cross-cultural adaptation which comprises existing approaches and the five important keys omitted in the conceptual literature:

1. *Macro and micro level.* To understand the process of adaptation of individuals completely, one should take into consideration not only macro-level factors (culture, institutions and the ethnic community of the host country), but also micro-level factors (personal history and inner features of the individuals).

2. *Short- and long-term adaptation.* Because these issues are closely related, they should not be treated separately.

3. *New learning and psychological growth.* These two important aspects of adaptation should be taken together for a full interpretation of the experiences from individuals in an unknown environment.

4. *Cross-cultural adaptation process.* The various factors which may influence the adaptation process should be selected with more consistency to reach a necessary coherence when explaining the different degrees of adjustment in individuals.

5. *Conditions of cross-cultural adaptation.* The divergent ideas behind 'assimilation' and 'pluralism' should be integrated into a pragmatic conception of cross-cultural adaptation 'as a condition of the host environment as well as of the individual adapting to that environment'.

However, the success – or otherwise – of a merger between companies at international level depends not only on managers who are well prepared for this cross-cultural adaptation and who have the interpersonal skills necessary. Success depends also on the motives and strategies of the companies wishing to co-operate with or take over another firm.

Company strategy

The current company is no longer what it was nor is it what it will be. This applies just as much to national as to international companies. The media report daily on mergers and acquisitions in every country and every business sector. In 1998, Paul Koster (1998: 37) was predicting that mergers and acquisitions would go on for decades: 'It is not a wave. There are only more or less intense episodes.' Today, the intensity is evident, particularly in Europe, where consolidation in many business sectors is rife. The hostile nature of some takeover battles has received considerable publicity, as has the increasing number of acquisitions made by 'foreign' private investment companies. 'Companies have cash to spare and the prey is cheap. It is a question of swallow or be swallowed' (Hendriks, 2004: 27).

As the examples below show, the forming of these kinds of co-operation, ranging from mergers and takeovers to joint ventures, alliances and partnerships, does not occur without difficulty:

In the acquisition of KLM by Air France there are also American partnerships to be integrated. However, the American competition authority does not accept that they want to make international agreements in Europe. It is not yet clear to what extent this dispute can further delay the takeover. Neither Air France nor KLM want to comment. 'We do not comment on matters happening on the other side of the Atlantic Ocean', was the official reaction from Air France in Paris.

NRC Handelsblad, 22 March 2004

The Swiss pharmaceutical company Novartis mentions in public a potential merger with Aventis. Novartis is only prepared to discuss a merger or takeover with the French–German company Aventis after an official invitation from the board of directors of Aventis. Furthermore, Novartis demands that the French government keeps out of the negotiations, or, at least, remains neutral. Earlier this month, the French government announced its opposition to a takeover of Aventis by Novartis.

Het Financieele Dagblad, 24 March 2004

The post-merger period often shows companies taking the opposite direction to that planned. The case of the British–Dutch steel company Corus illustrates this:

Two years ago, two years after the merger between British Steel and Hoogovens, Corus decided that the British part would continue to produce for the British market, even though production in the Netherlands was cheaper. According to CEO Philippe Varin, it is too expensive to close the existing plants and to expand in IJmuiden. Instead there will be capital investment in modernization in England.

Het Financieele Dagblad, 29 March 2004

As we see above, not only is the study of management after cross-border acquisitions of interest, but also during the acquisition phase, when the alliance forged on paper is being given shape.

What are then the implications of this globalisation for cross-border relations? What impact can this culture phenomenon have on the internationalisation of business, on marketing or on human resources?

The merger of two companies presupposes a change of 'culture' in the new organisation. If, in addition, the companies are established in two different countries, the complexity of the exchanges, of the interactions between cultures increases and gives rise to other problems than those in a merger between two national companies. What can be observed is an organisational situation being transformed, along with all the accompanying elements of cultural change. A merger is by no means a simple process but a complex evolutionary process due to the inevitable change of culture(s) involved.

Mergers and acquisitions: a strategic or cultural issue?

In this area of mergers and acquisitions, the company becomes integrated into the management's process of globalisation and internationalisation. Therefore, as Pierre (2001: 141), emphasises, this requires 'a permanent adaptation of the manager' because 'the environment is in perpetual change and the international executives appear continuously "under construction" through a never-ending professional maturation'.

What are the reasons compelling companies to seek an alliance? According to the protagonists the reason is purely economic, particularly financial, whatever the sector.

'Ahold looks for takeovers after 2006. Company directs focus on Europe', is a headline from a financial newspaper (*Het Financieele Dagblad*, 1 June 2004). The article explains: 'the objective of the current takeovers is to reduce the imbalance in income'. Others have acted similarly: 'Scottish Bank makes large takeover in US. Royal Bank of Scotland (RBOS) buys the American bank Carter One for $10.5 billion in cash. This makes RBOS the seventh-largest American bank' (*Het Financieele Dagblad*, 6 April 2004).

What role does the cultural element play in these forms of cross-border alliance? As mentioned before, this element is usually completely ignored when plans are being drawn up for a merger, as well as at the start of the alliance. When KLM and Air France had just completed their merger (to create a stronger position for themselves in the market), cultural issues were far from their minds. This was suggested in their reactions to a question concerning EasyJet's latest results:

> Without saying it aloud, the disappointing results of EasyJet are for both parties the proof that they were right about their plans to merge. Problems for EasyJet? 'We have our own problems to solve', they both said, laughing.
>
> *Het Financieele Dagblad*, 6 April 2004

Sorting out financial questions resulting from the merger was clearly the priority for both parties.

SPOTLIGHT 9.3

The case of KLM and Northwest Airlines

By Ard-Pieter de Man, Nadine Roijakkers, Henk de Graauw

While alliance formation is typically associated with high-tech firms and R&D-intensive industries, the airline industry is an example of a service-oriented sector where various kinds of alliances have also proliferated. One of the first and most successful ongoing alliances formed in this industry is the agreement between the Dutch airline KLM (now part of the Air France–KLM Holding Company) and the US-based Northwest Airlines (NWA; at the time of writing involved in a merger with Delta Airlines), the start of which dates back to 1989.

For many airlines the formation of alliances has constituted an important tactic to generate additional revenue and realise some cost savings. Alliances serve to accomplish these goals in the following ways:

Through alliances airlines gain access to a larger network of flight routes and final destinations as they connect their own network to that of their partners. Specifically, on the basis of a hub-and-spoke system partnering airlines transport their passengers between major airports (or hubs) where they board connecting flights to final destinations (spokes). Partnering airlines can increase their income substantially by increasing the number of final destinations on offer through connecting their flight networks.

By delivering passengers to each other's networks and by combining flights (that is by jointly operating flights, a phenomenon called code-sharing) the occupancy rate of the planes increases. Fewer empty seats mean a better use of capacity and revenue growth.

Source: de Man *et al.*, 2010, extract.

It is often the case that cultural factors come to the fore only when mergers and acquisitions do not meet strategic expectations, or necessitate a change of strategy. Even then, cultural factors may not be explicitly referred to:

> The board of directors of the British–Dutch steel company Corus has to offer, at short notice, positions to Dutch directors. This was stated by the Russian steel baron Alisher Usmavov (a shareholder in Corus, who has a 12% interest in the company).
>
> *Het Financieele Dagblad*, 29 March 2004

Nevertheless, as Thévenet (1999: 10) remarks, the cultural element in companies is to be found everywhere: 'In all our investigations, not one company has ever showed itself to be interested in culture per se, but everybody works on culture to resolve concrete problems: problems of strategy, mergers, mobilization of the staff, reorganization, even communication.' This explicit attention to culture is all the greater when a company is operating across borders.

This does not necessarily mean, however, that the cultural problems occurring in mergers are related solely to national cultures. This is confirmed by Trompenaars (2004) when describing the Sony/Philips alliance: the problems that had arisen were less to do with differences in national culture and more to do with the strong market orientation of Sony coming up against the technical orientation of Philips.

All the same, it remains obvious that those advocating a merger of some kind often underestimate the differences in the local cultures that have been brought together under one roof. Moreover, they tend to ignore the cultural confrontations that take place and which, in many cases, provoke resistance to any changes on both sides. This resistance is often the manifestation of collective fears intrinsic to the merger or takeover. These fears are often justified, because not only does the organisational culture change, but also the company's strategy. That is why any change needs to be managed carefully in such a way that the fears can be identified and monitored. The phenomenon of change in relation to culture will be developed in the next chapter.

Conclusion

This chapter has dealt with the close relationship between the organisational culture and the corporate strategy of a company. The organisational culture is actually a part of the strategy in the sense that it influences not only the formulation of a strategy, but also the way it is implemented in the company. Furthermore, as Schneider and Barsoux point out, in the process of strategy development lie the same levels as in culture: artefacts, values and assumptions.

This relation is particularly obvious in mergers and cross-border acquisitions since both involve not only the companies themselves, but also their cultures. Companies may well believe that such actions offer a strategic way of dealing with globalisation, but more often than not fail to take into account the cultural problems inherent in the emergence of a new culture in the new organisation.

Points for reflection

1. Strategy is often linked to change. Globalisation compels companies to internationalise, so they must choose a strategy that enables them to remain competitive in the global market. Strategy is also linked to the future. It is a question of choosing strategies

appropriate for enabling them to achieve long-term objectives. Having to face an environment often perceived as hostile and unstable, a company needs to redefine its strategy, to give it a new orientation.

Are these attitudes towards strategy common to all companies?

What role can culture play in defining strategy?

2. What is important in the process of creating a global culture is dealing with diversity, opposite poles and the complementarity of ideas. This means that the creation of a global culture in cross-border organisations has to do with the opposition between ideas.

The question therefore arises: **how can the local cultures of two organisations with their different forms of logic and principles be united while ensuring that their duality is maintained?**

Further reading

Deresky, H. (2003) *International Management: Managing Across Borders and Cultures*, 4th edition, Upper Saddle River, NJ: Prentice Hall. The author takes a global perspective in foreign environments while taking into account the variables of culture. Cross-cultural management is evaluated in the context of global changes.

Fatehi, K. (1996) *International Management: A Cross-cultural Approach*, Upper Saddle River, NJ: Prentice Hall. This work uses the concepts of managing from an international perspective while emphasising the cultural differences and the difficulties of working with people from diverse cultural backgrounds.

References

Bartlett, C.A., Ghoshal, S. and Birkinshaw, J. (2003) *Transnational Management*, 4th edition, New York, NY: McGraw-Hill Education.

Black, J.S., Gregersen, H.B., Mendenhall, M.E. and Stroh, L.K. (1999) *Globalizing People Through International Assignments*, Harlow: Addison-Wesley.

Browaeys, M.-J. (ed.) (1996) *The Challenges of Cross-Cultural Management*, Breukelen, Netherlands: Nyenrode University Press.

Cartwright, S. and Cooper, C.L. (1993) 'The role of culture compatibility in successful organizational marriage', *Academy of Management Executive*, 7(2); quoted by Delavallée, E. (2002) *La culture d'entreprise pour manager autrement*, Paris: Editions d'Organisation: 55–70.

Delavallée, E. (2002) *La culture d'entreprise pour manager autrement*, Paris: Editions d'Organisation.

Deresky, H. (2003) *International Management: Managing Across Borders and Cultures*, 4th edition, Upper Saddle River, NJ: Prentice Hall.

Fatehi, K. (1996) *International Management: A Cross-cultural Approach*, Upper Saddle River, NJ: Prentice Hall.

Hendriks, P. (2004) *FEM Business Magazine*, Amsterdam, Netherlands: Reed Business, 6 March: 27.

Kim, Y.Y. (2005) 'Adapting to a new culture: An integrative communication theory', in Gudykunst, W.B. (ed.) *Theorizing about Intercultural Communication*, Thousand Oaks: Sage: 375–400.

Koster, P. (1998) *FEM Business Magazine*, Haarlem, Netherlands: NVU Media, 19/6/1998: 37.

Marx, E. (1999) *Breaking Through Culture Shock*, London: Nicholas Brealey.

Man de, A.-P., Roijakkers, N. and Graauw de, H. (2010) 'Managing dynamics through robust alliance governance structures: the case of KLM and Northwest Airlines', *European Management Journal*, 28: 171–181.

Oberg, K. (1960) 'Culture shock: adjustment to new cultural environments', *Practical Anthropology* 7: 177–82, quoted by Marx, E. (1999) *Breaking Through Culture Shock*, London: Nicholas Brealey: 5.

Pierre, P. (2001) 'Eléments pour une réflexion critique sur le management interculturel', *Sociologies Pratiques*, 5: 119–143.

Schneider, S.C. and Barsoux, J.-L. (2003) *Managing Across Cultures*, 2nd edition, Harlow: FT Prentice Hall.

Schoenberger, E.J. (1997) *The Cultural Crisis of the Firm*, Oxford: Blackwell.

Tayeb, M. (2003) *International Management*, Harlow: Prentice Hall.

Thévenet, M. (1999) *La culture d'entreprise*, Paris: PUF Que sais-je?

Trice, H.M. and Beyer, J.M. (1993) *The Culture of Work Organizations*, Upper Saddle River, NJ: Prentice Hall.

Trompenaars, F. (2004) 'HRM moet verzoenen in plaats van uitsluiten', in Verbakel, F. (ed.), *Gids voor Personeelsmanagement*, 83(4): 20–22.

Chapter 9 Activities

Shell's reorganisation

In 2005, two companies, Royal Dutch Petroleum Company and Shell Transport and Trading Company merged to form one company: Royal Dutch Shell plc.

Read the two articles below. These describe the developments in the organisation of Shell. Then answer the questions that follow.

Our strategy in action: creating the culture and organization to deliver

We have made significant progress in changing our culture and organization to ensure that we can deliver our strategy. The unification of the parent companies under Royal Dutch Shell plc in 2005 has provided us with a clearer, simpler, more efficient and accountable form of governance.

The chief executive now reports to a single board comprising 10 non-executive directors and five executive directors and a key advantage of this single, smaller board is that it provides a very clear and direct line of accountability to shareholders. Royal Dutch Shell now has a single headquarters in The Hague (the Netherlands). The centralization of a number of activities in the headquarters is helping to reduce duplication and helping us to operate in a more streamlined and efficient way.

The structural changes are also helping to reinforce our work to simplify and standardize many of our business processes. In particular, the integration of the oil products and chemicals businesses into one down-stream organization has so far been very successful in creating a more dynamic, responsive and effective organization. We have seen particular benefits at sites which contain both refineries and chemicals manufacturing plants.

By sharing services and integrating their activities we can operate much more efficiently. It also means we have been able to share and adopt best practice more quickly and so improve operational performance.

Source: Royal Dutch Shell 2005 annual report, www.shell.com/annualreports.

Marriage after a century of cohabitation: Shell prepares for the next merger round

On the top floor of London's towering Shell Centre, a cavernous boardroom looms over the Houses of Parliament, filled with high-backed chairs and rows of angled microphones. For decades, British and Dutch directors from two separate companies have held eight 'conferences' a year, alternating between there and the Netherlands, to decide on the business of Royal Dutch/Shell Group. But if shareholders today approve the most radical restructuring in its history, the London room will fall into disuse. Instead, board members will assemble each time in the more intimate surroundings of a gabled building topped by a clock tower in The Hague.

After nearly a century of quirky cohabitation, shareholders of Royal Dutch Petroleum and Shell Transport and Trading will today be asked to approve the formal marriage of the two, which together make up the world's biggest publicly traded oil company after Exxon-Mobil and BP.

The union will put the relationship on a new footing and fundamentally alter the way the company is governed. Shell's eccentric corporate governance structure – long a source of befuddlement to outsiders – will be scrapped in favour of a modern, 'Anglo-Saxon-style' system designed to bring it into line with Exxon and BP, its more successful rivals.

Executives say the shift represents a dramatic transformation of the company's conservative and consensus-driven culture – changes they say are badly needed if it is to compete in a rapidly changing oil industry. But critics ask why it took them so long to accept the need for change and why Shell had to be forced into it by shareholders following a scandal last year in which the group was forced to slash what it had recorded as proved reserves of oil and gas no fewer than five times. That reduced the level of reserves by one-third, led to a boardroom purge and brought $150m in fines imposed by US and British regulators. Investors question whether the merger will do enough to alter the ponderous way in which the group operates.

'We changed a lot of the culture of this company', insists Jeroen Van der Veer, appointed as Shell's first-ever chief executive following the reserves scandal and the decision to streamline the group. A soft-spoken Dutchman with a kindly manner, Mr Van der Veer – still eager to show that he and the other executives have taken a firm grip following one of the worst crises in its history – adds: 'We were very much a "bottom-up" company. Now there is certainly more direction from the top. I try to give very high clarity on where to go.'

He makes it clear that the direction the group is headed will include takeovers. Shell had missed out on the wave of mega-mergers in the late 1990s that saw Exxon merge with Mobil and BP buy Amoco. The failure to participate was prompted largely by a prediction that oil prices would remain low – at about $10 a barrel instead of the $60 seen today. But Shell's dual structure also meant it would have been hard for the group to use its stock as currency to finance takeovers, as its rivals were doing.

With today's high oil price, the cost of any deals is much higher. But Mr Van der Veer says the company must be ready for the next wave of consolidation in the industry. 'If you study – and I do that fairly regularly – the last 100 years of the oil industry, it is one long story of consolidation', he says. 'So you [had] better [be] prepared. You must have the tools in your toolkit.'

The necessary tools were absent when the reserves crisis hit. Shell seemed paralysed. It took some measures to improve the way in which it booked reserves and addressed other compliance issues. But investors were unhappy about the speed at which it was moving after Mr Van der Veer and his new team took over in March last year. Advisers intervened on behalf of large institutional investors to try to press their views about the need for a thorough overhaul of the company's structure. Shareholders wanted an end to the company's dual-board system which, they maintained, hamstrung the company with a cumbersome decision-making process and obstructed accountability.

At first, the group resisted the calls. 'They thought the structure was doing well and when the reserves debacle hit, to some extent they were in denial,' says one senior adviser to the company. 'They quickly went away from that into a phase where I quite frankly realized they didn't know what to do.'

Shell had periodically considered altering its structure, most recently during the 1990s. At that time, the company was doing well and there was little support for change. But things had now changed and reformers saw their opportunity.

Two broad options were on the table. The first was to create a single unified board while maintaining separate Dutch and British companies – a so-called 'dual-header' company such as Rio Tinto or BHP Billiton. This choice represented a tidying-up of the existing arrangement and had the advantage of being easier to do. But the big-bang approach of a full merger had the virtue of simplicity and would do away with the complex corporate structure that so bothered investors.

Any changes also had the potential to upset the delicate balance of power within the group that had existed for 98 years. Royal Dutch was in the ascendant when they joined forces in 1907. The then troubled Shell side was forced to join up with Royal Dutch on somewhat humiliating terms – a 60/40 split in the Dutch company's favour.

Under the new plan, however, the merged company will be incorporated in Britain and listed on the London Stock Exchange. 'For some people in the Netherlands, seeing by far the largest company in the Netherlands become a plc with its primary listing in London is quite a difficult issue', says one director.

To offset the perception that it is becoming too British, the company will be headquartered in The Hague and will be a tax resident of the Netherlands. The 60/40 split will also be maintained. A senior adviser to the company says: 'The idea was to try to preserve the Anglo-Dutch heritage in as many ways as possible. There was a tax advantage to having the headquarters in The Hague, which made no sense to give up. To the extent that you needed to pacify political

interests in the Netherlands that clearly served the purpose. Equally, having a UK listing played to the UK gallery.'

Shell executives insist the changes are not cosmetic. Mr Routs, head of downstream operations, says he is already seeing tangible benefits. 'If I compare differences in the team in terms of operating, it is night and day', he says. 'We are now a more transparent, supportive, action-orientated executive team that makes things happen. There is not a lot of consensus-seeking in the old way of expressing it. We come to conclusions faster. We come to deals faster.'

The reorganization of the company would not have happened without the reserves crisis, many believe. But Shell still does not accept that the reserves crisis was a result of its management structure. That has left investors baffled. If there is no connection between the reserves crisis and the structure, then why change at all? Conversely, if much of what is proposed is 'common sense', as Mr Routs now says, then why was it not done sooner?

Some believe that the directors of Royal Dutch/ Shell agreed to the restructuring not because they really believed in it but as a sop to disgruntled investors. As a senior adviser to the company says: 'The reserves debacle had seriously dented shareholder confidence and I suppose [the big-bang approach] was ultimately also a way of demonstrating to shareholders that we can deliver.'

At the height of the scandal last summer over the level of oil reserves it had booked, Jeroen Van der Veer, the group's lead executive, held a number of meetings with shareholders in the US, The Hague and the City of London. The discussions centred on investor demand for a structure that would foster accountability and transparency in decision-making.

Investors say it took several meetings for Shell executives to accept that the status quo was not an option. A year on, investors hope the combined structure will help prevent any future scandal. Few are entirely satisfied, though, and remain watchful lest Shell slip back into its secretive previous ways.

1. How would you characterise, in cultural terms, the nature of Shell when it was a 'cohabitation' of Royal Dutch Petroleum and Shell Transport and Trading?

2. What changes in the culture of Shell are the 'marriage' of the two companies expected to bring?

3. What were the reasons for the strategic decision to merge the two companies?

4. How did the reserves crisis precipitate the changes? If necessary, refer to Concept 8.2.

5. What do you consider to have been the key managerial and cultural factors involved in the merger process?

6. What evidence can you find in the text to suggest the possible emergence of a 'third culture' within the new company?

ACTIVITY 9.2

The text below is an adaptation of an article written by a lawyer (a specialist in company reorganisation, mergers and acquisitions) when he was working for an international group of tax consultants. Once you have read the text, answer the questions that follow.

Cultural differences during international takeovers and mergers

Cultural differences have played an important role in many of the cases I have been involved in. Sometimes they have helped to speed up a transaction, sometimes they have delayed a transaction – and even prevented a deal being made.

Some of the differences I have experienced are, in my opinion, to do with language. By language I do not mean the use of different mother tongues but also the use of the professional language prevalent among consultants. In our profession, it is easy to forget that not all our clients and others involved in our cases will understand the language terms we use. This goes not only for our international clients, but also for one group of specialists communicating with a different group of specialists in the same company.

Other differences have to do with customs, different ways of doing things. I have been involved in several cases where such [cultural] differences have played a crucial role. A number of these are outlined below.

A British baker's takeover

A British concern wanted to take over a Dutch family baker. Although the former used internationally recognised norms when determining the value of the Dutch firm (these differed considerably from the norms used by the Dutch side), the deal was more or less finalised. All that had to be done was to work out how best to keep on managers of the Dutch bakers for a while once the takeover had taken place. The British buyers, aware of the family's considerable knowledge of and experience in the market, were keen to keep its members in position for a few months.

The takeover was completed, but it soon became clear that the Dutch managers could not come to terms with the regime of the new owners. The strict accounting procedures coupled with the new bookkeeping approach gave them a number of headaches, as did the new company's answerability to its shareholders.

In the end this all proved too much for the Dutch family and their stay-on was reduced from one year to six months.

A Finnish–Norwegian merger

I represented a Norwegian oil company in its discussions with a Finnish oil company over the integration of their respective plastic divisions. The Finns used the services of an American lawyer; the Norwegians used my firm since, apparently, it was considered large enough and with enough international experience to do a good job. The idea of using a British firm had been considered but eventually rejected: British lawyers were considered to be too expensive, complicated and drawn out in their dealings.

The intended merger itself was on a very large scale: one hundred companies were involved in several countries. Many external parties were also involved, including a British investment bank, which was in charge of the whole project. It relentlessly pushed the project forward knowing that if the merger did not come off it would receive no fee for its efforts.

Once a letter of intent had been agreed upon and 'due diligence' reports completed, the real negotiations began, with co-operation on an equal footing being the main goal. The Norwegian party had noticed during its 'due diligence' investigations that several of the Finnish companies involved had caused environmental pollution. This would involve a costly clean-up operation and, along with other issues, would make it difficult for a 50–50 deal to be reached. Nevertheless, after a number of long, drawn-out negotiations in several European cities (to underline the European character of the merger), the contracts were signed in England.

During the process, clear differences in working practice between the American and Dutch lawyers emerged. The Finn's American lawyer made a note in detail and required every point to be covered – preferably twice – in the agreement. This slowed down the whole process, particularly when the American lawyers acted as if they were the spokespersons of the company and even appeared to be making decisions on the company's behalf. The Dutch lawyers behaved as they usually do: they are there to advise the client along with other advisers (accountants, tax consultants, etc.). They consider it natural that in the end it is the company's directors who determine policy and take the decisions.

Further differences emerged in behaviour during the negotiations. The lawyers representing the Finnish partners showed a rather aggressive attitude throughout and this contrasted strongly with the quieter, more modest approach of the Norwegians' lawyers. The Norwegians were somewhat intimidated by the American lawyers and had to be reassured that the less contentious approach in no way undermined the justness of their cause.

A French takeover of a Dutch concern

Language turned out to be a barrier when a French group of companies decided to take over a Dutch company. During the research phase prior to the negotiations, the French sent several employees from the Alsace region of France to carry out interviews in the Netherlands. They assumed that the dialect spoken by these colleagues would enable them to communicate with their Dutch counterparts. When this did not turn out to be the case, everyone involved started using English.

English was used during the negotiating phase, but its role in the actual written agreement was hotly disputed. The French preferred to have the takeover contracts written in French, the Dutch in Dutch. In such a situation, a contract written in a neutral language is the best solution, especially since legal terms written in one language can have a very different meaning in another. If both sides can agree on a neutral language, then agreements can be reached on what the legal terms used actually mean.

In this particular takeover, neither side would back down and, for a while, the language question threatened to scupper the whole deal. Eventually, however, after a further round of protracted negotiations, an agreement was reached and the deal went through. The takeover contract was drawn up in French for the French group of companies and in Dutch for the Dutch concern. An English version was made for reference during face-to-face encounters.

Source: adapted from Browaeys, 1996: 41–50.

Questions

1. The author of the article above mentioned some cultural differences he has encountered in dealing with companies abroad: language (different mother tongues and professional language) and customs (different way of doing things). Note the kinds of cultural differences – language, customs or others (say what they are) dealt with in the three cases:

   a) a British baker's takeover;

   b) a Finnish–Norwegian merger;

   c) a French takeover of a Dutch concern.

2. Describe the differences in attitudes and working practices of the lawyers and the people involved in the process of the three mergers/takeovers.

3. Write a conclusion to this article: make a synthesis of the three cases and answer the question: what have I learnt from this account about the cultural aspects in international mergers and acquisitions?

Chapter 10

Cultural change in organisations

So far, this book has examined organisational culture in terms of the various models put forward by researchers, the concepts of leadership and the cultural contingencies and variables involved. Furthermore, it has looked at the question of company strategy and corporate culture. All these elements come together when it is a question of a company needing to adapt its culture to ensure its success or even survival.

Concept 10.1 examines the process of adaptation, the starting point for any real cultural change in an organisation. Concept 10.2 tackles the issue of changing the underlying culture of global organisations.

Learning outcomes

After reading this chapter, you will gain an understanding of:

● Certain mechanisms for changing an organisation's culture as well as an instrument for diagnosing the changes required.

● The tensions between national culture and organisational culture in the change process, particularly the emergence of a so-called international corporate culture.

Concept 10.1 Organisational change as a cultural process

Whether an organisation thrives, survives – or otherwise – depends on numerous factors, both within the company and outside it. There are, of course, external factors to which a company needs to respond, or circumstances to anticipate in the way it organises its operations. Rapid technological change, changes in industries and markets, new deregulation policies, increased competition and the development of the global economy can all be seen as potential threats to a company's survival, or potential opportunities.

But success has also to do with internal factors. How can an organisation adapt? Is it able to change its behavioural practices and structures, to deal with external pressures? Admittedly, the culture of a company is dynamic. However, does it need to change its core values to survive or will changing cultural artefacts suffice? It is generally acknowledged that successful change has to do with maintaining both continuity and change, retaining the cultural foundation on which the company rests while changing its strategies and practices. In short, can essential elements of culture be brought in line with responses to the external forces pushing on the company?

The process of change

André Laurent (1989) addresses the difficulties involved in the process of change. The way workers view organisational change, and the management thereof, is inhibited by their own assumptions and conceptions. For a start, they may have fixed ideas as to how an organisation should be structured. They may not, for example, consider any alternatives to the hierarchical pyramid, where movements up and down are clearly defined. The idea of unity of command may also be taken for granted. Such concepts, the products of classical (Western) management thought, may not be appropriate when the organisation has to take on fresh tasks or technologies, or deal with new people or environments. Moreover, the whole idea of change may be naive, if well-intentioned. People focus too much on the benefits from change without giving consideration to the idea that change is not an organisational shift from A to B, but a transformation from A into B.

These two differing concepts of change, shift versus transformation, reflect the 'doing' orientation of Anglo-Saxon cultures and 'being' of many Eastern cultures mentioned in Part One. In 'doing' cultures, people and groups are mostly defined in terms of what they do, what they achieve. In 'being' cultures, people and groups are defined more in terms of affiliation, the relationships they have with others in the organisation. In 'doing' cultures organisational change is perceived more in linear fashion, a question of putting the past state of affairs behind and pushing on with the new. In 'being' cultures, however, the past state of affairs undergoes gradual transformation so that it eventually becomes a new state of affairs.

Laurent (1989) advocates a dual approach to organisational change: both the instrumental and social nature of the organisation must be considered. Managing change in the sense of ensuring the continuing running of the organisation, re-assigning tasks and maintaining overall stability, may well be necessary in the process, but it is not enough. What is also needed is inspirational guidance, a leader who engages people's minds through vision. According to Laurent, our minds are the receptacles of culture, and as such give meaning and guidance to our experiences. Minds cannot be managed, but they can be transformed through inspiring leaders who spread visions that advocate new meanings and new lines of thinking.

Such concerns are shared by Deal and Kennedy (2000: 158). Many company managers, they maintain, are concerned about change, but do not pay attention to the cultural issues involved. They may go about dealing with tangible factors, such as changing job descriptions, replacing managers, changing the company structure even, but essentially, 'the business of change is cultural transformation'.

> These actions . . . are not the kind of long-term, all-encompassing behavioural and cultural changes we are talking about. When we speak of organizational or cultural change we mean real changes in the behaviour of people throughout the organization.

In their view, the decision to become, for example, more marketing-oriented or to become cost-effective cannot be taken without subjecting the company to a fundamental cultural change that involves everyone. The change is not just a matter of changing routines but also of identifying with role-models who embody a new purpose or goal. Such fundamental change does not occur overnight; it is often a gradual and sometimes painful transformation.

The mechanisms of change

Schein (2004) described several ways which enable a leader to implant and maintain the corporate culture. Such means can be used to change the culture of an organisation. He also lists what he calls 'secondary' means. These are mechanisms for shaping and reinforcing the culture that are only effective if consistent with the primary means:

- the design and structure of the organisation;
- the systems and procedures used;
- the 'rites and rituals' used in an organisation;
- the design and layout of the organisation's physical space;
- stories of important events and people;
- formal statements of the organisation's philosophy.

When a manager is intent on getting employees to perceive things differently, all the primary mechanisms must be used. Moreover, according to Schein, they must all be consistent with each other.

Schein's model refers to the group-learning process when responding to problems externally and internally. External problems are concerned with responding to the environment. Internal problems arise from managing the internal development of the organisation. For Schein, culture plays an important role in determining not only how environmental developments are perceived by members of organisations, but also how members of the organisation react to the strategies designed to respond to those environmental developments.

In his article 'Organizational culture: what it is and how to change it', Schein (1989) presents what he believes to be the culture issues predominating at each phase of a company's growth. In addition, he discusses the change mechanisms that could be operating during each phase of growth. These phases only apply to private organisations and the kind of change possible depends on the extent to which the organisation is ready for change as a result of either an external crisis or an internal push for change. Table 10.1 summarises Schein's insights and Table 10.2 outlines how he believes the cultural change mechanisms work.

Can organisational culture really be changed?

Table 10.2 triggers an important question: is it possible to bring about fundamental transformations? An analysis by Deal and Kennedy (2000) reflects the belief that the culture of an organisation is deep-rooted, particularly if, in Schein's terms, it is in a mid-life or maturity stage. A culture that has developed along with the organisation and been passed on from generation to generation will be difficult to change and involves all kinds of relations between individuals and subgroups.

If the external factors referred to in Chapter 7 are believed to have a strong influence on the organisational culture, the values, beliefs and behaviours that employees bring to the organisation, then there is little conviction that an organisation can be changed unless the external environment changes in line with the desired changes. If organisational culture

Table 10.1 Growth states, functions of culture and mechanisms of change

Growth stage	Function of culture/issue
I. Birth and early growth Founder domination, possible family domination	• Culture is a distinctive competence and source of identity • Culture is the 'glue' that holds organisation together • Organisation strives towards more integration and clarity • Heavy emphasis on socialisation as evidence of commitment
Succession phase	• Culture becomes battleground between conservatives and liberals • Potential successors are judged on whether they will preserve or change cultural elements
Change mechanisms 1. Natural evolution 2. Self-guided evolution through organisational therapy 3. Managed evolution through hybrids 4. Managed 'revolution' through outsiders	
II. Organisational mid-life • Expansion of products/markets • Vertical integration • Geographical expansion • Acquisitions, mergers	• Cultural integration declines as subcultures are spawned • Loss of goals, values and assumptions creates crisis identity • Opportunity to manage direction of cultural change is provided
Change mechanisms 5. Planned change and organisation development 6. Technological seduction 7. Change through scandal, explosion of myths 8. Incrementalism	
III. Organisational maturity • Maturity or decline of markets • Increasing internal stability and/or stagnation • Lack of motivation to change	• Culture becomes a constraint on innovation • Culture preserves the glories of the past, hence, is valued as a source of self-esteem, defence
Transformation option	• Culture change is necessary and inevitable, but not all elements of culture can or must change • Essential elements of culture must be identified, preserved • Culture change can be managed or simply allowed to evolve
Destruction option • Bankruptcy and reorganisation • Takeover and reorganisation • Merger and assimilation	• Culture changes at fundamental levels • Culture changes through massive replacement of people
Change mechanisms 9. Coercive persuasion 10. Turnaround 11. Reorganisation, destruction, rebirth	

Source: Schein (1989).

Table 10.2 **Mechanisms of cultural change**

Natural evolution	The culture will evolve a culture of what works best if the organisation is not undergoing too much stress from the environment. This may also involve what Schein calls a 'general evolution' to the next stage of the organisation's development through diversification and growing complexity. It may also involve 'specific evolution' where subcultures may emerge around the increasing number of subunits in the organisation
Self-guided evolution through organisational therapy	The organisation gains insight into own strengths and weaknesses, e.g. by using an outside consultant to 'unfreeze' the organisational culture and so allowing dramatic changes to occur
Managed evolution through hybrids, 'revolution' through outsiders	This approach is useful where the culture needs to change, but the organisation may lose its identity as a result. People from inside the company are used in key positions, people who realise there is a need for change but may meet less resistance than outsiders
Planned change and organisational development	Differentiation through growth and increasing complexity may lead to increasing sub-cultures coming into conflict. A consultant initiates a change programme to reduce conflict, one that involves some sort of culture change
Technological seduction	Technological changes may bring about cultural change because they change behaviour patterns and compel the organisation to examine the way it carries out business
Change through scandal, explosion of myths	Change may occur through discrepancies between the values that are espoused by the organisation and the practices that it actually performs. 'Whistle-blowers' may reveal, for example, how ethical standards are being bypassed in certain operations, safety procedures ignored, promotion policies undermined. Such exposures often lead to assumptions being reconsidered and cultural changes being made
Incrementalism	Cultural change is implemented gradually over several years and is hardly noticed. Recruitment and selection policies, for example, may result in all key positions in a company being filled by people who act according to assumptions that are different to those of the old culture
Coercive persuasion	A culture turnaround, usually in a mature culture, where change agents – possibly senior managers – challenge old assumptions, put forward new ones and give key managers psychological safety by rewarding them for embracing the new assumptions
Turnaround	A turnaround individual or team has a clear idea of where the organisation must go and how it is to get there. Some or all of the above mechanisms may be used while the present culture is unfrozen and psychological safety offered to reduce resistance
Reorganisation and rebirth	An unusual occurrence, whereby the group that bears the old culture is removed and replaced by a new group and a fresh culture

is seen as dependent on internal factors, then there is a belief that culture can be directed and changed. Ideas as to how these changes are brought about vary: some concentrate on the role of the leader as instigator of changes or as facilitator, others focus more on how to initiate change at the three levels of corporate culture as defined by Schein (norms, values and beliefs; then behaviours and norms; then symbols and artefacts).

The notion that cultural change is easier to implement in an organisation with a 'weak' culture rather than a 'strong' culture is contested by Laurent (1989). In a way, both are doomed to extinction. The organisation with a weak culture may eventually crash, even if there is an initial burst of creativity from its disparate body of workers. With employees who each give the organisation a different meaning and who each have a different view of what needs to be done, an organisation with a weak culture is poorly coordinated, lacking direction and consistency. An organisation with a strong culture, however, may be throttled by rigid norms and behaviour and the resulting dearth of innovation.

Rather than the strong–weak paradigm, Laurent advocates a more conceptual differentiation, which takes account of the extent to which an organisation knows itself and the environment in which it operates. The higher the degree of awareness, both internally and externally, the better an organisation can interpret its environment and deal with it.

Schein (2004) takes this awareness-raising issue further. He suggests that one way of trying to 'grasp' the corporate culture is for members of the organisation to examine their culture together and assess some of the main assumptions. One or more of these may need to be abandoned or re-defined so that those involved can help decide the way the organisation needs to evolve. The leader can play a key role here in getting the 'self-guided' evolution under way and by managing the process.

SPOTLIGHT 10.1

Steadfastness in turbulent times

By Rob Goffee and Gareth Jones

In turbulent times steadfastness is a leadership virtue. Not in the sense of having a fixed view of what will happen next, but by being true to a set of core values. A naïve reading of this point would suggest that all the leader has to do is be their authentic self. But that is not enough. Change will require that leaders play different roles in different contexts. In our previous book, *Why Should Anyone Be Led By You?*, we noted that effective leadership involves a complex balancing act between using your authentic differences and adapting your behaviours to context. Being authentic is not about being the same all the time. The most effective leaders are authentic chameleons. The chameleon always adapts to context but remains a chameleon.

 Source: 'The challenges facing leadership', *Financial Times (FT.com)*, 12/11/2009 (extract).

A degree of culture change will almost always be necessary, Schein maintains, because what has been learned has become routine. Bringing unconscious values and norms to the surface, then questioning and redefining them, may lead to a considerable anxiety: the subjects involved may feel that their sense of identity or integrity is threatened. Everything must be done to reassure those involved, to show them that changes are possible and that they will not be humiliated in the process.

This brings us back to the role of transformational leaders, discussed in Chapter 8. Their role is to provide that reassurance through communicating a vision of how things should be, of convincing those who feel under threat that there is a brighter, happier future for the organisation.

An inquiry into secret accounts held by the European Commission is an example of the sort of crisis that can trigger organisational change. Consider Mini-case 10.1.

Change in an organisational culture does seem possible, but the effort involved may be considerable and time-consuming. Apart from needing to be motivated to undergo change, those involved need to go through a process whereby they can gain clear insight into important cultural assumptions and then work out which of these help or hinder the organisation's future. A 'transformational' leader can be critical to such a process.

MINI-CASE 10.1

Irregular practices at the European Commission

Brussels launches probe into secret accounts

A widespread inquiry into secret bank accounts and fictitious contracts across the European Commission has been launched.

There is fear that the 'vast enterprise of looting' that fraud investigators found at Eurostat, the Commission's statistical arm, may exist elsewhere in the European Union's executive. Although problems were identified at Eurostat by trade unions in 1997, by internal Commission audits in 1999 and 2000 and by Paul van Buitenen, a whistle-blower, in 2001, they were not taken seriously until newspaper reports surfaced in May 2003.

Neil Kinnock, EU administration commissioner, has since revealed the 'relatively extensive practice' at Eurostat until 1999 of setting up secret and illegal accounts, into which millions of euros are thought to have disappeared. The secret bank accounts at Eurostat were set up by Commission officials to hold money paid through inflated contracts to sub-contractors.

The commission has responded by initiating three disciplinary proceedings, suspending all directors and ordering an investigation into the work of some thirty heads of unit.

 Source: from 'Brussels launches probe into secret accounts', *Financial Times*, 16/7/2003, © The Financial Times Ltd. All Rights Reserved.

Progress in the implementation of the reform within the Commission

Extract from the 2003 annual report dealing with protection of the European Community's financial interests and the fight against fraud.

The modernization of the European public service continued to progress during 2003, in parallel to the work relating to the deepening of the antifraud reform of May 1999. In particular, the financial and administrative reform conceived in the White Paper of March 2000 on the internal reform of the Commission is being completed with the entry into force of the new Financial Regulation on 1 January 2003 which changes in particular the internal control system, and the decision of July 2003 on the Specialised Financial Irregularities Panel. As a result of the political agreement reached on 19 May 2003 in the Council and the opinion of the European Parliament of 19 June 2003, the Commission adopted an amended Proposal for the Staff Regulation. As from its entry into force on 1 May 2004, this staff reform will have a major impact on the managing practices of departments and will contribute in particular to the prevention of irregularities . . .

In response to the irregular practices detected at Eurostat, the Commission adopted complementary horizontal reinforcement measures: the September 1999 Code of conduct on the relations between the Commissioners and their services was revised in order to improve the information transmitted to Commissioners and to enable them to assume their political responsibility. To this end, a group of Commissioners including the President ensured that all the relevant information and/or allegations of fraud, irregularity and other reprehensible acts coming in particular from OLAF, IDOC and the Internal Audit Service are the subject of a rigorous follow-up. The group of commissioners is assisted by a high-level interdepartmental group.

Source: Report from the Commission Protection of the European Communities' financial interests and the fight against fraud, Annual Report 2003, (http://eur-lex.europa.eu/LexUriServ/LexUriServ.do?uri=CELEX:52004DC0573:EN:NOT), accessed 1/9/2010.

Questions

1. How would you describe the effect that the whistle-blower's actions had on the European Commission?
2. In what way do you think the 'culture' of Eurostat might have been changed as a result of the actions?

Concept 10.2 Organisational change in a global environment

So, organisational change in companies operating across a number of cultures is not just instrumental (becoming more cost-effective or market-oriented) but also transformational (giving new ways of thinking). How, therefore, does a multinational deal with change if it not only has to deal with policy changes, but also internal factors that may vary considerably from one part of the company to another? Equally important is how the multinational can handle the external factors that are said to have such an influence on the culture of the organisation (Laurent, 1989).

The tension between organisational and national cultures

The first issue to be addressed is the one briefly described in Part One: the tension between organisational culture and national culture. Adler (2002) wondered whether organisational values in some way pushed aside or diluted the national culture of the organisation's environment. She refers to the seminal research carried out by Laurent in the 1980s. The conclusions of this research were that cultural differences among managers working for a multinational company were significantly greater than those cultural differences among managers working for companies in their own (native) country. Although restricted to Western managers, Laurent's investigations showed that 'nationally bounded' collective perceptions of organisations did not appear to be diminished in any way through international business. On the contrary, as Adler indicates, these appear to be reinforced through the international exposure.

The conclusion is that the national companies of multinationals are likely to prefer different ways of bringing about the organisational changes that headquarters wish to implement. To use the terms adopted in Concept 10.1, the transformation of an organisation from A to B may involve following a different path in one part of the multinational than in another, even if the end-result (B) is the same. The means used to reach the desired change will also depend on how the national organisation determines what the starting-point should be. In other words, the outset of the transformation to B will depend on how the national organisation interprets its own present situation (A).

Does an international corporate culture exist?

Despite the all-important influence of national cultures, the opinion is often expressed that there is a growing class of transnational business people who share a similar education, similar work experience and who are developing their own global business culture. Moreover, it is argued that the companies for which these people work are themselves developing commonalities in terms of efficient production processes, quality control, workers' rights and environment issues. More and more international norms concerning business are being established through various agencies and these are being followed by an increasing number of globally active companies. So, the argument runs, both the increasing homogeneity among international managers and the increasing convergence of business practices is leading to the establishment of a common management culture among more and more international companies and their national constituents, a common culture which has no roots in any particular national culture.

These arguments appear to be supported by investigations done by Despharde *et al.* (1997). They investigated whether there were any commonalities when comparing the organisational performance of multinationals based in Japan, the US, England, France and Germany. They found that, although the companies operated very differently, the most successful businesses surveyed used a similar organisational strategy. Whatever the country of origin, each successful multinational was most likely to foster competitive, entrepreneurial values. In particular, they found that those companies where innovation was most valued were the most successful.

Their findings may indeed highlight values that account for the success of the companies investigated, but to suggest that these companies have adopted an organisational culture at the expense of national cultures is considered by many in the field to be wishful thinking. There may indeed be a growing consensus among multinationals as to what best practice is for international business. However, the idea that a shared organisational culture of many multinationals is pushing aside national cultures not only downplays the deep-seated nature of national cultures, but also discourages the transfer of know-how between the culturally different subsidiaries of the company, particularly when it comes to organisational change. Moreover, there is always the risk that multinational constituents become estranged from their national roots and that local relationships of all kinds are put under strain.

In short, a true multinational does not subordinate national cultures, but regards them as a source of learning and increased synergy within the company. To return to the analysis made by Laurent (1989: 93) and summarised at the start of this concept, this increased learning and synergy:

> [. . .] cannot be the result of a rational management decision. It requires an evolution in ways of thinking – from a parochial and ethnocentric conception of management and organization to a world view.

Mapping corporate culture change

At this stage it is worthwhile looking at the framework of reference used in the survey carried out by Despharde *et al.* (1997) to allow the issue of corporate culture change to be taken further. Cameron and Quinn (1999) categorise organisational effectiveness perspectives and associated types of organisation (Figure 10.1). They emphasise that this categorisation should not be seen in any way as comprehensive. It is, however, based on many scholarly analyses of corporate culture and has, they claim, proved its value in many subsequent investigations into corporate culture change.

As can be seen in Table 10.3, two dimensions are used to differentiate effectiveness criteria: one emphasises either flexibility and discretion or stability and control; another emphasises either internal orientation (integration and unity) or external orientation (differentiation and rivalry). These two dimensions produce four quadrants, which each represents a set of values that are at the base of judgements about organisations. The quadrants are contradictory or competing on the diagonal. Hence, the name of the model, the competing values (CV) framework.

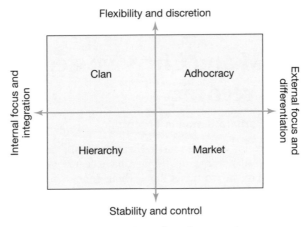

Figure 10.1 **The competing values framework**
Source: Cameron and Quinn, 1999: 32.

Table 10.3 **The characteristics of the CV framework quadrants**

Hierarchy culture	Values tradition, continuity, rationalisation and regulation. It focuses more on internal than external (market) issues, and values stability and control over flexibility and discretion. This is the traditional 'command and control' model of organisations, which can work effectively if the goal is efficiency and the organisational environment is stable and simple
Market culture	Also values stability and control but is more focused on external rather than internal issues. This culture values profit, productivity, competitive advantage and achievement
Clan culture	Focuses on internal issues and flexibility and discretion rather than seeking stability and control. It values team spirit, participation, consensus and mutual support
Adhocracy culture	Focuses on external issues and values flexibility. Its values are adaptability and innovation

The characteristics of these quadrants, as described by Cameron and Quinn (1999), are summarised in Table 10.3.

This categorisation is not clear-cut: all organisations have aspects of all four cultures. An 'adhocracy', for example, which is intent on creativity and flexibility, still needs to contain some 'hierarchy' values if it is not to run out of control; a 'market' culture may be so focused on making profit that individuals – and their health – may become secondary to the whole operation; a 'clan' culture may allow for so much uncontrolled individualism that the company's tasks become secondary. However, over time, one type of culture tends to predominate. High performance entails, therefore, balancing conflicting and competing demands.

The elements in the competing values framework, as well as the language used, can be used to discuss organisational culture and change. As such, the framework serves as a basis for diagnosing the predominant culture of an organisation and for assessing whether it is responding appropriately to the challenges and changes in the environment. Equally important, the framework helps in the diagnosis and management of the interrelationships, congruencies and contradictions in the organisation. Altogether, the framework helps leaders to improve in a comprehensive way the organisation's performance and value creation.

MINI-CASE 10.2

GM and Chrysler steer different paths to recovery

By Bernard Simon in Toronto

Detroit's two embattled carmakers, General Motors and Chrysler, have been a study in contrasts since their emergence from court-supervised restructurings in recent months. The 'new' GM has galloped out of the gate with a slew of announcements on management shuffles, new vehicles and other initiatives. Meanwhile, Chrysler has been relatively silent apart from run-of-the-mill sales promotions.

Fritz Henderson, GM's chief executive, has hosted numerous web chats and media conferences lately, in an attempt to persuade car buyers, especially Americans, that the dinosaur of old is managing to turn itself into a nimble, cutting-edge enterprise. He and his colleagues on Monday invited about 100 consumers, including some of GM's fiercest critics, to a face-to-face feedback session about the company and its vehicles.

This week, GM cemented a joint venture with Ebay to sell vehicles online,

outlined plans for a new Cadillac model and trumpeted the fuel efficiency of its new Chevy Volt plug-in hybrid, to be launched at the end of next year.

'We're changing the culture of GM', Mr Henderson said at the Volt briefing on Tuesday.

By contrast, Chrysler, now under the day-to-day control of Italy's Fiat, has discontinued its monthly sales data briefings. Its sole representative at a motor industry conference in Traverse City, Michigan, last week was a public affairs manager. Toyota's president, GM's vice-chairman and Ford Motor's chief financial officer were among other speakers present.

It is too early to judge which of the two companies is on the right track. Some outsiders question whether the flurry of activity at GM is more representative of style than substance.

Questions

1. **Using Figure 10.1, describe how GM is attempting to bring about changes to the GM culture.**

2. **Which of Schein's 'mechanisms of change' do you think are being applied at GM?**

The 'organisational culture assessment instrument' used to carry out the diagnosis is described in detail by Cameron and Quinn (1999). It takes the form of a questionnaire in which respondents complete questions covering six items. The questions are answered first in terms of the organisation's current culture, then answered again in terms of what the respondents think should be developed in the culture to respond to future challenges.

Once the present and future profiles of the organisation have been drawn up, they can be examined from several angles:

- What type of culture is most heavily emphasised (what basic assumptions, styles and values are dominant)?
- What discrepancies are there between the present and future profiles (what needs to be done to close the gap)?
- What is the degree of congruence between the individual responses to the questions (to what degree are the values and assumptions shared)?

An organisation's profile can also be measured against an average industry profile. Cameron and Quinn (1999) provide a range of these, mostly from the US but also in Europe, South America, Africa, Australasia and Asia. Comparing the two profiles allows insights to be developed concerning the cultural changes needed: is the organisation out of line with the requirements of the sector's environment, or is the mismatch itself a source of competitive advantage?

SPOTLIGHT 10.2

Decision-making and competing values

Here is a short extract from an article written by John Kay, founding Director of the Said Business School at Oxford University, in which he examines the question of decision-making, the theory and the reality.

We do not solve problems in the way the concept of decision science implies because we can't. The achievement of the great statesman is not to reach the best decision fastest, but to mediate effectively among competing views and values. The achievement of the successful business leader is not to articulate visions of the far future, but to match continuously the capabilities of the firm to the changing market environment. The test of financial acumen is to navigate successfully through irresolvable uncertainties.

[. . .]

Our approaches are iterative and adaptive. We make our choices from a limited range of options. Our knowledge of the relevant information and of what information is relevant, is imperfect. Different people make different judgments in the same situation, not just because they have different objectives, but because they observe different options, select different information, and assess that information differently; even with hindsight it will often not be possible to say who was right and who was wrong.

 Source: from 'Decision-making, John Kay's way', *Financial Times*, 20/3/2010 (Kay, J.),
© The Financial Times Ltd. All Rights Reserved.

As a final point with regard to the competing values framework, it is worth returning to the survey by Despharde *et al.* (1997). Although the authors came to the conclusion that successful international companies were likely to foster very similar competitive, entrepreneurial values, they also noted differences of emphasis when it came to categorising these companies according to the CV framework. They found, for example, that the Japanese companies under investigation fostered 'hierarchy' and 'clan' values while at the same time stressing competition and performance. English companies, although fostering values associated with 'adhocracy', also displayed 'clan' values of loyalty and cohesiveness. French companies embraced many values associated with 'hierarchy' cultures, but also embraced the virtues of entrepreneurship and innovation associated with the 'adhocracy' culture. These findings confirm the 'competing' nature of the framework, but also clearly imply that congruity between an organisation's cultural values and national cultural values are a measure of a company's success.

Conclusion

Chapter 10 has described the role of culture in organisational change. It has outlined the cultural issues which, according to Schein, are prevalent at the various stages in a company's development, and it has summarised the actions he proposes as mechanisms of change.

One crucial factor in any change process is the extent to which a company is aware of its culture and of the operational environment. Using the competing values framework devised by Cameron and Quinn is one way of assessing whether a company and its employees are responding appropriately to the environment; this framework has been outlined in the chapter.

Chapter 10 has also shown that, even if the culture of a multinational organisation needs to be changed, any transformation carried out will need to reflect the national culture while at the same time ensuring that the subsidiaries involved remain integral parts of the whole multinational.

Points for reflection

1. As the text indicates, companies tend not to give explicit attention to cultural issues when planning and implementing organisational change. Laurent advocates a dual approach to address this situation.

   What type of leader is required in this approach and what does that leader need to do? Where does this approach belong in Table 10.2 (Schein's 'mechanisms of cultural change')?

2. Concept 7.2 summarised a classification of the types of cultures, made by Deal and Kennedy (2000) on the basis of a study they made of various firms and their business environment.

   What are the similarities between this and the cultures defined in the competing values framework presented in Figure 10.1? What differences do your perceive between the two – and how do you account for these?

Further reading

Schein, E.H. (2004) *Organizational Culture and Leadership*, 3rd edition, San Francisco, CA: Jossey-Bass. This is the third edition of the book published originally in 1985. Schein offers his readers considerable insight into the dynamics of organisations and change. Using the findings of contemporary research, as well as referring to many of the organisations with whom he has worked, Schein examines occupational cultures as well as the ways in which leaders apply the principles of culture to achieve organisational goals. He also addresses the question of cultural change within an organisation, specifically the role of the leader in this process. One aspect that Schein considers indispensable – and which he says is almost completely ignored in most leadership books – is the question of organisational growth and the different role that culture plays during each stage of growth.

Cameron, K.S. and Quinn, R.E. (1999) *Diagnosing and Changing Organizational Culture*, Upper Saddle River, NJ: Prentice-Hall. This book provides an instrument for diagnosing organisational culture and a framework for understanding organisational culture. It then describes a step-by-step process for producing an organisational culture profile, identifying the ways in which the culture of the organisation should change, and formulating a strategy for accomplishing that change. The book contains an assessment instrument that readers can use to determine their own cultural profile as leaders/managers/employees in an organisation.

References

Adler, N.J. (2002) *International Dimension of Organizational Behaviour*, Cincinnati, OH: South-Western.

Cameron, K.S. and Quinn, R.E. (1999) *Diagnosing and Changing Organizational Culture*, Upper Saddle River, NJ: Prentice Hall.

Deal, T.E. and Kennedy, A.A. (2000) *Corporate Cultures: The Rites and Rituals of Corporate Life*, Cambridge, MA: Perseus.

Despharde, R., Farley, J.U. and Webster Jr., F.E. (1997) 'Factors affecting organizational performance: a five-country comparison', *Harvard Business School Working Paper*, 98–027.

Laurent, A. (1989) 'A cultural view of organizational change', in Evans, P., Doz, Y. and Laurent, A. (eds), *Human Resource Management in International Firms*, London: Macmillan: 83–94.

Qi, L. (2005) 'Learn to agree to differ', *The Link*, autumn, Chinese Europe International Business School on its website (www.ceibs.edu/link/index.shtml).

Schein, E.H. (1989) 'Organizational culture: what it is and how to change it', in Evans, P., Doz, Y. and Laurent, A. (eds), *Human Resource Management in International Firms*, London: Macmillan: 56–82.

Schein, E.H. (2004) *Organizational Culture and Leadership*, 3rd edition, San Francisco, CA: Jossey-Bass.

Chapter 10 Activities

ACTIVITY 10.1

The summary of events given below concerning Michelin's joint venture in China is based on the detailed account given in the autumn 2005 issue of *The Link*, the learning interface of China European Business School, Shanghai, accessed 1 June 2008 (www.ceibs.edu/link/index.shtml).

Answer the questions that follow the summary.

Michelin in China implementing a human resources strategy

In 2001, Michelin, the world's leading tyre manufacturer and based in France, set up a joint venture in Shanghai, China, with Shanghai Tyre and Rubber Company. The Chinese tyre market was expected to almost treble within three years, so Michelin was happy to invest $200 million in the company.

The new company, in which Michelin had a 70 per cent stake, was mostly made up of employees from the Chinese partner plus a small team of expatriate managers and managers recruited from other international ventures in China. The expatriates were used to lay the foundation for future operations and to support the management team that had originally run the Chinese company. This team was kept in place to facilitate the integration process.

Michelin wished to implement its well-established personal management philosophy in the new company. This was the way to develop the personal and professional effectiveness of the workforce as well as help individuals develop their career in the company. The company badly needed managers who could work in a joint venture environment, so this active approach to human resource development compensated for the dearth of suitable managers available in China.

The management approach Michelin wished to have adopted was based on Michelin's five core values which were founded on respect for: customers, people, shareholders, the environment and facts. See the company's corporate website: http://www.michelin.com/corporate/front/templates/affich.jsp?codeRubrique =74&lang=EN.

These values were immediately recognisable and not difficult for the Chinese employees to accept. But were they aware of what the implementation of these values through the management approach entailed?

The personnel department in Shanghai, as well as its counterparts in other Michelin production plants, was responsible for creating and maintaining a strong, open and shared company culture, one that was a source of social cohesion and motivation. The department encouraged individual employees to advance themselves professionally according to their performance, skills and ambitions. Just as on other Michelin sites, the department was set apart from the business units. The personnel managers had no formal position in the hierarchy but worked closely with partners, the managers of the business units. During the employees' progress within the company there was continual evaluation and face-to-face dialogue involving the employee, the unit manager and the career manager from the personnel department.

In her analysis of the personnel situation in the Shanghai plant, the human resources director of Michelin China described the difficulties that the integration of this approach into the joint venture would cause (Qi, 2005). Clearly, this could not be done overnight. The concept of appraisal and the role of career managers did not fit into the concept that the Chinese have of management and the importance given to hierarchical relationships. Other elements of the HR approach that would be difficult for the Chinese to accept included the notion that support functions such as human resources were as important as functional departments and the expectation that employees should speak openly about themselves and the working environment.

The starting point of any integration needed to be for both sides to understand each other's ways of thinking. In this way initial fears and suspicions could be removed and the process of building mutual trust set in motion. The employees who had been recruited from other joint ventures and who had become familiar with Western practices acted as a bridge between the expatriates (who were mostly involved in the technical process) and the line managers (who were Chinese). In addition, considerable resources were dedicated to training courses and study abroad for (potential) managers.

Four years after the creation of the joint venture, the HR director saw some progress, but that integration was by no means complete. Although some employees were unable to adapt to the changing environment and left, the majority appeared to be willing to accept Michelin's approach to human resources. The career management system was 'taking shape' and the process of dialogue between employees, career managers and line managers was under way. At the same time, the expatriates had gained a deeper insight into how the Chinese culture works.

As the writer indicates, one core value of the Michelin culture – respect for people – lies at the core of the integration process. Respect by both sides of both sides. The process, therefore, was not about establishing the Michelin way, or the Chinese way; it was about establishing the Michelin China way.

Questions

1. Summarise what you believe to be the 'Michelin China way'.
2. Which of the values, as described in the competing values framework, do you recognise in the case with regard to Michelin and its Chinese partner? How do you account for any similarities or differences?

ACTIVITY 10.2

The article below describes the changes which an Asian company is attempting to bring to its R&D department in order to improve the company's position in the global market.

Read the article and answer the questions follow.

Samsung sows for the future with its garden of delights

By Anna Fifield

Samsung Electronics executives often feel uneasy when they enter the company's 'value innovation programme' (VIP) centre south of Seoul, where grass sprouts from the ceilings, the doors are covered with funfair mirrors and the walls covered with chalk drawings of ideas.

South Korean offices typically feature grey computers on grey desks inside grey walls, where workers adhere to strict Confucian traditions and would never dream of questioning a superior or making wacky suggestions. But here, in the Samsung idea incubator, they are encouraged to put on Viking and bumblebee hats, lie on the floor and throw round ideas without regard for rank, play with Elmo toys and inflatable dolphins, all the while taking polaroids of themselves. Such an environment might be commonplace in the information technology companies of California but it is revolutionary in Korea.

'Some people come here because their manager tells them to, and when they arrive they say "I can't work in this environment"', says Chung Sue-young, one of the 'VIP' centre coordinators. 'The engineers immediately start tidying up and stacking all the magazines in date order, the R&D people only want to talk with Americans, and the designers just stand there and don't say anything', she says.

But this kind of change is crucial as Samsung, which has made a remarkable transformation from copycat manufacturer to become Asia's most valuable technology company, now finds itself in something of a rut. Many of its products – such as semiconductors and flat screens – are becoming commodities, and it has yet to produce a killer product, as Sony did with the Walkman and Apple with the iPod.

So Samsung is increasingly sending employees to the VIP centre for weeks at a time, encouraging them to think outside the box, and outside the office. They go to department stores to watch people shopping, or to museums to think about space and light.

'In our Samsung culture, it looks like the people here are slacking off', Ms Chung explains in one of the VIP centre rooms, which is incongruously housed in a run-down old dormitory at its main research and development centre. 'But there are more and more people who recognize the value of creative slacking', she adds.

Chairman Lee Kun-hee recognizes the need for creativity if Samsung is going to make the next leap forward.

'An unexpected but tremendously rapid change will occur by 2010', he said last year at the Samsung Electronics research centre. 'In all areas from design, marketing and R&D, we have to be prepared for the future by implementing creative management schemes.'

The value innovation programme – which essentially boils down to providing the things that a customer wants, at the lowest cost – is central to that drive. It was here that three engineers, a designer and a marketing specialist came up with the 'Bordeaux' flat-screen television. With its focus on design – the speakers are hidden and the lines are supposed to be reminiscent of a wine glass – the Bordeaux became Samsung's first LCD television to sell more than 1m units.

'People often complain that the TV takes up lots of space and that it doesn't go with the other furniture. What the Bordeaux team did was simply to sit down and say, we're going to make the kind of pretty TV that customers want', Ms Chung explains. 'This is common sense but when you work with technology and are very product oriented, sometimes you are too specialist to see these kinds of things', she says.

While the VIP centre is a kind of hotbed for creative thinking, Samsung is trying to develop a more creative culture across its R&D centre, which is now home to more than 39,000 employees.

'Traditionally we have been workaholics, spending very long hours in the office, but now the emphasis is moving to efficiency and the number of people coming in at weekends has drastically decreased', says Eugene Pak, vice-president of the technology planning team.

In Mr Pak's department, executives are gathering for morning '10-minute talks', chatting about things such as their hobbies or current events – topics that would be water-cooler talk in other countries but which could be deemed frivolous here.

Samsung is also changing its recruiting priorities.

'Before, we looked for loyalty but these days we are increasingly also looking for creativity and a knack for doing something unique, something a little bit crazy. We now look for people that have that extra dimension', Mr Pak says.

'We have good talent but we are maybe 2 per cent short – we just need the extra push to make it to the top', he says. 'We need that extra insight that I think we can get from bringing people from abroad to help change the corporate culture.'

 Source: adapted from 'Samsung sows for the future with its garden of delights', *Financial Times*, 4/1/2008 (Fifield, A.), © The Financial Times Ltd. All Rights Reserved.

Questions

1. How does the environment of the 'idea incubator' encourage those working there to change their behaviour?

2. Using the Competing Values framework outlined in Concept 10.1, describe the changes that Samsung is attempting to bring to the R&D department.

3. The author of the article refers to Samsung as having once been a 'copy-cat' manufacturer. To what extent to you consider the creation of the VIP centre to be an example of 'copy-cat' behaviour?

Chapter 11

Culture and international marketing management

Marketing is no longer an isolated function of the organisation. This means that its activities such as creating markets and satisfying consumers can no longer be realised without the contribution of the whole organisation. The focus of this approach is principally on the consumer. Marketing is the integrating part of the organisation, linking it to its environment. International marketing is more complex. It needs not only the knowledge of foreign markets, but also an understanding of cultural differences among countries.

Concept 11.1 goes beyond the boundaries of the domestic firm to examine relationship marketing management in an international and social networking environment, with all the adaptations this requires, especially in marketing research.

Concept 11.2 focuses on communication in an intercultural environment, especially advertising in commercial and social marketing, as well as on management of meanings related to brand names and messages for international markets and to country of origin images.

Learning outcomes

After reading this chapter, you should have an understanding of:

- The cultural differences in marketing management practices in the world.
- The nature of cross-cultural research in marketing and its components.
- The role of communication in international marketing.
- The impact of culture on advertising.

Concept 11.1   Marketing in a cross-cultural environment

Figure 11.1 **Marketing in a cross-cultural environment**

Since the new approach to marketing is seen as the most appropriate and effective way of dealing with consumers within the expanding and increasingly integrated market, there are several problems which marketers must face with cross-border markets. The question of adapting products and marketing strategies to suit the needs and wishes of the consumer lies at the heart of the intercultural marketing approach.

Marketing is an integral part of a company's activities. It tries to balance customer needs with the aims and resources of the organisation. Wall and Rees (2004) separate out marketing activities as follows:

1. Market analysis with at least three elements:

   - *environment analysis*: this involves making an inventory of the risks and opportunities in the company's environment;
   - *buyer behaviour*: the company needs to establish the profile of its (potential) customers and to know how and why they buy;
   - *market research*: this is the way information concerning the company's customers and environment is collected.

2. Marketing strategy. Once a market has been scanned using the above tools, the company has to develop a strategy to give a meaning and direction to its marketing activities. The following strategies are often used:

   - *market segmentation*: taking a group of (potential) customers who share certain characteristics (such as age or income range or occupational profile);
   - *marketing mix*: comprising, apart from the product itself, price, promotional activities and place.

The various marketing activities are integrated into the organisation through planning and management itself. Through planning, market opportunities can be evaluated in relation to the resources of the enterprise with a view to attaining its goals. Management is intent on running the whole process effectively so that the customers' needs and wishes are met.

However, this classification of marketing activities in terms of market, strategy, planning and management, as well as the strategy of the marketing mix, has its critics. Some experts see these approaches as being traditional ones that no longer meet present-day needs.

Traditional view and new ideas and concepts

As Welford *et al.* (2008) note, experts are increasingly questioning the effectiveness of the marketing mix approach. They argue that market-driven management should be more than a succession of 'ordered functions'. They see a modern concept of marketing with a stronger customer focus, one that entails not only the notion of anticipating and responding to customer needs, but also that of defining and delivering customer value through a market-oriented business strategy. This means that the whole marketing function of a company should no longer be a separate unit; the function should be seen as a collective one whereby departments link up to perform various tasks and processes.

This prescription is, according to Welford *et al.* (2008), closely linked to the development of relationship marketing. Here, too, the focus is less on the marketing mix and more on the development of relationships that firmly link the company to the market. These relationships comprise not just personal and organisational ones, but also the creation of networks that the authors define as 'sets of relationships and interactions performed within specific relationships'. Relationship marketing management is essentially about connecting with customers through continual transactions and exchanges whereby the expectations of customers are not only met but also, if possible, exceeded.

When looking for ways of establishing sustainable relations with and between consumers, companies are turning more and more to *social media* for marketing purposes. In fact, according to marketers worldwide, social network applications now receive priority over digital advertising and e-mail marketing. Enterprises are now setting up marketing strategies that bring not only change to corporate communication and marketing but also a real cultural revolution to the whole company. The switch from the 'mass media' to 'relational media' encourages companies to listen to consumers and to enter into dialogue with them.

SPOTLIGHT 11.1

Social network marketing: Facebook

An important concern for the marketers is to know where the (potential) consumers are. According to Shih (2009), this is now possible through the social networking sites across every continent. Social networks became a new powerful kind of marketing channel providing new ability to 'think global, act local' using 'hypertargeting' – defined by Shih (2009: 82) as 'the ability on social networking sites to target ads on very specific criteria'. The advertisers who know the demographic and psychographic profiles of the users can focus their ads on what will interest the viewers.

Having said this, Shih (2009: 89) adds that 'social media is a commitment, not a campaign'.

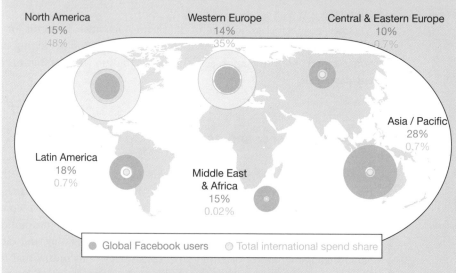

Figure 11.2 **Facebook users versus international spend share**

Source: http://searchenginewatch.com/article/2329906/Only-52-of-Facebook-Ad-Spend-is-Outside-the-U.S.-tuy

Along with their brands, marketers may join the interactive conversations between people participating in social sites. When this is done on Facebook, for example, members not only identify themselves with a particular brand, but are also encouraged to communicate this to their 'friends'. Shih calls this marketing approach 'appvertising'.

According to a report referred to by Marin Software (http://searchenginewatch.com/article/2329906/Only-52-of-Facebook-Ad-Spend-is-Outside-the-U.S.-Study, February 2014), global brands are spending less on advertising in regions such as Asia-Pacific (APAC) and Latin America (LATAM) than in North America. However, as shown in the figure below, 85 per cent of Facebook users reside outside North America, whereas only 52 per cent of ad spending share occurs outside the US. One of the conclusions of this report says that the APAC, with its considerable number of Facebook users, is among the most promising regions for reaching a target an audience through such social media. The report referred to by Marin Software, entitled 'Grow Your Business with International Facebook Advertising: A Greenfield Opportunity to Engage a Massive Global Audience', can be accessed on: http://www.marinsoftware.com/resources/whitepapers/international-facebook-advertising-a-greenfield-opportunity-to-engage-a-massive-global-audience?utm_medium=press&utm_source=publicrelations&utm_campaign=coverage&track-id=70150000000KHQhAAO

International marketing

According to Wall and Rees (2004: 306), 'international marketing can be simply defined as marketing activities that cross national borders'. They do add, however, that these activities occur at three levels in line with the focus of a company's operations:

- Companies whose sales for the most part are made in the domestic market and consider exports to be less important.

- Multinational companies selling throughout the world that consider their country of origin or host country in the same way as the other market environments in which they are involved.

- Those companies – usually multinationals – that want to adopt a global marketing strategy by identifying products or services with certain similarities in certain markets, and pursuing a single, global marketing strategy for them (Coca-Cola being an obvious example). Consumer products as well as industrial products are all potential candidates for the global market, particularly when there is little or no need to adapt them for local consumption (telecommunications and pharmaceuticals are examples).

The application of international marketing depends not only on the target market but also on the marketing orientation of the company. There are five common marketing orientations: production, customer, strategic marketing, sales and social marketing. The last two are described below.

Companies with a **sales orientation** try to sell the same product domestically and in a large number of countries where consumer characteristics are similar and, as Daniels *et al.* (2011: 640) point out, 'where there is also a great deal of spillover' between countries when it comes to product information.

Increasingly, however, exporting companies are having to adopt a **social marketing orientation**. This entails not only knowing how a product is bought, but also how it is disposed of, not only knowing why a product is bought, but also how it could be modified in some way to make it more socially desirable. Furthermore, for their international marketing to succeed, these companies have to take into account the effect of their products on all stakeholders – such as consumer associations – so that they have regard for the concept of social responsibility.

A change in orientation may be necessary because of legal, cultural or even economic reasons. Such a change may compel the enterprise to modify its products to meet the needs of local consumers. The real reason for a change in orientation is often a cultural one. A switch from one product to another, a change in colour preferences or choice of materials is difficult to predict. Marketers just cannot determine in advance what the consumer is going to buy – not even when they are surveying their home country. Making such predictions in foreign markets is as difficult, if not more so, when it comes to selling new products, or at least products that are unknown to the consumers there.

Intercultural marketing

The question of adapting products and marketing strategies to suit the needs and wishes of the consumer lies at the heart of the intercultural marketing approach. According to Usunier and Lee (2005), intercultural marketing is as much to do with localising as with globalising. The intercultural marketing approach takes account of criteria related to geography and nationality while, at the same time, using criteria to do with consumer attitudes, preferences and lifestyles related to age, class and ethnicity, as well as to occupation.

Intercultural marketing is made easier if the conditions for identification with the products are present in the target market. If consumers are to buy a certain product they need to identify with it in some way. Usunier and Lee (2005: 232) also maintain that consumers:

> buy the meaning that they find in products for the purpose of cultural identification, based on the desire for assimilation in a certain civilization.

The elements involved in the process of cultural identification are, according to the authors, twofold:

- the notion of *identity* (the need to reproduce the national culture such as it is, the desire to feel at home);
- the notion of *exoticism* (the desire to escape from one's culture and to experience other values, other ways of living).

These notions are closely interlinked in a rather ambiguous way in the identification process, so a straightforward description of the approach is difficult to make. That is why it is preferable to make clusters of countries or consumers who share 'meaningful cultural characteristics'.

There are, in their analysis, 'geographical cultural affinity zones' which, to a large extent, resemble national cultural groups; and 'cultural affinity classes', which are formed using different kinds of segmentation. Usunier and Lee (2005: 232) give an example of such a class composed of people between the ages of 15 and 20 from Japan, Europe and the US:

> They have a tendency to share common values, behaviour and interests, and tend to present common traits as a consumer segment; their lifestyles converge worldwide irrespective of national borders.

Such cultural affinity classes can be an ideal target for standardised products because they have a sense of belonging to a common age, gender or income group across different countries. They may also share a common channel of communication, particularly the web and satellite television.

Cross-cultural consumer behaviour

A certain understanding of cultural differences is indispensable for effective communication (see Figure 11.2) with consumers from different backgrounds. However, according to Kaynak and Jallat (2004), the importance of geographic frontiers and politics will gradually diminish because of changes in the economic environment and the evolution of consumer behaviour. Europe offers an example of such changes, as do the young generations of consumers in more and more countries. They increasingly behave in the same way. Even in China there is evidence of the influence of the Confucian system of values retreating among the young to make way for a more individualist attitude in their buying habits.

Although differences in the cultural and economic environment remain, there is increasing uniformity in consumer taste and consumer behaviour. This already appears to be having an effect on the marketing strategies of companies operating at an international level.

Nevertheless, Usunier and Lee (2005) maintain that there are limitations to the way behavioural intentions are determined. Significant differences in consumer behaviour may be determined and the need to adapt a product established, but this is not sufficient in itself because the intentions of the consumers need to be established. Models of behavioural intention, which were once assumed to be applicable universally, show different weightings between attitudes and norms.

To what extent, therefore, is it possible to talk of transposing theories to do with consumer behaviour? There are certainly similarities between cultures, but to really understand consumer behaviour, account must be taken of the characteristics of the consumers' culture and their underlying models. There remain, however, problems for marketers and market researchers. Europe being a prime example.

Problems with cross-border market research

Welford *et al.* (2001: 394–395) define these problems as follows:

- *Language barriers.* Language poses a real problem when it comes to identifying behaviours common to different nationalities. Translating from one language to another is one problem, but also assessing the differences between countries when it comes to the meaning of the translated words.

- *Sensitivity of questioning.* Europeans show differences in the information they choose to communicate. The Greeks, for example, may not be worried about revealing information on their income, whereas the British are.

- *Research techniques.* Most of marketing research techniques emanate from the US. They focus on the ability of individuals to express their sentiments and feelings. Some customers, whether in Europe or Asia, are reluctant to talk openly about such matters and prefer instead to be asked questions on more practical issues.

- *Cultural differences.* When surveys are being carried out across cultures about the way people live, behave and think, it is important to take into account the cultural context when responses to questionnaires are being analysed. If this is not done, the research findings may be misinterpreted and the real meanings undiscovered.

- *Suspicion.* People in certain countries are becoming increasingly suspicious about what happens to information gathered through marketing surveys. They are increasingly reluctant, therefore, to participate in such surveys.

- *Statistical comparisons.* Cross-country comparisons of statistics are difficult to perform since the data is established locally and is based on practices that differ between countries. Demographic information, educational qualifications and social groupings may be different, as well as the relative amounts spent on promotion and advertising.

- *Fragmentation.* Many multinational concerns have decentralised structures whereby operating companies enjoy considerable autonomy. Research done by a local company across different countries and markets may lack a consistent method, be fragmented and inconclusive.

An illustration of the problems defined above is given in Spotlight 11.2.

SPOTLIGHT 11.2

What is behind the question?

In his article on linguistic sensitivity in cross-cultural organisational research, Gales (2003) refers to the differences between France and the US with regard to the centrality of work in one's life.

He refers to research into job satisfaction across cultures. Researchers have used well-tried survey instruments in English, translating them into the languages of the cultures in question. However, as the author points out, a translation of this kind will not necessarily 'capture the nuances of work life and job satisfaction within a given culture' (Gales, 2003: 135). A question such as 'How satisfied are you with your salary?' translated into French may not adequately reflect the concern that the French give to the quality of life. Job satisfaction will probably have a different meaning to those living in a culture – such as that in France – where work does not play such an important role in self-fulfilment.

Marketing is also a process in which communication plays an important role. Consumers buy not only the product but the meaning that goes with it. This idea will be developed in Concept 11.2.

Concept 11.2 Marketing communication across cultures

Promoting brands internationally

Some say that the brand often sells better than the product. Among many products on the market, the buyer recognises 'his' or 'her' brand before actually buying the product. The seductive power of the name seems therefore to count as much as the way the product is made.

How can we define what a brand is? Well, for a start, it is the brand that identifies a product/service or range of products/services. In a legal sense, provided it is registered, this form of identification becomes a trademark. As such, the brand (eventually) becomes instantly recognisable and can to a certain extent market itself, so reducing promotional costs.

According to Daniels *et al.* (2011: 654), every producer and marketer working in an international environment must be very careful when making decisions about brands. They must decide 'whether to adopt a worldwide brand or to use different brands for a variety of country markets'. Using one uniform brand internationally makes economic sense, but problems can arise as a result, particularly when it comes to language. A name originally chosen for one particular market with a particular language may have a different association in other language areas. As Daniels *et al.* (2011) rightly point out, problems with promoting brands internationally are exacerbated by the lack of some sounds of a brand name in other languages. The name chosen may also be difficult to pronounce because the pronunciation of the name may create a meaning different to the original. Such problems may be all the greater if the brand is promoted using a different alphabet.

SPOTLIGHT 11.3

Jif and Cif

Unilever developed a liquid cleaning product that was first sold in France under the name 'Cif'. When it proved to be successful, it was introduced in other markets. For the British and Dutch markets it was renamed 'Jif' because, the story goes, the manufacturers were concerned that the name 'Cif' might be associated with 'syph', the slang word for the sexually transmitted disease syphilis. The word 'jif' is found in English phrases such as 'see you in a jif' or 'this won't take a jif' – implying that something will happen quickly. In 2001, however, Unilever decided to use just one brand name for the product across Europe – 'Cif'. Although it seems logical to have the same name for the same product for marketing purposes, the change may also reflect the fact that syphilis is no longer a common subject of discussion in the UK.

The name 'Jif' is still used in Australia, New Zealand, Norway and the Middle East. In Canada and India, it is called 'Vim', which was the name given to a similar product first manufactured by Lever Brothers in the UK in 1905.

Brands and national images

As we have seen, the brand name can provoke associations of ideas and emotions in such a way that consumers are not just buying a product but also the image it conveys. In terms of a consumer's purchase criteria, image is an important facet of the product, along with quality, innovation, design, and ease of use as well, of course, as price. In terms of international marketing, how do consumers perceive products from countries other than their own? What is the relationship between the nationality of a product and the image it evokes?

A number of authors, including Usunier and Lee (2005) see this relationship as a very important one, not only in terms of the 'made in' label, but also in terms of other elements that contribute to the consumer's perception of product nationality. These include:

- the image of national products as compared with imported or international products;
- national images of generic products;
- the national image of the manufacturing company;
- the image diffused by the brand name.

Such elements are not necessarily related to one country (e.g. pasta to Italy), but to several countries (e.g. wine), or even to a geographical area (yoghurt to the Balkans). Moreover, there are many perceptions of products which are not shared by consumers from different national cultures; consumers from one country do not always have the same image of a product from their own country as do consumers from another country.

Usunier and Lee (2005: 289) note the role of stereotypes (Chapter 14) in associating a product with the national image of a country. There are, they maintain, a small, but important number of consistent stereotypical images:

> [. . .] the image of the robustness of German products, the image of France as associated with luxury goods, the image of Korean products as being cheap.

SPOTLIGHT 11.4

Skoda transformed

The perception of the brand name 'Skoda' has undergone a massive change since the early 1990s. Skoda was originally the name of a Czechoslovakian car manufacturer nationalised by the new communist regime after World War II. The cars it made before the 1989 'Velvet Revolution' were available in western as well as east Europe. Although behind the Iron Curtain they were considered to be superior to cars from other communist countries, they were seen in the West as cheap but poorly made and unreliable. Jokes about the car – along with those made by the Russian equivalent, 'Lada' – were heard frequently:

How do you double the value of a Skoda? Answer: Fill it with petrol.
Why does a Skoda have a heated rear windscreen? Answer: To keep your hands warm when you push it.

Once the German car maker Volkswagen had taken a 30 per cent stake in the company in 1991 (eventually taking total control of the company in 2001), things changed. Through intensive training and extensive investment in the plant, research and product development, the quality of Skoda products improved considerably. The cars were soon earning high praise from the motoring press. However, the accolades the company received were not immediately reflected in sales figures in the West. Nevertheless, through clever marketing campaigns in Europe (and parts of Asia and Latin America), consistently positive reviews from the motoring press and multiplying word-of-mouth recommendations from satisfied buyers, sales started rising rapidly.

In the UK, marketers found it particularly difficult to shake off the old Skoda image. Commercials were made, however, that faced up to this image in an honest but humorous way. In one of these, for example, a Skoda driver returns to his car where a parking attendant is waiting. The attendant says: 'I'm afraid some little vandal has stuck a Skoda badge on the front of your car'. The commercial ends with the picture of the handsome new Skoda (Fabia or Octavia) and, beneath it, the slogan 'It's a Skoda. Honest!'

Market researchers found that this and other similar commercials, in which the 'new' image played with the 'old' image, had a very positive effect on consumer awareness. They helped boost sales during the eighteen-month promotion period. Moreover, the percentage of British consumers who said they would not consider buying a Skoda fell by more than a third after one year into the campaign.

Source: 'Skoda goes from trash to treasure', American Marketing Association, 18/2/2002 (www.marketingpower.com/content16161S1.php), accessed 1/6/2008.

Such shared perceptions, however, do change, as Usunier and Lee (2005) conclude from their investigations, and seem to do so rapidly. This is particularly the case for products from Japan and the newly industrialised countries of Asia. This applies also to countries that have cultural and language similarities through their colonial past, but which have very differing perceptions of the meaning of products.

Country of origin

Another factor that can change shared perceptions is the matter of 'country of origin'. As Usunier and Lee (2005) indicate, multinationals sell the same products under the same brand worldwide. These products may, however, differ considerably from one economic zone to another, containing components from the company's country of origin as well as from the areas where they are sold. For example, how 'French' is a Peugeot that has been assembled in the UK or Spain, containing parts from different European countries – including France – as well as from Asia?

Some multinationals underplay the country of origin and focus on the 'country-of-brand'. So, Daimler-Benz talks in its corporate advertising of the company 'being home in more than 200 countries' (Usunier and Lee, 2005: 292).

Related to this change of focus is the increasing appearance of products that are 'made in the European Union'. What sort of associations are this label expected to evoke among consumers within the EU – and those buying the product outside the EU?

MINI-CASE 11.1

Changing cultural habits in India: Cadbury to raise India's role

By Joe Leahy in Mumbai

Cadbury is looking to build on its dominant position in India's chocolate market by making the country a regional centre for cocoa production. The UK-based producer of brands such as Cadbury's Dairy Milk and Bournville said India was proving one of its most resilient markets, with profit continuing to grow at about 20 per cent a year and sales at 30 per cent – in spite of the global recession.

'Cadbury should be in a position to sustain the growth we have had in the last three years', said Anand Kripalu, president, Asia and managing director of Cadbury India.

The challenge for Cadbury, which has been in India for 60 years, has been to change cultural habits in a country that has traditionally not eaten chocolate.

Cadbury has also been forced to become more self-sufficient in cocoa beans in India than in other countries because of a 30 per cent import duty on the commodity, mostly grown in Ghana and Ivory Coast.

The company hopes to source all of its beans domestically by 2015 rather than from the traditional overseas markets, which are also less politically stable. Cocoa seedlings grow alongside coconut palms in southern India and, therefore, do not require fresh clearing of forests for plantations.

Cadbury believes that, if it can persuade 20 per cent of Indian coconut farmers to include cocoa trees in their plantations, it could increase national output of the beans from 10,000 tonnes to 150,000 tonnes a year, or 3 per cent of world production, by 2020.

287

'As a company, we believe we want to derisk cocoa', said Mr Kripalu.

Cadbury controls more than 70 per cent of the chocolate market in India with a presence in 1.2m stores while Nestlé controls about 25 per cent. Annual revenue is about £200m, small compared with the UK but growing rapidly. This growth has come partly through extensive advertising campaigns, including 'Celebrate with Cadbury Dairy Milk' in 2004.

This was aimed at convincing Indians to eat chocolate alongside traditional sweets, known as mithai, which are made of milk, sugar and flavouring. They are eaten by Indians to celebrate or to mark an event.

Cadbury's light-hearted ads in India show a middle-aged man who is celebrating after finally passing his final grade at school. 'Bringing a cultural context to chocolates by associating with traditional sweets & occasions' is how Cadbury describes the message of the ads.

 Source: from 'Cadbury to raise India's role', *Financial Times*, 1/6/2009, p. 19 (Leahy, J.), © The Financial Times Ltd. All Rights Reserved.

Questions

1. **Why does Cadbury want to persuade Indians to eat chocolate?**

2. **How did Cadbury proceed in order to reach its goal?**

Impact of culture on advertising

To communicate with the customer and the outside world – whether the focus is on the organisation in question or on its products – marketing uses advertising as its principal channel. Internet technology offers a number of opportunities for international marketing. Being on the Web, however, also creates a number of strategic challenges for global companies. Company websites allow not only information to be given about the products or services sold, but also online advertising and sales promotion worldwide. However, despite these advantages, dealing in the same way with all the markets and consumers in different countries still remains a difficult task.

Advertising is often defined as the channel of communication used not only to inform the public, but also to persuade the consumer to buy a product or service. Some consider advertising as a universal phenomenon, an indispensable part of everyday life; others focus on its power, the power not only to persuade people to buy, but also to create a need. In any case, advertising in its simplest form is information intended to create a link between the producer and consumer. But there is clearly a purpose behind this, namely to sell! Its essential purpose is to publicise a product and so create a demand for it. And when a product has become known, advertising maintains the recognition and reputation it has acquired while maintaining the consumer's wish to buy the product.

In the end, of course, it is all about the consumer. Those busy with international marketing must go beyond questions of language and behavioural differences to try and find out the meanings that consumers in different cultures give to products, brands, messages and behaviours. Even 'lifestyle' research and other investigations to determine market segmentation pay increasing attention to the way culture affects consumers' perception of products and services.

Taking a cultural approach in marketing and advertising gives added value in the sense that it provides indispensable information to the marketers. The product or service is therefore no longer presented to the public as it is, but presented in a symbolic way to create adhesion. The advertising presents the product in such a way as to attract the consumer and when doing so, focuses its message on the benefit the product brings the consumer, not on its qualities. Advertising and other promotional campaigns adapted to the local market allow the image of the product in question to be directly associated with the product concept in the mind of the consumer.

The *meaning* of brands and messages across cultures

Incorporating understanding of a consumer's culture takes into account the emotional element, necessary if a product is to be successfully launched in a new market. As Hoecklin (1995) observes, companies operating internationally are managing the meaning of brands across cultures while building the strength of their brand and extending the number of markets in which they are selling and promoting their brand. Their attempts to adapt to the cultural differences in communication and product use have reached a sophisticated level: companies are increasingly intent on making sure that the *intended meaning* of the brand coincides with the *perceived meaning* of the message.

This approach underlines the importance of the notion of perception. In psychological terms, perception is a complex act whereby the individual is not just observing but also reconstructing his environment. He is not just discovering, but also interpreting it by applying shapes or patterns. If cognitive theories of perception are applied to advertising, they indicate that a product must always involve the receiver to a sufficient degree. If this does not happen, the information given will not retain the consumer's attention, even if the information is considered shocking. Generally speaking, consumers will avoid everything that contradicts their system of thought, or will reduce its importance when interpreting it. One can deduce from this that differences in cultural systems also determine what is seen and how it is perceived.

SPOTLIGHT 11.5

Sensodyne toothpaste

To illustrate this 'glocal' strategy, consider the information to be found on a tube of Sensodyne bought in Holland and on a tube bought in France:

Same product: both tubes show identical ingredients (in English) and the same product description ('Sensodyne for sensitive teeth') in their respective languages.

Same message: the Dutch tube gives the following message in Dutch: 'Daily use of Sensodyne protects sensitive teeth and prevents the pain from returning.' The French tube gives the following message in French: 'If used daily, it prevents the sensitivity from returning.'

The difference: on the Dutch tube: 'Brushing twice a day brings a lasting result.' On the French tube: 'After three weeks' use you will be able to notice the improvement in your dental sensitivity and regain the pleasure of savouring everything you like.'

According to Hoecklin (1995: 111), for effective communication to take place, 'consumers' *perceived* meaning of a product or service must coincide with the advertiser's *intended* meaning' (Figure 11.3).

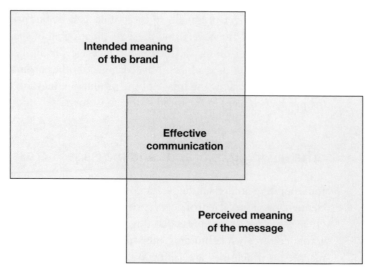

Figure 11.3 **Effective communication**

From a cultural viewpoint, this means that 'the intended meaning of products brands' must coincide with 'the perceived meanings' of consumers who come from different cultures. The most cost-effective way of ensuring that this happens is to standardise the product or service concept globally, but at the same time allow for local adaptation of the message. Figure 11.4 illustrates this approach.

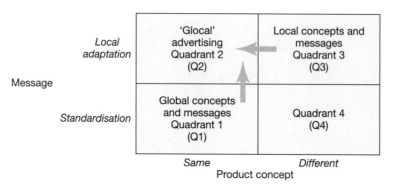

Figure 11.4 **The managing meaning matrix**
Source: Hoecklin, 1995: 101.

In Figure 11.4, quadrant 1 contains truly global products and services. The product concept is the same everywhere and the advertising is standardised. This approach allows considerable economies of scale and cost savings in the marketing of the product.

Quadrant 2 contains products and services where the brand concept is globalised (as in quadrant 1) but the message – the promotion – is adapted to the local culture. Sales are increased globally by matching the perceived meaning and intended meaning in each particular country/culture.

The success of the approach in Q1 is limited: few products and services can be marketed this way. Hence, the tendency to go for the 'glocal' approach in Q2, as indicated by the upward arrow from Q1. The arrow from Q3 to Q1 shows the move by producers of local product concepts to create a larger market through standardising the product concept but using differently coded messages to ensure its success in different countries/cultures.

The approach in quadrant 4 applies to products for which the global message is the same, but which contain different ingredients corresponding to the particular preferences of a country. An example is a soft drink that is promoted using global marketing, but which contains a different amount of sugar in a certain country where local taste differs slightly from the 'mainstream' taste. Spotlight 11.6 illustrates the unfortunate consequences when it is assumed that a product with the same name and function is assumed to be the same in one country as in another.

SPOTLIGHT 11.6

Vicks inhaler

British skier Alan Baxter finished in third place at the Winter Olympics in Salt Lake City in 2002. Two days later, when he was still celebrating his victory, he was told by the Olympic authorities that he had tested positive for drugs. He was eventually disqualified and had to return his bronze medal. All this because he used an American inhaler rather than a British one.

While preparing for the big event, Alan bought a Vicks inhaler stick to help him breathe more easily and so improve his sleep. The packaging and the product looked exactly like the one he used regularly in the UK. When he went for the doping control it did not cross his mind to declare his use of the product. Unfortunately for Alan, the US product differed significantly. It contained a substance that is on the proscribed list of the International Olympic Committee: levmetamphetamine.

Despite his appeal that he had no idea that the US stick contained the substance – and that the substance itself would not have improved his performance anyway – the IOC stuck to its decision: the substance was detected and an offence had been committed.

Source: 'The Highlander laid low' by Steven Downes, *Scotland on Sunday*, 10/3/2002 (http://scotlandonsunday.scotsman.com/sport.cfm?id=268802002), accessed 01/06/2008.

Managing the meaning of brands across cultures is not so much to do with presenting the products themselves, but the value they communicate. The basic values attached to the products are supplemented by values specific to each cultural group enhanced by the messages.

Message framing in social marketing campaigns

In non-commercial marketing – social marketing – other techniques need to be used in advertising or promotion, particularly with regard to how the message is framed. Social marketing is about complex social problems, such as smoking or alcohol consumption. Ethical issues must be taken into account in social marketing interventions. Thus, 'social marketing is not simply selling – or advertising'; it is 'a holistic approach to behaviour change' of individuals and groups (Eagle *et al.*, 2013: 5).

As suggested above, an important aspect of developing social marketing campaigns for specific topics or population segments is message framing – which can be positive or negative (fear-based appeals), rational or emotional and related not only to behaviour but also to beliefs and norms. According to Eagle, Dahl *et al.* (2013), there are differences in perception, interpretation and reaction to appeals used in advertising across cultural groups. According to the results of some research, a negative message framing would be more effective in a collectivist than in an individualistic culture. Whatever the case, it is always essential to check whether the message framing is acceptable/appropriate to an intended target group.

Conclusion

This chapter presented ideas about international marketing management and pointed out problems involved in cross-border marketing research. The focus is more on the consumer than on marketing methods, because it is the consumer who first presents the most important cultural differences. Even if there is a certain standardisation in consumer behaviour, manufacturers still continue to adapt their products to suit the consumer markets where they are sold.

Another element of international marketing which deserves special attention is communication. To succeed, communication through the various channels of commercial and social advertising needs to create a balance in the relation between the product itself, the message and the perception that people in a certain country may have about this product.

Points for reflection

1. The cultural differences in the behaviour of the consumer appear to be diminishing, competition is becoming more global than national, the marketing function of an enterprise involves not only the complete organisation but also its environment, and multinationals are selling their products under the same brand.

   Is it necessary, as marketer, to make a choice between global marketing and intercultural marketing?

2. Although advertising has been around for a long time, techniques have certainly evolved and the channels used have multiplied, with websites now playing an important role alongside television and radio, the press and posters. Nowadays consumers – in Western Europe at least – seem to appreciate advertising more than they used to. This is because it reflects the expectations of the consumer: more and more advertising is less to do with pushing the consumer into buying a product or service at any cost and more to do with keeping the consumer up to date on new products and services, providing more information and, most importantly, acting as a form of buying guide. The messages given are also clearer, more relevant and believable.

How do you account for this change? Use the concepts to support your arguments.

How is advertising perceived in your country? Do you see the same evolution as that described above?

Further reading

Usunier, J.-C. and Lee, J.A. (2005) *Marketing Across Cultures*, 4th edition, Harlow: Pearson Education. The first edition of this book, written by the French professor Jean-Claude Usunier with the title *Commerce entre cultures* was published in 1992 and translated into several languages. The author's cultural approach offers a major contribution to international marketing. The influence of culture on relevant aspects of marketing in an international environment is given a comprehensive analysis in the book. The fourth edition updates the subjects and cross-cultural cases, but more importantly the book deals more thoroughly with the phenomenon of globalisation, thanks to the contributions of its Australian co-author Julie Lee.

References

Browaeys, M.-J. and Trompenaars, F. (eds) (2000) *Cases Studies on Cultural Dilemmas*, Breukelen, Netherlands: Nyenrode University Press.

Daniels, J.D., Radebaugh, L.H. and Sullivan, D.P. (2011) *International Business: Environments and Operations*, 13th edition, Upper Saddle River NJ: Prentice Hall.

Eagle, L., Dahl, S., Hill, S., Bird, S., Spotswood, F. and Tapp, A. (2013) *Social Marketing*, Harlow: Pearson.

Gales, L.M. (2003) 'Linguistic sensitivity in cross-cultural organizational research: positivist/post-positivist and grounded theory approaches', *Language and Intercultural Communication*, 3(2): 131–140.

Hoecklin, L. (1995) *Managing Cultural Differences: Strategies for Competitive Advantage*, Wokingham: Addison-Wesley.

Kaynak, E. and Jallat, F. (2004) 'Marketing in Western Europe: a monolith or a multidimensional market', in Kaynak, E. and Jallat, F. (eds), *Marketing Issues in Western Europe: Changes and Developments*, Binghamton, NY: International Business Press: 1–14.

Shih, C. (2009) *The Facebook Era*, Boston, MA: Prentice Hall.

Usunier, J-C. and Lee, J.A. (2005) *Marketing Across Cultures*, 4th edition, Harlow: Pearson Education.

Wall, S. and Rees, B. (2004) *International Business*, 2nd edition, Harlow: Pearson Education.

Welford, R., Mercado, S. and Prescott, K. (2001, 2008) *European Business*, 4th edition, 5th edition, Harlow: Pearson Education.

ACTIVITY 11.1

Read the case and answer the questions that follow.

Coping with variables: a comparison of Indian and European hauliers

Hauliers in India and Europe both face a competitive environment, and buying the best lorry for the job is just half the battle. Both have to contend with a number of variables if they are to generate a healthy profit. And the variables for the Indian haulier are very different from those faced by his European counterpart.

The main difference between these haulage sectors is the room to manoeuvre which these variables afford. In European countries, many variables are fixed: some are set by government regulations and others offer almost no choice. In terms of infrastructure, for example, when it comes to road conditions and speed limits, there are very few variables to be found. Equally importantly, every competitor can take full advantage of these facilities, so they offer no competitive advantage at all. In India, however, the road network shows many differences: some four-lane highways are available in the urban areas, while single lane potholed dirt roads are the only option for lorries in rural areas.

Figure 11.5 indicates the differences in management tools for the hauliers between both continents. The 'crossed' variables are fixed in the market. These clearly limit a haulier's management decisions regarding investment in one area of variability to extract greater economies from another.

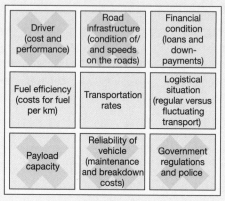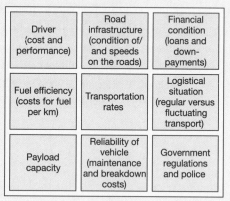

Figure 11.5 **Differences in hauliers' management tools**

There are, for example, many variables attached to the lorry driver in India. A haulier could decide to employ either a trained and experienced truck driver (who knows the ins and outs of the lorry and how to use it profitably), or to hire an inexperienced driver (who has only worked as a co-driver and knows little about profitable lorry use). Either driver could be put to use in Europe and India, although the European haulier would doubtless incur a loss if he used the inexperienced driver (assuming this driver had been able to get a driver's licence in the first place). If the Indian haulier employs an experienced driver, he can make more profit on account of the driver's reliability and efficient use of fuel. On the other hand, he knows this driver will ask for higher pay. If he uses an inexperienced driver, he can compensate for any loss of efficiency by overloading the driver's lorry or by putting him on a very old lorry. In that way the haulier can still make a profit.

Both India and Western Europe have government-imposed restrictions on vehicle design and the use of lorries, although European regulations are generally a lot stricter. The few regulations that India does have can be manipulated easily because they are not being strictly enforced. Corruption among police officers is common and both hauliers and drivers frequently use this as a way of escaping regulatory restrictions.

Payload capacity is strictly fixed in Europe. Lorries are free to transport as long as they keep to the limits imposed by law. Lorry manufacturers and the trailer and body building industry have come up with lighter vehicles so that heavier payloads are possible, but these new lorries are available to the whole transport industry, so the payload is not a variable. The picture is very different in India. Here, government regulations and manufacturers' maximum payloads do not 'count'. The sky is the limit when it comes to load volumes: any load can be transported, as long as it stays on the vehicle.

The power – or otherwise – of government legislation has considerable influence on the thinking process of an Indian haulier. Unlike his counterpart in Europe, a haulier in India cannot claim financial compensation from a business supplier if the contract is discontinued without proper reason. Most transport contracts in India contain a clause allowing the supplier to discontinue the contract if he believes he can get a better deal elsewhere. Therefore, in contrast to his European counterpart, who is sure he has a deal when a contract is signed, the Indian haulier still has to face some uncertainty and insecurity, especially if he is saddled with high monthly financial instalments over and above his normal living costs. The Indian haulier, therefore, will want his vehicles on the road as much as possible to pay off these costs. No wonder, then, that drivers have to work long hours driving overloaded lorries.

Source: adapted from Engelaer, F. and Vloet, D. (2005) *Analysis of the Indian truck market*, Nyenrode Business University.

Questions

1. Consider the following statement about variable 'legislation and legal liability':

   Legislation can have a serious impact on market developments and the performance of current business models all over the world. The Indian government has announced its intention to bring legislation on transportation up to European levels. By doing this, it clearly demonstrates its appreciation of European developments in the industry. However, the implementation of such legislation does not necessarily result in a change of mentality or a change in the process. One needs to take into account the thinking process of an Indian lorry owner.

   Using the information given in the case (and/or your experience), give your opinion on the above statement.

2. Consider Table 11.5 which compares marketing communication in the European and Indian lorry markets.

   Notice the differences between Europe and India concerning:

   - communication flow;
   - responsibility of the dealers, manufacturers, importers;
   - marketing strategy; and
   - marketing activities.

Table 11.5 **Marketing in Europe and India**

Europe	India
The flow of marketing communication starts with and is directed by the manufacturers. They set the marketing boundaries with which an importer has to comply; the importer in turn controls a large part of the marketing flow of a dealer. Manufacturers and importers are mainly responsible for mass communication, while dealers account for most relational marketing activities. They visit their 'accounts' (as they are called) and organise test drives and demonstrations. The marketing strategy of European lorry brands focuses on existing customer relations rather than on new prospects	The communication flow is comparable to Europe, with manufacturers controlling the process. Dealers might be less proactive than in Europe, but this is certainly no longer the case for all dealerships. The main difference is that, in the Indian lorry market, the focus is more on new prospects and first-time users, and less on existing customers than in Europe. Indian sales brochures focus on functionalities, while European brochures focus more on visual aspects

ACTIVITY 11.2

When it comes to launching a product in another cultural environment, there are obstacles, even when the country in question seems to have a business culture similar to that where the product is already being sold.

Read the case and answer the questions that follow.

Product launch in Uruguay

A few months after an Argentinian food manufacturing company had launched a number of product categories in Uruguay, it decided that the next launch would be cake and dessert mixes. The sale of these products would help to build the brand rapidly and would contribute high volumes to the company's operations.

It was entering a market where there was only one competitor, and it had a 90 per cent market share. The company thought the launch would (literally) be a 'piece of cake': the country's culture was similar to its own, so what could go wrong? The products were launched together with a TV commercial where the only change was to give the voice-over a Uruguayan accent.

About three months later, the products were still on the shelves. The distributor was not sending any new orders but calling instead to ask what should be done next.

The company decided to run focus groups to find out what was happening. What it discovered was surprising. Consumers, women aged 20 to 45, middle class mothers who were the purchase decision-makers for this type of product, explained that it was a disgrace to buy a pre-packaged cake or dessert. The true identity of a mother or a wife was only proven when she could cook something delicious for her loved ones. These women even prepared gelatine at home out of chicken bones (a very time-consuming and disgusting process). Making cakes from packets was out of the question: only the housewives could give them the right flavour and ingredients – and cakes were easy to make anyway. There was a market for pre-packaged ingredients, but only a small one, for those occasions when the housewives had no time to prepare cakes in the normal way.

The company was not prepared for this feedback and started wondering whether its main competitor was aware of this. It was time to start a campaign to educate the customer.

Source: adapted from Browaeys and Trompenaars, 2000: case 6.

Questions

1. Analyse the case using Trompenaars' framework (see Chapter 5).
2. What should the company have done to make the launch of its cake mixes a success?

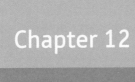

Chapter 12

Cultural diversity in organisations

The word 'diversity' is ambiguous, especially when associated with the term 'organisation'. An organisation can be a domestic one, with many of its employees who have their roots abroad – reflecting the social diversity of the country in question. It can also be an international organisation whose cultural diversity is reflected in its foreign subsidiaries. At the same time, diversity can refer to the collection of groups who form the organisation: groups differentiated in terms of gender, mother tongue, education, as well as their position or salary.

Moore (1999: 212) analysed the attitudes of organisations towards diversity generally and identified four different perspectives:

1. *Diversity blindness*: no provision is made within the organisation for addressing the problems and/or opportunities relating to diversity.
2. *Diversity hostility*: the organisation attempts to 'homogenize' its employees and actively suppresses expressions of diversity.
3. *Diversity naïveté*: the organisation views diversity positively and encourages diversity awareness, but is probably unable to cope with any problems which diversity may cause.
4. *Diversity integration*: the organisation addresses diversity in a pragmatic way. It helps its employees to develop skills in diversity management and creates the preconditions needed for effective communication between the different groups in the workforce.

The concepts in this chapter will focus specifically on the management of cultural diversity in multinational operations. Concept 12.1 first examines how managers can deal with cultural diversity and how they can turn this diversity to their advantage. It then considers the question of how to take account of ethical values in a culturally diverse workforce.

Concept 12.2 takes an initial look at the notion of transcultural competence, the term used to describe the attitudes and behaviour needed to manage cultural diversity effectively. These elements will be developed further throughout Part Three.

Learning outcomes

After reading this chapter, you will gain insight into:

- The features of management culture required in multinational companies.
- The skills managers need to manage cultural differences in a global environment.
- The importance of ethical values in a context of cultural diversity.

Concept 12.1   Managing diversity in a global environment

Globalisation is one of the most discussed topics in business. International business research is directly affected by a globalisation process that does not seem to end. Furthermore, researchers of other disciplines are also being urged to reflect on this process, which concerns all institutions of human society.

Compared with political, social and educational institutions, however, businesses appear to be the most suitable candidates for globalisation, particularly those in the industrial, financial and service sectors. According to de Woot (2000), companies in these sectors have cleared most obstacles in the globalisation process: that of size (with multinationals), that of time (with long-term strategies), that of complexity, and finally that of information and communication. The globalisation of companies seems to be linked to the cultural diversity of organisations, which in turn is connected to the internationalisation of organisations.

Management culture and multinationals

As many writers on the subject indicate, one fundamental problem which the globalisation of the economy causes organisations is the management of cultural differences. Steinmann and Scherer (2000) raise some fundamental issues with regard to the effects of the globalisation process on managerial functions. These include the way the executives of a company conceive the interaction between the different cultures present. If, for example, a multinational embraces operating companies in Asia, should it advocate Western values (what Steinmann and Scherer call a 'strategy of proclamation'), or should it embark on the new process of intercultural learning, based on the application of reasoning (a 'strategy of learning')? This last option seems to them the best way of settling the intercultural conflicts in multinational companies.

What sort of management culture is to be found in multinationals? Théry (2002) distinguishes three types:

- a dominant management culture that is a copy of the multinational's home country (e.g. American management in a US multinational);
- a dominant transnational management culture created by the mother company's founders using clearly defined specific values, a culture present in all the multinational's operating companies;
- a minimum management culture, leaving considerable room for national cultures in all their diversity.

In all three cases, the multinational must perform two roles at once: an integrating role and an adapting role. It not only has to ensure that the companies forming the group remain integrated and thus able to continue as a multinational; it also has to ensure that it respects the different national groups of clients and employees by making the necessary adaptations.

Transnational organisation

That globalisation has become a reality and that it is still progressing at high speed is not in doubt. The same holds true for the increase in cultural diversity in domestic and international companies where people from different cultural backgrounds are working together more and more. In view of these changes, Bartlett and Ghoshal (1989) propose a model for the organisation of the future: the transnational company (see Concept 7.1). The 'transnational' is a management mentality combining the abilities of the multinational, global or international firm: flexibility, efficiency and the transfer of expertise. The managers at the headquarters and in the subsidiaries abroad are responsible for co-ordinating these capacities throughout the different units of the organisation. For Trompenaars and Hampden-Turner (1997: 188), 'the transnational corporation is polycentric rather than co-ordinated from the centre'.

Bartlett *et al.* (2003) go further. They believe that top management must bring added value to the transnational company in the same way as the executives operating at all levels of the organisation. This means that the top managers are not just content to create an operational framework in which the responsibilities of the functional and geographic groups are clearly defined. They also have a federating role by integrating the different influences of these groups in the management process. While recognising that diversity and internal tensions can be the source of new ideas, it seems that the role of top management is rather to create a common vision for the future, a shared set of values to reflect managers' goals.

Ethical values and multicultural diversity

When working with a culturally diverse workforce, managers must take into account the values and associated norms inherent in the cultures involved, particularly when it comes to ethical issues. Ethical values, as depicted in the work of many cross-cultural researchers, can be compared and may assist the international managers when deciding on the implementation of a particular business practice. Their making such comparisons, however, almost inevitably involves making implicit judgements about the ethicality of values which differ from their own.

Jackson (2011) argues that what managers need to do is not just focus on what differences there are, but also attempt to discover *why* the ethicality of culture may differ from their own. He suggests examining not just norms (the notions of right/wrong – what Jackson refers to as 'rules') and values (the notions of good/bad), but also the various elements of society which reflect these norms and values in more concrete form. According to Jackson, the questions which international managers might ask are:

1. What choices are available to individuals and organizations in the decisions they make?
2. What values influence or govern these choices?
3. What rules are followed (or not followed) in order to make such choices?
4. How do these rules control the levels and nature of choice in a society or an organization?
5. What are the power relations among the different stakeholders within the organization or society that control the rules and the values that influence choice?

6. **What different objectives do the different stakeholders have that influence choice in decision making?**

Jackson, 2011: 14

Jackson (2011) suggests that these questions relate to three broad areas of investigation:

a) **context** (e.g. governmental practices, organisational governance and structure, the social/economic/educational background of a society;

b) **content** (including national and organisational cultural values and the degree of homogeneity involved, as well as work–home/individual–group value conflicts;

c) **conduct** (e.g. international interactions, interorganisational interactions and interpersonal interactions).

Figure 12.1 shows how these three areas integrate to determine ethical conduct.

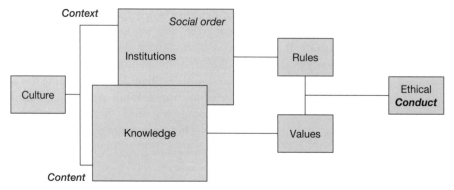

Figure 12.1 **Culture and ethical conduct**
Source: Jackson, 2011: 22.

'Interface' is the term Jackson uses to denote the coming together of these three facets (Jackson, 2011: 26). The integration of different levels of interaction is a dynamic phenomenon whereby power plays a crucial role. This is a factor which, Jackson argues, needs to be considered when understanding cross-cultural relations in a transnational organisation. Power dynamics are at play, he suggests (Jackson, 2011: 33) at both context level (structures, strategies and principles) and at content level (values, beliefs, attitudes, perceptions and knowledge). Through globalisation a 'crossvergence' of cultures may be considered which leads to 'hybrid forms of societies, organizations, values and institutions'.

What is corrupt behaviour?

Issues to do with ethicality are centred on the question of what is considered to be corrupt behaviour. Corruption can be defined in many ways, but the simplest is probably that given by Transparency International, a non-governmental organisation whose aim is 'to stop corruption and promote transparency, accountability and integrity at all levels and across all sectors of society' (http://www.transparency.org/whoweare/organisation/mission_vision_and_values). The definition it uses is 'the abuse of entrusted power for private gain' and covers

behaviour that might arguably be considered unethical, which involves money, privileges, or favours in payment for a particular action, and through which someone is directly or indirectly harmed.

Eicher, 2009: 4

SPOTLIGHT 12.1

Companies 'apathetic' about corruption

Multinational companies are failing to keep pace with tougher corruption laws in high-risk countries, putting them under threat of prosecution, the security consultancy, Control Risks, has warned.

Richard Fenning, head of the consultancy, has voiced his dismay at the 'apathy' he has seen among firms working in countries with high levels of corruption, blaming the 'desensitisation' of employees who have operated in these environments for long periods.

He cautioned that political regime changes, such as last year's Politburo hand-over in China, can bring about sudden shifts in the business environment, for which companies are underprepared.

With increasingly tough corruption enforcement in overseas markets, as well as far-reaching anti-bribery laws in the US and UK, companies could face hefty fines, exclusion from public contracts and, in some cases, imprisonment of senior executives if found guilty of wrongdoing.

'The most dangerous words in the corporate vocabulary are, "You have got to understand that's how business is done in this country"', he said. 'What was acceptable a generation ago is no longer acceptable. We hear that all the time.'

He added that part of the reason for boardroom complacency was down to a mistaken belief that authorities only count significant payments in return for lucrative contracts, and not smaller day-to-day sweeteners, as bribery.

Source: 'Companies apathetic about corruption', *Telegraph* 8/9/2013 (Roland, D.), http://www.telegraph.co.uk/finance/globalbusiness/10294957/Companies-apathetic-about-corruption-risks.html, accessed 1/2/2014.

All manner of behaviours can be accounted for, both at personal and organisational level whereby the company and/or individual can increase profit, wealth and power. As seen in Chapter 3 when the nature of Russian 'blad' was described, bribery – the act of taking or providing something whereby the provider influences the behaviour of the receiver in some way favourable to the provider – is a frequent topic of discussion when it comes to ethical behaviour in an international context. As Eicher (2009: 6) says:

> In many cultures, people may require that a relationship be developed before business transactions occur. One way that this occurs is often through socializing and gift-giving that denote respect and appreciation or gratitude [. . .] Cultural differences regarding such norms as gift giving make articulating international anti-corruption strategies difficult.

When offering a (possible) client a free lunch to establish or strengthen a business relationship, is a business person involved offering a bribe? Moreover, if the (possible) client accepts the offer is that client accepting a bribe? Is this in any way different from offering and accepting a much larger gift of some sort? Some societies perceive no difference, others do.

> What part of such practices is cultural, what part is acceptable, and what part constitutes an ethics violation?

Eicher, 2009: 6

This is an uncomfortable point of discussion for many, particularly since no over arching set of international ethical principles exist to which reference can be made.

MINI-CASE 12.1

Oil and gas has highest bribery rate

By Guy Chazan

The oil and gas industry was subject to the most prosecutions for bribery and graft in the UK of any sector over the past four years, according to a new survey.

The study by Ernst & Young found that of 26 completed cases since 2008, oil and gas made up nearly one-fifth of prosecutions. The industry saw five completed cases, compared to three each in the medical goods, insurance, and engineering and construction sectors.

Most of them involved payments made abroad, or kickbacks to foreign government officials.

With most oil and gas produced in third-world countries, the industry is far more exposed to the risk of corruption than other kinds of business. To cite one example, Nigeria, Africa's biggest oil producer, and a place where western oil majors such as Shell, Total and ENI have been operating for decades, comes 143 out of 182 in Transparency International's 2011 corruption perception index. Angola, another big African crude exporter where BP has a number of big projects, is at 168.

Western oil companies are particularly exposed to the risk of corruption because they usually operate in joint ventures with state-owned entities or foreign governments and 'are at risk of being liable for any bribes or corrupt activity by any partners acting on their behalf', Ernst & Young said.

The issue of corruption has taken on added urgency with the advent of the UK Bribery Act, which came into force in 2010. The act bans facilitation payments, which are widespread in developing countries and seen by many companies as an indispensable means of expediting often painfully slow bureaucratic processes.

Many oil companies have instituted rigorous internal procedures to root out corruption. But Jonathan Middup, UK Head of Ernst & Young's anti-bribery and corruption team, said they often got their priorities wrong.

'Companies spend a disproportionate amount of time and effort on compliance around corporate hospitality and facilitation payments', he said, 'and not enough on the issue of third-party due diligence – what agents, intermediaries, introducers and joint-venture partners are doing in their name.'

Third-party risk, he said, is 'constant and ongoing'. 'You can't prevent other people breaking the law, but you are liable if they do', he said.

The issue is particularly acute for oil companies because of the importance of multimillion dollar procurement contracts in big oil developments. Constant vigilance is required to make sure contracts are not awarded to parties related to the companies' joint-venture partners.

Questions

1. Why is the UK Bribery Act not proving to be effective in the oil and gas industry?

2. In what way do you consider 'facilitation payments' to be unethical?

Concept 12.2 Diversity and transcultural competence in organisations

What is diversity? Gómez-Mejìa *et al.* (2001) see in the notion of diversity a human characteristic that allows a differentiation to be made between people. On the one hand there are individual characteristics, such as race, age or gender, over which the individual has no or little control. On the other hand there are characteristics an individual can act on during his life, such as work background, geographical situation and education. In everyday business life, managers may well see their employees as individuals. However, they should also be aware of the diversity and the characteristics inherent in each specific group. In fact, diversity among employees may well not only cause misunderstandings but also obstruct team work and productivity. Good management is therefore crucial to prevent this happening.

How do the managers in a transnational organisation perceive cultural diversity? Adler (2002: 157) refers to a survey (Adler and Ghadar, 1990) to show that it can be a source of both problems and advantages.

Problems caused by cultural diversity are to do with communication and integration, particularly when the organisation requires its employees to think and act in the same way. The more an organisation demands transparency and convergent opinions, the greater the ambiguity, complexity and confusion. Problems with diversity also arise when certain practices and procedures are adopted by the organisation across the board. Export managers may use the same marketing campaign across countries without taking account of the different cultures involved.

As for the possible advantages of cultural diversity, Adler (2002) notes that some managers describe multicultural organisations as being more flexible and open to new ideas. Other managers find such organisations to be more aware of consumer needs. Diversity is also considered an advantage when the concern needs to reposition itself, to generate ideas, to develop projects, to open itself up to fresh perspectives.

Within organisations operating in an international environment, partners, collaborators and co-workers will be brought into intercultural situations that need to be turned to their advantage to prevent failure of the strategy of internationalisation. This means that knowledge, tools and working methods need to be acquired to help develop the attitude and behaviour desirable in a specific cross-cultural context.

Transcultural competence

Managing diversity in this kind of organisation and its environment demands, at all management levels, a competence that is often referred to as 'transcultural'. To develop the capacity to act effectively at international level, companies must opt for intercultural management, in other words management that adapts its way of communicating, negotiating and leading to the cultural context of the country in question. According to Théry (2002) imparting recipes or dos and don'ts is not the answer: such quick fixes are too anecdotal and offer no insight into the situation at hand. Nor is providing instruments for 'cracking' cultural codes the answer on its own. What is needed is the application of a global approach across the board, or a country-by-country approach. Moreover, the managers

303

involved must become aware of their own cultural preferences and, case by case, look for ways of working that are adapted to those of another culture.

Trompenaars and Woolliams (2000) argue that cross-cultural comparisons are helpful to demonstrate the different ways in which dilemmas are approached. In particular, they have observed that some cultures begin from their own orientation and accommodate the opposing dimension in a process of reconciliation. In contrast, some cultures (managers) are quick to abandon their own orientation and to start from the opposing viewpoint before returning to their initial orientation to ensure it is accommodated in the reconciliation process (see Concept 5.2).

SPOTLIGHT 12.2

Gender and reconciliation

Trompenaars and Woolliams (2000) found that women in American/Anglo-Saxon middle management tend to have a higher propensity to reconcile than their male counterparts. Women also appear to be more synchronic than men. However, when severely challenged and unable to reconcile a dilemma, women also show a certain readiness to adopt a compromise, whereas men – in this case Americans/Anglo-Saxons – tend to fall back on their own comfort zone, which may be dogmatic in nature.

In an article, Trompenaars and Woolliams (2000: 20–21) explain their viewpoint on transcultural competence:

> Over the last ten years, many business school researchers, consultancies and organizational psychologist groups have developed a range of competency frameworks that claim to delineate effective behaviours of high performing managers. They often form a reference for job design, person specification, organization structuring and training needs analysis. These models often seek the same end but often differ considerably as they each try to encapsulate the existing and traditional body of knowledge. Often, these are only prescriptive lists, like a series of ingredients for a recipe.
>
> Many of the derived underlying behaviours owe their origin to observations of business practice or research in American/Anglo-Saxon studies. Their often ethnocentric nature can cause managers operating internationally additional problems. These prescriptions for behaviour, we increasingly find, do not transfer to other countries or other types of organization from where they were originally developed and tested. At first sight they seem to prescribe a change of behaviour in new destinations as in 'When in Rome, do as the Romans do'. A different set of competencies or framework seems, therefore, to be required for a different destination culture – and even for working with a diverse workforce or in a transcultural team. As a consequence, it becomes like trying to impress on your first date. Our approach is completely different.

The approach used by Trompenaars and Woolliams (2000) is what they call 'the new framework of transcultural competence'. This framework, described in Chapter 5, entails the ability to bridge the differences between the native and destination culture through developing the propensity to reconcile seemingly opposing values. This principle of reconciliation is what lies at the heart of transcultural competence. The extent to which managers display this competence is, on the basis of feedback received by peers on their business performance, closely correlated to the degree of success these managers achieve in business abroad. The amount of experience working on international assignments and with a diverse workforce is also closely correlated to their degree of success.

Hypercultural competence

When putting forward a general framework of competence for what they call 'today's global village', Trompenaars and Woolliams (2009) consider transcultural competence to be one of a number of sublevels of competence which together form hypercultural competence. Hypercultural competence involves meeting challenges at many levels when interacting with the numerous and diverse stakeholders involved. Maak and Pless (2006: 101) highlight a number of essential challenges facing managers:

- A diversity challenge: leading local and global people, both inside and outside the company in an environment where 'people find meaning, feel valued and respected and can contribute to their highest potential'.
- An ethics challenge: dealing with the interests of stakeholders which reflect diverse expectations and values.
- A 'business in society' challenge whereby managers take account of their company's impact on the social and natural environment.

According to Trompenaars and Woolliams (2009), preceding transcultural competence are:

- *Cross-cultural competence* – the ability to function according to the rules of more than one cultural system and to respond in a culturally sensitive and appropriate manner.
- *Intercultural competence* – the ability to communicate and collaborate successfully and effectively with those from other cultures by recognising and respecting differences as well as other points of view.

Intracultural competence

Following on from transcultural competence is intracultural competence which Trompenaars and Woolliams (2009: 443) define as 'the capability to leverage cultural and/or ethnic diversity within teams'.

Contrary to what would have been expected, internationalisation has reinforced the importance of cultural diversity, rather than reducing it. It is, therefore, a question of a company having a management that can actually manage this diversity in some way. This means having managers who are able to adapt and who can use the intercultural situations present both within and outside the company to the company's advantage. Managers need to acquire tools and working methods to allow them to develop sufficient competence in the cross-cultural context to turn diversity into a competitive advantage.

Intercultural competence is everyone's business. It is not just a requirement for expatriates, but also for managers who work in multicultural teams. The question as to how this competence can be acquired, or at least developed, is partially addressed in the introduction to Part Two. The particular skills relating to the all-important communicative component of intercultural competence are examined in Chapter 18.

Conclusion

This chapter has examined how managers in multinationals can best deal with cultural diversity and do so to the company's advantage. One problem was addressed: how can managers embrace the values of the country in which each subsidiary is operating while ensuring that the subsidiary remains an integral part of the multinational? Bartlett and Ghoshal's concept of the transnational organisation, with its flexibility, efficiency and transfer of expertise, was put forward as a way of resolving the local/global issues because it allows the integration into the management process of the influences of the diverse culture groups within the organisation. This chapter also addressed the particular problems at an ethical level which can occur in a multicultural environment. Managers should not only be aware of any differences regarding the ethicality of differing values, but also try to discover why these differences exist.

The chapter finally put forward the notion of transcultural competence as exemplified in the process of reconciliation (referred to earlier in Chapter 5). Using the reconciliation approach can turn cultural diversity into a competitive advantage.

Points for reflection

1. Certain companies regard the management of cultural diversity as a way of developing new competencies that give them certain advantages. They are, for example, able to recruit and hold on to good employees, to diversify their markets and to promote creativity and innovation. For most of the time, however, it is just a question of managing differences between genders and ethnic minorities.

   What, in your opinion, are the reasons for companies adapting their recruiting, training and communication policies to the cultural diversity of their personnel?

2. Managers in international companies increasingly find themselves in situations where they encounter representatives of many different cultures with which they are totally unfamiliar or of which they have only superficial acquaintance. Rather than using a country-by-country approach in such encounters, they are compelled by circumstances to adopt a global stance, as Théry points out in Concept 12.2.

   What do you consider to be one key element in this global approach?

   To what extent do you consider it possible to adopt a global stance when it comes to addressing ethical issues in a multicultural context?

3. Transcultural competence is considered to be an essential element when managing diversity of whatever kind.

   To what extent do you believe this competence can be developed, one which a number of observers claim is essentially innate?

Further reading

Adler, N.J. (2002) *International Dimensions of Organizational Behaviour*, 4th edition, Cincinnati, OH: South-Western Thomson Learning. This book, devoted to cross-cultural management, examines what Nancy Adler calls 'the international dimensions of people's behaviour in organizations' and which she defines as 'a new field relative to the traditional study of management'. This work is particularly interesting because it deals with studies of human behaviour carried out in essentially North American organisations while, at the same time, adopting an approach to take account of the diversity and complexity involved in the globalisation of present-day organisations.

References

Adler, N.J. (2002) *International Dimensions of Organizational Behavior*, 4th edition, Cincinnati, OH: South-Western Thomson Learning.

Adler, N.J. and Ghadar, F. (1990) 'International strategy from the perspective of people and culture: the North American context', in Rugman, A.M. (ed.), *Research in Global Strategic Management: International Business Research for the Twenty-first Century; Canada's New Research Agenda*, Vol. 1, Greenwich, CT: JAI Press: 179–205.

Bartlett, C.A. and Ghoshal, S. (1989) *Managing Across Borders*, Boston, MA: Harvard Business School Press.

Bartlett, C.A., Ghoshal, S. and Birkinshaw, J. (2003) *Transnational Management*, 4th edition, New York, NY: McGraw-Hill Education.

Eicher, S. (2009) 'What corruption is and why it matters', in Eicher, S. (ed.), *Corruption* in *International Business: the Challenge of Cultural and Legal Diversity*, Burlington, VT: Gower.

Gómez-Mejìa, L.R., Balkin, D.B. and Cardy, R.L. (2001) *Managing Human Resources*, 3rd edition, Upper Saddle River, NJ: Prentice Hall.

Jackson, T. (2011) *International Management Ethics: a Critical, Cross-cultural Perspective*, Cambridge, UK: Cambridge University Press.

Maak, T. and Pless, N.M. (2006) 'Responsible Leadership in a Stakeholder Society – a Relational Perspective' in *Journal of Business Ethics* (2006) 66: 99–115.

Moore, S. (1999) 'Understanding and managing diversity among groups at work: key issues for organizational training and development' in *Journal of European Industrial Training*, 23/4/5: 208–217.

Steinmann, H. and Scherer, A.G. (2000) 'Considérations philosophiques sur le pluralisme culturel et le management', in Ricciardelli, M., Urban, S. and Nanopoulos, K. (eds), *Mondialisation des sociétés multiculturelles*, Paris: PUF: 99–130.

Théry, B. (2002) *Manager dans la diversité culturelle*, Paris: Éditions d'Organisation.

Trompenaars, F. and Hampden-Turner, C. (1997) *Ridings the Waves of Culture*, 2nd edition, London: Nicholas Brealey.

Trompenaars, F. and Woolliams, P. (2000) 'A new unified competency framework for the millennium manager' in Browaeys, M.-J. and Trompenaars, F. (eds), *Case Studies on Cultural Dilemmas*, Breukelen, Netherlands: Nyenrode University Press: 21–28.

Trompenaars, F. and Woolliams, P. (2009) 'Towards a general framework of competence for today's global village', in Deardorff, D.K. (ed.), *The Sage Handbook of Intercultural Competence*, Thousand Oaks, CA: Sage: 438–455.

Woot, Ph. de (2000) 'Ambiguïtés de la globalisation', in Ricciardelli, M., Urban, S. and Nanopoulos, K. (eds) *Mondialisation des sociétés multiculturelles*, Paris: PUF: 155–170.

Chapter 12 Activities

ACTIVITY 12.1

Diversity versus localisation within a telecommunications company in Latin America*

Read the case study below and answer the questions that follow it.

INTRODUCTION

This case study is related to the field of cultural management and focuses on a large international telecommunications company, which has operations in Latin America. It is specifically related to the networks division of this company.

The telecommunications industry has seen huge growth during the last couple of years in this part of the world. One important factor is that the GSM technology has been adapted as the standard in most Latin American countries and the local operators have adapted their mobile networks to this technology. The operations of the company in question consist of providing equipment and services for the local operators so they can build, operate and maintain a GSM mobile network. During the last few years there has been important growth in terms of revenues, personnel and offices. The company is present in most Latin American countries (Figure 12.2).

Figure 12.2 **Company's presence in Latin America (2005)**

To manage the growth of the personnel in this region efficiently and effectively, the company is using two approaches. First, existing employees of the company are moved to Latin America and offered positions for a fixed period ('expatriates', often abbreviated to 'expats'). Second, employees are being hired from the country itself ('locals'). With regard to this second

* Case study adapted from a case written by Roberto Danker (2006), Nyenrode Business University.

approach, the network division of this company is facing a cultural dilemma: should it maintain a diversified organisation in the specific country or should it 'localise' the organisation?

Diversity can be defined as a mixture of people with different groups of identities, such as gender, age, education, ethnicity, language or marital status. Diversity can also be related to work, such as seniority, management status, income or functional level of an employee. The advantages of diversity might be that it increases creativity, generates different opinions and opens the mind-set. This element of diversity plays an important role in the company. In fact, it sees itself as a multicultural company in which diversity is an important asset that enables the company to achieve extraordinary results. On the other hand, 'localisation' of personnel is also an important driver as it can, for instance, bring down costs and so make the company more competitive in the market. Another advantage of localisation can be that it increases cultural awareness within the company of the country within which it is operating. Locals naturally understand their customs, behaviours and language better than outsiders do.

COMPANY VALUES AND DIVERSITY

The corporate culture of the company is embedded in its culture and values. Despite the company's rapid growth, including that of the network division, it has continued to stress a corporate culture more typical of an independent, innovative and creative start-up. The objective has always been to maintain this culture, no matter how large the company might become. The company believes the best way to achieve this goal is through leadership rather than traditional management. This first entails the leaders disseminating the company's four values, defined in the 1990s, to everyone in the organisation. These values are: customer satisfaction, respect, achievement and renewal. They are applied worldwide and form the core element of the company culture as well as the basis for operations.

Furthermore, the company has defined goals with respect to diversity, a concept it defines as: 'Any demographic and individual attribute that defines each person as a unique individual. It means all the ways we are different from each other.' First of all, the company wants to encourage innovation which, it believes, can best be achieved by well-managed teams whose members come from diverse cultures. These teams are usually more creative and find better solutions than homogeneous teams. The company also aims to improve its understanding of customers. This can be best achieved through it mirroring a diverse marketplace to meet customer needs and so anticipate future opportunities. Finally, the company wants to maximise the pool of talent available. This entails attracting and retaining the best people within a competitive environment.

QUALITATIVE RESEARCH

To identify the corporate culture embedded in the company's values, qualitative research was conducted among forty middle managers of the company in Latin America. An investigation was also carried out to identify the company's corporate diversity policy and the attitude of the employees in this particular region towards it. Topics were analysed such as 'the (dis)advantages of diversity' versus 'the (dis)advantages of localisation' in Latin America and the extent to which the company should 'localise' different functions. The total group was further split into three subgroups to identify any differences in views between certain types of employees. The following subgroups were made (Figure 12.3):

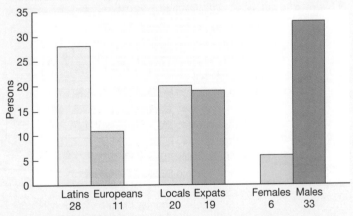

Figure 12.3 **Subgroups of respondents to the questionnaire in the Latin American region**

● Latins and Europeans;

● locals and expats; and

● females and males.

RESULTS OF THE RESEARCH

Cultural dimensions of the company in Latin America

From the research comes the identification of the characteristics of the corporate culture and the cultural dimensions of the company in Latin America. Figure 12.4 shows the characteristics of the corporate culture (using Trompenaars' model; each shade represents a different type of corporate culture). The three most dominant characteristics of the company culture in Latin America are 'commitment to tasks', 'personal relationships' and 'task-oriented'. On the other hand, a characteristic such as 'person-oriented', which basically means that a company exists only to serve its employees, is a characteristic with which the respondents of the company are not identified.

The results were based on the entire group: no distinction was made between different subgroups. It is interesting to look at each subgroup and analyse how people in it identify themselves with, for instance, cultural dimensions. Figure 12.5 shows the trends among the three subgroups in Latin America in terms of cultural dimensions. The 'diffuse' dimension, for example, which is the degree of involvement in personal relationship among colleagues, is a cultural dimension valued much more highly by Europeans and expats than by Latins and locals. This might seem to be atypical since Latins naturally value this dimension more highly than Europeans. An explanation for this result might be that all the Europeans are also expats in Latin America and therefore are much more open to having close personal contact among their colleagues. The results might have looked different for Europeans when based in their own country in Europe. Another example is that the females do not see the company as 'diffuse',

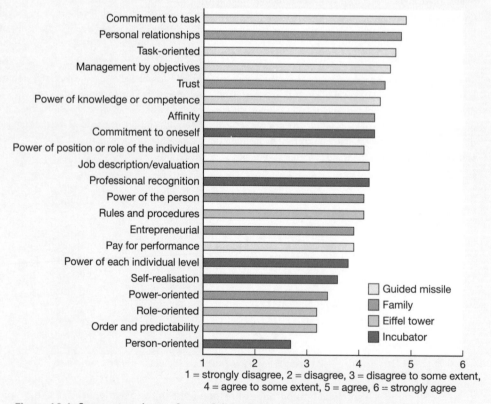

1 = strongly disagree, 2 = disagree, 3 = disagree to some extent,
4 = agree to some extent, 5 = agree, 6 = strongly agree

Figure 12.4 **Corporate culture of one of the company's divisions in Latin America**

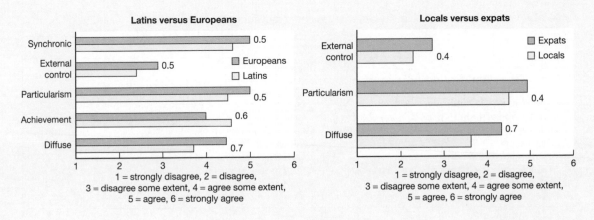

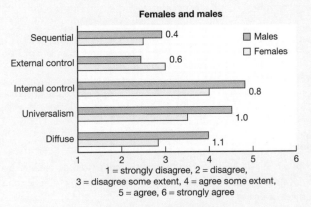

Figure 12.5 **Large differences among the three subgroups regarding cultural dimensions**

which means that the females do not tend to share many personal issues among their colleagues. Their male colleagues, on the other hand, see 'diffuse' as a dominant cultural dimension of the company in Latin America. Males tend to share their personal life and issues much more easily among colleagues.

Advantages and disadvantages of localisation versus diversity

The research also consisted of open questions by which those interviewed were asked to identify advantages and disadvantages of localisation and diversity. Table 12.1 summarises the responses.

It is also interesting to see the differences in opinion within each subgroup regarding the (dis)advantages of localisation and diversity. A Latin might have a different perception or preference from a European. The same can be said about a local person compared to an expatriate (who may be either a Latin or a European). Some typical 'quotes' show the different perspectives within each subgroup:

Advantages of localisation

Local: 'Knowledge of the local situation can be very important in particular places like Latin America.' 'The cost of these resources is significantly lower.' 'The deep knowledge, contacts, behaviour, networking and cultural aspects bring potentially better positions for dealing with the local culture of the customers and suppliers. Also the roles that do not add value to the overall business are better contracted locally to reduce the cost of the operation.'

Expat: 'Apart from minimising the disadvantages of diversity, localisation in general matches the cost levels our customers can accept. Also, certain jobs, especially in the field and customer support functions, would prefer local personnel for language and cultural reasons. The company will additionally have access to the local ways of doing things, which are most often the most efficient.'

Table 12.1 **Localisation versus diversity: advantages and disadvantages**

Localisation	
Advantages	**Disadvantages**
• Cost reduction and cost efficiency • Knowing the local culture, better insight, understanding of the local reality, local way of thinking • Customer intimacy and understanding customer needs • Language • Locals are able to solve things faster • Everybody understands each other's position when discrepancies arise • More realistic approach to solving problems	• Lower awareness of company culture or company way of working. Local culture cannot be appropriate for company culture • Limited experience, lower exchange of experience • Lack of global connections and global guidance • Less control • Certain local habits may not be supportive to business • Local people tend to create their own rules • Creation of small political groups • It creates too narrow a mind-set
Diversity	
Advantages	**Disadvantages**
• Different opinions, mind-sets, points of view • Stimulates more creativity • Brings in more experience • Puts flavour in work environment	• Cultural barriers and distance might lead to misunderstandings • Language (difficult to understand and communicate) • Higher costs • More difficult to manage • Adaptation of foreigners to local culture might be a risk • Locals are not as well respected as they should be

Disadvantages of localisation

Latin: 'The company culture is still based on its European background (transparency, respect, flat organisations, etc.). If key positions are localised without there being a good understanding of the person's background, there is a high risk of basic principles being lost.'

European: 'Less possibility of ensuring that the local organisation stays in line with the way the company works.'

Advantages of diversity

Local: 'People with different experiences in other projects in which our company participated enriched others with a broader knowledge of the mobile business around the globe. Diversity itself motivates tolerance. This means that people of different nationalities, education and language working together is itself a challenge that creates an environment of co-operation and flexibility to work under potentially difficult circumstances.'

Expat: 'Having foreigners keeps the company's way of working alive, and ensures that our company does not become too "localised" in terms of behaviour. A diverse organisation also impresses our customers: they have the feeling that they are getting the best of the company's global reach.'

CONCLUSIONS

On the basis of the research findings, conclusions can be made with respect to the cultural dilemma: why should the company have a diversified organisation and what are the main reasons for having localisation?

The main incentives for having a diversified organisation in Latin America can be summarised as follows.

a) Having cultural differences and multicultural teams in the organisation in Latin America can lead to more creativity and better solutions.

b) Diversity is necessary for remaining in business. This is because the organisation in Latin America has been growing fast during the last two years with a lot of new local employees, so experienced employees (mostly foreigners) must be kept inside the organisation for it to remain successful and competitive. With regard to its customers, the company feels that it needs strong international back-up support in Latin America to ensure that its customers get the best possible attention.

c) Diversity keeps the company way of working alive.

As for localising resources in the region, this is needed to reduce costs to stay competitive in the market. Furthermore, the company should have local knowledge in Latin America to gain a deep understanding of the market and to be close to the customer. Localisation also helps to remove possible language barriers and to gain a closer cultural match with local circumstances (customers, suppliers, customs, etc.).

Questions

1. Look at Chapter 5 for a description of Trompenaars' seven dimensions, and then examine how the author in his case study describes the results for the 'diffuse' dimension with regard to the three sub-groups (Figure 12.5).

2. Do the same analysis for the two dimensions 'external control' and 'particularism', using the information given in Figure 12.5 and Trompenaars' definitions of these dimensions.

3. Read the quotes from the different sub-groups and then decide which (dis)advantages of localisation and diversity are most referred to.

4. Discuss the conclusions given by the author at the end of the case study.

5. Below is the author's answer with respect to the cultural dilemma: 'Which positions should be localised, and which not?'

Author's analysis

The cultural dilemma comes down basically to the following question: which positions should be localised in Latin America and which not? The results of the survey show that the organisation does not have a clear answer to this question. All respondents, whatever subgroup they belonged to, replied that the localisation 'policy' was not clear. However, if we look at the issue of localisation in terms of different job grades, and the percentages involved, the survey findings show that for positions such as assistants and engineers the localisation is around 90 per cent. Furthermore, the survey shows a tendency whereby the higher the position inside the company, the less localised it should be. For higher management positions the localisation is at least 75 per cent or more. Considering the 'Latin–European subgroup', the Latins believe there should be higher localisation for high management positions (around 75–80 per cent). The Europeans would like to see a lower localisation percentage (50–75 per cent). The reason for this might be that Latins believe that higher management also has to deal with political issues in the country, in which case a local person is more suitable. The Europeans believe that the company headquarters needs to keep control of local subsidiaries such as the one in Latin America, and that the localisation should therefore be less.

a) Discuss the author's analysis with your peers.

b) Using the information given in the case and/or your knowledge of the area in question, what other alternative(s), if any, could you put forward?

ACTIVITY 12.2

Defending IKEA's culture

As IKEA, the world's largest furniture retailer, pursues its global expansion, a number of events have occurred which threaten the company's long-cherished culture. In this activity you will first be asked to determine the values at the heart of IKEA's culture and then to respond to questions on an article which examines the problems which the company has experienced in maintaining its values while expanding its operations globally.

A) Read the following extract from IKEA's website and another from its 2012 Annual Report, then answer the questions following on from the extracts.

Our Responsibility

Our businesses are guided by our values and by our Småland legacy to make the best possible use of the limited resources available.

We have a long term perspective on our business. For us there is no contradiction between profitability and responsibility. On the contrary, we see responsibility and profitability depending on each other. We can only ensure long term profitability by acting in a way that creates trust among stakeholders, and we can only ensure our ability to take long term responsibility by being profitable.

We strive to create shared value in relation to our primary stakeholders—franchisees, employees, customers and suppliers, and in relation to society.

We've come a long way. We do however realise that our journey has just started and that most things still remain to be done. We cannot solve everything at once, but we are committed to be part of the solution.

Source: http://inter.ikea.com/en/about-us/responsibility/, accessed 1/2/2014.

In practice, our values encourage a constant desire for renewal and a willingness to make change, as well as a cost-conscious mind-set in all areas of operation. Trying new solutions, daring to be different, humbleness in approaching our task and simplicity in our way of doing things are also cornerstones of the Inter IKEA culture. Our spirit is based on a belief that no method is more effective than a good example. We believe that each co-worker is important, that all of us have a responsibility, and that it is by working together, 'tillsammans' in Swedish, that we really make a difference.

IKEA values have proven to be viable in an international context and we strongly believe that they are one of the most important factors behind our achievements. By keeping them alive and well-rooted, it will help us continue to turn future challenges into opportunities.

Source: Inter IKEA Group Annual Report 2012: 3.

Questions:

1. How would you define the values alluded to in both extracts?

2. In what way could IKEA's culture be described as unique?

3. In the final paragraph of the website extract is the statement 'We cannot solve everything at once'. What do you think IKEA is trying to solve exactly? What impediments to a solution are implied in the two extracts?

B) Now read the following article written at a time when IKEA had been encountering a number of assaults on its corporate culture. Then answer the questions which follow on from the article.

Ikea: against the grain

By Richard Milne

Mr Kamprad founded [IKEA] in 1943 just to the north of Älmhult, a community surrounded by dense forests and little else. Fifteen years later he opened the first shop in the town in what would become a global empire of flat-pack furniture.

Ikea is one of the most extraordinary success stories in postwar European business. Famed for its Scandinavian chic but cheap tables, bookcases and beds, its self-assembly wares inspire admiration and frustration in equal measure.

Now the privately held group is looking to cement its status as the world's biggest furniture retailer by increasing the number of stores by 50 per cent by the end of the decade and almost doubling its sales and customer numbers.

But the expansion raises questions of whether the unique corporate culture forged in Älmhult is fully steeled for such rapid growth from China to the Dominican Republic. Ikea has suffered a series of high-profile stumbles, ranging from a corruption scandal in Russia to allegations of spying on staff and customers in France and airbrushing women out of its catalogue in Saudi Arabia.

Steen Kanter, a senior executive at Ikea from 1971 to 1994, says: 'I'm concerned about Ikea's culture. I think the foundation of Ikea is its culture and I hope it doesn't go by the wayside.'

Mr Kanter, who now runs Kanter International, an advisory firm, says he was in an Ikea store in Boston this month. 'I don't feel the same spirit when I go into Ikea. There is a danger that Ikea just turns into another big impersonal company', he adds.

Christopher Bartlett, an emeritus professor at Harvard Business School who has written several case studies over three decades on Ikea, has similar concerns: 'In any company that is as large and diverse as Ikea it does become a challenge [to maintain the culture].'

The way in which Mr Kamprad built up the company has entered folklore. As a schoolboy he used a milk float to deliver goods to farmers. Becoming more sophisticated, he offered pens and watches by mail order before opening first a showroom and then a store for furniture in Älmhult.

Culture soon became important and stories – some apocryphal, some not – abounded of Mr Kamprad's penny-pinching nature. He is said to have cut coupons from in-flight magazines to save on car-hire costs and replaced drinks he had consumed from a hotel minibar with the same items from a supermarket. Perhaps such tales offer some explanation of the company's reputation for cutting prices, which fall by an average of 2 per cent a year: the Lack table, which sold for SKr259 in 1990, now retails at just SKr49.

Critics have derided the Älmhult culture, with Johan Stenebo, a former personal assistant to Mr Kamprad, portraying the company as a cult-like dictatorship within the province of Småland, seemingly filling in for North Korea. Most of its chief executives, including Peter Agnefjäll, who will take over next year, have worked as Mr Kamprad's personal assistant and they seem to echo one another over the decades. Mr Agnefjäll himself says that Älmhult is 'in many ways the heart of Ikea'.

But the culture goes much deeper. Mikael Ohlsson, Ikea's chief executive, says: 'We always recruit through values. We spend an enormous effort in strengthening the values: togetherness, down to earth and hard working.' An article in MIT Sloan Management Review corroborates this, noting how Ikea's standard jobs questionnaire plays down skills, academic credentials or experience to focus on values and beliefs. Would-be employees can even take a culture quiz on Ikea's website to gauge their suitability.

Mr Ohlsson contends that such a strong culture allows senior executives to have deep trust in country or store managers. 'We can have a very decentralised organisation with the culture as a foundation. We can have a very flat and un-bureaucratic organisation', he says.

Fredrik Håkansson Lund, Älmhult's store manager, has 'big freedom within frames', Mr Ohlsson says. Mr Lund has the biggest range of Ikea products in the world – some 10,000 of them – at his disposal. He can use these as he wants to decorate showrooms in a way that inspires local customers. On the other hand, Mr Lund cannot customise products or branch out of the set product ranges.

Tina Petterson-Lind, the head of Ikea's range which is designed for the world from Älmhult, says products are split into three categories: the vast majority are global; some have local differences such as a darker wood in one market than another; while a few are designed specifically for a set country.

Tailor-made products are very much the exception because Ikea takes little notice of the modern management tenet of 'think global, act local' by imposing similar store design and product offering whether in Bangkok or Baltimore. That allows Ikea to save on costs on volume and logistics.

But it has caused problems in some parts of the world, says Mr Kanter, who ran part of the Swedish group's operations in the US in the 1980s and 1990s. He recalls how Ikea's launch ran quickly into trouble in the US because the mattresses were too hard, drinking glasses too small and kitchens not big enough for the Thanksgiving turkey.

Still, as Mr Kanter says: 'Ikea is relatively good at admitting when they screw up'. The US business was turned around by changing the products to suit local tastes. Even for that seemingly obvious step, Mr Kanter says he had to guarantee he could generate enough work for an entire factory with the new, larger kitchen units before he received approval to change it.

The recent mistakes have had more serious implications. In Russia, Ikea fired two senior executives in 2010 for tolerating bribery, while this year a man with apparent connections to another top manager was jailed for corruption. The case attracted particular attention because Ikea had adopted a tough stance against corruption. But as Prof. Bartlett notes: 'There is often a tension between the corporate culture and a national culture.'

Another case came to light when it emerged that women had been airbrushed out of certain pictures in the Saudi catalogue over several years. Amid global media interest, the Swedish group admitted that this was partly due to its production guidelines and promised a change.

Perhaps most serious was the case in France where Ikea sacked the country head, finance director, risk manager and head of human resources following allegations the company had gained illegal access to police files and used private detectives to pry into the home lives of employees and dissatisfied customers.

Ikea responded with workshops on its code of conduct over the summer with its 9,000 French

staff encouraged to discuss what happened, and by appointing an ethical committee.

Mr Ohlsson says the problems are isolated, not a sign of the culture buckling as the company expands. 'The culture has been an anchor for a long, long time. It is really the inner strength of Ikea. In our co-worker survey, spirit and culture are voted as one of the real assets of Ikea. We are very much against prestige and hierarchies. [But] with 140,000–150,000 co-workers there can always be an exception', he says.

One worry is about the pace at which Ikea plans to grow. It wants to open 20 to 25 stores a year until the end of the decade, rising to 500 in 2020 from 338 today. It opened just seven last year. The plans could mean up to €20bn of investment and 100,000 jobs in the next eight years. Sales are planned to almost double from €27bn in the year to August.

Mr Kanter recalls an expansion in the late 1970s when Ikea went from 35 to 50 stores in one year. 'I remember how scary that was. That resulted in a big corporate initiative in 1980 where we didn't open a single store.'

But Prof. Bartlett says that, for all his concerns, Ikea has been one of the most successful companies at preserving its culture as it grows. Returning to visit Ikea in 2006, a decade after a previous case study, he saw little difference: 'The culture had been remarkably robust and well maintained and it is very well embedded. It tends to be transferred mouth to ear.'

Älmhult plays a critical role in that process with managers from around the world arriving to exchange ideas and hear the latest thinking from Småland. Mr Agnefjäll says the expansion makes the focus on culture all the more important.

'Every company needs something that glues it together. For some companies it is an organisational chart. For other companies such as Ikea it's our culture. If we share the same values and the same vision we can put more trust in people working in the organisation', adds the future chief executive.

Questions

1. The text refers to Mr Ohlsson's contention that 'such a strong culture allows senior executives to have deep trust in country or store managers'. **Why can this culture be called 'strong' and how do you think it engenders trust among senior executives in their managers?**

2. Mention is made in the text of the tension between IKEA's corporate culture and national culture. **Which of the 'high-profile stumbles' mentioned in the text do you think offer the clearest indication of this tension in terms of cultural values? Explain your choice.**

3. IKEA is said to pay little attention to the tenet 'Think global, act local'. **To what extent do you think the company's attitude is justifiable bearing in mind its strong global presence in the furniture market?**

Making cultural profiles of brands

A strong brand is reflected in the culture of the organisation, which is itself a reflection of the people working in it. This relationship is the focus of the study below.

The authors of the original study on which the text below is based, examined and compared a number of different brands of one company. To assess the extent to which the brands differ from each other, they developed a model which is an adaptation of the model used in Part One to determine a cultural profile. The model used in their study maintains the layout and some of the values of the Part One model, supplemented with others conceived by the authors. Using this model, the authors drew up a cultural profile for each of the brands in question in line with the authors' observations and perceptions.

Learning outcomes

After completing this activity you should be able to:

● Indicate cultural differences used in the marketing of brands.

● Determine the cultural profile of your choice of brands using an adapted version of the model used in Part One to determine a person's cultural profile.

YOUR ASSIGNMENT

Read the paper below and answer the questions that follow it.

Brands and their cultures

This paper is based on the Master's thesis written by Erik Sierkstra and Robert Stal (2005, Nyenrode Business Universiteit). The company and brands used in the original thesis have been fictionalised.

Cherlon, with its headquarters in New York, is an international manufacturer of cosmetic products. It has brand teams in each of its operating companies responsible for the sales and marketing in their specific country. Within Cherlon Germany, it is said that the employees radiate the characteristics of the brand they are currently working with. This paper will consider four brands and their respective teams at the operating company's Berlin headquarters. The important features of each brand will be discussed and then contrasted.

METHODOLOGY USED

The cultural profile model used by Browaeys and Price (Part One, Chapter 6, Figure 6.3) will be applied, but in amended form to enable research into brands in general, and the differences between them in particular. The first element added to the model is that of *Control*: the extent to which head office exercises control over the different brands (flexible/rigid). Two other elements, *Appearance* and *Behaviour* (formal/informal), have been added to the profile model to enable the degree of formality in people's behaviour to be assessed. Two further additions have been made to assess the *Fashion* sense in the brand (trendy/classical) as well as the *Affinity* of the brand with the parent company – the extent to which the brand is associated with Cherlon (weak/strong).

The three values used in the original cultural profile are adhered to: *Time Focus* (monochronic/polychronic), *Power structure* (hierarchy/equality) and *Action* (doing/being). These values are aspects of a brand's culture and can be extracted easily from interviews. They are all artefacts, as it were, of a brand culture and the values of one brand can be easily compared with those of another.

To gain insight into each of the brands, interviews were carried out with employees working for one of these brands. All of these employees had worked for other brands, mainly at Cherlon's head office. The questions asked of each interviewee were focused on how the culture of the brand which the employee was currently busy with differed from other brands he knew or had worked for. Other questions were also asked to determine how the culture of the employee's brand in the country in question differed from the same brand's culture in another country's subsidiary.

THE BRANDS

Four brands were chosen for analysis from Cherlon's products. They each occupy a unique position in the company's portfolio and the images they radiate are different to each other's.

The brands described below were chosen from the:

- women's professional products division
- men's professional products division
- luxury products division
- consumer products division.

To show the difference between these brands, a cultural profile was made of each.

Brand A: Mara from the women's professional products division

Mara stands for passion for fashion. The products are manufactured specifically for use by hairstylists and colourists. This division tries to create a strong bond with its clients by ensuring that a brand representative visits its main professional clients at least once every five weeks.

Apart from this intensive contact, the brand also has a foot in the door in the fashion world. As a hairstylist at fashion shows and a sponsor of young talent in the industry, Mara stays in close contact with the market.

Mara's cultural profile

The first feature of the brand that emerged from the interviews was its obvious flexibility. The way the product is to be marketed is left entirely to the subsidiary. This is because the division's marketing is based on door-to-door (salon-to-salon) and must therefore be adjusted for each market (Figure A2.1.1).

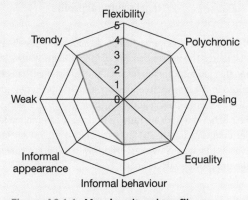

Figure A2.1.1 **Mara's cultural profile**

Mara seems to have a polychronic time focus. This means that the people working with the brand do many things at once and do not always stick to a planned schedule. Furthermore, the culture appears to be both a being and a doing culture. Although the brand truly 'lives' in the team (being), its members also have to come up with their own ideas about how to market

319

and sell the product (doing). The hierarchy of the brand team appears to be quite flat, despite the expectations for German organisations. While the behaviour seemed to be neither formal nor informal, the team members who were seen walking around were dressed in stylish suits (rather formal). The affinity with the mother company seems to be strong since the people in the brand team look neat, stylish and fashion-aware, reflecting head office culture. Finally, the style seen within the Mara team was very trendy in terms of hairstyle and, even though people were wearing suits, as mentioned earlier, they were trendy suits, giving the impression that the people were representing a trendy brand rather than a classical one.

Brand B: Ragel from the men's professional products division

The men's professional products division was recently acquired by the company. Although it has been integrated into the company, the head office is still in London, where Ragel is originally from. The image of Ragel reflects the trendy, life-in-the-fast-lane of London's young inhabitants. The brand offers consumers a high-priced luxury hair-care product. This is offered to both men and women, although the focus at present seems to be on men. Ragel is a product for a younger market.

Ragel's cultural profile

From Figure A2.1.2, one can see differences between Ragel's cultural profile and that of Mara. The parent company's control over this brand seems relatively rigid. The brand team involved can decide for themselves where they want to place posters, advertisements and TV commercials. All these, however, have been designed in London where Ragel's head office is found. Since the team is not directly involved in the design process, one would expect its members to be dissatisfied with the inflexibility of their task. The interviews, however, did not reveal any discontent.

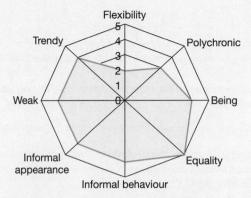

Figure A2.1.2 **Ragel's cultural profile**

The timing seems to be a mix of polychronic and monochronic. Although any planning is strict, some leeway is offered to allow the team to apply their personal touch. The impression emerged that Ragel was more a being brand rather than a doing brand: it appeared to be more a brand that judges a person for what they are rather than how they perform. The brand conveys a certain sense of equality as evidenced in the way the team's work area has been designed (no closed-off rooms, only glass divisions) and in the way the members mix when having lunch together (marketers with salespeople, administrators with art designers). Their attire as well as their behaviour appears rather informal: the brand manager as well as the rest of the team walk around the office in jeans rather than suits (internally). In terms of its overall style, Ragel is trendy.

Of all of Cherlon's brands, Ragel seems to have the weakest affinity with its parent company. It gives the impression of being a brand on its own, separate from the group while still belonging to it.

Brand C: Lussu from the luxury products division

Lussu is the only daughter of a vigilant father, an eternal beauty who seems so fragile that she must be handled with great care. This image is reflected in the culture of the brand. Cherlon's head office is the 'father' of Lussu's beauty and Lussu is the flagship of the Cherlon group, a treasure well-guarded by head office. This is why it seems so difficult for anyone to make any changes within this brand until they have proved themselves worthy of doing so.

Lussu's cultural profile

The profile in Figure A2.1.3 clearly differs from those of the other brands. Because of its value, Lussu is a rigidly controlled brand. It has a planning system that works according to strictly regulated launch times and controlled tasks and targets. The brand seems to be a strong 'doing' brand, one that is focused on meeting targets and reaching goals rather than using to the full the personal qualities of its team members. Lussu seems to be one of the most hierarchical brands within the company, where every step seems to be controlled by head office. It appears also to be a very formal brand, both in terms of attire and behaviour. Lussu's affinity with its parent company is very strong: it is a proud image of the company. Finally, Lussu seems more of a classic brand than a trendy one. Though it is up to date with fashion, as all brands of the company should be, it seems to target mature, 'classy' ladies who are willing to spend money on their looks.

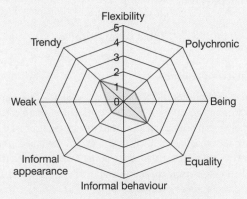

Figure A2.1.3 **Lussu's cultural profile**

Brand D: Tifla from the consumer products division

Tifla is what one could call the young face of the company, a brand based on high sales and strong image. This brand is used to sell products such as haircare, skincare, make-up and styling products to young people. Brand D is based on high sales and a good image. This seems to be company's representative brand in the consumer products division.

Tifla's cultural profile

Tifla seems to be more tightly controlled than the other brands discussed (Figure A2.1.4). This is a brand based on high volume sales for revenues and, for this reason, control from head office is considerable. The divisional manager at the local subsidiary does, however, have certain discretion over the launch price of a new product and in-store promotions. For this reason, the timing involved can be considered more monochronic than polychronic. This brand seems to have a rather 'soft' hierarchy: attire seems relatively informal, as does the behaviour. This ties in with the brand being the young face of the company, even though it is not the most informal. Tifla's affinity with the company group is very strong and this is visible on the packaging where the name of the parent-company appears in slightly smaller letters below the brand name. Tifla is also trendy: it needs to spot the newest fashion in the market and mass produce it. Those working for the brand wear trendy clothes, reflecting the brand's image and showing once again that those working with the brand live up to its image.

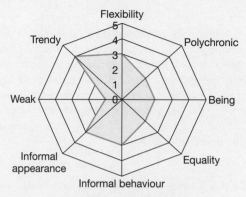

Figure A2.1.4 **Tifla's cultural profile**

Concluding remarks on brands across cultures

There are some large differences in the cultures of the brands described above. One can see, brand by brand, what cultural values are important within these brands and how these differ. One can imagine, therefore, how problematic the transfer of an employee from one brand team to another can be: the employee will be expected to dress differently, communicate with people differently, act differently and make other adjustments to become 'a part of the brand'. This just shows how much the brands 'live' in the company as a whole. Were this not the case, then any transfer from one brand to another would entail simply selling a different product. However, at Cherlon, a person changes along with the change of brand. That is why the differences between the brand cultures described above are so important.

Questions

1. By referring to Figure 6.3 'Model of culture' and Activity 6.2 in Part One, make a similar 'model for brand cultures' using the parameters chosen by the authors of this study.

2. Re-read the definitions of the topics in Concept 6.1: Time focus (polychronic/monochronic); Activity (being/doing); and Power (hierarchy/equality). Define in the same way the five new values of the model used by the authors' paper in making the profile of the brands.

3. Summarise the differences and similarities between the profiles of the four Cherlon brands.

4. Using a similar procedure, make a cultural study of brands in cosmetics or other industries:

   a) Choose a real company on the internet that works with several brands.

   b) Look at the information available – text as well as images – and choose some of contrasting brands within the company. If possible, talk to people familiar with the brands in question and, if possible, with people working for the brands.

   c) Develop a cultural profile for each brand using the models referred to in question 1. If necessary, you may adapt some of the values used in the models.

This activity is based on a case study into how two chemical companies in South Africa addressed the strategic and cultural issues involved in a joint venture. The author was involved in setting up the joint venture and ends his case with a critical assessment of the measures implemented to ensure the venture's success on the cultural front.

Learning outcomes

After completing this activity you will:

- Gain insight into the issues involved when two companies that are culturally different, but in the same country, set up a stand-alone joint venture.
- Be aware of the issues of power involved in such a venture and the difficulties in resolving them.
- Understand how active measures can promote the creation of a new organisational culture within such a joint venture.

YOUR ASSIGNMENT

Read the following case study and then answer the questions that follow it.

Creating chemistry – a case study

This case is adapted from one written by Fain Ferguson in Browaeys, M.-J. (ed.) (1996) *The Challenge of Cross-Cultural Management*, Nyenrode University Press.

WHY A JOINT VENTURE?

A couple of years ago, two large chemical manufacturers in South Africa – AECI Limited and Sasol Limited – agreed to combine certain operations and to form a separate entity as a joint venture. The new venture formed was called Polifin. As the company now stands, AECI and Sasol own 80 per cent of the shares with the remaining 20 per cent being traded on the stock exchange or held in employee share benefit schemes. Although the company is now run as a separate entity, it is still effectively controlled by the board of directors and shareholders of both AECI and Sasol.

The objective of the project was to combine complementary manufacturing plants from the two separate companies to benefit from the effects of internal transfer pricing and the synergies that would be created. It was felt that greater economies of scale, better production scheduling, more efficient customer service and the creation of a monopolistic niche could be achieved by the joint venture. The reason for creating such a joint venture, and not just a sales agreement, was to create a company that was separate from the other two companies and one that could grow and develop products and processes that would not be achieved with just a sales agreement. Furthermore, the size of the combined forces would give credibility to the operation in the market place.

BRINGING ABOUT THE JOINT VENTURE

From inception, a separate management team was created to run this project. The team included managers and staff from both founding organisations as well as new staff. It was expected to co-ordinate, create and manage the changeover of functions and staff to the new company. Decisions had to be made to match reporting methods, to resolve personnel issues (such as staff grading, pension benefits, medical aid and staff pre-requisites) and to determine the type of control given to divisions. The project was made more complicated than the start of a brand new operation by the fact that these functions already existed and now had to be modified or changed to fit with the new strategies and directions taken.

A new plant was built to increase the capacity of the organisation and a completely new head office was created, with sales, some division heads and corporate administration being included. This move, again, provided management with a number of decisions as to where to locate, the type of offices and the size required and allocation to be given to the various divisions.

The two companies involved (AECI and Sasol) had very different reporting requirements as well as information needs. Information had to be supplied at different times to each during the month and the information-gathering process often had to be duplicated to supply exactly the information requested. The fact that these two companies had different year ends also complicated life within Polifin. Fortunately, the product flow was in a linear fashion with most divisions only being reliant on one other division. Consequently, there were not a lot of serious cultural issues that the divisions had to address.

CULTURE ISSUES

As already mentioned, a large percentage of the staff came from AECI and Sasol. The companies were run differently, with AECI being used to much more informal management and decentralisation of power to the divisions. Sasol on the other hand was a fairly hierarchical company with protocols that were written and unwritten law within the organisation (for example office sizes were determined by the specific level of seniority in the organisation, with formal titles being used and staff having to go through the 'right' bureaucratic channels to get issues addressed). The cultural issues will be addressed at various levels.

National culture

Two of the subcultures within South Africa are English and Afrikaans. The English culture is based on open and informal communications, whereby the nature of authority is frequently challenged. The Afrikaans culture on the other hand is characterised by distinct respect for elders and discipline (especially within a school environment) and the need to obey this discipline and not to question authority at all stages.

Professional culture

As is typical of the chemical industry, senior management mainly had backgrounds in chemical engineering and in this respect found it easy to understand one another. Other functions, such as accounting, were staffed by people with similar backgrounds. Consequently, the issue of professional culture did not appear to have much effect on the joint venture.

Organisational culture

The existence of two subcultures led to a problem in defining the best corporate culture for the venture. The culture of the AECI staff was informal with a number of business issues being discussed over a 'beer' in the evening and an informal, open-door, first-name basis. On the other hand, the Sasol staff were characterised by a head of the division controlling all the information flows in and out as well as being the representative with senior management. The culture was hierarchical and formal with much empire building behind the scenes.

The analysis above reveals the problem faced at Polifin. Two distinct operating styles needed to be satisfied and supported, or even modified to create a new culture.

POWER ISSUES

The need to win the confidence of senior managers, as well as the need to assert power over other divisions, led to power issues. A couple of examples are required to illustrate this:

● The corporate accounting division had the task of co-ordinating and reporting financial information monthly, quarterly and annually. Because of the stringent requirements of the controlling shareholders and the fact that the head was second in charge of the joint venture, and responsible for the day-to-day running of the organisation, the division was given a lot of power to force compliance with their reporting requirements. The problem was that the divisions that came from the AECI group were used to their own standards and deadlines and refused to co-operate. The result was that at the end of each month, a couple of telephone calls were required to ensure compliance.

- Senior staff from Sasol wanted their own parking bays and would really create a stir if anyone else was found using them. The need to affirm their seniority was strong.

- Ex-Sasol division heads would only pass on information about their figures on 'a need to know' basis. They protected their information base, apparently hoping to be able to use informational advantages as leverage during the year. It reflected the culture of hierarchy and forcing of reliance so that they were noticed.

A **frontstage** to the organisation could be identified, showing it to be fairly dynamic without too many formal procedures in place, one which was undergoing a few teething problems in its rush to meet consumer demand. However, there was also a **backstage** where the culture was definitely one of power struggles. The environment had an adversarial feeling in which ex-Sasol employees faced ex-AECI employees, both sides supported by 'their' divisions. Clearly the full benefits of synergy were not being obtained.

BRINGING THE CULTURES TOGETHER

Measures had to be taken to bridge the two regimes and to define a new culture to go with the new stand-alone business.

Bridging culture

Occasions were created whereby employees had the opportunity to interact. A number of annual events (such as the annual managers' conference) were arranged to bring the two regimes together and to create a new sense of belonging. Management tours of plants were arranged to meet the staff and to let staff know who the managers were. Sporting events and social activities helped create interaction among staff and to create healthy competition among divisions.

Other instruments were used:

- in-house magazines were introduced to create a feeling of internal culture as well as to enable the 'people' within the organisation to get to know each other;

- computer systems throughout the organisation were eventually harmonised;

- a new logo was created and a distinctive image of the company portrayed to the public, giving the employees something to work towards and feel part of;

- once the stock was listed, shares were awarded to staff throughout the company;

- new policies and procedure manuals were written to define the expectations of the new company.

NEUTRALISING POWER IMBALANCE

The method used to stop the creation of power empires was to instigate job rotation. Managers who previously operated in a hierarchical manner were suddenly thrown into situations that required a different approach. This would, it was hoped, lead to a change in management approach and would help to modify the structural inefficiencies. Furthermore, this rotation could lead to a good bridging of the backstage cultures: new managers could develop a deeper understanding of the underlying issues.

Power was also removed from division managers. Divisions had previously been allowed to handle their own cash and run separate bank accounts. This was now done centrally to simplify the cash position of the organisation.

Managers had also to complete newly formatted reports. They now had to comply with the new information requirements and learn how to present their information in a different way.

THE RESULTS OF THE MEASURES

The outcome of the project was the eventual creation of a new identity and culture that could definitely be identified from the outside (frontstage culture). However, there was still a way to go to achieve a new internal culture (backstage culture). The divisions insisted on maintaining their own way of collating information and, for example, often supplied information to the corporate accounting division in different formats and with varying degrees of detail. The efficiency of the organisation still needed improvement because lack of total compliance increased the time spent making enquiries at the divisions.

In economic terms, the project appeared to be successful: the results exceeded expectations and surprised the controlling shareholders. The synergies achieved created a monopoly within the South African market that was able to undercut internationally competitive prices. The market became a price taker and this resulted in impressive profits and cash flows. The funding of new projects could be made from cash rather than from borrowings.

The combination of the various divisions created benefits, with raw material inputs being more efficiently used to create the finished goods at a cheaper price and better quality. There were fewer stock failures through increased understanding of the flow of products. Managers who had previously worked on a seller/purchaser basis now had closer contact to each other and understood each other's needs better.

BOUNDARY-SPANNING PERFORMANCE

An important lesson to be learnt from this exercise was that a better awareness of the cultural differences (and how culture affected the various operations) could have led to fewer conflicts. Cultural issues could have been addressed in advance instead of being left to simmer until conflict brought them to the surface. Perhaps better planning at the start-up phase would have negated the culture differences. This could have involved reviewing the structure of divisions, defining a new, company-wide standard that allowed employees to start at similar levels, and organising cross-cultural workshops to create awareness. Furthermore, the development of policies, procedures and practices could have been defined at the start instead of being developed in an ad hoc manner.

The focus of not just the functional aspects but also the interpersonal aspects could have been addressed a lot better than they were. Up-front discussion and negotiations with staff members could have assuaged a lot of their worries.

Finally, there is a saying that 'time heals all wounds' – and this seems to be relevant here. As time goes by, people will create their own culture within an organisation and will slowly drop/adapt their old cultures. Eventually, staff will retire and be replaced with new staff who will become socialised to the new culture.

Questions

1. What were the reasons compelling the two companies to set up a joint venture?

2. What do you consider to have been the main cultural issues at the outset?

3. How were these issues addressed at the start? What was done later to deal with the cultural problems?

4. The author suggests how the cultural conflicts could have been addressed from the start of the venture and suggests that a new culture will eventually replace the previous ones. Give your opinion of his suggestions and propose any other actions that could have been taken both at the start and during the development of the joint project.

Part Three

CULTURE AND COMMUNICATION

Introduction to Part Three

Setting the scene

The relationship between culture and communication is an intriguing one. Although the process of communication can be seen as a way of transmitting the beliefs, attitudes, behaviours that identify a certain culture, this very process can also be regarded as an agent in shaping this identity. Although people, when communicating, draw on the meanings of the culture to which they belong, this very culture owes its existence to the exchange of information between its members.

Communication between cultures is culturally determined to a considerable extent. The cultural factor has come to be considered as the prime cause of difficulties in the interaction between individuals and groups who perceive themselves as belonging to different cultures. This explains to some extent the considerable amount of literature devoted to intercultural communication generally and to communication in international business in particular. Rather than attempting to summarise all the theories and empirical studies in this area, Part Three will focus on those ideas which we consider particularly relevant.

At this point, however, it is worth considering two key terms used in studies on communication and culture. One has been used in the previous paragraph – **intercultural communication**. Another term, **cross-cultural communication**, is also frequently used in the same context. Gudykunst (2004) explains the differences between what may appear to be terms with similar meanings. Intercultural communication is to do with communication between people from different national cultures and comprises all aspects relating to the study of culture and communication. Cross-cultural communication has to do with the comparison of the various ways people communicate across cultures. Cross-cultural communication is therefore a 'sub-domain', which means that understanding intercultural communication is a prerequisite to understanding cross-cultural communication.

Part Three will not stick rigidly to the distinction between intercultural and cross-cultural communication; the intention is to deal with those subjects relevant to communication both in and between cultures without necessarily classifying them.

Before examining these subjects, however, it is appropriate to first consider the process in graphic form when two representatives of different cultures are communicating. Figure III.1 displays the communication process between the two, including the frame of reference each communicator uses, as well as key filters through which messages sent and received must pass.

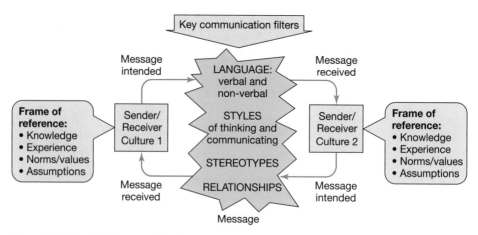

Figure III.1 **Model of communication**

Frame of reference

When communicating, each sender/receiver is unconsciously referring to a framework consisting of:

- their knowledge of the subject under discussion;
- their experience in professional or individual terms;
- their norms, i.e. the norms of the society in which they live;
- their assumptions, i.e. what is taken as fact or believed to be true.

Communication filters

Where the sender/receivers do not share the same culture, the particular filters through which the messages pass can lead not just to incomprehension of the messages, but also to their distortion and misunderstanding. The elements that act as barriers to communication will be examined in Chapter 14. Suffice for the moment to outline/define the filters involved.

Use of language: verbal and non-verbal

Language can be seen as part of the social process, a systematic framework for handling events. As such, its use allows entry into a social organisation, which is at the same time a sort of language community. Its members share certain language habits which are formalised in grammars and dictionaries.

Cultural groups can differ in the way they distribute the total information involved in an interchange between verbal and non-verbal language. The **verbal** use of language has to do with sounds, intonation, idiom, grammar, slang and dialects, both regional and occupational. It also has to do with the assumptions of the language community with regard to the meaning of words and idioms it uses, the connotations attached. The use of **non-verbal** language is a necessary concomitant of any spoken interchange. Although determined by the social groups using it, **non-verbal** language may cut across the boundaries of language communities. Non-verbal language has visible elements, such as gestures, facial expressions and eye contact, as well as body posture and physical distance between those involved in conversation. Non-verbal language has also audible elements such as the tone of voice and (the nature and frequency of) interjections. The assumptions underlying the various elements of non-verbal language may differ from one language community to another, even if these elements look or sound the same. Particular attention is given to non-verbal language and differing cultural contexts in Chapters 13 and 14.

Styles of thinking and communicating

How people think and how they express their thoughts appears to be determined not just individually but also socially. Patterns of thought involved in discussing the fortunes of a company, for example, may be problem-solving in approach, using a cause/effect analysis. Equally, the subject can be approached without the idea of a 'problem' being in mind, but rather the contradictions and complexities inherent in running a concern.

The way such thoughts are communicated depend on a number of factors, including:

- Context – the spoken word may or may not be the primary means of communicating. As we saw in Part One, high-context and low-context styles of communication (Hall and Hall, 1990) show the importance or otherwise for the interlocutors of the situation they are in and their relationships. Here is an example from life at home which shows how, within the given context and the relationship between partners, very few words can convey a lot of meaning.

The husband is reading his newspaper and his wife is having a bath. The doorbell rings.

The wife shouts 'Darling!' and the husband, getting up from his chair and heading for the door shouts 'OK!'

Only a couple of words have been spoken, but a lot has been said.

When the wife says 'Darling!' she probably means 'The door bell has rung, I'm in the bath, so I can't answer it. Please could you go to the door?' When he replies 'OK!' his message is probably 'I realise you're in the bath and can't go to the door, so I'll go.'

Whenever something is said, an act of communication is being performed. But is the act always understood by the other? Is the intention behind the spoken word always clear to the other party?

This matter of context is in turn related to:

- **Directness** – the extent to which communicators wish to 'get to the point'. Do they cut straight to the perceived 'truth', or do they imply, suggest, understate matters? Is assertiveness seen by the other as aggression, indirectness as being submissive?
- **Face** – is related to the previous two aspects: is exchange of information and opinions the primary goal of a conversation, or is it more to do with saving face, maintaining the relationship, showing respect for an elder or superior, avoiding confrontation and promoting harmony?

These elements will be dealt with in various chapters, particularly Chapter 14 on communication barriers and Chapter 17 on dealing with conflict.

Stereotypes

Stereotypes are beliefs based on generalisations made about another group of people or their individual members. Such generalisations can be true, but they are often wrong because they are based on inaccurate information and resistant to change. As such, they reflect one or more prejudices, a prejudice being an attitude that is often negative towards another social group.

The source of prejudice, according to social identity theory, is to do with the idea that a person's identity is created primarily through their membership of a group (the in-group). Group members tend to regard their own group as superior, have prejudicial attitudes towards other groups and may be prepared to discriminate against out-groups, even though there are no obvious reasons extrinsically.

Chapter 14 will deal further with stereotypes as one of the main barriers in intercultural communication.

Management of relationships

This has to do with how those communicating perceive each other's social standing. A range of factors may be involved, including the degree of (in)formality, respect and intimacy considered appropriate by one or the other, and the way this is reflected in the interactional behaviour. Hierarchical considerations can also come into play: when employees from different hierarchical levels and cultural backgrounds have to work together, status may be a barrier in communication between them. However aware interlocutors may be about the question of managing working relationships, there are unconscious behaviour elements that can support or contradict spoken communication, such as (lack of) eye contact, or tone of voice.

Aspects of relation management will be dealt with in various chapters, including Chapters 13, 15 and 16, while Chapter 18 will focus on the components of intercultural communication competence.

As stated earlier, Part Three is by no means comprehensive. Readers who wish to go into more depth on the areas chosen should turn to the list of further readings. This introduction also contains a selection of literature on the general area.

Chapter and concept overview

Chapter 13 Business communication across cultures

This chapter introduces the concept of communicating in and between cultures. In dealing with people from other cultures within a company, or with cross-border business clients, a manager will use the normal channels of communication. However, in this communication process the identities of the cultures in question, and the resulting interactions, will play an important role. A number of factors can affect the process of communication. The concept is divided into four main sub-concepts:

- A model of communication.
- Forms of communication in business practice.

- Language during business encounters.
- Face-to-face management relations across cultures.

Chapter 14 Barriers to intercultural communication

Perception is the key word in communication and is largely determined by culture. When business is being done with other cultures, communication is the most important cause of misunderstandings. The filters mentioned in the introduction will now be regarded more closely in terms of barriers to cross-cultural communication. Particular attention is paid to stereotypes because of their important role in relations between cultures. This applies across the board – from one-to-one encounters to marketing campaigns. It is important to know where stereotypes come from and how best to deal with them.

The concept is divided into four sub-concepts:

- What are communication barriers?
- Non-verbal behaviour as a barrier.
- Assumptions and culture.
- Perceptions and stereotypes.

Chapter 15 Negotiating internationally

This chapter introduces the concept of approaches to negotiating in an intercultural context. The concept is divided into three main topics:

- The nature of negotiating from both a Western and non-Western perspective.
- Key facets of negotiation in an international business context and the various types of interaction that may result.
- The issue of strategy adaptation when negotiating with counterparts from other cultures.

Chapter 16 Working with international teams

This chapter introduces the concept of group processes during international encounters. After defining the word 'team' and the elements involved (types and roles), this concept will focus on a common phenomenon of global business, namely international teams and their functioning. The final part of the concept will deal with the management of multicultural teams, with particular reference to Afro-Western teams.

The concept is divided into three sub-concepts:

- Teams in organisations.
- Team tasks and processes.
- The management of multicultural teams.

Chapter 17 Conflicts and cultural differences

This chapter introduces the concept of understanding and dealing with conflicts. This concept will first give a general overview of conflicts and their sources before looking at the role emotions can play in different cultures. It will then examine the management of conflicts, particularly the different approaches used in Eastern and Western cultures.

The concept is divided into five sub-concepts:

- The nature of conflict: when conflicts happen and factors involved.
- A model of conflict styles: how modes of communicative behaviour during conflict can be classified.
- Culture, emotions and conflict: how different cultural values influence the role of emotions in conflict situations.
- Management of conflict (with particular attention to the Asia-Pacific region): the culture-based views of effectiveness and appropriacy in conflict resolution.
- Mediation and cultural transformation: how third party intervention and/or the practice of mindful communication skills can transform the perception of conflict and the attitudes of those involved.

Chapter 18 Developing intercultural communicative competence

This chapter examines how an individual can meet the challenges involved in communicating with different cultures through developing an intercultural communication competence. It has the concept of becoming a competent intercultural communicator at its core. This concept is divided into four elements:

- The main components involved in adapting and developing communication skills appropriate to a cultural context.
- How intercultural competence can be achieved through collaboration between those communicating interculturally.
- The ethical component as a component of intercultural communication competence.
- Developing a third culture between parties to allow the emergence of a shared system of values.

Final activities

Part Three contains two extra activities:

1. **A simulation:** *negotiating internationally.* You will be taking part in a meeting of department heads within a newly merged company. You are required to decide on company policy, particularly with regard to the location of production facilities.
2. **A group-project activity:** *Vechtel: adapting an international approach to the local market.* This presents a series of events in the recent past of a company on the international takeover path and describes the perceptions of those involved. You are asked to prepare a report together with a number of your colleagues, to be used as a basis for an oral presentation and class discussion.

What you will gain

After working through Part Three you will gain more insight into:

- How culture affects communication.
- How intercultural communication can be affected by the cultural differences between those involved.
- How intercultural communication can be made more effective.

References

Gudykunst, W.B. (ed.) (2004) *Cross-Cultural and Intercultural Communication*, Thousand Oaks, CA: Sage.

Hall, E.T. and Hall, M.R. (1990) *Understanding Cultural Differences*, Yarmouth, ME: Intercultural Press.

Chapter 13

Business communication across cultures

As seen in Part Two, the development of globalisation in business has compelled managers, employees and customers to take increasing account of intercultural relations. The increasingly global nature of business and the growing interaction between cultures is adding to the complexity of doing business.

The composition of staff and clientele is changing as companies start up operations in countries across the globe. Managers in such companies, therefore, must be able to operate on an international level and deal with other cultures. It is no longer enough for them to be aware of the existence of cultural differences; they must also be able to communicate, negotiate and work together with business partners from other cultures.

These requirements go far beyond the standard recipes for management from early business studies where the emphasis was very much on a universal approach, one which took no account of relativity or diversity. New management skills are necessary, particularly in the area of communication skills.

The concept in Chapter 13 first examines the elements involved in intercultural and intra-cultural communication before looking at communication in business. Chapter 14 follows on with an analysis of a number of barriers, both verbal and non-verbal, to intercultural communication.

Learning outcomes

After reading this chapter, you will have acquired an overview of theories on communication between cultures, as well as gained an understanding of:

- The different components that have an influence on the process of communication.
- The role of communication in business practices.

Concept 13.1 Communicating in and between cultures

As discussed in the introduction to Part Three, intercultural communication comprises all forms of communication both within and between cultures. This concept should be considered not just in terms of comparisons between cultures, but also in terms of the process of interaction and exchange between different cultures. As Ladmiral and Lipiansky

(1989) indicate, the term 'intercultural communication' could imply that it is the cultures and identities that are in contact. This is not really the case. Instead, it is individuals who are interacting and it is they who bring their culture's way of thinking, feeling and living into the interaction. These authors therefore argue that intercultural communication can be seen as a 'fabric of relations', a fabric created by the individuals or groups from different cultures and woven from the perceptions they have of each other, as well as the values, codes, lifestyles and thought processes belonging to their respective cultures.

Intercultural communication can be better defined as an interactive phenomenon rather than one involving comparisons between cultures. These cultures are non-homogeneous social groups that are forever evolving. Their interaction should not just be seen in terms of a set of relations between the cultures, but also as a dynamic process (therefore one implying change) whereby the cultures are defined both through their own characteristics as well as through their interaction with each other. This definition therefore takes both a systemic perspective (involving sets of interrelations between individuals) and a dynamic one (whereby the interrelations can change).

This approach to communication brings us to the model which we presented in the introduction to Part Three (Figure III.1).

A model of communication

The schematic representation of the model in the introduction emphasises the actors involved in the communication, namely the addresser and the addressee. When they communicate, they unconsciously make use of a frame of reference which, in general terms, consists of:

- knowledge (about the subject under discussion);
- experience (in professional or individual terms);
- norms (i.e. the norms of the society in which they live) and values; and
- assumptions and prejudices (with regard to each other).

Communication theories

However, according to a model proposed by researchers known as the Palo Alto Group, human communication does not emphasise the addresser and the addressee. These researchers, who were based at the Mental Research Institute in Palo Alto in the US, collaborated in the 1950s and 1960s on the theory of communication and the relationship between the individuals. They maintained that since both addresser and addressee are in perpetual interaction, they cannot be isolated. The emphasis is not on the message, but on the whole system of communication involved, including a network of relations that cannot be broken up. Everybody is involved in a network of relations woven by the cultural group (the ethnic group or society in question). Communication does, of course, require a message (form and content), but more important than the message in the exchange between protagonists is the interaction, i.e. the relation between the persons communicating and the context of the communication. This determines the information exchanged. Furthermore, the information in the message does not have an absolute value; it is subject to interpretation due to the interaction itself. That is why in human communication – and even more so in intercultural communication – the question of interpretation remains crucial (Donnadieu and Karsky, 2002).

Other relevant communication theories are those in which culture and communication are both integrated (see: Further reading). However, it should be kept in mind that most of these theories have been developed in the Western world and that, for example, Asian conceptualisations of intercultural communication may lead to different patterns of communication than Western approaches (Gudykunst *et al.*, 2005). While appropriate theories are constructed in the native language, a translation into English will, of course, be necessary to allow indigenous non-Western theories to be included in the body of Western thought (on communication). However, their inclusion will not fully resolve the problem. To keep the Asian setting, for example, social scientific research using Western methods is not always appropriate when studying Asian cultural factors. Therefore, as we discussed above, it is preferable to use a theory which incorporates both Western and non-Western approaches. Nonetheless, when doing so, cross-cultural communication researchers should be aware that they might face problems especially on account of inconsistencies and contradictions between the two kinds of theories – or systems – and the phenomena studied within traditional Asian cultures (Prosser, 2009).

SPOTLIGHT 13.1

A harmony theory of Chinese communication

Guo-Ming Chen (2001: 58) sees harmony as being the core value of Chinese culture. The more Chinese are able to achieve harmony in communication, the greater the degree of communicative competence attained.

According to Chen (2001), three sets of abilities need to be developed in order to realise harmony in interaction:

1. to make the following an integral part of one's beliefs: *jen* (humanity/benevolence), *yi* (righteousness or appropriateness) and *li* (rite/courtesy);
2. to accommodate *shi* (temporal contingencies), *wei* (spatial contingencies – social context and communication environment), and *ji* (the first imperceptible beginning of movement);

3. to make strategic use of *guanxi* (inter-relations), *mientz* (face) and power.

On the basis of these three sets, Chen developed his harmony theory of Chinese communication which in turn generated four propositions, 23 axioms and 23 theorems.

Harmonious interaction, however, cannot always be expected to be attained or maintained. As Chen (2002) points out, when the balance of power (both visible and invisible) inherent in Chinese communication is threatened, the participants may become emotional and express themselves in a very candid and aggressive manner. This is what Chen calls the 'dark side' of Chinese communication (2013: 277).

Without going more deeply into the theories on communication between cultures, it can be concluded that not only do the interpretations made by individuals when communicating play an important role, but also the role played by the (cultural) context. It is this role, already referred to in Part One, to which this chapter now turns, with particular reference to the business environment.

The role of the 'context' in communication

Context can be defined as the environment in which the communication process takes place and which helps to define the communication. Knowing the physical context, one can predict much of the communication to a high degree of accuracy. The choice of the environment, the context, helps assign the desired meaning to the words communicated. Culture is also context. Every culture has its own world view; its own way of thinking of activity, time and human nature; its own way of perceiving self; and its own system of social organisation. Knowing each of these helps people assign meaning to the symbols. The component of context helps identify the extent to which the source and receiver have similar meanings for the communicated symbols. Similar understandings of the culture in which the communication takes place is critical to the success of the communication.

Hall and Hall (1990) established two groups of cultures, called *high context* and *low context*. The difference between them was the degree of importance attached to the context of any message. In low-context cultures, the information of any message is contained in the message itself, i.e. in the words used. The message is explicit. In high-context cultures, most of the information is contained in the context where the message is being sent, i.e. in the relationships between the people involved and the situation where people are communicating. The message is implicit.

When representatives of high-context and low-context cultures are doing business, the one may have a very different idea as to what is important in their communication. For example, when the Swiss and the Japanese meet, the former may prefer to come quickly to the point and get down to business. The Japanese, on the other hand, prefer not to talk directly about the business at hand; they are inclined to talk generally about this and that, about life in general, and to do so in order to get to know each other.

As Figure 6.4 in Chapter 6 shows, the Swiss are placed in the low-context group and the Japanese in the high-context group. These two cultures lie at the extreme ends of a continuum.

Another aspect of the process of communication raised by Hall, one often neglected but also important in the relation between cultures, is what he called 'proxemics'.

Proxemics and cultures

The term **proxemics** was coined by Hall (1966) to describe the study of how people perceive their social and personal space. Hall maintains that awareness of the differences between cultures with regard to proxemics is indispensable when interacting with other cultures. This entails being able to work out the 'silent' messages being communicated through the distance separating people when they are interacting, as well as in terms of the senses (touch, smell, sight and sound). Different cultural frameworks define the information received by our physical senses, not only in terms of what can be perceived, but also in terms of what can be eliminated. According to Hall, individuals learn from childhood which types of information they need to retain and which they can dispense with. As soon as these perceptive models have been developed, they appear to be fixed for life.

Personal space is characterised by an invisible zone with distinct boundaries. When an intruder enters this zone, people may feel uncomfortable. This space is a sort of personal territory, a zone of protection or even of defence. The main factors influencing personal space are: gender, age, personality, the degree of sympathy towards the individuals concerned, the situation in which the individuals are confronted, and also the culture(s) involved.

Corraze (1988) reports on investigations made by Hall (1966, 1969) and Watson (1970) into the differences between cultures with regard to the notion of 'personal space'. Hall postulates that the distance between individuals is related to the preferences each culture has with regard to the sensory inputs used. Each culture has a preference for certain sensory receptors. Take, for example, the differences in personal space between Arabs and Americans: Arabs, it seems, prefer a smaller personal space than Americans because the former are more susceptible to the olfactory dimension, including skin odour. Hall, in fact, makes a link between smell and a person's disposition in the Arabic-speaking world.

> When couples are being matched for marriage, the man's go-between will sometimes ask to smell the girl, who may be turned down if she doesn't 'smell nice'.
>
> Hall, 1969: 149

Watson compares the distances between people in conversation in different cultures and makes a ranking according to the differences in the size of their personal space. The ranking, from small to large is illustrated in Figure 13.1. Research supports the hypothesis that if someone's personal space is violated, this can impair communication because of an increase in anxiety.

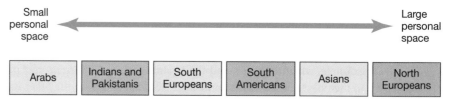

Figure 13.1 **Distances during conversation**

Proxemics also relates to the places where people move and the places where they work. If tables in a restaurant are placed in a way that does not respect personal space, the occupants may well apologise to their neighbours for sitting so close, or display non-verbal behaviour (such as deliberately looking away). If managers do not take the concept of personal space into account when seeing to the organisation of offices and the arrangement of desks, the ensuing anxiety among staff can hamper communication and thus the efficient running of a business. This is a non-verbal aspect of communication in the working environment to which managers pay little attention.

Communication also refers to the meaningful exchange process by which verbal and non-verbal information is shared through messages, and it can take many forms. Even if managers use all these forms in their business practices, they each have different perceptions of the effectiveness of these forms of communication and may therefore prefer some over others. The question of which forms of communication to use is one that should receive more attention in business as well as in research into communication generally.

Forms of communication in business practice

Many channels of communication are available to managers. Electronic mail, for example, is becoming the most common form of written communication within many companies. The e-mail is used for many purposes, both externally and internally: from their smartphone, tablet or computer, managers write e-mails to call a meeting, or give their colleagues

Table 13.1 **Channels of business communication**

Medium	Oral	Written	Electronic/digital
(Telephone) conversations	✗		
Conference calls	✗		
(Online) meetings	✗		✗
Online forums/blogs/social networks		✗	✗
Voice mail (asynchronic)	✗		✗
Video teleconferences (synchronic)	✗		✗
Electronic mail (asynchronic)		✗	✗
Instant messaging (synchronic)		✗	✗
Training sessions	✗	✗	✗
Presentations, speeches	✗	✗	✗
Press conferences	✗	✗	✗
Press releases		✗	
Memos		✗	
Proposals		✗	
Letters		✗	
Reports		✗	
Fax		✗	

NB: any of the written documents listed above, if attached to e-mails, could also be considered as communication by means of the electronic channel.

and subordinates feedback and instructions, or correspond with customers and clients. Some managers, however, prefer to communicate by talking face-to-face in a meeting or informally, by making phone calls (including conference calls), or by using video tele-conferences. These ways of communicating in turn involve the use of some or all of the non-verbal elements of communication, such as gestures, tone of voice, facial expressions, and body language generally.

Culture and choice of communication mode

The choice of communication mode can be influenced by cultural factors. Mead (1990: 84) gives an example with regard to telephoning. A US businessman would consider it quite normal to make a 'cold call', to phone a stranger with whom he thinks he could do business. A Japanese businessman, on the other hand, would consider this to be intrusive or aggressive, preferring instead to find a third party who can 'vouch for your credibility and make a formal introduction'.

This is, of course, related to the cultural dimensions discussed in earlier chapters. A business from an 'individualist' culture, for example, may be intent on what it considers 'efficient' communication when dealing with a business in a 'collectivist' culture. It puts forward a comprehensive business proposal and expects a similar response. If the company asked to respond is not accustomed to such direct approaches, it may well decide not to deal with the proposal directly in writing, but to request instead a face-to-face meeting with representatives of the company concerned. In this way, a good relationship can be established before any discussion of the proposal is entered into since, in the eyes of the possible business partner, efficiency and speed are less important than establishing trust and confidence. The oral mode is used to set the conditions for co-operation, whereafter the written mode can be considered as a means of communication, provided the relationships established are scrupulously maintained.

Computer (or mobile)-mediated communication (CMC)

As was said earlier, electronic mail is being increasingly used as a way of sending documents, requests and information generally to colleagues and (potential) clients. However, even though it offers many advantages in terms of speed and efficiency, it can also contain many pitfalls when used interculturally. Problems of comprehension may arise, of course, through inaccurate language and poorly structured text. (These points are discussed in the next sub-section with reference to using English as the medium of communication.) Also, cultural issues can lead to misunderstanding and even antagonism. The recipient of an e-mail may consider its style too formal or informal depending on what their expectations are. They may take offence, for example, if they are not addressed at the start of the e-mail or if the style of the message is too direct or casual, particularly if it contains careless language. Others who consider e-mails to be more conversational in nature may dislike the distancing effect of a formal written style and the lack of explicit information or opinion, particularly if direct answers are not given to direct questions. As with any written form of communication, there are no facial expressions to mitigate or clarify messages.

It could be argued that the use of e-mail, just as other forms of computer-mediated communication (CMC), blurs the distinction between the oral and written messages for many of its users. A sender or recipient may expect an e-mail to be the equivalent of a letter or memo, meeting the formal requirements of language accuracy and text cohesion of a written text. Another sender/recipient, however, may regard the message sent as being the start (or continuation) of a conversation in writing, of a thread of messages. The style will reflect more the spoken word with its slips of the tongue, false starts, hesitations and inaccuracies. Any resulting misunderstanding or incomprehension can be communicated and dealt with in later messages.

Such differing expectations, be they intracultural or intercultural, need to be recognised and managed by the communicating parties. However, CMC can help to alleviate discrepancies because both sender and receiver have, in theory, time to reflect upon and discuss the process as they are communicating.

Differences in expectation and resulting behaviours in both the intracultural and intercultural context are discussed in a literature review, in which Waldvogel (2001) found that many of the gender differences in face-to-face interaction were carried over into CMC and even accentuated:

> There is evidence that women and men communicate in different ways on the net. A study of two academic groups conducted by Herring (1996) reveals that 'Both men and women structure their messages in an interactive way and that for both, the pure exchange of information takes second place to the exchange of views. Significant gender differences are found in how

electronic messages are oriented [. . .] Although messages posted by women contain somewhat more interactional features they are also more informative, in contrast with male messages which most often express (critical) views.'

Herring found that while women value politeness, men operate in accordance with competitive values which result in violations, including flaming, of conventional politeness norms. Men dominated the 'talking' time. They participated at a higher rate than their numerical representation justified, and their messages were considerably longer. They took little interest in what women had to say, which seems to have resulted in a decline of female participation. In this supposedly liberal academic environment, CMC was found to be male-dominated, power-based and hierarchical.

Waldvogel, 2001: 7–8

Language during business encounters

The previous discussion assumes that the two business representatives are able to communicate even though their native languages are different. When this is not possible, a number of options present themselves:

- Both sides could insist on using their native language when communicating, necessitating the use of an intermediary to translate. This may remove the obligation of managers to learn their counterpart's language and ensure that communication runs efficiently. However, apart from practical problems (including the availability of interpreters and the cost involved), there is always the question of reliability: is the translation accurate? Is the interpreter able to convey the full nuance of what is being said? Moreover, the presence of an intermediary can hamper the establishment of a relationship between the parties. Interaction is necessarily delayed and the role of non-verbal communication reduced. The focus of interaction may well become the interpreter who, in a way, is controlling the whole exchange without bearing the responsibility for the outcome.

- One interlocutor uses the mother tongue of the other. Many regard this as the best solution: by becoming truly bilingual, the manager is able to 'tune into' the other's culture, pick up all the nuances, understand the cultural references and respond appropriately. An 'expat' manager who has worked and lived for a long time in one country or region may well be in a position to perform this role optimally. However, managers who are operating across many cultures and making forays into new countries cannot be expected to acquire the language of every culture with which they are (about to be) involved.

It is worthwhile mentioning here problems experienced by interlocutors who share the same language, whether they come from different cultures or not. Within an English-speaking country, such as the UK, there can be enormous differences in the level of expression in both written and spoken language, and this can affect communication generally. Between English-speaking countries, such as the UK and the US, there may be a shared language, but British and US managers must sometimes check the meanings of words that their counterparts use. Differences in pronunciation can also add confusion. This goes also for speakers of other dialects of English such as Indian English, Singapore English and South African English.

Spotlight 13.2 shows how native speakers of English in the UK can be confused by the plethora of business terms taken from American English.

English: a neutral language?

A third possibility for managers who cannot communicate with each other through their mother tongues is for them to share a neutral foreign language. History shows how the use of a 'lingua franca' (common language) has been indispensable to the development of trade in many parts of the world. Nowadays, English frequently serves as a means of communication between companies whose managers have acquired the language as part of their education and have been exposed to it through various media. This language is often referred to as 'international English', but is difficult to define exactly because it has evolved organically on the basis of how non-native speakers use English. It is said to contain words and phrases that are generally understood across the world. It appears to be devoid of complex grammar constructions and of all but the most common idiomatic phrases. Those using it may often need to readjust their use of the language while using it to accommodate differences in knowledge and understanding between the speakers concerned. The differences in pronunciation may also need to be considered, especially when it is heavily influenced by that used for the mother tongue.

SPOTLIGHT 13.2

Meeting-room jargon: just fuel for buzzword bingo?

By Michael Quinion

If you can't understand half of what your colleagues are saying in meetings, take heart – you are not alone.

A survey of a thousand office workers in Britain was published last week by the firm of recruitment consultants Office Angels. It reported that two-thirds of office staff used unnecessary jargon terms, for the usual reasons of wanting to confuse opponents and seem superior. But 40 per cent of those surveyed found it irritating and distracting, and 10 per cent thought it made the most frequent users sound pretentious and untrustworthy. Nothing very new or startling so far. But the list of buzz phrases that were reported as being at the same time most common and least understood was intriguing:

Low-hanging fruit, e-tailing, talk off-line, blue-sky idea, win–win situation, think outside the box, holistic approach, level playing field, sanity check, put to bed, whole nine yards, helicopter view, gap analysis, touch base, rain check, sing from the same hymn sheet, finger in the air, get in bed with, big picture, benchmark, ball park, ticks in all the right boxes, strategic fit, bread and butter.

It's clear that jargonisers in British offices are picking up terms from American English, some from the standard language, but mostly from business jargon. The survey suggests

they are doing so because more business people have access to the American-dominated internet.

You can see that phrases like rain check, ball park and touch base could confuse hearers in Britain, because we literally don't play the game. (But one supermarket in Britain uses rain checks as its name for the vouchers it gives out when special offers are in short supply, so some of us have been exposed to it.)

Some terms are odd and would stop almost anybody for a moment – low–hanging fruit, for a target that's easy to reach, helicopter view, for an overview, and gap analysis, for assessing untapped opportunities. But several – such as level playing field, benchmark, and blue-sky – have been in British English for many years. And are strategic fit or bread and butter really so hard to figure out, in context? It would seem so, from the survey.

Jargon is all right in its place. But what the survey shows is that people are easily confused by the unfamiliar, good enough reason for sticking to plain English the rest of the time. Giving bored attendees at meetings the chance to play buzzword bingo is hardly a substitute.

Source: www.worldwidewords.org/articles/jargon.htm, accessed 1/9/2010.

Even here, however, there are problems. A speaker using English as a neutral foreign language may well suffer similar problems to native speakers using English to communicate with non-native speakers. This is particularly the case when the speaker in question is from a country where English is used as the second language of communication in, for example, education and business. The speaker may not be aware of the breadth of his vocabulary compared with that of his counterpart, and may be unable to modify his pronunciation since it is part and parcel of the way English is used in his country of origin.

Some observers regard international English as a move towards cultural neutrality, a way of shedding the cultural connotations of British English or American English. However, as a sort of default language, it has considerable limitations: discussion can be superficial and communicating thoughts difficult. The basic problem is that language is the very expression of a culture, be it Canadian English, Hong Kong English, Caribbean English or African English. Stripping culture off any language, let alone a particular sort of English, can impoverish the semantics of the language and reduce its whole power of expression. There may be less room for nuance and subtlety, for saying something that expresses much more than the words used. The language can be deprived of its deeper meaning.

This goes equally for written English. A report in writing in a 'stripped down' English – particularly one using 'bullets' of information – may not in itself prove easy to understand by a non-native speaker of English. A noble attempt to simplify English may cause more problems than those it was intended to solve. The connections between thoughts, ideas and information may become more diffuse or even non-existent. Deprived of proper cohesion, clear context and any oral explanation, the adapted text may have lost a good deal of the intended meaning of the original. Such problems frequently occur during exchanges of e-mails when messages sent in simplified telescopic form can result in misunderstandings or incomprehension. This goes particularly for e-mails written in idiomatic, telegram-style language that may be appropriate for an office colleague, but not for a client in Bangladesh.

Over and above such problems, there is, of course, the question of language as a potent way of expressing cultural identity. How motivated are people to use a language that is not theirs and which does not allow them to assert their own personal or cultural identity? Mini-case 13.1 shows what can happen when a company, which was once a Chinese state-owned enterprise, adopts English as its official language.

Face-to-face management relations

This brings us to the question of face-to-face business encounters. Whatever the language chosen, encounters occur in situations and contexts where the expectations of the inter-locutors may be very different, where the pressure of differing social norms can disturb the communicative relationship.

The first encounter

The way different cultures pursue the formality mode indicated earlier reflects tendencies within the cultures concerned. The very start of an encounter can indicate clear differences, even if it takes place in a shared language. A formal first meeting between a US manager and a German manager, for example, may show how the one is intent on establishing an open, friendly and eventually informal relationship whereas the other is more reserved

MINI-CASE 13.1

Straight-talking, English-speaking culture brings communication problems

By Justine Lau

When a Hong Kong-based analyst recently called computer-maker Lenovo's Beijing office and asked for an employee by the English first name on her business card, he got a puzzling response. The operator told him the person did not exist.

Baffled, he called back and asked for the same person in her Chinese name. He was put through to her office immediately.

What the analyst encountered was a Lenovo in flux where the transformation of a corporate culture has yielded occasional moments of confusion even within the company.

Some employees at Lenovo, which acquired IBM's PC unit last year, now receive internal e-mails from a 'John' or 'Mary' whom they struggle to identify until they find out their Chinese names.

'In the past, we used to call each other by Chinese names. But now since a lot of our communications involve our US colleagues, some people may find it easier to have an English name', says one Lenovo employee.

The spontaneous move by staff to adopt English names may be causing slight confusion, but it underlines broader changes in the company's culture that analysts see as key to its success in managing the acquisition of the IBM unit.

Shortly after the deal, Lenovo hired Bill Amelio, a former Dell executive, to be its chief executive. It moved its headquarters from Beijing to North Carolina and changed the official company language from Chinese to English. It is also establishing a straight-talking culture inside the company.

'Lenovo used to behave like any state-owned enterprise. [But] it has realised that in order to become a true global company, the first step is to drop some of the old habits', said Randy Zhou, an analyst at Bank of China International.

 Source: from 'Straight-talking, English-speaking culture brings communication problems', *Financial Times*, 9/11/2006: 31 (Lau, J.), © The Financial Times Ltd. All Rights Reserved.

Questions

1. How do you think the adoption of English by the company would help establish a 'straight-talking culture'?

2. What else do you think would need to be done for this new culture to be established?

in exchanging information, particularly with regard to their respective positions and responsibilities. The very exchange of names ('Hi! I'm Ron Smith.' – 'Hello. Stoldt, Dr Peter Stoldt.') can be the start of a precarious scenario, particularly when English is being used: using 'you' goes hand-in-hand with informality for the American, whereas the German may use 'you' as the equivalent of '*Sie*', the formal version of 'you' in German which establishes a certain distance between speakers. Two conflicting functions of the meeting (cultivating social ties and exchanging information) may well be pursued with growing unease by the two parties. The German possibly does not share the optimism and (superficial) friendliness of the other; he is more intent on establishing the other's credentials and clarifying the potential of a business deal. Any attempt by the American to break through what he considers to be the rather cold reserved manner of his counterpart could have an adverse effect, with the German developing an antipathy towards persistent affability.

The context of meetings can determine the nature of such encounters. For example, it will become apparent to any foreign visitor in a Japanese setting that addressing a Japanese manager by his first name is inappropriate: office relationships retain a formality not experienced in many Western business cultures. Any attempt to counter this can result in extreme embarrassment for the Japanese manager and his colleagues. In another (Western) setting, however, first-name terms may be the norm and insistence on using a title and surname may prove a barrier to establishing trust and confidence in that setting.

Conversational styles

If a business relationship develops, some kind of negotiated communication mode may be established, whereby the context involved plays a decisive role. Once the Japanese manager has deemed it appropriate for business with his Western counterpart to be pursued, then he may be prepared to drop his guard and enter into a less formal style of communication. However, if other, less involved, Japanese colleagues are present, the more formal style will be retained, and the American will adapt his (verbal) behaviour correspondingly. On the other hand, the Japanese may well be prepared to communicate (and possibly behave) more informally in a Western setting – as long as his authority is not questioned.

Once the relationship between managers from different cultures has been established, the maintenance of such a relationship can be fraught with difficulty, particularly when different styles of conversation are used. One interlocutor may expect those involved in a meeting, for example, to be able to take turns when speaking, the other may assume it is his right to interrupt as and when necessary; one interlocutor may be focused on his particular take on matters, the other may involve his 'ego' much less; one may tend to make assertive, conclusive statements, the other may prefer to make more negotiable contributions and be less conclusive; one may consider pauses in the conversation to be appropriate for reflection, the other may shy away from silence and fill up a gap as soon as it appears.

Listening is, of course, a crucial element of any conversation: understanding not only what is being said but evaluating the meaning of what is being said. Taking turns to speak, rather than interrupting each other, may certainly ease the process of understanding, as will asking questions to check on understanding. The use of a shared second language will probably necessitate a check on the intended meaning of words or phrases used, and possibly a rephrasing of statements to clarify understanding. Listening carefully to what is not said is just as important. As Mead (1990: 118) indicates in his list of habits a good listener needs to develop:

> Listen for what is *not* said; that is, for what the sender thinks is so obvious as to be redundant or what is so new as to be outside his or her experience. This means processing the message in terms of the differences between your and the speaker's personal and cultural priorities.

Another element to take into account when evaluating the contributions of other interlocutors is their facial expressions.

Facial expressions during interaction

Facial expressions have been analysed more frequently in terms of the emotions expressed than in terms of their effect on human relations. However, such expressions give important signals in social and business interaction. They are totally linked to the context and differ according to whether the context is clear or ambiguous. A persistent look can make the interlocutor feel like escaping or responding with signals of aggression. Such looks are therefore often associated with feelings (unease, embarrassment) which, according to the context, will express attitudes that are diametrically opposed (such as aggression and friendliness).

Facial expressions are also connected to the status of the interlocutors. In social and business encounters they can play an important role when expressing the degrees of dominance between people with different levels of status. Any perceived degree of status can, however, have causes unrelated to a person's actual social position. We sometimes arbitrarily attribute a dominant status to someone because they are able to talk very fluently and knowledgeably during a discussion.

Cultural differences can play a significant role in the way facial expressions function. The length of visual contact, for example, depends to a great extent on the cultural origin of the interlocutors. When someone actually averts their gaze, this can be interpreted differently. In some cultures this act can have a negative connotation, but in others it may be seen simply as a sign that the speaker is changing direction in the discussion. The act of smiling might be assumed to have a similar function across the world as a signifier of happiness. Trumble's (2004) book, *A Brief History of the Smile*, reveals many of the nuances attached to this physiological process. Through his enlightening account Trumble shows that smiling intersects not just with happiness, but also with piety, sex and corruption. Here is an account of how a Russian smile can be interpreted (Sauer, 2007: 13):

> Anyone who has been to Russia knows how unbelievably sullen the people look. They hardly ever smile but instead give all the signs that life for most Russians is just hell. I maintain that a smile actually has another function – an observation that has been scientifically corroborated. My teacher of Russian, Maria, obtained her doctorate from Moscow University with a dissertation entitled: 'A comparison between the function of the smile in Russia and its function in Western cultures, together with the historical background'. My teacher spent over three years researching the subject and interviewed hundreds of Russians and non-Russians. A smile in Russian culture, sends a totally different message to that sent by a smile in the West. According to Maria, a smile in Russia – when shown to a stranger – has a negative connotation: 'He's pulling my leg!', or 'He's criticizing me!' In Russian, the word 'smile' often evokes a negative feeling. Maria: 'We use the phrase "Enough smiling!" meaning "Cut it out!", while in English you say "Keep smiling" – which means the opposite.'

Interaction through interpreters

English may be the working language during many international encounters, but many executives still rely on interpreters to explore and develop business opportunities abroad particularly in regions of the world where local companies have not yet been able to develop sufficient English language skills within their workforce.

Having a third party involved in encounters with (potential) agents or clients is fraught with difficulty. An interpreter is essentially an outsider who is most probably not familiar with the company for whom he/she is working, nor with its culture, nor with its expertise in the area under discussion. Moreover, at a personal level, the interpreter may end up becoming the focus of any interaction between parties; rather than establishing eye contact and developing a rapport with each other, they may well tend to concentrate on the interpreter who is speaking directly to them. Even if the interpreter manages to translate expertly, the actual communication may still be unsuccessful because signals in a translated utterance may not be picked up by the receiver since he/she is unaware of the cultural context, of the 'loading' which the words contain.

SPOTLIGHT 13.3

Dealing with a Japanese subsidiary

In her article 'A matter of interpretation',[1] Alicia Clegg gives an account of the problems which Gaelle Olivier, vice president of Axa, the French insurance group, encountered when dealing with a Japanese subsidiary which was struggling to survive in the market.

Ms Olivier was sometimes told that a task would be 'muzukashii'. Her interpreter translated this as 'difficult', which Ms Olivier took to mean tough but do-able. Only when her team repeatedly missed deadlines did she begin to understand that *muzukashii* is a cultural euphemism for saying 'It is impossible and we cannot do it'.

Misunderstandings prompt the question of whether it is better to work with interpreters who translate word for word or with those who sacrifice literal accuracy to get across the spirit of what is being said. Ms Olivier, who has since learned Japanese, prefers the literal approach. She believes that relying on the interpreter's potted version is risky and makes you even more of an outsider. 'If you are living in a country, it is important to make yourself knowledgeable about its culture', she adds.

 [1] From 'A matter of interpretation', *Financial Times*, 2/2/2010, p. 16 (Clegg, A.) . © The Financial Times Ltd. All Rights Reserved.

This concept has presented the main forms of communication exchange and addressed some of the issues involved in the choice of language in business encounters. The management of relations during such encounters has also been examined and this has shown the many facets of communication that people from different cultures need to be mindful of during face-to-face meetings.

The tendency to use stereotyping is also ever-present during such encounters and these will be discussed in Chapter 14. The question of interaction between people from different cultures will be examined further in Chapter 18.

Conclusion

This chapter has given a brief outline of the theory of communication, which is indispensable to a better understanding of intercultural communication. Even if language remains the dominant factor in communication situations, there are other elements that come into play, including the context, proxemics and facial expressions.

Even if they share a common language (English being increasingly used in business by non-native speakers), interlocutors may still experience problems because of their cultural backgrounds. Developments in computer (or mobile)-mediated communication in particular are changing the way people communicate. The numerous examples given in this chapter allow a better understanding of the new framework of intercultural business communication.

Points for reflection

1. The concept examined three possibilities with regard to the use of language during a business encounter. A fourth possibility is for the manager in question to learn the target language and employ translators.

   What advantages does this combination afford those involved?

2. When two people from different cultures meet in a business situation, the interaction, which is specific to each situation, does not allow the protagonists to be certain of the outcome of their encounter.

   What, in your opinion, are the factors that can influence the outcome of an intercultural interaction? Explain how these factors can influence the outcome.

Further reading

Asante, M.K., Miike, Y. and Yin, J. (eds) (2014) *The Global Intercultural Communication Reader* 2nd edition, New York: Routledge. As the publishers proudly proclaim, this is the first anthology which takes a distinctly non-Eurocentric approach to the study of culture and communication. It brings together contributions from across the world which deal with the processes and politics of intercultural communication using critical, historical and indigenous perspectives. As well as examining key issues to do with the nature of research into cross-cultural and intercultural research, this reader also focuses on intercultural competence in a multicultural society, the effects of globalisation and ethical considerations.

Gudykunst, W.B. (ed.) (2004) *Cross-Cultural and Intercultural Communication*, Thousand Oaks, CA: Sage. In his role as editor, W.B. Gudykunst has chosen to classify the contributions from experts in the field into two distinct categories: cross-cultural communication and intercultural communication. The difference lies essentially in the subject area being researched. Intercultural communication includes all aspects of the study of culture and communication. Cross-cultural communication research tends to be comparative and focuses on cultural communication – the role of communication – and cultural identities. The book covers such topics as: language and verbal communication across cultures; non-verbal communication across cultures; cultural influences on the expression and perception of emotions; identity and intergroup communication; communication in intercultural relationships; and adapting to an unfamiliar culture.

Littejohn, S.W. and Foss, K.A. (eds) (2009) *Encyclopaedia of Communication Theory*, Thousand Oaks, CA: Sage. This two-volume book presents an overview of communication theory, offering current descriptions of theories as well as the background issues and concepts that comprise these theories. In addition, it summarises the diversity of theory in the communication field.

References

Chen G.-M. (2001) 'Towards transcultural understanding: A harmony theory of Chinese communication', in Milhouse V.H., Asante, M.K. and Nwosu, P.O. (eds), *Transcultural realities: Interdisciplinary Perspectives on Cross-Cultural Relations*, Thousand Oaks, CA: Sage: 55–70.

Chen, G.-M. (2002) 'The impact of harmony on Chinese conflict management', in Chen, G.-M. and Ma, R. (eds), *Chinese Conflict Management and Resolution*, Westport, CT: Ablex: 3–19.

Chen, G.-M. (2013) 'The Two Faces of Chinese Communication', in Asante, M.K., Miike, Y. and Yin, J. (eds), *The Global Intercultural Communication Reader*, 2nd edition, New York: Routledge: 273–282.

Corraze, J. (1988) *Les communications non-verbales*, 4th edition, Paris: Presses Universitaires de France.

Donnadieu, G. and Karsky, M. (2002) *La systémique*, Rueil-Malmaison, France: Editions Liaisons.

Gudykunst, W., Lee, C., Nishida, T. and Ogawa, N. (2005) 'An Introduction', in Gudykunst, W.

(ed.), *Theorizing about Intercultural Communication*, Thousand Oaks: Sage: 3–32.

Hall, E.T. (1966) *The Hidden Dimension*, New York, NY: Bantam Doubleday Dell.

Hall, E.T. (1969) *The Hidden Dimension: Man's Use of Space in Public and Private*, London: Bodley Head.

Hall, E.T. and Hall, M.R. (1990) *Understanding Cultural Differences*, Yarmouth, ME: Intercultural Press ANC.

Herring, S. (1996) *Computer-Mediated Communication: Linguistic, Social and Cross-cultural Perspectives*, Amsterdam: John Benjamins. Quoted in: Waldvogel, J. (2001): 7–8.

Ladmiral, J.R. and Lipiansky, E.M. (1989) *La communication interculturelle*, Paris: Armand Colin.

Mead, R. (1990) *Cross-Cultural Management Communication*, Chichester: John Wiley.

Prosser, M.H. (2009) 'Cross-cultural communication', in Littejohn, S.W. and Foss, K.A (eds), *Encyclopaedia of Communication Theory*, 2 Volumes, Thousand Oaks, CA: Sage: 248–252.

Sauer, D. (2007) 'Glimlach', *Het Parool*, 16/6/2007: 13.

Trumble, A. (2004) *A Brief History of the Smile*, New York, NY: Basic.

Waldvogel, J. (2001) *Email and Workplace Communication: a Literature Review*, Wellington, New Zealand: Victoria University of Wellington, accessed 1/6/2008, www.vuw.ac.nz/lals/research/lwp/docs/ops/op3.htm.

Watson, O.M. (1970) *Proxemic behavior*, The Hague: Mouton. Quoted by Corraze, J. (1988) *Les communications non-verbales*: 179.

ACTIVITY 13.1

Read the article below and then answer the questions that follow it.

English names catch on among Chinese: young bridging a gap with West

By Jehangir S. Pocha

Di, Chao, Xu and Wentao now answer to Eddy, Super, Promise and Wendy

For pragmatic Chinese, adopting English names has long represented a way for them to bridge the linguistic and cultural gap. Now, as China widens its reach abroad and as the number of foreigners living in mainland China swells, picking an English name has become a rite of passage for most young, urban Chinese.

When students enrol in Chinese universities, they routinely are required to pick English names as a way to prepare themselves for life in their increasingly Westernized world. Students race to snap up the 'best' English names on a list the schools circulate.

'Popular names like Michael and Alex go quite fast, and Eddie was already gone before I could choose it', said Eddy Wu, 19, a student at Beijing Forestry University, explaining that he wanted the name because it sounded like his Chinese name, Di. 'So I said "OK, let me take Eddy with this other spelling."'

People usually adopt only English first names and retain their Chinese family name. The practice is informal and has no legal significance. Sometimes, the results can be quirky, with Chinese names that potentially mystify foreigners often being replaced with English aliases that amuse them.

Super Zhang, 25, a paralegal in Beijing, said he chose his English name because it is a literal translation of his Chinese one, Chao. 'I like to see myself as a great and extraordinary person', Super said. 'People wonder about my name all the time and are always asking me to explain it. But I still enjoy having it.'

Most Chinese take their English name – its meaning, its sound, and its associations with historic figures – very seriously. Promise Hong, a 30-year-old writer in Beijing, said her English name was a rough translation of her Chinese one, Xu, and that she saw a philosophical connotation in it.

'Promise has more profound meanings especially with the biblical background of the promised land', she said. 'I began to use it when I was a freshman in college, 12 years ago, and some people I've met have expressed their kind appreciation and curiosity about my choice.'

In nineteenth-century China, choosing an English name was the privilege of only a handful of elites. Possessing one was a status symbol indicating that a person had been to college and rubbed shoulders with the 'laowai', the Puntonghua word for foreigner. The process of picking the name often involved weeks of discussions between the person, English tutors and foreign friends. Chinese sages would then vet the short list of names for their tonal qualities and astrological powers.

That English names are now ubiquitous in urban China is a sign of the country's progress, Eddy said. 'My parents tell me how once any foreigner on the street would be stared at, they were so unusual', he said. 'Now, China is developing very fast and Chinese are becoming very modern.'

While most Chinese with English names reserve their use for times when they are in the company of foreigners, Eddy said more people, especially young women, prefer using their English names. This is particularly true for Chinese immigrants in the US and other English-speaking countries, who use their Western names to help them fit into their new world.

Wentao Zhang, 40, began calling herself Wendy while living in New Jersey for 15 years. 'It just makes things easier', she said. 'People (in the US) used to find it really hard to say my name, so I began saying "Just call me Wendy" and it worked really well.'

This phonetic approach, picking a new name that sounds like your original one, sidesteps the pitfalls of trying to find English translations of Chinese names.

Of course, not every Chinese person has an English name. In the sleepy hamlets that dot the countryside, farmers and workers look surprised at the thought of taking an English name. And sometimes, name changes alone are not enough to bridge the cultural gap.

Apple Li, 21, a travel agent in Beijing, said she chose her English name because her Chinese name is Ping and the Mandarin word for apple is 'pingguo'. But one problem remains: her business card reads Li Ping, since the Chinese write their family name first and given name second.

Many foreigners accustomed to the Western format assume that Li means apple in Mandarin, she said. Adding to the confusion is that Li, when written using a certain character, means pear.

Source: *Boston Globe*, 1/10/2006, accessed 1/6/2008, www.boston.com/news/world/asia/articles/2006/10/01/english_names_catch_on_among_chinese.

Questions

1. What are the reasons given for young Chinese adopting an English first name?

2. Do you think that this custom can help to improve communication between China and Western countries? Explain why.

3. What changes, if any, do you think the use of English names brings to the Chinese way of doing business? Explain your point of view.

ACTIVITY 13.2

The article below highlights the problem of cultural identity by describing developments in France, a country proud of the historical importance of French as the language of politics and culture. The behaviour of Jacques Chirac, born in 1932, president of France at the time, provoked many discussions on the role of English in French society. Read the article and answer the questions following it.

Why English is de rigueur in many French boardrooms

By Tom Braithwaite in Paris and Chris Smyth

When Jacques Chirac stormed out of a meeting at the European Union summit, he said it was because he had been 'profoundly shocked' to hear a French industrialist speaking in English. On this basis, the French president may wish to stay away from a number of his nation's boardrooms.

Mr Chirac's outrage was all too visible on Thursday night when he heard Ernest-Antoine Seillière, the head of the Unice employers' organization, explain he had decided to deliver his speech in English because it was 'the language of business'.

But in the boardroom of Air Liquide, the French industrial gases group, meetings are usually held in English. So too at the media group Thomson, once chaired by Thierry Breton, the French finance minister, who joined his president in boycotting Mr Seillière's meeting. At France Telecom – where Mr Breton was also once chairman – English is commonly used in internal memos.

French companies choose English because they do most business outside France and because of an increased foreign presence on their boards. Meetings at Total, the oil group, regularly take place in English, even when only Frenchmen are present. 'It's the language of the oil industry', explains a spokeswoman. English is also the lingua franca at Thales and EADS – the French government has stakes in both defence groups.

Air France-KLM holds meetings of 'the strategy management committee' in English, while competence in the language is compulsory for managerial recruits at Renault. Mike Quigley, the chief operating officer and heir apparent at the telecoms equipment maker Alcatel, is an Australian who does not speak French. 'The English language has connotations of liberalism', said Jean-Louis Muller, the director of Cegos, a management training school. 'The defence of the French language by politicians and unions is the defence of the French social model.'

Mr Muller said the rise of English in French boardrooms appeared unstoppable: 'I witnessed a meeting at [engineering group] Alstom where there were only French managers in the room but English was still the language.'

 Source: from 'Why English is de rigueur in many French boardrooms', *Financial Times*, 25/3/2008, p. 8 (Braithwaite, T. and Smith, C.), © The Financial Times Ltd. All Rights Reserved.

Questions

1. What may explain the sudden departure by the president of France when a French industrialist used English to address the summit meeting?

2. Why, according to the interviews, is English used more and more in French boardrooms?

3. What, according to Jean-Louis Muller, do French and English seem to represent in terms of cultural identity?

Chapter 14

Barriers to intercultural communication

Apart from the framework of reference examined in Chapter 13 and the context of the communication, other elements play an important role in intercultural communication. These are essentially barriers to the communication process, as described in Figure III.1 in the Introduction to Part Three. When the sender and receiver in this figure are from different cultures, the communication process may be impaired through misunderstandings and may eventually break down. The barriers involved will be examined in the concept of this chapter.

Concept 14.1 examines the obstacles preventing the effective flow of information within an organisation. These obstacles relate to either the failure of individuals to communicate effectively, or the failure of systems to make effective communication possible. The break-down in communication is often to do with either too much information (information overload) or too little information, or it can be caused by communication that is misplaced, inaccurate or incomplete. It may also involve the context: personal and environmental factors can impair the quality of the information received. The context of communication is often complicated by the question of culture, with misunderstandings occurring when the sender and receiver do not share similar meanings for the communicated symbols.

Learning outcomes

After reading this chapter you will gain an understanding of:

- Those components of communication that can create obstacles in intercultural communication.
- The importance of the effects that barriers have on communication in business.

Concept 14.1 Barriers in cross-cultural management communication

What are communication barriers?

Ideally, for communication to take place, the frameworks of reference being used – with regard to norms and values, for example – should not be in conflict. However, since a framework of reference is to a considerable degree culturally determined, it is to be expected that the communication between individuals from two different cultures will be disturbed.

Some problems of this nature can occur when doing business with foreign partners, working with foreign colleagues in the same company, or within a joint venture with a foreign company. Communication problems may happen not only during meetings or negotiations, but also during informal situations. A barrier can lead to a business opportunity falling through and/or a business relationship ending up on the rocks.

Such disturbing factors between cultures are many in number and nature (see Figure III.1 in the Introduction). Breakdowns in communication commonly occur when the context of the message being communicated between the sender and receiver is unclear. Some barriers to communication originate from cultural misunderstandings between the speaker and receiver and these can clearly be of great importance for communication in business. Before looking at these barriers in detail, this chapter will discuss some notions that offer insights into the causes of misunderstandings in communication between cultures.

Non-verbal behaviour as a barrier

Is non-verbal behaviour natural or cultural? Is it productive (monologue) or communicative (dialogue)? Is it done voluntarily or spontaneously? We know from the many researchers who have investigated this phenomenon that antiquity was also fascinated by it and, moreover, that non-verbal communication plays an important role in communication as a whole. What this term encompasses is so large that this discussion must confine itself to gestures, facial expression (including affective expressions such as laughter or showing anger), posture and the distance between sender and receiver. These are all closely allied to, or indeed replace, verbal communication in terms of producing messages. They may even contradict the accompanying verbal messages. In short, all these also have a communicative value over and above verbal communication.

Meta-communication and non-verbal behaviour

In its basic form, a meta-communication is an act of communication between two protagonists that also communicates something about the communication itself, or about the relationship between the two protagonists, or both.

In terms of non-verbal behaviour, meta-communicative functions can also include:

- making gestures to complete messages when information is missing (e.g. when gesturing to indicate someone's height or size);
- making hand gestures and modulating the voice by adding rhythm and emphasis to reinforce the verbal message;
- replacing spoken language when it is impossible for some reason (physical barriers, the dominance of other sounds, unknown foreign language).

The nature of this meta-communicative behaviour is determined by personal, social, relational and cultural factors. The nature of the interaction itself may be modified by the intended character of the non-verbal signal of the sender on the one hand, and by the way the receiver reacts to the signal on the other.

The cultural dimension of non-verbal behaviour is apparent once the body language used by interlocutors from different cultures is compared and contrasted. The interactional nature of face-to-face communication therefore takes on an intercultural dimension. All cultures use forms of body language to communicate, but the meaning of these forms is subject to different interpretations according to the cultural background of the interpreter.

Non-verbal interaction

Although facial expressions communicating anger, sadness and fear are considered to be universal, the causes of these expressions may be different. Other gestures, however, may not be so universal: a nod of the head may well be expected to indicate affirmation and a shake negation, but some cultures nod to negate and shake to affirm (for example, the Greeks give a shake of the head to say 'yes'). When a speaker raises his shoulders, this could convey indifference, resignation or ignorance, depending on the cultural context. Furthermore, to convey the idea that someone is stupid can be conveyed in several ways, depending on the cultural context. If the gesture or expression made is unknown in another culture, then its meaning will not be understood. Communication could be interrupted or, if an incorrect meaning is applied by the 'receiver', diverted.

When those interacting come from different cultures, the non-verbal signals used in a certain context may therefore not only differ but also necessarily influence other consequent non-verbal signals. Furthermore, the question of the intention behind non-verbal language must also be addressed. How is it possible to determine whether the sender (if from another culture) has intentionally chosen to transmit a non-verbal message with an exact purpose or whether he is pretending to do so? The receiver is expected to respond to the signal given by the sender who in turn may need to re-adjust his communicative goal, vary the non-verbal messages so that the desired goal is eventually reached. Non-verbal behaviour therefore can be crucial in face-to-face interaction.

Those communicating across cultures, therefore, must be careful not to assume that certain gestures have the same meaning as in their own culture. In France, for example, pulling one's eyelid down with the forefinger means 'I don't believe you!' In Italy, however, the same gesture means something very different: 'I'm keeping an eye on you!'

Since gestures are a purely cultural acquisition, they also reveal certain characteristics of a culture's collective mentality. Let us compare the expression 'to be fed up with . . .' or 'have had enough of . . .' in France and the Netherlands (Figure 14.1).

Figure 14.1 **'I've had enough!'**

The gesture for these words is made in the same way by raising one's hand to the head. However, there is a crucial difference as to where the hand movement stops. In France, the hand stops at the top of the head but in the Netherlands it stops earlier – at the neck. Therefore, in this example, it is more than only a difference of gesture: the gesture represents a cultural attitude that here expresses the limit of exasperation or of patience.

We can only make tentative explanations about how certain gestures and body language generally came into being. This is due to the unstable nature of the values of gestures associated with a language. If, for example, we look at the past with Cresswell (1968), he reminds us that in the eighteenth century there was disapproval of the tendency of the English to use gestures when speaking. A century later, however, the English were characterised for their 'phlegm', their calm self-possession!

Non-verbal communication barriers in business

Although verbal communication is essential in business contacts and can be the main source of misunderstandings between cultures, language differences can be a dominant factor in any communication barrier and can even be an insurmountable one. Just as with translating from one language to another, it can be difficult to convey the full meaning and nuances of expression. As seen in Chapter 13, using English as a means of communication can make the situation easier when doing business, but this does not mean, of course, that misunderstandings do not occur. This applies even to native speakers of English who come from different countries.

However, non-verbal communication can also be a source of misunderstanding and irritation. For example, research carried out into the use of body language by Dutch and French people from a similar business environment showed how great the differences were. When using gestures, for example, the French are very expressive and use the whole upper part of their body. The Dutch, on the other hand, usually limit gestures to the use of their arms – or just one arm – to emphasise the rhythm of their speech. When the Dutch are interacting with the French they can easily come to the conclusion that their interlocutors are very emotional and excited since, in the Dutch culture, such 'exaggerated' use of gestures is only witnessed when very strong emotions are at play (Browaeys, 1989).

Silence can also be a cause of misunderstandings, particularly between Western and Asian cultures. In Western cultures, silence marks pauses in a discourse. These pauses must not last too long, unlike those in oriental cultures where any time without a word being spoken is an integral part of communication. In Thailand, for example, silence is not only a sign of respect, of agreement or disagreement, but it is also highly appreciated as a style of discourse. Asian cultures discourage verbalisation since it contradicts the principle of modesty. In Korea, silence is preferable to the improper use of words. Japan, however, appears to be the exception: even if silence is preferred to verbalisation, it can also be considered as being impolite in situations where active participation by the interlocutors is expected. This is especially the case where an interlocutor is a stranger; remaining silent 'is considered more negative than it is in America' (Tae-Seop Lim, 2003: 62).

It should be said at this point that such examples of non-verbal communication are simply styles of communication and do not indicate that a particular culture experiences more or less emotion. However, the way all sorts of feelings are expressed can be so different between cultures that it can result in representatives of one culture having negative feelings towards another. The creation of such prejudices is not the differences in themselves but the way in which the differences are interpreted.

Assumptions and culture

Cultural assumptions evolve as basic human responses to fundamental problems. Usunier and Lee (2005) provide a framework for the evaluation of the problems and combine three dimensions. Assumptions may have: a cognitive dimension, related to presumptions as to how people think that things work; an affective dimension, related to the presumed likings of people; and a directive dimension related to the presumed choices of people.

Cultural assumptions can be related to time, space or identity. Time-related cultural assumptions relate to four common questions:

- Is time considered as a scarce good (economy of time)?
- Are tasks performed simultaneously or one after the other (monochronic versus polychronic)?
- Is life seen as a continuity or as cyclic episodes?
- Is the orientation in time towards the past, the present or the future?

Cultural assumptions that are space-related have to do with being 'in' or 'out'; being a member or not; belonging or not belonging. The strict opposition defines the content of the 'out-group' and 'in-group' whereby the group space includes – or excludes – families, nations and cultures. Out-group orientation is based on the assumption that there is a unity of mankind beyond the borders of in-group spaces. In-group orientation does not completely exclude out-group orientation. This can be seen, for example, in Nordic European cultures, where a strong sense of national identity goes along with a strong commitment to the development of the poorest nations and international organisations.

Identity-related assumptions relate to self and others and are about the ideal conduct in certain social contexts. They are related to the main socio-demographic categories (age, sex, social class), as well as to particular roles in society (such as the perfect politician, or successful businessman).

Cultural assumptions are difficult for foreigners to detect because they are not easily expressed and are, for the most part, hardly understood by the insiders. As seen in Part One, statements may be given about values and ideas, but the underlying assumptions are generally unclear. There is a gap between the explanations that people give for their behaviour and the real motives for the behaviour. In the same way, there is a difference between what people say and what people want to say (Schneider and Barsoux, 2003). That is why assumptions can generate a lack of understanding and misunderstandings when people from different cultures are communicating.

Barriers

Apart from a system of values, every culture has assumptions that are seldom tested for their justifiability. These are affirmations, mostly normative in nature, about what is true and what is not. To be accepted in a culture or subculture, one has to respect these assumptions. What 'should be done' is generally close to what is believed to be the 'nature of things'. However, assumptions about 'how things are' are often disguised suppositions about 'how they should be'. Moreover, once the values of a group are institutionalised and assimilated, they acquire a kind of existential validity for the members of the group. Sometimes, a value acts as a self-fulfilling prophecy and causes behaviour that complies with the idea, e.g. 'men don't cry' (Oomkes, 1987).

As such, assumptions can create all kinds of problems. A simple example from the business world shows how they can even lead to conflict (Spotlight 14.1). Imagine you receive an order confirmation from a supplier stating that the delivery date of the order will be two weeks. The question is: what does a Dutch supplier mean by 'delivery date' compared with a French supplier?

SPOTLIGHT 14.1

Delivery date: two weeks

Paul had recently begun working as the purchasing manager of a French-owned company in the Netherlands. He was in a bad mood because of a delay resulting from a bottleneck. His mood worsened when he read a memo on his desk. The memo informed him that an order to be supplied by the parent company had not yet been delivered, although it should have arrived two weeks previously.

Delivery delays had almost become a routine problem in his dealings with the parent company. He sent a very business-like reply stating briefly, in English, that he had not yet received the goods on order and that they must be delivered as soon as possible, otherwise he would have to turn to an outside supplier.

The reply came by e-mail, three pages of it, written in French by Jacques, the production manager. His tone was friendly:

We have done everything possible, but you see – what with the renovation of the production area and the holiday period, as well as the specifications of your order – there has been a delay. But don't worry: it's only a question of time now – a little patience and all will be fine.

Paul was flabbergasted by what he considered to be French arrogance. His reaction was as follows:

Firstly, I don't understand French, and secondly, the delivery date had been clearly indicated in the order, namely in two weeks' time. The two weeks have elapsed and now it's a simple matter of whether the goods are here or not. That's the only thing that counts here.

A Dutch supplier will in all likelihood think that the product must be delivered within two weeks: he feels contractually bound to this delivery time. A French supplier, however, may well think that he will do everything he can to dispatch the goods by the date given. For him this date is a promise that is still subject to reconsideration.

This problem of interpretation is not a language issue but a cultural one. The words are clear, but the assumptions underlying the words may differ from culture to culture. This can also be seen in the use of words describing time such as 'soon' or 'straightaway'. Does that mean in one minute or an hour? These words can have a very different meaning in Indonesia than in Germany.

Perceptions and stereotypes

Table 14.1 is an example of an introduction to the question of stereotypes. In the right hand column is a list of stereotypical remarks made by or about a number of Western cultures given in the left hand column. Can you work out which nationality says what about whom?

Table 14.1 **Who is saying what about whom?**

Who/about whom?	What?
Germans	*They're pretentious*
British	*They've got no sense of humour*
Americans	*They're chauvinist*
Spaniards	*They're hypocritical*
Dutch	*They're arrogant*
French	*They're individualistic*

Source: based on Gruère and Morel (1991).

The French could be the subject of all the stereotypical remarks in Table 14.1. The Germans consider the French to be showy, the Americans see them as chauvinistic, the Spanish as hypocritical, and the Dutch view them as the embodiment of arrogance. The British may even see them as having no sense of humour. And the French see themselves as individualistic.

However, all the comments given on the right could be applied to each other by all the nationalities in question. Some generally perceived stereotypical characteristics may well emerge from such an exercise: the British could consider that the Germans have no sense of humour. They are very serious and any humour a German displays does not fit into the British concept of what is funny. The Dutch could well consider the French as chauvinist. They see themselves as being much more tolerant of other nationalities than the French and do not so readily express their feelings of superiority. All the European nationalities could well consider the Americans to be arrogant. In their eyes, the Americans may come over as people who wish to impose on others what they think is best for them. Europeans may consider themselves superior to the Americans, but do not express their feelings of superiority so crassly.

Every culture sees its own system of values in a positive light. So when asked to apply a stereotypical characteristic to itself, every culture listed above could, for example, refer to itself as being individualistic because in the West this is generally considered to be a positive trait.

However, if individuals of a specific nationality within a multicultural group are confronted with negative rather than positive stereotypes of themselves by other nationalities, these individuals will, according to Lipianski (1992), not recognise themselves in the profile made. They will react strongly because they feel personally under attack and deny belonging to the group being characterised. They will defend their own personal identity and see their national identity more in terms of 'them' rather than 'us'.

Identity as an obstacle to communication

National identity therefore appears first as a compulsory image imposed by the outside world. It may characterise people with the same nationality, but it is an identity that the people may not recognise in themselves. In intercultural encounters, this identity dimension influences communication. Indeed, there is no communication without identity and identification of the persons present. According to Ladmiral and Lipianski (1989: 145), when people meet for the first time it is difficult to avoid asking and answering questions to do with identity (Who are you? Where do you come from?). For these authors, 'It is a question of knowing at the same moment the identity of my interlocutor and what elements of my own identity (sexual, social, professional, national, ideological) are going to be required during our exchange.'

However, identity can also appear as an obstacle to communication because the identity of both interlocutors defines and sets the limits of the exchange. The conflicts of ideas, opinions and interpretations – also in the interpersonal relations between individuals of different nationalities – refer to identity conflicts: on the one hand there is the alter ego, namely the double who reflects our own image, and on the other hand the opponent for whom we feel aversion (Ladmiral and Lipianski, 1989). The perception of the other always has a projective nature and can only have one's own culture as base and reference. This phenomenon is called **ethnocentrism** and refers to the values of one's own culture even when dealing with others who cannot share these values.

> Likewise, the tendency exists to describe and judge the value systems and dominant practices of other cultures from the standpoint of one's own. Such an attitude has connections with the stereotyping of others.
>
> Edgar and Sedgwick, 2002: 133

Ethnocentrism is inherent to any membership of a socio-cultural, ethnic or national group. It is the intrinsic mechanism of distinction separating mine from yours, relatives from foreigners, people here from people elsewhere. Ethnocentrism is both a cultural feature and a psychological phenomenon. It leads to any perception being made through a barrier that is unconsciously made up of our own values. Ethnocentrism, in its most simplified and elementary form, is responsible for forming prejudices and stereotypes – 'ready-for-use judgements' (Ladmiral and Lipianski, 1989: 138).

Consumer attitudes and perceptions about foreign products are highly influenced by ethnocentrism, the belief in the superiority of one's own ethnic group. Usunier and Lee (2005) report that highly ethnocentric consumers, who are usually older people, are likely to believe that purchasing imported products harms the domestic economy and causes unemployment. Younger consumers, they found, were less affected by ethnocentricity. This means that domestic companies may benefit to a certain extent from ethnocentrism. However, they also found that the resistance experienced by foreign companies to their products depends on the product category (e.g. wine, cars) and the consumers targeted.

Stereotyping in advertising

Stereotypes can be a disturbing factor not only in communication, but also in other areas of management. As seen in Chapter 11, it is advisable in marketing to tread very carefully when it comes to stereotyping across consumer nationalities.

MINI-CASE 14.1

Unleash the power of the Hispanic market by avoiding these pitfalls

By Mary Baroutakis

While writing this article, I tried to narrow down the number of pitfalls that marketers encounter when advertising to the Hispanic market. There are many, but for the sake of brevity, I will address the three that I come across most frequently:

- overusing Hispanic traits in ads;
- cloning a general market strategy for use in the Hispanic market; and
- keeping Hispanic advertising less ambitious and far more conservative than that aimed at the general market.

Overusing Hispanic traits

We have all heard again and again that Hispanics are very family oriented; that they are very close to their extended family; that they take care of their elders; that children tend to live at home after they reach 18. We've also heard that Hispanics tend to be emotional and sentimental. They listen to their hearts a lot and value relationships. This brings me to the first common mistake: the overuse of the above traits in Hispanic advertising and how this can sometimes weaken or cloud a selling message.

A few years ago, a telecommunications company aired a commercial introducing a new plan for international callers to Latin America. The commercial was absolutely beautiful. It was shot on location in many parts of Latin America and the scenery was breathtaking. It showed vignettes of people abroad receiving calls from their family in the US. The background music score was very nostalgic.

The research company that pre-tested this commercial uncovered very positive findings for the client. After a couple of months on the air, however, the amount of calls to the free phone number in the commercial seeking more information was very disappointing. The client was perplexed. What happened? Why was there was so little interest?

The client contacted us because they wanted another firm to re-test the spot. We did so and found, to the client's and agency's amazement, that the first research company had misread the results. Even though the target audience understood the main message and liked the spot, all they retained were the bittersweet images of the people back home, the beautiful scenery and the feeling of nostalgia for their family and country. The execution had gone overboard using warm-and-fuzzy family scenes and nostalgia to sell its product. After people saw this commercial at home, they made a call – but not to the free number to inquire about the calling plan. Instead, they called their mother, or their grandmother or their sister in Latin America. They had been distracted by these warm scenes and completely forgot about the calling plan!

Our client decided to start from scratch. A new commercial was shot based on our findings and recommendations. In this new spot, the calling plan was 'the hero' – not the family or the scenery. It was a happy commercial but also one that provided factual information about the calling plan. This new commercial broke all previous records in number of calls received and new subscribers to the plan.

Cloning the general market

The next pitfall is using a general market strategy for the Hispanic market. Generally, marketers like to do this because it keeps everything nice and organized. It is also the path of least resistance: upper management will buy into their plans faster and it's easier to deal with one strategy.

Using a general market strategy may be effective but this can only be determined after testing various options. I can't count the number of times that marketers have decided to use a general market approach before any testing has been conducted among the intended Hispanic target.

Before taking this step, advertisers must be sure that this will be the most compelling strategy. It isn't that the general market strategy is plain wrong, it's just not the one that will attract most Hispanic consumers. An even worse scenario is forcing the use of a general market commercial (re-shot with Hispanic actors) to target Hispanics.

Here's an example of both pitfalls. A while back, we tested a commercial for a drink that was being sold as 'offbeat and wacky' in the general market. The client wanted to define the brand the same way in the Hispanic market, so a number of commercials were produced using this strategy. By the way, this was the first time this client had advertised to the Hispanic market and this was the first piece of Hispanic research it had conducted. In other words, without knowing if this wacky, offbeat personality would sell in the Hispanic market, the client and the agency had already produced five radio commercials, which we were going to test.

The focus group participants rejected this strategy. Unfamiliar with this drink's general market spots, Hispanics had their own image of the product – they saw it as fun and friendly – and what was being presented went against that perception. They felt that this product, as presented in the radio executions, was for weird, confused people!

We also tested a commercial for an ice-cream brand that was a word-for-word adaptation of the general market spot. In this case, the spot used humour to make its point – American humour translated into Spanish.

The spot features a couple of vignettes. One tested well, the other did not. It shows a little boy telling his father that he's going to wash the family car. What he neglects to say is that he intends to use a scouring pad. When the father finds out, the announcer comes on and tells him: 'Relax, and enjoy some of our ice cream.' No one saw the situation as funny. And, everyone agreed that this would not be the right time to enjoy this product.

Inordinate caution

Another mistake advertisers make quite frequently is 'holding back their horses', in other words, running more 'in-the-box', less ambitious advertising in the Hispanic market. Hispanic consumers complain about this phenomenon all the time.

Why does this happen? Many reasons are cited. The one we hear most often from Hispanic agencies is that Hispanic production budgets are much lower than those allocated for the general market. But we all know that big budgets don't always lead to great commercials nor do low budgets result in poor advertising.

There is another possible reason, however, for creating less-ambitious Hispanic ads – the idea that simplistic, innocuous commercials are good enough for the Hispanic market or even worse, that 'out-of-the-box' commercials do not appeal or are not understood by Hispanic consumers. How many times have we heard the phrase 'Hispanics take everything literally'? This is generally true in instances where the audience is looking for concrete information. It should not be used as an excuse, however, to lower standards in the Hispanic market.

Less ambitious, more run-of-the-mill advertising falls short of achieving goals, especially with Hispanic teenagers and young adults who are bilingual and also watch American TV and tend to compare the Spanish with the English language ads.

For example, we tested some commercials for a sports drink that strongly appeals to Hispanic male teens and young adults. They complained that the Hispanic commercials for this product constantly showed young males like themselves playing different sports (basketball, soccer, baseball) in different venues (the park, the beach, the gym). These commercials may be new but they always come across as old and tired. These consumers couldn't help comparing them with the general market commercials, which they described as cutting-edge. And the question remains: why does a leading-edge product use tired, run-of-the-mill commercials to attract its Hispanic target?

Unfortunately, the root of many of these marketing mistakes is the result of preconceived notions or impressions about ethnic markets. When it comes to the general market, no client expects its agency or researchers to be experts on Americans and the American way of life. Think for example what you would say as an American if someone asked you 'What are Americans like?' You probably wouldn't even know where to start or what to say. The American market is not a static market. New things happen all the time and that's why studies are conducted every day. You would never ask such a general question of your agency or researchers. Yet this question is asked every day of Hispanic agencies, consultants and primary researchers. What is odd is that there are people who answer this question, ignoring the fact that things are constantly changing in the Hispanic market as well.

Source: *Quirk's Marketing Research Review*, April 2000, article 20000402, accessed 1/9/2010,
http://www.quirks.com/articles/a2000/20000402.aspx?%20searchID=2071341.

Questions

1. How would you summarise the suggestions made by the author for avoiding the three pitfalls mentioned?

2. Regarding your own country, give some principles for avoiding cultural mistakes in situations similar to those described in the case.

Having seen how stereotypes can be a disturbing factor in marketing as well as communication, we need to examine the way stereotypes are formed.

Building stereotypes

In specifically cultural terms, the starting-point for building stereotypes is the norms and values of the culture concerned. When someone from that culture judges someone from another culture, the tendency is for that person to do so using his/her norms and values. If the person being judged does not conform to these in some way through their behaviour – or simply appearance – then a negative judgement will probably be made.

A stereotype is a series of images created in our minds with regard to a group or groups of people, in this context: cultural groups. These images are over-generalisations made through selective perceptions (self-perceptions) and information that corresponds with our beliefs. The development of prejudices, which are a 'distinct combination of feelings, inclinations to act and beliefs' (Myers, 2005: 333), is supported or provoked by our cultural environment; family, friends and the media can fill us with stereotyping images of all kinds. A stereotype is therefore a confirmation of prejudices rather than the result of accurate observations of reality.

Comments, jokes, commercials and anecdotes can create and perpetuate stereotypes, categorise nationalities in a way that sustains a culture's norms and values.

Spotlight 14.2 illustrates how a prejudice can lead to unjustifiable behaviour of one group towards another.

SPOTLIGHT 14.2

The misunderstood marketing manager

A Dutch company wanted to introduce a new product into its range. On-site production would be too costly and, besides, there was a US company already manufacturing this product.

The marketing manager decided to phone this supplier. 'Yes' was their reaction, but only if a large quantity were to be ordered. The minimum amount they stated was much more than the Dutch market would warrant. When told this, the US manufacturer suggested the Dutch company contact a partner of theirs operating in France.

So the marketing manager phoned the French company. Talking in French to the manager of the production department, he gave the name of this company in the usual way, explaining that he would like to buy this product because the US company was unable to supply the small amount which they required. The Dutchman was told to put his request in writing.

The Dutchman was really shocked by this reaction and accused the French of being odd. Why could they not simply give him the information he required over the phone?

The French manager had asked for a request in writing because the Dutch marketing manager had put forward his query without any preliminaries and had not fully introduced his company. The Frenchman could not therefore 'place' the person on the other end of the phone. He needed to know exactly which company he was doing business with and the identity of the man proposing the co-operation in the first place.

After he had put down the phone, the Frenchman wondered: 'Who the hell was this guy with the funny accent?'

To summarise the building process of stereotypes, it can be said that prejudices, which may be positive or negative in nature, are basic, irrational reactions that depend simply on how someone views the group in question in terms of their own cultural preferences. People may be classified in some way socially on the basis of a perception of common attributes: people may perceive them as members of an 'in-group', sharing a system of values or as members of an 'out-group' whose values counter theirs in some way. As prejudices are confirmed over and over again through such selective perceptions, people develop stereotypical images that come quickly to mind and which serve to legitimise the statements people make about another culture. However, as indicated earlier, cultural stereotypes may also display positive traits, particularly when people perceive that there are aspects of another culture's norms and values that reflect their own and in an exemplary way.

This issue of prejudices and stereotypes is illustrated in Spotlight 14.3. Most people regard the information and computer technology (ICT) sector to be a male preserve. This is indeed the case, since the majority of ICT workers in most countries are male. Malaysia, however, is an exception.

SPOTLIGHT 14.3

Delete stereotypes!

ICT is a male profession! In Malaysia, such a statement raises smiles. In the faculty of information technologies of Kuala Lumpur, the capital, all those in positions of responsibility in the department are women, including the dean. In Penang, 65 per cent of the ICT students and seven of the ten ICT professors are women, as well as the dean. The head of the department says she has never considered ICT as a male discipline: 'I do not see anything male in ICT!' The reasons she gives are that ICT is clean work, does not require much physical strength, is an activity exercised in the service sector, and allows those employed in it to work at home. In contrast, outside Malaysia, ICT is a very masculine sector. In France, it is the only scientific profession where there has been a very large fall in the proportion of females employed.

Source: extract from 'L'informatique a-t-elle un sexe?', *Le Monde Diplomatique*, 3/6/2007: 3 (Collet, I.).

However, stereotypes are not always based on prejudices. A stereotype may have an intrinsic quality as shown in the passage below on the perception of Confucianism in the world of business.

Stereotypes in the Confucian business world

Cazal (1993) raises the question of stereotypes in business relating to Confucianism. This system of thought was referred to in Chapter 4 when the importance of loyalty in Chinese business relations was being discussed. Cazal wonders how present-day Confucianism, which he defines as 'a specific discourse constructed to maintain the economic development and performance of [Asian-run] companies' (Cazal, 1993: 188), is perceived in the West and in Asia. He reminds us of an important characteristic of Confucianism whereby formal value is attached to status in the sense that a person in a subordinate position must behave in a way that conforms to that of his interlocutor. Nowadays, however, a subordinate is not expected to adhere to these Confucian principles.

Foreigners, especially those who have lived in South Korea, observe that Confucianism still survives in social relations, such as those within the hierarchy based on age, gender and qualifications. Although these people still see that it reflects a philosophy that rests on the principle of harmony, they consider the majority of the stereotypes resulting from it as being negative in nature. Some Asians are critical of Confucianism, seeing it as a 'cultural alibi for political, social and managerial abuses' (Cazal, 1993: 190). Cazal ends up by questioning whether present-day Confucianism is itself a stereotype since its principles are far from the founding precepts in the teachings of Confucius. Even if classic Confucianism serves as a reference, this doctrine as applied in countries such as China, South Korea and Japan lacks unity and homogeneity.

Several articles have commented on and misrepresented Confucian thought. That explains why doubt can be cast on the unity of Confucianism as a doctrine in countries such as China, South Korea and Japan, even if this unity is to be found at a practical level.

Dealing with stereotypes

The question remains: what is the best way of dealing with prejudices and stereotypes? Is it best to try and suppress them, fight against them or simply ignore them? The best route may lie in the views of those anthropologists (including Caroll (1987) and Hall (1983)), who approach the question of cultural differences without battling against stereotypes or without creating stereotypes to replace the old ones. It is better when dealing with other cultures not to fight against stereotypes and prejudices. A stereotype is, after all, the first stage in the process whereby the existence of another culture is acknowledged.

Furthermore, it can be argued that stereotypes are a necessary way of establishing one's own cultural identity. If a cultural group cannot compare itself with other groups then it cannot become aware of what it is. All its characteristics must be perceived in terms of those characteristics of others. In this context, a stereotype can be seen as an articulation of this differentiation, even though it is based on prejudices and imperfect information.

Moreover, if stereotypes were to be somehow set aside, the vacuum created would inevitably be filled by those who had set them aside. In other words, the culture of these people would be perceived as the one and only culture in the world – the worst of all prejudices.

Nevertheless, cross-cultural researchers are attempting to find perception areas that cultures share, rather than the differences. In the best of all possible worlds, people would be able to place another culture in its own context and so avoid judging a culture on the basis of their own. Only then would stereotypes eventually disappear.

Finally, it should be noted that there is a dynamic element present when two people are communicating, namely interaction. Not only do the specific characteristics of the speakers play a role, but also the structure of the situation and the context, as well as time and space (see Chapter 13). If you are aware of the barriers when communicating with your interlocutor, this does not mean that you are able to conduct the conversation well. The variable nature of the interaction makes every communicative situation unique and therefore unpredictable.

Every culture proposes a structure which, even if it is not unchanging, forces its members to conform to it, and it is by the process of communication that it succeeds in doing so. Furthermore, as seen in this chapter, the encounters between cultures often destabilise the process of communication, create barriers and lack of understanding between the interlocutors. At the same time, thanks to these intercultural contacts, the expression of a culture – and thereby the way it communicates – evolves without any loss of identity. On the contrary, this identity is maintained because, according to Todorov (1986: 16), 'what happens between cultures is *per se* an element of culture'.

The concepts described in Chapters 13 and 14 can be used as a basis for any form of communication in the professional domain. The following chapters will deal with the application of these concepts in specific domains such as international negotiation and international teamwork.

Conclusion

This chapter has elaborated the model of communication given in the introduction by looking at barriers to intercultural situations in general and in those in business in particular. The culture of the interlocutors filters the information and interprets it according to their own reference framework. Barriers can build up at various levels: badly interpreted gestures, a smile expressing the opposite of satisfaction, concrete words having an implicit meaning. Stereotypes, however, remain the most important barrier in communication. They are very difficult to deal with since they are formed by the identity and the perceptions of individuals.

Points for reflection

1. Stereotypes appear in all cross-cultural situations. When you are doing business with other cultures, stereotypes particularly arise in meetings and negotiations. If you are aware of the stereotypes of the group you are dealing with, it may help you at the beginning of the interaction.

   What is your opinion of this statement?

2. You have just read about barriers to communicating with other cultures. Some of these can lead to misunderstandings, others can degenerate into conflict.

   Which of these barriers, in your opinion, can lead to misunderstandings and which of them can lead to conflict? Explain your choice.

Further reading

Mead, R. (1990) *Cross-Cultural Management Communication*, Chichester: John Wiley. This book explores the many aspects and problems of cross-cultural communication encountered by managers. It focuses on understanding management cultures, and explores how situations within the context of different cultures and markets can be interpreted accurately. The author shows how management priorities are decided and communicated in different cultures and examines the organisational problems managers may face when operating in other cultures. Despite its age, this book remains a useful reference work.

References

Browaeys, M.-J. (1989) *Les gestes conversationnels et les différences culturelles en France et aux Pays-Bas*, Amsterdam: Universiteit van Amsterdam.

Browaeys, M.-J. and Trompenaars, F. (eds) (2000) *Cases Studies on Cultural Dilemmas*, Breukelen, Netherlands: Nyenrode University Press.

Caroll, R. (1987) *Evidences invisibles*, Paris: Editions du Seuil.

Cazal, D. (1993) 'Ethique et management interculturel: le cas du confucianisme d'entreprise', in Bosche, M. (ed.), *Le management interculturel*, Paris: Editions Nathan: 181–192.

Cresswell, R. (1968) 'Le geste manuel associé aux langages', *Langages*, 10: 119–127.

Edgar, A. and Sedgwick, P. (eds) (2002) *Cultural Theory: the Key Concepts*, London: Routledge.

Gruère, J.-P. and Morel, P. (1991) *Cadres français et communications interculturelles*, Paris: Editions Eyrolles.

Hall, E.T. (1983) *The Dance of Life*, New York, NY: Anchor Press/Doubleday.

Ladmiral, J.R. and Lipianski, E.M. (1989) *La communication interculturelle*, Paris: Armand Colin.

Lipianski, E.-M. (1992) 'Identité, communication interculturelle et dynamique des groupes', in *Interculturel: groupe et transition*, Toulouse: Editions Erès: 59–70.

Myers, D.G. (2005) *Social Psychology*, 8th edition, New York, NY: McGraw-Hill.

Oomkes, F.R. (1987) *Communicatieleer*, Amsterdam: Boom Meppel.

Schneider, S.C. and Barsoux, J.-L. (2003) *Managing Across Cultures*, 2nd edition, Harlow: Pearson Education.

Tae-Seop Lim (2003) 'Language and verbal communication across cultures', in Gudykunst, W.B. (ed.), *Cross-Cultural and Intercultural Communication*, Thousand Oaks, CA: Sage: 53–71.

Todorov, T. (1986) 'Le croisement des cultures' in *Communications*, 43: 5–24.

Usunier, J.-C. and Lee, J.A. (2005) *Marketing Across Cultures*, 4th edition, Harlow: Pearson Education.

ACTIVITY 14.1

Read the text below which describes how Germany tried to improve its image during the 2006 World Cup which was held in Germany. Answer the questions that follow the text.

Germans aim to spring a World Cup surprise: they're fun

Soft power: The nation long seen as dull is plotting an image overhaul that could help it punch its weight on the international stage

By Hugh Williamson

For the host country Germany, next month's football World Cup is about a lot more than its (pretty slim) chances of lifting the trophy. An image overhaul for Europe's largest economy is the prize in its sights.

Robert Rode, a Berlin bus driver, understands the scale of the challenge. A stocky man with a strong local accent who speaks little English, he was one of 4,000 drivers who recently struggled through a 'World Cup language course'. Taking a break from learning how to guide fans through Berlin, he says that, despite the tongue-twisting, the course was worth it. 'When people arrive in Berlin, say at the airport or main station, and the first German they talk to is a bus driver who either cannot understand them or tells them to go and ask someone else, then that doesn't create a very good impression.'

Mr Rode is in good company. True to the tournament motto 'A time to make friends', chancellor Angela Merkel and her government, leading companies and cultural organizations and dozens of local authorities, have planned thousands of initiatives in the most ambitious attempt by a country to alter the way it is viewed. Ms Merkel heralded the tournament as 'a unique chance for Germany to present itself as a welcoming, tolerant and modern country, bursting with ideas'.

But as teams arrive in Germany this week ahead of kick-off on June 9, a senior German official is disarmingly candid. 'The world generally sees us in a positive, but one-sided way. A bit like the cars and household goods for which we are famous, Germans are seen as efficient, reliable but a touch boring. We need to show we are more than this: friendly, surprising and fun.' At stake is more than national *amour propre*. The transformation is seen as vital if Berlin is to maximize the country's post-reunification potential on the world stage.

The business community alone has invested more than €10m ($12.8m, £6.8m) to promote Germany as a 'Land of Ideas'. 'An opportunity of this kind will not return for another 50 years', says Franz Beckenbauer, president of the German tournament organizing committee.

Since 1990, Germany has stepped up its public diplomacy, as it has increased its role in international peacekeeping operations and intensified efforts to gain a permanent United Nations Security Council seat. Its World Cup campaign marks not only a new milestone in its engagement with the world but also a form of laboratory experiment in whether image offensives work.

Many are sceptical. A German ambassador, who declined to be named, argues: 'You can't market a country like a washing powder. To believe you can just tell others that, all of a sudden we [Germans] have become funny and good looking, is wrong. You can't deceive people.'

Germany's endeavour, which started three years ago, includes a €30m arts programme linking soccer and culture: a 'friendly service campaign' involving handbooks on how to welcome foreign guests; and giant sculptures in Berlin of football boots and aspirins to illustrate the wonders of German creativity.

Attempts to stir national pride raise some discomfiting parallels, however. 'You can't conquer history, or wash it away by just being happy', says Ulrich Maly, mayor of Nuremberg, the city infamous for Hitler's Nazi party rallies where England is due to play one of its games.

Meanwhile, Volker Perthes, director of Berlin's Institute for International and Security Affairs, points out that in 20 years, (*former*) West Germany went from post-war international pariah to economic beacon – only to see its attempt to present a more open face to the world go 'terribly wrong' when Israeli athletes were murdered at the 1972 Munich Olympics.

Germany's campaign is part of a broader debate on the value of public diplomacy and 'soft power' – the tools increasingly used by national governments to deepen their influence without resorting to economic and military might.

Joseph Nye, a Harvard professor and author of *Soft Power: The Means to Success in World Politics*, argues that it can be used to complement traditional diplomacy. 'Tangible threats or payoffs' are replaced by initiatives to influence stereotypes about a country, for example.

According to an internal German government strategy paper seen by the *Financial Times*, this approach was partly behind the decision to use the World Cup to alter Germany's image abroad. 'States are increasingly in competition for markets, tourists [...] value systems and political influence', and in this context 'Germany must take a position', the paper argues. It notes that foreigners' images of Germany often 'lack emotion' and 'exclude the [country's] more dynamic developments over the last 20–30 years'. 'Emotional aspects, such as street cafes in Munich [...] [German] lifestyle brands such as Adidas and Boss, and the happiness of reunification in 1989/90' need to be emphasized, the paper concludes. In a section on 'Germany's Image Abroad', Michael Reiffenstuel of the foreign office enthuses that the World Cup provides a 'unique communications opportunity'.

Germany is not the first country to attempt a national makeover. Britain tried – with limited success – to repackage itself as 'Cool Britannia' early in Tony Blair's premiership. Japan, co-host with South Korea of the 2002 World Cup, ran a less elaborate image campaign than Germany's. But visitors were surprised to find a country more vibrant and accessible than many had expected. The Japanese government has since deployed 'soft power' to exploit the popularity of manga cartoons and Japanese design and fashion. The number of tourists has noticeably increased – in part the result of an official tourism campaign but also reflecting a 'word-of-mouth' effect from the World Cup.

In Germany the jury is out on the campaign's impact. Nathalie Thiemann-Huguet, of the business-led Land of Ideas programme, says the giant sculptures in Berlin have become a 'major tourist attraction', while about 2,000 foreign journalists have registered to use pictures and TV footage on 'positive aspects of Germany's economy and society'.

Yet a series of organizational and other problems that have blighted tournament preparations have brought negative media coverage. Most recently, Ms Merkel was forced to allay concerns in the United States Congress that Germany was ignoring an alleged rise in illegal trafficking of prostitutes for the tournament. Worst of all was last month's apparent racist attack that left a young Ethiopian man in a coma. Experts argue that such incidents are unlikely to undermine

Germany's broader campaign, but that this must in turn be seen as only one element in reshaping its image. Ulrich Sacker of the Goethe-Institut, Germany's overseas cultural agency, says the World Cup will remain in the minds of tens of millions of global television viewers. 'We have to surprise people, make them think: "Germany is different to the country I imagined"', he says.

Mr Perthes believes government campaigns can only ever have a modest impact, given the post-Cold War complexity of public diplomacy. But rhetorically posing the question 'will the country's image after the World Cup return to the cliché about the ugly German?', he provides his own, upbeat answer: 'I don't think so. At least something from the campaign will stick.'

 Source: from 'Germans aim for a World Cup surprise: they're fun', *Financial Times*, 22/5/2006, p. 19 (Williamson, H.), © The Financial Times Ltd. All Rights Reserved.

Questions

1. Referring to Concept 14.1, comment on the statement made in the text: 'You can't market a country like a washing powder.'

2. Find expressions in the text that characterise the Germans. Consider whether each of these reflects your own individual perception or rather stereotypes of German culture.

ACTIVITY 14.2

Read the following account of an Indian's experiences when inspecting a local bank in India. Then answer the questions below.

Meeting a brick wall

I was working in the inspection department of the Central Bank of India and was given an assignment a few years ago to inspect a branch of a private commercial bank. I was assisted by a junior officer. One of our main tasks was to get some important information about a fraud, determine the chain of events, establish accountability and pass on the information to the team which was inspecting the head office of the bank.

The branch was in a small town which was very different to what I was used to: they spoke a different language there, ate different food and enjoyed a very different climate. The people working there were very old compared to employees of other banks I had visited and they behaved towards me in an indifferent and uncooperative manner. They claimed they had no idea how the fraud was committed and were reluctant to show me the relevant records.

Many of the staff members had been working in the branch for decades and had developed close relationships with each other. Their former branch manager had already been suspended for his suspected involvement in the fraud. My colleague, who was from the same region and of a similar age, managed to mix with the staff but was unable to get hold of the information needed. Eventually, he also became rather reluctant to get items of information requested, giving delays and unavailability as reasons for their non-appearance.

I was proud of my experience in inspections, my analytical skills, my management education and my past success in meeting deadlines. I followed the code of behaviour expected of someone in my position and kept the staff at a distance. I declined offers of lunch or even tea or coffee so that these should not be considered as some sort of bribe. I felt that the local staff were making one excuse after another not to come up with the right information. Were they perhaps trying to protect their colleagues, or were they afraid of being reprimanded by their bosses? The information I needed was crucial and could be obtained only from this branch. The days passed, but nothing substantial emerged. Time was running out.

Source: adapted from Browaeys and Trompenaars, 2000: case 11.

Questions

1. To what extent is the problem presented in the case a communication problem?
2. How do you think the author could try to get hold of the information needed?

Chapter 15

Negotiating internationally

Having given some attention to theories concerning cross-cultural communication, Part Three will use the following two chapters to examine two particular aspects of intercultural communication: negotiating and teamwork.

This chapter examines one crucial component of international business dealings – negotiating. First, the nature of negotiating from a Western perspective is considered and compared with a non-Western viewpoint. Thereafter, facets of cross-cultural business negotiation are described and applied to an examination of possible problems in the interaction between two negotiating parties, one from the US, the other from China. The chapter then moves on to examine a framework that can be used to address the issue of strategy adaptation when negotiating with counterparts from other cultures. Finally, the question of an international negotiating (meta-) culture is briefly discussed.

Learning outcomes

After reading this chapter you will:

- Understand how the perception of negotiating can differ from culture to culture.
- Be aware of how these different perceptions can affect the negotiating process between parties from different cultures and the eventual results.
- Be familiar with strategies of negotiation that are culturally responsive and which, at the same time, take account of the skills of the individuals involved.

Concept 15.1 Approaches to negotiating in an international context

The nature of negotiation

Negotiating is essentially regarded in the West as a problem-solving exercise. It is seen as a process whereby a problem is deliberated, ideas are put forward for resolution and where a solution of some kind is eventually reached. As Fisher (1980) indicates, the literature on negotiation is preoccupied with tactics and strategies that can be applied universally to achieve a result. Implicit in these works is the assumption that the participants share similar approaches, attitudes and principles.

The Western approach focuses on what happens between parties. This is evident in the way negotiating is dealt with by Whetten *et al.* (2000). The authors address the subject in a chapter on constructive conflict management whereby they distinguish two types of negotiation strategy predominant in Western culture: the distributive and integrative strategy. The distributive approach involves trying to get a piece of what they call a 'fixed-sized cake'. The negotiators are adversaries, trying to gain the best deal for themselves, which usually means that others lose out in some way (i.e. the result is 'win–lose'). Those adopting integrative strategies are trying to expand the 'cake' by collaborating in a problem-solving approach to try and get a 'win–win' result.

However, if negotiations are taking place between societies/cultures, rather than between groups from the same culture, then those involved need to try and work out what is going on in the minds of their counterparts. Negotiators in an international context are participating in a communicative event where assumptions and expectations may not be shared. Participants cannot assume that the 'opposite party' will have motives that chime with their own view of the world, or that the behaviour displayed by both parties – even if similar in nature – reflects similar motives.

As Fisher (1980) points out when recounting the words of a Japanese business executive, even the very act of negotiating can be an alien concept to other cultures. He makes it clear that the Japanese do not have in their culture the idea of a meeting where a conflict is resolved through a compromise acceptable to all sides, where the persuasive delivery of rational arguments is all-important. For the Japanese such a meeting of parties is a ceremonial occasion where a seal of approval is formally applied to what has been put together in a patient consensus-generating process 'behind the scenes'. This contrast of views reflects the possible perils of negotiating across cultures.

Facets of negotiation

This section aims to outline some key aspects of negotiating in an international context. First, though, some facets of negotiating need to be established as a framework of reference. Usunier (2003: 104) sees three facets of cultural differences affecting international marketing negotiations. These facets incorporate all the variables given in the 'Model of Culture' introduced in Part One of this book. They are presented here in a way that allows the cross-cultural process of negotiation to be more clearly perceived. Table 15.1 presents an overview of these facets, each of which will be briefly examined and exemplified below.

Behavioural predispositions of the parties

- *Interpersonal orientation.* One fundamental issue has to do with how the negotiating parties relate to each other and to the context of the negotiation. The individualism/ collectivism dimension, referred to in Chapter 2, is an appropriate method of analysis in this respect. Negotiators from cultures deemed to be 'collectivist' tend to avoid open conflict and prefer to maintain formal harmony during negotiations. Those from cultures deemed to be 'individualist' are expected to act more in self-interest and will not shy away from being overtly competitive and confrontational. With the former, the focus is on establishing good relations with negotiating counterparts, developing mutual respect

Table 15.1 **Facets of negotiation**

Negotiation facet	Elements	Concepts
Behavioural predispositions of the parties	Interpersonal orientation	Harmony, self-interest
	Power orientation	Formal power, (informal) influence
	Willingness to take risks	Negotiating party's degree of delegated decision-making, and (lack of) uncertainty
Underlying concept of negotiation	Negotiation strategies	Trust or mistrust as basis
	Strategic time frame	Logical, finite process or ongoing dialogue
Negotiation process	Styles of negotiation	Work towards specific, concrete goals, or more towards principles, concepts
	Outcome orientations	Iron-cast deal or less explicit agreement

Source: Usunier (2003).

and trust as a basis for a deal. With the latter, relationships certainly play a part, but respect may tend to result from the skills shown in reaching a good deal. Coming to a satisfactory conclusion – the deal – is for them the main objective.

- *Power orientation.* Also examined in Part One, this dimension relates to the question of who has formal influence and who has actual influence on the negotiating process. Are the people involved able to negotiate, how are they chosen and what is their role in the company? What qualities are attributed to the person in that position, and who is actually calling the shots?

- *Willingness to take risks.* This is in one sense closely related to power orientation. Negotiators from strictly controlled bureaucracies, where approval for any deal involves the approval of a number of bodies or committees, may well be reluctant to take as many risks as negotiators who need to consult their superiors less often, having been delegated negotiating power and a certain room for manoeuvre. This has clearly to do with the (lack of) uncertainty avoidance tendencies of certain cultures.

However, it should be noted that uncertainty and risk avoidance do not necessarily go hand-in-hand. Japan, for example, although renowned for its high degree of uncertainty avoidance, is not averse to taking risks. However, unlike other countries who are more willing to face risk and the consequent ambiguity, Japan pays considerable attention to risk-management. Rather than dealing with risk in a cavalier fashion, Japan takes very well calculated risks and its industry has benefited considerably as a result.

Underlying concept of negotiation

- *Negotiation strategies.* The integrative approach described earlier, whereby negotiation teams collaborate to get the best result, may be regarded as the most effective form of negotiating in Western business literature. The context, however, is implicitly an intra-cultural one, whereby both sides agree to work together to get a so-called 'win–win' result. In an intercultural situation, however, the oppositional nature of negotiating may come to the fore if one or both sides do not trust their counterparts, or if one or the other team does not feel that the best deal is necessarily the best for them. The establishment of trust may precede any discussion of details, with principles being established by which an agreement is eventually reached.

- *Strategic time frame.* The idea of following a 'logical' process, starting with orientation, then coming to a series of agreements, possibly in some form of package, and then closing a deal within some agreed-on time-limit, will contrast strongly with what could be called the dialogue approach. Negotiating is considered to be just part of a dialogue between business parties whereby any deals made are not necessarily regarded as immutable, but as a reflection of the wish to initiate or continue co-operation. Changes may well be needed later on to improve the situation for all those involved. The establishment of trust as the starting point enables such flexibility and improves the nature of the collaboration.

Negotiation process

- *Styles of negotiation.* With different concepts of negotiation come different styles. This is where the universalism–particularism dimension referred to in Chapter 5 can be reflected in the way negotiations are made. Is the focus on general issues or is there a concern for dealing with (a range of) specific issues? Is negotiating more to do with feelings than facts, opinion rather than evidence? If present in a negotiation, this stark opposition of styles can cause both sides headaches, with the 'universalists' frustrated by the concern for details rather than the more important principles and concepts, and the 'particularists' frustrated by the very broad approach taken by their counterpart which, in their eyes, makes it difficult for practical decisions to be taken.

  The high/low context dimension, covered in Chapters 6 and 13, plays a key role in the style of communication during negotiations. Low-context negotiators are more explicit, exact and direct than high-context negotiators. Their outspokenness will not necessarily be appreciated or accepted and the reciprocity they may expect from being explicit in their dealings is unlikely to be realised. High-context negotiators tend to infer, allude and do not always feel compelled to take turns in the discussion. The long pauses or silences which they bring to the discussion allow for consideration of what has been said and of the circumstances surrounding the discussion. A concrete decision or statement, however, is unlikely to be made as a result of their reflections.

- *Outcome orientations.* It will come as no surprise that the polarities described above are reflected in two types of outcome: a rather vague statement in which the parties involved express their mutual trust and desire for mutual co-operation, or a detailed account of the agreements reached and the ways in which these are to be implemented. Between these extremes lie agreements that will vary in terms of detail and explicitness.

  However detailed a conclusion, the interpretation of the 'document' may well differ since the wording will not necessarily refer to all the assumptions underlying any agreement. Moreover, the status of the document for negotiators may vary: it may be seen either as a cast-iron document determining exactly how matters should proceed, or as a statement of good intentions, which may not be realised. The very idea of preparing some sort of final document following on from a negotiation phase concept of an outcome may even be seen as superfluous. Any business relationship involves continuing negotiation at all levels: a statement of some kind after a negotiation phase is not the end of the story.

Cross-cultural negotiation in practice: the US and China

The facets of intercultural negotiating outlined above will now be used to profile two contrasting cultures. Imagine them facing each other across the negotiating table (an image that is itself culture-determined!) and imagine how they are likely to react to each other's approach to the task at hand.

Behavioural predispositions

Interpersonal orientation

In the US, the deal is seen as the objective of any negotiation while for the Chinese a negotiation is just part of the process of forming a life-long relationship. A focused, bottom-line approach is at odds with the Chinese need to establish a good rapport before talking of a deal. However, Americans might feel that the wish by their Chinese counterparts to establish friendship is one way of getting a better deal later on in the negotiation(s).

Power orientation

It is usually clear where the power lies in a US negotiating team. The deference shown by subordinates and experts towards the boss reflects the hierarchy within the team, even if the language used between them is informal. The boss will probably have been delegated considerable leeway in the negotiating process, although this will have been carefully discussed with headquarters beforehand. Risk-taking is part of the game and seen as inherent to getting the best deal possible.

The US team may find it difficult to determine who is leading the negotiation on the Chinese side, particularly if there are a large number of people in the delegation. For the Chinese, the consensus-building process is undergone not only between the negotiating teams but also within the Chinese team where a number of interested parties both from within the company as well as outside the company (essentially government bureaucrats) are involved. Pressure from the US side to get a deal will be stonewalled until all interested Chinese parties are satisfied. This dependence on consensus within the negotiating team means that any risk-taking behaviour within or before negotiations needs to be carefully orchestrated.

Underlying concept of negotiation

Negotiation strategies

There are two main approaches used in the US towards negotiations: the competitive ('win–lose') approach and integrative ('win–win') approach. The former approach involves taking up an initial position and then making concessions if necessary to reach a compromise agreement. The latter approach involves both 'sides' focusing on mutual interests rather than pre-determined positions, achieving joint profits using an objective standard. Both approaches, however, should lead to a definitive contract to which both sides are expected to adhere.

The Chinese will probably find it difficult to take such a linear approach. For them, a negotiation is just one of many encounters whereby the principle is to build a business partnership for the long term. Establishing a relationship entails getting to know your partner well. Hence, a lot of questions will be asked to do with the interests and personalities of the other team rather than dealing directly with the details of any deal or joint project. Detailed terms of any agreement need this strong consensual basis. However, a number of observers, including Faure (1998), note that there is also another side to their strategic behaviour, namely a persistence whereby the negotiator does all he can to exploit his opponent to the maximum. The style is what Faure sees as a combination of 'joint quest' and 'mobile warfare' which the Chinese negotiator uses to try and outflank the opponent (a reference to the tactics of Sun Tsu, the notorious ancient Chinese warrior). In US terms this could be seen as a combination of affiliative, integrative behaviour (the affective dimension) and competitive, forcing behaviour (the cognitive dimension).

Strategic time frame

For the Chinese, therefore, a negotiation is not a one-off event but a step along the path to a harmonious and mutually beneficial relationship in the long term. A deal made at the end of a negotiation remains in their eyes negotiable in the long-term since both parties could benefit more from an improvement of some kind in an agreement made. Moreover, all agreements are based on trust and goodwill, so a firm contract is superfluous. This attitude can be frustrating for Americans since for them time is of the essence.

Negotiating process

Style of negotiation

US negotiators will be concerned with specifics, eager to get a lot of information to enable them to pursue their way of negotiating. Only when they have sufficient input can they gain a clearer idea of the other party's concerns and interests and so establish or modify their negotiating goals. They, in turn, are willing to give a lot of information as long as this is part of an exchange. The Chinese reluctance to give information is noted in the literature on this area as well as the resulting frustration among Western negotiators. However, as Kumar and Worm (2003) discovered during research on business negotiations with the Chinese, the majority of their Western respondents noted that their Chinese negotiating partners were willing to disclose information – provided they had it! As another respondent remarked: 'Chinese firms are not accustomed to collect(ing) information' (Kumar and Worm, 2003: 276).

This raises two interesting issues in relation to the negotiating process. First, the importance of face to the Chinese: asking for information they do not have could be seen as an unintentional way of causing the Chinese to lose face. Second, times are changing in China: a freer exchange of information is now being applied in negotiations, presumably because a more systematic collection of information has been developed in Chinese companies.

Having said that, co-operation with the Chinese still has trust as its bedrock. However successful information exchange may be, the process of gaining trust and confidence remains, for the Chinese, of greater import than facts and figures.

A word of reservation is appropriate here. On the basis of a finding made by Kumar and Worm (2003) in their survey, younger managers who are involved in negotiations are more in tune with Western behavioural norms. One implication of this (although it is not tested in this study) is that Western managers may be able to conduct their negotiations more effectively/efficiently when dealing with Chinese who are younger.

Perhaps younger Chinese are also more comfortable with a lower position on the high/low context dimension referred to earlier. Although the explicit, direct, fact-oriented, cause-effect nature of discussions as favoured by the Americans contrasts strongly with the generally consensus-focused, relationship-developing nature of the Chinese, some younger Chinese may be more comfortable than their older colleagues when negotiating with Americans.

Outcome orientations

For the US negotiators a detailed contract is the ideal conclusion to a negotiation, one which is signed, sealed and delivered. Detailed points are hammered out in the final phase of the negotiation, particularly with regard to the implementation of the deal. The legal aspects are also given considerable attention.

The Chinese tend to avoid getting tied up in what they may consider to be Western legalistic details, preferring short, vaguer contracts that signify the willingness of both sides to commit to a joint project of some kind. Rather than being the last word on the deal, a contract is a formal moment in the development of a relationship; further negotiations will take place on the basis of the goodwill and friendship established.

All in all, therefore, the Chinese and Americans face innumerable difficulties around the negotiation table. The opposition in expectations and attitudes are clear, the expected frustrations and irritations evident. How can both sides resolve this dilemma? A framework for dealing with apparently conflicting cultural values is presented in the next part of this concept.

When in Rome, do as the Romans do?

Much of the literature on negotiating internationally tends to focus on the rituals of negotiating in other countries and, particularly in the case of non-Western countries, gives a convenient outline of the systems of values they embrace. Little attention appears to be given to the question of the extent to which a negotiator should adapt to the cultural values of the other party. Are international negotiators expected to adapt totally? Is the maxim 'When in Rome, do as the Romans do' appropriate?

The simplistic nature of this approach raises issues. First, it does not take account of the dominant role of one or the other partner: the Rome in question may well yield culturally to its counterpart. Second, is it ever possible to 'do as' the Romans? However much we try to behave as the other party does during negotiations, will they ever really consider us to be a member of their culture? Try as people may, behaving as the Romans will not make them Roman. Finally, there is a questionable assumption underlying this maxim – that a 'Roman' will always act as a Roman with a non-Roman in Rome!

This last point is one of a number put forward by Weiss (1994a) when examining cultural aspects of negotiating. He sees that international negotiators in today's global business cannot resort to a 'one-size-fits-all' approach when confronted with a variety of situations and individuals. Weiss advocates instead approaches that reflect the skills of the individuals involved. He proposes strategies that, while being culturally responsive, reflect the negotiators' own skills and the circumstances in which they are working.

In any communicative situation between two parties, one aim is to make sense of the interaction. In negotiations this means that the least both parties must be able to do is:

- recognise each other's ideas and the types of behaviour that form an international part of the negotiating process;
- interpret these in such a way that they can detect common and differing standpoints as well as changes made to these during the negotiating process;
- ensure that communication is maintained as the negotiation proceeds.

However, as indicated earlier, the knowledge and skills required to perform these crucial acts is often limited. What is needed, Weiss says, is a strategic framework allowing the parties to make sense of the negotiating process as best they can, using their own attributes and, where necessary, the skills of others.

SPOTLIGHT 15.1

Rice and nemawashi

Blaker (2002) presents a case study which highlights American and Japanese behaviour when both countries needed seven years to come to an agreement on importing US rice into Japan. Rice was, and still is, a highly sensitive issue since the Japanese consider it to be an indispensable part of their culture, a product embedded in the country's development. The US demand made in 1986 for access to the Japanese rice market was considered in essence as an attack on Japanese culture.

Blaker (2002) describes in considerable detail the long, tortuous path towards a settlement. He considered that the US set the negotiating agenda, and that the Japanese essentially reacted defensively throughout the whole process, starting from an initial refusal to even discuss the issue. The Japanese became very active outside the negotiating arena, however, when it was clear that the question of rice imports was more a multilateral issue, that refusal to make some sort of deal in this area could have a serious effect on Japan's trading activities generally. A consensus had to be created within the country that would allow discussions with the US to actually go ahead. This consensus-building process, called *nemawashi*, involved not only politicians, but also the whole bureaucratic machine as well as private groups of individuals who wielded considerable power in business and society. At every negotiating step the interested domestic parties were consulted, and even delegations and personal envoys went to the US to explore possible agreements. Towards the end, a Japanese group of people not officially involved in the negotiations paid a visit to the US Rice Millers Association to see whether the final compromise plan was likely to succeed.

The Weiss strategic framework

The framework that Weiss drew up is given in Figure 15.1. It shows in an organised form the culturally responsive strategies that can be adopted according to the level of familiarity that each negotiator has with the other's culture. The strategies in brackets reflect a co-ordinated approach between the parties involved.

Before the strategies are briefly described, two of the terms used need to be explained:

- 'Familiarity' is the term Weiss uses to denote not only one party's knowledge of the other party's culture, but also the ability to apply this knowledge effectively to the interaction.

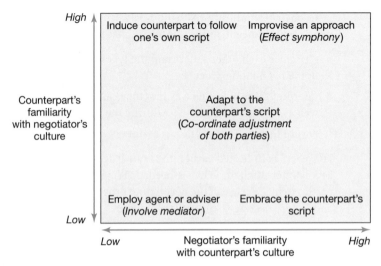

Figure 15.1 **Strategic framework for negotiating**
Source: Weiss, 1994a: 54.

High familiarity entails fluency in the predominant language, extensive exposure to the culture concerned and previous successful social interactions with those from the culture in question.

- 'Script' is the term that Weiss uses to denote a standardised sequence of behaviour expected by the person concerned.

According to Weiss (1994a), negotiators may consider using not only the strategies appropriate for their degree of familiarity, but also any strategies that correspond to lower degrees of familiarity.

The strategies proposed by the framework are:

- If a negotiator has *low familiarity* with the counterpart's culture, a third-party of some kind can be introduced to help out. This can be an agent who takes over the negotiating role (thus creating other possible problems, especially with regard to accountability and trust), or an adviser to help in preparations and during the process. The negotiator may also explicitly persuade the counterpart to adapt his approach, pleading ignorance with the other's culture and language, but every respect for them. The result may be further hindrance to agreement if the counterpart regards this as arrogant behaviour which results in a disadvantageous situation.

- If the negotiator has a *moderate familiarity* with the counterpart's culture, then the negotiator has two other options, provided the counterpart shares a similar familiarity. The negotiator can go some way towards making a compromise by altering his usual negotiating approach. This could include, for example, following the etiquette used by the counterpart, modifying the usual time frame, or being more 'upfront' with providing information. Tinkering with just part of the process, however, may create more confusion – and it may be exacerbated if the counterpart finds this half-hearted approach unacceptable. More promising is the idea of *co-ordinating adjustment*, whereby both parties negotiate as to how the negotiating is to proceed. This can be done explicitly at the start, or implicitly through a gradual blending of elements from the respective cultures. Weiss refers in particular to the medium of discussion and gives an example of a third language being used (presumably with some of its cultural baggage) in a high-level negotiation.

- Those parties that are *highly familiar* with each other's culture may improvise during the negotiating process, focusing on each other's attributes and skills as well as the circumstances. Weiss (1994a) is careful to point out that this does not allow an impromptu free-for-all, but rather a sensitive dialogue whereby both parties take account of each other's individuality as well as culture. It allows aspects of each other's culture to be brought to the foreground or pushed into the background as appropriate, pushing stereotypes aside and encouraging the development of a relationship that is not just based on the deal. Weiss takes this approach further by talking of *effecting symphony*. Here, both parties go beyond their home cultures and create their own approach, which may draw on their familiarity with both cultures but is unique to their relationship.

This final strategy takes further the idea of a synergistic approach to negotiating as proposed by Adler with Gunderson (2008: 237). They see the limitations to what they term 'principled approach' in complex international business negotiations and call instead for a collaborative, cultural, therefore synergistic style of negotiating. While recognising the extra problems caused through cultural differences, they argue that the very diversity of culture could help to increase the search for creative options for mutual gain. This collaborative approach is considered further in Chapter 18.

In his follow-up article to the one already outlined in the concept, Weiss (1994b) presents a step-by-step procedure for deciding which of the strategies put forward is:

- the most feasible, i.e. the extent to which it will fit with the counterpart's possible approach;
- the most appropriate in terms of the relationship and circumstances surrounding the interaction;
- the most acceptable in terms of the manager's own values.

This involves considerable reflection on one's own culture as well as careful investigation into the counterpart's culture. Moreover, it calls for both parties to consider their relationship as individuals as well as members of different cultures. Finding a balance between culture group and individual considerations is difficult, particularly as the degree of variation within a particular culture group can be considerable. The five steps Weiss (1994b: 86) proposes for selecting a negotiating strategy take account of these complexities.

1. Reflect on your culture's negotiation script.
2. Learn the negotiation script of the counterpart's culture.
3. Consider the relationship and circumstances.
4. Predict and influence the counterpart's approach.
5. Choose your strategy.

This approach highlights a regular message in this book: reflect carefully on your own culture while investigating others. The concept in the next chapter takes this approach further when considering international team-work.

Conclusion

Chapter 15 has examined three facets of cultural differences in international negotiations. One very important facet is the concept of negotiating: do people consider it to be more to do with problem-solving within a given time-frame, or is it just one aspect of a continuing dialogue between parties who are beginning or continuing a harmonious, mutually beneficial relationship? People's perception of negotiating colours their style of negotiating, as well as their expectations about the outcome. And, of course, it influences the way they tend to behave during the negotiations.

This chapter has also addressed the question as to what international negotiators should do when having to contend with such differences. The strategic framework of negotiations presented is a culturally responsive instrument, taking account of the negotiators' own skills and the circumstances of the negotiation.

Points for reflection

There are many books, articles and websites on international negotiations that offer 'dos and don'ts' on how to negotiate with parties from different cultures. For example, negotiators in China are urged not to say or do anything to embarrass the Chinese participants, or to point at anyone, or to raise their voice. Another guide to negotiating suggests that those negotiating in the US should be prepared to partake in preliminary small talk with their counterparts at the start of a meeting, and not to be surprised if a gift cannot be accepted.

1. To what extent do you think such prescriptive advice is useful?

2. What other ways of preparing for a cross-cultural negotiation do you consider to be (more) useful?

Further reading

Fisher, G. (1980) *International Negotiation: a Cross-Cultural Perspective*, Yarmouth, ME: Intercultural Press. This book focuses on the factors that affect the negotiating process between parties from different cultural and national backgrounds, with particular reference to Japan, France and the US. Fisher puts forward a conceptual framework for the negotiating process that allows negotiators to manage the process more effectively.

Ghauri, N. and Usunier, J.-C. (eds) (2003) *International Business Negotiations,* 2nd edition, Oxford: Elsevier. This book aims to enhance understanding of the effect of culture and communication on international business negotiations. It explores the problems faced by Western managers while doing business abroad and provides guidelines for international business negotiations. In particular, the book discusses negotiations for different types of businesses, using examples from different parts of the world.

References

Adler, N.J. with Gundersen, A. (2008, 2002) *International Dimensions of Organizational Behaviour*, 5th edition, Mason: South-Western Cengage Learning.

Blaker, M. (2002) 'Negotiations on rice imports', in Blaker, M., Giarra, P. and Vogel, E.F. (eds), *Case Studies in Japanese Negotiating Behavior*, Washington DC: US Institute of Peace Press.

Faure, G.O. (1998) 'Negotiation: the Chinese concept' in *Negotiation Journal*, 14(2): 137–148.

Fisher, G. (1980) *International Negotiation: a Cross-cultural Perspective*, Yarmouth, ME: Intercultural Press.

Kumar, R. and Worm, V. (2003) 'Social capital and the dynamics of business negotiations between the northern Europeans and the Chinese', in *International Marketing Review*, 20(3): 262–285.

Usunier, J.-C. (2003) 'Cultural aspects of international business negotiations', in Ghauri, N. and Usunier J.-C. (eds), *International Business Negotiations*, 2nd edition, Oxford: Elsevier: 97–136.

Weiss, S.E. (1994a) 'Negotiating with "Romans"': part 1, *Sloan Management Review*, 35(2): 51–61.

Weiss, S.E. (1994b) 'Negotiating with "Romans"': part 2, *Sloan Management Review*, 35(3): 85–99.

Whetten, D., Cameron, K. and Woods, M. (2000) *Developing Management Skills for Europe*, Harlow: FT Prentice Hall.

ACTIVITY 15.1

Negotiating with the Japanese

Table 15.2 below gives a brief description in note form of the typical approach by the Japanese to negotiating, using the framework given in Concept 15.1.

Table 15.2

Behavioural predispositions	
Interpersonal orientation	Wish to establish personal rapport: essential for building trust – the basis for doing any business. Time-consuming entertainment as part of that process. A negotiation is a face-to-face ceremonial and very formal moment when a stage of partnership development has been rounded off
Power orientation	Any decision requires consultation and support at all levels of the company. The leader of the negotiating team will probably be the motor behind this consensus-building. Others will be experts who have talked in great detail to the counterpart
Willingness to take risks	The concern for consensus will make the Japanese unwilling to take risks: intensive pre-negotiation preparation, reviews before and during the negotiation, no impulsive response to proposals from the other side
Underlying concept of negotiation	
Negotiation strategies	Doing business is a continuing affair, based on mutual trust and confidence. A negotiation is part of the process of developing a relationship. Once the base for the relationship has been established, details can be discussed and agreed upon, often before formal meetings between the two sides where the focus is less on problem-solving and, as Fisher (1980: 32) calls it, 'direction-taking'
Strategic time-frame	Patience is the key. Considerable care in preparation of a deal will allow its implementation to take place quite quickly
Negotiation process	
Styles of negotiation	No confrontation, disagreement or haggling involved – face-saving a key requirement. Highly indirect, highly formal communication. High-context negotiators: many allusions and inferences to the situation
Outcome orientations	Prefer a short written agreement to a definite, detailed contract. The establishment of a (further) stage in the relationship is what really counts: inevitable changes in the circumstances of both companies will necessitate later amendments anyway

Questions

1. Choose another culture with which you are familiar and note what you consider to be the similarities or differences with regard to the Japanese approach to negotiating.

2. Imagine how a Japanese party and a party from the other culture chosen would react to each other over the negotiating table.

ACTIVITY 15.2

Selecting a negotiation strategy

The aim of this activity is for you to use the five steps Weiss puts forward as a way of selecting a strategy for a particular negotiation with counterparts from another culture. For ease of reference these steps are given again below:

1. Reflect on your culture's negotiation script.
2. Learn the negotiation script of the counterpart's culture.
3. Consider the relationship and circumstances.
4. Predict and influence the counterpart's approach.
5. Choose your strategy.

Imagine that you are about to take part in an international, cross-cultural negotiation. You represent a company from your own country and are about to meet either a US or a Japanese negotiating team.

Questions

1. Sketch out the scenario for the negotiation that allows you to determine the degree of familiarity that both sides may have with regards to each other's culture. You will need to:
    *   Describe the circumstances of the negotiation (including the experience of both teams in international business and the nature of any possible agreement).
    *   Describe the relationship, if any, that you have developed with your counterparts.
2. Using the information from your response to question 1:
    *   Choose one negotiating strategy from those proposed by Weiss in his strategic framework (outlined in Figure 15.1 of this chapter's concept) that you believe to be appropriate.
    *   Describe the negotiation process as you envisage it, using the strategy chosen.

Chapter 16

Working with international teams

Having considered communication barriers in cross-cultural management and aspects of negotiating internationally, attention now focuses on an increasingly common phenomenon of global business, the international team. Knowing that cultural backgrounds have an enormous influence on how people behave, how do teams composed of people from different cultures operate?

After defining the word 'team' and the elements involved (types and roles), this concept will focus on global teams, their processes and the effect of cultural differences on these teams. The final part of Concept 16.1 will deal with the management of multicultural teams, with particular reference to Afro-Western teams.

Learning outcomes

After reading this chapter, you will gain an understanding of:

● The cultural factors that influence teams working in organisations.

● The importance of communication in the management of teams.

Concept 16.1 | Groups processes during international encounters

Teams in organisations

The word 'team' can be defined as a small number of people who work together for a common purpose and hold themselves collectively responsible for what they do. Senge *et al.* (1995: 354–355) define the word as 'any group of people who need each other to accomplish a result'. The word 'team', which comes from the Indo-European *deuk* (to pull), has always been understood in terms of people 'pulling together'. It was not until the sixteenth century that the word took on its modern meaning of 'a group of people acting together'.

This recent definition includes all those who are working both inside and outside the organisation, even if they are not regular participants. Senge *et al.* (1995) give us the example of large, technologically oriented organisations that have learnt to design their infrastructures on the basis of this broad definition of a team. This is because a team can also be a global network of specialists who communicate with each other digitally, or occasionally meet.

The teams found in organisations can differ in kind according to their objectives. Robbins (2000: 106) proposes four types:

- *Problem-solving.* Such teams meet regularly to discuss and put forward suggestions such as to how to improve work processes and methods.
- *Self-managed.* Such teams have no supervisor. Employees in these teams are directly involved in the decisions made concerning work.
- *Cross-functional.* The members of these teams come from different departments and work together to complete a task. Their position in the hierarchy is usually the same, even if they come from different domains.
- *Virtual.* These teams can do the same as the other types mentioned – exchange information, take decisions, accomplish tasks – but can also increase in size by co-opting members from other organisations such as suppliers or joint partners.

In business, companies are becoming more and more dependent on virtual teams. Most international virtual teams exist only through necessity, to overcome geographic distance or time differences. Although there seem to be fewer problems nowadays on the technical front, this modern way of working in international teams has generated other problems, or at least amplified them. Consider Spotlight 16.1.

Spotlight 16.1 makes it clear that trust is a prerequisite for working effectively in a team, but also shows that developing a climate of trust is a challenge for multicultural teams. To establish trust, team members must have an attitude of co-operation, which includes sharing common norms and values. However, as Schneider and Barsoux (2003) point out, this condition is difficult to realise because people from different cultural backgrounds seldom have common norms and values. Moreover, the concept of trust – and ways of developing it – varies from culture to culture. Such variations rest on differing cultural assumptions about relationships to nature, the environment and to other people. This explains why people from some cultures react more positively than those from others when they are asked if they trust other people. Figure 16.1 shows the results of a survey showing the degree of trust in other people in different cultures.

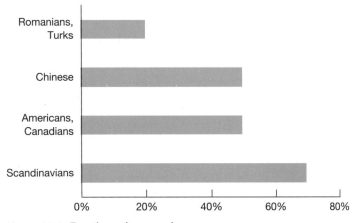

Figure 16.1 **Trusting other people**

Source: based on Inglehart (1997) as quoted by Schneider and Barsoux (2003).

SPOTLIGHT 16.1

'Virtual teams' endeavour to build trust

Global communication: Alison Maitland looks at how companies create corporate harmony between colleagues in different parts of the world.

Jenny Goodbody's team of six people is spread across six continents. Once a week, they meet through a teleconference, which means that she must be wide awake by 6.30 a.m. in New Jersey while her colleague in Sydney, Australia, has to stay in work mode until well past 8.30 p.m. This would mean that at least two of the team would be less tired. On the other hand, some of them might feel more isolated if they had fewer opportunities to talk as a group.

It is the kind of dilemma that faces any geographically dispersed team that has to communicate through email, telephone calls or video conferences rather than face-to-face. While trust is crucial for every team to operate effectively, it is harder to build that trust among people who rarely, if ever, see each other.

Part of the problem is that people working in a virtual team often assume that trust will come about automatically. 'The teams that were more successful put in an effort to try and build trust,' she says. 'They had short-term activities for people to work in pairs or threes, getting to know each other in smaller groups.'

A face-to-face group meeting at the start is important. 'The teams that got together once could kick off that trust-building much more quickly. With the

ones that didn't meet face-to-face, it was slower.' 'An important aspect of management behaviour, identified as supporting the development of trust, is consistency and its encouragement among other team members,' they add. 'Managers can also act in a sensitive way to the stage of development of team trust.'

Ms Goodbody found that the first stage, when the team is actually formed, is the most important in determining success. Team leaders can help to build relationships in different ways. 'They can try and get people to share some level of social information, for example about their country or their family.' As team co-ordinators, they also need to know how to summarise relevant information from the conversations that they have with individual members for the rest of the group. 'There's a fine line between making sure everybody is aware of what's going on and inundating people with emails they don't need,' she says.

Virtual teams need a strong 'sponsor' from the start – someone who is not involved in everyday team activities but who represents their interests at a senior level in the parent organization. 'One of the key things for the sponsor is to show interest in the team's progress and be involved in solving major issues.'

Cultures also have different assumptions as to the purpose of groups and teams: these are to enable the dissemination of information and discussion of problems, or they enable decisions to be made and action to be taken or, lastly, they enable the creation of social relations. These assumptions will in turn determine the frequency of the meetings and contacts and the time needed for the group to function, as well as determine whether the meetings will take place face-to-face or by telephone through conference calls.

When the members of a team display complementary skills to achieve a certain goal, then we can talk of teamwork. That is the reason why the concept of the 'team' goes further than that of the 'group'. While the term 'group' usually refers to two or more individuals who share a collective identity, and have a common goal, the term 'teamwork' implies a synergy from working together that increases the performance of the work being done collectively.

Team roles

What types of roles need to be performed within a team? There are two roles for each member of a team. First, as representative of a profession, a team member must show his professional aptitudes as a *specialist* in his area, such as a personnel manager or sales manager. Second, each member should also demonstrate personal characteristics, thereby performing an *interpersonal* role within the team. This should reflect the style in which each member works.

For Senge *et al.* (1995), it is also important for the team itself to clarify how decisions are taken and by whom. A *facilitator* could play an important role in this, thereby improving the team's whole performance. This facilitator should preferably come from outside the team and be someone who is trained in techniques for developing the team's reflection and inquiry skills while stimulating dialogue among its members. The authors argue that the members of a team 'often collude to misrepresent reality to each other' in a deceitful way, and do so without being aware of what they are doing. Only a facilitator who is not part of the team can see the team's shortcomings clearly and get the team to work on their behaviour. That is why a member of the team, even if competent to take on the role, is not the most suitable facilitator.

The role of team members and their performance as a team brings us to the Belbin (1993) model. This is used by many organisations to measure the influence of team member diversity regarding the different roles played in a team at work. Aritzeta *et al.* (2007: 99) emphasise that Belbin's team role model mainly concerns the way the roles evolve and that it defines the team role as a 'pattern of behaviour characteristic of the way in which one team member interacts with another to facilitate the progress of the team as a whole'.

Besides the stages of development of the team – identifying needs, finding ideas, formulating plans, executing ideas, establishing team organisation, following through – this model highlights the team roles (Table 16.1) which should each dominate in a particular stage of development. In addition, a good representation of all team roles is a guarantee of a team performing well (Aritzeta *et al.*, 2007).

Cultural background may have an influence on the choice of role in teams. Schneider and Barsoux (2003) suggest that some cultures may also have a preference for certain roles. They mention a study (Inglehart, 1997) carried out in Europe from which it appears that bringing up good ideas would be the domain of the French, structuring tasks would be that of the Germans and obtaining the necessary means to perform would be the task of the Swedes.

These preferences for team roles could have important implications for multinationals where managers with different cultural backgrounds form teams to help run their global business.

Table 16.1 **An overview of team roles**

Team role	Descriptors and strengths
Completer-finisher	Conscientious, introvert, delivers on time
Implementer	Conservative, reliable, turns ideas into practical actions
Team worker	Extrovert, co-operative, avoids friction
Specialist	Serious, provides knowledge and skills in rare supply
Monitor evaluator	Introvert, open to change, judges accurately
Co-ordinator	Dominant, good chairperson, delegates well
Plant	Trustful, creative, solves difficult problems
Shaper	Emotional, impatient, has the drive to overcome obstacles
Resource investigator	Diplomatic, persuasive, communicative, develops contacts

Source: Belbin, 1993: 22.

Global management teams

This term refers to a group of managers from different countries who work together to achieve common goals of an international enterprise. Deresky (2003) gives the example of a US–Dutch joint venture whose headquarters are in Italy. This company is managed by a Swede and has a management team composed of six people from Sweden, Italy, the Netherlands, the US, Belgium and Germany. To realise the goals the enterprise has set itself, the international teams must develop a global perspective and communicate a corporate culture while paying attention to the needs of the local market.

While the work of cross-cultural teams in domestic companies is restricted to internal activities and a few external contacts, the role of a multicultural team in an internationally operating company is important in establishing and maintaining relations with suppliers, sales people and other intermediaries. This goes also for multinationals, which have teams composed of managers and technical people who work together in local operating companies in different parts of the world. The ability to work together is vital to the company's success.

For global organisations, internal interactions at all levels go on at the same time as interactions with the external environment. That is why it is vital for an organisation to have not only global teamwork but also what Deresky (2003: 425) calls 'pockets of cross-cultural teamwork and interactions that occur at many boundaries'. These allow account to be taken of the organisation as an entity and local operations and their markets at one and the same time.

On an individual level, the members of a global management team share a multitude of identities derived from their national and professional cultures. Culture influences, for example, the way members see the role of the leader, the relations between superiors and subordinates, participation in meetings, the use of deadlines, as well as decision-making and problem-solving generally.

Team tasks and processes

The next part of the concept focuses on the human dynamics of group behaviour, particularly the roles and contributions made by group members in the process of team interaction.

Group members display many kinds of behaviour and the group itself will develop properties that are more than the average of the properties of the individuals composing it. Individuals influence group and team life, but their behaviour in turn is changed through the dynamics within the group.

Cultural differences can be seen in terms of what the organisation expects from a group, as well as how a group is expected to operate. Some of those expectations are related to *task strategies:* how the tasks are planned, who does what and when, how decisions are taken. Other expectations are related to *process-group building:* language, participation, ways of managing conflict and group evaluation. These expectations have to be negotiated in terms of both task and process.

Differences between task-oriented cultures (such as Germany, Switzerland, the US) and relationship-oriented cultures (such as Latin America, the Middle East and Southern Europe) were noted by Adler with Gundersen (2008, 2002). During the initial stage of team formation, the time when team members get to know each other and start building a long-lasting relationship, it was observed that those from task-oriented cultures spent little time getting to know each other before getting down to business. Those from relationship-oriented cultures, however, spent much more time establishing a personal relationship. It is not surprising, therefore, that when members of two such cultural groups meet together as a team they may find it more difficult to build strong relations with each other than single-culture teams.

Strategies for global teams

Whatever type of global team an organisation wishes to create, these teams face a complex task to reach their objectives. Gluesing and Gibson (2004) classify these in terms of:

- task;
- context;
- people;
- time (the amount of time which the team has to work together); and
- technology (information sharing and collaboration).

Task and context may be closely linked when the contexts in which the members of a team are working – such as climate, nationality, education, political and economic systems – are the same or very similar. Global teams, however, are based on the complexity of different contexts. Therefore, cross-cultural competence and the ability of the team to adapt appear to be just as necessary as professional expertise for the realisation of its task.

Before examining the effect of differences on global teams, it is useful to review the elements that are essential to team dynamics. Davison and Ekelund (2004) describe three aspects:

- *Task and social processes are closely linked.* The task process directly influences the performance of the team while the social process is related to the ability of the team to work together over a longer time.
- *Emergent states.* Through interacting, members of a team create a collective mental environment in which the predispositions and assumptions of each member 'set the stage for the dynamics'. The most important emergent states are 'mutual trust, collective team identity and confidence in the team's ability to achieve its tasks'.

- *Co-ordinating mechanisms.* The mechanism most frequently used by teams for co-ordination purposes is the face-to-face meeting. Thanks to developing technology, online meetings are also becoming increasingly important.

Differences between team members, particularly in global teams, can be seen at several levels: profession, culture, personality, style and role, as well as organisation. These differences can help improve the performance of the team, but can also be the source of conflict, depending on the way the team deals with these differences. Table 16.2 gives an overview of the ways in which differences can affect global teams.

Table 16.2 **The effect of differences on global teams**

This table lists the possible sources of difference, together with the opportunities they may offer, where the differences may have an effect and how they may be experienced within the team. The final column describes ways in which the whole group must integrate to choose a process which it considers appropriate as a response to the source of difference given. This can be negotiating the problem, finding a compromise, achieving consensus or just voting – whatever the team agrees on.

Source of difference	Opportunity presented	Effect on	Experienced as	Integrated mechanisms
Preferred leadership styles	To make leaders and members actively search for the most effective leadership role(s) and style where both adjust and align their expectations	Effective leader/team member interaction, decision-making, levels of satisfaction	Frustrations, disagreements on form. Disappointment due to failed expectations	Openness about leader style and leader–team member expectations. Identification of conflicts and the best ways to handle them
National and organisational culture of origin and leadership of the organisation	Can give core identity and sense of cohesion that can be adjusted/improved through experience in other cultures	People who share the nationality of the organisation and its leadership are perceived as more influential than others	Perceived bias in accepted norms and levels of influence and access to resources. Glass ceiling based on nationality	Well-structured participative processes and inclusive policies
Preferred ways of resolving conflicts	Confronts team with need to find synergistic solutions	Ability to address difficult challenges and conflicts	Denial of conflict. Displaced frustrations. Lack of trust. Lack of group efficacy	Joint definition of which conflicts need to be addressed and how. Also which conflicts are to be avoided
Preferred ways of making decisions	Creates variety; highlights need to make decision-making processes explicit and suitable for different contexts	The quality of, involvement in, and follow up/implementation of decision-making processes	Lack of loyalty to decision and team. Dissatisfaction and lack of respect	Collective training on which type of decisions
Different languages yet working in one (often English)	May force native speakers to improve communication styles. May be a hindrance for second-language speakers	Interruption patterns. Use and interpretation of silence. Meaning of gestures and body language. Use of in jokes/humour. Dominant patterns of logic	Inability to participate. Frequent misunderstandings. Exclusive patterns of humour. Translation can be clumsy when building relationships	Choosing a working language and/or translators; maintaining steady rhythm and active listening skills

Table 16.2 *continued*

Source of difference	Opportunity presented	Effect on	Experienced as	Integrated mechanisms
Different professions	Brings requisite variety of knowledge, skills and approaches to complex problems. Speeds things up. Improves quality, relevance of output	Values and where to focus. Common professions can act as a large integrating factor	Power struggle. Ignorance. Misunderstanding	Definition of the uses of different functions in relation to the goal. Respect and positive acknowledgement
Expectations and values around interaction and team behaviour	Forces awareness of differences, assumptions, the tensions that they bring and the need to acknowledge and work with them	Levels of participation. Misunderstandings	Missed timing, anger at inappropriate reciprocity. Feeling misunderstood. Things not happening 'in the right way'	Value checklist-type exercises to make differences explicit and legitimate and then negotiate them
Cultural preconceptions	Increased awareness of these. Approaching them with humour, not acting on them. A learning opportunity that there are many ways of seeing the world	Preconceived perceptions of more or less relevant experience, education	Stereotypical comments or implicit behaviour towards 'disadvantaged' people or about those 'in charge'	Highlighting team members' strengths and relevant experiences up front and using the strengths
International experience	Can bring empathy, flexibility, humbleness, and self-reflection. People with international experience can act as bridges between core and local sites	Ability to understand implicit rules and working norms. Ability to speak different languages. Ability to empathise with other team members	Bias that wide international experience and linguistic skills are more essential for people from 'other' nationalities than for those whose mother tongue is the working language of the firm	Insist on international experience as part of international career path and selection criteria for international team leaders
Different geographical locations	Allows global efficiencies, local responsiveness, and knowledge transfer and learning across the organisation	Who meets face-to-face and who does not. Co-ordination, timing understanding of importance of required actions	Impenetrable in groups in certain locations. Lack of loyalty, invisible agendas	Stress integrated team model spread across geography, not hub and spoke. Create hyper-attractiveness and virtual team visible locally and globally

Source: Davison and Ekelund, 2004: 232–234.

Den Hartog (2004) suggests that teams whose leaders encourage reflective processes (i.e. discussions on subjects such as the work of the team and who is more likely to come forward with suggestions) will function better than teams where such processes are not to be found. Other aspects of the team context can reinforce such processes when the team is working as a virtual one, with members who come from diverse cultures. Such members may have different rules and expectations in communication. Seeking harmony, using implicit (high context) communication and saving face are the norms for certain cultures, while other cultures consider open criticism and disagreement with their superiors to be the norm. The degree to which the communication process is expected to be structured and formal is also influenced by culture.

However, some writers think that the importance of the cultural dimension in the management of multicultural teams is over-stated. They believe that having clear objectives and a good allocation of roles and responsibilities among individual members of the team is enough to create teams that can work together. The synergy may not be present, but such teams do not create problems, and even produce good results.

SPOTLIGHT 16.2

Below is a short extract from a lecture given by Professor Martha Maznevski on leading diverse teams.

Diversity in teams

Professor Martha Maznevski

These are teams that engage their differences and use them, as we'll talk about in a minute. These are teams that really destroy the differences. The most frequent response to diversity in teams, so when a group of people are sitting around the table and they notice how different they are, wow we come from different countries, different companies, different departments, different professions, they see how diverse they are, their first reaction is to actually suppress that diversity to say you know, we're not all that different, we're really all the same. And what that does is it moves them from here, on the left side, where they're afraid of being, into the middle. It's a better place to be, but there are two problems with it. One is that you're leaving money on the table; you're really missing out the opportunities that diversity has to offer. These are the teams that really outperform expectations, so you're missing out that opportunity that comes from globalisation. The other thing is that people whose differences are suppressed, so people who are not the same as the dominant norm of the team, but they have to act as if they are, become demotivated and frustrated, and they don't actually give everything that they can offer to the team. So, this is actually a very unstable place to be, and most teams that do this end up right back here again. So, the two messages from that: one, if you've got diversity you should use it, the second is that if you want high performance you should use the diversity you have to get there.

 Source: from 'Diversity in teams', *Financial Times*, 27/3/2007 (Maznevski, M.), © The Financial Times Ltd. All Rights Reserved.

The management of multicultural teams

For Chevrier (2004), managing teams composed of people from several cultures is the essential task of intercultural management. This type of management has become necessary as a consequence of the development of transnational companies and the globalisation of economies.

However, as Chevrier (2004: 31) remarks, the teams formed with members from different countries have to face intercultural difficulties. She therefore presents four strategies aimed at overcoming cultural barriers:

A firm can:

1. count on the international team members' openness
2. contribute to developing interpersonal relations among the participants to help them establish efficient routines
3. bank on international occupational or organisational cultures
4. establish a coaching process to help the teams build intercultural synergies.

The way management deals with the cultural diversity of these teams can vary. Some managers will appeal to the professional culture of its members to bring an international team together. This appeal is not part of a Japanese manager's strategy since Japan does not attach the same value to professional culture as the West. Other managers lay stress on the communication between the actors, such as making the unspoken rules explicit, or using an approach that conforms either to what Chevrier calls American culture – or to the corporate culture.

According to Chevrier (2000), multicultural groups with the most harmonious relations are those whose members:

- have the same status;
- do not have contradictory interests;
- do not feel that their identity is threatened.

Such a team will not necessarily be prevented from reaching its goals, if the process is prolonged, or if it does not have detailed insight into other cultures, or even if it causes irritation.

Another characteristic of multicultural teams is their potential to be creative. Adler with Gundersen (2008, 2002) argue that, thanks to their diversity, such teams can work in a more creative way than homogeneous teams. Although multicultural teams encounter more process problems, they produce more divergent ideas, so favouring creativity, and propose more solutions for problems. Thus, it remains the challenge for the leaders of these teams to balance creativity (divergence) and cohesion (convergence).

The word 'multicultural' can also refer to the issue of multiculturalism, observable in the working relations between members of a team composed of people who come from countries (large or small) or companies (large or small) or of people with unequal power. This is explained by Mutabazi and Deer (2003) when referring to Afro-Occidental teams.

Afro-Western teams

In their study, Mutabazi and Deer (2003: 3) show that 'the problem associated with multiculturalism comes from pre-existing attitudes about relations between Africa and the West'. The dominant partner is the West, with its ideals and concepts of the world. This has repercussions on the relations in a team where one notices the indifference towards the values and perspectives of the other members, as well as the inability to have spontaneous interactions. Perfect integration between Western expatriates and local executives also appears to be impossible.

However, when the conditions regarding multiculturalism disappear, it is possible to achieve a high degree of integration, to go beyond the superficial relations work requires.

This integration results in a mutual commitment that allows skills within the teams to be developed rather than just what Mutabazi and Deer (2003: 11) call 'the opportunist addition of know-how techniques'.

One particular point in the authors' conclusions to their research on the African experience of intercultural team management deserves particular mention: the importance of time. According to Mutabazi and Deer (2003), time is needed for a group composed of people from different national and professional cultures to develop a real team spirit. Without it, the manager of the team loses his credibility and the ability to mobilise all the team members. Enough time also needs to be given to the members of a cross-cultural team to gain a clear perception of the project they are undertaking. This will help them individually to grasp exactly what the purpose of their work is, to understand how it is to be achieved and in what period of time. All these elements can then be incorporated into their own particular reference system.

Working in a team implies change not only in the way of doing, but also in the way of thinking. This teamwork pre-supposes the creation of common values and ideas, a delicate process in multicultural teams and organisations. This will be developed in Chapter 18. Teamwork also involves learning to deal with conflicts. This is what Chapter 17 will cover.

Conclusion

After giving Senge's definition of the word 'team', this chapter presented the range of roles that, according to Belbin, individuals can play in a team. When considering how teams work in an international context, it can be seen that the culture of each individual involved not only influences their role, but also the dynamic process within the team. The 'culture' variable therefore can increase the difficulty of managing global teams, which may be composed of task-oriented and relationship-oriented cultures, high-context and low-context cultures, or even different ethnic groups, such as in Afro-Western teams.

The success of teamwork is crucial to all international organisations. Whether they meet face-to-face or online, teams must address problems that go far beyond the field of communication. Creating common ideas and defining one's own values remains a challenge for those working in cross-cultural teams.

Points for reflection

1. To what extent is it necessary for the leader of a multicultural team to be very familiar with the culture of each team-member?

2. To what extent do you think the leader of a global team can ensure its success by just resolving any communication problems within the team, such as the choice of language?

3. Some researchers in team dynamics argue that cultural differences have less influence on the effective functioning of a multicultural team than a good combination of team members. They maintain that the effective distribution of roles within the team is more likely to ensure its success. **Discuss this standpoint.**

Further reading

Lane, H.W., Maznevski, M.L., Mendenhall, M.E. and McNett, J. (eds) (2004) *The Blackwell Handbook of Global Management: a Guide to Managing Complexity*, Oxford: Blackwell. This has been written for global executives and managers who are dealing with global complexity. The most important findings in the field – and their implications – are given in five areas: people and context, global competencies, leading and teaming, executing strategic initiatives globally, and special issues in developing and transitioning economies. The section on leading and teaming is of particular interest because the articles consider the importance of global teams, a relatively recent phenomenon in the world of business. Their diverse nature, in terms of function, organisation as well as cultural composition, necessitates the development of both relational and cross-cultural competences among its members and those managing such teams.

References

Adler, N.J. with Gundersen, A. (2008, 2002) *International Dimensions of Organizational Behaviour*, 5th edition, Mason: South-Western Cengage Learning.

Aritzeta, A., Swailes, S. and Senior, B. (2007) 'Belbin's role model: development, validity and applications for team building', *Journal of Management Studies*, 44(1): 96–118.

Belbin, M. (1993) *Teams Roles at Work*, Oxford: Butterworth-Heinemann.

Chevrier, S. (2000) *Le management des équipes interculturelles*, Paris: Presses Universitaires de France.

Chevrier, S. (2004) 'Le management des équipes interculturelles', *Management International*, 8(3): 31–40.

Davison, S.C. and Ekelund, B.Z. (2004) 'Effective team processes for global teams', in Maznevski, H.W., Mendenhall, M.L. and McNett, J.M.E. (eds), *The Blackwell Handbook of Global Management*, Oxford: Blackwell: 227–249.

Den Hartog, D.N. (2004) 'Leading in a global context: vision in complexity', in Maznevski, H.W., Mendenhall, M.L. and McNett, J.M.E. (eds), *The Blackwell Handbook of Global Management*, Oxford: Blackwell: 175–198.

Deresky, H. (2003) *International Management: Managing Across Borders and Cultures*, 4th edition, New Saddle River, NJ: Prentice Hall.

Gluesing, J.C. and Gibson, C.B. (2004) 'Designing and forming global teams', in Maznevski, H.W., Mendenhall, M.L. and McNett, J.M.E. (eds), *The Blackwell Handbook of Global Management*, Oxford: Blackwell: 199–226.

Inglehart, R. (1997) *The Silent Revolution: Changing Values and Political Styles in Advanced Industrial Society*, Princeton, NJ: Princeton University Press. Quoted by Schneider, S.C. and Barsoux, J.-L. (2003) *Managing Across Cultures*, 2nd edition, Harlow: Pearson Education.

Mutabazi, E. and Deer, C.B. (2003) 'The management of multicultural teams: the experience of Afro-Occidental teams in Africa', in *Cahiers de recherche* 13, accessed 01/09/2010, http://www.em-lyon.com//ressources/ge/documents/publications/wp/2003-13.pdf.

Robbins, S.P. (2000) *Essentials of Organizational Behaviour*, 6th edition, Upper Saddle River, NJ: Prentice Hall.

Schneider, S.C. and Barsoux, J.-L. (2003) *Managing Across Cultures*, 2nd edition, Harlow: Pearson Education.

Senge, P.M., Kleiner, A., Roberts, C., Ross, R.B. and Smith, B.J. (1995) *The Fifth Discipline Fieldbook*, London: Nicholas Brealey.

Before reading the case study and answering the questions, read through the concepts of Chapters 13 and 14 again.

Global harmony is their dream

Virtual teams: Sarah Murray considers collaboration between dispersed staff of different cultures

If managing diversity in the workplace is a tough task for business leaders, the challenges of keeping executives from different backgrounds working together efficiently in various parts of the world is even more difficult.

However, virtual working presents some unexpected benefits to teams whose members come from a variety of backgrounds. For executives whose first language is not English, for instance, working by means of e-mail or online chat rooms can eliminate many of the communication inequalities that might exist were the group to be working together face-to-face in the same location. People tend to be more comfortable reading and writing in their second language than speaking it, and email technology provides those less sure of the language with an opportunity to reflect before communicating.

'It certainly suggests that one of the things you should take into account is whether your team includes members who don't speak English well,' says Joanne Yates, a professor of management at MIT Sloan, who has studied the use of communication and information systems in companies. 'Any good virtual team has a communication plan that includes weekly conference calls or email check-ins, but with a virtual team where not everyone speaks English well, the regular

report-ins should be in written mode rather than by phone or conference call.'

The other advantage of email communications is that, for those working in different time zones, group messages can be responded to when it is convenient, reducing the need for early morning or late night calls.

At the same time, using email for work exchanges can remove much of the hierarchy of professional communications, since many executives find it far less intimidating to send an email to someone in a senior position than to telephone them. 'In many organizations that are fairly hierarchical, the lower and middle management executives often won't communicate with senior managers if it means picking up the phone', says Emma Kirk, a psychologist at Pearn Kandola, a UK-based research business and consultancy of occupational psychologists. 'Email removes that barrier because of its informality and immediacy, so it encourages people to communicate that might not otherwise', says Ms Kirk. 'And it's now accepted that people will send off ideas to each other via email.'

However, cultural or behavioural differences that can manifest themselves in face-to-face working situations can be exacerbated in virtual team working, particularly when the group has members from different backgrounds. One reason for this is that, when one is physically immersed in a new culture, it takes less time to adapt to the social norms and become aware of cultural sensitivities. So those trying to do this at a distance may find it tougher to fit in, increasing the potential for misunderstandings between team members. 'You don't build the relationships in the same way as you do working face-to-face, and you don't have those water cooler chats', says Martin Galpin, a psychologist at Pearn Kandola.

He argues that the differences can become more problematic when people are not working in the same location. 'When you have a group of people who are more diverse, there's a danger of increasing the chances of conflict if you don't manage it effectively.' For this reason, experts advise that those managing virtual teams organize face-to-face meetings at the start of a project or the formation of a new team of executives who will be working together remotely.

While this is true for all virtual teams, it is even more important for those with cultural differences. 'If a team is newly formed, there's huge value in bringing that team together', says Mr Galpin. 'Or if a new person joins the team, they need to be able to build new relationships. There's always a need for the social side – even if that's just setting aside time for more informal chats during the conference calls.'

Prof. Yates points out that, when people in professional groups come from different backgrounds or cultures, it is often useful to appoint someone in the team who knows both cultures as the person responsible for setting the norms of working behaviour during a project that is being carried out from different locations.

And virtual working certainly does not eradicate the sort of cultural misunderstandings that can arise in a face-to-face situation. Prof. Yates cites an online mini-conference she recently observed that took place between a group of US and Japanese executives working in the research and development unit of a Japanese company. 'A Japanese executive was putting text into a window for instant messaging when one of the Americans started asking questions in the middle of the presentation', she explains. 'That was not culturally familiar and required an instant response, which caused real problems. So [virtual communications] have a cultural element as well.'

 Source: *The Financial Times*, 12/5/2005: 8, Copyright © The Financial Times Ltd.

Questions

1. According to the article, what are the advantages of virtual communication compared with working face-to-face in with people from different backgrounds? What other advantages can you think of?

2. The text does suggest, however, that virtual working groups should meet at the start of a project or when a new team of executives is to work together remotely. Why is this thought to be necessary?

3. What are the specific problems that multicultural teams experience when they are communicating with each other virtually?

ACTIVITY 16.2

The following case study illustrates what may happen in the first meeting of a team that has been brought together to improve a company's fortunes.

A meeting of minds?

The Indian owners of an agricultural machine company, with a growing number of subsidiaries around the world, were determined to improve the productivity of their operations in Europe. To this end, they sent a managing director (MD) from its headquarters in Bombay to head its recently acquired company in Italy and to spearhead changes in the running of the European operations. Before his departure, the MD had persuaded the owners that a cross-subsidiary team of key managers needed to be created which, under his leadership, would harmonise the decisions made by the two European companies they owned (one in Italy and another in Lithuania). This team would eventually serve as a basis for integrating decision-making across all of the company's operations in Europe and Asia.

The initial team was to consist of managers from the technical, production, quality control and client relation departments of the Italian and Lithuanian subsidiaries. The team would have its first meeting in Rome, with later meetings in Vilnius and Bombay. The company's infrastructure would be updated to allow the team to meet virtually between their regular face-to-face meetings.

The MD from Bombay regarded his first meeting with the team-members as an opportunity for them to get to know each other and to share information about day-to-day operations. Once he had explained his aims to his Italian management team, he left them to organise the meeting.

This get-together was conducted in English, which was the operating language of the concern. After the MD had explained his plans and the importance of the team in improving the company's fortunes, he asked the individual members to take it in turns to introduce themselves. The Lithuanian members each talked very briefly about their positions and responsibilities. The Italians, however, found it difficult to restrict themselves to introductions and started talking in detail and with great eagerness about all the machinery they were producing. There was only an outline agenda for the meeting, so the introductions quickly became a disorganised discussion dominated by the Italians. They talked about the manufacturing process ('we were the leaders in automated production ten years ago, but now we are a long way behind our competitors'), and complained vociferously about the working conditions ('our main priority must be to renovate the factory. We cannot go on like this!'). They deplored the motivation of the employees ('absenteeism is a terrible burden . . . but you people must have the same problem in your country'), and speculated about future products ('we wonder whether the company is going to continue with tractor production').

Unable to get a word in edgeways, one or two Lithuanians in the team now and again asked the MD if they could add to the discussion, but their requests were frequently drowned out by the loud comments of the Italian participants. All the Lithuanians really managed to do was to ask occasional questions about certain products that they were also making.

Afterwards, when the team-members were drinking an aperitif before dinner, the MD wandered among the rather quiet Lithuanians on one side of the room, and asked them how they felt the meeting went. They were rather reluctant to respond at first, but eventually volunteered a few comments that showed their disappointment. One of them had this to say: 'We didn't really get the information we needed. We didn't find out enough about what is going on in your company – certainly not enough to write a decent report. Our management will wonder what we actually achieved here.' The MD then went over to the Italians on the other side of the room who were still continuing the discussion they had had during the meeting. When he asked one manager for his impression of the meeting, he was deluged with comments by everyone standing nearby. The reaction of one Italian participant reflected the general feelings of his fellow-countrymen: 'I don't understand why the visitors are so cold; they really didn't want to know anything about us and told us nothing about themselves. It should have gone much better – after all we speak the same technical language!'

Questions

1. Using the information given in the case study, as well as Table 16.2, make an analysis of the situation. Use the following questions as a guideline:
   - What are the 'sources of differences' in this case?
   - Which responses – appropriate or inappropriate – to the sources of these differences were used during the preparation for the meeting as well as the meeting itself?

2. How could the first meeting of the team have been more successful? Consider the suggestions below and add any ideas you may have.
   - The new managing director of the Italian subsidiary from Bombay could have asked the Italian participants to organise a meeting some days before the one planned with their Lithuanian counterparts. This internal meeting could have functioned as a rehearsal for the 'real' meeting, with the managing director (as chairman) allowing the participants to speak as they wanted and not organising the discussion in any way.
   - Those who were to attend the first meeting of the team could have been required to get to know each other beforehand, either through some kind of social/team-building event, or through telephone (conference) calls to each other, or even through video conferences.

Chapter 17

Conflicts and cultural differences

Chapters 15 and 16 examined intercultural communication in negotiating and working in teams. This chapter examines an aspect of intercultural communication that is often a feature of both these activities, as well as of interaction between cultures generally, and that is conflict. Cultural differences can be a cause of conflict, and the way conflict is dealt with is influenced by the cultural background and experience of those involved. The ambiguous nature of intercultural conflict may compel those in dispute to deal with the situation by using approaches – or styles of communication – learned from their own culture; these may only serve to exacerbate the conflict.

Concept 17.1 will first look at the question of the styles of communication in conflict situations and the tendencies displayed by certain types of culture. It goes on to examine emotion in conflict and its role in different cultures. Approaches to the management of conflicts will then be surveyed, with examples taken from conflicts between Eastern and Western cultures. Finally, a more radical approach to managing conflict, the notion of conflict transformation, will be addressed.

Learning outcomes

After reading this chapter you will:

- Be aware how culture influences the way people communicate in conflict.
- Understand how different cultural values affect the way people perceive and manage conflicts.
- Realise how particular communicative skills can transform the way people perceive the nature of conflict and the attitudes of those involved.

Concept 17.1 Understanding and dealing with conflicts

The nature of conflict

To gain a clearer insight into what conflict entails, it would be useful to define the very term in relation to managing and resolving disputes, whether within or between cultures. Yet, as Saphiro and Kulik (2004: 177) indicate, there seems to be no comprehensive definition of conflict because the many disciplines involved – psychology, sociology, anthropology and communication – each have their own. However, these definitions all agree on the moment when a conflict appears. That is when people with differing needs or goals are prevented – or perceive that they are being prevented – by others in achieving these needs or goals.

Incompatibility of goals in terms of material resources is referred to in relatively recent social psychology theory as the source of inter-group conflict. As Liu (2002) indicates, this realistic group conflict theory sees struggles over (limited) structural resources such as land, oil, gold and labour as the source of inter-group conflict, not personal characteristics. These insights were developed by social identity theory, whereby conflict between groups is seen to be the result of perceived identities. As noted in the introduction to Part Three, if one group perceives itself as being different to another, then prejudicial attitudes and discriminatory behaviour can result in favour of the in-group against the out-group. Both theories, however, stress that it is the situation that causes the conflict rather than the personalities of those involved.

Ting-Toomey (1999) also sees conflict as involving (cultural) groups protecting their own self-image, as well as intercultural perceptions, which are coloured by ethnocentrism and stereotypes. However, she sees conflict as involving not just the situation but also communicative behaviours which are profoundly shaped by the way individuals in a culture conceptualise the sense of self. Those who regard themselves as having an *independent sense of self* 'value individualism, personal achievement, self-direction, and competition'. Those who see themselves as having an *interdependent sense of self* 'want to fit in with others, act appropriately, protect others' goals, and value conformity and co-operation' (1999: 77). Ting-Toomey maintains that both types of self-construct are to be found within each culture, but that the independent self-concepts are to be found more often in individualist cultures, and interdependent self-concepts are more prevalent in collectivistic cultures.

Those with an independent sense of self will view communication in the conflict process as welcome, provided both parties address the issues in an open, honest manner. In this way, the chance to talk openly about thwarted needs or goals may prove very productive, with tangible results and even creative solutions. Those with an interdependent sense of self tend to see conflict as negative and unproductive, particularly if the other party is assertive and does not properly address issues or relational feelings. A conflict process is only satisfactory if the 'faces' of both parties have been saved in addition to a productive agreement.

A model of conflict styles

Several models have been proposed to predict and explain communicative behaviours during conflict. Reference is often made to a person's conflict style, which Hocker and Wilmot define as 'patterned responses or clusters of behaviour that people use in conflict' (1985: 96). The term 'style' is being used here to denote a way of communicating that reflects not only a person's cultural traits and personality, but also the situation in which the conflict takes place.

A number of these models emanate from a typology proposed by Blake and Mouton (1964) which is based on two dimensions defining the negotiators' concerns: 'concern for production' and 'concern for people'. This dual concern model was originally prescriptive in nature, but through it being validated by many empirical studies it is now considered to be descriptive. Other researchers have re-labelled the two orientations, but maintained the original opposing notions of concern for self and concern for others, echoing the distinction made earlier between independent and interdependent sense of self.

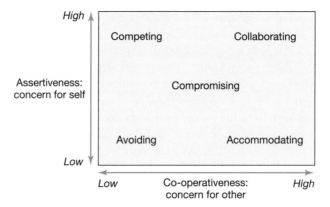

Figure 17.1 **Two-dimensional taxonomy of conflict handling modes**

Source: Thomas and Kilmann, 1974: 11.

Consider the model in Figure 17.1 devised by Thomas and Kilmann (1974). A questionnaire based on this model (see www.pyschometrics.com) is used extensively by consultants to assess how conflict-handling styles affect personal and group dynamics. The model allows individuals to be placed in five categories on the assumption that there are two factors in a person's conflict style which are defined as follows:

- assertiveness – the degree to which a person is concerned with his or her own interests; and
- co-operativeness – the degree to which a person is concerned with the interests of others.

If someone is low on both dimensions, then that person is an avoider, unassertive and unco-operative, rather withdrawn, preferring instead to put off an issue (possibly to save face). Someone who is high on the assertiveness dimension but low on the co-operative dimension is competitive, preferring to pursue their self-concern rather than the concern for others. An accommodating person, low on assertiveness but high on co-operativeness will be concerned more with the other party's needs rather than their own. Those in the middle will try to compromise between their own needs and those of the other party, trying to find a solution that, although not fully satisfactory, may resolve the issue in the short-term. A person high on both the assertiveness and co-operative dimensions works actively to develop a solution to a conflict in order to satisfy the needs of both parties. This collaborative, or integrative, approach involves attempts to reveal the underlying concerns of the other party.

Apart from the 'avoiding' style, the strategic choices imply willingness to make concessions by at least one of those involved in the dispute. The collaborating style is seen as being the most beneficial for those concerned. Unlike 'compromising', it is about working out a problem together, often by brainstorming, a method that responds best to the needs of both parties. The 'avoiding' style means that those involved in a conflict do not overtly recognise that there is any dispute.

Originally, the model was to be seen as predictive, and experimental studies appear to support its predictions. However, one of the original designers of the model, Thomas

(1992), has downplayed the predictive nature of the model by referring to it more as a classification of modes.

The effectiveness of such a model is questioned by some researchers. Saphiro and Kulik (2004) doubt whether it can be applied to the increasing complexity of modern-day disputes. Such a model needs to take account of the following elements:

- The parties in dispute do not always know each other. This applies particularly to situations where organisations rather than individuals are in dispute. If it is impossible for one party to identify the other in some way, then taking action to resolve differences can be very difficult.

- The strategic choices for the disputing parties are not always 'free'. Circumstances such as previous dealings with the parties concerned, government legislation and financial restrictions could narrow any room for manoeuvre.

- Modes of communication used during conflict: the model assumes that communication between the parties is direct. A number of modern-day disputes, however, take place over large distances, without any resort to face-to-face resolution.

Another objection is that raised by Leung *et al.* (2002). They point to the fact that a dual concern model such as this is focused solely on instrumentality because conflict behaviours are driven by concerns for the outcome of the conflict, either in terms of concern for self or concern for the other. They propose the introduction of harmony into the model. As a goal in itself, rather than a means to an end, harmony can be seen as a value perspective concerned with the relationship between self and the other rather than focusing on concern for self or the other. At the same time, harmony can be an instrumental perspective whereby the focus is on using a conflict-free relationship to achieve a goal.

The proposal by Leung *et al.* (2002) to introduce harmony into the dual concerns model is made in the light of their investigation into conflict avoidance, a feature common in East Asia, and one associated with collectivistic cultures. Conflict avoidance, they argue, can in the end be just as dysfunctional in the long run as competing (or dominating) behaviour. The harm caused by the competing style to relationships may be more apparent and given more attention in conflict management literature, but an avoiding conflict style can cause equal harm to relationships in a more subtle manner by replacing genuine problem-solving with superficial harmony.

These considerations invite an examination of conflict management in Eastern cultures where the conflict styles used are not fully accounted for in dual concerns models.

Before this, however, some attention will be given to one particular element that affects all types of behaviour relating to conflict management.

Culture, emotions and conflict

The culture value systems examined in this book have a profound effect on the ways in which emotions are experienced, expressed and controlled.

Kumar (2004) has investigated the theme of culture and emotions in intercultural negotiations, but his findings are also relevant in general to conflicts between cultures for which a resolution of some kind is needed. He has adopted the definition of emotions as 'high-intensity affective states that stem from the focal actors' ability or inability to achieve their goals' (2004: 96). The nature of the goals pursued, however, varies across cultures according to the value systems of the cultures concerned. The greater the distance between cultures and their value systems, he hypothesises, the more likely it is that perceived dissimilarity will cause negative emotions to emerge, particularly when cross-cultural encounters are ambiguous and unpredictable.

SPOTLIGHT 17.1

Anger when negotiating

US President Clinton was reported to have taken a very aggressive stance during trade negotiations with the Japanese Prime Minister Hosokawa in 1994. The American government was intent on opening up the Japanese market to its country's products and, according to Schoppa (1997: 262), had decided to adopt a 'results-oriented' approach in its negotiations with Japan. In other words, Clinton wanted a 'get-tough-with-Japan' policy, in part to secure his political base at home.

Adam *et al.* (2010) describe how Clinton made a point of using very strong language during the drawn-out encounters with his Japanese counterpart but, in the end, was able to gain only minor concessions. His tough approach yielded few results. The authors contend that the president's behaviour reflected the idea prevalent in the US that showing anger during negotiations could elicit large concessions from the other side. However, this notion was based solely on research into negotiation behaviour in Western countries.

Adam *et al.* (2010) carried out what they consider to be the first investigation of its kind into how the emotions of anger affect negotiations across cultures, particularly between Europeans/Americans and (American) Asians. They used what they call a 'hypothetical negotiation scenario' as well as a computer-mediated negotiation simulation as part of their method. No method involving actual face-to-face interaction was employed. Nonetheless, the investigators found that showing anger, rather than not showing it, produced larger concessions from European/American negotiators, but smaller concessions from Asian and Asian American negotiators.

When, in a further study, the expressions of anger were manipulated in such a way as to be appropriate to cultural norms, the Asian and Asian American negotiators used in the experiment made larger concessions to their angry opponent. According to the investigators, these concessions were as large as those typically made by the European/American negotiators. In contrast, when expressions of anger were manipulated further so that they were inappropriate to cultural norms, European/American negotiators made smaller concessions, as did the Asian and Asian American negotiators.

Kumar (2004) uses the individualist/collectivist cultural dimension to put together the findings of research as to typologies of emotion. 'Ego-focused' emotions such as anger, frustration, pride and guilt are linked to the (non-)fulfilment of individual goals, whereas 'other-focused' emotions such as shame, anxiety and fear are related to the (in-)ability to promote the interdependent self, to show oneself as belonging to the social context. The difference is essentially that ego-focused emotions reflect the need for individuals to show their particular identity, whereas other-focused emotions reflect the need to 'fit in'. Although some research findings do not always confirm this hypothesis (possibly because of contextual factors in the measurement process), the distinction is an appealing one.

As for the behaviour associated with emotions, clear individualist/collectivist differences can be discerned. Individualist, ego-focused emotions can cause individuals to try harder to reach their goals. Collectivist, other-focused emotions can cause individuals to repair the damage done to relations. As Kumar (2004: 102) points out, the association between certain emotions and certain actions has important implications for intercultural interaction, particularly the discovery that 'different negative emotional states have different motivational implications'. In negotiation conflict, for example, those undergoing negative ego-focused feelings will put pressure on their opponents to make concessions, whereas those experiencing other-focused feelings may adjust their expectations to get an agreement. However, in some cultures, it seems that those experiencing other-focused emotions will be very reluctant to take any action. Kumar recounts his own finding that Japanese negotiators do not feel any compulsion to come up with new proposals if the negotiation process has hit a roadblock.

This last observation from Kumar (2004) reflects the first of three points he has to make concerning the extra dynamics which can arise during an encounter between disputants from different cultures:

- People from individualistic cultures are less constrained in their ability to overcome an impasse than negotiators from collectivist cultures. The latter are more likely to share the same perception of a given event and unlike their individualistic counterparts will find it difficult to suggest a way round an obstacle.

- Those from collectivist cultures are unlikely to respond overtly to emotion. Their obligation to maintain group harmony and conform to its ways may not allow them to express their frustration openly or make emotional responses individually. Expressions of strong feelings provoke unseemly attention to a person's individuality and distinctness. They must be countered with attempts to restore personal composure in a way that restores harmony and prevents embarrassment.

- People from collectivistic societies are more sensitive to emotions that arise from a contravention of relational norms than from failure to attain desired goals. If emotional behaviour within such a society is felt to threaten harmony, the person exhibiting that behaviour tends to be regarded as unreliable and untrustworthy. Should a person who is not from the 'in-group' behave in such a way, collectivists may be less reluctant to respond aggressively.

This final point raises the issue of behavioural incompatibility. What if conflict occurs between people from individualistic and collectivistic cultures? Emotions could drive them further apart, with one side attempting to force a resolution to the dispute and the other withdrawing from any interaction. In short, as Kumar (2004: 104) says, 'emotions reflect who we are as individuals and within relationships'. Emotions, in short, can exacerbate the in-group/out-group distinction and make any resolution of the conflict even more difficult.

Nicotera (1993) sees the need for an emotion component to be present in models of conflict styles such as the Thomas–Kilmann model (Thomas and Kilmann, 1974) referred to earlier in Figure 17.1. She suggests the inclusion of 'emotional intent' as a third dimension. This would, she argues, allow the model to take account of the basic mechanisms driving behaviour. Avoidance behaviour, therefore, might not just be to do with low concern for the other, but also because the person concerned is unwilling to deal with the emotional discomfort involved in the conflict. This suggested affective component is examined in Chapter 18.

Ting-Toomey *et al.* (2000) also advocate the inclusion of emotional expression. They recognise that a model such as the Thomas–Kilmann model (Thomas and Kilmann, 1974)

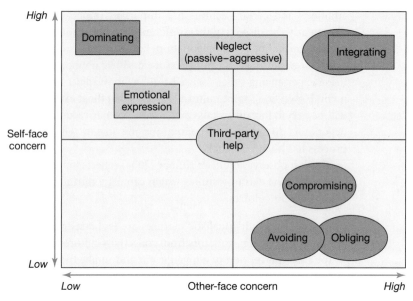

Figure 17.2 **An eight-style conflict grid: an intercultural approach**
Source: Ting-Toomey and Oetzel, 2002: 160.

cannot account for the many subtleties in conflict management, particularly with regard to cultural and ethnic differences in conflict. The model which Ting-Toomey and Oetzel (2002) propose is one based on their critical review of studies in the area of cultural conflict and includes emotional expression as well as neglect and third-party help. The model is given in Figure 17.2.

The inclusion of neglect accounts for responses that the authors call 'passive–aggressive' and which side-step the conflict at hand. Such responses receive an indirect reaction from the others in conflict. Another element proposed is third-party help, using an outsider who is acceptable to both sides to act as mediator. Use of mediation is not to be regarded as a form of avoidance, but rather a reflection of concern for both self and the other. Indeed, its employment is one possible way of overcoming the behavioural incompatibility referred to earlier.

The third-party conflict style is given more attention later on in this concept when the notion of conflict transformation is examined as a radical way of resolving incompatibilities between those in conflict.

Management of conflict

Although a manager is expected to resolve conflicts as part of his general brief, the task is nevertheless a difficult one. When confronted with a conflict he has to make sure that a local dispute does not damage the whole organisation. The importance of conflict management increases in an international context where organisations and people from different cultures are at work. Here, immense complications can arise whose knock-on effect can impinge severely on an organisation's performance. If well managed, however, conflicts can improve relations between partners, customers and employees.

Having said that, attitudes towards conflicts can vary considerably from culture to culture, as can the ways in which conflicts are addressed. These differences relate to:

- the degree to which disagreement is acceptable and therefore the extent to which conflict is tolerated;
- the strategies to be adopted when dealing with conflicts; and
- the moment when the manager needs to intervene and the way he or she intervenes.

The discussion below reflects considerations from Chapter 15 on the issue of distributive and integrative strategies in negotiating. The reader will recall that negotiating in Western management literature is often dealt with in terms of conflict management, that negotiating is essentially seen as a formalised way of resolving a conflict, a carefully managed problem-solving process whereby a number of techniques can be applied such as:

- win–lose: the competitive approach, whereby the goals of one party are achieved at the expense of the other;
- win–win: the co-operative approach, whereby the two parties collaborate to bring about a resolution to the conflict which is of benefit to both.

According to Covey (1989: 206), each of these approaches is 'a philosophy of human interaction', rather than being just a technique. He regards the 'win–lose' approach as an authoritarian one whereby people use their position, power, credentials or some other influence to get their way. The 'opposite' approach – 'lose–win' – is seen as total acquiescence to a situation, capitulation, doing anything to keep the peace. When two competitive – 'win–lose' – personalities interact, the outcome may well be a 'lose–lose' outcome. Both sides become so fixated by the behaviour of the other that all they want is for the other to lose, even if the result is that they lose as well. As Covey sees it, this is adversarial conflict, during which both sides can be annihilated.

When there is no context of competition, the 'win' approach is the most common. The only thing being considered here is the need to accomplish one's own goals. Nothing else is taken into account – others must look out for themselves.

The win–win approach is what Covey (1989) considers to be the healthiest form of interaction. A conflict is resolved with mutually beneficial outcomes for all parties. No one person or side needs to win or 'be right'. However, if a beneficial outcome cannot be achieved for both sides, there is 'no deal' and both can walk away.

As noted earlier, Ting-Toomey (1999) also considers such a win–win approach as being satisfactory, but only if the 'faces' of both parties have been saved in addition to a productive agreement. Unlike Covey, she explicitly addresses the culture-based factors in any intercultural conflict, including the perception of what is effective and what is appropriate in conflict resolution according to the self-construals of the individuals concerned.

Those with an independent sense of self will, she argues, consider a conflict effectively resolved if there has been a frank and open discussion of opinions, clarification of interests and goals reached or compromised – and plans made for avoiding future conflict. The conflict will have been appropriately resolved if the parties concerned have shown themselves to be sensitive towards the circumstances and causes of the conflict. Those with an interdependent sense of self will see the conflict as effectively resolved if faces have been saved and substantive consensus reached. For them, appropriate management involves meeting 'face' need during the conflict and settling any 'face' debts or obligations in the longer term.

When such different perceptions of effective and appropriate resolution are in play, any management of conflict involves each party making a great effort to bear in mind the cultural perspectives and personality factors. Ting-Toomey (1999) suggests a number of skills which can be developed to enhance conflict management, most of them linked to the idea of **mindfulness**. This notion, described by Langer (1990), involves being able to develop new categories (i.e. applying culturally sensitive concepts such as high/low context communication styles) and being open to new information. One particular skill Ting-Toomey (1999: 221) refers to is **mindful reframing**. To manage conflict, those involved must 'learn how to "translate" each other's verbal and non-verbal messages from the context of the other's cultural viewpoint'. Furthermore, mindful reframing means also that those involved need to 'reprioritize their goals after mindfully observing and listening to the viewpoints and expectations of their opponents'.

One strategy which can be followed to facilitate this process is what Ting-Toomey calls **collaborative dialogue**. This is an inquiry process during which the parties try to grasp the cultural and personal elements involved in the conflict by inviting the other involved – either directly or through example – to tell their stories and talk in some way or other about their expectations and issues to do with face. Time and patience are of the essence, as well as the eventual willingness of the parties to suspend their own assumptions regarding the conflict.

Mindfulness as illustrated above can be seen as an approach not just to conflict management but to communicating generally. It involves monitoring the communication process, tailoring messages in line with the expectations of the receiver, finding the right wavelength on which to communicate. As such, mindfulness is relevant to effective and appropriate communication both within and between cultures. Chapter 18, which examines intercultural communicative competence, will examine this and other related skills.

Skills in the area of conflict management can be increased to some extent through developing cognitive awareness as to how other cultures perceive and manage conflict. To this end, this concept will now examine how three countries in the Asia-Pacific region deal with conflict.

Managing conflict in the Asia-Pacific region

The people in the Asia-Pacific region, just as in other regions, often come into conflict in negotiations on issues ranging from the very specific to questions on setting up industries or working conditions. What interests Leung and Tjosvold (1998) is that those involved often have very different views as to how such conflicts should be managed. What seems reasonable to one group can appear strange to another. Methods of conflict management that appear natural and effective to an American can seem totally unproductive and inappropriate to a Japanese. On the other hand, although Koreans usually prefer to deal with conflicts outside the office during social events, Singaporeans will consider a formal discussion more appropriate. When divergent interests cause a conflict in Indonesia, social norms requires that an individual be prepared to take second place and, if necessary, leave aside personal interests and seek a common agreement to maintain harmony.

The contributors to Leung and Tjosvold's (1998) book reveal stereotypes they hold about their own and other countries concerning conflict management. Although conceding that their compatriots do not always manage conflicts effectively, the contributors explain how this is done. Their articles on three particular countries in the Asia-Pacific region – Malaysia, Thailand and Korea – will be summarised below.

Malaysia

Malaysia is composed of several ethnic groups: 61 per cent of the population is Malays (and by constitutional definition Muslim), 27 per cent of Chinese origin and 8 per cent of Indian origin. There are also other Malaysians of European, Middle Eastern, Cambodian, Thai and Vietnamese origin. The presence of so many ethnic groups makes Malaysia a particularly interesting country in which to examine the management of conflict at an intracultural level.

The Muslim Malays are seen as being more pragmatic than Muslims in the Middle East and Pakistan. They have succeeded in maintaining their practice of Islam while being liberal and competitive in their commercial activities. They have managed to create their own economic system, which includes Islamic banks and insurance companies.

In his contribution to the Leung and Tjosvold's book, Mansor (1998) mentions that the Chinese, who have come in large numbers to Malaysia, have developed social structures and values that in a broad sense have become an integral part of Malaysian society. Values such as 'hard work' and 'practical sense' have allowed them to succeed in business, to set up many family companies and keep control of them.

For historical reasons – both commercial and religious (Hinduism existed in Malaysia before Islam) – the Indians have been part of Malaysian culture for many centuries. Their respect for authority and hierarchy is reflected in the status they accord people working in government service and in the professions.

Mansor (1998) goes on to analyse certain core values of the aboriginal Malays that are applicable to Malaysian society generally:

● *concern for face*: this is of importance across all ethnic groups and is related to the notion of dignity, to how people see themselves as well as how they are seen by others;

● *concern for others*: this has to do with generosity, respect, honesty and sincerity, as well as being upright and caring. Malaysians hope these qualities will be reciprocated by their interlocutors.

Expectation of reciprocity brings these two elements together. Reciprocity is seen as a sign of respect towards others; not showing respect amounts to losing face. This in turn is regarded as being worse than physical maltreatment. What is more, no redemption is possible.

Respect for seniority, one of the principles of Confucianism, is another value embraced by all major ethnic groups – aboriginal Malaysian, Indians and Chinese. It plays an important role in the workplace. When a conflict breaks out in a Malaysian context, it is always important to know which of the two parties is older. In some conflicts, a third person – preferably of a certain age – can serve as mediator: when two parties cannot come to an agreement, the only way to mediate, or at least to clarify the issues, is to call in a 'neutral senior', seniority being attributed either in terms of age or social status. That is why the intervention by the 'boss' is considered desirable, even when the conflict is seen as insignificant.

The core values outlined above explain why, for example, subordinates will never confront their superior, even if they do not appreciate his behaviour. Rather than disagreeing publicly, employees will behave in an unco-operative manner and eventually resign themselves to the way their boss behaves. The core values also account for the durability of personal relations: even if a strong divergence of opinion results in conflict, the confidence and loyalty developed between friends and colleagues will predominate. However, despite the importance given to friendship as a basis for business relations, the Malay businessman will still maintain a rational approach to his work.

Thailand

Thailand is relatively homogeneous compared with Malaysia, with 85 per cent of the population speaking Thai and sharing the same culture. According to Roongrengsuke and Chansuthus (1998), the name given to Thailand – 'the land of smiles' – faithfully reflects the social harmony in this country. They point out, however, that behind this collective smile hides a complex social web in which individualism is quite predominant. The result is behaviour that causes much confusion and disagreement among those non-Thais who have tried to do business in the country. Roongrengsuke and Chansuthus (1998: 168) give the following illustration (Spotlight 17.2).

SPOTLIGHT 17.2

A grim silence

A British manager, upset about the continued unauthorised borrowing of equipment between departments, burst in on a meeting being held by his Thai subordinates and loudly berated the responsible person in front of his peers. Unwilling to dignify the insulting behaviour with a response, the Thais remained silent, smiling grimly, until the offending manager left. The incident was followed, however, by a work slowdown and a spate of resignations of key personnel.

When faced with such an unpleasant situation, a Thai smiles. He smiles not only in pleasant situations, but also in stress-filled situations that could be a source of considerable conflict.

When conflicts do erupt between Thais and non-Thais, the causes are often to do with lack of respect for deadlines, reluctance to take responsibility for a task, the imprecise – or tardy – nature of information delivered, the lack of service available, in short a lack of co-operation all round. These difficulties seem to be symptoms of a more profound problem. The Thais are basically more 'relationship-oriented' than 'results-oriented'. Therefore, to get results, non-Thais need to spend a lot of time creating strong and reciprocal relations with their protagonists at all levels of an organisation. These relations will form the network on which the non-Thai will depend if he wishes to realise the objectives he has set himself. The Thais need to create an environment in their place of work that resembles the family circle.

Another aspect in the example (Spotlight 17.2) given by Roongrengsuke and Chansuthus (1998) is the lack of emotion displayed by the Thai head of department. For a Thai to show his feelings in public would be the sign of a lack of self-discipline, which could in turn result in his losing status, prestige and, above all, face. Thais have been educated from childhood to avoid situations where they could lose face, by neutralising their emotions and confining their problems to their private life.

This education reflects the teachings of Buddhism, the national religion of Thailand for more than seven hundred years. Its karmic law (see the notion of karma in Chapter 4) is the origin of practices such as moderation, tolerance and compassion. Any behaviour shown in situations of conflict that does not reflect karmic practices must be carefully avoided. If this is not possible, then a compromise is the preferred option. In fact, the values of the Thai culture encourage harmonious relations and discourage open conflict of any kind. The Thai concept of *'jai yen'* (meaning literally 'cool heart') and one that emanates from Buddhism, is a very efficient mechanism for ensuring this social harmony while preserving an individual's 'face'.

According to Roongrengsuke and Chansuthus (1998), the methods of conflict management – such as those outlined earlier in the Thomas–Kilmann model (Thomas and Kilmann, 1974) – could not be applied in Thailand. One fundamental reason for this is that conflict is rarely if ever regarded as either positive or negative, even by Thais who have taken management studies in Western countries. This accounts for why, if a conflict does arise, a third party – traditionally a respected elder – is called on to mediate.

Korea

Korea, with its very homogeneous population, reflects in a way the differences and similarities between Western and Eastern attitudes to conflict. On the basis of empirical research carried out by Cho and Park (1998: 31), four characteristics emerge with regard to South Korea:

- Koreans prefer a non-competitive (or non-dominating) strategy in face-to-face conflict.
- Koreans prefer resorting to a higher position or authoritarian personality to resolve conflict rather than trying to find an integrative solution.
- Koreans differentiate between in-group and out-group situations when handling conflict. When dealing with out-groups, their strategy is comparable to the competitive approach in Western culture.
- Koreans make efforts in managing conflict beyond those used in face-to-face conflict situations. This can be compared with what Cho and Park call the Chinese 'self-confining' approach.

Mediation and conflict transformation

This brief survey of approaches to conflict in three countries in the Asia-Pacific area highlights the ways in which culture influences the perception and management of conflicting objectives and incompatible ideas. One similarity is the process of mediation by someone in the group concerned whose legitimacy rests on their social status within the group, their knowledge of traditions, as well as their personal characteristics. The mediation will be wide-ranging, encompassing issues for the group as a whole. This type of mediation is often contrasted with that used in Western cultures. Here, the authority of the mediator is seen as being defined more in terms of their expertise and experience, and is frequently exercised within a legal framework. The process of mediation will be tightly focused and not pursue more general issues.

The skills involved in mediation include those already mentioned, particularly the idea of mindful reframing. By mindfully observing and listening to the viewpoints and expectations of the parties in dispute, the mediator can reframe the content and process issues of both parties and transform the whole conflict in terms of the attitudes and behaviour of those involved. If this is done, the conflict itself can be restructured to open up space for co-operation.

This idea of **conflict transformation** is receiving much attention in relation to conflicts between countries. Its advocates see it as a more radical way of dealing with conflict and its long-term effects. The process involves first transforming attitudes, then transforming behaviour, then transforming the actual conflict in question by pinpointing incompatibilities and removing them (Augsburger, 1992).

As Botes (2003) indicates, conflict transformation is more concerned with the underlying causes of conflict and that this involves carrying out transformations at personal, social and structural level. Its proponents see conflict management or even conflict resolution as being more to do with putting out fires, which will come to life again after a short time. Conflict transformation, on the other hand, is a radical process that changes the whole nature of the relationship between warring parties.

Mediation is put forward as a possible instrument of transformation, but third-party intervention is not necessary if the parties involved are prepared to perceive the conflict process in terms of their own assumptions as well as in terms of those with whom they are in contention. This again brings up the notion of *mindfulness* (explained earlier), particularly mindful reframing whereby an integrated long-term perspective can be developed through collaborative dialogue.

This chapter has considered the notion of conflict and the role of culture in the perception and management thereof. Consideration has also been given to some of the skills involved, not only in conflict management but also in the notion of crisis transformation. This transformational approach prepares the ground for the notion of third-culture building, which is dealt with in Chapter 18.

As will be clear from the last part of this concept in particular, attention is moving away from relations between cultures and turning more towards the interaction between individuals involved in intercultural communication. The skills required for handling intercultural conflicts are part and parcel of those skills which individuals need in order to interact effectively and appropriately with people from other cultures, as Chapter 18 will show when examining intercultural communicative competence.

Conclusion

This chapter has examined the way in which cultural values affect how we perceive and deal with conflicts. It presented two models to account for different conflict styles, which both essentially relate to the extent to which people are concerned about themselves and about those with whom they are in conflict. The way in which emotions are experienced and expressed according to cultural values was also explained.

The role of mediation as a way of resolving incompatibilities was considered and examples given of its use in the Asia-Pacific region. The chapter also showed how mediation-type behaviour, particularly 'mindfulness' (taking account of the different cultural perspectives and personalities involved), can promote conflict resolution without the intervention of a third party. In addition, this chapter also put forward the notion of cultural transformation whereby personal, social and structural factors can be transformed through mediation and/or collaborative dialogue.

Points for reflection

1. There are several strategies and methods for managing conflicts and each culture has its own preferences in this respect. The fundamental issue, however, is how each culture perceives the notion of conflict. For some, it can mean confrontation and hostility, for others it means no more than a difference of views. These differences are also reflected in the way people communicate in such situations: certain cultures create a tension, a climate of conflict during a discussion to force a debate on the issue in question.

   How do you perceive the notion of conflict?

2. The concept includes two proposed models (Figures 17.1 and 17.2) which account for different ways of handling conflict.

   What do you consider to be the essential similarities between the two models as well as the essential differences? How do you account for the positioning of the emotional component in Figure 17.2? Do you think this positioning applies to all cultures? If not, what change(s) would you make to the model?

3. When there are incompatible goals, practices and attitudes among the parts of an organisation, conflicts can arise. There are many possible reasons for conflict.

   What, according to you, are the conflict sources within an organisation?

4. It is considered normal for a dynamic company to have conflicts between those working in a team, and for a manager to manage these tense situations and the resulting emotions (such as aggression). However, it is considered preferable not to wait till a conflict degenerates and becomes a real crisis but to intervene beforehand.

   How, in your opinion, can a manager prevent a crisis from happening?

Further reading

Leung, K. and Tjosvold, D. (eds) (1998) *Conflict Management in the Asia Pacific: Assumptions and Approaches in Diverse Cultures*, Singapore: John Wiley. The book is about doing business globally and the chapters address not only the different ways in which nations manage domestic conflict, but also how they manage conflict in international business. The authors of the chapters draw upon a range of disciplines to document the attitudes to conflict in Asia-Pacific countries. This can help business partners, managers and employees to appreciate and prepare for the variety of methods by which people in these countries manage conflict.

References

Adam, H., Shirako, A. and Maddux, W.W. (2010) 'Cultural variance in the interpersonal effects of anger in negotiations', *Psychological Science*, 21: 882–889.

Augsburger, D.W. (1992) *Conflict Mediation across Cultures: Pathways and Patterns*, Louisville, KY: Westminster/John Knox Press.

Blake, R. and Mouton, J. (1964) *The Managerial Grid: the Key to Leadership Excellence*, Houston: Gulf Publishing.

Botes, J. (2003) 'Conflict transformation: a debate over semantics or a crucial shift in the theory and practice of peace and conflict studies?', *The International Journal of Peace Studies*, 8(2): 1–27.

Browaeys, M.-J. and Trompenaars, F. (eds) (2000) *Cases Studies on Cultural Dilemmas*, Breukelen, Netherlands: Nyenrode University Press.

Cho, Y.-H. and Park, H.-H. (1998) 'Conflict management in Korea: the wisdom of dynamic collectivism', in Leung, K. and Tjosvold, D. (eds), *Conflict Management in the Asia Pacific*, Singapore: John Wiley: 13–48.

Covey, S.R. (1989) *The 7 Habits of Highly Effective People*, New York, NY: Free Press.

Hocker, J.L. and Wilmot, W.W. (1985) *Interpersonal Conflict*, Dubuque, Iowa: William C. Brown.

Kumar, E. (2004) 'Culture and emotions in intercultural negotiations', in Gelfand, M.J. and Brett, J.M. (eds), *The Handbook of Negotiation and Culture*, Stanford, CA: Stanford University Press: 95–113.

Langer, E.J. (1990) *Mindfulness*, Cambridge, MA: Da Capo Press.

Leung, K., Koch, P.T. and Lu, L. (2002) 'A dualistic model of harmony and its implications for conflict management in Asia', *Asia Pacific Journal of Management*, 19: 201–220.

Leung, K. and Tjosvold, D. (eds) (1998) *Conflict Management in the Asia Pacific*, Singapore: John Wiley.

Liu, J.H. (2002) *A Cultural Perspective on Inter-group Relations and Social Identity*, Online Readings in Psychology and Culture (Unit 15, Chapter 10). © International Association for Cross-Cultural Psychology, http://orpc.iaccp.org/index.php?option=com_content&view=article&id=87:liu&catid =35:chapter&Itemid=15, accessed 1/9/2010.

Mansor, N. (1998) 'Managing conflict in Malaysia: cultural and economics influences', in Leung, K. and Tjosvold, D. (eds), *Conflict Management in the Asia Pacific*, Singapore: John Wiley: 147–166.

Nicotera, A.M. (1993) 'Beyond two dimensions: a grounded theory model of conflict handling behavior', *Management Communication Quarterly*, 6: 282–306.

Roongrengsuke, R. and Chansuthus, D. (1998) 'Conflict management in Thailand', in Leung, K. and Tjosvold, D. (eds), *Conflict Management in the Asia Pacific*, Singapore: John Wiley: 167–221.

Saphiro, D.L. and Kulik, C.T. (2004) 'Resolving disputes between faceless disputants: new challenges for conflict management theory', in Gelfand, M.J. and Brett, J.M. (eds), *The Handbook of Negotiation and Culture*, Stanford, CA: Stanford Business Books: 177–192.

Schoppa, L.J. (1997) *Bargaining with Japan: What American Pressure Can and Cannot Do*, New York, NY: Columbia University Press.

Thomas, K.W. (1992) 'Conflict and conflict management: reflections and update', *Journal of Organizational Behavior*, 13: 265–274.

Thomas, K.W. and Kilmann, R.H. (1974) *Thomas–Kilmann Conflict Mode Instrument*, Tuxedo, NY: Xicom.

Ting-Toomey, S. (1999) *Communicating Across Cultures*, New York, NY: Guildford.

Ting-Toomey, S. and Oetzel, J.G. (2002) 'Cross-cultural face concerns and conflict styles: current status and future directions', in Gudykunst, W. and Mody, B. (eds), *Handbook of International and Intercultural Communication*, Thousand Oaks, CA: Sage: 127–147.

Ting-Toomey, S., Yee-Jung, K., Shapiro, R., Garcia, W., Wright, T. and Oetzel, J.G. (2000) 'Cultural/ethnic identity salience and conflict styles', *International Journal of Intercultural Relations*, 23: 47–81.

Chapter 17 Activities

Crisis? What crisis?

During a visit to Japan, when the market was particularly bad, I was privileged to be witness to a peculiar incident that can only be explained in terms of cultural differences. The Japanese have a deserved reputation for being very tough negotiators. Our opposition on the occasion seemed to relish their position of strength and pummelled our suggested price down to a very low level indeed. The negotiations carried on for approximately an hour, when the Japanese gave us an ultimatum of either accepting their price or cancelling the deal.

My boss, a grey-haired British individual well-known and respected in the industry, is normally extremely polite when it comes to Japanese customers. The frustration of having a weak negotiating position, coupled with the pressure he felt at having to sell at a price that was hardly profitable, led to an uncharacteristic outburst. For a good fifteen minutes he harangued the Japanese team about their hypocrisy of criticising white South Africans for exploiting blacks, while at the same time buying at prices that would lead to mine closures and the retrenchment of thousands of black workers. It was apparent from his demeanour that my boss was prepared to lose the customer rather than compromise on price.

After he had concluded his monologue, a stunned silence followed. Our agent was aghast at the rudeness displayed and started to apologise in Japanese. He was abruptly cut short by a few curt words from the Japanese lead negotiator.

The customer's team engaged in a whispered consultation. After a short time they asked us and our agent to leave the room, and wait outside in the passage. There we were left to cool our heels for an uncomfortable 15 minutes, with our agent casting reproachful glances at my boss. At the end of the 15 minutes, we were summoned back into the room.

The Japanese team had recovered their composure, and regarded us with perfect inscrutability. Their chief negotiator, in a significant departure from protocol, dispensed with the traditional translator and addressed us in fluent English: 'Johnson, we appreciate your frankness in explaining the situation in South Africa to us for our better understanding. We have very seriously considered what you have said. We have therefore decided not to accept your offer.'

At this point, we felt the tension really growing. We were after all going to lose this customer. Then the Japanese negotiator continued: 'We will however make you another offer. We have decided to offer you an additional fifty cents per tonne above the price that you originally asked for.'

This took a few moments to sink in. After insulting the Japanese, we were going to receive even more than we asked for. We accepted the offer with alacrity and good grace and returned to our hotel to celebrate and marvel at the strange course of events that had unfolded.

Source: adapted from Browaeys and Trompenaars, 2000: case 1.

Questions

1. Why did the Japanese offer a higher price than originally required?
2. What is the conflict-handling style chosen by each party? Give evidence from the case to support your answer.
3. Extract from the text those moments when emotions (do not) appear. Which are typically Japanese or British? Can you explain why?

ACTIVITY 17.2

Restoring cross-border collaboration

Below is an extract from a *Financial Times* article written by Jean-François Manzoni and Jean-Louis Barsoux, entitled 'Untangling alliances and joint ventures'. The article focuses on conflicts in joint ventures, particularly those that have a cross-cultural dimension to them. In this extract, the authors give an illustration of conflict between US and Indian software developers and how it was resolved.

Read the extract then answer the questions that follow.

From bad to worse

In one disintegrating collaboration studied in detail by Anca Metiu of INSEAD, software developers in a US company became very critical of their counterparts as an Indian partner. A dramatic increase in time-to-market pressures had led the US team to neglect the (previously productive) relationship. The Indian developers started grumbling about the lack of guidance, severely delayed feedback on their work and sudden changes in direction. Their junior status in the relationship made them especially sensitive to any perceived lack of respect or consideration. Predictably, the quality of their contributions and practicality of their suggestions suffered.

Oblivious to their own role in the problem, the US developers sensed that their Indian counterparts were not fully engaged. The US developers became increasingly critical of the work coming out of India and started manoeuvring to take control of all the modules of the project. As the ownership of the project shifted to the US, the need to communicate with India decreased, intensifying negative interpretations of the US partner's intentions and encouraging some Indian developers to leave the project. This re-enforced the feeling among US developers that the project needed to be brought completely in-house.

When suspicions mount, collaboration partners often start sticking labels on one another, like unreliable, unreasonable, profiteering or paranoid. In this case, the Indian partner came to be seen as uncommitted, while the US partner was regarded as unhelpful, but also devious in its attempts to re-appropriate the project. Unfortunately, viewing each other through such lenses has a tendency to distort whatever new information is received – even if it happens to be contradictory.

Labels orient people's attention and the way they make sense of data or events. In particular, the US developers focused on any work from India that seemed below par – and systematically brought these lapses to attention. If one Indian developer put a foot wrong, the whole US team knew about it. Moreover, US explanations for inferior work invariably focused on individual factors such as effort or ability, while neglecting external factors entirely. These biases were accentuated by steady turnover on both sides of the project.

More surprising still, reports that the Indian developers were working long hours further re-enforced their poor image. It merely fuelled US suspicions that the Indian developers must be working on parallel projects. In reality, deprived of US input, they were spending inordinate amounts of time trying to figure out the documents, instead of building on the work they had received.

Such information processing biases and stereotypical thinking intensify under conditions of stress – and clearly the US developers were under severe pressure to bring the product to market.

[. . .]

The US company appointed a manager specifically to liaise with the Indian partner. Other measures included increasing personnel exchanges. Thus, a few US engineers visited India to help put faces to names and to get a better feel for the context.

Similarly, several Indian engineers were seconded to the US for overlapping periods of several weeks. The partners also introduced weekly conference calls (at rotating hours) and daily updates.

The relationship between the US business and its Indian partner was restored, but at no small cost. First, several experienced Indian developers had been lost to the project. Then, the US managers had to devote significant time and effort to getting the remaining Indian team members to re-engage with the process. They also had to work hard to make sure that scheduled conference calls were properly attended on the US side. Finally, they were obliged to grant matching holidays to the US developers for each day spent at the partner site.

Ultimately, the product was successfully launched. But a painful and costly process of reconciliation could have been avoided.

 Source: extracts from 'Untangling alliances and joint ventures', FT.com, 16/10/2006 (Manzoni, J.-F. and Barsoux, J.-L.), Copyright © The Financial Times Ltd.

Questions

1. Further on in the same article, the authors propose two ways of addressing the problems they describe: intervention and prevention. The intervention method they suggest is similar to a medical one in that it is concerned with:

   ● examining the symptoms: what are the difficulties exactly in terms of (non-) actions and expectations?

   ● making a diagnosis: how have both parties contributed to creating the situation (e.g. divergent work practices, altered contexts or interests)

   ● deciding on the treatment needed: resolve the issues on principles that both sides consider reasonable. Taking a step back to discuss these principles may well facilitate joint decisions that both understand, accept and implement, including decisions on how to handle future issues as and when they arise.

   Apply this intervention strategy to the account given in the text: determine as best you can what the symptoms were of the conflict, make a diagnosis and show what treatment was decided on.

2. The other way that the authors put forward for addressing the problem is prevention. Part of this approach involves being aware of the mechanisms already described in question 1. However, according to the authors, there is also one overriding principle that must be followed in order to avoid such situations and that is to invest time and effort into the collaboration from the start.

   In order to avoid conflicts, what concrete steps do you consider are essential from the start of such a cross-cultural collaboration, from the negotiating stage through to its implementation?

Chapter 18

Developing intercultural communicative competence

Other chapters in Part Three have put forward factors to do with interacting effectively and appropriately with members of different cultures. This final chapter will address the concept of intercultural communicative competence (ICC) and so bring together the factors referred to earlier and add other features seen as fundamental to the concept.

The definition of ICC by Kim (1991) can serve as a starting point:

> [. . .] the overall internal ability of an individual to manage key challenging features of inter-cultural communication: namely cultural differences and unfamiliarity, intergroup posture, and the accompanying experience of stress.

Such competence is not something people are born with, nor is it something that occurs by chance. People need to have an understanding of the information and actions necessary, the motivation to engage in the communication process, and also the skills to perform effectively and appropriately.

This chapter will examine the main components of ICC, addressing in particular the notions of empathy and uncertainty management, as well as the role of ethics in intercultural communication.

Learning outcomes

After reading this chapter you will:

● Gain further understanding of the difficulties inherent in intercultural communication.

● Be critically aware of the prerequisites of successful intercultural communication.

● Be able to reflect on the knowledge, motivation and skills required to become a competent intercultural communicator.

Concept 18.1   Becoming a competent intercultural communicator

Developing competence in international communication can be hard work. The process requires following many paths of investigation through other cultures, as well as one's own. It involves acquiring, analysing, sifting and interpreting considerable amounts of information from all manner of sources, including oneself. This information is not just to do with facts but also with perceptions and behaviours. Such interpretation demands both an insider's view of the values and beliefs underlying the behaviour of a culture (the so-called **emic** approach), as well as an external view (the **etic** approach) whereby such values and beliefs – and resulting behaviours – can be compared across cultures.

One way of conceptualising this development of ICC is in terms of a progression through the stages outlined in Table 18.1. These stages suggest a logical, linear process towards a high degree of intercultural sensitivity. Bennett (1993: 65) is anxious to emphasise, however, that this model is only a construct of reality, that having mastered these stages, 'the next task . . . is to construct new continua that stretch in directions beyond our current vision'.

Table 18.1 **A developmental model of intercultural sensitivity**

Ethnocentric stages			Ethnorelative stages		
Denial	Defence	Minimisation	Acceptance	Adaptation	Integration
• Isolation • Separation	• Denigration • Superiority • Reversal	• Physical universalism • Transcendent universalism	• Respect for behavioural difference • Respect for value difference	• Empathy • Pluralism	• Contextual evaluation • Constructive marginality

Source: Bennett, 1993: 29.

Nevertheless, those involved in such a process see it much more as a series of trials and errors, a (life-)long chain of experiences during which insights are developed, hypotheses drawn and tested, fresh insights gained and new hypotheses developed that in turn require testing and assessment. The learning is more cyclical in nature, reflecting Kolb's model of experiential learning whereby 'knowledge is created through the transformation of experience' (1984: 38), as seen in Figure 18.1.

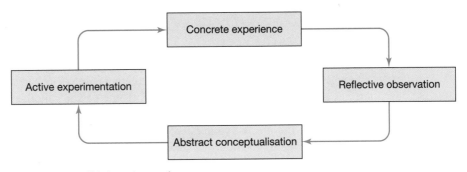

Figure 18.1 **Kolb's learning cycle**
Source: adapted from Kolb, 1984: 33.

Components of intercultural communicative competence (ICC)

By its very nature, communication generally, and intercultural communication in particular, involves people learning from interaction with others, seeking and developing ways of understanding, and responding to those around them. Three psychological components are involved in this process: cognitive, affective and behavioural. These will be reviewed and a fourth (ethical) component will be considered.

Cognitive

This is to do with knowledge about the people from the other culture(s) involved, their values, beliefs and expectations, knowledge of the language they use (even if the person in question is not fluent in that language) and the communicative strategies they tend to employ. Without this knowledge, the communicators in question may well make wrong assumptions, choose an inappropriate communication strategy and/or cause loss of face for themselves or the others. Obtaining the knowledge required has also to do with learning by doing, being open – or **cognitively flexible**, as Gudykunst (1992) calls it, to receiving and processing feedback. This flexibility also entails being able to take a perspective, to differentiate between describing, interpreting and evaluating behaviour. The skill of perspective-taking, according to Gudykunst and Kim (2003), reduces the possibility of attributing incorrect motives to another's behaviour, allowing instead a search for other interpretations, which may well allow a more accurate prediction of how others will behave. Linked to this is the notion of accumulating a repertoire of 'scripts' referred to in Chapter 15 for occasions when guidance is needed for communicative interaction. These scripts, which have proved to be successful in other encounters in achieving certain goals, can be referred to, applied and/or adapted to cope with unfamiliar encounters.

The notion of **ethnocentrism**, explained earlier in Chapter 14, is often referred to in this context, a term meaning that one's own group or culture is at the centre of everything. Being ethnocentric entails the belief that one's own culture is the most important and that other cultures are judged in relation to one's own. Although ethnocentrism may be seen as an inherent part of any culture's make-up, the degree to which it colours an individual's view of other cultures can vary considerably. The more willing and able a person is to move beyond this ethnocentrism, the more capable that person is of assimilating the knowledge required to be a competent intercultural communicator.

Affective

This component relates to the feelings, needs and general motivation of an individual with regard to interacting with others from different cultures. If fears and prejudices cloud feelings about communicating with another, then a person's motivation will be negative and they may tend to avoid interaction, even though they have the knowledge and skills to communicate. The affective component is about applying the cognitive elements described above, having the motivation to interact with other cultures and the confidence to deal with any anxiety or stress involved in dealing with those from another culture.

Indeed, managing **anxiety and uncertainty** is the fundamental ability of an effective communicator (Gudykunst, 2002). According to his anxiety and uncertainty management theory, there is a direct link between the anxiety and uncertainty of the communicators and the extent to which communicators experience their interaction as effective. An individual in a high state of anxiety tends to rely on simplistic information (by, for example, making excessive use of stereotypes) and, therefore, cannot communicate effectively. In a high state of uncertainty, the person may be unable to explain or predict the attitudes, behaviour or feelings of others. If, on the other hand, a person feels little anxiety, he may not be motivated to communicate and, if uncertainty is low, may feel confident enough to predict too eagerly – and inaccurately – the behaviour of others. Those, therefore, who engage in intercultural communication must consciously exercise anxiety and uncertainty management.

According to Gudykunst (2002), one way to reduce anxiety and uncertainty is to minimise misunderstandings through effective communication. This involves employing **mindfulness**, a notion referred to in Chapter 17 when conflict management was being discussed. For Gudykunst, mindfulness entails people thinking about their communication and continually working at changing what they do to become more effective. Langer (1990), who used the term to encapsulate a number of ways of thinking and behaving prevalent in Eastern cultures, identifies a number of characteristics:

- *Making more categories and distinctions when categorising others.* As already noted, categorising is a natural behaviour; effective intercultural communicators use more specific sub-categories and more personalised information to make predictions.
- *Being aware of more than one perspective.* People cannot assume that their interlocutors interpret their messages the same way as they intended.
- *Focusing on the process of communication as it is happening* – people being mindful of their own behaviour as well as the situation.

One aspect of being mindful involves **empathy**, defined by Casse (1981: 139) as:

> [...] the ability to see and understand how other people construct reality, or more specifically how they perceive, discover and invent the inner and outer worlds.

In a sense, empathy and perspective-taking ability are concepts that overlap: empathy has more to do with the emotional capacity to understand another's situation, while the latter is more to do with the cognitive skill of seeing the world from another's perspective.

When interacting with others, people are not only listening to what others say, but also trying to work out what they are actually feeling and thinking. People naturally tend to think that what is going on in someone else's mind is the same as what is going on in theirs. However, the ability to put oneself in the shoes of the other, to try and discern the thoughts behind their words and actions is a major factor in ICC (Spotlight 18.1).

SPOTLIGHT 18.1

Empathic listening

Successful communication involves the parties listening actively and carefully to make sure they understand what the other person is meaning. This can be difficult because people are too busy planning a response to give active consideration to what the other is saying.

Klopf (1988) refers to active listening as empathic listening. This involves:

- Paraphrasing: rewording what the other person has said.
- Reflecting feelings: relating back to the other person those feelings that one thinks the other is experiencing.
- Reflecting meanings: restating what the other says to confirm its meaning.
- Summarising: restating briefly the main points of the other person's message.

Having a high degree of empathy means that a person has attained a high degree of awareness. Hanvey's (1987) proposed levels of awareness, as given in Table 18.2 in adapted form, highlights the levels of awareness that can be attained during the competence development process. Here again, be wary of the model's implication that someone can move logically from one level to another. Hanvey refers to four such levels of awareness,

Table 18.2 **Levels of awareness**

Level	Information	Mode	Interpretation
Level I	Awareness of superficial or visible cultural traits – stereotypes	Tourism, textbooks	Unbelievable, i.e. exotic bizarre
Level II	Awareness of significant and subtle cultural traits that contrast markedly with one's own	Culture conflict situations	Unbelievable, i.e. frustrating irrational
Level III	Awareness of significant and subtle cultural traits that contrast markedly with one's own	Intellectual analysis	Believable, cognitively
Level IV	Awareness of how another culture feels from the standpoint of the insider	Cultural immersion: living the culture	Believable because of subjective familiarity

Source: Hanvey, 1987: 20.

arguing that 'believability' is necessary if one group or individual is to accept the other. This believability can be achieved only at levels III and IV.

Reaching level IV, however, can be a lifetime's work. It may be possible for an 'expat' on a long assignment who becomes immersed in the culture where he is working to attain this degree of awareness. But what about a global manager who has to deal with a number of cultures? This problem was addressed earlier in Chapter 15. Can such a manager develop some of the aspects of awareness belonging to level IV and so allow the manager, when necessary, to empathise with counterparts from another culture?

Hanvey (1987) refers to the very different nature of today's society: unlike just a generation ago, more and more of its members are engaged in all sorts of interaction across the world. It has become much more outward-looking, more ready for change, more mobile, more participative, more interdependent and has developed a high empathic capacity. In his terms, this means being able to imagine oneself in another role within the context of one's own culture. He suggests that such a society can go a step further and go beyond empathy by developing the capacity for **transspection**. This involves trying to share the beliefs, assumptions and feelings of the other, not within the context of one's own culture, but within the context of the other.

SPOTLIGHT 18.2

Scanning the context

In her article on 'Cultivating Intercultural Competence',[1] Janet Bennett gives an account of an encounter a friend of hers had with a taxi-driver: The friend had just landed in Montgomery, Alabama, USA. Her flight had been delayed and her luggage had not arrived with her. She got into a taxi, ready to 'release her pent-up frustrations'. But then she considered the situation she was in, or, as the writer expresses it, she 'scanned her context'.

A driver identity card on the visor revealed a Moslem name, while prayer beads dangled from the mirror. His accent suggested Africa to her, and instead of sharing her litany of travel travails, she said it had been a fine day, and by the way, where was he from?

'I am from Africa', he responded.

'Northern Africa?' she asked.

'Why yes!' he said.

'From Sudan?' she asked.

And soon they were gently discussing the tragic events in Darfur that had led him to seek refuge in the United States. It occurred to her that she had nearly whined about lost luggage to a man whose family had been murdered before his eyes only months earlier.

[1] Bennett, J., 2009: 121.

Behavioural

This third component has to do with how the knowledge and affective components described above are enacted, the actual *performance* of the behaviour felt to be effective and appropriate in the communication context. As Spitzberg (2000) sees it, competence in intercultural communication is not just a set of skilled behaviours, since any given behaviour may be seen as competent in one context, but incompetent in another. In other words, the competence does not lie in the behaviour itself but in the 'social evaluation of behaviour'. According to Spitzberg (2000: 347) this evaluation is made in terms of:

- Appropriacy. Does the behaviour meet the norms and expectations of the relationship?
- Effectiveness. Does the behaviour achieve 'valued goals or rewards relative to costs and alternatives'?

A person's behaviour that is considered to be competent may have been accidentally produced. If reproduced in a different context it may well be poorly evaluated. Equally, if the person has no clear and appropriate rationale behind the behaviour, the result might well be hit or miss, so the behaviour cannot be considered as competent. In short, Spitzberg maintains that communicative behaviour is only really skilled when it can be repeated and can achieve a certain goal.

The many facets of intercultural communication behaviour have already been identified and commented on in Part Three. Worth mentioning again, however, are the following points:

- The ability to effectively communicate: again, the idea that the cognitive and affective skills referred to earlier can be used effectively and appropriately. This includes entering into meaningful dialogue, initiating interaction, dealing with misunderstandings and interpersonal conflict and using different communication styles. These styles can relate, in particular, to an individual's position and role in the foreign culture, e.g. the expected behaviour in terms of their occupation and sex. The appropriate and effective use of a nonverbal repertoire must also be mentioned.
- The ability to establish meaningful relationships (Hammer *et al.*, 1978). This has to do with being able to develop and maintain interpersonal relationships with those from other cultures. Such relationships require feelings to be accurately understood and any kind of collaboration to be effective and mutually satisfying. Empathy plays a vital role generally.

All these elements are an integral part of an individual's communication behaviour in dealing effectively and efficiently with the challenges of intercultural communication. However, a fourth component needs to be addressed, which concerns the way ethical issues are to be handled in one's dealings with other cultures and their members.

The ethical component

In our examination of intercultural communicative competence, we have already discussed the need to take a certain distance from one's own culture, to reduce one's ethnocentrism and be open to the norms and values of the culture whose representatives are being addressed. When addressing ethical values in the context of multicultural diversity, Chapter 12 highlighted the difficulty of maintaining that distance, of avoiding making implicit judgements about the ethicality of values which differ from our own. Although Jackson (2011) suggests not just focusing on any differences but on trying to find out why the ethicality of a culture may be different from our own, does this mean a competent cross-cultural communicator should withhold criticism of practices in another culture which are not only based on differing values but on values which (s)he finds unacceptable? Is it possible to make moral judgements across cultures while being aware that moral principles of behaviour can be culture-bound and may vary across cultures.

Gudykunst and Kim (2003) make a distinction between two approaches to this issue: an analytical one (which involves being committed to a specific view of what morality is) and a normative one (i.e. knowing what should be done). The analytical approach does not allow ethical judgements whereas the normative approach does. Moreover, they argue, a distinction can be made between making moral judgements on the behaviour itself and on the person(s) displaying the behaviour.

This normative approach can be applied to the question of making payments to company officials to ensure, for example, that a tender is accepted. This action or practice may well be regarded as unacceptable if the normative approach is taken. The people pursuing this practice, however, will not necessarily be 'blamed' since such an action is regarded as acceptable in the culture concerned. These people have not necessarily wandered off their own moral path: they may themselves regard their involvement in the payment of gratuities as morally wrong, but realise that this is a 'necessary evil' since those expecting gratuities do not know any better.

The conclusion made by Gudykunst and Kim (2003) is that people withhold any ethical judgements when interacting with those living in another culture until they have clearly described the behaviour and examined various interpretations. And this necessarily involves improving their ability to communicate effectively. It can be argued, therefore, that dealing with intercultural moral conflicts is a necessary – if difficult – test of intercultural communicative competence.

When examining ethical aspects of interaction with other cultures, Gudykunst and Kim (2003) quote Barnlund (1980), who states that the cross-cultural arena is an 'ethical void'. In such an environment, he maintains, there is a 'meta-ethic' lacking, one that can be used or applied when ethical issues are being dealt with by people from different cultures. When making ethical judgements, people either use their own cultural standards as a framework of reference or those of the other culture. This means, however, that the ethical premises of one culture are necessarily subordinated to those of another. There is no meta-ethic to embrace both sets of premises.

There have been attempts to outline such a meta-ethic. Martin et al. (2002), for example, use three principles to define a meta-ethic:

- The humanness principle, whereby peace is at the centre: respect for all, empathy and identification with others.

- The dialogic principle, which stresses the centrality of human relationships and the support people must give each other. It includes the principle of inclusion and mutual equality.

- The principle of speaking 'with' and 'to' instead of 'for' and 'about,' which usually reinforces oppression. Learning to understand oneself and others when engaging with others is a key principle. Engaging in a dialogue of any nature is being able to listen carefully as well as speaking.

These principles were touched upon earlier in Chapter 12 when the challenges of hyper-cultural competence were being discussed, particularly the notion of 'active dialogue' and 'discursive engagement'.

A third culture?

Building blocks of this nature could, it is argued, be created through collaboration between the parties involved in the intercultural communication process. Casrnir (1999) proposes that building a third culture would allow a shared system of values or ethics to emerge – addressed earlier in this book. Cross-cultural encounters create a context where those involved are not only trying to achieve outcomes desired by all those involved, but also to develop standards and methods for achieving those outcomes. The relationship developed during these encounters could enable a process by which mutuality evolves from which a third culture emerges – a framework designed by all those involved that ensures an enduring adaptation and survival. Value systems shared by the participants could emerge, as well as continuing personal relationships and an increasing interdependence. The third-culture building model he proposes represents:

> [. . .] a co-operative, communication, community building process which does not include the need for coercion by anyone, including outsiders.
>
> Casrnir, 1999: 111

The building process he describes takes account of the dynamic, changing, developing nature of the communication event. Figure 18.2 is the model devised by Casrnir to visualise the process.

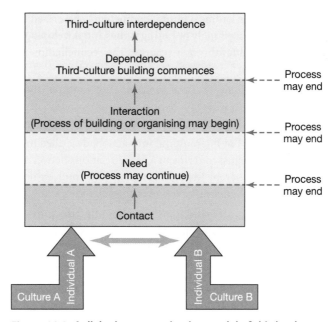

Figure 18.2 A dialogic communication model of third-culture building

Source: Casrnir, 1999: 109.

A model such as this can account for the evolutionary nature of intercultural interaction. Rather than focus on culture A and B, using etic categories, i.e. generalisations about larger entities, the emphasis should be on what actually happens when individuals 'representing' these cultures come together.

As Figure 18.2 indicates, any initial contact between the people involved may not progress because of many possible reasons, including fear, lack of time, or simply lack of skills for dealing with 'outsiders'. If, however, a mutual need is perceived, communication may continue, but those involved may well stick to their own rules of engagement and cultural values for a number of reasons (anger towards the other participants, fear of the unfamiliar, reluctance to take risks, missing interactional skills). Eventually, however, as the interaction continues, the people concerned enter into deeper dialogue and realise that some sort of change is needed to encourage the developing relationship, which could be of benefit to all concerned. It is here that a process of building or organising may well begin. Even here, though, the process may come to a halt when it eventually becomes clear to some or all those involved that a commitment to change is not really necessary, or that a meeting of minds is not possible. However, if the dialogue continues, the participants may show a dependence on each other to reach a goal that is mutually beneficial. If that happens, then the people can start developing the elements of a third culture, including their joint goals, interactional rules and their roles in the process. The final phase is based on interdependence: the groups and the individuals involved accept that cultural development depends on building mutual trust while constructing a third culture. As they are doing this, they need to develop their dialogic skills, these being a requisite for building the culture and maintaining it.

Casrnir's emphasis on the dialogic nature of third-culture building reflects ideas discussed elsewhere in this book:

- The notion of transcultural competence, described in Chapter 5, involves being able to reconcile seemingly opposing values and developing a dynamic equilibrium, an integration of values through synergy. The reconciliation approach opens the door to a third dimension.

- The possibility of 'crossvergence' of cultures through globalisation, mentioned in Chapter 12, whereby 'hybrid forms of societies, organisations, values and institutions' (Jackson, 2011: 33) could be considered.

- The nature of intercultural interaction, described in Chapter 13. Such interaction is not to be seen just in terms of a set of relations between the cultures, but also as a dynamic process whereby the cultures are defined both through their own characteristics as well as through their interaction with each other.

- The notion of crisis transformation, described in Chapter 17, has to do with coming to terms with the underlying causes of cross-cultural conflict through collaborative dialogue, thereby enabling transformations to occur at personal, social and structural levels.

These ideas, including Casrnir's, focus less on static comparisons between cultures and more on dynamic interaction between individuals from different cultures; less on the categorisations of cultures and more on the process of cultural transformation among people in a collaborative dialogue. People coming together, entering into dialogue and creating a togetherness form the basis of Casrnir's concept of building a third culture. Rather than focusing on the dichotomies that come from the distinction between 'self' and 'other', he argues, people can build something that is eventually 'theirs':

> [. . .] something which sooner or later becomes part of the changes which help new or changed cultures and their societal structures to emerge from it. To put it in other words, such changes can help assure our survival as humans.
>
> Casrnir, 1999: 113

This exhortation is perhaps a suitable way of rounding off the discussion of third-culture building as well as of completing the final concept of this book. It also indicates the direction of much research into intercultural communication, one that fully recognises the dynamic nature of all intercultural encounters.

Conclusion

Chapter 18 has examined the main elements of intercultural communicative competence (ICC). Developing ICC involves not only a lot of hard work on the cognitive and affective level, but also being able to perform appropriately and effectively. This chapter has highlighted the importance of (self-)reflection and cognitive flexibility, of being able to manage anxiety and uncertainty, and the need to develop empathy and mindfulness. It has also raised the question of dealing with intercultural moral conflicts, where all ICC skills are put to the test.

The final section has focused on the concept of building a third culture whereby those interacting apply their ICC skills in such a way that they can develop a mutually beneficial interdependence. This notion echoes similar ideas referred to earlier in this book, including reconciliation between seemingly opposing values, the dynamic nature of interaction and the notion of crisis transformation through mediation and/or collaborative dialogue.

Points for reflection

1. Empathy is put forward in the concept as a component of intercultural communication competence.

   To what extent do you think similarity among individuals is necessary to achieve empathy?

2. Casrnir proposes a model of third-culture building to account for the evolutionary nature of intercultural dialogue.

   What role do you think the many studies on cultural dimensions can play in the application of this model? Is it possible to anticipate how, for example, the inter-action could evolve between individuals from a 'low-context' culture and individuals from a 'high-context' culture?

3. If you were asked to design a training programme whose goal was to develop com-petence in intercultural communication, which of these components would you include? Explain your choice.

- Lectures with discussion on cross-cultural differences.
- Case studies dealing with (mis)communication.
- Simulations and role-plays (e.g. meetings or negotiations with participants from different cultures).
- Self-assessment instruments (e.g. questionnaires that allow participants to evaluate their skills in intercultural communication).

What other elements would you incorporate into an ICC development programme – and why?

4. If you incorporated an element on ethics into such a programme, what would it look like and what would be its main objective?

Further reading

Deardorff, D.K. (ed.) (2009) *The Sage Handbook of Intercultural Competence*, Thousand Oaks, CA: Sage. This handbook offers a number of articles written by a number of experts from around the world who work in a variety of fields, including communication, psychology, social work and conflict studies. The articles all address the question of intercultural competence in terms of both appropriate and effective behaviour, in intercultural situations.

Gudykunst, W.B. and Mody, B. (eds) (2001) *Handbook of International and Intercultural Communication,* 2nd edition, Thousand Oaks, CA: Sage Thousand Oaks, CA: Sage. The book gives a clear overview of the many aspects of this field. The authors examine cross-cultural communication, intercultural communication, international communication and development communication. It describes theories in each of these areas before dealing with detailed elements and current issues.

References

Barnlund, D. (1980) 'The cross-cultural arena: An ethical void', in Asuncion-Lande (ed.), *Ethical Perspectives and Critical Issues in Intercultural Communication*, Falls Church, VA: Speech Communication Association.

Bennett, J.M. (2009) 'Cultivating Intercultural Competence – a Process Perspective', in Deardorff, D.K. (ed.), *The Sage Handbook of Intercultural Competence*, Thousand Oaks CA: Sage: 121–140.

Bennett, M.J. (1993) 'Towards Ethnorelativism: A developmental model of intercultural sensitivity', in Paige, R.M. (ed.), *Education for the Intercultural Experience*, 2nd edition, Yarmouth, ME: Intercultural Press: 21–71.

Browaeys, M.-J. and Trompenaars, F. (eds) (2000) *Cases Studies on Cultural Dilemmas*, Breukelen, Netherlands: Nyenrode University Press.

Casrnir, F.L. (1999) 'Foundations for the study of intercultural communication based on a third-culture model', *International Journal of Intercultural Relations*, 23(1): 91–116.

Casse, P. (1981) *Training for the Cross-Cultural Mind*, 2nd edition, Washington, DC: SIETAR.

Gudykunst, W.B. (1992) 'Being perceived as a competent communicator', in Gudykunst, W.B. and Kim, Y.Y. (eds), *Readings on Communicating with Strangers*, New York, NY: McGraw-Hill: 382–392.

Gudykunst, W.B. (2002) 'Intercultural communication theories', in Gudykunst, W.B. and Mody, B. (eds), *Handbook of International and Intercultural Communication*, 2nd edition, Thousand Oaks, CA: Sage: 183–205.

Gudykunst, W.B. and Kim, Y.Y. (2003) *Communicating with Strangers*, 4th edition, New York, NY: McGraw-Hill.

Hammer, M., Gudykunst, W. and Wiseman, R. (1978) 'Dimensions of intercultural effectiveness', *International Journal of Intercultural Relations*, 2(Winter): 382–393.

Hanvey, R.G. (1987) 'Cross-cultural awareness', in Luce, L.F. and Smith, E.C. (eds), *Toward Internationalism*, 2nd edition, Cambridge, MA: Newbury House: 13–23.

Jackson, T. (2011) *International Management Ethics: a Critical, Cross-cultural Perspective*, Cambridge, UK: Cambridge University Press.

Kim, Y.Y. (1991) 'Intercultural communicative competence', in Ting-Toomey, S. and Korzenny, F. (eds), *Cross-cultural Interpersonal Communication*, Thousand Oaks, CA: Sage: 259–275.

Klopf, D.W. (1988) *Intercultural Encounters: the Fundamentals of Intercultural Communication*, Eaglewood, CO: Morton.

Kolb, D.A. (1984) *Experiential Learning: Experience as the Source of Learning and Development*, Englewood Cliffs, NJ: Prentice-Hall.

Langer, E.J. (1990) *Mindfulness*, Cambridge, MA: Da Capo.

Martin, J.N., Flores, L. and Nakayama, T.K. (2002) 'Ethical Issues in Intercultural Communication', in Martin, J.N., Flores, L. and Nakayama, T.K. (eds), *Reading in Intercultural Communication Experiences and Contexts*, 2nd edition, Boston: McGraw-Hill: 375–387.

Spitzberg, B.H. (2000) 'A model of intercultural communication competence', in Samovar, L. and Porter, R. (eds), *Intercultural Communication: a Reader*, 9th edition, Belmont, CA: Wadsworth: 375–387.

ACTIVITY 18.1

Identifying assumptions

Casse (1981) developed an exercise to encourage his students to develop their empathic skills. He asked them to listen to a recording of a dialogue between John Miller (a US project manager in Kenya), and Costa Maniatis (a Greek agronomist involved in the same project managed by Miller, his boss). Below is a transcript of the dialogue and comments from the narrator.

Costa Maniatis: (knocking on door) Did you call me Mr Miller?

John Miller: Ah, Costa, yes . . . come in. (door shuts) It is about the report required by the Ministry of Agriculture. How long will it take you to finish it?

CM: (surprised) I don't know, Mr Miller . . . umm . . . Do you think . . . ?

JM: No, Costa, no! You are in the best position to analyse time requirements.

CM: Well, let's say 10 days.

JM: Ten days . . . OK . . . let's say 15 – alright? Then . . . it is agreed you will do it in 15 days.

CM: Yes, Mr Miller.

Narrator: In fact, the report needed 30 days of regular work. So the Greek worked day and night, but at the end of 15 days he still needed one more day's work. The following dialogue took place 15 days later in Costa Maniatis' office:

JM: Well, Costa, where is the report?

CM: It will be ready tomorrow.

JM: But we agreed it would be ready today.

Narrator: From that day, the relationship between Costa Maniatis and Miller became more and more difficult, and three months later, Costa asked for his transfer to another project. Why did Maniatis leave?

To find an answer to this last question, the students were then asked to identify as many cultural assumptions as possible, assumptions underlying the words of Miller and Maniatis. These assumptions were to be based on the cultural frame of each protagonist, not of the students themselves. Which assumptions do you consider to be the most appropriate? **Write down the assumptions against each part of the dialogue given in the table below. You can give several answers against each.**

To help you determine the cultural profile of Miller and Maniatis, look at the following websites:

- http://international-business-center.com/geert-hofstede/index.shtml
- www.kwintessential.co.uk/intercultural-business-communication/tool.php

The first assumptions are suggested in Table 18.3.

Table 18.3

Who said	What	Meaning what? (cultural assumption)
Miller	How long will it take you to finish this?	I'm asking him to participate.
Maniatis	I do not know. Do you think . . . ?	His behaviour makes no sense. He is the boss; why doesn't he tell me? I'm going to ask for instructions.
Miller	You are in the best position to analyse time requirements.	
Maniatis	Ten days.	
Miller	Take fifteen. It is agreed you will do it in fifteen days.	
Maniatis	Yes, Mr Miller	
Narrator: In fact, the report needed 30 days of regular work, so the Greek worked day and night, but at the end of the fifteenth day, he still needed one more day's work.		
Miller	Where is the report?	
Maniatis	It will be ready tomorrow.	
Miller	But we had agreed it would be ready today.	
Miller	(The American is surprised)	
Maniatis	(The Greek is angry)	

Source: adapted from Casse, 1981: 140–141.

Table 18.4 gives the assumptions suggested by Casse (1981). Compare his answers with yours and tick if you gave a correct assumption.

Table 18.4

Who said	What	Meaning what? (cultural assumptions)	Tick here if correct
Miller	How long will it take you to finish the report?	(1) Employees should be involved in the decision-making process.	
		(2) Employees are accountable.	
		(3) Planning is important.	
Maniatis	I do not know.	(4) The question does not make any sense. The manager is accountable. To recognise that one does not know is OK.	
		(5) It is the responsibility of the manager to tell the employee what to do and how.	
Maniatis	Do you think . . . ?	(6) The manager is the one who is supposed to know. He should provide some instructions to the employee.	
Miller	No, Costa . . .	(7) The employee should take responsibility.	
Miller	You are in the best position to analyse time.	(8) Delegation of responsibility to those who know.	
		(9) It is the role of the manager to press the team member to take responsibility for his/her own actions.	
Maniatis	Well, 10 days.	(10) Since the boss insists, an answer has to be given. After all, he is the 'authority'.	
Miller	Ten days OK . . .	(11) The problem has to be assessed. In this case, it is the team member's lack of ability to estimate time (problem orientation).	
Miller	Take 15. It is agreed you will do it in 15 days.	(12) A contract is offered.	
		(13) Instructions are received.	
Maniatis	Yes . . .		
Miller	Where is the report?	(14) Part of a manager's role is to make sure that the contract is fulfilled.	
Maniatis	It will be ready tomorrow.	(15) Today or tomorrow is all right. Besides, the report needed 30 days and it will be done in 16.	
Miller	But we had agreed that it would be ready today!	(16) Importance of deadlines. A manager should teach his employees to respect deadlines.	
Maniatis		(17) The wrong instructions were given, so the boss is incompetent.	
		(18) The boss is insensitive. (He does not appreciate that the job was done in 16 days instead of 30.)	
		(19) One cannot work with someone who is incompetent and insensitive.	
		(20) No further discussion with the boss is possible. The only option left is to leave.	

Source: Casse (1981).

The key put forward by Casse is given in Table 18.5. Add up the ticks according to your empathy for the two protagonists.

Table 18.5 **Calculate your score**

	Number of correct assumptions given per protagonist
Empathy 1 (for Miller) = 1 – 2 – 3 – 7 – 8 – 9 – 11 – 12 –	
14 – 16	
Empathy 2 (for Maniatis) = 4 – 5 – 6 – 10 – 13 – 15 – 17 –	
18 – 19 – 20	
Total (Empathy 1 + 2) = 20	

Casse then illuminates the score, as in Table 18.6.

Table 18.6 **Interpret your score**

Empathy 1 (for Miller)
• A score between 7 and 10 shows that you understand some of the characteristics of US culture (managerial) quite well.
• A score of 4–6 shows an average empathic ability regarding US managerial culture.
• A score of 0–3 indicates a lack of empathic ability regarding US managerial culture.
Empathy 2 (for Maniatis)
• A score of 7–10 shows a good understanding of the Greek culture.
• A score of 4–6 shows an average empathic ability (could be improved).
• A score of 0–3 shows a need to improve one's own empathic ability.
Overall empathic ability
• A score of 14–20 shows you are able to put yourself into someone else's shoes.
• A score of 9–13 means your empathic ability could be improved.
• A score of 0–8 indicates a lack of empathic ability.

Source: Casse, 1981: 144–145.

When you have finished scoring your results, discuss with your colleagues the results and the validity of the exercise.

ACTIVITY 18.2

Resolving a dilemma: should I take the apartment?

Read the following account of an incident during a business trip to London. In the questions which follow you will be asked to put yourself in the role of the team leader and decide what you would do to resolve the dilemma posed in the account.

My team and I were in London for a short stay because of business we were conducting for a client of ours based in the UK.

As a part of the contract with our client, my team was to be reimbursed for our living expenses in London. Our contract, however, specified that we needed to make every 'reasonable effort' to sign a short-term lease (13 weeks) and reduce costs related to this expense. The contract did, however, have a clause allocating sufficient funding for us to sign a lease for 26 weeks if necessary.

To assist us in finding housing, my Indian colleague offered to contact a 'friend'. This 'friend' failed to find us a short-term lease, and was only able to find us an apartment with a 26-week lease. Additionally, the lease cost $8,880 in total, the exact maximum amount of money the client had allotted us for housing expenses. My Indian colleague was very happy with the apartment and suggested we sign a lease form 'immediately'.

However, according to information I had received from other professionals who had travelled to London, it should have been possible to find a short-term lease for far less money. For this reason, I suspected that the apartment transaction might be taking advantage of my client.

My dilemma was whether I should risk insulting my Indian colleague by not accepting the apartment arranged by his 'friend' because I believed that the transaction did not seem 'fair'. If I failed to do this, it seemed likely that my client would question the legitimacy of such an odd transaction. I believed this could cause my own integrity to be put into doubt. Additionally, even if their auditors did not notice the 'coincidental' nature of the transaction, I could not help but feel it would be unethical if we did not abide by the contract and make 'every reasonable effort' to reduce costs.

Source: adapted from Browaeys and Trompenaars, 2000: case 8.

Questions

1. If you were in the author's situation, what would you do? Explain why.

2. How would you interpret the notion of 'fairness' with regard to the transaction being considered?

3. Analyse the dilemma described using both the analytical approach and the normative one suggested by Gudykunst and Kim which are described in the subsection 'The ethical component'.

Part Three Final activity A3.1

Simulation: negotiating internationally

This simulation is best performed with the assistance of an instructor who can explain the exact procedure and any time limitations involved. However, the material can be adapted and/or extended in accordance with the reader's learning situation.

The value of this simulation – and any other simulation of its kind – depends on:

- the effort put into its preparation;
- the ability of team members to embrace the roles they are playing;
- the extent to which the observers are able to detect and describe behaviours that help or hinder effective interaction.

You are encouraged to apply, in a manner appropriate to the situation, those skills discussed in Part Three, particularly with regard to negotiating, conflict management and intercultural communicative competence generally. These factors should also form the framework for a post-simulation discussion, between the participants and observers, on the effectiveness of the interaction. Other concepts in the book could also prove to be relevant.

Learning objectives

After you have either performed the simulation and discussed the comments of the observers, or observed the simulation and discussed your comments with the performers, you should:

- Be more aware of the skills required to interact effectively, particularly with individuals from other cultures.
- Have a clearer insight into what it takes to be an effective team-member in such a situation.
- Have a deeper awareness of what intercultural communicative competence entails.

YOUR ASSIGNMENT

You will be taking part in a simulation of a meeting involving two teams of department heads within a company that was formed as the result of a very recent merger between two companies from different continents. The aim of the meeting is to decide on company policy and work out how best to implement the decisions made.

Some of you will be playing a role as department head in one or other of the teams; some of you will be acting as observers. If you are playing a role in the meeting, you are expected to identify with the points of view given in your brief. These should be supplemented during a preparatory meeting by other information and opinions that support your team brief. This meeting will allow the team to develop its standpoints and the arguments needed to support them, as well as to devise *negotiating tactics*. If you are observing, you will be expected to report your observations to the teams on how the preparation for the meeting went as well as the actual simulation. Your report will be based on the questions given in your own brief.

All those involved in the simulation should read the introduction below. The teams appointed to participate in the meeting should then study their particular brief before preparing for the meeting; those appointed to observe should read their own brief to determine exactly what their task involves.

Introduction

MHC is a North American manufacturer of household equipment. It has recently merged with another production company. This company is referred to below as MHC Europe, although your instructor may decide that another company, such as MHC India or MHC Australia is more appropriate to your learning needs.

- *MHC America* would prefer to keep control over the production of all products sold in the US, because of the specific characteristics of the home market. In this respect, the company opposes a policy drawn up by MHC Europe to market its products globally.

- *MHC Europe* believes in developing an international image for MHC in Europe. It argues that because the MHC brand has an international appeal, the company must adopt a global marketing approach, particularly on account of the financial benefits this could bring. It proposes that MHC America should only be involved with the production of kitchen equipment and that MHC Europe should take care of larger household products such as washing machines.

The meeting

MHC Europe has organised a meeting to discuss future company policy and to come to some working agreements. Two teams of division heads are meeting, one from MHC Europe and one from MHC America. Each team comprises the heads of (all or some of) the following divisions:

- production
- marketing
- sales
- finance
- corporate communications
- human resources.

Briefing for the representatives of MHC America

- You are a US national and you work at MHC America.

- MHC America wants its products to correspond to the needs of the North American consumer. MHC Europe's intention to switch from a local to a global marketing strategy could result in MHC America losing an important share of its own market in North America.

- The North American market for household equipment has particular characteristics:

  - The consumer may prefer to cook traditional dishes but wishes to use a very broad range of modern appliances that offers maximum convenience and versatility;

  - Storage is a concern: Americans tend to buy in bulk and so need large cupboards, refrigerators and freezers for storage;

  - Consumers prefer the washing machine/dryer combi-model (because there is always a lack of space in the bathroom) and top-loading machines (because they are safer);

- Advertising pays less attention to the purchasing price and more attention to the specific features of household equipment;
- Distribution channels: MHC America sells more of its equipment through hypermarkets and department stores than through specialist household appliance stores.

Your counterparts at MHC Europe have proposed that MHC should adopt a global marketing approach. Using the above information and other information or opinions you consider to be relevant, prepare arguments to put forward at your meeting with the representatives of MHC Europe. As a team, draw up *negotiating strategies* to help you and your counterparts to come to an agreement on MHC's future marketing policy.

Briefing for the representatives of MHC Europe

- You are a European national (i.e. you come from a European country of your choice) and you work at MHC Europe.
- Although MHC Europe is smaller than MHC America in terms of turnover, you believe that the Americans will ultimately have to accept your proposal to switch from a local to a global marketing approach. The arguments you intend to put forward include:
  - MHC Europe has coped very well with the many changes in the European market and has pursued a successful integration of its various national operations there;
  - MHC Europe has considerable know-how in terms of the specifications needed for international products;
  - The strategy used in Europe should be pursued on a global scale, bringing even more substantial cost reductions, particularly through the use of internationally oriented advertising and marketing channels;
  - The quality of MHC products in the global market will be enhanced through the incorporation of MHC America's prestigious brands;
  - Changes are taking place in consumers' purchasing patterns. Consumers are showing increasing preference for international rather than national products. Global consumers are emerging, characterised by their preference for similar kitchens with the same sort of appliances, such as microwave ovens, cookers, washing machines, all of a standard design. The quality and the safety of these appliances satisfy more or less the same standards.

Using the above considerations, as well as any other information or opinions you consider relevant, prepare your argumentation for a global marketing approach. As a team, draw up *negotiating strategies* to help you and your counterparts to come to an agreement on MHC's future marketing policy.

Briefing for the observers

Your goal is to prepare an account of your team's performance during the meeting, with particular focus on the verbal and non-verbal behaviour used towards the other team. The questions below are intended to guide you in your observations as well as to help you draw conclusions about your team's effectiveness during the interaction.

During the preparation

- How did the team make its preparations?
- How would you describe the team's attitude towards the other team? Note any relevant remarks made, particularly those you think reflect certain prejudices.

- How would you describe the negotiating strategy drawn up? Is it, for example, competitive or co-operative in nature?
- To what extent did the members of the team show willingness to work together and suppress or adapt their individual wishes?

During the meeting

- Watch how the interaction between your team and the other proceeds. Note examples of your team's behaviour that you felt helped or hindered the meeting to reach its goal.
- Pinpoint, in particular, a key moment where the interests of both parties came into conflict. Follow the interaction closely and describe as best you can the behaviour (verbal and non-verbal) of the group and/or individuals concerned. How effectively do you think your team handled that moment? What was the outcome?
- Note any examples from your team of empathy and/or mindfulness (see Chapters 17 and 18). What effect do you think they had on the proceedings?
- How closely did the group follow the negotiating strategy prepared beforehand? How do you account for any changes made to the strategy?
- To what extent do you think the goal of the meeting was reached by the end? What issues are still outstanding? How would you describe the relations between the two teams at the end of the meeting?
- What do you think should be the next step in the deliberations between the two parties? Explain why.

After the meeting

- Present a summary of your observations to both teams and add your comments on the general effectiveness of the teams in terms of their communication skills.
- Use this summary as the starting-point for a discussion with the participants.

Part Three Final activity A3.2

The account given below of Dutch brewer Vechtel's expansion in France focuses on the cross-cultural problems encountered by the company. The events described are based on the actual experiences of a Dutch brewer's endeavours to gain a foothold in the French brewing industry and take account of a number of observations made by key managers during interviews.

Many of the events which take place along Vechtel's takeover path are told through the eyes of one of the main protagonists in the story, to whom we have given the name Jean-Pierre Courbet. His actions, as well as the motives and perceptions behind them, reveal a number of vivid insights into factors which can play a key role in international takeovers, particularly those of leadership, cross-cultural communication and company cultures.

Learning Objectives

After completing the assignment, you should:

- Be in a position to identify typical cultural issues that companies and their managers can encounter when involved in an international takeover.
- Understand how such cultural issues can be effectively and appropriately managed.
- Be aware of how all the factors in this book relating to culture and management (Part One), culture and organisations (Part Two) as well as culture and communication (Part Three) can be present in one particular international takeover scenario.

YOUR ASSIGNMENT

After you have read the account, carry out the tasks requested. These will involve collaborating with your fellow students.

Vechtel

Adapting an international approach to the local market

1. BEFORE THE MEETING

The morning commuter traffic crawled through the suburbs of Lyons. **Jean-Pierre Courbet** sat at the wheel of his Renault, on his way to a meeting at Vechtel's headquarters. He had time, as usual, to contemplate his present situation. While doing so, he looked around at the name displays in the street and was encouraged by the ever increasing presence of the Vechtel name among the myriad signs.

He had an urgent meeting with **Jaap Harmelen**, Vechtel France's chief executive. The meeting had been hastily planned the evening before and the agenda was not too clear – Harmelen's secretary had been vague when questioned. Courbet thought he got on well with Harmelen, despite a feeling that Vechtel headquarters in Rotterdam was always looking over Harmelen's shoulder. For Vechtel had recently taken over the ramshackle group of breweries that Courbet himself had been trying to manage. Now the group was in the middle of a radical restructuring and it was causing him and many of the old guard considerable pain.

From time to time Courbet wondered whether he had made right decision to stay on and help Vechtel in its mammoth task. Events in Spain were giving him doubts. For it was there that Vechtel had bought its way into a huge brewery and, from what he had heard, read and seen, the takeover was not going well. For a start there was a basic communication problem at local headquarters: key figures did not share the same language and were using interpreters a lot of the time. Some local managers had been fired, including a key marketing executive, and they had been replaced by Dutch expatriates. This was, in Courbet's eyes, a recipe for possible disaster.

There were not too many communication problems in Lyons at least, thought Courbet. He himself could manage English, and his skills were improving by the day through contact with Rotterdam HQ. The younger managers were better trained and could more than cope. Harmelen himself was proficient in English and, perhaps more importantly, he could speak fluent French. On top of that he seemed to be a real Francophile, one who particularly relished France's dedication to food and drink.

As for the present organisational upheavals, Harmelen seemed to be doing his best in a very difficult situation. There had been dismissals of some of Courbet's French colleagues, but Courbet thought this was inevitable in a reorganisation where there were many overlapping parts – a consequence of previous mergers between rival breweries who had been thrown into each other's arms. Technical and financial experts had been called in from other operating companies belonging to Vechtel, but some key positions were still held by the French. Jean-Pierre Courbet was still there, advising the chief executive and helping to keep the train running while the rails were being changed. But what was going to happen next?

After taking over in Lyons, Vechtel had talked with great relish and persuasion about the power of Vechtel's brand name and the need to exploit this power as much as possible. This inevitably put a question mark over the future of some of the French brands the company was still promoting. Courbet realised there were too many of them and some rationalisation would eventually be necessary. So far, however, he knew of no concrete plans.

There was one component in the French acquisition that Vechtel seemed to have problems with – Inter-HRC, the distribution company. As director of Inter-HRC, Courbet had spent a lot of time justifying the way it operated, particularly since the company was distributing its rivals' products as well as those of Vechtel. Up to now Vechtel had been persuaded to keep its hands off Inter-HRC, but Jean-Pierre was not optimistic. After all, Vechtel had been quick to sell off the distribution arm of the brewery it had bought in Spain.

Jean-Pierre Courbet could not help feeling that eventually things would go the way they had gone in Spain. Although he had heard that the Spanish operation was supposed to become the jewel in the Vechtel crown, he could not help feeling that the ruthless approach being taken there was a recipe for disaster. Would Vechtel make the same mistakes in France?

Jean-Pierre had no illusions. Although the board of directors had expressed confidence in the future of its French operation, Jean-Pierre knew the venture was a risky one. He had heard that Arie van der Vecht himself, the son of the founder of the Vechtel brewery, had pushed for the takeover in France. This was seen as one of Arie's many whims – a capricious addition to Vechtel's portfolio of companies, one resulting from Arie's strong emotional attachment to France. In fact, Jean-Pierre had the feeling that Vechtel believed the venture in Spain would be more successful than the one he was helping to run in France.

Courbet was now queuing to turn right into the street where the headquarters stood. Which direction, he thought, would his career take? Would he continue to have a role to play in reviving the breweries' fortunes? Or was he going to be set aside along with other relics of the old breweries?

Jean-Pierre looked at his reflection in the rear-view mirror. 'You're not easy to get on with, are you?' he said to himself. 'The trouble with you is you're not afraid to speak your mind. Why don't you blah-blah like those other polished executives you've met?'

Jean-Pierre cringed at the thought. He wasn't ever going to be like those graduates from exclusive top business schools (the 'grandes écoles') who, as managers, still behaved as if they were analysing a business strategy case study. But he wasn't the blustering, domineering sort of old-style manager either: he simply saw no point in obsequious behaviour towards his new bosses. If he didn't agree, he said so. He wasn't looking for trouble; all that he wanted was the best for the company.

And the first signs were very encouraging. Since taking over, Vechtel seemed ready to learn, were dynamic, open, willing to take the long-term view. But did they want Courbet to stay on? He had been the key instigator in their taking over the company, but he knew that sentimentality or gratitude for past good deeds was not necessarily a reason for keeping him on. Spain had showed how mercilessly Vechtel could act.

Why did Jaap Harmelen want to see him so urgently? Had the time come for Vechtel and Jean-Pierre Courbet to go their different ways?

2. FROM VECHTEL FRANCE TO BRASSERIES VECHTEL

France: a beer-drinking country

France may still have the image of being a country of heavy wine drinkers, but beer has come to play an increasingly important role in French drinking habits. During the 1950s and 1960s there was a considerable increase in beer consumption and these years were the heyday of the many small breweries scattered throughout France. From the mid-1970s, however, the increase in beer consumption levelled off and started declining. From then on many of the small breweries were forced to merge and some even had to close.

The majority of the breweries in France are to be found in two regions – Alsace and le Nord. As any visitor to Alsace will discover, the region enjoys a long history of beer making – there were already nine brewers established in Strasbourg in the fourteenth century. Nowadays it accounts for about half of all beer consumed in France. The region Nord – with the city of Lille at its centre – is equally proud of its brewing skills. It dominated the brewing industry until after the Second World War, but now its position has gradually become less prominent.

Vechtel to the rescue

It seemed to Jean-Pierre Courbet that he had been battling with the precarious financial situations of all the breweries where he had worked as manager. As general manager of Union du Nord, a group of smaller breweries reluctantly forced to work together to keep their heads above water, he had had to cajole them into merging with their main rival, Brasseries Lilloises, to form Groupe du Nord. However, this merger did not produce the results expected and Courbet realised that outside intervention was necessary to pull together the motley bunch forming Groupe du Nord and to give it financial strength. He approached Vechtel BV in the Netherlands, as well as a Danish brewery, to discuss possible co-operation. The Danes appeared to be interested in a licensing agreement only, but Vechtel was ready to go further, particularly as Vechtel saw its increased involvement in France as a step to reaching its goal – to become a dominant company in the European beer market.

Vechtel BV took over Groupe du Nord and merged it with Vechtel France to form Brasseries Unies. This company therefore comprised three components: Brasseries Lilloises, Union du Nord and Vechtel France (see Figure A3.2.1). Relations between the three were strained: Brasseries Lilloises and Vechtel France were both full of resentment about being managed by the 'patron' of the third component – Union du Nord – of the new company: Jean-Pierre Courbet. Brasseries Lilloises took great pride in its very rigorous approach to the brewing of its beer, and was proud of its hard-working approach to the *métier*. Now it saw itself being run by the mercenary manager of the Union du Nord, who had fought tooth and nail to keep his own company afloat. Vechtel France, on the other hand, was proud of its role in developing the cult of the Vechtel brand in France and saw itself as Vechtel's torchbearer.

The original division between Vechtel France and Groupe du Nord soon showed itself to be unworkable. There were conflicting interests, particularly with regard to long-term plans. Vechtel wanted a freer rein and so, in 1997, it bought out the rest of Brasseries Unies' shareholding.

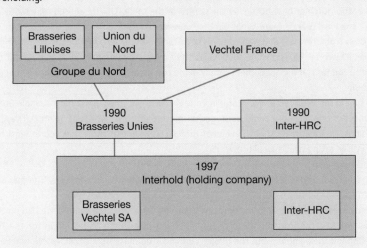

Figure A3.2.1 **The path to Brasseries Vechtel**

Apart from having to contend with internal friction, Vechtel also had to deal with a deplorable set of financial figures, an excessive number of breweries and an overloaded portfolio of brands. Restructuring was badly needed: several breweries would have to be closed, people laid off and the brand range revised to ensure that those brands remaining could be given sufficient support.

There was, however, one profitable company in the holding – the distribution company Inter-HRC. It was a major wholesale distributor in France and had around 70 subsidiaries scattered throughout the country. Despite it being a Vechtel company as well as an active promoter of Vechtel products, it also distributed the products of its competitors.

Although the French were naturally suspicious of their new owners, they soon discovered that Vechtel's approach to the company was intelligent and not too interventionist. A Dutch manager, Jaap Harmelen, was brought in by the corporate headquarters in Rotterdam to run Brasseries Unies. He turned out to be a considerate director, one who displayed dignity and sagacity, someone who respected the various brewery cultures within the company despite the friction they were causing. He trod carefully, slowly creating confidence among employees as to the future of the company, despite the urgent restructuring now being planned.

Harmelen was blown off course for a while, however, when it was decided to change the company's name – from 'Brasseries Unies' to 'Brasseries Vechtel'. The idea behind the change was to accelerate the integration of the loose elements in the company by creating a clear identity, a Vechtel identity, both within and to the world outside. There was a lingering resistance to the change at all levels of the work force, and Jaap Harmelen was told on many occasions, in very clear terms, what his employees thought of the new name. He could not expect an overnight change of name to create an immediate change of attitude.

It was Mr Harmelen with whom Jean-Pierre Courbet had his urgent appointment.

3. THE MEETING

Jean-Pierre Courbet walked quickly towards Jaap Harmelen's office. He was ten minutes late, but Harmelen's secretary offered him a cup of coffee while Harmelen was finishing a phone call. Jean-Pierre was eventually shown in, cup in hand, to be confronted by his very agitated boss.

'Have you heard the news?' asked Harmelen as he firmly shook Courbet's hand and showed him a chair at the same time. Before Jean-Pierre could answer, Harmelen exclaimed, 'The management team at the Spanish brewery has been sent back to the Netherlands!'

Jean-Pierre was not surprised. He said nothing, but sipped his coffee. Staring into his cup he said, 'I suppose we sort of saw it coming. After all, they had sold their distribution network – you don't just sell an invaluable asset like that. If you do, you're bound to lose market share.'

'Come on', said Harmelen impatiently, 'you know they had a great range of beer brands – that should have been enough, shouldn't it?'

Jean-Pierre looked at the clutch of beer bottles at the centre of the table. 'OK', he agreed reluctantly, 'they had the Vechtel brands. But what about the local brands, Jaap? What did they do with them?'

Harmelen got up slowly from the table and walked to his secretary's office, deep in thought. He returned with a jug of coffee. 'Vechtel's approach was all wrong', he said while topping up their cups. 'The company didn't understand the way the country was going. It wasn't up to the task. The management simply made too many mistakes. If the management is good, it will always find its way out of trouble.'

Jean-Pierre looked him in the eye. 'You know,' Jean-Pierre said scornfully, 'they didn't have a single Spaniard in the management team. What's more, not one manager could put together more than three words of Spanish. They had no idea about the way the Spanish do things. No idea about their feelings of pride! You've got to show that you at least have some idea about Spanish culture when you're taking over a local brewery!'

'You're right', sighed Harmelen.

'We're lucky here, you know', added Jean-Pierre Courbet before Harmelen could continue. 'The management here takes us seriously – you listen to us!'

'You're referring to Inter-HRC, the distribution company! Well, you were shouting so loud, we had no alternative but to keep it running! After all, as you say, the Horeca industry ('Horeca' being the Dutch abbreviation for the Hotel, Restaurant and Catering sector) is so difficult to segment – but the people running it do make up a considerable number of our customers in France – about 40,000 in all.'

'But that's not the only reason for keeping the distribution network', Jean-Pierre responded. 'It's more complicated than that. You've got to go along to these pubs and bistros, chat up the people running them, shake hands with the new boss, get to know everyone personally. That's the way to get your beer sold in this country!'

'That's what we should have done in Spain', said Harmelen, clearly annoyed. 'After all, they're the same sort of people as in France. They expect the personal touch, good contacts with the brewery.'

Harmelen pushed his coffee cup away and brought a smile to his face. 'Anyway', he said cheerfully, 'that's not really why I called you in, Jean-Pierre. I know we've got a pile of things to do on the restructuring, but first I want to talk about you!'

Jean-Pierre felt his heart thumping fiercely. He gripped his coffee cup while Harmelen continued.

'You know all about the bottom line, don't you, Jean-Pierre? Rotterdam wants as quick a turnaround as possible. We're still too top-heavy. We've still got to rationalise further. We can't just stop here.'

After a long pause, he continued. 'There is, however, another, more important consideration: our market share. Rotterdam agrees with me that we've got to do everything to push it up. What's the point of it all if we start losing our customers? We've got to keep them and find new ones. That's our priority number one.'

Jean-Pierre shuffled in his chair. He felt anxious and relieved at the same time.

'I want you to go after that market share', continued Harmelen. 'Yes, you! I'm going back to Rotterdam soon, to sit on the board, and I want you to take over here!'

Two hours later, after both had gone through the immense task that Jean-Pierre had been set, Harmelen and Courbet were walking to the café opposite the company's headquarters. They'd been talking beer all morning and now it was time to remind themselves of that Vechtel taste – and to celebrate Jean-Pierre's appointment to the position of chief at Vechtel's French operation.

4. SCHAEFFER FOR SALE

Expansion

After taking over from Harmelen, Jean-Pierre Courbet had quickly established his position. He had managed to calm the waters after the change of company name from Brasseries Unies to Brasseries Vechtel SA. This was essentially due to the immense respect he had already acquired within Vechtel.

Vechtel was now in full control of Interhold, the holding company, and had successfully introduced its main brands into France. The country had become a strategic market for Vechtel, one in which the Vechtel Group had become a dominant player.

Jean-Pierre Courbet was ever mindful of the question of Vechtel's market share in France and the need to improve it. Vechtel was doing well despite the tough competition. It was not yet market leader, but was rapidly improving its position, and was in fact beating its rivals in the Horeca sector. The own-brand beers sold by the large supermarkets were increasing in popularity and this was putting pressure on all branded beers. How could Vechtel improve its position in the French market?

The Schaeffer brewery, together with its subsidiary, Société Mundolsheim, came into the picture. Schaeffer, a family-controlled company, was quoted on the French stock exchange. It was one of the top five French brewers and was based in Alsace, where Vechtel had made its entry into the French market. Schaeffer was renowned for its speciality Alsatian beers, which sold well in the premium sector. Schaeffer's Mundolsheim subsidiary had built up its business by brewing *premier prix* beers – made for supermarkets to sell under their own name.

Long before the news reached the business press, Jean-Pierre Courbet had discovered that all was not well with the management of the company. Through his contacts in the brewery world he learnt that there were two factions within the management who were at each other's throats. As someone who had experienced similar boardroom battles when trying to manage an alliance of very different small breweries, he knew that this might be the moment for Vechtel to strike. If his company was to increase its market share in one fell swoop, a takeover of a strife-ridden company such as Schaeffer might be the answer.

Jean-Pierre realised that Vechtel had the power to manoeuvre. The mother company had plenty of cash in the bank as well as willing lenders. Moreover, it would be willing to invest the time needed to make the takeover a success. The other possible contenders in such a takeover would, he felt, be reluctant to pay what was sure to be a high price. They were so obsessed by the stock market that they would be unwilling to put their profitability at risk in the short term.

Key to Jean-Pierre's plans was the future status of Schaeffer. Although the takeover was intended to strengthen the Vechtel brand, he did not want to see Schaeffer absorbed into Brasseries Vechtel, but to survive as a separate operating company within the Interhold holding. He advocated this step not just to allow the families running the brewery to keep some control after the takeover – a demand they would certainly put forward in the negotiations, but also to acknowledge in organisational terms the ever increasing importance of speciality beers. Schaeffer was, after all, renowned as a brewer of special Alsatian beers.

Jean-Pierre also believed that Schaeffer's Mundolsheim subsidiary – which had built up its business by brewing *premier prix* beers for supermarkets to sell under their own name – should be hived off and designated as a further operating company under the Interhold umbrella. Again, this was the organisation taking account of an area of the beer market – own-label beers – that was developing at a fast rate and putting the sales of national and international beer brands under pressure.

Deliberation

As he put together this detailed strategy, Jean-Pierre knew that its realisation depended on his ability to convince the board in Rotterdam. He knew that the members had confidence in his judgement, but would still need to be presented with a solid case for the takeover.

Courbet raised the matter with the board at one of their frequent and regular meetings. Their initial reaction was lukewarm, to say the least. The questions and comments were many and Courbet had to explain in great detail the context in which the takeover was happening and the need for creating separate operating companies. One member of that board was his old sparring partner, Jaap Harmelen, the previous chief of Brasseries Unies. Harmelen, who frequently confessed to one and all that he had become a real Francophile, gave gentle backing to Jean-Pierre's plans, adding supportive points of information where needed. Harmelen eventually called upon the members of the board to give Courbet the green light and to allow him to prepare detailed plans for the takeover. The board agreed.

Jean-Pierre set to work on the dossiers. Not only would they have to stand up to Rotterdam's critical scrutiny, they would also have to go as far as possible towards meeting Schaeffer's financial demands. On top of all that, the dossiers would need to deal with the other concerns of the Schaeffer management and its employees. Schaeffer's family managers would be reluctant not only to lose control but also to see the Schaeffer tradition jeopardised. The unions who would doubtless be involved in negotiations would do everything to prevent redundancies. Unemployment was their greatest fear: the number of unemployed in France was high and rising. In this respect Vechtel was generally regarded as a good employer: it knew a cheque book in such a situation was not the only answer. Its approach was more philanthropic and long term.

There was also the possibility that the French government might throw a spanner in the works by raising objections. It might regard the move as one leading to an unhealthy domination of the market and use this as a reason for applying its anti-monopoly legislation.

Jean-Pierre set to work using not only his own vast experience but also that of the Vechtel group: Vechtel had recently created working groups relating to key areas of the business: logistics, purchasing, marketing – where the expertise of the various Vechtel companies were brought together. The resulting synergy helped to create various initiatives across the Vechtel group.

Despite initial resistance to Courbet's plans, the board gradually warmed to them. The weight of Jean-Pierre's experience in the French market and the tenacity of his conviction that the Vechtel organisation in France must develop in line with the market it was serving, made the directors think again.

Courbet presented his finalised dossiers to the board in Rotterdam and, once it had given its approval, the talks with Schaeffer could begin. The negotiation team consisted of Harmelen, Vechtel's lawyer and a Dutch banker. These were to be supplemented at certain stages of the talks by experts to discuss nitty-gritty details. Courbet himself did not want to participate actively in the process: he had no wish to get caught up in the intensive day-to-day, hour-by-hour negotiations. He wanted to keep a clear head and a clear overview of progress, so preferred instead to stay behind the scenes, discussing progress with his team during the many adjournments as well as talking informally to the other side.

EPILOGUE

Jean-Pierre was quietly sitting in his office. He had spent much of the last couple of days hovering around as the final round of negotiations took place. They had reached the finishing line, almost. He looked nervously at the phone. Why were they taking so long? The agreement was all but signed anyway!

He picked up a sheet of paper from one of the many piles on his desk. It was the organisational chart of the holding company Interhold, new-style. He drew a ring round the Schaeffer box, the one standing proudly between the Brasseries Vechtel and the other newly created company – Mundolsheim.

And there was also Inter-HRC – the grand survivor. In Spain, the company Vechtel had taken over had got rid of its distribution arm, and Jean-Pierre had felt under pressure to do the same in France. He had resisted. If he had not been able to make Vechtel understand the need to respect the French way of doing things, heaven knows what would have happened. In Spain,

Figure A3.2.2 **Organisational chart for Interhold**

the Dutch managers had not taken account of the Spanish context and of the dominant Horeca sector. Fortunately, he had been more persuasive, perhaps more credible as well. In the end they had listened to him, otherwise things would have gone the Spanish way.

Schaeffer had to be bought, he mused, not just to increase market share but also to develop synergies, reduce costs and improve productivity. But there was another important factor: the people involved. Large brewers, he thought to himself, couldn't really handle specialty beers. A key for success was not only the ability to adapt to the market but also to adapt to a state of mind. Why not allow beer brands their independence? Certain schools of thought advocated mergers and acquisitions because they allowed for all kinds of economies of operation. But what was often lost in the process was that vital commodity – innovation. The people working in companies that had been taken over should be allowed to give full rein to their creativity and not just follow the corporate line.

He thought back to that meeting with Harmelen where he had been told his fate. How time had flown by since then! Time, he thought to himself, is the essential component of management. It proves whether you're right or wrong. You can imagine what things will be like in 10 years' time, you can set your goal. But how can you reach it? It's not strategy that can make or break a company, it's the speed and manner of its implementation.

Absorbed in his thoughts, Courbet jumps when the phone rings. As he listens to Jaap Harmelen at the other end, a broad smile spreads across his face. Mission accomplished! After putting down the phone a few minutes later, Jean-Pierre mutters to himself: 'Well, the only real way to get results is to use us locals!'

The denouement

The outcome was successful, if expensive, for Vechtel. The acquisition of a majority of the shares held by the families involved was agreed on, and Schaeffer agreed to recommend to its remaining (public) shareholders that they accept Vechtel's offer to buy the remaining shares. So Interhold acquired a majority of the shares held by the family and made an offer to purchase shares held by the public. The same procedure was used for shares held by the public in Société Mundolsheim.

YOUR TASKS

Group-project activity

You are asked to prepare a report together with a number of your colleagues, to be used as a basis for an oral presentation and class discussion. Your instructor will give you details as to how you should proceed.

Task 1 Preparation of the report
In the report:

1) Summarise the events described in the account given above. Highlight what you consider to be the essential issues.

2) Draw up what you perceive to be the cultural profile of each of the two protagonists involved in the account. Use only the cultural values which you regard as relevant to the case (See Part One, Chapter 6, Model of culture). Compare and discuss the profiles which you have produced. Then answer the question: Where are the conflicting cultural values?

3) (a) Determine the internationalisation strategy of both Vechtel (Rotterdam HQ) and Brasseries Vechtel (Lyons), particularly with regard to the similarities and differences between the strategy of Rotterdam and that of Lyons.

(b) Using your answer to question 3a), try to answer the question 'Mergers and acquisitions: a strategic or cultural issue?', particularly in takeovers such as those described in the account of Vechtel's expansion. (See Part Two, Chapter 9, Concept 9.1.)

4) Make a critical evaluation of the negotiation process described in the account. (See Part Three, Chapter 15, Concept 15.1.) Consider in particular:

- Styles of negotiation.
- Outcome orientations.

5) Examine the interaction between Courbet and Harmelen using the model of communication (Part Three, Introduction, Figure III.1). Find in the account the elements describing:

- Their frames of reference.
- The communication filters which play a role in the interaction. Refer, for example, to the extent to which stereotyping is evident in the thoughts and words of the two protagonists.

Task 2: Presentation of your report

Include two questions which serve as the starting point for a class discussion of the issues raised during your presentation.

Further reading

Those who wish to gain further insight into aspects of the takeover process described in the case are advised to read the following articles:

Dijk van, N. and Punch M. (1993) 'Open borders, closed circles: management and organization in the Netherlands', in Hickson, D. (ed.), *Management in Western Europe*, Berlin/New York: Walter de Gruyter: 167–190. This chapter examines Dutch society and Dutch business, and attempts to find the source of what the authors call the mechanism of pragmatic accommodation, which permeates so many of the country's institutional arrangements.

Morden, T. (1995) 'Management in France', in *Cross Cultural Management: an International Journal*, 3 (3): 31–38. This article examines the nature of work relations in France before giving particular attention to the character and role of the *cadre* (the manager) and the professional status such people enjoy.

Trompenaars, F. (1996) 'Resolving international conflict: culture and business strategy', in *Business Strategy Review*, London Business School, 7 (3): 51–68. This article forms a basis for case analysis by giving an overview of seven dimensions by which cultures can be identified. The author also focuses on the question of reconciling cultural differences as an essential component of effective strategic management.

Index